FIDALGOS AND PHILANTHROPISTS

FIDALGOS AND PHILANTHROPISTS

The Santa Casa da Misericórdia
of Bahia, 1550-1755

A. J. R. RUSSELL-WOOD

Research Fellow of St Antony's College, Oxford

UNIVERSITY OF CALIFORNIA PRESS

Berkeley and Los Angeles

1968

First published 1968

© A. J. R. Russell-Wood 1968

Library of Congress catalog card no. 68–55798

Printed in Great Britain by R. & R. CLARK, LTD., EDINBURGH

Contents

Preface   ix

Acknowledgements   xv

Abbreviations and orthography   xvii

1. The Santa Casa da Misericórdia in Portugal   1
2. The Santas Casas da Misericórdia in Asia, Africa and Brazil   24
3. The City of the Saviour, 1549–1763   43
4. The Santa Casa da Misericórdia of Bahia
    A. THE FOUNDATION   80
    B. THE FIRST CENTURY, 1550–1650   86
5. The Administration of Charity   96
6. Class, Creed and Colour in Administration   116
7. Charity in Bahia
    A. THE PERSONALITY OF CHARITY   146
    B. THE CHARITABLE IMPULSE   159
8. Dowries   173
9. Burials   201
10. Justice and Charity   234
11. The Hospital of Saint Christopher   260
12. The Foundling Wheel   295
13. The Retirement House of the Most Holy Name of Jesus 320
14. Conclusion   337

Appendices
1. a. *Monarchs of Portugal and Brazil, 1500–1760*
    b. *Viceroys and Governors-General of Brazil at Bahia,*
      1549–1760   369

v

2.   Provedors of the Santa Casa da Misericórdia of Bahia,
      1560–1755   372

3. a. *Currency in circulation in Brazil, 1550–1750*
        i. 1550–1640
        ii. Reigns of Dom João IV (1640–1656), Dom Affonso VI
            (1656–1667) and the Regency of Dom Pedro (1667–1683)
        iii. Reign of Dom Pedro II (1683–1706)
        iv. Reign of Dom João V (1706–1750)
    b. *The price of labour, 1680–1750*   376

4.   *Weights and measures*   381
        i. Weights
        ii. Measures of capacity (dry)
        iii. Measures of capacity (liquid)
        iv. Measures of length

Glossary   383

Bibliography   386

Index   407

Illustrations

Between pages 206 and 207

Compromisso of 1516 of the Misericórdia of Lisbon

Reproduced from História de Portugal (*Barcelos, 1928–37) ed. Damião Peres*

A view of Bahia in 1714

Reproduced from Amédée François Fré^ier, Relation du voyage de la mer du Sud (Paris, 1716)

An ex-voto of the eighteen century

A painting in the church of Mont'Serrat, Bahia

João de Mattos de Aguiar

A painting in the Misericórdia of Bahia

Francisco Fernandes do Sim

A painting in the Misericórdia of Bahia

The Misericórdia of Bahia taking part in the Maundy Thursday procession

Tiles in the church of the brotherhood in Bahia

The 'procession of the bones'

Tiles in the church of the Misericórdia in Bahia

The funeral cortège of a brother of the Misericórdia

Tiles in the church of the brotherhood in Bahia

Punishment of a Negro at Feira de Santana

Reproduced from João Maurício Rugendas, Viagem pitoresca através do Brasil (5th ed., São Paulo, 1954)

A foundling wheel

In the convent of Sta Clara do Desterro, Bahia

The Santa Casa da Misericórdia of Bahia in 1958

Reproduced from Carlos Ott, A Santa Casa de Misericórdia da cidade do Salvador (Rio de Janeiro, 1960)

vii

MAPS

Santas Casas da Misericórdia founded before 1750   30-31

The Recôncavo of Bahia   42

Portuguese America in 1750   72

TABLES

I. The admissions of brothers to the Misericórdia of Bahia, 1665–1755   128

II. Legacies left to the Misericórdia for the saying of masses or for charitable purposes, 1600–1750   169

III. Legacies left to the Misericórdia for charitable purposes, 1600–1750   170

Preface

THE discoveries made by sailors serving under the flags of the Iberian kingdoms in the fifteenth and sixteenth centuries made the most dramatic impact on western Europe. They had been born, not of a dynamic western Europe eager for territorial expansion, but of an inward-looking Europe only just beginning to emerge from two painful centuries of social transition and economic and territorial decline. The peripheral outposts of Christendom had been lost in the latter part of the thirteenth century. The fourteenth century had seen the overthrow of chivalry, and the ideals it embodied, by a foot-slogging plebeian infantry. The feudal lords had yielded pride of place to speculators and financiers only for these, in their turn, to be ruined before the century had drawn to its close. Those cities which had been the commercial emporia of Europe during the eleventh, twelfth and thirteenth centuries had declined because of the fall in trade in the late fourteenth and early fifteenth centuries. Agrarian discontent had been rife throughout Europe. In 1347 and subsequent years the whole of Europe, from the Peloponnesus to Galway, had been ravaged by the 'Black Death'. It is against this sombre background of general depression in western Europe that the so-called 'Expansion' must be seen.

Portugal and Castile had been the leaders in this new age of discovery. Under the patronage of the somewhat mythical Prince Henry, 'The Navigator' (1394–1460), Portuguese captains had gradually advanced down the west coast of Africa. In 1488 Bartholomeu Dias had rounded the Cape of Good Hope. In 1492 the discoveries made by the Genoese Christopher Columbus in the service of Castile, had opened up the new world of the Americas. In 1498 Vasco da Gama had arrived in Calicut. In 1500 Pedro Álvares Cabral had discovered Brazil. From these tentative, and sometimes fortuitous landfalls, Spain and Portugal achieved the virtual territorial monopoly of the Americas and much of the profit to be made in commerce between Asia and Europe and within Asia itself. Only after 1600 was the

ix

Iberian supremacy in America and Asia to be challenged by the Dutch, English and French.

It is all too easy to reduce Portuguese participation in this territorial and commercial expansion of Europe to a calendar of dates of landfalls, naval engagements, battles and the capture of cities. It is often regarded as a history of the Sword and the Cross: of cruelty against native peoples, piracy, arson, unjustified offensives against local potentates and a total disregard for prevailing social and religious customs; of missionary zeal, ranging the world from Japan to Brazil, with the Jesuit fathers providing a spiritual counter-weight to the heavy bloodshed of conquest. Portuguese chroniclers of the fifteenth and sixteenth centuries dwelt on these two aspects. Their example has been followed by modern writers of standard histories, who censure the alleged cruelty of Affonso de Albuquerque or wax lyrical over the achievements of St Francis Xavier or Father José de Anchieta. The vital factor in this great epic — the Portuguese themselves — has been largely ignored. The reader will learn much from such chronicles and histories about the viceroys, governors, marshals, admirals, saints and bishops of the Portuguese overseas empire. He will have gained no insight into the ways of life of the common soldier, sailor, merchant, lawyer, small-holder, priest and artisan who formed small pockets of Portuguese throughout Africa, Asia and Brazil.

As he wearily turns the final page of his chronicle or history he will doubtless feel relief at an end to tales of bloodshed and sanctity which have aroused feelings of revulsion and admiration in him. But many of his questions will remain unanswered. Who were these Portuguese who left kith and kin for the Orient or Brazil? What did they hope to achieve by so doing? What lure did Asia hold for the storekeeper of Viana do Castelo or Brazil for the peasant of the Minho? How did they react to their new environments? What stresses and strains did they have to endure? What were their prejudices? What legacies of Portuguese culture and administration did they preserve? These are the questions which must be posed and answered before any understanding can be reached of the true nature of the Portuguese expansion. The researcher will be led into many a historical cul-de-sac in his quest, but the results will prove infinitely more rewarding than those endless roll-calls of infamy and glory.

Viceroys, governors, chief justices and bishops were posted to Asia,

Africa and Brazil by the Portuguese Crown, served their terms of office and were then recalled to Portugal. Their influence on the subjects under their jurisdiction was slight and they contributed little (with some notable exceptions) to the social way of life of the various Portuguese settlements. It was the common people who transposed to the East and to Brazil a community structure such as had existed in the villages and towns which they had left in Portugal. The *Câmara*, or town council, and the lay brotherhoods were social institutions common to every town in Portugal. The Portuguese who travelled overseas took these institutions with them. Town councils were established in very different circumstances, but all were modelled on their continental counterparts in Lisbon, Évora or Oporto. Lay brotherhoods were founded in the overseas settlements and followed the statutes of the parent bodies in Portugal. The social significance of such institutions has not been sufficiently recognised by historians. Only recently has there come from the pen of Professor C. R. Boxer a comparative study of the municipal councils of Gôa, Macao, Bahia and Luanda in which emphasis is laid on their social importance. For their part the brotherhoods have been largely ignored by historians, yet the answers to many of the questions posed above are to be found in their archives.

The most important of these brotherhoods was the Brotherhood of Our Lady, Mother of God, Virgin Mary of Mercy, which had been founded in Lisbon in 1498. This brotherhood, commonly known as the *Misericórdia*, had fallen under the royal patronage and had received many privileges. It had grown rapidly in Portugal and branches had been founded overseas. By the end of the sixteenth century practically every settlement of Portuguese, from Nagasaki to Bahia, had boasted its branch of the Misericórdia. In view of the obvious importance of the Misericórdia it is curious that, of the overseas branches of the brotherhood, book-length histories have only been written of the branches in Rio de Janeiro, Santos, Gôa and Macao. Numerous articles deal with the artistic and religious aspects of the Misericórdia. In all cases these histories and articles have dwelt on the Misericórdia as an institution, but serious studies of the social significance of the various branches still have to be made.

My object in this book has been threefold. The first has been to describe in detail Portuguese society as it existed in one part of her far-flung empire. The society which I have chosen is that of Salvador, capital of the Captaincy of Bahia and capital of Brazil from 1549 to 1763. The name of the city founded in 1549 was Salvador, but king and viceroy alike referred to it as Bahia. This practice has persisted to the present day, and I have followed it except in those cases where there could be ambiguity between Bahia (city) and Bahia (captaincy). Bahia was one of the centres of the Brazilian sugar industry during the colonial period. The patriarchal society of the sugar plantations has been exhaustively described by historians, anthropologists and novelists. The importance of the city as an urban centre has been largely disregarded. This book is intended to remedy this deficiency to some degree by describing the society of the capital. Whereas on the plantations the social structure was limited to a slave-master relationship, in the city the interaction of economic, religious and racial factors contributed to a social structure of great complexity and flexibility.

My second object has been to describe an institution which was common to both Portugal and Brazil. The Misericórdia flourished in Portugal and the branch in Bahia was the most important in colonial Brazil. The private archives of the brotherhood in Bahia serve as an index to the economic and social changes which occurred in Bahia during the seventeenth and eighteenth centuries. The brotherhood drew its members from the more eloquent citizens, be these landed aristocrats, merchants, or prominent artisans. The minutes of the boards of guardians record not only decisions on the policy of the brotherhood but reflect the ideology of the colonial era in Brazil.

My third object has been to place the conclusions concerning Bahia and the Misericórdia within the wider context of Iberian expansion. This has led to comparisons with the Spanish empire in America and with the Portuguese settlements in Africa and Asia. Experts in these fields may well disagree with some of my conclusions, but it seems important that they should be made and that the society described should not be regarded as peculiar to colonial Bahia.

This history is based primarily on unpublished archival materials. The archives of Bahia are rich in manuscript collections for the eighteenth century, but less so for the seventeenth century. All records of the sixteenth century were destroyed by the Dutch during their occupation of Bahia (1624–5). The registers in the archives of the Misericórdia comprise some 100 volumes for the period under discussion. These registers are more or less complete from 1660, but there are occasional gaps in some of the less important series when a volume has been lost or destroyed. Thus sometimes one aspect of the activities of the Misericórdia can be more fully documented than another. The municipal archives of Bahia are rich in material dealing with local government. The most important series are the minutes of the city council, which are complete from 1625, and the correspondence between the city councillors and the Crown. These two archival sources have been complemented by the manuscript collections in the archives of the State of Bahia. These include copies of the correspondence between the Crown or the Overseas Council in Lisbon and the governor-general or viceroy in Bahia. This series is almost complete for the later seventeenth century and the eighteenth century. In all cases the manuscripts in these archives have been generally classified and bound and are in quite readable condition.

The printed material for this study has been sparse. The National Library in Rio de Janeiro has performed a valuable service in publishing documents of supreme importance for an understanding of the colonial period in Brazil in its series entitled *Documentos historicos da Biblioteca Nacional do Rio de Janeiro*. The city council of Bahia has published the minutes of the city council for the period 1625–1700 and some of the letters from the city council to the Crown in the late seventeenth century. Other printed sources include the writings of the early Jesuits and the contemporary histories of Gabriel Soares de Sousa, friar Vicente do Salvador and Sebastião da Rocha Pitta. In the case of Bahia we are fortunate enough to have the colourful, and on the whole accurate, descriptions of the city by European visitors such as Froger, Dampier and Frézier.

While writing this book I have been made uncomfortably aware of how I have wandered from the broad roads of history on to the narrow footpaths of disciplines such as medicine, sociology, anthropology, ethnology and economics. Each of these demands a formal training which I lack. Nevertheless I have pressed on over stiles and fences in the belief that such a study cannot be made within the narrow confines of any single discipline. The archives of Bahia contain much of interest for specialists in these disciplines — mortality rates, prevalent diseases, immigration, miscegenation, genealogies, slavery, demography and the economic history of Bahia. It was essential that reference should be made to these issues and that hypotheses should be advanced. Into one field alone have I not trespassed, the artistic. This has received excellent and exhaustive treatment in the monographs of Dr Carlos Ott.

The Misericórdia was only one of innumerable brotherhoods in colonial Bahia. These ranged from the white élites of the Misericórdia and the Third Orders to the slave brotherhoods dedicated to St Benedict and Our Lady of the Rosary. Their members formed a broad spectrum of Bahian society. No definitive social history of Brazil can be written until the private archives of these brotherhoods have been examined. The first step is to overcome the strong 'falta de confiança', or distrust, of historical researchers felt by guardians of these archives (sometimes with justification). The second step is to catalogue the manuscripts in these archives and, if possible, publish the fruits of these researches. Only after such preliminary investigations have been made can monographs be written on individual brotherhoods, and only then will it be possible to write a truly representative social history of Brazil.

This book is not addressed to any particular class of readers. Students of colonial history will doubtless find items of interest and will establish comparisons which have escaped the writer. Specialists in the disciplines mentioned above may find information on subjects within their own fields, which are here treated in a different perspective. But it may also appeal to the general reader whose interests lie in the broader themes of the influence of economic factors on social change, or the conflicts of race and society. Some may even be persuaded to follow the writer in the courses of the caravels through those (in the words of the Portuguese poet Luís de Camões) 'mares nunca d'antes navegados'.

A. J. R. RUSSELL-WOOD

Llangoed
Beaumaris
Isle of Anglesey
October 1967

Acknowledgements

THIS book has been made possible by the generous assistance I have received from governments, staffs of archives, and individual scholars. The British and Brazilian governments, through their respective Ministries of Education and Culture, provided funds which enabled me to spend eighteen months in Brazil in 1964–5. St Antony's College, Oxford, gave me a *pied-à-terre* during the period of writing and more recently elected me to a Research Fellowship. Directors of libraries and archives on both sides of the Atlantic have gone out of their way to procure obscure books or to facilitate the consultation of manuscripts. In England I wish to record my gratitude to the following: the staffs of the Bodleian Library and of the Taylor Institution, Oxford; the staffs of the British Museum, of the Institute of Historical Research and of King's College of the University of London. The welcome accorded me and the friendly co-operation I received in Brazilian archives and libraries could not have been surpassed. Dr Darcy Damasceno of the manuscript section of the Biblioteca Nacional, and Dr José Honório Rodrigues and Dr José Gabriel Calmon da Costa Pinto in the Arquivo Nacional, made my stay in Rio de Janeiro most profitable. In Bahia the staff of the Santa Casa da Misericórdia, under the Provedors Dr João da Costa Pinto Dantas Júnior and Mr Erwin Morgenroth, afforded me every facility during the many months I worked in the archives of the brotherhood. Dr Luís Henrique Dias Tavares, director of the Arquivo Público, and Dr Affonso Rui, director of the Arquivo Municipal, cut away much bureaucratic red tape and permitted me to consult their manuscript collections freely. The nuns of the convent of Sta Clara do Desterro were extremely gracious in allowing me to study in their archives. The officers of the Instituto Geográfico e Histórico da Bahia gave me full facilities to use their library and did me the honour of electing me as a corresponding member towards the end of my stay in Bahia.

My gratitude is due to many people who have contributed to this book

xv

in various ways. I am particularly grateful to Professor C. R. Boxer, who awoke my interest in Brazil initially and whose enthusiasm has spurred me on during the period of research and writing. At all times he has shared his deep knowledge of the Portuguese seaborne empire and has allowed me to consult books in his library, which are otherwise virtually unobtainable on this side of the Atlantic. My thanks are also due to Professor H. R. Trevor-Roper, whose illuminating comments have suggested comparisons and encouraged me to view the Bahian situation within a wider context. I should also like to record my gratitude to the following *Bahianos*: Dr Thales de Azevedo, whose own researches have contributed to our knowledge of Bahian society; Dr Frederico Edelweiss, for much stimulating conversation on the foundation of the city of Salvador and for permission to roam freely around his magnificent library; Dr Carlos Ott, who suggested archival sources; Dona Marieta Alves, who facilitated my entry into the archives of the Third Order of St Francis. Mrs Agnes Neeser contributed much towards making my stay in Bahia so happy and Mr Erik Loeff's kindness enabled me to visit the Recôncavo and see many of the places described in this book. Father Michael Cooper, S.J., and Dr D. A. G. Waddell put me on the track of references to Japan and New Mexico respectively. Professor Raymond Carr made helpful editorial suggestions. While acknowledging my gratitude to these people for their assistance and encouragement, I must make it clear that they are in no way responsible for the opinions expressed in this book, nor for any errors of fact or interpretation which it may contain.

Miss Georgina Best and Miss Rosemary Hunt placed their technical skills at my disposal, the former in typing the manuscript, and the latter in devoting many hours to the drawing of the maps. My greatest debt is to my parents who meticulously checked the manuscript and made many valuable suggestions for improvements: this book is dedicated to them.

A. J. R. R.-W.

Abbreviations and Orthography

THE following abbreviations have been used in the footnotes to refer to archives which have been consulted.

ACDB   Archives of the Convent of Sta Clara do Desterro, Salvador, Bahia.

AMB   Archives of the Municipality of Salvador, Bahia.

APB   Public Archives of the State of Bahia.

ASCMB Archives of the Santa Casa da Misericórdia, Salvador, Bahia.

ANRJ   National Archives, Rio de Janeiro.

BNRJ   National Library, Rio de Janeiro.

The Portuguese language over the last 500 years has been characterised by its conservatism in morphology and syntax, but presents problems of orthography. In the transcription of documents of the seventeenth and eighteenth centuries I have preserved the original spelling and punctuation. This accounts for scribal inconsistencies such as Sousa–Souza, Sá–Saa, Fernandes–Fernandez, Crasto–Castro, esquiffe–esquife, cidade–sidade, sanctos–santos. Orthographic reforms have done little to solve inconsistencies of accentuation and transliteration in modern Portuguese and Brazilian. Common variants are annaes–anais, historia–história, geográphico–geográfico and archivo–arquivo. Proper names and place names are similarly inconsistent, e.g. Antonio–António–Antônio, Vasconcellos–Vasconcelos, Macao–Macau, Loanda–Luanda and Baía–Bahia. In general I have used the English forms of place names where these are in common usage, e.g. Oporto not Pôrto, Lisbon not Lisboa, and Mozambique not Moçambique. In other cases I have employed the Portuguese forms to avoid possible ambiguities.

I

The Santa Casa da Misericórdia in Portugal

THE Brotherhood of Our Lady, Mother of God, Virgin Mary of Mercy was dedicated on 15 August 1498 in a chapel of the cathedral of Lisbon. The traditional founders were a group of laymen and a Trinitarian friar. The new brotherhood was approved by the Regent Dona Leonor and confirmed by her brother, the King Dom Manuel I. Statutes were drawn up, and the initial membership was limited to fifty nobles and fifty plebeians. The avowed object of the brotherhood was to afford spiritual and material aid to all in need. From this modest origin the brotherhood, popularly known as the *Santa Casa da Misericórdia* or simply the *Santa Casa*, spread throughout the Portuguese-speaking world. Branches ranged from Nagasaki in Japan to Ouro Prêto in the interior of Brazil. The story of the Misericórdia is comprehensible only against the background of the older story of charitable assistance in Europe.

Poverty is the result of many related factors — physical, economic and social. The Middle Ages in Europe was a period of physical hardship for the lower classes. Famine was frequent, because of inadequate reserves of food supplies. An agrarian economy supported communities at subsistence level. Failure of a crop meant hunger. Deficient communications and transport made the movement of foodstuffs from one area to another impossible. Marginal wage-earners lacked financial resources to sustain physical set-backs. Cyclical poverty resulting from a single disaster often became endemic poverty. Malnutrition and hardship made whole communities ready victims of the other scourge of the Middle Ages — plague. Despite the great mortality resulting from famine and plague, there was an increase in the population of western Europe between the tenth and fourteenth centuries. This brought its own problems. An increase in the labour

I

force did not imply an increase in productivity. In fact, the opposite was the case and in some areas the disruption of the ecological equilibrium resulted in impoverishment.[1]

Economic and social changes in the twelfth and thirteenth centuries also disrupted the life of the lower classes. The gradual decline of feudalism from the late twelfth century placed greater onus on the individual. Although the manorial system had resulted in much exploitation, it had also afforded a degree of protection to the serf. The decline of feudalism was hastened by the increasing importance of the cities and the development of international trade. Venice was the wealthiest city in Europe in the eleventh century because of its commercial links with Constantinople. Capital gained by trade was invested in light industries such as weaving and spinning. This professional attitude towards industry ousted 'cottage' crafts in the rural areas. Migration to the cities resulted in highly competitive labour and forced wages down to the minimum. For the first time Europe faced the problem of urban poverty.

Societies were formed to protect the interests of artisans and to provide social relief. From the outset a distinction must be made between the artisan groups, which multiplied in the twelfth and thirteenth centuries, and the confraternities whose prime function was to afford mutual assistance. The former — known variously as *jurés*, *scuole* or *Zünfte* — were designed to protect the interests of a professional group. Religious observance was a prominent characteristic of these corporations. Members were obliged to attend mass in the corporation's church and the annual celebrations in honour of the patron saint. Social services for members and their dependents took the form of dowries or outright alms. Some corporations even maintained their own hospitals.[2] The confraternities shared the characteristic of religious observance. Unlike the corporations, their

---

[1] G. Duby, *La société aux XIᵉ et XIIᵉ siècles dans la région mâconnaise* (Paris, 1953), p. 64. For a general study of the relationship between population increase and productivity see David Herlihy, 'The Agrarian Revolution in Southern France and Italy, 801–1150' in *Speculum*, vol. 33 (1958), pp. 23–41, which modifies the over-optimistic portrayal given by H. Pirenne, *Mediaeval Cities: their origins and the revival of trade* (Princeton, 1946), p. 81.

[2] For a study of these artisan groups in France see E. Martin Saint-Léon, *Histoire des corporations de métiers depuis leurs origines jusqu'à leur suppression en 1791* (4th ed., Paris, 1941), especially pp. 171–4 on mutual assistance.

membership was not taken from one class of society. It was composed of lay men and women who wished to perform works of Christian charity towards their neighbours. Administration was in the hands of a governing body with a term of office up to one year. The governing body allocated duties to members who fulfilled different charitable services in rotation. A factor common to all these brotherhoods was provision for the social well-being of brothers and their families. This consisted of dowries, alms, prison aid, hospital treatment and burial. In some brotherhoods one aspect predominated: for example the Confraternity of St Leonard at Viterbo, famous for its hospital in the twelfth century, and the fifteenth-century Confraternity of S. Giovanni Decollato of Florence, specialised in the accompanying of the condemned to the scaffold and the subsequent burial of their bodies.[1]

Nowhere did brotherhoods founded for charitable ends multiply so profusely as in northern and central Italy. Venice, Milan and Florence counted such societies by the hundred. All social classes reacted to the stoic doctrines of St Francis and St Dominic. Some lay men and women chose the spiritual essence of renunciation and formed secular groups of tertiaries allied to the mendicant orders. Others chose a more worldly vocation and established brotherhoods specifically to assist the urban poor. The circumstances surrounding the foundation of one of the oldest brotherhoods of Florence, the Confraternity of Our Lady of Mercy (*Confraternità di Santa Maria della Misericòrdia*), illustrate how social preoccupations were felt by all classes and contribute to our knowledge of the foundation of its namesake in Lisbon.

In the thirteenth century Florence was famous for its manufacture of woollen goods and a trade fair was held twice a year. A large number of porters were employed on such occasions and passed their free time in a cellar on the south side of the present Piazza del Duomo. In 1244, one Piero Borsi, shocked by the blasphemies of his fellows, instituted a swear box to which all offenders contributed a *crazia* (about a halfpenny). All fines went towards the purchase and upkeep of six litters, kept in different parts of the city, for the transportation of the sick to hospital and the removal of the

---

[1] For a complete study of the Italian brotherhoods see G. M. Monti, *Le confraternite medievali dell'Alta e Media Italia* (2 vols., Venezia, 1927), especially vol. 1, chapters 4–7.

bodies of victims of sudden death from the streets. This was the origin of the Confraternity of Our Lady of Mercy.[1]

The brotherhood grew in prestige and wealth. A private oratory was built on land over the cellar, given to the Misericòrdia by the governor in 1248 in recognition of its valuable services to the community. The humanitarian activities of the brothers in the great plague of 1325, in which some 100,000 Florentines died, brought much credit to the Misericòrdia. The number of brothers, originally limited to seventy-two porters, was increased. Nobles were also admitted for the first time on payment of the usual subscription. The only conditions were that they should be of the Catholic faith and of good repute. With this larger membership the Misericòrdia was able to expand its social services. Seven groups, each of fifteen brothers, visited all parts of the city twice daily to care for the needy. There was also an increase in the governing body to seventy-two members, known as the *Capi di Guardia*. These were chosen from different social strata — ten prelates, fourteen nobles, twenty priests and twenty-eight labourers. Each member had equal voting powers. The governing body elected a *Provveditòre* to serve as President for four months. He was assisted by a Vice-President and a Chancellor.

The success of the Misericòrdia aroused the jealousy of other brotherhoods. In 1425, when the Misericòrdia was at its apogee, Cosimo de Medici, a powerful voice in Florence and a member of the governing body of the *Compagnia Maggiore di Santa Maria del Bigallo*, suggested the amalgamation of this ailing brotherhood with the prosperous Misericòrdia. The protests of the Misericòrdia were over-ruled and the union took place. The results were fatal for the Misericòrdia which suffered loss of prestige and had to reduce its charitable activities because of lack of co-operation from its unwelcome partner. Only in 1475, after a body had been left in the street for several hours, were measures taken by the municipal authorities to revive the Misericòrdia. The prominent rôle played by the brotherhood during the plague of 1494 firmly re-established its reputation.

The need for social assistance, which had given rise to the foundation of

---

[1] The outline history which follows is based on Placido Landini, *Istoria dell'Oratorio e della Venerabile Arciconfraternita di Santa Maria della Misericordia della città di Firenze* (Firenze, 1843) and Maria Zucchi, 'The Misericordia of Florence' in *The Dublin Review*, no. 229 (1894), vol. 114, pp. 333–45.

charitable brotherhoods in Italy in the eleventh, twelfth and thirteenth centuries, was no less present in Portugal. Nor was the response less great, although generally there were fewer financial resources available for charity than in the commercial emporia of Italy. The need can be reduced to the trilogy of plague, famine and war. To these may be added agrarian depopulation as a result of the overseas expansion in the sixteenth century.

There were twenty-two recorded outbreaks of plague in Portugal between 1188 and 1496. Many more local outbreaks probably went unrecorded or were not recognised as such. The 'great pestilence' of 1310 was so devastating that burial of the dead was a physical problem. The grim story was repeated in 1333; even mass burials in communal graves could not clear the streets of corpses.[1] Although serious, these local outbreaks were insignificant in comparison with the great tragedy of the Middle Ages: the Black Death. This bubonic plague had originated in Crimean Tartary and had been brought to Europe by Genoese ships in early 1347. It had spread rapidly throughout Europe and reached Portugal in September 1348, causing widespread mortality.[2] During the fifteenth century there were further intermittent outbreaks affecting both the countryside and the cities. An account of the visit of the Bohemian Baron, Leo of Rozmital, to Portugal in the 1460s was written by a member of his suite and described the havoc wrought by plague on the villages of northern Portugal:

> We left the Counts and rode through a great mortality from plágue, such as I have never heard of. We rode through a market or village which was quite deserted and desolated. Not another soul was to be seen. What wretched experiences we had there no one would believe. We had to buy wine and bread from people who lay ill, or had sick people in the house, and lodge with them. But for the most part as long as we rode through that country I lay with my horses in the open.

---

[1] F. da Silva Correia gives a full list of outbreaks in *Portugal sanitário* (Lisboa, 1937), chapter 37.

[2] Estimates of the extent of the mortality vary between 90 per cent (José F. de Macedo Pinto, *Medicina administrativa e legislativa* apud F. da Silva Correia, *Estudos sôbre a história da Assistência. Origens e formação das Misericórdias portuguesas* (Lisboa, 1944), p. 245 and from 35 to 50 per cent (Marcello Caetano, *A administração municipal de Lisboa durante a I^a dinastia, 1179–1383* (Lisboa, 1951), p. 80.

In many places as we rode through the world, we saw nothing but sky, water and heath.[1]

In the cities the situation was equally bad. Plague prevailed in Lisbon from 1477 to 1497, despite sanitary measures ordered by Dom João. II.[2] A contributory factor was the large number of Jews who had sought refuge in Lisbon after having been expelled from Spain in 1492 and had been carriers of plague.[3] The courts of Dom Manuel I (1495–1521) and Dom João III (1521–57) moved constantly between Lisbon, Almeirim, Sintra and Évora in an attempt to escape outbreaks of plague.

Plague and famine were constant fellows. Portugal suffered at least five outbreaks of famine within the first four centuries of its nationhood. The earliest recorded famine was in 1122 and extended from the Minho to the Tagus, lands only recently conquered from the Moors.[4] An outbreak in 1202 was common to all western Europe and was especially severe in Portugal, killing man and beast alike. The years 1267, 1333 and 1356 were years of famine, often linked to plague. Local outbreaks of famine could not easily be remedied. This was largely because of the excessive number of privileges granted to municipalities, villages, castles, churches and private owners of bridges and roads for the levying of crippling taxes on all food-stuffs passing through the area of their jurisdiction. Many municipalities imposed sumptuary laws, and refused to permit the export of foodstuffs or the import from other regions of any commodity produced locally. The difficulty of finding suitable transportation also made it virtually impossible for prosperous areas to send help to their neighbours stricken by famine.[5]

To these natural misfortunes must be added the devastating effects of war, a constant factor in Portuguese life from the twelfth to the fourteenth

[1] *The Travels of Leo of Rozmital through Germany, Flanders, England, France, Spain, Portugal and Italy 1465–1467*, edited by Malcolm Letts for the Hakluyt Society (Cambridge, 1957), p. 110.
[2] Eduardo Freire de Oliveira, *Elementos para a historia do municipio de Lisboa* (19 vols., Lisboa, 1882–1943), vol. 1, p. 363; cf. vol. 1, p. 318 for municipal measures as early as 1437.
[3] Rui de Pina, *Crónica de El-Rei D. João II* (Coimbra, 1950), chapter lxv.
[4] Henrique da Gama Barros, *Historia da administração publica em Portugal nos seculos XII a XV* (11 vols., 2nd ed., Lisboa, 1945–54), vol. 5, p. 125.
[5] Henrique da Gama Barros, op. cit., vol. 5, p. 130.

centuries. Agriculture was disrupted and villages destroyed. The re-conquest of Portugal lasted over a century before the national territory was finally established by the conquest of the Algarve in 1249. The reigns of Dom Diniz (1279–1325), Dom Affonso IV (1325–57) and Dom João II (1481–95) were troubled by civil wars. Castile was a constant threat until the battle of Aljubarrota (1385) ended the pretensions of Juan I to the Portuguese throne. Fernão Lopes, the chronicler of the siege of Lisbon by the Castilian troops in April 1384, provided an insight into the miseries of war for the common person, accompanied by the abandonment of agri-culture and the ravages of plague and famine. He described the peasants flocking into Lisbon from the neighbouring countryside, parents with their children in their arms and their worldly possessions on a mule. This sudden influx resulted in a chronic shortage of food and water, despite heavy provisioning by John of Aviz. All those unable to serve in the defence of the city were expelled, but even this measure could not avoid exorbitant prices for food and wine. Many resorted to scavenging and eating roots. From famine to plague was but a short step. Ironically enough, the Castilian army succumbed first to this evil. In March 1384, when leaving Santarém, Juan had been advised against besieging Lisbon because of plague victims in his ranks. The static and cramped living conditions in the encampments around the walls of Lisbon aggravated the situation and the deaths of some 200 soldiers daily finally compelled Juan to withdraw.[1]

In addition to plagues of continental origin, there were those born of the African campaigns. The first Portuguese overseas offensive against Ceuta in 1415 had resulted in the transmission of plague to the Algarve by the returning soldiers. The fifteenth-century chronicler, Zurara, referred briefly to this negative aspect of the conquest and listed the names of noble-men who had died from plague.[2] The overseas conquests were later, and especially after 1500, to disturb the ecological equilibrium of the rural areas of Portugal. At first, they provided a safety valve for rural overpopulation but excessive migration of peasants to Lisbon and overseas finally resulted in the depopulation of large areas of northern Portugal. The ludicrous

---

[1] Fernão Lopes, *Crónica de D. João I* (2 vols., Porto, 1945–9), vol. 1, chapters lxx, lxxxvi, cxxxvi, cxlviii and cxlix.

[2] Gomes Eannes de Zurara, *Crónica da tomada de Ceuta por El Rei D. João I* (Lisboa, 1915), chapter ciii.

character of the *ratinho*, or country bumpkin, of the plays of Gil Vicente typified the hopes of rapid social advancement which induced peasant lads to go to Lisbon and supplied makeshift seamen for the Indiamen.

Social philanthropy in Portugal, in its most primitive form, had originated in *albergarias*, or inns, situated on the pilgrim routes as early as the eleventh century. Local shrines were common in the Douro and Minho and the cult of St James brought pilgrims from all over Europe to Santiago de Compostela.[1] Hostelries had been established on royal or monastic foundations, or simply by individuals for commercial gain. Essentially these hostelries offered shelter for pilgrims, but sometimes provision was made for the poor and there was even a rudimentary medical service. In fact, some of these inns later became hospitals. The famous *Albergaria dos Mirléus* in Coimbra became a leper house and an enquiry by Dom Diniz in 1321 revealed that the inn at Pampilhosa housed nine lepers.[2] The word *hospital* was often used as a synonym for *albergaria* but did not always imply medical assistance, the degree of social philanthropy varying from one inn to the next.

The line of distinction between the different types of hostelries is not clear, but the following brief description will indicate their form and functions. The hostelries gave a roof and a bed for three days and a small ration of food and water. In the larger inns there were special quarters for the gentry. In the small isolated hostelries of the Beira Alta and Alto Douro, which rang bells to guide weary travellers through the mountains, the accommodation was no more than a straw mattress and a heavy blanket. The majority of these inns were situated along the old Roman roads between Lisbon, Coimbra, Oporto and Braga, with a heavy concentration in the mountainous regions of the Minho and Alto Douro. South of Lisbon there were only twenty-seven inns, of which half were in the district of Évora, out of a total for the country calculated at 186.[3] Not all these inns were situated on the highways and byways. Two of the most famous were the *Albergaria de Payo Delgado* in Lisbon and the *Albergaria de Rocamador* in Oporto, both

[1] For a general description of these pilgrimages see Mário Martins, S.J., *Peregrinações e livros de milagres na nossa Idade Média* (2nd ed., Lisboa, 1957).

[2] *História de Portugal. Edição monumental* (8 vols., Barcelos, 1928–37, ed. Damião Peres), vol. 4, p. 532.

[3] F. da Silva Correia, *Estudos sôbre a história da Assistência*, pp. 406–20 and figure 76.

dating from the twelfth century. A reconstruction of the latter illustrates the ambivalent nature of these establishments. Annexed to the main hostelry was a hospital with eighteen beds for the poor and five private rooms for 'distinguished gentlemen'. There was also a kitchen, an orchard, a private chapel and a cemetery.[1] Although only one inn in four was in a city, over half of the 211 hospitals were in the cities of Lisbon, Oporto, Guimarães, Coimbra, Évora and Santarém. Lisbon itself counted some fifty hospitals providing for its citizenry and foreign travellers, many of these hospitals being linked to hostelries.

Allied to the hostelry-hospital complex were the leper houses, about which there is more information because they were under royal or municipal jurisdiction. The Moorish invasions and the return to Portugal of infected crusaders had led to an increase in leprosy in the eleventh and twelfth centuries. Since it was regarded as incurable, the authorities made no attempt to provide any medical care. It was up to the individual to seek alleviation in the sulphur baths, of which those at Lafões were the most famous. Nor was there any law forbidding lepers from circulating freely in the cities and along the roads. The number of leper houses in Portugal has been calculated at seventy-five, a conservative estimate considering the prevalence of this disease in the twelfth and thirteenth centuries.[2]

Leper houses fell into three administrative groups. First there were those under royal jurisdiction, where the warden was nominated by the Crown. Such was the leper house of St Lazarus in Coimbra, whose first director had been appointed by Dom Diniz and which received numerous privileges from other kings. Secondly, came those leper houses under the jurisdiction of municipal councils, such as the leper house of St Lazarus in Lisbon. A third group were those houses run by the lepers themselves, who had formed an association and built their own leper house. One of the oldest leper houses in Portugal was of this type, having been founded in Santarém possibly in the time of Dom Affonso Henriques. The earliest extant statutes date from 1217 and were drawn up by the lepers themselves who elected their own director and board of guardians. The Crown encouraged such initiative by concessions of land well outside the municipal

---

[1] Magalhães Basto, *História da Santa Casa da Misericórdia do Pôrto* (Porto, 1934), p. 327.

[2] F. da Silva Correia, *Estudos sôbre a história da Assistência*, pp. 435–42.

limits to prevent any risk of contagion.[1]　A typical leper community consisted of a chapel and some seven to ten small houses for the lepers within a walled patio.　It was self-supporting with garden and orchard, and relied on alms for financial support.　In the larger establishments there was a resident warden, cellars, a wood-burning stove, a wine or olive press and a dispensary.　A leper colony in Coimbra in 1452 even included a prison! The rules for admittance to such colonies were rigid.　An entrant contributed a part of his possessions to the community and was only allowed to leave with the permission of the warden, granted only for begging or pilgrimage.　Usually leper houses catered for both sexes, single and married, but heavy penalties were enforced for concubinage.　The lepers received a daily ration of food and wine, with special allowances on saints' days and religious festivals.　The lepers guarded their privileges jealously, examining all new applications to ensure that no healthy person, or a cured leper, should benefit without justification.[2]

The philanthropic stimulus for the foundation and maintenance of these inns, hospitals or leper houses came from a variety of sources, individual and collective, ecclesiastical and lay.　The monastic orders played an important rôle in assisting the indigent and infirm on a national scale.　Pride of place must go to the Cistercian monastery at Alcobaça, founded in the second half of the twelfth century.　This maintained a hostelry and a hospital with wards where not only monks but poor people were cured free of charge.　From the fifteenth century it possessed the first regular pharmacy in Portugal with a resident pharmacist.　The monastery was aided in this social welfare by royal privileges to defray expenses.　Such privileges included the right to a portion of the corn crop and to fish from the nearby village of Pederneira.

The smaller Orders of St Antão, Saint Mary of Rocamadour and the Trinitarians followed this example.　The first was dedicated to the care of victims of ergotism, a disease produced by eating bread made with diseased rye, and present in Portugal from the twelfth century.　By the fourteenth century the Order had five main monasteries and several small monasteries, with wards for the sick.　The origin of the Order of Our Lady of Rocama-

---

[1] Damião Peres, op. cit., vol. 4, pp. 548–56.
[2] F. da Silva Correia, *Estudos sôbre a história da Assistência*, pp. 369–74, publishes summaries of the statutes of the leper houses of Santarém (1261) and Coimbra (1329).

dour is obscure. It appears that the charitable brotherhood which maintained a hospital for pilgrims to Rocamadour was brought to Portugal by
the crusaders. The Order established its seat at Sousa-a-Velha on land
endowed by Dom Sancho I (1185–1211). Other royal favours followed and
the Order established hospitals in Lisbon, Oporto, Coimbra, Santarém,
Leiria, Braga, Tôrres Vedras and Guimarães. The Trinitarians catered for a
different charitable purpose — the ransom of Christians captive in Moorish
hands. In addition to collecting alms with which to pay the ransom, the
Order maintained hospitals in Lisbon and Santarém for the ransomed and
for the poor.

In comparison with the monastic orders, the charitable rôle played by the
Templars and the Hospitallers in Portugal was small. The Templars had
their main sphere of activity in the region between the Mondego and the
Tagus, founding some hostelries and hospitals and endowing others. The
action of the Hospitallers was insignificant, despite encouragement from the
first king of Portugal, Dom Affonso Henriques (1139–85), who had handed
over to them the administration of a hospital he had founded in Évora.[1]

Portuguese royalty vied with the monastic orders in founding hostelries,
hospitals and leper houses. In his will Dom Diniz provided for lepers, the
ransom of captives, the clothing of the poor and dowries, and made grants
towards the upkeep of inns and leper houses. The most famous royal
benefactors were Dona Isabel, Queen of Dom Diniz, and Dona Leonor,
Queen of Dom João II. The generosity of Dona Isabel in the distribution
of alms led to accusations of extravagance by king and courtiers. The
common people attributed miraculous powers to her. In Lent she washed
the feet of lepers and fallen women and on one occasion she healed the foot
of a crippled woman. Contemporary chroniclers praised her Christian
humility and charity, whatever the criticism levelled against her at court.[2]
Dona Leonor was more practical, founding a hospital at Caldas in 1485.
A resident medical staff of physician, surgeon, 'barber' (for bleeding),
pharmacist and nurses cared for a hundred sick. This foundation was

---

[1] For a survey of the monastic and military orders and the social action of the
clergy in Portugal see Fortunato de Almeida, *História da igreja em Portugal*
(4 vols., Coimbra, 1910–24), vol. 1, pp. 264–340 and pp. 541–9, vol. 2, pp. 103–85
and pp. 439–43, vol. 3 (2nd part), pp. 467–88.

[2] *Crónica de D. Dinis* (Coimbra, 1947), chapters 3–4.

the first step towards the reform of hospital conditions in Portugal. Charity towards the needy and infirm on the part of the laity was not limited to royalty. As had been the case in other European countries, groups of laymen were formed for mutual assistance and charitable acts. Once again the distinction must be made between associations of a professional nature and lay brotherhoods. Some historians have considered that the professional associations presented two fronts; the civil, consisting of economic interests and the protection of these interests, and the religious, corresponding to the brotherhood.[1] This is too narrow an interpretation, implying a connection between the association and the brotherhood which does not exist. The Portuguese historian, Marcello Caetano, gave two definitions for associations of artisans: first 'a grouping of those exercising the same trade', and secondly 'a corporation, formed of more than one profession'.[2] While true for groups of artisans such unions would have been extremely rare between brotherhoods, who were jealously proud of their independence. The distinction between the association and the brotherhood is clear from the respective statutes. The associations of artisans followed a *regimento*, or set of rules, approved by the municipal council or the Crown, whereas the brotherhoods enjoyed the flexibility of a *compromisso*, or statutes, based on mutual trust.

The charitable activities of the associations were limited to their own members. Many had their own hospitals, such as that of the carpenters of the Ribeira of Lisbon, that of the cobblers of Tôrres Vedras and that of the weavers of Leiria.[3] As for brotherhoods, their presence in Portugal from an early date is as indubitable as it is undocumented. Brief consideration of the functions of two early brotherhoods will provide the historical context of social philanthropy in which it is essential to view the Misericórdia.

The *Confraria dos Homens Bons* ('Brotherhood of the Worthy Men') was founded in Beja in 1297 and authorised by Dom Diniz on condition that its

---

[1] Paul Viollet, *Histoire des institutions politiques et administratives de la France* (3 vols., Paris, 1890–1903), vol. 3, pp. 143–76, and especially pp. 164–5; L. Lallemand, *Histoire de la charité* (4 vols., Paris, 1902–12), vol. 3, p. 333, n. 1 and p. 334, n. 7.

[2] Marcello Caetano, 'A antiga organização dos mesteres da cidade de Lisboa' in Franz-Paul Langhans, *As corporações dos ofícios mecânicos-subsídios para a sua história* (2 vols., Lisboa, 1943–6), pp. xi–lxxiv.

[3] Damião Peres, op. cit., vol. 4, pp. 542–3.

wealth and property remained in lay hands. Essentially aristocratic, it is reminiscent of Germanic guilds for mutual defence in battle. The statutes provided for the replacement of a dead horse in battle, mutual assistance for brothers in the king's service, and ordered that the fifth part of all booty be given to the communal coffers. If these clauses are not typical of Portuguese brotherhoods, those dealing with medical assistance, financial aid and the saying of masses were common to more plebeian brotherhoods.[1] The Brotherhood of the Immaculate Conception of Sintra (1346) was such a brotherhood. The statutes included clauses on the weekly mass of the brotherhood, the annual dinner, visits to the sick, the reconciliation of discordant elements, funeral arrangements and the saying of masses for the souls of dead brothers and their families.[2] These two brotherhoods and the Third Order of St Francis (1289) are the oldest lay brotherhoods in Portugal for which there are details. There are vague accounts of the existence of a brotherhood dedicated to Our Lady of Mercy in the cathedral of Lisbon before 1230. Its functions were to bury the dead, visit and console the sick, assist prisoners, and accompany to the scaffold criminals sentenced to death.

By the fifteenth century there existed in Portugal not only a social conscience but the charitable mechanism to satisfy this feeling. Indeed, there was such a profusion of leper houses, hospitals and charitable brotherhoods, that considerable overlapping of activities was inevitable. This was especially so in Lisbon and resulted in much abuse in the application of alms. In the 1420s, Dom Pedro had written to his brother Dom Duarte suggesting royal intervention in the administration of inns. The 1446 legal code known as the *Ordenações Affonsinas* had advocated that lawsuits over legacies to brotherhoods should be heard in civil and not ecclesiastical courts. By the end of the fifteenth century two attitudes towards social philanthropy were apparent: first, the necessity for an official policy on social welfare; secondly the desire on the part of the Crown to lessen ecclesiastical jurisdiction over charitable lay brotherhoods.

The first positive action was in 1479, when the future Dom João II, while still a prince, secured a papal bull authorising the fusion of all the small hospitals of Lisbon into a single building. This centralising policy was

---

[1] F. da Silva Correia, *Estudos sôbre a história da Assistência*, pp. 288–9.

[2] A. Braamcamp Freire, 'Compromisso de confraria em 1346' in *Archivo Historico Portuguez*, vol. 1, no. 10 (Lisboa, 1903), pp. 349–55.

extended to all cities in Portugal by a bull of Pope Innocent VIII in 1485. The first result of this policy was the Hospital of All Saints, founded in Lisbon in 1492. This building incorporated forty-three small hospitals of the city and environs. When it was finished some ten years later, it had five main wards with a hundred beds, subsidiary wards outside the main building, a foundling home and a hostelry.[1] Dom Manuel followed the policy of his predecessor and secured a papal bull in 1499 for the amalgamation of hospitals in Coimbra, Évora and Santarém. By the time of his death in 1521 this was standard practice throughout Portugal.

There is no concrete evidence that the foundation of the *Santa Casa da Misericórdia* in Lisbon in 1498 constituted another aspect of this official centralisation of social assistance. The fact that the brotherhood later came to fulfil this rôle was the result of its immediate success and royal patronage. Nor is there any evidence to support the view that the Misericórdia of Lisbon was influenced by charitable brotherhoods in Italy. This assertion is based on two facts: first, the similarity of name and function of the Misericórdia in Lisbon and the Misericòrdia in Florence; secondly, a clause in the will of Dom João II commending the administration of the hospital of Florence as a model for the new Hospital of All Saints in Lisbon.[2] Certainly there were close links between Portugal and Italy. The relationship had been established by the marriage (1146) of the first King of Portugal, Dom Affonso Henriques, to Mafalda, daughter of Amadeus III, Count of Maurienne and Savoy; had been fostered by the European contacts of Dom Diniz and his appointment of the Genoese Manuel Peçanha as High Admiral to reform the Portuguese navy; and had been confirmed by Dom Affonso IV (1325–57) and Dom Pedro I (1357–67) who granted charters giving freedom of trade and movement to many Italian families in Lisbon. Nevertheless, certain facts must be borne in mind. Brotherhoods dedicated to Our Lady of Mercy existed all over Europe. Moreover, a tradition of charitable brotherhoods had been firmly established in Portugal before 1498.

---

[1] The date of completion varies between 1501 and 1504 and estimates of the number of beds available between 103 and 150, Eduardo Freire de Oliveira, *Elementos*, vol. 1, p. 379, n. 2; Damião Peres, *História*, vol. 4, p. 558; F. da Silva Correia, *Estudos*, p. 524.

[2] Damião de Góis, *Crónica do Felicíssimo Rei D. Manuel* (4 vols., Coimbra, 1949–55), part 1, chapter i.

Comparisons between hospitals and brotherhoods are not valid as there was not a parallel development between these two forms of social aid. Finally, it is extremely doubtful if Italian interests in Portugal went beyond the purely commercial, centred on the strategic position of Lisbon on the long sea route between Italy and the ports of northern Europe. In short, the Misericórdia of Lisbon continued a Portuguese tradition of charitable brotherhoods which was already in existence within the wider framework of social philanthropy in Europe.

The basic facts of the foundation of the Misericórdia of Lisbon have already been presented. Lack of contemporary evidence leaves many questions unanswered. Principal among these is the personality of the founder or founders. The initiative for the foundation has been variously attributed to Dona Leonor, the widow of Dom João II, the Trinitarian friar Miguel Contreiras, and a group of six laymen. My purpose here will be to present the evidence briefly and discuss the views advanced by different historians.

The mysterious figure of friar Miguel Contreiras is the central character in all discussions on the foundation. A native of Valencia (or Segovia according to some sources), he had come to Portugal in 1481 at the age of fifty and settled in Lisbon. He soon became famous for his charitable works and was popularly known as 'the father of the poor'. He toured the city daily collecting alms in the saddlebags of a donkey driven by a dwarf. At the end of the day he returned to the chapel of Our Lady of Mercy in the cathedral, where the alms were distributed to the poor. He founded a primitive hospital for the poor in a house near to the cathedral given to him by the city council. He also became famous as a preacher. It was inevitable that his charitable acts should commend him to Dona Leonor, herself a notable philanthropist, and she chose him as her confessor in 1498.

Historians are divided as to the precise rôle played by Contreiras in the foundation of the Misericórdia. There are two broad schools of thought. The first supports the theory that Contreiras suggested the foundation to Dona Leonor; that she established the brotherhood and that Contreiras drew up the statutes and was the first *Provedor*, or President of the board of guardians. The bulk of the evidence for this theory is supplied by the enquiry of 1574 made by the Trinitarians precisely in order to gain official recognition for Contreiras as the prime motivator of the foundation.

B

Although the Misericórdia agreed in 1575 that all banners of the branches of the brotherhood should carry the letters *F.M.I.*, signifying 'Frei Miguel Instituidor', this was diplomatic rather than historical recognition. The second school of thought plays down the importance of Contreiras and Dona Leonor, reducing the former to the position of priest to the brotherhood and the latter to that of royal sponsor. The evidence for this view is the prologue of the first extant *Compromisso*, or statutes, which refers to 'some good and faithful Christians' as the founders. The *Estatística de Lisboa* of 1552 suggests that a group of laymen were encouraged to found the brotherhood by Dona Leonor. These were: Mestre Miguel, possibly a doctor; Gonçalo Fernandes, a bookseller; João Rodrigues, a waxchandler; João Rodrigues Ronca; a Fleming, Contim do Paço, and a Valencian embroiderer. The two schools of thought are born of differences of interpretation; whereas the first regards the foundation of the Misericórdia as a unique event, the second places it in the historical context of lay social philanthropy in Portugal.[1]

Discussion of the identity of the founder has been centred on the respective rôles of the queen and the friar. The part played by the king, Dom Manuel I, has been neglected, although it was in his jurisdiction that the final authorisation of the brotherhood lay. Certainly he was not the direct instigator of the new brotherhood. In 1498 he was absent from Lisbon between 29 March and 9 October, the inauguration of the Misericórdia occurring on 15 August.[2] There is no reason for attributing significance to the fact that the Misericórdia was founded during the king's absence — if anything, it reinforces the spontaneous nature of the foundation by the group of laymen. There can be no doubt that within the first year of the existence of the Misericórdia, Dom Manuel recognised its possibilities as furthering the policy of centralisation of charitable services. On 14 March 1499 he wrote to the city elders of Oporto commending to them the foundation of a Misericórdia. At about the same time he petitioned the Pope for authorisation to merge small hospitals in Coimbra, Évora and Santarém into single

---

[1] The first view is held by Costa Godolphim, *As Misericordias* (Lisboa, 1897) and Vitor Ribeiro, *A Santa Casa da Misericordia de Lisboa* (*subsidios para a sua historia*) *1498–1898* (Historia e memorias da Academia Real das Sciencias de Lisboa, Nova Serie, 2ª Classe. Tomo ix, parte ii, Lisboa, 1902). Protagonists of the second are Magalhães Basto, op. cit., and F. da Silva Correia, *Estudos*.

[2] Damião de Góis, op. cit., part 1, chapters xxvi and xxxii.

large hospitals. The papal bull *Cum sit carissimus* sanctioning this was granted on 23 September 1499. On 12 September 1500, Dom Manuel wrote to the elders of Coimbra suggesting the foundation of a Misericórdia in that city.[1] In the mind of Dom Manuel, the policy of centralising hospital services came to include the fusion of other forms of social philanthropy into a single body — the Misericórdia. To further this policy he granted numerous privileges to the Misericórdia in its early years as a brotherhood.

During his lifetime Dom Manuel granted some thirty privileges to the Misericórdia, of which half were in the first three years of the brotherhood's existence. Prominent among the early privileges were those dealing with prison welfare. The *mordomos*, or stewards, of the Misericórdia had freedom of access to prisoners (13 September 1498) and were responsible for the cleanliness of the prisons in the city of Lisbon (15 April 1499). The brotherhood's duties also included the general assistance and sustenance of poor prisoners (10 September 1501). The course of Portuguese justice was sluggish. Prisoners spent long periods in jail before being brought to trial. This was especially the case of poor prisoners who could not meet the financial demands of petty officials, each determined to take his 'cut' of the legal costs. The true victim was the Misericórdia which had to feed such prisoners, and privileges were granted to the brotherhood to lessen this burden.

These privileges fell into two groups — legal and financial. To expedite the course of justice, court sessions to hear prisoners' cases were held weekly in the actual jail by the criminal judges, and fortnightly by the *corregidor* (10 October 1500). Legal costs of criminals exiled to S. Tomé, Príncipe or further afield were waived if a ship was available for their immediate transportation (16 October 1501). Also abolished were the rights of petty officials to claim gratuities before presenting a prisoner's case to the judge (22 January 1512) or for accompanying exiles from prison to the ships (29 February 1499). Special provision was made for slaves imprisoned in the Limoeiro, the principal jail of Lisbon. In cases where the owners refused to feed them, these were fed by the jailer from a daily allowance of 15 rs. In the event of the death of a slave, all costs were met by the master; if he were acquitted all costs had to be paid by the master before he was freed (27 February 1520). The Misericórdia was helped by the concession of

[1] F. da Silva Correia, *Estudos*, pp. 557 and 579–80.

rations of free meat supplied daily by the municipal officials for the imprisoned and sick assisted by the brotherhood (25 June 1513). Legal privileges were granted to the brotherhood. The *escrivão*, or scribe, had the status of a public notary during his year of office (10 October 1500). The attorney of the brotherhood had the privilege of speaking first in all court sessions (24 July 1499). It is easy to reduce the rôle of the Misericórdia to that of an association for prison aid. Possibly the king himself regarded this activity as the most important for he stressed this aspect in his letter of 1499 to the elders of Oporto. If so, the immediate success of the brotherhood led the king to modify his attitude and to cast the Misericórdia in a more general rôle. After 1500, privileges covering a wide range of charitable fields were granted to the brotherhood, thereby establishing the Misericórdia as the leading charitable brotherhood of Portugal.[1]

Indicative of this change of attitude by Dom Manuel were privileges which virtually gave the Misericórdia the monopoly of collecting alms in Lisbon, thereby sounding the death knell for the multitude of small brotherhoods in the capital. Only the Misericórdia was permitted to circulate collecting boxes in Lisbon (15 February 1499), and this privilege was extended in 1501 to the Ribatejo as far as the town of Alenquer.[2] In 1513, the Misericórdia was authorised to have fourteen assistants within the urban confines and fourteen in the neighbouring districts for the collection of alms for the charitable activities of the brotherhood. Infringement of these privileges by other brotherhoods resulted in fines payable to the Misericórdia (5 July 1517). At a time when Lisbon was teeming with collectors for papal bulls, the ransom of captives, dowries, orphans and the poor, the importance of these privileges granted to the Misericórdia cannot be overestimated.

Portuguese bureaucracy never has been notable for inter-departmental co-operation. Authorities resented the expanding activities of the Misericórdia and ignored its privileges. The Misericórdia complained to the king that legacies made to the brotherhood by Portuguese soldiers dying in Guinea and India were never received but remained in the hands of the Treasurers of the Captives. This was remedied by a royal privilege of 3 September 1507 ordering payment of such legacies to be made to the

[1] These privileges are recorded in the archives of the Misericórdia of Bahia (henceforth abbreviated to ASCMB), vols. 206, 207 and 209.

[2] Damião Peres, op. cit., vol. 4, p. 567.

Misericórdia. Even in continental Portugal, civil judges were remiss in informing the Misericórdia of legacies due to the brotherhood. Dom Manuel ordered that such lapses be punished and that public notaries be fined for such negligence (27 October 1514 and 17 April 1518). Privileges were granted to the officers of the brotherhood. During their year of office they could not be compelled to give lodging to soldiers in the king's service, nor were their houses, clothing or horses subject to confiscation. They were also exempt from municipal duties and taxes (3 May 1502). The Misericórdia enjoyed total autonomy and its brothers could not be ordered to take part in processions organised by the associations of artisans (15 February 1499). The privileges granted by Dom Manuel were confirmed by his successors. With the foundation of branches of the Misericórdia overseas, they were extended to provide for these new branches and frequently brought the brotherhood into conflict with the municipal, juridical and ecclesiastical authorities.

If the privileged position of the Misericórdia made it exceptional among Portuguese brotherhoods, the same cannot be said of its *Compromisso*, or statutes. The *Compromisso* was entirely traditional, both in concept and application. The loss of the original *Compromisso* of Lisbon makes it impossible to reconstruct the scope of the brotherhood as it was initially conceived. The earliest extant *Compromissos* are of the Misericórdias of Évora and Oporto and show only minor variations from the first printed *Compromisso* of Lisbon (1516).[1] This *Compromisso* and later reforms were followed by all branches of the Misericórdia both in continental Portugal and overseas.

The *Compromisso* of Lisbon of 1516 contained nineteen chapters. It opened with a summary of the seven spiritual and seven corporal works of charity to be practised by all brothers. These were:

Spiritual.
 1. Teach the ignorant.
 2. Give good counsel.
 3. Punish transgressors with understanding.

---

[1] The *Compromisso* of Évora differed from the 1516 *Compromisso* of Lisbon in having two additional chapters, the first nineteen coinciding in both sets of statutes. The earliest *Compromisso* of Évora is printed in Costa Godolphim, op. cit., pp. 434–57.

4. Console the sorrowful.
5. Pardon injuries received.
6. Suffer our neighbours' shortcomings.
7. Pray to God for the living and the dead.

Corporal.

1. Ransom captives and visit prisoners.
2. Cure the sick.
3. Clothe the naked.
4. Give food to the hungry.
5. Give drink to the thirsty.
6. Shelter travellers and the poor.
7. Bury the dead.

The brotherhood consisted of 100 members initially.[1] These were divided into two classes, numerically equal. The first was of *irmãos nobres* ('noble brothers'), sometimes known as *irmãos de maior condição* ('brothers of higher standing'). Nobility in this case did not necessarily imply nobility of blood, but included members of the gentry, the professional classes and ecclesiastics. The second was of plebeians, known as *oficiais mecânicos* ('members of the mechanical trades') or *irmãos de menor condição* ('brothers of lower standing').[2] All had to be of good repute, God fearing, serve the brotherhood without question, and congregate when summoned by the bell of the Misericórdia. Attendance at the Misericórdia was obligatory on three occasions during the year: the election of the *Mesa*, or board of guardians, on the day of the Visitation; the Maundy Thursday procession of penitents; the All Saints' day procession to the scaffold at St Barbara to collect the bones of the hanged and give them decent burial in the private cemetery of the Misericórdia. Expulsion from the brotherhood — except in blatant cases — could only be enforced after three admonitions by the

---

[1] The 1618 *Compromisso* fixed the number of brothers at 600 and some historians have taken this to apply to the initial membership, António da Silva Rêgo, *História das Missões do Padroado Português do Oriente. India. 1500–1542* (Lisboa, 1949), pp. 237–8.

[2] For further discussion of the finer distinctions between the two classes in Bahia see pp. 124–6.

Provedor. In return for his allegiance, the brother and his family received financial and medical aid if they were in need and a funeral attended by the brotherhood.

The *Mesa*, or board of guardians, consisted of thirteen brothers, six from each class. The *Provedor*, or President, was always chosen from the upper class. The election was indirect, viz. by an electoral committee of ten brothers chosen by the body of the brotherhood. In addition to the Provedor, the board of guardians consisted of the *escrivão*, or scribe, nine counsellors and two *mordomos* or stewards. All were elected for a yearly term of office, except the stewards who were elected monthly because of their heavy duties. The results of the election were announced on 3 July when the new Mesa took the oath.

The Provedor was always a person of good social standing and of financial means. He defended the Misericórdia against the incursions of civil and ecclesiastical authorities on the privileges of the brotherhood. He also delegated duties to the brothers, but only in minor decisions did he have independence of action. He was obliged to convene the Mesa on all matters of policy, the dispatching of petitions and financial transactions. To keep in touch with the brotherhood's activities, he was obliged by statute to make monthly visits to the prison, the hospital and the needy maintained by the Misericórdia, to ensure that the alms were being properly applied.

The scribe was responsible for the supervision of the ledgers of the brotherhood and the minutes of the Mesa. He and the remaining nine guardians formed five pairs, each composed of one noble and one plebeian, to each of which was allocated a specific duty. The first visited the sick at home and in hospital, providing food, medicine and bed-clothing where necessary. The second also visited the sick in their homes and in prison, distributing medicine and clothes, but devoting more attention to the spiritual welfare of the sick. The third provided for the material welfare of prisoners: on Sundays they distributed to the most needy a meat chop, a pint of wine and bread; on Wednesdays the ration consisted of bread and wine. The fourth pair, the scribe and one guardian, gave alms to people who had fallen on evil days and had been recommended to the Misericórdia by parish priests. The fifth dealt with financial matters, collecting alms, rents and legacies. The duties of the stewards were distinct. The *mordomo da capela* was responsible for the fabric of the chapel, alms, burials and masses. The *mordomo de fora* provided legal aid for prisoners and paid any fees necessary before they could be released.

All the brothers assisted in the activities of the brotherhood, but the Misericórdia also employed a small staff. A chaplain and two assistant chaplains officiated at mass, gave the sacraments to the dying and conducted funeral services. Other employees included servants to clean the chapel and for general duties. The brothers were helped by volunteers in the collection of alms and bread for the prisoners after Sunday mass. The fabric of the brotherhood consisted of the chapel silver and vestments, the banner of the Misericórdia, the bell to call the brothers, two coffers for money and clothes, a bier for the funerals of brothers and a litter for the funerals of poor people. The brotherhood had two more litters to carry the bodies of the hanged or the remains of criminals who had been quartered and placed on the city gates, back to the Misericórdia cemetery for burial.

The *Compromisso* of 1516 was modified by later reforms. In some cases the functions became out of date; in others the Misericórdia took on new obligations. Administrative experience also dictated amendments. The historian of the Misericórdia of Rio de Janeiro, Felix Ferreira, proposed numerous reforms within the first century of the brotherhood's existence. He suggested the first reform as occurring between the date of foundation and the date of the printed *Compromisso* of 1516. Basing his suppositions on royal decrees designating new duties to the Misericórdia, for example, the administration of the Hospital of All Saints in 1564, he indicated further reforms in 1564, 1577, 1582 and 1600. These decrees did extend the activities of the Misericórdia but it is rather exaggerated to regard them as reforms. The greatest single reform of the brotherhood was in 1618. A new *Compromisso* was formulated, modifying not only the administration but the spirit in which the Misericórdia had been conceived.[1]

The rapid growth of branches of the Misericórdia was the result of the happy coincidence of royal aspirations and popular sentiment. It is difficult to estimate accurately the date of foundation of many branches, in part because of the common usage of the title *Misericórdia*, and in part because many brotherhoods tried to benefit from the popularity of the *Santa Casa* and adopted this name. Within the year 1498, ten branches were founded in addition to the Misericórdia of Lisbon. Of these, eight were in Portugal

[1] For a discussion of conflicting opinions see Vitor Ribeiro, op. cit., pp. 53–4.

and two in Madeira. By 1524, when Dona Leonor died, every town and many villages of Portugal had a *Santa Casa da Misericórdia*, making a total of sixty-one following the *Compromisso* of the parent house in Lisbon.[1]

This rapid growth of the brotherhood was not limited to Portugal. The development of commercial routes to India and the Far East and the opportunities offered by the lucrative interport trade based on Nagasaki–Macao–Malacca–Gôa led to the establishment of Portuguese colonies in all these cities. When the glitter of the golden East was waning, royal interest turned to Brazil, where the founding of Misericórdias often coincided with the establishment of the first townships.

[1] F. da Silva Correia, *Estudos*, pp. 581–2 corrects some of the dates given by Costa Godolphim, op. cit., pp. 85–423.

2

The Santas Casas da Misericórdia in Asia, Africa and Brazil

PORTUGUESE chroniclers went to great lengths to stress the divine nature of the expansion. But even they became confused by the increasing presence of Mammon. The crusading zeal, not to say obsession, which had led to the capture of Ceuta in 1415, became blended with the realisation of the profits in gold and slaves to be gained from the regions of the Niger and Senegal rivers. Although the sixteenth-century chronicler, João de Barros, affirmed that the fort of S. Jorge da Mina (started in 1482) was the 'foundation stone of the Church in the Orient', in reality it was never more than a trading post.[1] Exploratory probings along the west African coast and the psychological as well as physical passage beyond Cape Nun, culminated in the rounding of the Cape of Good Hope by Bartholomeu Dias in 1488. This maritime achievement had its terrestrial counterpart. Pero de Covilhã left Lisbon in 1487 and travelled overland to the coast of Malabar, returning *via* the Persian Gulf, the Red Sea and the east coast of Africa where he was possibly the first European to visit Sofala. While in Cairo he managed to send to Dom João II a report containing details of the spice trade. He then went on to Abyssinia where he was held by the legendary Prester John. It is not certain if Dom João II ever saw this report; if he did the details of the spice trade must have weighed as heavily on the mind of the king, if not more so, as the physical achievement of the rounding of the Cape.

[1] João de Barros squared his conscience by saying that the Negroes found most alert in trade would be most suitable for conversion, *Ásia. Dos feitos que os portugueses fizeram no descobrimento e conquista dos mares e terras do Oriente. 4 Décadas* (4 vols., 6th ed., Lisboa, 1945–6), primeira década, livro 3, capítulo 1. For a description of this fort see A. W. Lawrence, *Trade Castles and Forts of West Africa* (London, 1963), pp. 103–15.

The preparations made by Dom João II were to result in the voyage of Vasco da Gama to India in the reign of Dom Manuel I, 'The Fortunate'. What Vasco da Gama had discovered, Affonso de Albuquerque consolidated by the capture of Gôa (1510), the chief port of the India trade, and Malacca (1511), the key port of the spice trade. The Portuguese built a fort on Socotra in 1506 but this had little effect in reducing trade through the Red Sea.[1] The decline of the Levant only started after the capture of Hormuz in the Persian Gulf by Albuquerque in 1515. In addition to these key centres the Portuguese maintained trading 'factories' at Calicut (1500), Cochin (1500), Cannanore (1502) and Kilwa (1503). These were often threatened by attack and a fort had been built in Cochin in 1503; in 1506 the Viceroy, Dom Francisco de Almeida, replaced this by a stone structure. Forts were built in the other trading centres and, with the sense of protection they offered, small Portuguese settlements formed in and around them. In 1508 Cannanore boasted a fort, a hospital, two churches, warehouses and a powder factory. These fortified settlements were complemented on the east African coast by the fortresses at Mozambique, Sofala and, in the last decade of the sixteenth century, Fort Jesus at Mombasa. Beyond Malacca the Portuguese never enjoyed the monopoly of trade they achieved in the Indian Ocean. They profited from the Sino-Japanese trade embargo by acting as carriers for Chinese gold and silk and Japanese silver and copper. The granting of extra-territorial rights at Macao (1555–7) and the trading centre at Nagasaki completed a commercial cycle of inter-complementary wares reaching from Sofala to the Moluccas, with the accompanying colonies or pockets of Portuguese.

Portugal faced a chronic shortage of manpower in the East. The Viceroy, Dom Francisco de Almeida (1505–9), tried to solve this by encouraging his soldiers to marry respectable local girls. The response on the part of the women, willing to embrace Christianity wholeheartedly in return for the perquisites offered by the viceroy, was so overwhelming that Almeida was compelled to abandon this policy. Affonso de Albuquerque (Governor, 1509–15), faced by a lack of soldiers and trained artisans, advocated marriage as a means of stabilising the floating Portuguese population. He offered

---

[1] G. W. F. Stripling, *The Ottoman Turks and the Arabs,* 1511–1574 (Illinois Studies in the Social Sciences, vol. 26, no. 4; Urbana, Illinois, 1942), overstates the importance of the Portuguese capture of Socotra in hastening the decline of the Levant.

privileges and financial rewards to soldiers marrying the daughters and widows of Brahmins or Muslims converted to Christianity. The results were disappointing.[1] Albuquerque failed to understand the caste system and was opposed by the Portuguese clergy. Moreover, most Portuguese soldiers preferred casual sexual alliances with Kaffir imports and the local dancing girls.[2] The motives of Albuquerque were misinterpreted at court and Dom Manuel ordered such marriages to cease. Later governors and viceroys followed a modified marriage policy and small colonies of married Portuguese were formed in the major ports and trading posts.

These men followed the traditional way of life of communities in Portugal. Brotherhoods had played an important rôle in community life in the villages and towns of Portugal. Portuguese soldiers and artisans who had gone to the East founded new branches of these brotherhoods with statutes modelled on the parent bodies in Portugal. Misericórdias were established throughout the East and followed the *Compromisso* of Lisbon with minor amendments dictated by local conditions. The activities of these brotherhoods and of the Jesuit missionaries counteract the unedifying picture of the Portuguese expansion which can all too easily, and even often justifiably, be reduced to a struggle for trading supremacy west of Malacca and brazen piracy in the South China Sea and beyond.

Portuguese chroniclers and historians themselves have done little to correct this impression of rapine and bloodshed. The only two histories of Misericórdias in the East are of the branches at Gôa and Macao. In Africa only the Misericórdia of Luanda has been described in a small monograph.[3] An outline of these branches of the Misericórdia in Asia and Africa will place their Brazilian counterparts in greater perspective.

---

[1] By April 1512 there had been 200 marriages in Gôa and 100 in Cochin and Cannanore. Marriages were suspended in the latter part of the year because of lack of money for dowries, Affonso de Albuquerque, *Cartas* (7 vols., Lisboa, 1884–1935), vol. 1, cartas ix and xl.

[2] C. R. Boxer, 'Fidalgos portuguêses e bailadeiras indianas (séculos xvii e xviii), in *Revista de História*, no. 45 (São Paulo, 1961), pp. 83–105.

[3] J. F. Ferreira Martins, *Historia da Misericordia de Goa (1520–1910)* (3 vols., Nova Goa, 1910–14); José Caetano Soares, *Macau e a Assistência (Programa médico-social)* (Lisboa, 1950); Pe. António Brásio, 'As Misericórdias de Angola' in *Studia*, vol. 4 (July 1959, Centro de Estudos Históricos Ultramarinos, Lisboa), pp. 106–49.

The Misericórdia of Gôa was probably founded during the governorship of Lopo Soares (1515–18), although the first documents, referring to fines being allocated to the brotherhood, only date from 1519.[1] The Misericórdia of Gôa followed the *Compromisso* of Lisbon. This had been so modified to provide for local conditions that in 1595 three equally valid *Compromissos* governed the brotherhood, giving rise to much administrative confusion. The Mesa of 1595 formulated yet another *Compromisso*, which was a compilation of its predecessors. This remained in force until the adoption by Gôa of the 1618 *Compromisso* of Lisbon. The privileges enjoyed by the Misericórdia of Lisbon were extended to the branch in Gôa by a royal decree of 31 January 1605.

The brotherhood developed rapidly from 100 members initially to some 600 in 1609. The brothers were divided into the two classes of nobles and plebeians, as in Lisbon. This balance was not always maintained with harmony because of the dearth of artisans. Different Provedors tried to restore the balance in various ways. The Count of Alvor (Provedor, 1686) simply elected brothers of the upper class in excess of the number stipulated by the *Compromisso* to serve on the board of guardians. Thomé Freire (Provedor, 1685–6), who completed the term of office of the Count of Alvor after his recall to Portugal, arbitrarily transferred some brothers from among the gentry to the lower class of the plebeians. This aroused great opposition and many brothers of higher standing were expelled from the Misericórdia because of their refusal to accept this indignity.

The Misericórdia of Gôa was to the East what that of Bahia was to Brazil. Positions on its Mesa were strongly contested. The frequency of 'rigged' elections led the Archbishop, Dom Aleixo de Meneses, in 1608 to threaten to excommunicate any brothers of the Mesa found guilty of electoral dishonesty.[2] Here, as in Bahia, threats of excommunication were disregarded and in 1742 the governor ordered the imprisonment of Pedro da Silva Alva after he had been elected Provedor by dubious means. Membership of the

[1] J. F. Ferreira Martins (op. cit., vol. 1, pp. 100 et seq.) attempts to credit Affonso de Albuquerque with the foundation, but the documented arguments for a later foundation presented by António da Silva Rêgo, *História*, pp. 237–42 are more convincing in the absence of definite proof of the date of foundation.

[2] The alert soldier-chronicler Diogo do Couto remarked on the rigged elections of the Misericórdia, *O soldado prático* (Lisboa, 1937) ed. Rodrigues Lapa, Iª parte, cena x, pp. 118–19.

Mesa ranked with a post on the *Câmara*, or city council, as a testimonial of integrity and ability. Viceroys and governors often chose the incumbents of these positions for higher offices such as the command of a fortress or the controllership of a 'factory'.

The prestige of the Misericórdia was such that governors, viceroys, archbishops, inquisitors and ministers of justice served as Provedors. A governor as Provedor was a boon and a bane for the brotherhood. He defended the interests of the Misericórdia, but it was to the coffers of the brotherhood that he turned when those of the Treasury were empty. The defence of Malacca against the Dutch was a case in point. Indifferent success by the Viceroy, Dom Martim Affonso de Castro, turned to despair with the Dutch attack on the fleet of Nuno Pereira. The viceroy sent to Gôa for money to rebuild the armada. The coffers of the Treasury were empty and the acting governor, the Archbishop Dom Aleixo de Meneses, made a compulsory loan from the Misericórdia of 25,026 *xerafines* in 1607, pledging the archiepiscopal crosier and cathedral silver as securities. This enforced loan was made in direct defiance of a royal decree forbidding the Misericórdia to place on loan money left to the brotherhood by soldiers who had died in India for transmission to relatives in Portugal. Despite the royal indignation at the action of the archbishop, the funds of the Misericórdia were to be further depleted by loans for defence and trade. In 1621 the city council borrowed 100,000 *xerafines* from the Misericórdia to fit out galleons for the relief of Hormuz. In 1653 another loan of 15,000 *xerafines* was made by the Misericórdia to the city council for the relief of Colombo. Nor did the Crown ignore this source of finance. In 1642 Dom João IV wrote to the board of guardians of the Misericórdia of Gôa requesting the loan of 220,000 *xerafines* to buy pepper for the homeward-bound fleet. This loan was to be repaid to the Misericórdia of Lisbon as trustees of soldiers who had died in the Orient.[1] The policy of the Misericórdia on the granting of such loans was ambivalent. Boards of guardians usually complied in cases where the national interest was at stake, such as the defence of Ceylon, Gôa or Mombasa. They were more reluctant to grant loans for unspecified purposes. In the final analysis, such loans depended on the Provedor. Fernão de Albuquerque, who as Provedor in 1607 had resisted the compulsory loan for the defence of Malacca, later tried to browbeat the Misericórdia

[1] J. F. Ferreira Martins, op. cit., vol. 1, pp. 312–16 and vol. 2, pp. 41, 48 and 72.

into lending money for the help of Hormuz when he was viceroy.

Gôa was of vital importance to the Portuguese as the final port of the *carreira da India*, or India run, and as a wayport for the Far East. A hospital had existed in Gôa from shortly after the conquest in 1510, but it is not clear if this was administered by the Misericórdia or the municipality at this early date. Later these two bodies were to have their own hospitals. The Misericórdia maintained the Hospital of All Saints and the municipality the Hospital of Our Lady of Mercy (*Nossa Senhora da Piedade*). Until the Jesuits founded a hospital in 1630, the Hospital of All Saints was the only hospital in Gôa to cater for all, irrespective of race or creed. Increasingly heavy expenditure on the hospital in the seventeenth century placed the Misericórdia in severe financial difficulties. In 1680 agreement was reached with the city council for the amalgamation of the Hospital of All Saints with the Hospital of Our Lady of Mercy. The Misericórdia received a small grant from the municipality towards the expenses of running the combined hospital. The complete amalgamation was only realised in 1706 and from this date the hospital was known as the Hospital of the Poor.[1] A subsidiary of the hospital was the leper house, maintained by the Misericórdia from its own funds. Independent of these hospitals was the Royal Hospital of the Holy Spirit, a state institution for the treatment of Portuguese on the royal service. In 1542 the administration of this hospital was handed to the Misericórdia. The financial terms were extremely favourable to the brotherhood, and the Misericórdia was exempt from all civil or ecclesiastical interference in the administration of this hospital. This transfer of the administration from state authorities to a private body is indicative of the prestige of the Misericórdia. In 1591 the Viceroy, Mathias de Albuquerque, handed over the administration to the Jesuits. Whether this action was born of personal antipathy towards the Misericórdia or was the result of administrative deficiencies by the brotherhood, is not clear. In 1608 the French traveller, François Pyard de Laval, was lavish in his praise of the hospital while still under Jesuit jurisdiction.[2] Another Frenchman, Jean-Baptiste

---

[1] J. F. Ferreira Martins, op. cit., vol. 2, pp. 69 and 338–41.

[2] He described it as 'un Hospital, vrayement Royal, excellent et magnifique', *Voyage de François Pyrard de Laval, contenant sa navegation aux Indes Orientales, Maldives, Moluques, Bresil* (2 vols., 3rd ed., Paris, 1619), vol. 1, chapter xxix and vol. 2, chapter i.

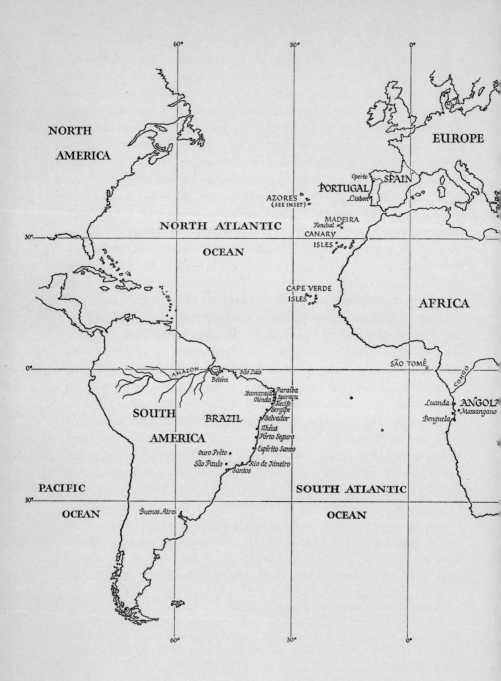

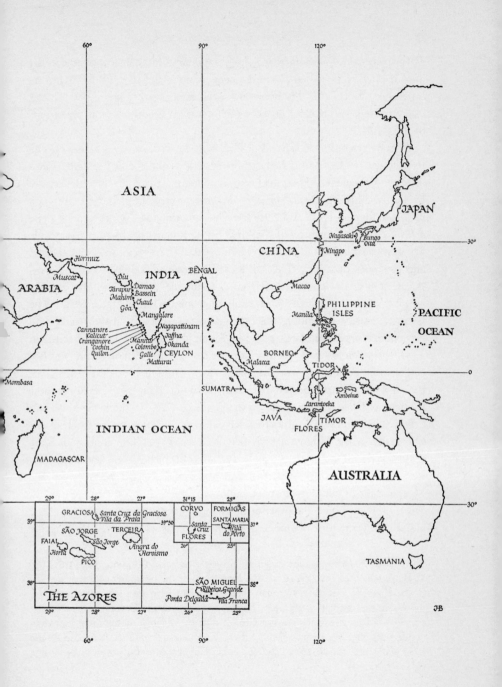

Tavernier, who visited Gôa for the second time in 1648, commented that the hospital at Gôa had formerly been famous throughout India for its excellence, 'but, since this hospital has changed its managers, patients are badly treated, and many Europeans who enter it do not leave it save to go to the tomb'.[1]

The Misericórdia of Gôa also administered two retirement houses, the Retirement House of Our Lady of the Mountain and the Retirement House of Mary Magdalene. These had been founded in 1598 and 1610 respectively by the Archbishop Dom Aleixo de Meneses. Orphan girls were always a problem for the local authorities. The situation was aggravated by the *orfãs del Rei*, or 'orphans of the king'; these were orphans of marriageable age sent from Lisbon to India to be married. The Crown paid all expenses and provided dowries. The Misericórdia arranged lodging with a Portuguese family, the city council found a suitable partner and the viceroy arranged a dowry usually consisting of a minor bureaucratic post. The Crown persisted in sending these girls despite protests from the viceroy and city councillors that nobody could be found to marry them. The promise of a post in some isolated 'factory' or fortress in the distant future was not sufficient inducement to woo the soldiers away from their doxies. Moreover, the orphan girls prejudiced the chances of the daughters of Portuguese soldiers who had died in India on the king's service, although the king later granted the latter equal rights to receive dowries. The Retirement House of Our Lady of the Mountain provided for such girls. The conditions were that they should be white, Catholic and of good birth. The last stipulation was often ignored and viceroys and governors exerted pressure on the Misericórdia to admit women of dubious virtue. After the foundation of this retirement house the practice of giving offices as dowries was abolished and all dowries were in money, and paid by the Treasury. Respectable

---

[1] *Travels in India by Jean Baptiste Tavernier* (2 vols., London, 1889; trans. by V. Ball), vol. 1, p. 198. In 1675 John Fryer praised the treatment of the sick in the Royal Hospital, but observed that 'The Physicians here are great Bleeders, insomuch that they exceed often *Galen's advice, ad deliquium*, in Fevers; hardly leaving enough to feed the Currents for Circulation; of which Cruelty some complain invidiously after Recovery', John Fryer, *A new account of East India and Persia being nine years' travels 1672–1681* (3 vols., Hakluyt Society, London, 1909–15), vol. 2, p. 14.

widows and wives abandoned by their husbands were also admitted as paying lodgers.

The morality of Indo-Portuguese womanhood left much to be desired. The Dutch navigator Linschoten (1563–1611) commented on the difficulties facing a chaste woman and the prevalence of adultery in Gôa. The Retirement House of Mary Magdalene was intended for 'women who have repented and been converted from their evil way of life'. Only white women were admitted and the regulations were strict. By offering a place of refuge the Misericórdia provided an alternative to flight into Moslem territory and conversion to Islam. The brotherhood contributed to the national marriage policy by contacting branches in Malacca, Macao, Angola and even Brazil. Women were sent from Gôa to these branches, travelling under the supervision of a guardian and with their expenses paid by the Treasury which also supplied a dowry in the event of marriage.

The ransom of captives and care of prisoners were included in the obligations of all brothers of the Misericórdia. Branches of the Misericórdia co-operated in the ransom of Portuguese who had fallen into enemy hands, be these in Arabia or India. Priority was given to white captives and to women and children because they were more likely to be converted to Islam. In 1623 the Misericórdia of Gôa contacted the branch in S. Tomé de Meliapor on the Coromandel coast to arrange for the ransom of captives of the Pegu war. On many occasions Jesuit missionaries were used as intermediaries. The care of prisoners by the Misericórdia evoked the praise of François Pyrard de Laval and will be fully treated in Chapter 10. The French traveller was also favourably impressed by the action of the Misericórdia of Gôa as trustees for Portuguese who died in India or the Far East. There can be no doubt that the Misericórdia of Gôa fulfilled the obligations of the *Compromisso* to the full and was the most powerful branch of the brotherhood in the Orient.

Frequently it is easier to establish the date of extinction of a Misericórdia than the date of foundation. This is the case of the branches at Colombo, taken by the Dutch in 1656, and Jaffna which suffered a similar fate in 1658. The money and jewels of both branches were sent to Gôa. The treasure of the latter was captured by the Dutch while in transit but representations by the Misericórdia of Gôa led to complete restitution by the Dutch. Certainly by 1600, Misericórdias had been established at Cochin, Chaul, Diu, Malacca, Bassein, Hormuz, Cannanore, S. Tomé and Mannar.[1]

The Misericórdia of Macao was the most important branch in the Far East. It was founded with a hospital in about 1569 by the Bishop, Dom Belchior Carneiro, so horrified was he by the brutal manner in which the Chinese treated their sick.[2] At a later date the Misericórdia refused to admit heathen Chinese to the hospital, in part because of the large numbers needing medical aid, and in part because if a Chinese died in the hospital the mandarins would sue the brotherhood for compensation to be made to the family. One eighteenth-century Provedor, Francisco Rangel, went to jail rather than accede to the demands of the Governor Francisco de Melo e Castro for the admission of a seriously sick heathen Chinese. The brotherhood also maintained a leper house with regulations reminiscent of similar houses in Portugal in the thirteenth century.

Macao also had its female problem. Kaffir girls, Malayans and Chinese *bichas* scrounged alms from the Misericórdia by such subterfuges as holding animals under their robes to appear pregnant, or sending their transvestite lovers to collect the alms. There was much illegitimacy. The Misericórdia paid for the upkeep of foundlings for seven years and then stopped further aid. In some cases wet-nurses, who had relied on this source of income, had no alternative to prostitution once the foundling was raised. During the seventeenth century the brotherhood made casual provision for older female orphans and even offered dowries valid for four years. Only in 1727 was an orphanage established by the Misericórdia. This catered for twenty orphans and accepted some widows as paying lodgers. Within ten years the brotherhood was compelled to close this orphanage because of financial straits.

The Misericórdia of Macao made its own *Compromisso* in 1627. In 1639 the privileges of the Misericórdia of Lisbon were extended to the branch in

---

[1] J. F. Ferreira Martins, op. cit., vol. 1, p. 174 lists the following additional branches of the Misericórdia as sixteenth-century foundations — Calicut, Bengal, Damao, Mahim, Mangalore, Manila, Muscat, Tarapur, Negapattinam and Sena. A more comprehensive list of branches in the Orient is in *Actas do IV Congresso das Misericórdias* (3 vols., Lisboa, 1959), vol. 1, p. 173.

[2] José Caetano Soares, op. cit., p. 12. This contrasts with the praise of Galeote Pereira and Gaspar da Cruz for the hospitals of mainland China about the same time, C. R. Boxer, *South China in the Sixteenth Century* (London, 1953), pp. 30–1 and p. 123.

Macao 'in view of its extreme remoteness and its situation among un-
believers'.[1] As had been the case in Gôa, elections were 'rigged' and capital
was lent on poor securities. Money to finance the Japan voyages was often
borrowed from funds earmarked for the care of orphans.[2] Little is known
of the Misericórdias beyond Macao. In the annual Jesuit letter of 1585,
Padre Luís Frois referred to the foundation of a Misericórdia at Nagasaki,
with 100 brothers and following the *Compromisso* of Macao.[3] There may
also have been branches at Bungo and other places in Japan where there
were small nuclei of Portuguese. There are similarly vague references to
branches at Amboina and Tidor in the Moluccas. The Spanish Brotherhood
of Mercy (*Hermandad de la Misericordia*) at Manila in the Philippines, which
financed the Acapulco galleons, was closely related to its Portuguese namesake.[4]

On the east coast of Africa the strategic position of Mozambique as a
waystation for Indiamen and later as a trading centre for the Monomotapa
gold mines, had demanded a hospital for the care of soldiers. This evoked
the praise of successive generations of Jesuit visitors, but it appears that the
Misericórdia did no more than administer it on behalf of the Crown. The
brotherhood must have enjoyed a position of importance because it possessed the same municipal administrative privilege as the branch in Diu in
the election of the *almotacés*, or weights and measures inspectors.[5] Elsewhere on the Swahili coast the pockets of Portuguese at the 'factories' of
Kilwa, Mafia, Pemba, Zanzibar and Patta were never sufficiently numerous
to form brotherhoods. Mombasa was the exception, being the commercial

1 Royal letter of 15 January 1639 in *Arquivos de Macau* (Macau, 1929 in progress), 3ª Série, vol. 2, no. 2, August 1964, p. 127.

2 C. R. Boxer, *The Great Ship from Amacon, Annals of Macao and the Old Japan
Trade, 1555–1640* (Lisboa, 1963, reprint of work first published in 1959), p. 51.

3 *Cartas que os padres e irmãos da Companhia de Jesus escreverão dos reynos de
Iapão e China aos da mesma Companhia da India, e Europa, desde anno de 1549 até o de
1580* (2 parts, Évora, 1598), part 2, ff. 129–30 apud C. R. Boxer, *The Great Ship*,
p. 48. João Rodrigues Giram, S.J., referred to 1500 *cruzados* received in alms by the
Nagasaki Misericórdia in his *Carta anua da vice-província do Japão do ano de 1604*
(ed. António Baião, Coimbra, 1933), p. 43.

4 For details of the financial dealings of this branch of the Misericórdia, see
W. L. Schurz, *The Manila Galleon* (New York, 1959, new edition of work first
published in 1939), pp. 167–72.

5 J. F. Ferreira Martins, op. cit., vol. 3, pp. 446–7 and pp. 460–1.

centre for the coast. After the building of Fort Jesus in 1593, enough Portuguese settled there to form a Misericórdia.[1]

On the west coast of Africa Portuguese interest was directed to Angola. Initially, Portuguese activity was limited to illegal slave trading and a futile expedition to report on mineral sources. In 1557 an ambassador from the Ngola arrived in Lisbon and the Portuguese became aware of the possibilities of the country. A commercial attitude gave way to the desire for conquest. A charter of 1571 divided Angola into two parts under the administration of Paulo Dias de Novais in the dual capacity of governor and hereditary ruler. He arrived in Luanda in 1575 and moved the city from the island to the continent in the following year, founding a Misericórdia on the advice of the Jesuit priest Garcia Simões. The Misericórdia achieved its greatest prominence in the seventeenth century. The brotherhood found a powerful ally and protector in the Bishop and Governor (1621–4), Dom Frei Simão Mascarenhas, who reformed the hospital. Another Bishop of the Congo and Angola, Dom Francisco do Soveral, was a benefactor to the brotherhood. He donated money for alms and his generosity enabled work to be finished on the four wards of the hospital. In 1679 a new church was built. By the 1680s the Misericórdia counted some seventy brothers, was financially prosperous with alms from private donors and grants from the Treasury and cured some 400 sick each year in the hospital. This prosperity did not last. The cost of treating soldiers, prison visits and distributing alms reduced the brotherhood to dire straits. In 1695 the Misericórdia was granted the preference in the sale of 500 slaves annually — an unusual concession to a charitable body! But even this measure failed to restore the brotherhood and by 1750 the Misericórdia of Luanda was totally decadent.

A continuous thorn in the flesh of the Luanda Misericórdia was the branch established at Massangano about 1660. The principal bone of contention was the hospital run by the Misericórdia of Massangano, serving the garrisons of Muxima, Cambembe and Ambaca. The Misericórdia in Luanda alleged it was suffering a severe loss of income from fees normally received for the treatment of these soldiers. Moreover, the branch at Massangano received alms previously given to the Misericórdia in Luanda and by its very presence reduced the authority of the parent body. These

---

[1] António da Silva Rêgo, *Documentação para a história das Missões do Padroado Português do Oriente. India* (12 vols., Lisboa, 1947–58), vol. 12, no. 2, cap⁰ 33.

complaints were born of self interest and the Misericórdia survived in Massangano because of the immediate medical treatment it offered to soldiers wounded in the campaigns.

On the other side of the Atlantic the discovery of Brazil (1500) had made little initial impact on Dom Manuel. The reports of Cabral and Vespucci had not been sufficiently attractive to woo the king away from his obsession with the Golden East. Dom Manuel had committed himself to the task of justifying the title he had assumed of 'Lord of the Conquest, Navigation, and Commerce of India, Ethiopia, Arabia and Persia'. Nor, indeed, had the small population of Portugal permitted the deployment of manpower in the Americas as well as throughout Africa and Asia. The Portuguese Crown had simply leased parts of Brazil to individual speculators on a contract basis. The first such concession had been granted to a group of New Christian businessmen under Fernão de Noronha. This group had agreed to send six ships annually to Brazil, undertake exploration and provide for the defence of the newly discovered territories. In return they had been granted the monopoly on all exports, including Brazil wood. If Dom Manuel, blinded by the glitter of the Orient, had ignored his new discovery, other European nations had not dismissed its importance so summarily. Breton and French corsairs who had attacked Portuguese shipping in the North Atlantic had now turned their attentions south of the equator. They had established friendly relations with the Tupinambá Indians in Brazil and soon the illegal French trade in Brazil wood had showed a larger turnover than that of the official Portuguese contractors. Free of the restrictions and taxes imposed by the terms of contract, the French had out-bid their Portuguese rivals in the purchase of Brazil wood. They had been able to offer this commodity at lower prices on the European market, especially in Flanders where the dye was important in the textile industry. Despite diplomatic representations by the Portuguese Crown, these traders had continued their activities mainly in Pernambuco and Bahia. In this piracy they had received the semi-official support of the French Crown which challenged the validity of the Treaty of Tordesillas (1494) dividing the new-found world between Spain and Portugal with papal sanction.

The continued incursions by French traders along the Brazilian coast had led to a deterioration in diplomatic relations between France and Portugal. In 1526 a fleet of six ships had left Lisbon under the command of Cristóvão

Jacques with the specific object of attacking and destroying any French pirates in Brazilian waters. After establishing a 'factory' in Pernambuco opposite the Island of Itamaracá, Cristóvão Jacques had sailed south with a squadron of four ships and had entered the Bay of All Saints in 1527. He had surprised and captured three French ships loading wood in the interior of the bay near the mouth of the River Paraguaçú and had taken some 300 prisoners. In 1530 Dom João III had dispatched a fleet of five sail under Martim Affonso de Sousa to dispel the French raiders and re-establish Portuguese superiority. Martim Affonso de Sousa had captured three French vessels at Pernambuco and then patrolled the coast southwards, stopping at the Bay of All Saints, and the bays of Guanabara and Cananéia. His plans to reconnoitre the River Plate were frustrated by shipwreck, and he returned to the Island of São Vicente. He established two townships, one on the island itself and the other some leagues inland on the edge of the plateau of Piratininga. Before the report of Martim Affonso de Sousa on his successful colonisation had reached Portugal, a single incident had brought home to Dom João III the need for a definite policy towards Brazil. This incident had been the capture of the French vessel *La Pèlerine* by a Portuguese squadron in the Straits of Gibraltar in 1532. Investigation had revealed that *La Pèlerine* was carrying a cargo of Brazil wood and had landed some seventy men in Pernambuco with a view to colonisation. The Portuguese 'factory' there had been destroyed. On the safe arrival of *La Pèlerine* at Marseilles, a fleet of between ten and thirty vessels would be dispatched to Brazil. This episode had compelled Dom João III to consider the colonisation of Brazil.

In 1532 Dom João III decided to grant hereditary captaincies in Brazil to anyone capable of raising sufficient capital and who would guarantee to defend the area under his jurisdiction. In the years 1534–5 captaincies were allocated to twelve donatories. Each donatory had wide jurisdiction. He could establish townships, levy taxes, appoint municipal officers and allocate grants of land for cultivation. The Crown reserved for itself only the right to impose export taxes and the monopoly on Brazil wood. The criteria for selection of the donatories favoured men brought up in the cut and thrust atmosphere of Portuguese India. One notable exception was the historian João de Barros, a partner in the captaincy of Rio Grande. This form of colonisation failed. Soldiers seldom made good civilian administrators and many donatories never even visited their captaincies. The only successful donatories were Martim Affonso de Sousa in São Vicente and Duarte Coelho in Pernambuco, both of whom established sugar cane plantations.

The overall failure of the donatory system and renewed French interest led Dom João III to appoint Tomé de Sousa as Governor-General of Brazil in 1549. He had served with distinction in the campaigns in Morocco and India. His *Regimento*, or brief, was comprehensive. Clauses dealt with the broad issues of defence, colonisation, the propagation of Catholicism and commerce. A fortified administrative centre was to be established in Bahia and the Tupinambás subjugated. Grants of land in the Recôncavo were to be made to suitable settlers for cultivation and the building of sugar mills was to be encouraged. Once this had been done, Tomé de Sousa was to make a visit of inspection to the other captaincies. He was to ensure that the law was enforced and enact measures designed to help commerce. He was also to assure himself of the adequacy of the defences against attack from the land by Indians and from the sea by pirates. Every effort was to be made to convert the Indians to catholicism. Once a degree of public order had been established in the coastal areas, expeditions were to be sent to explore the interior. Dom João III had reminded his governor-general that his overall aim should be 'the exaltation of our Holy Faith and profit of my Realms and Dominions and the subjects thereof'.[1] The measure of success achieved by Tomé de Sousa and following governors was readily apparent in the rapid establishment of towns along the Brazilian littoral and increasing colonisation of the interior.

The honour of the first Misericórdia to be founded in Brazil is disputed by the Captaincies of São Vicente and Pernambuco. Historians are generally agreed that pride of place should go to the brotherhood in Santos, founded by Bras Cubas in 1543.[2] This foundation was confirmed by royal *alvará*, or charter, of April 1551. In many cases the foundation of a Misericórdia was

---

[1] This *Regimento* is published in I. Accioli–B. Amaral, *Memorias historicas e politicas da provincia da Bahia* (6 vols., Bahia, 1919–40), vol. 1, pp. 263–74.

[2] F. A. de Varnhagen, *História geral do Brasil* (2 vols., Rio de Janeiro, 1854–7), vol. 1, p. 303; Robert Southey, *History of Brazil* (3 vols., London 1810–19), vol. 3, p. 850; Ernesto de Sousa Campos, *Santa Casa da Misericórdia de Santos* (São Paulo, 1943); Serafim Leite S.J., *História da Companhia de Jesus no Brasil* (10 vols., Rio de Janeiro–Lisboa, 1938–50), vol. 1, p. 262, agrees with the date of foundation but doubts the existence of a hospital before 1549.

contemporary with, or shortly after, the establishment of towns. The date of foundation of the Misericórdia of Espírito Santo is uncertain but it was in existence by 1551 when it moved to the new city of Vitória.[1] Olinda and Ilhéus boasted Misericórdias in the 1560s.[2] The Misericórdia of Rio de Janeiro was functioning in 1582 when the fleet of Diogo Flores Valdés arrived in the bay of Guanabara with many sick aboard. Felix Ferreira in his history of the Misericórdia of Rio de Janeiro attempted to sustain the argument for a foundation before the arrival of Estácio de Sá in 1565, but this is unconvincing. Other historians have attributed the foundation to the Jesuit priest, José de Anchieta. From the evidence it appears more likely that Anchieta's participation was limited to providing additional hospital accommodation, consisting of *pau-a-pique* huts built by the Indians, for the sick of the Castilian fleet.[3] By the end of the sixteenth century there were also Misericórdias in São Paulo[4] and Pôrto Seguro.[5]

In the early seventeenth century Misericórdias were founded in many parts of Brazil — Sergipe, Paraíba (1604), Itamaracá (1611), Belém (1619) and

[1] Lycurgo Santos Filho, *História da medicina no Brasil* (2 vols., São Paulo, 1947), vol. 1, p. 350.

[2] The staunch defender of the primacy of the Misericórdia of Olinda was F. A. Pereira da Costa, *Anais pernambucanos* (7 vols., Recife, 1951–8), vol. 1, pp. 213–15, but this is doubtful.

[3] In addition to Felix Ferreira, *A Santa Casa da Misericórdia Fluminense* (Rio de Janeiro, 1898), see Duarte Nunes, 'Notícia da fundacão da Santa Casa da Misericórdia' in *Revista do Instituto Histórico e Geográfico Brasileiro*, tomo 21 (Rio de Janeiro, 1858), pp. 158–60 for a 1567 foundation. Jozé Vieira Fazenda, 'A Santa Casa da Misericórdia do Rio de Janeiro', idem, tomo 69 (1908), pp. 7–51, attributes the foundation to Anchieta. For a review of the evidence and the publication of a letter of Anchieta of 1584 which clarifies his rôle, see Serafim Leite, op. cit., vol. 2, pp. 577–8; his assertion that the Misericórdia existed since the foundation of the city, based on the dubious premise that this was the case elsewhere, must be qualified (op. cit., vol. 2, p. 578, n. 2).

[4] Ernesto de Sousa Campos, 'Santa Casa da Misericórdia de São Paulo' in *Revista do Instituto Histórico e Geográfico de São Paulo*, vol. 64, 2ª parte (São Paulo, 1949), p. 25.

[5] The only evidence for an earlier foundation is a letter from Dom João V dated 17 March 1718 granting financial aid towards the cost of finishing the church and hospital of the Misericórdia, 'a primeira e mais antiga que houve, e há naquelle Brazil', cited by Carlos Ott, *A Santa Casa de Misericórdia da cidade do Salvador* (Rio de Janeiro, 1960), p. 124, n. 14.

Igarassú (1629). The date of foundation of the Misericórdia at São Luís de Maranhão is unknown, but the Jesuit missionary António Vieira referred to it in a letter of 1653. Here, as elsewhere, the Jesuits stimulated the Portuguese settlers to establish a hospital. Vieira exhorted the local Misericórdia to build a hospital, but a change of Mesa and the accompanying change of policy delayed the foundation. Finally, in 1654 Vieira had the satisfaction of accompanying the officers of the Misericórdia when they chose a site for the hospital.[1]

The importance of the Misericórdias in Asia, Africa and Brazil was recognised by ecclesiastical and lay authorities. The Jesuits, who worked with the brothers of the Misericórdia in many hospitals, praised the activities of the brotherhood in the field of social welfare. Francis Xavier, the founder of the Japan mission, wrote enthusiastically about the Misericórdia in his letters to Jesuit Colleges in Portugal. The Crown acknowledged the rôle played by the brotherhood. Privileges granted by Dom Manuel I were confirmed by his successors, who added new concessions. Dom Pedro II, while Prince-Regent, in his instructions to Roque Barreto on assuming the Governorship of Brazil in 1678, reminded him specifically to give special protection to the *Santas Casas da Misericórdia*. The most important branch of the Misericórdia in Brazil was in Bahia and the time has come to study its history within the wider context of the establishment and development of the City of the Saviour.

[1] *Cartas do Padre António Vieira* (3 vols., Coimbra, 1925–8), vol. i, carta lxiv of 22 May 1653 and carta lxvi of 1654.

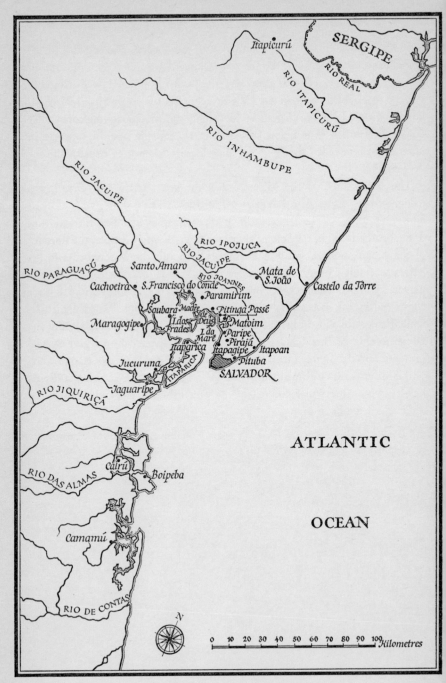

The Recôncavo of Bahia

3

The City of the Saviour, 1549-1763

THE Bay of All Saints is on the Atlantic seaboard of Brazil, 13° south of the equator. A promontory separates the bay, a deep natural harbour twenty-eight miles wide and twenty-two miles long, from the ocean. Entrance to the bay is from the south. Although the mouth of the bay is some twenty-five miles wide, access is reduced to two channels, one on either side of the Island of Itaparica. This fertile and hilly island extends across much of the mouth of the bay and projects into the bay itself. In conjunction with the promontory to the east, it affords protection for ships within the bay from south-easterly gales. The passage for deep-water vessels is some five miles wide between Itaparica and the promontory on the eastern extremity of the bay. In colonial times considerable care was necessary because sandbanks reduced the width of this channel to some two miles. Visitors to colonial Bahia agreed unanimously that this 'little Mediterranean' was one of the best anchorages in the world, with a firm bottom and protection from the pre-vailing winds. The inner part of the bay is considerably shallower than the roadstead and there are numerous islands. The largest of these are the Ilha da Maré ('the Island of the Tide'), the Ilha dos Frades ('the Island of Friars') and the Ilha da Madre de Deus ('Island of the Mother of God'). In colonial times galleons running too far to the north risked grounding on the numerous shoals in this part of the bay or of being caught in the treacherous crosswinds between the islands. The French traveller, François Pyrard de Laval, homeward bound from India, had been marooned in Salvador for two months when his ship had foundered on a sandbank.[1] Although today the first hazard has been largely eliminated by constant dredging, even experienced yachtsmen often find themselves in difficulties in the interior part of the bay.

[1] François Pyrard de Laval, op. cit., vol. 2, chapter xxv.

The territory behind the Bay of All Saints falls into three distinct geographical regions. The coastal plain, or Recôncavo, is characterised by a semi-tropical rain forest with high humidity and luxuriant vegetation. The fertile soil favours the extensive cultivation of crops, especially of sugar cane and tobacco. This fertile region is some fifty miles wide and is crossed by numerous navigable rivers which were of vital importance, in colonial times, for communication and transportation. The largest is the River Paraguaçú which rises in the Serra do Espinhaço and was widely used by the plantation owners of Cachoeira for shipping their crates of sugar to the city of Salvador. Beyond the Recôncavo is a zone of rising broken lands which extend for a further fifty miles inland. Beyond this is the *sertão*, a semi-barren plateau about 3,000 feet above sea-level. The monotony of this desert region is broken by granite rocks rearing out of the plain in weird shapes and totally devoid of vegetation. This is the region of the *caatinga*, or scrubland, with cacti and other xerophilous plants hardy enough to survive the scorching summer which kills vegetation and cattle. This plateau comprises much of the interior of the state of Bahia. Some 325 miles from the coast it is traversed by the River São Francisco. This river, navigable for much of its course, rises in Minas Gerais and descends through the *sertão* from the south-west to the north-east, before turning abruptly to the east and forming the boundary of Bahia with Pernambuco. In the early seventeenth century cattle ranches had been established along its banks, and with the discovery of gold the River São Francisco was one of the principal routes to the mining areas.

At the time of the discovery of Brazil the indigenous inhabitants were the Tupí Indians who occupied the coastal region from the mouth of the Amazon to São Vicente. Although speaking a common tongue, the Tupís were divided into several nations, often at war with each other. In Bahia there were two principal tribes, the Tupinambás and the Tupiniquins. The Tupinambás occupied the Recôncavo and the territory to the north as far as the River São Francisco. The Tupiniquins lived in the area extending southwards from the Bay of All Saints to Pôrto Seguro. The latter group had been described in glowing terms by Pedro Vaz de Caminha, chronicler of the fleet of Cabral, in his letter of 1 May 1500 to Dom Manuel relating the discovery of Brazil and the customs of the people. Most of the Indians living in the interior of the captaincy of Bahia were known as the Tapuyas, a generic term for some seventy tribes inhabiting this region at the time of discovery.

Cabral had not visited the Bay of All Saints on his voyage of discovery, but it is likely that the supply vessel which was dispatched to Portugal announcing the discovery had done so. This vessel had followed the Brazilian coastline northwards from Pôrto Seguro to Cabo de São Roque, making soundings and charting the coast. It is almost inconceivable that the captain had failed to note the largest bay on this part of the coast at a point where the Brazilian coastline turns sharply towards the north-east. The first European fleet to anchor in the bay had probably been that carrying the Florentine cosmographer Amerigo Vespucci, commissioned by Dom Manuel to make astronomical observations and charts. This squadron of three ships had entered the bay on All Saints' Day 1501 and historians are generally agreed that the name of the bay derives from the date of landfall. On this occasion the fleet had remained less than a week, but Vespucci may have revisited the bay in 1503 and made several trips into the Recôncavo.

The Bay of All Saints had been one of the main centres for Gallo–Portuguese commercial rivalry. The first recorded visit of a French ship to the bay had been in 1504. The French traders had not established 'factories', as had been current Portuguese practice. They had preferred to leave an agent who had gone native and had encouraged the Indians to trade with the French. This had been in marked contrast to the Portuguese who had lorded it over the Indians and had attempted to establish small trading posts, as stipulated in their terms of contract. Whereas the French had become assimilated, the Portuguese had remained objects of suspicion. There had been one notable exception, concerning one Diogo Álvares Correia. Little is known of his antecedents but it appears that he had been shipwrecked on the reefs of Rio Vermelho about 1510. He had been named Caramurú (moray) by the Indians and had taken a native wife, Catharina de Paraguaçú. With his numerous offspring, both legitimate and illegitimate, Diogo Álvares had lived in a small settlement composed of Europeans and Indians on the south-eastern promontory of the bay. Such had been the general disregard shown by the Portuguese Crown towards Brazil that when Dom João III had decided in 1532 to divide his new territories into captaincies, he had been totally unaware of how Diogo Álvares had been living in harmony with the Indians for the previous twenty years and had acquired considerable prestige.

The Captaincy of Bahia had reached initially from the right bank of the River São Francisco to the Ponta do Padrão at the entry of the Bay of All Saints. Later it was extended to the Morro de São Paulo, thereby including the bay itself. This captaincy had been granted to Francisco Pereira Coutinho. He had had a good military record in Asia, had been with Affonso de Albuquerque at the taking of Gôa in 1510, and had had the curious distinction of bringing back to Europe a rhinoceros sent by the King of Cambay to Dom Manuel as a present. Francisco Pereira had equipped seven ships and had arrived in Bahia in 1536. His first act had been to build a fort of wattle and daub with a surrounding palisade to afford protection to the Portuguese who had accompanied him. This settlement had been known as the Vila Velha and had been on the hill overlooking the earlier settlement of Diogo Álvares. Diogo Álvares had been confirmed in the possession of the lands he already owned. Other *sesmarias*, or concessions of land, had been made in the Recôncavo to suitable settlers for cultivation. Francisco Pereira had also started to build two sugar mills for the grinding of the cane.

This promising start had soon been marred by discord. The advanced age and uncertain temper of Francisco Pereira Coutinho had made him unsuitable as the civil administrator of a new colony. Discord had been sown among the Portuguese by a priest claiming that he had received orders from the Portuguese Crown to imprison Francisco Pereira. French pirates had renewed their activities in the Bay of All Saints, encouraged by Francis I who in 1540 had revoked his order of 1538 forbidding French ships from trading in Brazilian waters. The French had also contributed to unrest among the Indians. In 1545 Francisco Pereira Coutinho and the other Portuguese had been compelled to flee from Bahia and seek refuge in Pôrto Seguro. When returning to Bahia in 1547, Francisco Pereira had been shipwrecked on the Island of Itaparica and killed by Indians. Diogo Álvares had been saved because of his ability to make himself understood to the natives. During the absence of the donatory a French corsair had stripped the fort of its cannons. The Bay of All Saints had seen considerable discord and bloodshed in the years preceding the appointment of Tomé de Sousa as Governor-General of Brazil in 1549.

Tomé de Sousa had landed on 29 March 1549 in the sheltered cove on the south-eastern shore of the Bay of All Saints with orders to establish a capital. His fleet had consisted of six vessels — three ships, two caravels and a small two-masted barque. This expedition had represented a triumph of organisation by Dom João III and his advisers, and the careful planning had been in marked contrast to that of the fleets leaving the Tagus annually for India. The detailed *Regimento* had been backed by some 1,000 men who had been carefully selected for the building of the new city and, once this had been done, the establishment of civil government. The defence of Bahia had been entrusted to some 320 soldiers — a mixed bag of nationalities on mercenary service. A handful of qualified bombardiers, pikemen, crossbow-men and musketeers made up the military contingent. The civilian population consisted of carpenters, stone-masons, tile-makers, whitewashers, and workers in wattle and daub. Unskilled manual labour had been provided by some 600 *degredados*, or exiles. The construction of the new capital had been in the hands of these men under the authority of the well-known architect and engineer Luís Dias. The health of the expedition had been cared for by the doctor Jorge de Valadares and the apothecary Diogo de Castro. A small party of six Jesuits under Manoel da Nóbrega had been charged with the propagation of Catholicism and the conversion of the Indians. Dom João III had also provided the new capital with a body of bureaucrats to establish public law and order. The most important had been Dr Pedro Borges, the chief justice, and António Cardoso de Barros, the commissioner of the Treasury. These officials had staffs to deal with all aspects of administration — commerce, law cases, the collection of taxes and customs' dues, and the formulating of rules for coastal shipping.[1]

Tomé de Sousa had been ordered to find a site more suitable for the building of a fortress and future capital than that chosen by Francisco Pereira Coutinho. The new site was to afford a safe anchorage, good defensive possibilities and a healthy position. During the month of April 1549 Tomé de Sousa concentrated on strengthening the stockade of the Vila Velha and examining possible sites for the new city. The site finally chosen had also been on the south-eastern shore, but further within the bay than

---

[1] Inventories of men on this expedition are in Theodoro Sampaio, *Historia da fundação da cidade do Salvador* (Bahia, 1949), pp. 178–81, and Pedro Calmon, *História da fundação da Bahia* (Bahia, 1949) pp. 123–31.

C

the Vila Velha. Uneven ground at the top of steep cliffs with a narrow waterfront had made this an ideal location for the new city. The Jesuit, Manoel da Nóbrega, had described this site as being in a 'very good position on the beach in the vicinity of many springs, between the land and the sea'.[1] Here was to be founded the City of the Saviour (*Cidade do Salvador*), capital of Brazil from 1549 to 1763.[2]

The tools and many of the building materials for the new city had been brought from Europe. Tomé de Sousa had gained the confidence of the Indians and they had helped to construct a warehouse on the seashore. A small settlement of at least temporary houses for artisans had grown up around the warehouse and had been known casually as the 'povoação da praia' ('settlement on the beach').[3] One of the first buildings to be constructed by Tomé de Sousa had been a small chapel, dedicated to Our Lady of the Immaculate Conception, situated probably on the site of the present church of the same name at the foot of the cliff. This shanty town on the shore had meant that the workmen had no longer been obliged to commute daily from the Vila Velha.

With the king's orders in mind, Tomé de Sousa had set to work clearing the scrub from the area on the top of the cliff and building mud walls as a defence against possible Indian attacks. These had been the primitive defences of what was still little more than an encampment for the troops who had been moved from their temporary billets in the Vila Velha. During this period of construction the two medical men had been kept constantly on the alert. Sudden changes of climate had resulted in numerous cases of dysentery.

[1] 'muito bom sitio sobre a praia em local de muitas fontes, entre mar e terra', Manoel da Nóbrega, *Cartas do Brasil* (*1549–1560*) (Rio de Janeiro, 1931), carta iv of 1549.

[2] The name of the city founded by Tomé de Sousa was Salvador and the captaincy was known as the Captaincy of Bahia. In their correspondence viceroys and kings referred to the city as Bahia, as is also common practice today. I have followed this practice using the designation Salvador only when there could be ambiguity between the terms Bahia (city) and Bahia (captaincy). The whole question is discussed by Frederico Edelweiss, 'Estudos Bahianos' in the *Revista do Instituto Geográfico e Histórico da Bahia*, no. 73 (1946), pp. 283–9.

[3] A payment cheque for the freight of building materials was made out to Francisco Pinto, 'morador na povoação da praia', *Documentos historicos da Biblioteca Nacional do Rio de Janeiro* (Rio de Janeiro, 1928, in progress), vol. 37, p. 237, doc. 593.

Many of the exiles had been in poor physical condition and practically naked, making them highly susceptible to insect and snake bites incurred while clearing the area for the upper city.[1] Once the primitive defensive walls had been finished there had been a move of population from the settlement on the beach to the cleared area at the top of the cliff.

The choice of site for the new city had been dictated by the topography of the area at the top of the cliff. The builders of the walls had taken advantage of the natural strategic benefits. The triangular encampment had been bordered on the west by an escarpment some sixty metres high, separated from the sea by a narrow strip of beach. On the north and south sides there had been natural depressions and on the land side (the east) the ground had fallen away to a valley along which flowed a river. Four gates in the walls covered access from the cardinal points. The primitive defences had been replaced by stronger walls reinforced with bastions, two facing the sea and four facing towards the land. By the beginning of 1551 the walls and defences of the city had been more or less completed.

Although Tomé de Sousa had been primarily concerned with defence, he had not ignored the administration of the new city. A municipal council had been in operation by June 1549 and the Treasury slightly earlier.[2] In August 1551 the works foreman had reported with justifiable pride: 'And thus we built a very good and well finished prison with a court room and municipal offices over it, and on the waterfront at the place known as the *Ribeira de Goes* we built the Treasury, Customs house, warehouses and smithies; all these buildings were of stone and clay, whitewashed and with tiled roofs'.[3] By this date the city had also boasted many houses, three churches, a hospital and a Jesuit College, the last situated just beyond the north wall.

[1] On 22 June 1549 a payment order was made to clothe men working on the construction of the walls, *Documentos historicos*, vol. 13, p. 284, doc. 33.

[2] *Documentos historicos*, vol. 37, p. 2, doc. 4 and vol. 13, p. 283, doc. 30. For further discussion of the date of the foundation of the new capital see 'A fundação da cidade do Salvador' in *Revista do Instituto Geográfico e Histórico da Bahia*, no. 72 (1945), pp. 295–312, and *29 de Março, data simbólica da fundação da cidade do Salvador* (Bahia, 1952).

[3] 'E asy fezemos cadeya muito boa e bem acabada com casa daudiencia e camara em syma e na ribeyra de Goes casa da fazenda e alfandegas e almazens e ferarias, tudo de pedra e baro revocadas de cal e telhados com telha' (*História da colonização portuguesa do Brasil* (3 vols., Porto, 1921–4, ed. Malheiro Dias), vol. 3, p. 363.

A papal bull of 25 February 1551 had instituted the Bishopric of Salvador and the Church of the Saviour had been raised to the status of a cathedral.

During the next half-century the City of the Saviour had grown in importance, size and prosperity. Brazil had been largely a self-governing colony. The governors of the various captaincies had reported in the first instance to the governor-general in Bahia. In many cases he had acted on his own authority without referring the matter to the Crown. This authority of the governor-general and the prestige of Bahia as the seat of government had not been reduced by the union of the Spanish and Portuguese Crowns in 1580. As the first bishopric to be created in Brazil, Bahia had been of supreme importance in ecclesiastical administration. Although the Jesuits remained the most powerful religious order in Brazil, the Benedictines, Carmelites and Franciscans had all established houses in Bahia in the late sixteenth century. Increased immigration had also contributed to the growth of the new city. The city had expanded beyond the limits of the walls of Tomé de Sousa and new districts had been established.

The ethnic composition of the population of Bahia had changed drastically in the half century following the establishment of the capital. In 1584, the Jesuit Fernão Cardim had estimated the population of the city at 3,000 Portuguese, 8,000 Indians converted to Christianity and from 3,000 to 4,000 slaves from Guinea.[1] The number of white immigrants had increased significantly. Although in the early years there had been a predominance of bachelors, towards the end of the century whole families were emigrating to Brazil from the over-crowded Atlantic islands and from the north of Portugal. The Iberian union had resulted in the emigration of many New Christians or crypto-Jews to Brazil, where no branch of the Inquisition had been formally established. These had contributed much to the commercial importance of Bahia by their enterprise and initiative. The number of Indians in the urban area had decreased and had been limited to *indios mansos*, or 'tame Indians'.

The greatest influx had been of Negro slaves brought from west Africa for work on the sugar plantations or in domestic service. Initially these slaves had mostly been bought on the Guinea coast and the islands of S. Tomé and Príncipe. These slaves had been of Sudanese descent. The foundation of

---

[1] Fernão Cardim, *Tratados da terra e gente do Brasil* (Rio, 1925), p. 288.

Luanda in 1575 had offered a much shorter sea-passage to Bahia for the slavers and there had been a shift from Sudanese slaves to Bantu slaves from Angola. The relative merits of the two types of slave were much disputed. It was generally accepted that whereas the Sudanese were stronger and more hardworking, they were also more rebellious. On the other hand the Bantu were more susceptible to disease, less intelligent and more suited to domestic duties than the sweated labour of the plantations. Bantu slaves predominated in Bahia throughout the seventeenth century.[1]

The position of the City of the Saviour divided it naturally into two parts, the upper and the lower. Each developed its own atmosphere. The upper city was the residential area. Here were the governor's palace, the college of the Jesuits, the Benedictine, Carmelite and Franciscan monasteries, the cathedral, the Misericórdia, the bishop's palace and the city houses of the sugar planters or the more prominent civil servants and noblemen. Here too were the municipal offices and the Treasury. The lower city was the commercial zone with warehouses and loading wharves. The steepness of the cliff made communication between the two cities difficult. Four steep *ladeiras*, or paths, were suitable for pedestrians or lightly loaded carts, but all heavy merchandise had to be hauled up on a windlass operated on a counter-poise system.

One of the few descriptions of Bahia at the beginning of the seventeenth century made by a foreign visitor is that of François Pyrard de Laval, stranded there for two months in 1610. The French traveller had been returning from Golden Gôa, then at the height of its prosperity. Nevertheless he had been well impressed by the City of the Saviour and described it in the following terms:

> The city of St. Salvador is high-pitched on the summit of a mountain of difficult ascent, which on the seaside is sheer. Everything brought to the town or exported in gross has to be raised or lowered by a certain engine. No waggons are used, because it were too troublesome and expensive, whereas by this machine the cost is slight.
> At the foot of this mountain, for more than a quarter of a league, are

---

[1] General surveys of the slave trade in Bahia are Luiz Vianna Filho, *O negro na Bahia* (Rio de Janeiro–São Paulo, 1946) and the more closely documented monograph of Pierre Verger, *Bahia and the West Coast Trade (1549–1851)* (Ibadan University Press, 1964).

well-built houses on both hands, forming a long and handsome street, well crowded with all manner of merchants, craftsmen, and artisans. There also are the cellars and warehouses for the receipt and despatch of merchandise, whether of the king or of private persons. And by this engine whereof I have spoken the merchandise is raised up into the town, according as it is sold for distribution. To lift a cask of wine costs 20 sols, and the same to lower it; that is 40 sols a turn; for every time a cask or other weighty thing is raised, another of the same weight is lowered. It is like the two weights that ascend and descend a well, and is in the fashion of a crane.

The city is walled and well built; it is a bishopric, and contains one college of Jesuits (besides others in the country), a monastery of Franciscans, another of Benedictines, another of Carmelites: all these have handsomely built churches. Great numbers are continually converted to the Christian religion, albeit they are not so firm in their faith as are the East Indians after their baptism, but remain as fickle and hare-brained as before.

There is a hospital in the town, ordered after the manner of Spain and France. Also a Misericórdia and a very fine cathedral church or *Assee*, with a dean and canons, but no Inquisition, for which cause there are there great numbers of *Christianos nuevos* that is, Jews, or Jews turned Christian. It was said the King of Spain desired to establish it, whereat all these Jews took great fright. For the rest, the Portuguese in Brazil conduct themselves in all respects as in Portugal, and not as in the East Indies. The King of Spain maintains in the town of St. Salvador three companies of infantry of 100 men each, whereof one is on guard every day at the residence of the viceroy, or Governor of Brazil.[1]

Sugar had replaced Brazil wood as the major product of the new colony. During the fifteenth century sugar had been successfully cultivated on Madeira and S. Tomé. Dom Manuel and Dom João III had encouraged the transplantation of sugar canes to Brazil. São Vicente, Pernambuco and Bahia had been the areas most suitable for their cultivation. Brazil had rapidly ousted the Atlantic islands as the leading supplier of sugar to western Europe. In 1550 there had been five sugar mills in Brazil. In 1584 there had been about 118 in the whole of Brazil, of which thirty-six had been in the Recôncavo of Bahia.[2] The annual output of these mills had

[1] I have used here the translation by Albert Gray in *The Voyage of François Pyrard of Laval to the East Indies, the Maldives, the Moluccas and Brazil* (Hakluyt Society, 2 vols., London, 1887–90), vol. 2, pp. 310–11.

[2] Fernão Cardim, op. cit., p. 288.

been about 120,000 *arróbas*. During the next forty years the number of sugar mills and the annual output had doubled and in 1623, on the eve of the Dutch invasion, there had been some 350 sugar mills in Brazil.[1]

Sugar had been the life's blood of Bahia in the sixteenth and early seventeenth centuries, and its cultivation and processing deserve a more detailed description. The *senhor de engenho*, or plantation owner, leased much of his land to smallholders in exchange for part of their crop. These smallholders cultivated their lands at their own expense but all the sugar cane was brought to the central mill for grinding and for a division of the profits with the plantation owner. The cultivation and processing were succinctly described in an anthology dealing with the New World compiled in 1671 by John Ogilby, the cosmographer of Charles II of England, and dedicated to His Majesty:

The Sugar-Canes, by the *Brasilians* call'd *Viba* or *Tacomaree*, grow better in a clayie and fat Soil, over which the Rivers flowing leave their Mud, than on High-Lands, Hills, or Mountains; they are Planted after this manner: They first plough their Fields, weed them, and make Holes at an exact distance one from the other, into which they plant their Canes in such a manner, that the tops touch one another. The Holes before mention'd require more Earth to fill them in Summer than in Winter, that the violent Heat of the Sun may not dry up the Root, and that the Rain may the freelier come at them to moisten them, for the more moisture they have, the better they grow; they attain to their full ripeness in ten, or at most in twelve Moneths; *February* and *March* being the two last Winter Moneths, are accounted the best to Plant in, because the Earth softened by Rains, suffers the Root to shoot forth the better. The ripe Canes being cut off, are left in the Field till the following Year; during which time new Canes growing, are often ground in the Mill with the old ones; but if they stand two years, then the sweet Liquor dries up, and the Cane withers. The young Plants carefully planted in good Ground may last forty, nay fifty years; but in a barren Soil they set new every five years. Sometimes in great Droughts and extraordinary hot Seasons, the Canes are scorcht to nothing, which being burnt in the Winter, the Ashes serve to Dung the Ground; and so in like manner when the Water, overflowing the Fields, drowns the young Plants. In moist Grounds the black-wing'd Worm, call'd *Guirapeacopa*, (by the *Portuguese* nam'd *Pao de Galeuba*) gnaws the Roots in such a manner, that the Canes die, and sometimes it

---

[1] C. R. Boxer, *The Dutch in Brazil, 1624–1654* (Oxford, 1957), p. 18.

happens also that the Weeds choak the young Plants; wherefore the Ground is to be weeded four times a year, till such time as the Canes are strong enough to bear against the Weeds: they cut off the ripe Canes at the lowermost Joynt, and, all the Leaves being first pull'd off, tie them up in Bundles, and bring them to the Mills, which consist of three great Iron Bars, between which the Canes are squeez'd. The Water-Mills are turn'd by the force of the Water, which in great Gutters led from high Mountains falls with exceeding force into Pools made for that purpose; after which manner, though they wind the Canes much faster, yet they get not so much Sugar as when they grind them in the Mills turn'd by Cattel: The places through which the Juice runs must be cleans'd twice in twenty four hours; the Canes put in behind between the first Bar, are turn'd into the second, and thence into the third, which successively squeezes out all the remaining Juice: The Canes thus press'd, serve for Fewel to burn; but they constantly keep such a great Fire both Night and Day, that besides those press'd Canes, they burn forty Fathom of Wood in twenty four hours, insomuch that whole Woods are consum'd in a short time: The Liquor, nam'd *Caldo*, runs along woodden Gutters into great Kettles, in which it is boyl'd, but if it happen to be over-boyl'd they put Water amongst it, whereby it becomes excellent Food for Horses; then they put the Liquor into a second Kettle, where it is boyl'd afresh, and also scumm'd; and for the better cleansing of it, Lime-Juyce and other things are put amongst it; then they strein it through Clothes, and give the Dross which remains in the same to the Slaves, which work for half a year together Night and Day like Horses. The Dross mix'd with Water makes also good Wine. Out of the great Kettles, by the *Portuguese* call'd *Caldero de Mellar*, the *Caldo* runs into the lesser nam'd *Tachas*, where it is boyl'd a third time, and continually stirr'd till it comes to be thick like a Syrrup, and at last to the consistence of Sugar: It may be accounted amongst the Mysteries of Nature, that while the Sugar boyls in the *Tachas*, which are the little Kettles, they must drop Oyl amongst the Liquor, which if they should do whilest it is in the great Kettel, the Liquor would not turn to the consistence of Sugar; as on the contrary, if they should put their Lye into the little Kettles as they do into the great, the Liquor would be quite spoil'd. In their Boyling-houses stand several hundreds of Earthen Pots one by another on Planks full of Holes; which Pots they cover with moist clay, and after fourteen days knocking it out of the Pots, they separate the brown Sugar from the white, both which are laid to dry in the Sun, and put into Chests.[1]

---

[1] *America, being the latest and most accurate description of the New World containing the Original of the Inhabitants, and the Remarkable Voyages thither. The*

Other European nations had tried to horn in on the prosperity of Brazil. Holland had been the most prominent. The seven northern provinces of the Netherlands had been joined by the Union of Utrecht (1579). In 1581 they had seceded from Spain and in 1588 the Republic had been declared. By the turn of the seventeenth century Holland had emerged as the major commercial power in the world, with trading interests from the Baltic to the Philippines. Jews who had emigrated from Spain and Portugal to Amsterdam, where they enjoyed religious freedom, had contributed significantly to this prosperity. They had maintained cultural and commercial ties with relatives and acquaintances throughout Europe, Asia and South America. Ships from Amsterdam had traded along the north Brazilian coast and the west African ports in Guinea, Angola and S. Tomé. This trading had not been affected by a twelve-year truce made between Philip III of Spain and the Republic in 1609. Dutch ships with false papers had continued to trade directly between Angola and Brazil with cargoes of ivory, cotton and slaves which they sold for tobacco and other commodities.

The evident success of these freelance pirateers had encouraged the foundation of the East India and West India Companies in 1602 and 1621 respectively. These companies had received state support in the form of troops, but had been responsible for raising their own capital. The West India Company had been founded primarily for colonisation and commerce. Its board of directors, known as the *Heeren XIX*, had chosen Brazil as their first objective. As a military exercise this had presented few difficulties and it had been assumed that once Pernambuco and Bahia had been captured the whole country would fall into Dutch hands. The operation had been economically attractive because of the flourishing sugar industry. The proceeds would not only be sufficient to enrich the company but would also finance the upkeep of the new colony. The invasion of Brazil by

Conquest of the Vast Empires of Mexico and Peru, and other Large Provinces and Territories, with the several European Plantations in those Parts (London, 1671), pp. 503–5. The most extensive description of all aspects of the sugar industry in Bahia is by the Jesuit priest André João Antonil, *pseud* (i.e. Giovanni Antonio Andreoni, S.J.), *Cultura e Opulencia do Brasil, por suas Drogas, e Minas, com varias noticias curiosas do modo de fazer o Assucar; plantar e beneficiar o Tabaco; tirar Ouro das Minas e descubrir as da Prata* (Lisboa, 1711), parte i.

the Dutch has been described in detail elsewhere and here I will limit myself to an appreciation of its effect on Bahia.[1]

As the capital of Brazil, Bahia had been chosen as the first point to be attacked. An expedition of twenty-six ships, carrying 3,300 men and 450 guns, had arrived in the Bay of All Saints on 8 May 1624. This had been commanded by Admiral Jacob Willekens and Vice-Admiral Piet Heyn, with Jan van Dorth in charge of the troops. Under cover of a naval barrage, troops had been landed and had taken the city virtually unopposed. Despite the exhortations of the governor-general, Diogo de Mendonça Furtado, most of the populace fled the city with the bishop, Dom Marcos Teixeira, in the van. The governor-general and his supporters who had remained in the city had been sent to Holland as prisoners. The news of the fall of Bahia had caused great alarm in Lisbon and Madrid. The Portuguese had feared that the capture of Bahia heralded the fall of Brazil. The main worry of the Spaniards had been that the Dutch might advance westwards and reach the silver mines of Peru.

For once the authorities in Lisbon and Madrid had acted in concert. A liberating force of fifty-two warships with 1,185 guns and a complement of 12,566 men under the Spanish naval Commander-in-Chief Don Fadrique de Toledo y Osorio had been dispatched post-haste to Brazil and had landed on the Bahian coast on 29 March 1625. The task of the expeditionary force had been made easier because the Dutch had depleted their troops by sending Willekens to Holland with eleven ships and Piet Heyn to Angola with a further seven ships. The remaining Dutch force had lacked effective leadership after the death of van Dorth in an ambush soon after arrival. The command of the garrison had fallen to the Schouten brothers, one of whom had drunk himself to death while the other had been totally incompetent. Moreover the initial demoralisation of the Portuguese had worn off and been replaced by effective guerrilla tactics. After a siege lasting one month the Dutch had capitulated on 30 April and the victorious expeditionary force had entered the city on 1 May. The terms of surrender had compelled the Dutch to hand over all arms and supplies, ships, prisoners, slaves and booty such as gold, silver and jewels. They had then been packed

---

[1] Two authoritative studies in English using Dutch, Portuguese and Brazilian sources are C. R. Boxer, *The Dutch in Brazil* and, for the Bahian campaign, *Salvador de Sá and the Struggle for Brazil and Angola, 1602–1686* (London, 1952) by the same author, pp. 47–63.

off to Holland with provisions for the journey and weapons for their defence.

The occupation of Bahia by the Dutch had lasted eleven and a half months. Although failing to hold Bahia, the Dutch expedition against Pernambuco in 1630 had been successful. Olinda and Recife had been taken on 16 February 1630. Then had begun a slow war of attrition throughout the north-east of Brazil with bush fighting and guerrilla skirmishes. The plantations of Pernambuco, Paraíba, Goiana and Rio Grande had been fired. The tedium of this war had been largely due to division of leadership, both in civilian and in military administration. In 1636 the *Heeren XIX* had appointed Johan Maurits van Nassau as Governor-General of Brazil. During his term of office (1637–44) Dutch Brazil had come to include the Maranhão, Ceará, Rio Grande do Norte, Paraíba, Itamaracá, Pernambuco and Sergipe. His capital had been at Mauritsstad on an island off Recife.

The Dutch had realised that their influence in Brazil would be limited as long as there remained in Bahia the Portuguese seat of government. In 1638 Johan Maurits had besieged the city unsuccessfully and had only narrowly failed in a frontal assault. He had returned to Recife without making further offensives. More serious to Bahia had been the attacks on the Recôncavo during the later period when Dutch supremacy had been severely challenged. In 1640 Admiral Lichthart had destroyed twenty-seven sugar mills in the Recôncavo. In 1647 General Sigismund von Schoppe had driven the Portuguese garrison from Itaparica. He had made several sallies against the Recôncavo, but had not succeeded in dominating the sea-going channel giving access to the bay. Nevertheless his presence had constituted a threat to the city. Dom João IV had sent a fleet to retake the island under the command of António Telles de Meneses (Count of Villa-Pouca de Aguiar) who had been nominated as the new governor-general. He had arrived in Bahia on 22 December 1647, only to find that the Dutch had evacuated the island a week earlier. The final act of aggression of the Dutch against Bahia had been in December 1648 and January 1649. A fleet under Michiel van Goch and Colonels van den Brande and Haulthain had raided the Recôncavo and had fired twenty-three sugar mills and made off with considerable booty in sugar and valuables. This had been the last assault on the Bay of All Saints by a foreign force during the colonial period.

With the proclamation of Dom João IV as King of Portugal and the removal of the threat of further invasions, Bahia had settled down to an era of peace and prosperity. Bahia had become the most important city in the Portuguese overseas empire in the seventeenth century and was to enjoy its Golden Age from 1650 to 1700. As the administrative capital of Portuguese America, it was the seat of the governors-general and viceroys. A papal bull of 1676 had raised the bishopric to the standing of a metropolitanate, the only archbishopric in Brazil.[1] Bahia was also the seat of the only *Relação*, or High Court, in Brazil for much of the colonial period. This had been established in 1609, suppressed because of the Dutch invasion, and re-established in 1652.[2] In military terms Bahia was of considerable strategic importance. Although the garrison was rarely up to strength, soldiers from Bahia were employed in the defence of Sacramento against the Spaniards and in replenishing the garrisons of S. Tomé and other forts in Africa and Asia.

In 1699 the English adventurer William Dampier described Bahia as 'the most considerable Town in *Brazil*, whether in respect of the Beauty of its Buildings, its Bulk, or its Trade and Revenue'. The prosperity of Bahia was reflected in the number of new buildings erected during the second half of the seventeenth century. Like most visitors to colonial Bahia, Dampier was impressed by the number of churches which he placed at thirteen. Many of these were recent constructions at the time of his visit. The religious orders had also benefited from the city's prosperity. The Jesuits, Franciscans, Benedictines, Carmelites and Dominicans were all in the process of building, or rebuilding, their churches. The convent of the Desterro also dated from this era. Civilian reconstructions included the governor's residence, the archbishop's palace, the city council's offices and the Misericórdia. The rebuilding of the fortresses of Sto António da Barra, S. Diogo, and Sta Maria had been due to the drive and enthusiasm of Dom João de Lencastre during his governor-generalship from 1694 to 1702. He had also constructed the mint and the High Court and rebuilt the municipal prison. Dampier commented favourably on the well-built houses in the city and the wide paved streets.[3]

---

[1] Sebastião da Rocha Pitta, *Historia da America Portugueza desde o anno MD do seu descobrimento até o de MDCCXXIV* (2nd ed., Lisboa, 1880), livro vi, §99.

[2] Sebastião da Rocha Pitta, op. cit., livro v, § iii.

[3] William Dampier, *A Voyage to New Holland &c. In the year 1699. Wherein are described the Canary-Islands, the Isles of Mayo and St. Jago, the Bay of All Saints, with the Forts and Town of Bahia in Brazil* (London, 1703), pp. 51–2.

Commerce was the key to this prosperity. There was a flourishing triangular trade of inter-complementary wares between Portugal, the west coast of Africa and Brazil. This was a trade of supply and demand. Portugal relied for its economic survival on the agricultural products of Brazil and the gold and ivory of Africa. Luanda and Bahia needed manufactured goods of all sorts, foodstuffs unobtainable in the tropics, and certain luxury items. The sugar mills and plantations of Bahia depended on African slaves from Guinea and Angola for their man-power. The cargoes of ships outward bound from Portugal included linens, woollens, baize, serge and domestic utensils such as iron tools, pewter vessels, dishes, plates and spoons. Whereas ships bound for Luanda tended to carry goods suitable for barter such as mirrors, beads and trinkets, those bound for Bahia carried more luxury items such as silks, brocade and china. Wines, olive oil, butter, cheese, salt beef and pork were greatly in demand, whether in Bahia or Luanda. In Luanda the proceeds from the sale of these goods bought gold, ivory and slaves. In Bahia they bought sugar, tobacco, cattle hides, dye woods, whale oil, and such curiosities as monkeys and parrots. The slave ships leaving Bahia for Luanda carried tobacco, rum or brandy. This trade worked in both directions or between two of the three terminals. The latter was especially true of the slave traders whose boats plied between Bahia and Luanda without touching a European port. On the other hand a Lisbon businessman might dispatch a boat to Angola, sell or barter the cargo for slaves which he would transport to Brazil, and then invest the proceeds derived from their sale in the purchase of sugar or tobacco for sale in Lisbon.

Sugar remained the largest Bahian export throughout the seventeenth century. The industry had recovered rapidly after the Dutch invasions and reached the height of its prosperity between 1650 and 1680. Brazilian sugar was more highly regarded in Europe than its counterpart from the West Indies because of its finer quality. The planters of the Barbados simply left their sugar in the unrefined state as brown sugar cakes, known as *mascavado*. The Brazilian sugar was refined by mixing it with very white clay and water and leaving the concoction to stand for ten to twelve days. The hard clay was then removed from the top and the sugar underneath was found to have been whitened by the liquid passing through it.[1] Secondary products of the sugar industry were rum and brandy, much of which were exported to west Africa.

[1] Dampier, op. cit., pp. 55–6.

The cultivation of sugar was not an independent, self-supporting industry. The plantation owner relied on horses to work his sugar mill and on oxen for the transportation of the boxes of sugar from the mill to the nearest river. Cattle corrals were an essential part of any large plantation. Whereas the establishment of a sugar plantation and mill demanded capital, the rearing of cattle demanded hard work and a willingness to forsake the pleasures of the city or the *casa grande* for the scrub and cactus of the inhospitable *caatinga* region of the interior.

Cattle raising was not a seventeenth-century development in Bahia. A minor nobleman, Garcia d'Avila, who had been in the fleet of Tomé de Sousa, had established cattle corrals in Itapoan and in the valley of the River Joanes. He had built a fortified manor house at Tatuapara to be able the better to defend his cattle against Indian attacks. But it was only in the seventeenth century that cattle raising became a major factor in the Bahian economy, and was recognised as a financially rewarding alternative to sugar. Intrepid *bandeirantes*, or pioneers, had pushed inland by land and water from the sugar centres of Pernambuco, Bahia and São Vicente. The development of the hinterland of Maranhão, Piauí, Paraíba, Rio Grande do Norte and Ceará had been undertaken from Pernambuco. The *bandeirantes* from Bahia had advanced northwards to the River São Francisco and had then turned inland to Goiás and Mato Grosso. From São Vicente in the south they had penetrated the hilly regions of Minas Gerais and had joined up with their counterparts from Bahia. Ambition, independence of spirit and hard work had been rewarded by success. In the early eighteenth century the Italian Jesuit Giovanni Antonio Andreoni (writing under the pseudonym of André João Antonil) described herds of up to 300 head of cattle arriving at Capoâme, the cattle mart eight leagues from the city of Bahia, every day during certain seasons of the year. Here the cattle were sold as draught animals for the plantations, or slaughtered for their meat and hides. These hides were exported to Lisbon as wrappings for the rolls of tobacco and for shoe leather. In 1711 Bahia headed Brazilian leather exports to Portugal with some 50,000 hides annually, valued at 99,000$000.[1]

Tobacco had only been grown in commercial quantities in Bahia in the early seventeenth century. Peasants from the north of Portugal or the Atlantic islands had emigrated to Brazil with few assets apart from the know-

---

[1] Antonil, op. cit., parte iv, capítulo iv.

ledge gained from tilling crops.   The cultivation of tobacco, which demanded small capital outlay and few slaves, had been especially suitable for
such settlers.   Cachoeira had become the centre of the Bahian tobacco
industry.   Royal decrees ordered that the best quality tobacco should be
sent to Portugal and the worst to west Africa.   In fact, there was a good deal
of smuggling and agents in Lisbon frequently complained of the deplorable
quality of the tobacco they received.   This industry boomed in the seventeenth century.   By the end of the century tobacco rivalled sugar as the
major agricultural export from Bahia.   In 1711 Antonil noted that 'If sugar
has made Brazil known in all the kingdoms and provinces of Europe,
tobacco has made it more famous in the four corners of the world.'

The cultivation of sugar and the raising of cattle had been the foundation
of the Bahian economy in the seventeenth century.   There had been many
differences between the two cultures.   Generally speaking, the sugar
planters were often descended from families of the minor nobility who had
emigrated from Portugal to Brazil in the sixteenth century, and had been
granted lands in the Recôncavo.   Less frequently did the cattle owners come
from noble stock, although there were some notable exceptions.   Geographi-
cally too, there had been a split between the two cultures.   The one had been
linked to the fertile littoral region of the Recôncavo — essentially a static
culture.   The other had been characterised by its mobility, as shown by the
penetration of the interior.   Naturally there had been exceptions in both
cases.   In the early eighteenth century many plantation owners spent most
of the year in their city houses rather than on the plantations.   Similarly,
whereas some cattle owners were preoccupied with extending their lands in
the interior and never visited the capital, other families rarely stirred from
their houses in the city and left the supervision of their estates in the hands
of an overseer.

Whatever their differences, these cattle barons and sugar planters constituted the landed aristocracy of colonial Bahia.   A sugar plantation was far
more than a centre of commercial activity with cane fields, crushing machines,
coppers, vats and stills.   It was a community with its own chapel, resident
chaplain and a social hierarchy at once staunchly rigid yet curiously flexible.
Slave labour was the basis of this community, be it outdoors as cultivators
of the cane, herdsmen, shepherds, fishermen and boatmen, or in the domestic
duties of the house.   The carnivalesque festivity of the *senzala*, or slave

quarters, was rivalled by the traditional hospitality of the *casa grande* (lit. 'big house'), the residence of the plantation owner. All administrative decisions concerning the commercial and social life of the community were the responsibility of a single man, the *senhor de engenho*, or plantation owner. His authority was absolute. Antonil described the prestige of such a figure in these words: 'To be a plantation owner is an honour to which many aspire because such a title demands servitude, obedience and respect from many people. And if he should be, as he must be, a man of wealth and administrative ability, the esteem accorded to a plantation owner in Brazil can be equated to the honour in which a titled nobleman is held in Portugal.'[1]

The dominance exercised by the cattle barons was no less great. In the seventeenth century the Crown had attempted to limit the extent of the vast tracts of land owned by a few families. Royal edicts and threats of expropriation had been totally ineffective. The interior of Bahia was largely owned by two families, the Guedes de Brito of the House of Ponte and the Dias d'Avila of the House of Tôrre. These *poderosos do sertão* ('powerful men of the backlands') abused their power and were frequently accused of oppressive measures against subjects too frightened to protest. Religious orders, who had inherited lands in wills, often found on laying claim to such properties that they had been surreptitiously incorporated into larger estates.

This landed aristocracy dominated the administrative and social life of Bahia in the seventeenth century and, to a lesser degree, in the eighteenth century. Inter-married to a high degree, the leading landowning families constituted the most powerful pressure group in national and local politics. Governors-general and viceroys took good care to placate such families as far as possible, well aware of the influence they could exert at court. Self-appointed advisers to governor-general and viceroy alike, these landed aristocrats had no qualms about addressing themselves directly to the Crown when opposing royal decrees running counter to their own interests. The members of the city council of Bahia were chosen almost exclusively from this class. Although positions on the city council did not pass from father to son and the annual elections resulted in a rapid turn-over of personnel, in fact this was no more than an illusion of representative democracy because

---

[1] Antonil, op. cit., parte i, livro i, capítulo i.

of the high degree of inter-marriage and coincidence of interests.[1] This
was also the case among the socially prestigious brotherhoods and Third
Orders of Bahia. We shall have occasion to discuss this matter again with
reference to the Misericórdia. Suffice it to say here that the governing bodies
of the Misericórdia and the Third Orders of St Francis and the Carmelites
were virtually monopolised by the landed aristocracy.

In 1699 William Dampier commented on the active business community
of Bahia. He distinguished between merchants engaged in trade by sea
from Bahia to west Africa and Portugal on the one hand, and on the other
those craftsmen and tradesmen who had achieved considerable wealth by
their industry. A third class were businessmen engaged solely in financial
dealings. There was always a demand for capital in Bahia, were it to finance
the sugar crop, the purchase of slaves, the purchase of cattle, or simply a
house in the city. This capital was lent at an interest rate of $6\frac{1}{4}$ per cent and
the guarantee was usually the sugar crop, slave cargo, cattle or house whose
purchase it was financing. Bahia offered great possibilities for young
bachelors who had emigrated from Portugal, married local girls, made some
capital by acting as middle-men and then placed this capital on loan.

The most successful story of financial speculation concerned João de
Mattos de Aguiar, the financial leviathan of colonial Bahia. Little is known
about his life. Born in Ponte de Lima in the north of Portugal, he had
emigrated to Bahia where he had married but had no offspring. Possibly he
had originally come out to Bahia to help his uncle, João de Mattos, in the
administration of his sugar plantations in Patatiba. Whether this had been
the case or not, João de Mattos de Aguiar was already a rich man in his own
right at the time of the death of his uncle in 1685 because the latter's will
offered his nephew the option on the purchase of these plantations for
30,000 *cruzados*.[2] João de Mattos de Aguiar died in 1700, leaving enormous
bequests to be administered by the Misericórdia. The manner in which João
de Mattos de Aguiar acquired his fortune was described by the contemporary
chronicler Sebastião da Rocha Pitta:

> From humble and poor estate he rose to become a man of very great
> wealth. This wealth had been acquired by much application and was

---

[1] A more or less complete list of councillors is published by Affonso Ruy,
Historia da Câmara municipal da cidade do Salvador (Bahia, 1953), pp. 347–74.

[2] ASCMB, vol. 41, ff. 239v–244.

preserved by his carefulness in the employment of money. He was very austere in his way of life, both in his diet and his dress. All his wealth (with the exception of two houses, and a few cattle corrals) was placed on loan and so great were the returns that not even he himself knew the exact amount of his fortune.[1]

The success story of João de Mattos de Aguiar was exceptional, but there is every indication that in the eighteenth century considerable wealth could be acquired without possessing cattle or sugar plantations. Businessmen first appeared as such among the brothers of the Misericórdia about 1700 and we shall have occasion to analyse in detail the increasingly important rôle they played in the social life of Bahia during the next fifty years. The consolidation achieved by this class was indicated by the foundation of a brotherhood, that of St Anthony of the Barra, for businessmen. Its 'coming of age' as a class was recognised by a royal order of 1740. Dom João V told the viceroy to solve the problem of finding suitable people to serve as city councillors by entering the names of businessmen on the electoral rolls, since this class was now firmly established and fit to hold public office.[2] The economic change from the real estate tradition of the seventeenth century to commerce and financial speculation was recognised by the Count of Galvêas who wrote to Dom João V in 1744: 'There are few people (I am not referring to the vulgar populace) who fail to recognise and acknowledge that commerce is the very soul of the state, and the treasury on which ruling princes rely in the event of a national crisis.'[3]

The prosperity of Bahia declined in the 1680s. Sugar had been the basis of the Bahian economy. A fall in the demand for Brazilian sugar meant the decline of Bahia. Brazil had been able to maintain its lead in the world sugar market up to about 1650. After this date it had come under increasingly severe pressure from the Dutch, French and English planters in the West Indies. By the 1680s the increased production from the West Indies had reduced the demand for Brazilian sugar and had lowered the price

[1] Sebastião da Rocha Pitta, op. cit., livro x, § 17.
[2] Royal letter of 6 May 1740, APB, *Ordens régias*, vol. 36, doc. 60.
[3] 'Sam poucos os que deixão de conhecer, e advertir (não falo com a gente popular) que o Comercio hé Alma dos Estados, e o Erario em que depozitam os Princepes que os dominão as esperanças de poderem acudir ao reparo de qual quer urgencia publica e repentina' (letter of 9 March 1744, APB, *Ordens régias*, vol. 41, doc. 6a).

of this commodity on the European market.[1] A contributory factor in favour of sugar from the West Indies had been the regularity of the fleets, whereas those to Brazil were notoriously unreliable. In some years no fleet at all called at Bahia. The advantage of the superior quality of Brazilian sugar noted by Dampier was out-weighed by its deterioration in damp warehouses for two years. In 1687 the municipal councillors of Bahia had informed the Crown that firms in Portugal had ordered their representatives in Brazil to send money and not sugar because of the decline in the market for sugar.[2] Five years later the councillors wrote to the Crown that Brazil, 'the finest jewel in the royal crown', could only be saved from economic ruin by swift official action.[3]

This blow to the Bahian economy from external sources had come at a time of internal crisis. A smallpox epidemic from 1680–4 had coincided with a drought lasting three years. Slaves had died, cattle had starved, crops had been ruined.[4] The elements had not been the only factors in the depressed economy. The citizenry of Bahia had laboured under the burden of excessive taxation. Sugar had been taxed at the rate of seven *vintens* the *arróba* and tobacco at one *vintem* the pound. In 1687 the city council had complained with justification that these taxes had been levied in the period 1645–55 to meet war requirements and that the price of sugar had then been at 3$500 the *arróba*.[5] In addition to taxes on commodities, Bahia was paying off its share of an indemnity to the Dutch and a contribution to the dowry of Catherine of Braganza who had married Charles II of England. In 1691 the total bill for taxes and donations to be met by the city council had come to more than 100,000 *cruzados*. Reminders to the Crown that Bahia had contributed generously to the conquest of Angola, the retention of Rio de Janeiro and the defence of Pernambuco in the seventeenth century fell on deaf ears. In 1691 the councillors commented bitterly that the king only paid any attention to Bahia when he was about to levy new taxes, 'all to the damnation and ruination of this state which will be bled white as was India

---

[1] Roberto C. Simonsen, *História econômica do Brasil (1500/1820)* (4th ed., São Paulo, 1962), p. 114.   [2] Letter of 12 August 1687 (AMB, vol. 174, f. 79).

[3] Letter of 18 July 1692 (AMB, vol. 174, f. 104).

[4] Letter of 2 July 1685 (AMB, vol. 174, f. 59).

[5] An *arróba* at this period was slightly more than the English quarter. Letter of 12 August 1687 (AMB, vol. 174, f. 79).

on the pretext of the alleged desire for the increase in the power of the Crown'.[1] In the following year the councillors of Bahia, who did not mince words in their correspondence with the Crown, told the king bluntly that he and his ministers were following a policy of 'taking blood from the arms to give relief to the head'.[2]

These complaints by the city council to the Crown continued throughout the eighteenth century. It is possible that the councillors (many of whom were plantation owners) were guilty of exaggeration in their estimate of the seriousness of the situation. More than once their correspondence has a note of panic. This may well have been the case on some occasions, but other reliable sources draw a similarly depressing picture. William Dampier noted the decline of the sugar industry in 1699, although praising the quality of the refined sugar: 'When I was here this Sugar was sold for 50s. *per* 100 lb. and the Bottoms of the Pots, which is very coarse Sugar, for about 20s. *per* 100 lb. both sorts being then scarce; for here was not enough to lade the Ships, and therefore some of them were to lie here till the next Season.'[3] In the eighteenth century the level-headed Count of Sabugosa and the Count of Galvêas repeatedly wrote to the king about the critical economic situation in Bahia. Three internal factors contributed to this — a series of bad harvests, a dearth of slaves and a shortage of ready cash.

The Bahian winter lasts from about mid-March to mid-August. Sugar canes and tobacco plants depend on equal amounts of rain and sunshine for their successful cultivation. Sugar cane is less susceptible to minor climatic variations than tobacco plants, which can be ruined by a heavy dew or rain at a crucial period of growth. The eighteenth century was characterised by a series of irregular seasons with unusually long winters and short summers. The viceroyal correspondence to the Crown on the state of the colony was a chronicle of prolonged droughts, heavy downpours and laments on the 'desigualdade dos tempos'. By 1724 a long drought had reduced the populace to a state of total dejection. An earth tremor on 4 January produced panic and wild speculation. Prayers for rain were said in the churches.

---

[1] 'tudo em damno e Ruina deste Estado, que se pertende atenuar como o da India com o pretexto do fingido zello do aumento da Coroa' (letter of 14 July 1691, AMB, vol. 174, ff. 100v–101).

[2] 'pretendem tirar o sangue dos braços para come elle se acudir a cabessa' (letter of 18 July 1692 in AMB, vol. 174, f. 104).   [3] Dampier, op. cit., p. 56.

In March a procession carrying the statue of the patron saint of Bahia, St Francis Xavier, paraded the streets with the same intent. These supplications were ineffective and the crops were totally ruined by the continuing drought. Other regions of Brazil were similarly affected. In Pernambuco lack of flour made the price soar to eight *patacas* for an *alqueire*. In Paraíba, sickness and death resulted from the starving populace eating unknown roots. Two years later torrential rains plunged Bahia into despair again. The sugar plantation owners chose Balthazar de Vasconcellos Cavalcante as their spokesman to present a petition to the viceroy asking that the sailing of the fleet be postponed. They alleged that there had only been three full working days in the whole winter because of deluges which had brought the sugar mills to a halt and killed oxen and horses. The task of drying the sugar was hopeless. Rains had washed out roads and made the rivers impassable for the transportation of the crates of sugar to the city. Very small quantities of sugar in bags had been carried by horses and slaves for boxing at the ports, but as many of the plantations were five to six leagues inland such an expedient had been impracticable for the majority of plantation owners. Large amounts of sugar had been reduced to pulp in the warehouses on the plantations.[1] This story of misfortune was repeated in 1728, 1733, 1736, 1739, 1742 and 1746 when immoderate rains or prolonged droughts disrupted all forms of agriculture.

Slaves were the *mãos de obra* ('working hands') of the plantation owners. Epidemics had killed many slaves in the 1680s. The plantation owners could not compete with the prices offered by the miners from Minas Gerais who came to Bahia to buy their slaves. In June of 1710 the city councillors of Bahia took the extraordinary step of asking the king to close down the gold mines because the cultivation of crops in Bahia was being neglected for want of manpower. In vain did the councillors remind Dom João V of the example of his predecessors, Dom Sancho and Dom Diniz, in the protection of agriculture as the basis of a stable economy.[2] By 1723 shortage of slave labour had caused the closure of twenty-four sugar mills in the

---

[1] The departure date for the fleet had been fixed for 20 July 1726. The planters were successful in their petition of 1 July because the letter from the viceroy to the king explaining the reason for the delay was only written on 22 August (APB, *Ordens régias*, vol. 20, doc. 103 and accompanying documents).

[2] Letter of 14 June 1710 (AMB, vol. 176, f. 81).

Recôncavo. A slave who had formerly cost 40$000 to 60$000 now fetched 200$000. Only the miners could afford the prices demanded by slave traders who exploited the financial situation.[1] A second reason for the high cost of slaves was a change in slave fashions. In 1700 the slaves from the Mina coast were held in low repute and plantation owners refused to buy any but Angolan slaves. In the 1730s the opposite was the case and slaves from the Mina coast were preferred to those of Angolan origin.[2] In Africa the attacks by the King of Dahomey on neighbouring rulers had disrupted trade. In the 1730s ships from Bahia frequently remained in African ports long beyond their scheduled sailing dates in the hope of achieving a reasonable cargo of slaves. Nevertheless, they often returned half empty to Bahia.[3] Plans were proposed by the city council of Bahia for the purchase of slaves from beyond the Cape of Good Hope. The Count of Galvêas, who had assumed the office of viceroy in 1735, effectively put an end to these proposals. He pointed out to the councillors supporting the measure that if the ten to twelve ships already engaged in trade with west African ports were straining the resources of the slavers to the utmost, there could be no hope of their financing the construction of the stronger vessels necessary to round the Cape of Good Hope and trade in east African ports.[4]

[1] Letter from the city councillors to the king, 15 November 1723 (AMB, vol. 176, ff. 142v–143v).

[2] This change was mentioned by the viceroy in a letter to the secretary of state, probably written in 1738. Referring to the discovery of the gold deposits, the Count of Galvêas wrote: 'Quando ellas se comessarão a descobrir que haverâ trinta e sete para trinta e oito annos, herão muito poucos os escravos que vinhão da Costa da Mina, e esses tão mal reputados, que os Senhores de Engenho, os Lavradores de tabaco, e todos os mais que se empregavão na cultura da Companhia, lhes preferião os de Angolla, de tal sorte que comprando estes por cincoenta mil rs pouco mais, ou menos, não querião os da Costa por nenhũ preço; mas o tempo que tudo altera, e tudo muda, trocou as couzas de maneyra que hoje regeitão totalmente os de Angolla, pello mesmo vallor q' então os compravão, e comprão os da Costa por cento e vinte, e cento e cincoenta mil reis, e dahy para sima; desta alteração de preços com o excesso de quazi duas partes mais do seu antigo vallor, foi a primeira origem da decadencia em que ao prezente se achão as Lavouras do Brazil' (APB, *Ordens régias*, vol. 34, doc. 15).

[3] Letters from the viceroy to the king of 22 April 1733 and 18 April 1736 (APB, *Ordens régias*, vol. 29, doc. 74 and vol. 32, doc. 126).

[4] APB, *Ordens régias*, vol. 34, doc. 15.

A shortage of ready cash was the third reason for the decline in the prosperity of Bahia in the eighteenth century. In 1694 a mint had been established in Bahia to coin money of a value lower than that existing in Portugal in order to discourage the practice of Bahian merchants sending currency to Lisbon. This measure was ineffective because, once the demand for Brazilian sugar diminished, companies in Lisbon ordered their agents in Bahia to send currency rather than sugar. This money, although of a lower value than the continental coinage, still offered a better return than sugar. The result was a shortage of currency in Bahia. In addition, the more mobile way of life of the cattle ranchers and gold diggers meant that these sought payment in cash rather than in kind. Much of the provincial money which had been coined in Bahia was taken by the miners to Minas Gerais and Jacobina, or by the ranchers to Maranhão or Piauí. In 1712 the city council estimated that the total amount of currency circulating in Bahia did not exceed 500,000 *cruzados*.[1] Thirty years later the councillors of Bahia informed Dom João V that the silver coins minted fifty years previously were extinct and requested authorisation for the minting of a new issue to provide the means of commerce.[2]

This lack of currency ruined the possibility of good relations existing between the merchants and sugar planters. In the eighteenth century, the price of sugar was settled each year at a meeting between two representatives of the sugar planters and two representatives of the mercantile community. If they failed to agree on prices for refined and unrefined sugar within the statutory period of three days, the matter was referred to the viceroy, who made the final decision. Increasingly frequently in the eighteenth century the merchants offered rates which the planters refused, alleging that the price would not even cover their rising production costs. The year 1743 was one of crisis for both sides. A drought lasting three and a half years had ruined the soil and made the harvests so small that the produce of two years was sent by a single fleet.[3] The merchants had been unable to sell in Lisbon even a tenth of the crop they had bought in Bahia for the previous fleet of 1741. Thus they had been unable to pay off outstanding debts. Many

[1] Letter of 22 June 1712 (AMB, vol. 176, f. 88).
[2] Letter of 30 September 1743 (AMB, vol. 182, ff. 2v–3).
[3] Letters from the viceroy to the secretary of state in Lisbon dated Bahia 4 March 1743 and 30 September 1743 in APB, *Ordens régias*, vol. 39, docs. 7 and 47.

sought refuge in monasteries rather than face their creditors. Others were refused loans even at the exorbitant interest rates of 20 to 24 per cent in addition to the usual securities in kind, and were compelled to pawn their wives' jewels to the brotherhoods and Third Orders in return for loans.[1]

A contributory factor to the decline of Bahia had been the discovery of gold in Minas Gerais in the 1690s. This ended what little official interest there had been in the agriculture of Bahia. The Crown's attention was directed to the collection of the *quintos*, or royal fifths, on this gold. Within the frontiers of the captaincy of Bahia, gold strikes had been made at Jacobina and Rio de Contas at the beginning of the eighteenth century and in 1727 further deposits were found at Arassúahy and Fanado.[2] These strikes were not sufficiently rich to reawaken the interest of the Crown in Bahia. While searching for gold in the rivers of Minas Gerais, the early speculators had found sparkling stones in large quantities. These were identified as diamonds by the Governor of Minas Gerais, Dom Lourenço de Almeida, in 1726. This new development in the Brazilian economy benefited Bahia no more than had the discovery of gold. The smuggling of diamonds was even easier than that of gold. Dom João V was only interested in Bahia as one of the ports for a large illegal traffic in precious stones between Brazil and Portugal.

All branches of the Bahian economy were adversely affected by these factors. The plantation owners were the most severely hit. Their wealth lay in their cane crop, slaves, houses and sugar mills. In many cases they lacked sufficient reserves to replenish their stock, once this had been destroyed. The Bahian sugar economy was to a large extent self-contained. The planters sold directly to the merchants who exported the sugar to Lisbon. The price was settled in Bahia and the outcome of negotiations did not depend on the proceeds the sale realised in Portugal. This contrasted with the West Indies where the factor in Bristol or Holland sold the sugar

---

[1] In his letter to the secretary of state, written from Bahia on 30 September 1743, the viceroy noted that there had been a delay of a month and a half in the departure of the fleet, but that nevertheless so little cargo had been loaded 'advertindo tambem ao mao conceyto que formarião as Nações Estrangeiras das nossas frotas, perdendo totalmente a opinião em que athe agora estiveram das riquezas do Brazil' (APB, *Ordens régias*, vol. 39, doc. 55).

[2] C. R. Boxer, *The Golden Age*, p. 152.

at the best price he could obtain and placed any profit to the credit of the planter after deducting his commission for making the sale. Moreover, slave breeding was more common in the West Indies than in Brazil. In the case of Brazil, no capital was drawn out of the metropolitan economy to finance the sugar planters. During the eighteenth century sugar did pick up, but for many plantation owners the crisis of the 1680s had been decisive.[1] Cattle ranchers and tobacco planters likewise suffered a set-back but speedily recovered. Least affected were the businessmen and merchants whose capital was not invested in real estate. Despite the diminished demand for Brazilian sugar, they could continue trading in other commodities. Moreover, many of them had salted away their profits in Lisbon.

Culture came a poor second to commerce in colonial Bahia. Throughout the colonial period the Crown refused all the petitions of the city council of Bahia for a foundation of a university in the Brazilian capital. The intellectual life of the city was centred on the Jesuit College, until the expulsion of the Order from Brazil in 1759. Already in the sixteenth century the college had offered a primary education and a degree course in arts. The curriculum had consisted of three courses: Letters (Latin, grammar, rhetoric, poetry and history) for three years; Arts (philosophy and science) for another three years. Students intending to enter the Church took a further course in theology. The first degrees had been awarded in 1575.

Early writings on Brazil and Bahia had tried to answer the demand for information about the new continent. The Jesuits Manoel da Nóbrega and José de Anchieta had written letters to the colleges in Portugal describing the new capital and the flora and fauna of Brazil. Another Jesuit, Fernão Cardim, who had come to Bahia in 1583 and was to be the Provincial of the Order, had written treatises on the climate and land of Brazil and on the Indians. The honour of being the first native Bahian historian goes to the Franciscan friar, Vicente do Salvador. He had been born in Matoim in 1564 and published a history of Brazil in 1627. This had consisted of five books and traced the history of the colony from 1500 up to the governorship of Diogo Luís de Oliveira (1627–35). The most important description of

---

[1] In the absence of a complete set of bills of lading for each fleet leaving Bahia at this time, it is difficult to verify the extent of this improvement in the sugar industry. For the situation in 1758 in Bahia and the Recôncavo see *Anais da Biblioteca Nacional do Rio de Janeiro*, vol. 31 (1909–13), no. 3924.

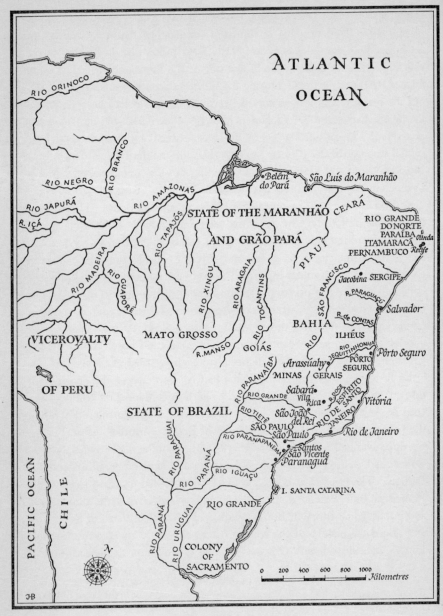

ATLANTIC OCEAN

RIO ORINOCO

RIO NEGRO

RIO BRANCO

RIO JAPURÁ

R. IÇÁ

RIO AMAZONAS

Belém do Pará

São Luís do Maranhão

STATE OF THE MARANHÃO   CEARÁ

AND GRÃO PARÁ

RIO GRANDE DO NORTE
PARAÍBA   Olinda
ITAMARACÁ   Recife
PERNAMBUCO

RIO MADEIRA

RIO GUAPORÉ

RIO TAPAJÓS

RIO XINGU

RIO ARAGAIA

RIO TOCANTINS

PIAUÍ

Jacobina   SERGIPE

R. PARAGUAÇÚ

R. de CONTAS

RIO SÃO FRANCISCO

Salvador

VICEROYALTY

MATO GROSSO

R. MANSO

GOIÁS

BAHIA

ILHÉUS

RIO JEQUITINHONHA

PÔRTO SEGURO

Pôrto Seguro

OF PERU

RIO PARANAÍBA

Arassúahy

MINAS   GERAIS

R. DOCE

ESPÍRITO SANTO

Vitória

STATE OF BRAZIL

RIO GRANDE

Sabará

Vila

Rica

RIO DE JANEIRO

São João del Rei

RIO TIETÊ

SÃO PAULO

São Paulo

Rio de Janeiro

RIO PARANAPANEMA

Santos

São Vicente

Paranaguá

RIO PARANÁ

RIO PARAGUAI

RIO IGUAÇU

I. SANTA CATARINA

RIO PARANÁ

RIO URUGUAI

RIO GRANDE

PACIFIC OCEAN

CHILE

N

COLONY OF SACRAMENTO

0   200   400   600   800   1000

Kilometres

Portuguese America in 1750

Bahia in the sixteenth century had come from the pen of a layman, Gabriel Soares de Sousa. Born in Portugal about 1540 he had emigrated to Bahia in the late 1560s. During a residence of eighteen years in Bahia he became a successful sugar plantation owner and had served on the city council in 1580. His brother, João Coelho de Sousa, had discovered mineral deposits in the interior of the captaincy. He had died before being able to exploit these deposits but had left to Gabriel a map indicating their whereabouts. In 1584 Gabriel had gone to the court in Lisbon to petition for the concession of these and any further strikes. This had been granted in 1590 and he had been given the patent of Governor and Captain-Major of the Conquest and Mines of the River São Francisco. Returning to Bahia with 360 followers he had led an expedition to the upper valley of the River Salitre seeking the headwaters of the River São Francisco. He had died on the return journey and had been buried in the Benedictine monastery in Bahia under a tomb-stone with the inscription 'Here lies a sinner'. He had taken with him to Lisbon a detailed description of Brazil divided into two parts. The first was a 'General Itinerary' of the Brazilian coastline, treated captaincy by captaincy. The second was a 'Memorial on the greatnesses of Bahia' and described the city and captaincy in detail. This work is of the greatest value because of the wealth of its descriptions at a time for which many of the official records have been destroyed.[1]

The Bahian literary scene in the seventeenth century had been dominated by two dynamic, headstrong, but totally dissimilar figures. The first had been the Jesuit missionary and preacher António Vieira. The second had been the satirical poet Gregório de Mattos. António Vieira had been born in Lisbon in 1608, but had studied in Bahia and had been ordained there in 1634. He soon revealed himself as a formidable scholar and a most eloquent preacher. Some of his more forceful sermons on the Dutch war and slave

---

[1] Fernão Cardim, S.J., *Tratados da terra e gente do Brasil*. Introduções e notas de Baptista Caetano, Capistrano de Abreu e Rodolpho Garcia (Rio de Janeiro, 1925); Vicente (Rodrigues Palha) do Salvador, *História do Brasil, 1500–1627*. Revista por Capistrano de Abreu e Rodolfo Garcia (4th ed., São Paulo, 1954); Gabriel Soares de Sousa, *Notícia do Brasil*. Introdução, comentários e notas pelo Professor Pirajá da Silva (2 vols., 8th ed., São Paulo, 1949). For bio-bibliographical details of Gabriel Soares see Rubens Borba de Moraes, *Bibliographia brasiliana* (2 vols., Rio de Janeiro–Amsterdam, 1959) and Accioli–Amaral, *Memorias*, vol. 1, pp. 452–6.

conditions were preached in Bahia. For his sermon in the church of St Anthony in Bahia on this saint's day in 1638, on the occasion of the failure of the Dutch in their siege of the city, Vieira took as his text the verse from the Book of Kings, 'For I will defend this city, to save it, for mine own sake, and for my servant David's sake'. By a play of concepts in which he compared Bahia to Jerusalem, Vieira attributed the salvation of the city to divine intervention. He went further in the analogy, comparing the high ground where the church of St Anthony was to Mount Zion, the city of David, and making St Anthony a second David and servant of Our Lord in the defence of the City of the Saviour and the Bay of All Saints.[1] Vieira was also a champion of human rights and preached against the exploitation of the Negro and the Indian to the intense annoyance of the white colonists. In 1633 in a sermon to a Negro brotherhood on a Bahian plantation, Vieira told his audience:

> In a sugar mill you are re-living the crucifixion of Christ — *Imitatoribus Christi crucifixi* — because your suffering is very similar to the suffering of Our Lord on the cross and with the same passion. His cross was formed of two beams of wood, and yours in a sugar mill has three. In the same way as the two cane crops bring you tribulation, so did he too suffer the double agony: once on account of the crown of thorns and a second time on account of the sponge with which they gave him vinegar to drink mixed with gall. The passion of Christ embraced a night without slumber and a day without rest, and so are your nights and your days. Christ naked, and you naked; Christ without food, and you famished; Christ illtreated in everything, and you illtreated in everything. The irons, the imprisonment, the lashes of the whip, the scores, the abusive names — in all these constitutes your imitation, which if it were accompanied by patience would also be deserving of martyrdom. All that is lacking for a complete and perfect comparison to the cross is the name of the mill; but Christ himself provided this, not with another word, but the very word itself. Your mill or your cross is called *Torcular*, and Christ himself by his very lips called his own cross *Torcular*: *Torcular calcavi solus*.[2]

The power of the hard-hitting rhetoric of António Vieira was rivalled by the bitter satire of Gregório de Mattos. He had been born in Bahia in 1633,

---

[1] António Vieira, *Obras* (4 vols., Lisboa, 1940, with a biographical study by Hernani Cidade), vol. 2, pp. 5–37.

[2] António Vieira, op. cit., vol. 3, pp. 30–1.

had attended the Jesuit College in Bahia and had then gone to the University of Coimbra. After graduating in law he practised in Lisbon and was a magistrate. He had found a protector in Dom Pedro who had promised him an office in the Supreme Court of Appeals in Lisbon, the *Casa da Suplicação*. This had been on condition he should go to Rio de Janeiro and make the official enquiry into the governorship of Salvador de Sá, who had been recalled in 1661. Gregório de Mattos had refused to accept this condition and had lost the royal favour. In 1678 he had returned to Bahia. He had been appointed judge in the ecclesiastical Court of Appeals, but his loose living brought about his dismissal. During his days at Coimbra the violence of his satire had earned Gregório de Mattos the name of 'Boca do inferno' and he now turned the full power of his invective against the authorities. The governors António de Sousa de Meneses (1682–4) and António Luís Gonçalves da Câmara Coutinho (1690–4) were targets of his verses as, too, were the ecclesiastical dignitaries. In view of his constant needling of authority it was rather surprising that he should have been elected to the Misericórdia in 1691 as a brother of higher standing.[1] Although the new governor-general in 1694, Dom João de Lencastre, had been favourably inclined to the poet initially, he was later compelled to deport him to Angola because of the bitterness of his pen. When the poet returned to Brazil, he sought refuge in Recife where he died in poverty in 1696. The poetry of Gregório de Mattos remained unpublished for a long time after his death, but is of great importance as providing a picture of Bahian society in the late seventeenth century.[2]

In the eighteenth century the arts in Bahia received considerable incentive from the dynamic Count of Sabugosa, Vasco Fernandes Cesar de Meneses. The son of Luís Cesar de Meneses, Governor-General of Brazil from 1705 to 1710, Vasco Fernandes had served as Viceroy of Portuguese India (1712–1717) before his appointment as Viceroy of Brazil in 1720. During the next fifteen years he gave every stimulus to the arts in Bahia. He encouraged the foundation of a literary academy in Bahia. The first meeting was in 1724

---

[1] The term recording his admission is dated 8 April 1691 at the beginning and 10 April 1691 at the end. The autograph signature of Gregório de Mattos is almost entirely destroyed (ASCMB, vol. 2, f. 324.)

[2] Gregório de Mattos, *Obras completas* (6 vols., Rio de Janeiro, 1923–33, edited by the Academia Brasileira).

and the members called themselves 'The Forgotten'. The historian Sebastião da Rocha Pitta referred to 'the most erudite people' who presided over the meetings, the 'serious and learned subjects' there discussed, and 'the verses full of elegance and wit' produced by its members.[1] In fact the Academy's activities produced many lengthy eulogies, perorations, euphuistic poetry and the discussion of trivia. The only work of importance to be produced by any of its forty-four members was Rocha Pitta's *Historia da America Portugueza*. Sebastião da Rocha Pitta was a product of the Jesuit College in Bahia and then studied at Coimbra. Returning to Bahia he wrote a considerable amount of poetry but concentrated on a study of Brazilian history. In 1720 Dom João V founded the Royal Academy of History in Lisbon and asked the Count of Sabugosa to acquire all information relative to Brazil. Sebastião da Rocha Pitta's work was already near to completion and he was charged with the task of accumulating details of the history of the colony.[2] His *History* covered the period from the discovery of Brazil up to 1724 and was published in Lisbon in 1730. The Count of Sabugosa commissioned selected authors to write volumes on natural history, ecclesiastical history and military history. These either remained in manuscript or were published long after the short-lived academy had foundered.

An 'Academy of the Re-born' was founded in Bahia in 1759 by José Mascarenhas Pacheco Pereira Coelho de Melo. His harsh persecution of the Jesuits in Oporto had brought him to the notice of the Marquis of Pombal and he had been sent to Brazil to carry out the expulsion of the order from Bahia. During the voyage a storm threatened to destroy the ship in which José Mascarenhas was travelling and he had solemnly vowed not to persecute the Jesuits in Bahia if he should be saved. The vessel survived the storm and José Mascarenhas arrived safely in Bahia. He fulfilled his vow. Although ostensibly continuing to harass the Jesuits in fact he did not do so and turned his interests to the arts. Revealing an unexpected literary streak he established the *Academia dos Renascidos* which counted forty full members and eighty supernumerary members. It was not long before the changed attitude of José Mascarenhas was reported to the court in Lisbon. The Marquis of Pombal immediately ordered his arrest and José Mascarenhas

[1] Sebastião da Rocha Pitta, op. cit., livro x, §112.
[2] Secretary of state to viceroy, 14 May 1723, and the reply of the Count of Sabugosa in APB, *Ordens régias*, vol. 17, docs. 93 and 93a.

was sent in chains to the fortress of Sta Catharina where he remained for seventeen years. The Academy did not survive the disgrace of its founder and was dissolved on 10 November 1759 after an active life of only six months. The literary production of the Academy was limited to the *Historia militar do Brasil* (*1549–1752*) of José de Mirales, the *Culto metrico* of José Pires de Carvalho e Albuquerque and some minor poetic works. Publications by former members after the dissolution of the Academy included the *Nobiliarquia paulista* of Pedro Taques and the chronicle of the Franciscan order entitled *Novo Orbe Serafico Brasileiro* of friar António de S. Maria Jaboatão. Another academician was José António Caldas, author of a *Notícia geral desta capitania da Bahia*. He was a student and later a teacher at the Military School founded at Bahia on the royal order in 1699. His descriptions and drawings of Bahia are of high quality and complement the largely statistical survey entitled *Estatística da Bahia* (1757) carried out by his colleague at the Military School, Manuel de Oliveira Mendes. It was ironical that the year of the foundation of the 'Academy of the Re-born' should also be the year of the expulsion of the Jesuits from Bahia. The closing of the Jesuit College marked the end of an era in the cultural and intellectual life of Bahia.[1]

Drama and music in colonial Bahia also owed much to the Jesuits. The early Jesuits had written short plays of a moralising content and the Jesuit College had put on tragicomedies on saints' days and holy days. The Count of Sabugosa had established a secular theatre in Bahia and the municipality had presented plays commemorating royal anniversaries and celebrations. This had been short lived.[2] From the early days of colonisation the Jesuits had used music to convert and teach the Indians. Sacred operas were presented in the Jesuit College and possessed considerable dramatic qualities. Secular music in Brazil was scarcely influenced by the musical tradition of the Indian which was primarily ritualistic. More important was the transference

[1] A survey of Bahian literature in this period is contained in Pedro Calmon, *História da literatura bahiana* (Bahia, 1949), pp. 13–73. For details of the *Academia dos Renascidos* see Arthur Viegas, *O poeta Santa Rita Durão. Revelações históricas da sua vida e do seu século* (Brussels–Paris, 1914) and Alberto Lamego, *A Academia Brazileira dos Renascidos. Sua fundação e trabalhos inéditos* (Brussels–Paris, 1923).

[2] An account of the theatre in Bahia is contained in the article by Affonso Ruy in the volume *História das artes na cidade do Salvador* (Salvador, 1967). See also *Anais do Arquivo Público da Bahia*, vol. 32 (Bahia, 1952), pp. 303–10.

of the Negro music from west Africa to Bahia with the slaves. This was characterised by the use of percussion instruments of wood or metal and the all-pervading rhythm. During the eighteenth century the dance known as the *lundú* of entirely African origin and the Brazilian *modinha* enjoyed great popularity and contributed to the creation of the *fado* in Portugal.

Bahia was the leading city in Portuguese America during the sixteenth and seventeenth centuries. Here was the seat of government, the only archbishopric in Brazil and the only High Court of Appeals. The city was a flourishing commercial centre for imports and exports. In the eighteenth century Rio de Janeiro gradually ousted Bahia from its position of supremacy. The discovery of gold in Minas Gerais had heralded the decline of Bahia. The increasing exploitation of mineral resources resulted in the shift of the economic centre of the colony from the north-east to the south. Bahia had been one of the original outlets for this new found wealth but rapidly Rio de Janeiro became the major export centre for gold and diamonds. Rio de Janeiro grew in prosperity and importance in the eighteenth century. Its public buildings and richly decorated churches evoked the admiration of foreign visitors. Dom João V recognised the increasing prestige of Rio by giving additional administrative responsibilities to the governor. In 1750 the jurisdiction of the Governor of Rio, Gomes Freire de Andrada, extended over the captaincies of Rio de Janeiro, Minas Gerais, São Paulo, Goiás, Mato Grosso, Santa Catharina, Rio Grande do Sul and the colony of Sacramento in the River Plate. He was more powerful than the viceroy in Bahia and his authority was felt throughout a larger part of Brazil. The inadequacy of the High Court of Appeals at Bahia to deal with law and order throughout Brazil was recognised by the foundation of a High Court of Appeals in Rio in 1751, totally independent of the judiciary in Bahia. The final blow to the supremacy of Bahia was fortuitous. In 1761 France drew Spain into the Seven Years War and it was readily apparent that both countries would invade Portugal. Pombal invoked the English Alliance but in April 1762 Spanish troops invaded the north of Portugal. This had repercussions in Brazil. In September 1762 the Colony of Sacramento in the River Plate was invaded by a Spanish force under Don Pedro de Ceballos and surrendered the following month. English intervention was late and ineffective. Ceballos then invaded Rio Grande do Sul but was held in check. This military challenge on the southern frontiers of Brazil enhanced the strategic importance of Rio de Janeiro. This was fully appreciated in Lisbon. By a royal letter of 27 June 1763 Dom José I sounded the death knell of Bahia by ordering the transfer of the capital of Brazil from the City of the Saviour on the Bay of All Saints to the City of St Sebastian on the River of January. It is against this background of the rise and decline of the first capital of colonial Brazil that we must view the history of the Brotherhood of Our Lady of Mercy in Bahia.

4

The Santa Casa da Misericórdia of Bahia

A. THE FOUNDATION

THE earliest reference to the existence of a branch of the Misericórdia at Bahia is in 1552. Writing from Bahia in late August, the Jesuit Manoel da Nóbrega referred to the difficulty of maintaining an orphanage which 'I gave to the Misericórdia of this city so that the brothers could look after the children, but neither they nor anyone else were willing to accept this responsibility'.[1] The destruction of the archives of the Misericórdia by the Dutch and the ravages of time and ants have removed the possibility of stating precisely the date of foundation of the brotherhood in Bahia. The nineteenth-century auditor and historian of the Misericórdia, António Joaquim Damázio, cautiously placed the foundation as occurring between the arrival of Tomé de Sousa in 1549 and the death of the third governor, Mem de Sá, in 1572. The subsequent publication of documents in the National Library in Rio de Janeiro dealing with the early history of Bahia and of letters written by the first Jesuits in Brazil to the colleges in Portugal has enabled modern historians to reduce this span. In the light of the new material scholars such as Theodoro Sampaio, Ernesto de Sousa Campos, Serafim Leite, Pedro Calmon and Carlos Ott have moved back the date of the foundation of the Misericórdia in Bahia.[2] The Bahian historians Pedro

---

[1] '...da casa, a qual eu dava á Misericordia desta cidade, e que tivessem cuidado dos meninos, o que nem elles, nem ninguem quizeram acceitar'. Although un-dated, internal evidence shows that the letter was written after 15 August, Manoel da Nóbrega, *Cartas*, p. 140.

[2] António Joaquim Damázio, *Tombamento dos bens immoveis da Santa Casa da Misericordia da Bahia em 1862* (Bahia, 1865), part 3: Ernesto de Sousa Campos, 'Santa Casa de Misericórdia da Bahia. Origem e aspectos de seu funcionamento', *Revista do Instituto Geográfico e Histórico da Bahia*, no. 69 (1943), pp. 213–52;

Calmon and Carlos Ott have even asserted that as early as 1549 a branch of the Misericórdia was functioning in Bahia. We may commence our history of the brotherhood by examining the evidence, albeit fragmentary, relating to the foundation.

The advocates of the foundation in 1549 base their assertions on three documents. Two of these are orders for fines incurred by sailors to be paid to the hospital. The first is dated 5 October 1549 and orders payment of 900 *rs.* in merchandise to be made to the 'Provedor of the Hospital of the City of the Saviour . . . for the works of the aforesaid Hospital'. The second is of 6 November 1549 and orders payment of two fines to 'Diogo Moniz, Provedor of the Hospital of this City of the Saviour . . . for the aforesaid Hospital'.[1] The third document is dated 14 December 1549 and is an order for payment to be made to '. . . Diogo Moniz, Provedor of the Hospital of this City of the Saviour, as executor of Estevão Fernandes de Tavora, a sailor of the caravel *Leôa* who died in this City, 1$800 *rs.* in merchandise due to the aforesaid dead man for the months of June and July at the rate of 900 *rs.* monthly'.[2] These documents have given substance to the belief that a hospital of the Misericórdia existed as early as July 1549 and that the brotherhood was fully organised with a Provedor and board of guardians. Carlos Ott even suggests that a brotherhood was formed, under the direction of Manoel da Nóbrega, in April or May at the latest. This is based on the assumption, unsupported by documentary evidence, that a hospital was built before the May rains (cause of much illness) and was administered by the Misericórdia. When the sailor Estevão Fernandes de Tavora died after treatment in this primitive hospital he left the wages due to him for June and July to the Misericórdia for improvements to be made to the hospital.

This thesis embodies a series of misconceptions of the administrative structure of the Misericórdia and its social functions. The first is the assumption that the presence of a hospital, *ipso facto*, infers a Misericórdia. This was not the case. In Gôa, Cochin and Cannanore, hospitals had

---

Theodoro Sampaio attributes the foundation to Mem de Sá, *Historia da fundação*, p. 255, n. 3; Pedro Calmon, *História da fundação*, pp. 169–70; Carlos Ott, *A Santa Casa*, pp. 17–19.

[1] *Documentos historicos*, vol. 37, doc. 269, pp. 96–7 and doc. 281, pp. 100–1.

[2] *Documentos historicos*, vol. 37, doc. 146, p. 60.

existed since the earliest days of the Portuguese settlements and long before the foundation of the respective branches of the Misericórdia. It must also be remembered that although the *Compromisso* catered for the care of the sick, it made no provision for the administration of a hospital. When such responsibility was given to, or forced on, the Misericórdia the brotherhood usually stipulated that it should incur no financial loss in fulfilling this obligation, or that a liberal grant should be made to the brotherhood by the Crown. The second misconception concerns the spirit in which the Misericórdia was founded in Lisbon. Although Catholic in religion, the Misericórdia was entirely secular. Members of the religious orders were not admitted to the brotherhood and the Misericórdia jealously defended its autonomy from any form of interference by the secular clergy or ecclesiastical authorities. Manoel da Nóbrega may have encouraged the formation of a branch in Bahia but it is extremely unlikely that he was the founder. The third misconception concerns the title — 'Provedor'. This title was an inherent part of the Misericórdia, but was not limited to the Misericórdia. It was a general administrative title applied to Crown and municipal officials, or simply to individuals in charge of institutions.[1] It is easy to be led astray by the nobility demanded of the Provedor of the Misericórdia and the aristocracy of Diogo Moniz Barreto. Of noble family, he was appointed *alcaide-mór* of Bahia in 1554 and acted for Mem de Sá as governor during the latter's absence in Rio de Janeiro in 1560. Pedro Calmon suggests that Diogo Moniz Barreto passed from the post of Provedor of the hospital (and therefore of the Misericórdia) to that of *alcaide-mór*.[2] This suggestion does not take into account that the Provedor was elected annually and that the Misericórdia was never a bureaucratic institution under civil jurisdiction.

A solution to the problem of the date of foundation of the Misericórdia can be reached by using different documentation. This clarifies the erroneous equation of hospital-Misericórdia, examines the true relationship of the one to the other, and establishes the topographical position of the Misericórdia.

[1] Pedro Calmon quotes the title of 'Provedor' of the hospital of Caldas founded by Dona Leonor and of the Hospital of All Saints in Lisbon founded by Dom João II to justify the equating of hospital—Misericórdia in Bahia. This is a totally false equation (*História da fundação*, p. 169, n. 8).

[2] Calmon, *História da fundação*, p. 128, n. 31. He only took the oath on 22 June 1556, *Documentos historicos*, vol. 35, pp. 353–5.

There can be no doubt that a Misericórdia did not exist before the arrival of Tomé de Sousa on 29 March 1549. The activities of the donatory Francisco Pereira Coutinho had been limited to allocating some *sesmarias*, or grants of land, and the building of a stockade round the encampment. After landing, the first concern of Tomé de Sousa had been the choice of a site for the new city. Thus it is safe to say that the Misericórdia of Bahia was founded between April 1549 and August 1552.

The problem of the hospital can only be understood within the wider context of the foundation of the city. The Vila Velha served as a base for the expedition, at least during the month of April. It is probable that a make-shift hospital was built there to cater for those still sick after the sea journey. Once the site of the city had been chosen it was essential to have a doctor readily available to deal with accidents while unloading, dysentery and snake and insect bites.[1] It was not practicable for him to travel daily from the Vila Velha, nor for the sick to be transported there. A mud and wattle shack on the beach was converted into a primitive hospital. This was where Jorge de Valadares worked initially under the general supervision of Diogo Moniz Barreto. Here it was that Estevão Fernandes de Tavora died at the end of July or beginning of August, leaving the wages due to him to Diogo Moniz whom he nominated as his executor. There is no basis for the assertion that Estevão Fernandes made a legacy to the hospital. It was perfectly natural that a dying man should nominate as his executor the director of the hospital, whom he could trust to forward his small bequest to relatives in Portugal. When the stockade of the upper city had been built there was a shift of population from the cramped quarters on the beach to the defended area of the upper city.

A hospital was built just outside the north wall of the upper city, to prevent possible contagion. Building lasted from October 1549 to January 1550 and the final structure was solid and permanent.[2] By mid-February all interior work and whitewashing was complete. On 25 February Tomé de

[1] The first wage-packets for work on clearing the site date from 1 May 1549, *Documentos historicos*, vol. 37, docs. 8, 9, 10 and 11, *inter alia*, pp. 4–5.

[2] Orders for fines to be paid 'for the works of the hospital' cover the period 5 October 1549 (*Documentos historicos*, vol. 37, doc. 269, pp. 96–7) to 12 January 1550 (vol. 37, doc. 408, pp. 149–50). This is a later date for the conclusion of the works than that suggested by Calmon, *História da fundação*, p. 169, n. 7.

Sousa ordered some thirty-five metres of hemp cloth to be given to the hospital for draw curtains.[1] Whether the cloth was used for protection against the sun or for partitioning off a dispensary or surgery is immaterial. The important point is that for such an order to have been made all building works must have been finished.

At first sight this does not advance our conclusions as to the presence of a Misericórdia, were it not for an alteration in the phrasing of this last grant. The two orders for payment of fines to the hospital specified that payment be made to the Provedor, be he Diogo Moniz Barreto by name or not. The order of Tomé de Sousa for cloth to be given to the hospital stated expressly that this be handed to the 'Stewards (*Mordomos*) of the Hospital of the City of the Saviour'. The order also stated that the cost of this cloth was 'to the account of the 100 *cruzados*, given by His Majesty as alms for the expenses of the aforesaid Hospital'. This order of 1550 was followed by further payments in 1552.[2] These orders referred to the stewards and the royal gift but omitted any mention of a Provedor. This seems conclusive evidence that there was at least a change of administration once the hospital had been completed.

A strong case can be made for the existence of a Misericórdia in Bahia in 1550. It was common Portuguese administrative practice to pass the obligation for the provision of social welfare from the Crown or municipal authorities to private organisations such as brotherhoods or religious orders. It appears that this happened in Bahia because if the hospital had been administered by the Crown all costs would have been met by the Treasury and there would be no reference to alms. There were numerous examples elsewhere of the Portuguese authorities building a hospital and then entrusting the administration to the Misericórdia, e.g. the Hospital of All Saints in Lisbon and the Royal Hospital of the Holy Spirit in Gôa. When the administration of a hospital was accepted by the Misericórdia it was on the condition that the brotherhood should incur no financial loss thereby. Possibly the 100 *cruzados* was a sum agreed on by the Crown and the

[1] 'trinta, e cinco varas, e terça de panno de Canhamaço de preço de oitenta reis vara para umas corrediças para o dito Hospital', (*Documentos historicos*, vol. 37, doc. 469, pp. 178–9).

[2] *Documentos historicos*, vol. 38, doc. 1134, pp. 56–7, and doc. 1222, p. 97, of 15 July and 5 November 1552 respectively.

Misericórdia for the costs of administration of the hospital of Bahia. Finally, the 1516 *Compromisso* of Lisbon had made provision for two *conselheiros* to visit the hospitals. These were members of the board of guardians and frequently known as *mordomos*. The brotherhood in Bahia was governed by these statutes.

The case for the Devil's advocate is simple — the total absence of any reference to the Misericórdia in the reports of Tomé de Sousa or in the Jesuit correspondence, before the letter of Manoel da Nóbrega in August 1552. The fact that individual orders for payments were made suggests that the total sum of 100 *cruzados* was not handed to the treasurer of the brotherhood as was the usual practice in such cases. It would have been interesting to know if this grant was made annually or on a single occasion, but this is not stated. Gabriel Soares de Sousa in his *Notícia do Brasil* referred to the poverty of the brotherhood and the small hospital wards in 1584. He added that this was because the Misericórdia received no royal grant towards the upkeep of the hospital.[1] In the absence of any conclusive evidence on the date of foundation of the Misericórdia of Bahia all that can be said is that there are strong grounds for the belief that it existed in early 1550.

The hospital was known as the Hospital of the City of the Saviour at least until the end of 1552. But three years later the governor, Dom Duarte da Costa, referred to the Hospital of Our Lady of Candles in a letter to Dom João III. The governor suggested to the king that sentences of exile be commuted to financial penalties and the proceeds allocated to this hospital.[2] There can be no doubt that there was still only one hospital in Bahia because Dom Duarte da Costa stated that all the sick, both from the ships and the city, were treated there. The only possible conclusion is that the hospital was renamed after completion. The name is significant. It indicates that the hospital was not administered by the Crown as it would then have been known as the Royal Hospital or Hospital of the King, as was the case elsewhere. It is also sufficient indication that the Misericórdia did not include the hospital within its own patrimony in 1555, as it would then have been referred to as the hospital of the Misericórdia. If the stewards mentioned in 1550 were brothers of the Misericórdia, then the relationship of the

---

[1] Gabriel Soares de Sousa, *Notícia*, vol. 1, pp. 256–7.
[2] Letter of 3 April 1555 (*História da colonisação do Brasil*, vol. 3, pp. 371–2).

Misericórdia to the hospital at that date can only have been purely nominal consisting of general supervision. The Misericórdia only came to possess a hospital at a much later date, possibly during the governorship of Mem de Sá (1558–72), Provedor and benefactor of the brotherhood.

B. THE FIRST CENTURY, 1550–1650

If the circumstances surrounding the foundation of the Misericórdia are clouded in mystery, no less so is the history of the brotherhood in the next decade. In 1556 we find the brothers collecting alms for the many sick of the Indiaman *São Paulo*, which had put into Bahia after being blown off course.[1] Nine years later there is a further reference to the Misericórdia performing one of the more picturesque duties ordered by the *Compromisso* — the accompanying of the condemned to the scaffold. In 1565 the fleet of Francisco Barreto, former Governor of India, arrived in Bahia on its way to the conquest of Monomotapa. A sailor, Medeiros by name, had been condemned to death for murder. The sentence was carried out in Bahia but on three occasions he fell from the gallows because friends had tampered with the ropes. After the third occasion the Misericórdia appealed to the chief justice for his acquittal on the grounds that his escape was the will of God. This appeal was rejected and Mem de Sá secretly ordered the unfortunate wretch to be hanged in the early morning outside the prison. This time the rope did not break![2]

By the 1560s the Misericórdia had achieved a position of social importance in Bahia. Mem de Sá served as Provedor and assisted the brotherhood financially. He built, or completed, the first church of the Misericórdia, made of stone and whitewashed. Towards the end of his term of office he listed this among the more notable achievements of his governorship. This was confirmed by an independent witness who also referred to wards and care of the sick.[3] It seems likely that Mem de Sá made improvements to the hospital which by this time was administered by the Misericórdia.

[1] Pedro Calmon, *História da fundação*, p. 212.
[2] Vicente do Salvador, *História*, pp. 182–3.
[3] *Documentos relativos a Mem de Sá* (Rio de Janeiro, 1906; extract from *Anais da Biblioteca Nacional*, vol. 27), pp. 4 and 11.

A travelling companion of Medeiros had been Gabriel Soares de Sousa. From his account of Bahia it is evident that in 1584 the administrative offices, church and hospital of the Misericórdia existed in the same place as the present *Santa Casa*. This is the first description of the Misericórdia and is of sufficient interest to be quoted:

> A fine street, known as the *Rua dos Mercadores*, runs northwards from the principal square to the cathedral. At the end of this street, on the sea side, is the *Casa da Misericórdia* with its hospital. Its church is not big but very well finished and decorated; and if this *Casa* does not have large offices and wards, it is because it is very poor and receives no income from the Crown nor from private people. It is maintained only by those alms given by local people. Although these are plentiful the need is even greater because of the many sailors and exiles who leave these kingdoms very poor and have no other help in their plight than that of this *Casa*. The alms amount to some 3,000 *cruzados* annually and this sum is spent meticulously in the treatment of the sick and aid for the needy.[1]

In 1587 the Provedor, Cristóvão de Barros, himself sought to remedy the dire financial straits of the brotherhood by personally visiting the sugar plantations of the Recôncavo to ask for alms.[2]

Information on the Misericórdia in the early seventeenth century is equally scarce. Pyrard de Laval passed through Bahia in 1610 on his return from India. He made casual reference to the Misericórdia and its hospital but this failed to arouse in him the enthusiasm he had felt for its counterpart in Gôa.[3] The Misericórdia featured prominently in the Dutch occupation of Bahia in 1624–5. During the eleven and a half months that the Dutch held the city they used the churches as powder stores and shops. The church of the Jesuit College was used as a wine cellar and, when the wines were exhausted, as an infirmary. When the relieving expedition, under Don Fadrique de Toledo y Osorio, established its two forward batteries in the Carmelite and Benedictine monasteries, the Dutch were using the wards of the Misericórdia as their main hospital post. Although the Misericórdia had escaped damage during the capture of the city by the Dutch, a freak shot from the Portuguese battery in the Carmelite monastery ricocheted off the

---

[1] Gabriel Soares de Sousa, *Notícia*, vol. 1, pp. 256–7.
[2] Vicente do Salvador, *História*, p. 273.
[3] François Pyrard de Laval, *Voyage*, vol. 2, p. 330.

ground near the Dutch battery at the door of the cathedral and smashed the hospital wall, killing two surgeons at work.[1] The most serious loss to the Misericórdia resulting from the Dutch invasion was the destruction of its archives.

After the restoration there was a wave of civic enthusiasm. The local governor, Dom Francisco de Moura Rolim (1625–7), was Provedor of the Misericórdia for the year 1625–6 and encouraged membership. By 1629 there were no vacancies in the brotherhood and potential candidates were refused admission.[2] This same enthusiasm led the scribe, Jorge de Araújo de Góis, to compile a list of brothers in 1625 to replace the records destroyed by the Dutch. This first book of brothers was lost in 1897 while being copied and the first extant membership register only dates from 1663.[3] Records of property owned by the Misericórdia had also been lost during the Dutch occupation. In 1652 the scribe, Gonçalo Pinto de Freitas, took testimonies from the former scribes Jorge de Araújo de Góis, Captain Francisco de Barbuda and Francisco de Castro in an attempt to establish legal rights to this patrimony. He calculated this at some twenty-six properties in the immediate vicinity of the Misericórdia, five shops and a butcher's shop, giving an annual income of 757$000 to the brotherhood. There was also a group of shops and houses in front of the cathedral which were rented for 90$000 annually.[4] The documentary material for a history of the Misericórdia between 1625 and 1650 is limited to two registers dealing with administration and one account ledger.[5] These records provide a one-sided picture of the Misericórdia's activities but do permit an insight to be obtained into its administration.

The Misericórdia derived its main source of income from legacies, either outright or with conditions attached to a property. Legacies were made to the Misericórdia with the obligation to say a stipulated number of masses over the year in the brotherhood's church. The after-life was a constant

---

[1] Vicente do Salvador, *História*, p. 434.　　　[2] ASCMB, vol. 195, f. 3.

[3] This register was consulted by Damázio, *Tombamento*, n. 54. In the catalogue of the archives of the Misericórdia made in 1940 there is the note: 'O Iᵒ Livro desta coleção não foi encontrado desde 1897, conforme consta do antigo Indice, parecendo que foi extraviado por ocasião de ser copiado'. The first index was also lost or destroyed because it is no longer in the archives.

[4] ASCMB, vol. 40, ff. 230–234v.　　　[5] ASCMB, vols. 13, 40 and 843.

preoccupation with the Bahian gentry, whose wealth was often gained unscrupulously and at the cost of exploiting their slaves. The first purchase by any white person was a slave. During his lifetime the master abused his slave. On his death-bed the master provided for his own salvation by leaving the slave to the Misericórdia so that the proceeds derived from the sale could be applied to masses for the soul of the dead master.[1] Even a humble music teacher, faced with the problem of exacting payment for lessons to the children of a wealthy citizen, satisfied his own conscience and benefited the Misericórdia by leaving the debt to the brotherhood which could enforce payment, by legal means if necessary.[2]

Such monetary legacies were pittances compared with those leaving houses and property to the brotherhood. By the seventeenth century the Misericórdia possessed properties not only in the city itself, but also in the Recôncavo. Mecia Rodrigues, the New Christian wife of the wealthy land-owner Garcia d'Avila, left substantial properties to the Misericórdia in the city near the Benedictine monastery, and in the Recôncavo lands in Itapagipe and Itapoan.[3] The latter were left to the Misericórdia and the Benedictines. An amicable solution was reached and the brotherhood paid compensation to the Order in the final division of property.[4] In his enquiry Gonçalo Pinto de Freitas discovered that the legacy of Mecia Rodrigues had financed the building of some houses on lands left to the brotherhood by another benefactor, Simão da Gama de Andrade.[5] In the city the Misericórdia had to compete with the Jesuits and Franciscans as recipients of legacies. When Jorge Ferreira, wealthy owner of a sugar plantation in Sergipe and a produce farm in the Serra, died in 1641, the Franciscans were the main beneficiaries receiving six houses in the main square where property values were high. The Misericórdia had to content itself with three houses and the shared administration of dowries, with an additional obligation to say masses.[6]

---

[1] ASCMB, vol. 40, ff. 142v–143 and f. 193, *inter alia.*

[2] ASCMB, vol. 40, f. 141.

[3] The lands in the city were of a leasehold value of 600$000, Pedro Calmon, *História da Casa da Tôrre* (2nd ed., Rio de Janeiro, 1958), p. 26, n. 16.

[4] The Misericórdia kept the lands in Itapagipe and the Benedictines those in Itapoan. The Misericórdia paid 100$000 in compensation because of the lower value of the lands in Itapoan, *Livro velho do tombo do mosteiro de São Bento da cidade do Salvador* (Bahia, 1945), pp. 230–3 and pp. 328–31.

[5] ASCMB, vol. 40, f. 230v.   [6] ASCMB, vol. 40, ff. 143v–153.

The prosperity of Bahia in the early seventeenth century meant that the plantation owners and cattle ranchers endowed the religious orders and brotherhoods liberally. In 1637 the Misericórdia took possession of houses in the main square of Bahia, the legacy of Pedro Viegas Giraldes, a brother and owner of a ranch in Pitinga with seventy head of cattle and sixty sheep. This legacy carried the obligation of saying two masses weekly in the Misericórdia's church.[1] The largest legacy of property received by the Misericórdia was from a priest, Francisco de Araújo, in 1650. Reference will be made to this legacy later; suffice it to say here that it comprised four corrals of cattle and a flock of sheep in Saboara as well as smallholdings of tobacco and cotton.

The brotherhood supplemented its income from legacies by investing in houses in the belief that these would not depreciate in value and that the legacy would be safe from loss by maladministration. The Misericórdia could drive a hard business deal. A prominent Bahian in the early seventeenth century, Captain Gonçalo de Morgade, and his wife were induced to part with two houses valued at 380$000 for a mere 200$000, the extent of a legacy received by the brotherhood.[2] The Misericórdia also exacted transfer fees, known as *laudémios*, from the sale of property on lands of which it was the owner.

The administration of properties and lands brought the Misericórdia into contact with other land-owning bodies. The most prominent and wealthiest were the Jesuits and the Benedictines. The Misericórdia enjoyed good business relations with the latter, but the Jesuits were more rapacious. Francisco de Araújo had inherited rich estates but had fallen foul of Jesuit demands. He had left his extensive properties to the Misericórdia on condition that the brotherhood would fight, without quarter or compromise, Jesuit claims to his lands. He had maintained that such claims were based on faulty land measurements. Failure to fulfil this condition on the part of the Misericórdia meant that the legacy would pass automatically to the Benedictines on the same terms. The Misericórdia took possession of the lands in 1652, which indicates that it was successful in this instance. The brotherhood administered the property with varying degrees of success until the nineteenth century.[3]

These lands were part of a larger property which involved the Misericórdia

---

[1] ASCMB, vol. 40, ff. 97v–105v and ff. 115v–118.
[2] ASCMB, vol. 40, f. 35 and ff. 36v–40.   [3] ASCMB, vol. 40, ff. 245–253v.

in a legal *cause célèbre* lasting almost a century. In his will (1569) Mem de Sá had stated that if his children, Francisco and Felippa, died without offspring, his lands in Sergipe should be divided into three parts between the Misericórdia, the Jesuit College in Bahia and the provision of alms and dowries. Francisco had died, unmarried. Felippa had married the Count of Linhares but there had been no children. A widow, she had founded the church of the Jesuit College of St Antão in Lisbon in 1613. In her will she had ordered that the lands in Sergipe should be sold and the proceeds directed to finishing this church. The share of the Misericórdia by the will of Mem de Sá had been valued at 80,000 *cruzados*. The brotherhood had challenged the will of Felippa in 1622, but without success. The legal question was whether Felippa had inherited from her father or from her brother, since in the latter case she would not be bound by the terms of her father's will. A three-cornered legal battle had developed between the Misericórdia and the two Jesuit Colleges. In 1644 the Misericórdia had refused an offer by the College of St Antão of 12,000 *cruzados* as final settlement. The brotherhood had insisted on 20,000 *cruzados* in cash in addition to adequate compensation for one Pedro Gonçalves de Mattos to whom the Misericórdia had sold its share for 15,000 *cruzados* in 1638.

There were several rumours that the Misericórdia of Bahia had won its case. In 1632 the board of guardians of the Misericórdia in Bahia, under the Provedor Diogo Luís de Oliveira (Governor-General, 1627–35), voted the sums of 1,000 *cruzados* to the Misericórdia of Lisbon and 300 *cruzados* to each of the two lawyers handling the case, if the outcome were successful. In October 1638 the money for the Misericórdia of Lisbon was paid to the retiring governor-general, Pedro da Silva, for delivery on his arrival in Portugal.[1] This generosity by the Misericórdia of Bahia can only have been born of a total misunderstanding or some partial settlement between the brotherhood and the Jesuit College of St Antão. On 12 June 1651 the brotherhood in Bahia was convoked by the ringing of handbells in the streets to hear the Provedor, the Count of Castelo Melhor, make an official announcement of the successful outcome of the case. This too was a false alarm and the legal wrangling continued.[2]

[1] Minute of 29 October 1632 (ASCMB, vol. 40, f. 36). Pedro da Silva signed a receipt for payment on 12 October 1638 (ASCMB, vol. 40, ff. 134v–135).

[2] ASCMB, vol. 13, ff. 23–4.

Initially the Jesuit College in Bahia had supported the Misericórdia, whose prestige had lent weight to its own claim. In 1655, under pressure from the General of the Order, the two Jesuit Colleges agreed to co-operate in the interests of the Order.[1] The Misericórdia recognised that the Jesuits could exert more influence in Lisbon and Bahia than it could. The accuracy of this assessment was shown by the Jesuit choice of spokesman to present their proposals to the Misericórdia — Salvador de Sá, Member of the Overseas Council in Lisbon, former Governor of Angola, former Governor of Rio de Janeiro and now Captain-General of the three southern captaincies of Brazil known as the *Repartição do Sul*. On 12 October 1659 the Mesa discussed his proposals and decided to accept any reasonable solution.[2] On 13 October 1659 representatives of the Misericórdia met those of the Jesuits and the heirs of Pedro Gonçalves de Mattos. The final outcome was that the Misericórdia received a paltry 13,500 *cruzados* and the heirs of Pedro Gonçalves de Mattos received full compensation.[3]

The dispute over the legacy of Mem de Sá was exceptional, but not unique. The Misericórdia found that legal disputes and the expense of maintaining properties made such legacies of doubtful value. Often the brotherhood was co-legatory with a religious order. The wealthy Jorge Ferreira left a fine property in the main square to the Misericórdia, but the Jesuits received part of the rents. The brotherhood found that it was a better economic proposition to sell its own holding for 250$000 and place this sum on loan at $6\frac{1}{4}$ per cent rate of interest than to rent the house for a mere 12$000 annually.[4] Monetary legacies which would have been profitable if placed on loan were squandered on repairs to property. Even estates outside the city proved a liability because careless tenants allowed the lands to deteriorate and were negligent in paying the rents. The Misericórdia was severely hit

---

[1] *Documentos historicos*, vol. 62, pp. 141–9.

[2] 'os R^dos P^es da Companhia de Jesus assim os do Colegio desta cidade como os de Santo Antão da cidade de Lisboa mandarão aesta Santa Casa pello general Salvador Correa de Saa e Benavides tratar de consertar sobre a demanda q' a tantos anos corria com os ditos padres sobre o legado q' aesta Sta Caza deixou o G^dor Mem de Saa sobre o eng^o de Sergipe do Conde e suas terras o coal general Salvador Correa de Saa e Benavides vieira a este Consistório tratar do ditto conserto' (ASCMB, vol. 13, ff. 118–119v.) Salvador de Sá enjoyed an amicable relationship with the Jesuits, C. R. Boxer, *Salvador de Sá*, pp. 125–7, 133, 154, 287, 369.

[3] *Documentos historicos*, vol. 62, pp. 159–88.   [4] ASCMB, vol. 13, f. 21.

by a fall in property values in the mid-seventeenth century. The brother-hood was often in debt to its own treasurers who generously paid the Misericórdia's debts from their own pockets in the belief that they would be reimbursed at the end of the financial year. Matters came to a head in 1652. The treasurer informed the Mesa that there were not enough funds to meet hospital expenses and he had already committed himself heavily from private means.[1] Faced by financial collapse the Mesa of 1652-3 decided to petition the Misericórdia of Lisbon for the granting of the privilege, enjoyed by the parent body, permitting the sale of houses and lands left unconditionally to the brotherhood. All proceeds were to be placed on loan with adequate securities.[2] This petition was authorised by the Crown in 1657.[3]

This change of policy did not mean that the Misericórdia was entering upon an unknown field. Many of the cash legacies it received for charitable purposes were placed on loan and only the interest used. The brotherhood stipulated that all potential borrowers must supply suitable guarantors and pledge property within the city limits. Although later this service of the Misericórdia as a primitive banking agency was to be abused by the borrowers and even the boards of guardians themselves, it appears that in the mid-seventeenth century the conditions were fulfilled. Small business men and plantation owners were regular borrowers and even the Secretary of State, Bernardo Vieira Ravasco, featured in the register of borrowers.

The Misericórdia always enjoyed the royal patronage. Privileges granted to the Misericórdia in Lisbon were extended to Bahia by Philip III of Portugal (IV of Spain) in 1622.[4] These enabled the Misericórdia to 'lord it over' lesser brotherhoods. Its only possible rivals — the Third Orders of St Francis and the Carmelites — possessed no royal privileges. One such privilege gave the Misericórdia the monopoly of burying the dead in Bahia. This was a lucrative source of income and the Misericórdia guarded this privilege jealously. Before another brotherhood could possess a bier the permission of the Misericórdia had to be obtained. The whole subject of burials will be treated in Chapter 9 and I will limit myself here to a brief reference to the first occasion on which this permission was sought. In 1649

---

[1] ASCMB, vol. 13, f. 31.
[2] The actual date of this minute is destroyed (ASCMB, vol. 13, ff. 37v-38v).
[3] Royal decree of 11 December 1657 (ASCMB, vol. 209, f. 48).
[4] Royal decree of 23 September 1622 (ASCMB, vol. 209, f. 36).

the slave brotherhood dedicated to Our Lady of Succour petitioned the Misericórdia for the use of a bier. This was granted by the Mesa; the slave brotherhood was permitted to have an *esquife* (little more than a bare board). Only slaves were to be carried on this *esquife* and the board of guardians of the Misericórdia was to be informed each time it was used.[1]

There are few details of the social activities of the Misericórdia during this early period. The hospital was functioning successfully. The first reference to medical staff was in 1645, and concerned the appointment of a surgeon. The actual nursing was superficial and rough. A male nurse was dismissed in 1650 for having abandoned his patients for games of chance with the soldiers of the garrison.[2] The spiritual needs of the sick were cared for by a resident priest appointed solely for this purpose.

The Misericórdia performed other social services. Legal assistance was provided for poor prisoners recommended to the Misericórdia. Perhaps the most remarkable of these was one Maria Ramos jailed for the murder of her fourth husband! She died in jail in 1645 but the Misericórdia cared for her child for a short time before entrusting it to a person nominated by the mother.[3] The Misericórdia also granted dowries to deserving girls. Testators such as Jorge Ferreira, Felippe Correia and Joanna Fernandes left legacies to the Misericórdia to finance the allocation of a certain number of dowries annually. At first the brotherhood allocated these dowries in advance before the money was available. A stricter administration was introduced in 1653 and a regulation was imposed compelling recipients of dowries to marry within the year or forfeit the dowry.[4]

By the mid-seventeenth century the Misericórdia had achieved a position of prestige in Bahia, and was fulfilling the terms of the Lisbon *Compromisso*. This eminent standing of the brotherhood was not reflected in its buildings. An organisation whose Provedors had included the governors Mem de Sá, Diogo Luís de Oliveira, the Count of Castelo Melhor and the bishop Dom Pedro Leitão, was not content to remain with the church and hospital of the 1560s. Once the fear of Dutch aggression had passed a desire for reform and the feeling of civic pride induced brothers to give generously for the renovation of the hospital and the reconstruction of the church. The cost of

---

[1] Minute of 25 July 1649 (ASCMB, vol 13, ff. 9–10).
[2] ASCMB, vol. 13, f. 15v. 　　　　　　　　[3] ASCMB, vol. 13, f. 6.
[4] Minute of 1 November 1653 (ASCMB, vol. 13, f. 42).

re-beaming the hospital in 1649 was borne by a brother, Captain Francisco Gil de Araújo.[1] A new church was built on the same site as the earlier church, but considerably larger. When the Provedor, António da Silva Pimentel, had suggested to the brotherhood that some unspent legacies should be allocated to improvements on the old church, he had been over-ruled and the general feeling was that a new church should be built. The legacy of the landowner António Dias de Ottões provided the means and the plan was drawn up by friar Macário de São João. The feeling of the age was shown in the phrasing of the minute approving the new construction which noted that this 'was in keeping with the authority of this Holy House'.[2]

These reforms were intended to impress on the Bahian populace the dual purpose of the Misericórdia, as an exponent of social philanthropy and a congregation of the faithful. They also reveal the pride, born of a feeling of ethnic and social superiority, which was to be the boon and the bane of the Misericórdia in the coming century. The brotherhood was to be led into embarking on grandiose plans and accepting new responsibilities in the field of social philanthropy without counting the cost in hard financial terms. The archives of the Misericórdia are more or less complete from this date and enable a clear picture to be drawn of the activities of the Misericórdia in Bahia during the 'Golden Age of Brazil'.

[1] ASCMB, vol. 13, f. 13.
[2] Minute of 1 November 1653 (ASCMB, vol. 13, f. 41). For a well-documented and detailed study of the construction of the church and its artistic aspects, see Carlos Ott, *A Santa Casa*, pp. 32–45.

5

The Administration of Charity

THE *Santas Casas da Misericórdia* in Asia, Africa and Brazil were governed by the *Compromisso* of Lisbon and shared the privileges granted to the parent house. The Misericórdia of Bahia had followed the 1516 *Compromisso* of Lisbon. This had been incorporated into the definitive statutes of 1618 with modifications and the introduction of twenty-two new chapters. A century of use had shown that the terms of reference of the 1516 *Compromisso* had been too general. The 1618 *Compromisso* had been characterised by its detail and lack of ambiguity, especially in the conditions of entry, the electoral procedure, and the responsibilities of brothers. It had catered for the expanding rôle of the brotherhood in Lisbon by appointing stewards for poor aid, legal affairs, the administration of legacies, the chapel and the dispensary. Additional commitments such as the administration of the Hospital of All Saints and the retirement house had also demanded special regulations. If the 1516 *Compromisso* had been a model of its kind, its successor had been no less so, as testified by its adoption until the nineteenth century.

The Crown favoured the foundation of brotherhoods in the overseas provinces but maintained strict control by insisting that the statutes be sent to Lisbon for approval. In most cases this was readily granted with slight amendments. A new branch of a brotherhood already existing in Portugal followed the statutes of the parent body. Thus the Brotherhood of the Most Holy Sacrament of the cathedral of Bahia followed the statutes of its counterpart in the cathedral of Lisbon until 1746, when a new *Compromisso* suited to local conditions was made.[1] For its part the Bahia Misericórdia

her I am indebted to the Bahian historian Marieta Alves for allowing me to examine
   [1] copy of this *Compromisso*.

had adopted the 1618 reform, whose terms it followed until 1896.[1] Although the 1618 *Compromisso* was frequently reprinted in Lisbon, it seems doubtful if it was ever printed in Bahia.[2] As late as 1870 the scribe made a copy by hand for the Misericórdia archives. The earlier copies which existed in Bahia (and judging from the general ignorance of the terms of the *Compromisso*, these were few) were brought from Lisbon and sold to brothers sufficiently interested to buy them.[3]

There were only two major attempts at reform during the 278 years that the 1618 *Compromisso* was followed in Bahia. Both of these failed. Major reforms were mooted in 1737 and 1832 but neither of these altered the administrative structure. In 1737 the controversial *alcaide-mór* Anselmo Dias, who had survived expulsion in 1732 and was then enjoying the first of his three terms as Provedor, proposed drastic reforms of the *Compromisso*. So notorious had the Misericórdia become for the 'rigging' of elections that many citizens suitable to serve on the board of guardians refused to be associated with the brotherhood. Loss of confidence in the administration of the Misericórdia had led many potential benefactors to leave legacies to other brotherhoods or the religious orders rather than to the Misericórdia. Anselmo Dias sought to remedy these abuses. He proposed that the indirect election of the Mesa by an electoral committee should be replaced by the direct election of its successors by the outgoing Mesa. He also wished to reduce the authority of the subsidiary governing body, known as the *Junta*. To eliminate petty discord he suggested the reduction of its members from twenty to twelve and that the Junta should no longer be concerned with the election of brothers. Finally, he proposed that the term of office of the Junta, which started on 10 August, should coincide with that of the Mesa beginning 3 July. In view of the radical nature of these proposals and the inadequacy of the 1618 *Compromisso* to provide for Bahian conditions, he suggested that a committee be set up to formulate a new *Compromisso*. Although Anselmo Dias received the unanimous support of his Mesa and Junta, these proposals were never implemented.[4] A further attempt in 1832

[1] The new *Compromisso* was approved on 31 May 1896 and printed in Bahia in that year.
[2] Vitor Ribeiro, *A Santa Casa*, pp. 86-7, lists further editions published in Lisbon.
[3] In 1748 two copies were sold for 320 *rs.* each (ASCMB, vol. 861, f. 1v and f. 16).
[4] Minute of 14 August 1737 (ASCMB, vol. 14, ff. 237-9).

to establish a local *Compromisso* was only slightly more successful. A revised *Compromisso* was submitted to the Mesa by a committee of three brothers, only to die a silent death.[1]

The absence of major reform does not imply dogged adherence to the 1618 *Compromisso*. New responsibilities demanded new administration, for example, the legacy of the philanthropist João de Mattos de Aguiar in 1700, or the turning wheel for foundlings established in 1726. Peculiarly Brazilian conditions such as the burial of slaves, or the acceptance of sugar in lieu of interest on a loan required special provision. Sometimes experience dictated modifications to the *Compromisso*. This was especially so in the administration of the financial affairs of the brotherhood.

The Misericórdia relied on private charity and legacies left in mortmain for its income. These legacies were made to the brotherhood on the understanding that they would be placed on loan and the interest used for charitable purposes. With the severe shortage of currency in Bahia in the late seventeenth century, it became increasingly common for debtors to fall into arrears in their payment of interest or to make payment in sugar rather than cash. Sometimes the financial crash of a plantation owner led to the loss of the capital he had borrowed from the Misericórdia. As the result of experience gained at heavy cost, the brotherhood took a series of measures in the 1690s aimed at avoiding such losses and ensuring regular payment of interest. The practice of transferring loans from one debtor to another was prohibited, unless total repayment of all capital and interest had been made to the Misericórdia.[2] The maximum sum for any loan was limited to 5,000 *cruzados*.[3] Book-keeping methods were more closely scrutinised. Decrees prevented treasurers from spending money out of bequests made to the brotherhood to be placed on loan. There were monthly checks of the accounts and the authorisation of the Mesa and Junta was required for all expenditure of capital.[4] In all cases the decrees were written into the *Compromisso* and approved by the king.

The *Compromisso* was the written law of the Misericórdia, but differed

---

[1] The committee reported in 1834 (ASCMB, vol. 16, ff. 226–229v and f. 283v).

[2] Minute of 28 May 1691 (ASCMB, vol. 14, ff. 20v–21).

[3] Minute of 22 March 1692 (ASCMB, vol. 14, ff. 24v–25).

[4] Minutes of 19 August 1682 and 30 April 1735 (ASCMB, vol. 14, ff. 7v–8v and ff. 211–12).

from the statutes of other brotherhoods only in its excellence. The Miseri-córdia owed its unique position among Portuguese brotherhoods to royal patronage. The example of Dom Manuel I in the granting of privileges had been followed by his successors. During the Spanish domination (1580–1640) the Misericórdia had benefited by the confirmation of old and the concession of new privileges. With his usual prudence and desire to render himself acceptable to his Portuguese subjects, Philip I of Portugal (II of Spain) had been prolific in granting favours to the powerful brotherhood. Some privileges had had no application beyond Lisbon, e.g. the exemption of the butcher supplying meat to the Misericórdia from a tax on meat payable to the health authorities for the cost of bringing water to the Rocio. Other privileges had been equally applicable to the overseas Misericórdias and were constantly cited by them.

The privileges of the Misericórdia of Lisbon had been extended to the brotherhood in Bahia by Philip III in 1622. This right was frequently challenged by the local authorities. Throughout the first half of the eighteenth century the correspondence of the Misericórdia of Bahia with its counterpart in Lisbon and its own attorney constantly asserted the need for the confirmation of these privileges by the Crown. The Lisbon authorities ignored these appeals of the Misericórdia. The Overseas Council, founded to relieve the Crown of the mass of paper work from verbose overseas bureaucrats, was tardy in transacting business. The complaints of the Count of Sabugosa echoed those of the Misericórdia. On one occasion a petition was delayed because the letter of enquiry had been sent to Maranhão instead of Bahia. On another the secretary of the Overseas Council denied all knowledge of appeals by the Misericórdia of Bahia — although these were repeated annually![1]

In the course of its history the Misericórdia of Bahia suffered continual opposition, because of the failure to observe its privileges. The opposition came from the judiciary, the city council and the ecclesiastical authorities. If this opposition is examined in some detail it is to illustrate that the charitable works of the brotherhood were performed despite the local authorities. The increasingly critical state of the brotherhood during the first half of the eighteenth century can be attributed, in part, to the lack of co-operation, let alone encouragement, it received from official circles.

[1] ASCMB, vol. 52, ff. 39–40 and f. 123.

The judiciary challenged the privileges of the Misericórdia in the courts and in financial matters. The *mordomos dos presos*, two brothers in charge of the welfare of prisoners, enjoyed a privileged position in the court room. In the early eighteenth century the Mesa complained to the king that this privilege was being ignored. Dom Pedro II ordered recognition of their privileged position and that in future these officials should sit immediately below and to the right of the *desembargadores*, or Crown judges, taking precedence over the district judge (*ouvidor da comarca*) and district magistrate (*juiz de fora*). Since it was not customary for the last two to attend court, considerable bitterness developed between them and the two brothers until the king relieved them of this duty.[1] The representative of the Misericórdia also had the privilege of speaking first in the Court of Appeals. This privilege was likewise ignored. Often prisoners defended by the Misericórdia never received a hearing simply because the representative of the brotherhood could not appeal on their behalf.[2]

The Misericórdia had been granted legal privileges in financial matters. These were also challenged by the judiciary. The greatest bone of contention was the right of the brotherhood to enforce payment of outstanding debts of capital or interest by the compulsory sale of property. This privilege was common to the Treasury and some religious orders. A legal loophole had been found whereby appeal could be made against orders for compulsory sale. The ensuing dilatory proceedings meant that it was no longer practicable for the brotherhood to contemplate legal action against its debtors.[3] These debtors were aided and abetted in their refusal to pay by local magistrates in the villages of the Recôncavo who chose not to enforce letters of subpoena rather than risk the ill will of powerful plantation owners. The Misericórdia tried to overcome these delays by asking Lisbon to authorise the appointment of a private judge, whose sole duties would be to examine pending law suits and institute legal proceedings against debtors. These petitions were ignored, but the justice of them was recognised by the 1755 report on the Misericórdia undertaken on the king's orders by the

---

[1] Royal letters of 27 February 1702 and 8 February 1704 (APB, *Ordens régias*, vol. 7, docs. 86 and 250).　　　　[2] ASCMB, vol. 52, ff. 151v–154.

[3] ASCMB, vol. 52, ff. 178–81. In 1824 there was a test case in Rio de Janeiro to establish if this privilege of the Misericórdia was applicable to liquid debts only, or also to legacies left to the brotherhood (ANRJ, *Caixa 129*, doc. 28).

visiting Crown judge, António José de Affonseca Lemos. He advocated such an appointment for the protection of the brotherhood's interests in the Court of Appeals and the enforcement of regulations dealing with regular examinations of the accounts of the Misericórdia.[1]

Despite the truth of the Alentejan proverb 'Quem não está na Câmara, está na Misericórdia' ('He who is not a city councillor is a brother of the Misericórdia') relations between the two bodies were often acrimonious. The city council impeded the Misericórdia at every turn, unless it were to its own immediate advantage. Indeed, when the Misericórdia was in a critical financial position in 1736, its chances of recovery were ruined by the city council pressing through legal action for the payment of 11,500 *cruzados* by the brotherhood.[2] The most severe dispute was over the debts of sugar planters to the brotherhood. By numerous decrees from 1663 onwards the Crown had protected the sugar industry, forbidding creditors from taking legal action against the buildings and equipment of plantations and ruling that they must be satisfied from the proceeds derived from the sale of the crop. The king had also forbidden the compulsory sale of the crop out of season for the payment of debts. Any valuation should be made only in the fortnight preceding the arrival of the fleet by two representatives of the municipal council. In the last two decades of the seventeenth century the sugar industry had been hit by falling prices, slave mortality and a succession of bad harvests. When the Misericórdia in 1715 secured the privilege of taking legal action against its debtors and enforcing the compulsory sale of the sugar crop out of season, the city councillors challenged this privilege.[3] The councillors brought embargoes against the Misericórdia in the Bahian judiciary but they were rejected. The municipal council appealed to Lisbon. In 1717 the rumour reached Brazil that the council had been successful in

[1] Chapter i of report, (BNRJ, *11–33, 24, 45*, doc. 10).

[2] The Mesa 'borrowed' this sum from the legacy of João de Mattos de Aguiar by a minute of 14 November 1736 (ASCMB, vol. 14, f. 231).

[3] There is doubt as to whether this privilege was granted in 1715 or 1716. In a letter of 3 August 1715 the Mesa in Bahia congratulated its counterpart in Lisbon on its success in obtaining a royal *provisão* allowing the Misericórdia of Bahia to enforce the compulsory sale of pledged sugar, despite municipal opposition. But in a letter of 22 August 1717 the Mesa in Bahia asked the board of guardians of the Lisbon branch to intervene officially to ensure that the *provisão* of 1716 be respected (ASCMB, vol. 52, ff. 73–76v and ff. 88–9).

quashing the privilege of the Misericórdia.[1] The brotherhood fought the
decision on the grounds that the royal decrees had been intended for the
business community and not for a charitable concern whose income was
derived from interest on loans.[2] The outcome of the dispute is uncertain.
Certainly infringements of the royal decrees continued. In 1729 the Count of
Sabugosa, replying to a plaintive letter from Dom João V on the collapse of
the Bahian economy, informed the king that the compulsory sales of property
to satisfy creditors meant that many plantations were being sold at three to
four times less than their market value. So severe was the shortage of ready
money in Brazil that sometimes there were even no bidders at all for good
plantations.[3]

In its relations with the Church the Misericórdia met with mixed success.
A distinction must be drawn between the local clergy and the papal authorities. Encounters with the local clergy over matters of protocol often resulted
in bad feeling and even led to excommunication. But such 'tiffs' were
infrequent and more than compensated for by the success of the brotherhood
in obtaining papal bulls. Friction with the Bahian ecclesiastical authorities
was caused by the infringement of the privileges of the Misericórdia. One
privilege exempted the Misericórdia from the jurisdiction of the diocesan
bishop. Although Dom João III had haggled over the concession of this
privilege it had been confirmed by the Council of Trent. When the
Misericórdia of Bahia had rebuilt its church in the 1650s the Ordinary had
infringed this privilege by visiting the new building. On the grounds that
he had not been consulted about the construction and that the altars were
not in the same position as the old altars, he had threatened the Misericórdia
with excommunication should mass be celebrated. The brotherhood had
ignored this threat and incurred excommunication.[4] Whether or not this
excommunication was later lifted is not stated, but the brotherhood continued
to celebrate masses in its new church.

Even if a compromise were reached on this occasion, it did not mean that
the contenders were willing to forgive and forget. Eleven years later (1669),
on the occasion of the Maundy Thursday procession, the vicar-general

---

[1] ASCMB, vol. 52, ff. 88–9.   [2] ASCMB, vol. 52, ff. 91v–93.
[3] Letter of 25 August 1729 by the viceroy (APB, *Ordens régias*, vol. 25, doc. 6a).
[4] The decree of excommunication had been published on 12 March 1658
(ASCMB, vol. 13, ff. 107–108v).

ordered the musicians not to perform unless accompanied by the Brotherhood of the Chapel of the Cathedral, or another brotherhood nominated by
the chapter of the cathedral.   This order directly opposed the papal bull
whereby the Misericórdia could elect a master of ceremonies from among its
own clergy, and not from those of the cathedral.   The board of guardians of
1669 decided to settle the question of exemption once and for all by pursuing
the matter through legal channels until a final ruling was obtained.[1]   In
1702 the Bahia Appeals Court published an order authorising the Visitor of
the archbishop to enter the sacrarium only of the Misericórdia, but no
mention was made of the more general issue.[2]   Certainly in the next half
century there were no further controversies.

The local clergy did not challenge the Misericórdia's privileges when
these did not deal with protocol.   Pope Alexander VIII had issued a bull
giving plenary indulgence to any condemned man who went to the scaffold
kissing an image of Christ held by a priest of the Misericórdia.   This
privilege was first applied in Bahia in 1690 and was respected on this and
subsequent occasions by the ecclesiastical authorities.[3]   So also was the
papal bull providing for a privileged altar in the church of the Misericórdia.
Terms of legacies were governed by canon law.   Charitable works were
assisted by the concession to the Misericórdia of all bequests not paid to the
legatees within the time stipulated by the testator.   The administration of
legacies applied to prison welfare was co-ordinated by all such legacies being
handed to the brothers in charge of prisoners.   We shall have occasion to
return later to the privilege of the Misericórdia to possess biers which brought
the brotherhood into conflict with local parish priests.

The most valuable papal concession to the Misericórdia of Bahia was the
reduction in the number of masses to be said by the brotherhood for the souls
of benefactors.   Over the years these masses had accumulated to the point
where it was simply a physical impossibility for the chaplains of the Misericórdia to say them all on the three altars of the church.   Moreover the
original legacies had declined in value, or been squandered by the maladmini-

---

[1] Minute of 2 June 1669 (ASCMB, vol. 13, ff. 157v–157Av).

[2] The governor-general had hesitated to publish the verdict, passed in 1701, and
referred the matter to the king who ordered its publication in a letter of 23 January
1702 (APB, *Ordens régias*, vol. 7, docs. 68 and 69).

[3] ASCMB, vol. 207, ff. 23–4.

stration of the brotherhood's treasurers. The normal number of masses had been swollen by the legacy of João de Mattos de Aguiar in 1700 providing for 11,000 masses to be said for his own soul and those of his relations. In 1729 the total commitment was some 2,000 masses to be said monthly. The Provedor and precentor in the cathedral, João Calmon, took steps to reduce this number.[1] Another ecclesiastic, Canon Francisco Martins Pereira, Provedor 1731–5, calculated the obligation of the Misericórdia in unsaid masses at 77,583 up to the end of 1734. Pope Clement 'wrote off' this backlog of masses once it was shown that the Misericórdia could not be accused of intent to defraud. In return for this favour, the Misericórdia made a contribution to the fabric of St Peter's in Rome, prayed for the Pope and promised to say an office every month for fifteen months in the Misericórdia church for the souls of benefactors.[2] Even this comparatively slight burden proved too much for the brotherhood. In 1739 all masses, for which the Misericórdia still had funds from the original legacies, were reduced by two-thirds in the majority of cases, e.g. two weekly masses were reduced to thirty-four annually. The extent of the reduction depended on how much of the original bequest still remained, or on the cost of the masses stipulated by the testator. In this manner 13,531 masses were reduced to 6,763 masses, costing 1,644$000.[3] This papal action removed the guilt complex which had troubled a generation of Provedors, but it could not avert the financial decline of the brotherhood.

The Misericórdia of Bahia adhered strictly to the *Compromisso* of Lisbon and was careful in the use of privileges. Mesas were well aware that any deviation from the letter of the *Compromisso* or the exploitation of a privilege would be pounced on by the local authorities. Thus the executive administration of the Misericórdia in Bahia was closely modelled on its European counterpart. The Mesa was the prime administrative body. Its composition and terms of reference have already been discussed (pp. 21–2) and had not been radically altered by the 1618 reform. An innovation of the 1618 *Compromisso* had been the introduction of an advisory body of twenty brothers, known as the Junta. The brothers were drawn equally from each class, and usually would have served on the Mesa or have comparable

---

[1] Minute of 10 April 1729 (ASCMB, vol. 35, ff. 9v–10v).
[2] Papal decree of 5 March 1735 copied in ASCMB, vol. 14, ff. 225–6.
[3] ASCMB, vol. 14, ff. 251–2.

administrative experience. The first recorded instance of a formal election of a Junta in Bahia had been in 1679 to decide on the admission of a brother of dubious qualifications.[1] From this date there was an annual election of what amounted to a secondary governing body. Previously the custom had been for the Provedor to invite the opinions of brothers of known administrative ability, for example to discuss the rumour of the successful outcome of the lawsuit with the Jesuits of St Antão in 1651.

Although elected annually, the Junta provided administrative continuum during the first month of the term of office of the new Mesa, between the elections of the Mesa on 3 July and those of the Junta on 10 August. The Junta also acted as a brake on a Mesa which could all too easily be swayed by the oratory of one powerful member. This happened over the siting of the retirement house when the selfish projects of the Secretary of State, Gonçalo Ravasco Cavalcante e Albuquerque, were defeated by the Junta. In financial matters the restraining influence of the Junta was all-important. A decree of 1735 ruled that any expenditure from capital must be authorised by the Junta, on pain of the culprits reimbursing the brotherhood from their own pockets.[2]

Despite the excellence of the Junta in theory, experience showed that it was subject to the same abuses as the Mesa. The absence of suitable candidates for the Mesa meant that the clause of the 1618 *Compromisso* forbidding re-election within three years of holding office was ignored in Bahia.[3] A member of the board of guardians one year often served on the Junta in the following year and regained his position on the Mesa in the third year. This reduced the representative power of the mass of the brotherhood because of the presence of the same individuals on one or the other of the governing bodies. Anselmo Dias had hoped to remedy this situation by his proposed reforms in 1737.

The Mesa was elected on the day of the Visitation, the main festival of the brotherhood. Previously a list of eligible brothers had been posted on the

[1] The Junta met on 1 March 1679 to debate the application for membership of Domingos Rodrigues Correia discussed on p. 137 (ASCMB, vol. 34, ff.14v–15v).

[2] Minute of 3 April 1735. This was approved by the Count of Sabugosa on 2 May 1735, who ordered its inclusion in the book of statutes governing the brotherhood (ASCMB, vol. 14, ff. 206v–207v and ff. 211–12).

[3] *Compromisso* of Lisbon of 1618, chapter 5, §6.

church door. On 2 July the brotherhood was summoned to the church. In the church were a round table, at which were seated the members of the outgoing Mesa, and two tables for the taking of votes. At one were the scribe in office, the treasurer of the previous Mesa and the president of the chapel. At the other were the treasurer in office, the scribe of the previous Mesa, and the master of the chapel. The clauses of the *Compromisso* dealing with the election were then read and the outgoing Mesa, followed by the brotherhood, cast votes for the ten members of the electoral panel. These votes were locked away for the night and on 3 July the names of the electors were announced. After mass these ten electors, five from each class, took the oath to put aside prejudices of 'relationship, friendship or hatred' in the choice of the board of guardians. They were then divided into groups of one 'noble' and one plebeian, each group voting for the most suitable candidates for each position to be filled on the Mesa. The results were announced the same day and the new Mesa was sworn into office.

A position on the board of guardians carried social prestige and could be personally profitable to the incumbent. Thus it was scarcely surprising that the electors should forget their oath, allowing their exalted ideals of impartiality to be tempered by more mundane considerations. 'Rigged' elections were frequent during the first half of the eighteenth century. In part, these were born of the economic situation in Bahia. There was a chronic shortage of ready money and loans were made on the dubious security of the coming sugar crop. Although the brotherhoods of Bahia never rivalled those of Manila in high finance, they did provide rudimentary banking services by making loans at an interest rate of $6\frac{1}{4}$ per cent.[1] The Misericórdia was prominent in this field, the interest, in theory, being applied to social assistance. In fact, not only did the brotherhood often not receive the interest but lost the capital investment also. Strict regulations on the securities for loans were relaxed. Many debtors found that the easiest way of concealing their own short-comings in the payment of debts was to be elected to the Mesa. Popularly known as 'castanhetadas', self-interested cliques imperilled the financial position of the Misericórdia and lowered its prestige.[2] Such were the administrative irregularities of the Misericórdia

---

[1] W. L. Schurz, *The Manila Galleon*, pp. 167–72.

[2] '... hum e dois mezes antes das Eleysoens todos os annos se fazião parcialides a que a vulgaride tinha posto o nome de castanhetada' (ASCMB, vol. 14, ff. 237–9).

that they could no longer be ignored by the Count of Sabugosa. During his viceroyalty in India he had chided the Misericórdia of Gôa for its failure to make loans without adequate securities.[1] In 1723 he notified the king of similar irregularities in the branch of the brotherhood in Bahia. He suggested an immediate enquiry into the Misericórdia's finances by a Crown judge and that brothers responsible for making loans on poor securities be compelled to reimburse the Misericórdia. Dom João's V reply was half-hearted, simply commending to the brotherhood the practice of electing to the board of guardians God-fearing men of integrity. The viceroy tartly retorted that moral recommendations would be totally ineffective — and so they were.[2] It must have been with considerable satisfaction that the Count of Sabugosa, embittered by the reluctance of the king to relieve him of his post, could report to Dom João V in 1729 that administrative abuses in the Misericórdia had led to losses of 61,428$240 from capital and 72,876$130 in interest which could not be collected. Moreover, almost all the capital of 4,432$960 left by testators to finance the saying of some 24,311 masses had been misappropriated and sent to Portugal.[3]

The election of the Mesa in 1729 caused a public scandal. The clergy played an active part in canvassing for votes, and even threatened members of opposing factions with violence. Complete strangers to the Misericórdia were enlisted to record their votes. The canvassing and threats produced the desired result. Cosme Rolim de Moura, in debt to the Misericórdia and reluctant to leave his plantation twelve leagues from the city, was elected Provedor. His lack of interest in the appointment could be gauged from the fact that it was only in September that he came into the city to take office.[4] His Mesa included the chief officer of the Court of Appeals, a Treasury official, and the clerk in charge of the welfare of orphans. All had full-time jobs in public administration and could not possibly fulfil their obligations as members of the board of guardians. Once again the

---

[1] J. F. Ferreira Martins, *Historia da Misericordia de Goa*, vol. 2, p. 93.

[2] King to viceroy, 28 June 1724. In his reply of 7 June 1725, the Count of Sabugosa said he had carried out the king's orders 'mas receyo que este remedio por brando não aproveyte a achaque tão inveterado' (APB, *Ordens régias*, vol. 19, docs. 62 and 62a).

[3] Letter of 6 August 1729 (APB, *Ordens régias*, vol. 24, doc. 55).

[4] The election of the Junta which was usually on 10 August was postponed until 4 September so that he could be present (ASCMB, vol. 35, ff. 15–16).

viceroy called for strong action but a decade passed before the king acted.[1]

In 1740 Dom João V ordered that a minister, or high-ranking judge, should attend the election of the board of guardians and take legal action against brothers found guilty of electoral canvassing. A list of debtors to the brotherhood was to be posted publicly before election day and those named were not to be considered eligible.[2] In the first decree Dom João V was merely giving royal approval to an already existing practice. As early as 1730 the viceroy had ordered the judge for civil affairs to attend the elections.[3] It was ironical that Anselmo Dias, the ardent proposer of reforms to curb electoral 'rigging', should be the first to fall foul of these measures when he tried for a third term of office as Provedor in 1739. Legal action was taken against him and his colleague in crime, Mathias Tôrres. This example led many possible candidates for the post of Provedor in future years to refrain from presenting themselves for election for fear of similar punishment. The embargo on debtors serving on the board of guardians was also a mixed blessing. So low was the repute of the brotherhood at that period that potential candidates incurred small debts expressly in order to become ineligible.[4]

These measures were ineffective. They did not end 'rigged' elections and they did not save the Misericórdia from financial decline. Dom João V was the victim of his own acute intelligence and width of interests, well illustrated by his requests for detailed reports on Brazilian flora and fauna. He was also the victim of the bureaucratic backlash of his policy of running an empire from Lisbon without delegating responsibility to local authorities. This policy was partly born of the fear that if local authorities were allowed to act on their own initiative, it would be the Crown who would have to bail them out of any financial crisis. For this reason the Crown demanded detailed reports and rigorously checked all petitions made to it. This plethora of paper resulted in frequent misunderstandings, delays and ineffective action. The Misericórdia was a case in point. Royal measures failed to stop dubious elections occurring. During the next fifteen years

---

[1] APB, *Ordens régias*, vol. 24, doc. 55.

[2] The king rejected outright the proposal of direct election by the outgoing board of guardians in his letter to the viceroy of 26 March 1740 (BNRJ, *11–33, 24, 45*, doc. 2).   [3] Viceroy to king, 14 August 1730 (BNRJ, *11–33, 24, 45*, doc. 8).

[4] Mesa to king, 10 September 1744 (ASCMB, vol. 52, ff. 208–9).

the Misericórdia was to become notorious for the number of Provedors who resigned. Between 1740 and 1754 the office of Provedor changed hands twenty times. But so scarce were candidates that in this same period Domingos Lucas de Aguiar and Domingos Borges de Barros each served three terms as Provedor and Salvador Pires de Carvalho e Albuquerque, António Rodrigues Lima and António Gonçalves Pereira each served twice. In 1741 the Count of Galvêas ordered a second election; such was the reluctance to serve as Provedor that the only person willing to hold office was Jerónimo Velho de Araújo, captain of an infantry company and a well-known agitator on the governing bodies of various Bahian brotherhoods.[1] In 1746 the viceroy again suspended the elections and forbade the election of the priest António de Brito as Provedor.[2] In 1750 the newly elected viceroy, the Count of Atouguia (1749–55), reminded the electors that they should elect secular members of the brotherhood to the posts of Provedor and scribe 'because experience in this city has shown the inconveniences and disorders which result from ecclesiastics holding administrative office in secular brotherhoods and confraternities'.[3] This ruling was not enforced. The final blow to any lingering pretence of social prestige came with the resignation of Dr Luís da Costa e Faria in 1754, forced on him by an unruly Mesa. No successor could be found and the desperate brothers even asked a fisherman at his nets, who was not a brother, to serve nominally as Provedor. He refused![4] Only under viceregal pressure was Domingos Borges de

---

[1] He resigned on 28 June 1742 (ASCMB, vol. 35, f. 65). For complaints about his ill-treatment of soldiers see the letter of the Count of Sabugosa to the king of 15 May 1729 (APB, *Ordens régias*, vol. 24, doc. 24a).

[2] The viceroy ordered the Mesa of 1745–6 to continue in office (ASCMB, vol. 35, f. 84). The king approved this action in a letter of 17 June 1749 (APB, *Ordens régias*, vol. 47, f. 90).

[3] 'Porquanto tem mostrado a experiencia nesta sidade os emconvenientes e dezordens q' se tem seguido de se emcarregar a preçidencia e governo das Irmandades e Confrarias seculares a pessoas ecclesiasticas . . .' Viceroyal brief of 3 July 1750 (ASCMB, vol. 35, ff. 103v–104).

[4] '. . . o ultimo remedio era chamarem os Electores pa lhes darem Provor tendo alias a certeza de que já naquelles tros não achariam facilmte Irmão que quizesse servir com elles se resolveram alguns já como dezemganados em hir fallar pa o ser a hum tal, qual homem que além de não ser Irmão ainda cuida nas suas redes de pescar e o peor hé q' nem este ainda bem se resolvia a fazer aceitação do convite' (APB, *Ordens régias*, vol. 73, doc. 49).

Barros induced to assume the reins of office for the third time in four years.[1]

There are several possible reasons for this reluctance on the part of Bahians to accept the post of Provedor. In their correspondence to the king, Mesas put it down to the financial burden which accompanied this office. In a letter of 10 September 1744 to Dom João V, the Mesa wrote that 'there is nobody who wishes to be Provedor or treasurer because the incumbents of these posts must be sufficiently well off to be able to meet the exorbitant expenses of the aforesaid *Casa* and be prepared to receive payment afterwards in boxes of sugar which comprise the income of the brotherhood'.[2] There was some truth in this assertion, because the decline in the prices of sugar and tobacco in the eighteenth century had hit the landed gentry. The case of the plantation owner António da Rocha Pitta provided a chastening example. While Provedor (1700), he had ostentatiously ordered a marble staircase to be sent from Portugal for the Misericórdia of Bahia at his own expense. When it arrived he was forced to ask the brotherhood to pay for the erection because of his own financial straits. Many potential candidates preferred to forgo the honour of being Provedor rather than risk exposure of their financial skeletons to the public eye. Anselmo Dias, who served the Misericórdia well in a high-handed manner, was obliged to resign as Provedor in 1751 to attend to his personal affairs and ward off impending ruin.[3] But financial difficulties explain only half the story of this reluctance. When somebody of the social standing of Francisco Dias d'Avila (the third of this name), heir to a tradition of family service on the municipal council and board of guardians of the Misericórdia, repeatedly asked for exemption from municipal duties and displayed no interest in the Misericórdia, it seems to indicate a contributory motive for this disinterest in public service.[4]

This lack of interest was not limited to service in the Misericórdia. Shortly before the letter of the Mesa in 1744 to Dom João V telling him of the difficulty of filling the post of Provedor, the viceroy had written a similar letter. He reported how people suitable for municipal service as councillors

---

[1] ASCMB, vol. 35, ff. 123v–124.

[2] '... nem hâ quem qr^a ser Provedor e Thezour^o porq^e ha de ser pessoa q' tenha cabedal com q' suprir as exorbitantes despezas da d^a Caza, para o depois se hir pagando pelos Rendimt^os della que sam caixas de assucar' (ASCMB, vol. 52, ff. 208–9).   [3] 21 September 1751 (ASCMB, vol. 35, f. 109v).

[4] Pedro Calmon, *História da Casa da Tôrre*, pp. 158–9.

sought to avoid such public duties, and that as a result the municipal council was often composed of individuals unsuited for public office.[1] This reluctance represented not just a natural reaction against the possibility of financial risk, but a complete change of spirit. The Bahian economy had been built on sugar. Sugar had created the landowning aristocracy and sugar had brought the Dutch to Bahia and Pernambuco in the early seventeenth century. Success against the invaders had given rise to a feeling of optimism and desire for positive action. This enthusiasm pervaded the seventeenth century. However the last decades brought financial crisis. The discovery of gold in Minas Gerais was the final blow to the prosperity of Bahia. Apathy set in. During the first years of the eighteenth century, Bahian society was in limbo, both spiritually and economically. The plantation families felt their position of dominance being undermined. The commercial community of the city was insufficiently consolidated to have produced a class of self-reliant business men. Gradually there was a transfer of power from the plantation owners to the business men and a shift in the centre of importance from the Rencôncavo to the city. This change was reflected in the incumbents of the post of Provedor of the Misericórdia, and even in the membership of the brotherhood.

The office of Provedor maintained its prestige throughout the seventeenth century and the first two decades of the eighteenth century. During this period elections were strongly contested. In 1715 the Marquis of Angeja (Viceroy, 1714–18) complained to Dom João V that Crown judges were monopolising the office of Provedor. The election of yet another, Dionísio de Azevedo Arvelos, the fifth in five years, had caused doubts to be cast on the probity of the election. The viceroy strongly urged that the holding of the offices of Provedor and Crown judge simultaneously should be forbidden. The Overseas Council in Lisbon adopted the attitude that experience gained in public service was beneficial to the Misericórdia. For once the king supported the viceroy, well aware of the opportunities for jobbery which could arise by the same individual holding two positions of influence in a society as small as was that of Bahia. Dom João V ordered that a

---

[1] Viceroy to king, 16 February 1739. In his reply of 6 May 1740 Dom João V commented on the difficulties of finding suitable candidates, 'por constar que os homens bons dessa cidade da Bahia procuravão izentarse de servir na Camera della, e de ocuparem os cargos de Almotacés' (APB, *Ordens régias*, vol. 36, doc. 60).

E

judge's participation in the affairs of the Misericórdia should be limited to serving on the board of guardians during his period of holding public office.[1]

The greatest clash of personalities for the post of Provedor was in the early eighteenth century and involved the lieutenant-general António Ferrão Castelo Branco and Gonçalo Ravasco Cavalcante e Albuquerque. The former was the son of Pedro de Unhão Castelo Branco, Provedor in 1693, and served in the Bahia garrison. He was related to the Master of the Field, Pedro Gomes, who had served as provisional Governor of Rio de Janeiro, and was a Knight of the Order of Christ. Gonçalo Ravasco was of noble lineage, of a family which had moved from Pernambuco to Bahia in the seventeenth century. He was the nephew of the Jesuit missionary, António Vieira, whose intelligence and impetuosity he shared, and the son of the secretary of state, Bernardo Vieira Ravasco, whose office he had inherited.[2] The struggle for power between these two influential citizens scandalised Bahian society, brought sharp rebuke from the king, and a viceroyal enquiry. The judiciary and the garrison were involved. António Ferrão threatened his subordinates with demotion unless they favoured his cause. Gonçalo Ravasco canvassed for votes among the legal officers. Justice triumphed in 1717 and 1720, the sword in 1718. The last of these affrays came to the notice of Dom João V who ordered stern rebuke for António Ferrão but merely a light reprimand for the secretary of state.[3] Such was contemporary feeling, that in neither case was the honesty and integrity of the offenders questioned. Gonçalo Ravasco remained as secretary of state until his death in 1725. António Ferrão was chosen to go to Lisbon to report on the mutiny of the Bahia garrison in 1728 and became Governor of S. Tomé in 1739.[4]

---

[1] Viceroy to king, 12 July 1715; decision of king in consultation with Overseas Council dated 10 September 1716 and communicated to the viceroy in a letter of 26 September 1716 (APB, *Ordens régias*, vol. 10, doc. 63 and *Documentos historicos*, vol. 96, doc. 124, pp. 251–4).

[2] For genealogical details see Fr. António de S. Maria Jaboatão, *Catalogo genealógico das principaes famílias* (Bahia, 1950; reprint from vols. 1–4 (1945–8) of the *Revista do Instituto Genealógico da Bahia*).

[3] King to viceroy, 17 April 1720 and 19 April 1723 (APB, *Ordens régias*, vol. 62, doc. 53 and vol. 17, doc. 30).

[4] He also carried samples of gold and silver from new strikes in the interior of Bahia. For his involvement in a scandal over dowries see pp. 189–90 (APB, *Ordens régias*, vol. 23, doc. 116).

Corruption in elections was not limited to the Misericórdia, nor to Bahia. Even the conventual peace was not immune to these disturbances. The abbess of the Convent of Sta Clara do Desterro of Bahia complained to the king on several occasions in the early eighteenth century of secular interference in elections. An extreme case was the election of a new abbess in September 1723. A group of laymen canvassed for votes; this group included a Crown judge, a sergeant-major in the garrison, a Benedictine friar and Gonçalo Ravasco Cavalcante e Albuquerque![1] The Third Order of St Francis was also subject to electoral disturbances. Ever since the contract in 1701 between the Third Order and the friars for the tertiaries to build a church, sacristy and cemetery on a plot of land known as the Genipapeiro in return for an annual rent of 30$000, the tertiaries had struggled to exempt themselves from the jurisdiction of the prelate. Matters came to a head when the tertiaries began the construction of a bell-tower, a status symbol among the brotherhoods who could then summon the people for processions and the brothers for funerals of their late colleagues. Work was halted in 1743, pending enquiry. Investigation revealed that the chief treasurer and canon of the cathedral, José Ferreira de Mattos, was the cause of these disputes during his second term of office as minister of the Third Order. During a similar disagreement in Rio between the tertiaries and the friars, the governor, Luís Vahia Monteiro (1725–32), had been indecisive and been reprimanded severely by the king for failing to support the prelate.[2] Mindful of this, the Count of Galvêas (Viceroy, 1735–49) laid the blame squarely on the dubious electoral methods employed by the tertiaries in Bahia.[3] An attempt by José Ferreira and his colleagues to appeal to the Roman Curia through their Lisbon attorney was frustrated by Dom João V.

[1] Gonçalo Ravasco's struggle for power on the city council and his pernicious influence in the administration of several brotherhoods had been censured by the king in 1720. In 1718 he had been expelled from the Third Order of the Carmelites (APB, *Ordens régias*, vol. 62, doc. 53). In a letter of 6 February 1725 the king ordered the viceroy to forbid further secular interference in conventual elections (APB, *Ordens régias*, vol. 19, doc. 91).

[2] The dispute was over the building of a hospital and chapel by the Third Order and the persistence of a clique of tertiaries in using these buildings despite orders to the contrary, ANRJ, *Códice 952*, vol. 22 (2nd part), ff. 273, 551, 582, 591, and vol. 23, ff. 112, 144, 316, and vol. 24, f. 248.

[3] Viceroy to king, 17 March 1744 (APB, *Ordens régias*, vol. 41, doc. 9a).

The canon resigned in 1745 protesting loyal allegiance to his Lord and Sovereign![1] The outcome was a royal order forbidding re-election within three years of holding office.[2] The 1618 *Compromisso* of Lisbon had contained an identical clause. In neither case was this ruling enforced or respected by tertiaries or brothers.

The municipal councils of Rio de Janeiro and Bahia echoed the Misericórdia in protests of impecuniosity, when faced by requests for the payment of debts. They too were subject to 'rigged' elections. In the very year (1746) that the Count of Galvêas suspended the elections of the Misericórdia in Bahia, the city council of Rio was accused of filling its offices with the sons and relatives of councillors. In Bahia, the malpractices of the municipal council rivalled those of the Misericórdia in their frequency. In 1737 Dom João V ordered that the three city councillors and the attorney of the city council who had served in 1736 should be imprisoned because of their malpractices during their term of office.[3] When the king sent out from Lisbon a Crown judge to take stock of the Misericórdia of Bahia in 1754, his terms of reference also included a full enquiry into the city council.[4]

The administration of charity in colonial Bahia left much to be desired. This was not because the administrative machinery did not exist — it did. It was because Brazilian administration at that period was dominated (and still is to some extent) by a minority of highly influential men. These men had received no formal training for public office, but belonged to an 'in' group formed of certain families who had intermarried. For them, administrative office was a family tradition and social duty. The actual every-day business was left to incompetent underlings. This lack of direct supervision resulted in poor decisions and negligent book-keeping, be it in the Misericórdia, city council or Treasury. A report on the Treasury in 1757 com-

---

[1] APB, *Ordens régias*, vol. 42, docs. 1 and 1a and vol. 43 docs. 55 and 55a.

[2] APB, *Ordens régias*, vol. 42, doc. 4 and accompanying documents.

[3] ANRJ, *Códice 952*, vol. 33, ff. 315, 360 and 362–3, and APB, *Ordens régias*, vol. 33, doc. 22.

[4] 'Fuy servido mandar que o Dezembargador Antonio Joze da Fonseca Lemos, fosse a essa cidade, e tirasse huma particular, e distincta devassa dos mesmos descaminhos, em cada huma das repartiçoens da Fazenda, fazendo a esse respeito, todos os exames, e averiguaçoens necessarias, e que da mesma forma, tomasse contas â Camara, e Mizericordia dessa cidade, para se descobrirem os excessos, que nessas duas cazas me consta se tem comettido' (APB, *Ordens régias*, vol. 51, f. 130).

mented that 'the world has never seen such a Babel of confusion and disorder as among the books, papers and records of the Treasury of Bahia'.[1] This was equally applicable to private and municipal archives, and the Misericórdia was simply at one with the age in this respect. A more detailed examination of the attitude to public service, as shown in the key posts of the Misericórdia — the posts of Provedor and treasurer — will reveal the extent to which an apparently administrative phenomenon was governed by social change.

[1] 'não tendo visto o mundo Babêl mais confuza nem mais desordenada do q' são os livros, papéis e estylos da Casa da Fazenda da Bª' (APB, *Ordens régias*, vol. 56, f. 449).

6

Class, Creed and Colour in Administration

THE *Compromissos* of the Misericórdia of Lisbon were followed by the overseas branches of the brotherhood. The living conditions in the settlements of Portuguese in Asia, Africa and Brazil differed markedly from those in the mother country. The social structure of these communities and the relations of the Portuguese with other ethnic groups and followers of other creeds, varied from country to country. The branches of the Misericórdia in Gôa and Macao made their own *Compromissos* to cater for local conditions. It has been seen that the Misericórdia of Bahia did not formulate its own *Compromisso*, but boards of guardians often found it necessary to interpret, rather than follow blindly, the clauses of the statutes of Lisbon. In this respect the archives of the Misericórdia afford a fascinating insight into the more elusive and least tangible aspects of Brazilian history — the infrastructure of society and the ethnic and religious stresses and strains present in colonial Bahia.

The Provedor of the Misericórdia was, by definition, 'a gentleman, of authority, prudence and virtue, of good repute and of such an age that the other brothers can recognise him as their head and can obey him the more easily'.[1] In Gôa the Misericórdia had sought the maximum degree of protection by the frequent election of the governor or viceroy to this office. In Bahia there had been some half a dozen such elections in the seventeenth century, but generally the Misericórdia preferred not to court official intervention.[2] In the eighteenth century the election of the viceroy to be

---

[1] *Compromisso* of 1618, chapter 8, §1.
[2] The Provedors of the Misericórdia of Gôa are listed in J. F. Ferreira Martins, *Historia da Misericordia de Goa*, vol. 1, pp. 385–400. In Bahia the records of Provedors are incomplete for the sixteenth and early seventeenth centuries, but the following governors-general served as Provedors: Mem de Sá (1560s?); Luís de

Provedor was only contemplated as an expedient to enforce payment of debts, but a motion proposing this in 1751 was defeated.[1] Even the Count of Sabugosa, who had served the Gôa Misericórdia admirably as Provedor in 1713 during his viceroyalty in India, was not asked to occupy the corresponding post in Bahia during his fifteen years as viceroy of Brazil.

There were three reasons for this difference of attitude between the Misericórdias of Gôa and Bahia. First, the membership of the Misericórdia of Bahia was drawn from a more highly-developed corporate social body than that existing in Gôa. Secondly, there had been established in Bahia a landowning aristocracy of plantation owners and cattle ranchers, the like of which never existed in the narrow confines of Gôa. Thirdly, the nationalistic spirit, which was to achieve Brazilian independence in the nineteenth century, was strongly in evidence a century earlier. The Count of Sabugosa was prominent in fostering this independence movement. He supported the Bahian business community in its efforts to maintain the monopoly of the slave trade to the west coast of Africa and the Gulf of Benin, against overtures from Dom João V and the merchants of Lisbon to 'cash in' on this trade. The landed aristocracy of Bahia had been born and bred in independence. Its members represented the human aspect of the dichotomy existing between the theory of royal decrees and the practice of enforcing them. This landed aristocracy financed the Misericórdia in the seventeenth century and monopolised the post of Provedor.

In 1726 Dom João V ordered the Count of Sabugosa to verify that the large tracts of land owned by certain families in the *hinterland* of Bahia were

---

Sousa (1617); Francisco de Moura Rolim, local governor with title of captain-major (1625); Diogo Luís de Oliveira (1632 and 1633); João Rodrigues de Vasconcellos e Sousa, Count of Castelo Melhor (1650); Affonso Furtado de Castro do Rio de Mendonça, Viscount of Barbacena (1671, ASCMB, vol. 34, f. 5: he was sworn in as a brother on 3 July, the day of his election as Provendor, ASCMB, vol. 2, f. 71).

[1] Minute of 13 October 1751 subsequently ruled null and void (ASCMB, vol. 15, f. 54). The Misericórdia of Rio de Janeiro sent a petition to Dom João V asking him to allow Gomes Freire de Andrada (Governor, 1733–63) to serve as Provedor 'porq' com o seu activo zello, e rectidão inflexivel fará com q' se paguem as numerozas dividas q' à mesma Santa Caza se devem'. The king passed the request on to the governor with a covering letter of 6 May 1746 encouraging his acceptance (ANRJ, *Códice 952*, vol. 33, f. 142).

being properly developed. He named the 'big five' landowners, or their heirs, as António Guedes de Brito, Domingos Affonso Sertão, António da Rocha Pitta, Pedro Barbosa Leal and Garcia d'Avila Pereira of the House of Tôrre.[1] He could have added the Silva Pimentel family to this list, because the marriage of a bastard daughter of António Guedes de Brito to António da Silva Pimentel had united these two powerful families.[2] It was no coincidence that these same names occur time and again in the records of the Misericórdia and that the post of Provedor often passed from father to son. An unwritten condition of the post of Provedor was that the incumbent should contribute generously to the expenses of the brotherhood. The electors were mindful of the fortunes to be made from the cultivation of sugar or the rearing of cattle when choosing a new Provedor. This obligation was recognised by the Provedors and the majority in the seventeenth century distinguished themselves by their generosity to the brotherhood. During their lives they sponsored artistic works and at death they left a legacy to the Misericórdia.

Some few examples will suffice to illustrate this. The pioneer and plantation owner, António da Silva Pimentel (Provedor, 1653), contributed towards the building of the new church of the Misericórdia in the 1650s. Another plantation owner, Francisco Fernandes do Sim (Provedor, 1656–9 and 1661), left 16,000 *cruzados* to the brotherhood to provide dowries for eight girls.[3] Manuel de Araújo de Aragão (Provedor, 1685) and the Master of the Field Pedro Gomes (Provedor, 1686) contributed towards the heavy costs of constructing a cloister, entrusted to one of the best stone-masons of Bahia, Manuel Quaresma. The greatest benefactor of the Misericórdia was João de Mattos de Aguiar, Provedor in 1684. When he died in 1700, he left vast legacies to be administered by the Misericórdia, providing for a retirement house, dowries and alms for the poor. The landowners Pedro Barbosa Leal (Provedor, 1703, 1704) and Domingos Affonso Sertão (Provedor, 1705) were the last Provedors to maintain the seventeenth-century tradition of supporting the brotherhood with open-handed generosity. Self-interest characterised the actions of the Provedors in the eighteenth century. This

---

[1] King to viceroy, 7 February 1726 (APB, *Ordens régias*, vol. 20, doc. 29 and accompanying documents).

[2] Jaboatão, *Catalogo*, p. 90, under 'Silva Pimenteis etc na Bahia'.

[3] He died in 1664 (ASCMB, vol. 41, ff. 91v–97).

was illustrated by António da Rocha Pitta, Provedor in 1700. His choice of a marble staircase as a gift to the Misericórdia satisfied his own vanity but did not greatly benefit the brotherhood. His inability to pay for its installation was indicative of the decline of the great plantation families of the Recôncavo.

There had been much inter-marriage between the families of the landed aristocracy of Bahia. Practically all the Provedors of the Misericórdia between 1660 and 1750 were related to a greater or lesser degree. Suffice it to quote the case of Gonçalo Ravasco Cavalcante e Albuquerque. Admitted to the brotherhood in 1686, he was the son of Bernardo Vieira Ravasco (Provedor, 1681) and Felippa de Albuquerque, daughter of the sometime Provedor Lourenço Cavalcante e Albuquerque. Gonçalo Ravasco married the daughter of the brother Aleixo Paes de Azevedo whose wife, Francisca de Vasconcellos, was the daughter of Gaspar de Araújo de Góis, Provedor in 1682.[1] For his part, Gonçalo Ravasco was Provedor in 1717 and 1720. This example was not exceptional and there were many similar cases among families represented on the Mesa and Junta. Among the noble Bahian families membership of the Misericórdia was nothing less than a family tradition.

Towards the turn of the seventeenth century there was a notable change and this became more apparent as the eighteenth century progressed. The landowning families were still represented on the Mesa and Junta, but increasingly rarely did they provide the Provedors and treasurers. The division of estates and the decline of the sugar industry had reduced the financial resources of such families, but such was their prestige that they continued to exert influence. The constructive energy of the post-restoration period, which had created the great estates of the Recôncavo and opened up the *hinterland*, was spent. António da Silva Pimentel, the driving force behind the building of the Misericórdia church in the 1650s, would have turned in his grave if he could have seen his son of the same name, Provedor in 1697 and 1698, leave a paltry 50$000 to the Misericórdia for the purchase of bedclothes for the hospital.[2] During the eighteenth century the Provedors regarded the Misericórdia rather as a milch cow for their own personal profit than as a charitable institution worthy of their favours.[3]

The decline in importance of the landowning class was a gradual process

---

[1] ASCMB, vol. 2, ff. 264v–265.   [2] ASCMB, vol. 42, f. 155.
[3] In a letter of 29 October 1739 the Mesa asked the king to refuse the petition of Balthazar de Vasconcellos Cavalcante (Provedor, 1723) for a royal

spread out over more than half a century. Prominent Bahian families did not sever themselves from all social intercourse, but tended simply to 'opt out' of public duties. These were to be assumed by business men, many of whom had come to Bahia as ambitious bachelors, married local girls and accumulated small fortunes by commerce. But on both sides there was a period of reluctance. The landowners were unwilling to renounce the post of Provedor to a class still tainted with semitic stigma in the popular mind. For their part, the business men still felt socially insecure and were not sufficiently consolidated as a community. Transition was painful and accompanied by a plethora of electoral abuses, resignations, expulsions and repeated interventions by the viceroy in the affairs of the Misericórdia. 'Caretaker' Provedors were needed until the business community was sufficiently established, financially and socially, to occupy executive posts in the Misericórdia. In the years 1710–50 an unusually large number of high-ranking public officials and ecclesiastical dignitaries served as Provedors, often under the auspices of the viceroy.[1] Generally speaking, these compromise Provedors did little for the brotherhood. Two exceptions were the precentor of the cathedral, João Calmon (Provedor, 1727, 1728) and Canon Francisco Martins Pereira (Provedor, 1731, 1732, 1733, 1734). Men of great integrity, they restored, to some degree, the prestige of the Misericórdia. They were also practical enough to obtain concessions for the brotherhood, such as the reduction in the number of masses.

The business men emerged as a social class from this period of transition and compromise. This process was accompanied by a shift in the distribution of wealth and by a gradual move from the rural areas to the city. Business men (*homens de negócio*) first appeared as such in the registers of admissions to the Misericórdia at the turn of the eighteenth century. From 1730 there was a significant increase in the numbers of these accepted as brothers. The position of the business man was ambiguous and difficult in the Portuguese overseas empire. He was scorned by the populace as a New

---

moratorium on a debt of 16,000$000 he owed to the brotherhood, 'porquanto he bem notorio e sabido a summa decadencia e mizeravel Estado em q' a tem posto seus devedores, e mayor mente os q' forão Provedores, como foi o supp^do p^a se proverem do Cabedal della' (ASCMB, vol. 52, ff. 185v–186v).

1 High Court judges were Provedors in the years 1711–15 and ecclesiastics in 1727–8, 1731–4, 1740, 1744, 1746 and 1754. See appendix 2 for a complete list of Provedors.

Christian, yet supported by the Crown as the means of replenishing the royal coffers. Financial success preceded social acceptance. Two business men who became Provedors, André Marques (1739 and 1749), and Domingos Lucas de Aguiar (1742, 1746 and 1747), show that the social 'breakthrough' took place in the 1740s. André Marques and Domingos Lucas de Aguiar had several points in common and possibly showed the pattern of behaviour of the business community. Both had emigrated to Brazil, André Marques from the commercial city of Oporto, and Domingos Lucas de Aguiar from a village in the archbishopric of Braga. They had married local girls of artisan families of some social position for the fathers had both served the Misericórdia as brothers of lower standing. André Marques and Domingos Lucas de Aguiar succeeded financially and were accepted into the Misericórdia as brothers of the upper class in 1718 and 1733 respectively.[1] They achieved sufficient prominence in the business community to represent the Board of Business Men (*Mesa dos Homens de Negócio*) in discussions on the plan of the Count of Galvêas for a fleet of twenty-four ships to cater for the west African trade. In 1743 and 1744 both submitted special reports on a trading company for slaves from the Mina coast.[2] Their success story was not unique and many more of their kind emigrated from the north of Portugal to Bahia, married into respectable working-class families, and went on to achieve considerable wealth.

It was in the office of treasurer that this change was more readily apparent. As early as 1641 the Misericórdia had been compelled to use a legacy in order to pay its treasurer.[3] In 1652 the board of guardians had been informed by the treasurer that he had no money in the brotherhood's coffers and that he had met the immediate expenses of the hospital from his own pocket and wished to be reimbursed. In 1682 the Misericórdia had implored the wealthy Pedro Barbosa Leal to serve God and the brotherhood by accepting this office.[4] This he did, but his successors in the treasury were less willing to place their personal fortune at the disposal of an often dubious administration. In the eighteenth century it became increasingly common for those

1 ASCMB, vol. 3, f. 225v and f. 379v respectively; details of the fathers-in-law are in vol. 2, ff. 234v–235 and f. 290.

2 APB, *Ordens régias*, vol. 41, docs. 6a and 6b.

3 Minute of 30 June 1641 (ASCMB, vol. 40, f. 142).

4 8 July 1682 (ASCMB, vol. 34, f. 24v).

elected at the first ballot to refuse, and those who did accept made it evident that they would sustain no personal loss. Anselmo Dias, treasurer in 1731 after José Rodrigues Pinheiro had been excused from office, was elected unconstitutionally on the express understanding that he would personally contribute to the Misericórdia's expenses. Later, the Mesa expelled him on the very grounds of his having been wrongfully elected, alleging that he had flaunted its authority. The truth of the matter was that he had refused to place his personal fortune at the disposal of the brotherhood and had disputed the authoritarian action of the scribe, Jerónimo Velho de Araújo, who had dominated the Provedor and was now infringing the privileges of the treasurer.[1] Anselmo Dias refused the customary method employed by the Misericórdia in reimbursing its treasurers by bags of sugar and insisted on a cash settlement for the 1,451$650 due to him.[2] Other treasurers were more demanding, not only on the Misericórdia's finances, but on its prestige by suing the brotherhood publicly for repayment. Caetano Buitrago fell victim of the tradition of the new treasurer taking on the debts of his predecessor. In this case his predecessor, Domingos Ramos da Cunha, had been expelled after only two months in office, but had incurred debts of 3,000 *cruzados* in this short time. Caetano Buitrago threatened the Misericórdia with legal action. Rather than be discredited the board of guardians took money from capital to satisfy the debt in 1724.[3] The Mesas in their financial plight did not limit themselves to the capital to satisfy creditors. Often they 'borrowed' from the funds of the legacy of João de Mattos de Aguiar.[4] Promises to replenish both funds from the first income to be

---

[1] ASCMB, vol. 35, f. 22 recording his election on 4 July 1731. He was expelled on 10 February 1732, the Mesa admitting in its letter of explusion that 'primeyro foi VM na nossa mente elleyto Recebedor das esmollas, do que tomasse o balandrao e juramento de Ir⁰; que sômente se lhe dava, não por outro algum pretexto mas q' para haver de exercitar o d⁰ cargo para q' o habilitava o poder suprir aos gastos da Caza com o seu dinheiro' (ASCMB, vol. 52, ff. 135v–136 and vol. 195, f. 83v). For Anselmo Dias' explanation see ASCMB, vol. 52, ff. 134–5. He was re-admitted and served as Provedor on three occasions. In 1751 he resigned 'por me livrar de hũa ocasião proxima da ruina á minha pessoa, caza e parentes' (ASCMB, vol. 35, f. 109v). [2] ASCMB, vol. 14, ff. 176v–177.

[3] ASCMB, vol. 14, ff. 134v–135v.

[4] In 1736 João Nunes da Cunha (treasurer 1724) received 1,900$000 from capital in settlement of debts incurred during his year of office (ASCMB, vol. 14,

received were never fulfilled. The loss of interest on the capital meant reduction in the social services of the brotherhood. If the board of guardians had complained in 1712 that it had to sweat blood to repay the 30,000 *cruzados* due to former treasurers and that brothers refused to hold this office, how much more did this become the case when sugar prices fell to the point where nobody would accept payment in sugar, except for the ailing Misericórdia whose debtors were usually plantation owners. In 1744 and 1753 a priest, Hilário dos Santos Fialho, was sworn into office because no other brother was willing to be treasurer.[1]

By using the post of treasurer as a bargaining instrument an ambitious young businessman could gain a position in the Misericórdia administration which, once achieved, was not easily lost. António de Castro, a native of Oporto who had emigrated to Bahia where he had married, became treasurer in the year of his election to the brotherhood (1722), and went on to serve as scribe in 1730, 1734 and 1743. José Álvares da Silva, a native of Viana do Castelo, had also emigrated, married a girl from Cachoeira, and became treasurer in 1750. Another émigré and business man, Paulo Ribeiro do Valle, was elected treasurer in 1754.[2] Apart from the characteristic pattern already noted in André Marques and Domingos Lucas de Aguiar, these three treasurers had in common the fact that previous to election they had only been members of the brotherhood for a few months — in fact they counted a total of only four years' service as brothers between them. This indicates how far the Misericórdia had moved from its position as a 'family' brotherhood based on tradition. It also shows how wealth was ousting heredity as a criterion of selection for officers. When the motives for promotion from a brother of lower standing to one of higher standing are discussed, it will be seen how the financial position of a brother could dictate

---

f. 231). In 1733 a debt of 645$750 to Belchior dos Réis Duarte (treasurer 1730) was paid from the legacy of João de Mattos de Aguiar (vol. 14, ff. 184v–185).

[1] 'obriga os nossos Irmãos Thezoureiros a meterem de suas fazendas muito drº; custando ao depois gottas de sangue o seu embolço pella qual rezam com difficuldade se acha quem queira servir a tal occupaçam' (ASCMB, vol. 52, f. 53 and ff. 59v–61). The elections of Hilário dos Santos Fialho are in ASCMB, vol. 35, f. 74v and ff. 116v–117.

[2] For António de Castro see ASCMB, vol. 3, f. 257v and vol. 34, f. 160; José Álvares da Silva, vol. 4, f. 135v and vol. 35, ff. 101v–103; Paulo Ribeiro do Valle, vol. 4, f. 184 and vol. 35, ff. 119–20.

his social promotion and that in some cases this promotion coincided with his election as treasurer.

The acceptance of the business fraternity as a class suitable for public office was one instance of a general change in the class structure of Bahian society in the eighteenth century. The prejudices attached to class were linked to religious prejudice and this, in turn, was often equated to racial prejudice. The 1618 *Compromisso* had followed its predecessor in general policy, but in one aspect — that of conditions governing the admission of brothers — it had radically altered the 1516 statutes. The *Compromisso* of 1516 had vaguely decreed that candidates for membership of the brotherhood should be 'of good repute and a pure conscience and leading a virtuous life, God fearing and the keepers of His commandments, meek and humble in the service of God and the aforesaid brotherhood'.[1] The 1618 *Compromisso* had revealed the greater social and religious consciousness which had pervaded the Portuguese mentality of the sixteenth century. It had stipulated seven conditions to be met by applicants for membership:

1. Purity of blood, without any taint of Moorish or Jewish origin, both in the applicant and his wife.
2. Freedom from ill-repute, in word and deed.
3. Of a suitable age and, in the case of a bachelor, over twenty-five years of age.
4. He should receive no payment from the brotherhood.
5. Owner of a shop, or be of a trade in which such possession was not customary: no manual labourer would be admitted.
6. Literacy.
7. In sufficiently comfortable circumstances to be able to assist the brotherhood without personal hardship and without giving rise to suspicions of embezzlement of funds to which he might have access.[2]

In all instances these stipulations were strictly enforced in Bahia and expulsion resulted from erroneous declarations made at the time of election to the brotherhood.

Three changes of a social nature merit closer attention. The first is the division of the brotherhood into two classes, laid down by the 1516 *Compromisso* and maintained by that of 1618. The second is the clause introduced in 1618 demanding religious purity of blood. The third is a local condition

---

[1] *Compromisso* of 1516, chapter 2.
[2] *Compromisso* of 1618, chapter 1, §3.

imposed by the Misericórdia of Bahia demanding ethnic (in this case white) purity of blood.

Although the 1516 *Compromisso* had catered for 100 brothers and that of 1618 for 600, both had maintained a class division into brothers of *maior* ('major') or *nobre* ('noble') standing and those of *menor* ('minor') or *mecânico* ('mechanic') standing. The equal representative power of both classes had been tipped in favour of the 'nobles' by the 1618 stipulation that the scribe and treasurer, as well as the Provedor, be selected only from the brothers of 'major' standing. In Bahia this class distinction was maintained. But the concept of distinction existing in Bahia differed radically from that present in Lisbon and a definition of 'major' and 'minor' is necessary.

In colonial Bahia the brothers of higher standing can be divided into two groups. The first was the landed aristocracy whose wealth and prestige had been gained from the cultivation of sugar cane or the rearing of cattle. Among the Provedors of the Misericórdia both types of settlers were represented: the sugar planters were the Silva Pimentels and Rocha Pittas; the cattle ranchers were João Peixoto Viegas, Pedro Barbosa Leal, Domingos Affonso Sertão, and the Dias d'Avila family of the House of Tôrre. The second group may be termed the *haute bourgeoisie*. Its representatives enjoyed many of the privileges of the aristocracy, but lacked the social prestige based on tradition of that class. The brothers of 'major' standing were professional men in the widest sense of the term — civil servants, ecclesiastics, inquisitors, military officers and university graduates. It is necessary to define the term 'business man' as opposed to 'merchant' in the context of the Misericórdia. Essentially the difference was that whereas the first was dealing in finance, the second was dealing in retail trade. In 1705 Dom Pedro II defined a merchant as follows: 'The word "merchants" is applicable only to those persons in an open shop who are actually engaged in measuring, weighing, and selling any kind of merchandise to the people'.[1] The classification adopted by the Misericórdia confirmed this distinction. Whereas a shopkeeper, no matter how prosperous, was accepted as a brother of lower standing, a business man automatically qualified for the higher ranking.

The brothers of minor standing were essentially those practising the mechanical arts. In Portugal each trade had had its own statutes but this

[1] C. R. Boxer, *The Golden Age of Brazil*, p. 110.

custom was not followed in Brazil and practically the only group of artisans who registered their trade were the goldsmiths, who did so in order to prevent falsification. The examinations of artisans, introduced in Portugal in the sixteenth century, were not enforced in Brazil before the eighteenth century. In 1701, the city council of Bahia decreed that all the city's artisans be examined. Payment of an examination fee was waived temporarily after protests by the artisans, but the council ruled that avoidance of the examinations would be penalised by a fine of 6$000 and the closure of the offender's shop.[1] In the institution of *cartas de examinação* ('certificates of examination'), Bahia was following the example of Lisbon, Braga and Madeira. Examiners were appointed to issue certificates to successful artisans, permitting the opening of a shop and the practice of their craft. In Bahia this class had been recognised as worthy of municipal representation in the seventeenth century. In 1641 all the artisans had been convoked in order to elect twelve *mesteres*, each representing a trade or group of trades. These representatives had elected a *juiz do povo*, or people's tribune, to represent working class interests on the city council. In the next sixty years this official was to do much good in reviewing the taxes, but the additional power represented by the appointment of a second people's tribune in 1645 had been resented by the councillors.[2] Although the election of a second tribune was later discontinued, there was considerable animosity between the councillors and the people's representative for the rest of the seventeenth century. This reached its climax in 1711 when the people's tribune incited the populace of Bahia to demonstrate in the streets against a price increase on salt and a proposed levy of 10 per cent on imported goods. The king, disturbed by news of rioting, abolished the posts of people's tribune and the representatives of the guilds in 1713.[3] Future attempts to revive them met with a stony silence from Lisbon. The 'brothers of lower condition' came from the more articulate members of this class and may be referred to as the *petite bourgeoisie*.

[1] Minutes of municipal council of 12 November 1701 and 26 November 1701 (AMB, vol. 22, f. 222v and ff. 223v–224).

[2] Affonso Ruy, *Historia da Câmara*, p. 178. For detailed studies of the *mesteres* and *juiz do povo* in Bahia, see C. R. Boxer, *Portuguese Society in the Tropics. The Municipal Councils of Goa, Macao, Bahia and Luanda, 1510–1800* (Wisconsin, 1965) pp. 73–7, 104–5 and 179–82; Affonso Ruy, op. cit., pp. 173–85.

[3] Royal order of 25 February 1713 (APB, *Ordens régias*, vol. 8, doc. 30).

The Misericórdia was the only Bahian brotherhood to preserve this mediaeval distinction, and its registers of members offer a unique source for a study of the class structure of colonial Bahia. Although all *Compromissos* of Lisbon had advocated equal numbers of brothers from both classes, it is highly unlikely that such a numerical equality was ever present in any of the overseas branches of the Misericórdia. There are no figures for the overall membership of the brotherhood in Bahia at any given date. Fortunately the registers recording the election of successful candidates to the Misericórdia are complete from 1663. Each entry specified whether the new brother was of higher or lower standing, but in some cases this detail was omitted or the relevant part of the page has been destroyed subsequently. A graphical presentation of the results of an analysis of these entries for the years 1665 to 1755 is presented in Table I. There are three obvious conclusions to be drawn. The first is that the number of entrants to the brotherhood varied considerably from year to year. The second is that there was a predominance of brothers from the upper class. The third is that the increase and decrease in membership affected both classes equally.

There are no grounds for thinking that fluctuations in the number of entrants were caused by cliques, or *ranchos*, of a family or professional nature.[1] The catastrophic fall in the number of admissions in the years 1685–90, the rise in the period 1730–5, and the decline in the 1740s and 1750s, are explicable by factors external and internal. In 1686 the city had been ravaged by the *peste da bicha* or yellow fever. Many applicants, or even those already elected to the brotherhood, had preferred not to leave the Recôncavo, where the plague had been less prevalent, to come to the city in order to take the oath without which they could not be accepted as brothers.[2] The climax in the 1730s and the decline in the following two decades can be explained by internal factors. The first of these was the successful Provedorship of Canon Francisco Martins Pereira. During his terms of office the

---

[1] The only recorded case of interference in the voting rights of brothers was in 1740. A member of the Junta, Manuel de Oliveira Correia, influenced the other members of the Junta and Mesa to the extent that, of sixty-one candidates for election as brothers, only one was accepted. The elections were suspended because the excessive number of voting beans being cast in each ballot was turning the election into a farce (ASCMB, vol. 195, ff. 108v–109v).

[2] Sebastião da Rocha Pitta, *Historia da America Portugueza*, livro 7, §45.

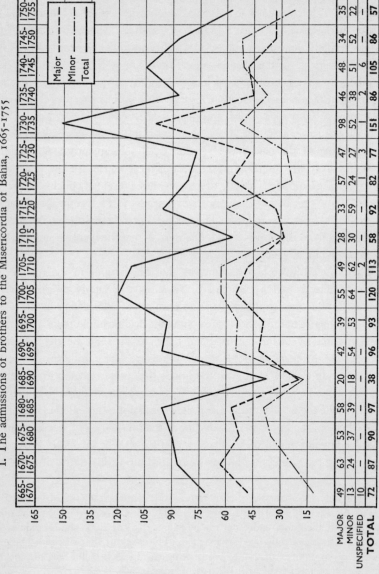

I. The admissions of brothers to the Misericórdia of Bahia, 1665-1755

	1665-1670	1670-1675	1675-1680	1680-1685	1685-1690	1690-1695	1695-1700	1700-1705	1705-1710	1710-1715	1715-1720	1720-1725	1725-1730	1730-1735	1735-1740	1740-1745	1745-1750	1750-1755
MAJOR	49	63	53	58	20	42	39	55	49	28	33	57	47	98	46	48	34	35
MINOR	13	24	37	39	18	54	53	64	62	30	59	24	27	52	38	51	52	22
UNSPECIFIED	10	–	–	–	–	–	1	1	2	–	–	1	3	1	2	6	–	–
TOTAL	72	87	90	97	38	96	93	120	113	58	92	82	77	151	86	105	86	57

Misericórdia reached the height of its prestige in the eighteenth century, exemplified by artistic works, such as the panelling of the *salão nobre* (lit. 'noble room'), the painting of the nave of the church and structural alterations to its exterior.[1] If the successors of the worthy canon had followed his example the Misericórdia might have avoided decline. Unfortunately these were not forthcoming and the brotherhood declined to the point when, in 1754, the king sent out a Crown judge to take stock of the Misericórdia. Economic decline implied a previous loss of social prestige. Loss of prestige in the socially conscious society of Bahia meant lack of membership. A fall in membership meant lack of financial support by gifts or bequests. The Misericórdia was inextricably enclosed within this vicious socio-economic circle.

The registers of the admissions of brothers to the Misericórdia provide information on the place of origin of the brother and his wife, the parentage on both sides, and the profession of the applicant. A study of the places of origin in Portugal and the Atlantic islands confirms the conclusions of Carlos Ott that the vast majority of the Portuguese emigrants to Bahia came from the provinces of the Douro and the Minho.[2] Despite official discouragement of foreigners, there was a *pot-pourri* of nationalities — Italian, French, German and even brothers of English and Irish descent. Fear of the Dutch had evidently subsided, for families of Dutch descent, such as the Guisenrodes, were accepted into the Misericórdia. The most significant fact to emerge from a statistical analysis of the admissions registers for these years is that there was a considerable difference in the ratio of immigrants from the two classes. The percentage of immigrants elected brothers of the upper class was 10 per cent higher than the number of Brazilian born brothers of the upper class, whereas the ratio of the immigrants elected as brothers of lower standing to those who had been born in Brazil was 6:1. The second fact is that the brothers of higher standing born in Brazil outnumbered those of the lower class, also born in Brazil, in the ratio of 4:1.[3]

These records also provide information on the deployment of the labour

[1] For a full description of these works see Carlos Ott, *A Santa Casa*, pp. 68–75.

[2] Carlos Ott based his conclusions on inquisitorial records for the years 1591–2 and burial records of the Misericórdia for the late seventeenth and eighteenth centuries, *Formação e evolução étnica da cidade do Salvador* (2 vols., Bahia 1955–7), vol. 2, appendix 2.

[3] From 1663 to 1755, 874 brothers of higher standing and 729 of lower standing are recorded in the admissions' registers of the Misericórdia. There is no class

force in the same period in Bahia. With regard to the professional brothers of higher standing it is difficult to reach firm conclusions. This is partly because of scribal negligence but also because then, as now, the Brazilian thrived on a multiplicity of different jobs. An official of the Inquisition combined the duties of this post successfully with commerce and a small plantation. The trades of the brothers of lower standing are more frequently stated and do not offer the same ambiguity. Of a total of 729 plebeian brothers admitted in the period 1663–1755, the vocations of some 350 are stated. Although these only represent 48 per cent of the total, the vocations listed may be regarded as indicative of the general deployment of labour, because there were no reasons for drastic changes in the conditions of the artisan within these ninety years. Slight changes occurred in the eighteenth century with increased numbers of goldsmiths and other workers in precious metals, drawn to Bahia as one of the official outlets for the gold from the Minas. The results are what one would expect. The basic needs of the community were satisfied by shoemakers, tailors, cutlers and smiths. The building trades were represented by masons, carpenters and decorators. A minority group were the lesser legal officials who were usually promoted to be brothers of the upper class.[1]

During the eighteenth century there was an increasing number of promotions to the upper class of brothers originally admitted as 'minors'. In the majority of cases these were not of a mechanical trade and it would have been almost inconceivable for any smith or cobbler to hope for such social elevation. João de Miranda Ribeiro, a carpenter from the bishopric of Oporto, was admitted to the Misericórdia as a brother of 'minor' standing in 1717. In the next three decades he was to gain great wealth and was a co-founder of the Lapa convent. Such was his prestige that his son, Agostinho de Miranda Ribeiro, was admitted to the Misericórdia as a brother of 'major' standing in 1754, but the father remained tied to the lower category by his trade as a carpenter.[2] Those who did achieve social promotion came from

---

reference for 27. Details are complete for some 75 per cent of these and are as follows: 'Major': Brazilian born, 301; immigrants, 368; total, 669 (45 and 55 per cent), 'Minor': Brazilian born, 83; immigrants, 510; total, 593 (14 and 86 per cent).

[1] A partial list of artisans in Bahia and their places of origin is in Carlos Ott, *Formação e evolução étnica*, vol. 1, pp. 46–7 and vol. 2, appendix 6.

[2] ASCMB, vol. 3, f. 220v and vol. 4, f. 182v.

the marginal professions — shopkeepers, minor civil servants, and solicitors — who had greater opportunities for coming into contact with the upper classes and of improving their social as well as financial position. In the final analysis the criterion was social acceptability. This was exemplified by the two surgeons Constantino de Sousa Ferraz and João Rodrigues Velloso. Both were admitted as brothers of 'minor' standing in the eighteenth century, but whereas the former was promoted to the social category customary for his profession, the latter remained in the lower class.[1]

The Misericórdia records offer an index of this social change. The reasons for promotion come under the general titles of public service and economic improvement. As had been the case in the Middle Ages, the concession of a royal benefice was accompanied by social promotion for the recipient. In the late seventeenth century António Rodrigues da Costa, admitted as a 'minor', petitioned the Mesa for promotion because he had been ennobled by royal grace.[2] War also had been a traditional method of gaining social promotion. The Dutch occupation of 1624–5 had offered the opportunity for plebeians to achieve representation on the municipal council and to obtain a higher social standing. The concession of military commissions in the local militia entitled the holders to certain privileges of the upper class. They were exempt from all public duties and taxes. In Maranhão the abuse of these concessions led to complaints by the city council of S. Luís. The councillors alleged that such appointments could only be made by the city council, but that some governors had taken this right upon themselves. In 1686 the Governor of Maranhão, Gomes Freire, reformed the criteria for selection. In 1685 the Misericórdia of Tapuytapera, across the bay from S. Luís, was abolished because of the large number of artisans ennobled by such commissions.[3] In Bahia there were several cases of artisans and minor officials being promoted to brothers of higher standing in the Misericórdia because of such appointments.[4] A third instance of public service bringing

---

[1] They were admitted on 13 June 1716 and 21 March 1717 respectively (ASCMB, vol. 3, f. 206v and f. 219v). Ferraz was promoted on 6 June 1717.

[2] He had been admitted on 14 November 1666 (ASCMB, vol. 2, f. 30). He was promoted on 21 June 1676 'pois que procedia e se tratava como homem nobre, e pelo alvará que offerecia, lhe fizera sua Alteza mercê do Foro de Cavalheiro Fidalgo com 1$200 de moradia . . .' (ASCMB, vol. 2, f. 112).

[3] Robert Southey, *History of Brazil*, vol. 2, p. 633 and vol. 3, p. 5.

[4] ASCMB, vol. 3, ff. 61, 192, 241, 362v and vol. 4, ff. 94v, 158, 185, 356v.

promotion was among the minor officials of the city council. At no time was there any official connection between the Misericórdia and the municipality. But in the small society of Bahia the municipal councillors belonged automatically to the Misericórdia, the Third Order of St Francis and half a dozen other brotherhoods. The same people were prominent in the Misericórdia and on the city council. Office in the former recommended the incumbent for an executive post in the latter. If the councillors enjoyed social prestige, the municipal office of *almotacé*, or weights and measures inspector, carried few benefits and was regarded with misgiving. The occupant of this post must often have been the butt of vocal disapproval by the councillors who wished their measures enforced, and possibly the more organic disapproval of the vendors. Perhaps the social promotion offered by the Misericórdia to the hapless occupant of this post served as a degree of compensation.[1]

The choice of brothers for the posts of Provedor and treasurer has indicated the gradual social acceptance of the business community in the eighteenth century. Such was the desperate plight of the brotherhood to find a brother of 'major' standing to occupy the post of treasurer as demanded by the *Compromisso*, that on several occasions Mesas fell back on the recourse of promoting brothers of 'minor' status whose financial means enabled them to assist the brotherhood in meeting its creditors. Manuel Antunes Lima, a collaborator of João de Miranda Ribeiro in the construction of the Lapa Convent, and an engineer by profession, was promoted to the upper class on the occasion of his election as treasurer in 1732.[2] Manuel Antunes Lima had already been nominated treasurer in 1729 but had refused and so had not been promoted, serving on the Junta as a 'minor' for the term 1730–1. Other brothers, originally admitted to the lower class and later promoted, who occupied the post of treasurer were Jacinto Barbosa (1717), Sebastião Dionísio da Costa (1718) and João Nunes de Figueredo (1725 and 1726).

The feeling of class prejudice was strong in colonial Bahia and the

---

[1] ASCMB, vol. 2, f. 122v.

[2] ASCMB, vol. 3, f. 237v and vol. 35, ff. 12–13v, 19–20. He was elected treasurer on 10 February 1732 and promoted on the same day, following the expulsion of Anselmo Dias. He was re-elected in July 1732 (vol. 35, ff. 25v–26 and 26v–27v).

privilege of belonging to the upper class was highly coveted and, once achieved, jealously preserved. Members of the upper classes sometimes refused to serve in the garrison simply because promotion from soldier to second lieutenant meant passing through the rank of sergeant. One of the duties of a sergeant was to accompany the *serpentinas*, or hand-carried chairs, of his superiors, and the nobles considered this duty out of keeping with their social position.[1] Often an applicant to the Misericórdia, on hearing that he had been elected as a brother of minor standing, refused to take the oath. On some occasions this refusal was justified and the candidate simply bided his time until a more accommodating Mesa would admit him to the upper class. On others it was not. When an upstart 'barber' insisted he should be admitted to the upper class in 1636, he was simply exemplifying the delusions of grandeur entertained by many of his social position.[2] Two duties of brothers were intimately linked to class and their allocation aroused bitter feelings. The first was the decoration of the church for the feast of the Visitation — a duty limited to brothers of higher standing. The second was the monthly stint as buyer for the hospital — a duty reserved for brothers of the lower class. Since the former involved considerable financial outlay it could well have been used as a lever for social advancement. The indignation felt by one 'minor' brother, João Baptista Carneiro, on being asked to undertake this task in 1708, was doubtless tinged by the hope of social promotion. It was to the credit of the Misericórdia that it refused to be blackmailed in this or similar cases and João Baptista and his successors who aspired to social elevation were unceremoniously expelled.[3] The office of buyer entailed a degree of financial risk, depending on the honesty of the treasurer in allocating sufficient funds for this purpose, without the compensations of social advancement. Indeed the reverse was the case and brothers of the upper class underwent expulsion rather than submit to this indignity.

[1] An additional objection was that they would be 'emparelhados com os negros que as carregão'. On 23 June 1710 the city councillors of Bahia asked the king to permit people of proved nobility to pass from the rank of soldier to lieutenant, or at least be excused the duties of accompanying the *serpentinas* (AMB, vol. 176, f. 83).

[2] ASCMB, vol. 195, f. 6, cf. ff. 55 and 81; vol. 3, f. 193.

[3] ASCMB, vol. 195, f. 37.

The casual attitude towards expulsion demands some explanation. The *Compromisso* had laid down seven conditions for expulsion which generally covered disobedience to the orders of the board of guardians and actions which would bring the name of the brotherhood into disrepute. Apart from some few occasions of public debauchery, drunkenness and prostitution of wives and daughters, there were few expulsions from the Misericórdia of Bahia on the second count. Whereas expulsion on the grounds of discrediting the brotherhood was final, that resulting from disobedience or insubordination was revocable and was often inspired by personal antipathy. In these cases expulsion by one board of guardians was annulled by the next and a brother preferred a year or two in the wilderness rather than undertake tasks below his position.

This outline of Bahian society as portrayed by the Misericórdia records reveals two distinct modes of life. On the one hand was the aristocracy who owned vast tracts of land in the Recôncavo and the Sertão, and whose children married within this society. On the other hand was a class of men who had advanced by personal effort to achieve financial and social position. The one was rural, the other urban. It was only among the bourgeoisie that there existed a class struggle. The aristocracy was unassailable. There are grounds for thinking that in the first half of the eighteenth century the distinction between brothers of 'major' and 'minor' standing was declining in its practical application. In 1718 the Crown attorney supported the recommendation of the city council to the king for an increase in the number of girls to be admitted to the Desterro convent. But he opposed the enforcement of any distinction between girls of the aristocracy and those of plebeian stock 'because such a distinction was scandalous in Brazil where a person of the most modest circumstances and birth puts on the airs of a great nobleman'.[1]

In the boom town of Vila Rica de Ouro Prêto Dom João V authorised the foundation of a Misericórdia in 1738 on the condition that there be no class distinction between brothers.[2] He was following the recommendation of the municipal council who had reviewed a draft *Compromisso* in 1736 and recommended to the king that the preservation of this distinction was no longer practicable because many men of good character, suitable to hold

---

[1] *Documentos historicos*, vol. 97, p. 190.
[2] C. R. Boxer, *The Golden Age of Brazil*, p. 136.

office in the Misericórdia, had dedicated themselves to commerce.[1] In the socially conscious capital of Bahia the distinction may have lasted longer. It was significant that in 1739 Dom João V had to issue a royal order against laxity in terms of address, threatening heavy punishments for abuse of the title *Senhoria*. The necessity of such a decree indicated that no longer was great importance attached to such matters in the colony.[2] The admissions registers of brothers to the Misericórdia of Bahia no longer referred to class within the text of the record of entry in the 1730s, although it was maintained in the title until the end of the century. After 1800 any record of class disappeared, with some casual exceptions. This lengthy formal preservation of an outmoded distinction doubtless owed much to tradition and ceremony. Cases of social promotion after 1750 tended not to be the result of social betterment so much as a change in personal status such as ordination for the ministry or military promotion. Similarly, examples of brothers being expelled on grounds arising from class distinction were rare after this date. The anomaly of any class distinction was shown in the board of guardians of 1807, composed entirely of business men.[3] A process of social change, which had started in the early eighteenth century, ended in the first decade of the nineteenth century.

The equating in the popular mind of business man with New Christian did not deter such families from settling in Bahia. In 1497 all Jews in Portugal had been forcibly converted to Catholicism. They had been known as New Christians. Many had continued to practise Jewish rites in secret

---

[1] Augusto de Lima Júnior, *A Capitania das Minas Gerais* (2nd ed. Rio de Janeiro, 1943) apud Gilberto Freyre, *Sobrados e mucambos* (3 vols., Rio de Janeiro–São Paulo 1951, 2nd ed.) vol. 2, p. 673.

[2] This order of 29 January 1739 enforced an old law of 1597 on protocol. This ordered that marriages should preserve the social standing of both parties and that any marriage contracted without parental permission would result in the loss of any title held by the husband. Abuse of forms of address carried heavy penalties. People between the ranks of *fidalgo* and *cavalheiro* faced fines of 100$000 for a first offence and 200$000 for a second. 'Pessoas de menor qualidade' would be fined 20$000 and suffer two years' exile from their place of residence for a first offence and 40$000 with five years' exile to Africa on the second occasion (APB, *Ordens régias*, vol. 35, doc. 107a).

[3] The last instance I have found was in the election of the Mesa in 1816. Class distinction was preserved among the electors, but the members of the actual Mesa were simply referred to as 'consultores' (ASCMB, vol. 36, f. 76).

and had been denounced. Brazil had been a place of refuge for judaizers escaping the inquisition in Spain and Portugal. Several European travellers to Bahia in the eighteenth century commented on the numbers of Jews engaged in trade. If the populace accepted these families with distrust, the brotherhoods went further in their antipathy and forbade entry. The clause of the 1618 *Compromisso* of the Misericórdia demanding purity of blood was common to the Third Orders. After receiving an application the Mesa appointed one of its members to undertake a special enquiry into the truth of the statements made by the applicant and to establish his suitability. In addition to this special enquiry, all the other members of the board of guardians made general enquiries into his social background and submitted a report to the Provedor should they hear of any defect. This was the practice in the Misericórdia of Bahia but the archives contain no actual report of this nature. Possibly the Misericórdia followed the custom of the Third Order of the Carmelites and burned these documents. Fortunately two examples of the manner in which information was verified and the extent to which this anti-semitic prejudice was evident do exist in the Book of Secrets of the Misericórdia.

The first concerned Francisco Ferreira who was refused entry to the brotherhood in 1629, ostensibly on the grounds that there was no vacancy. It was rumoured that the real reason was that he was suspected of being a New Christian. Considering his honour to be at stake, Francisco Ferreira re-applied for membership in the following year, stating that any such accusation was born of malicious intent and that he would submit evidence to establish his purity of blood beyond all reasonable doubt. To this end he produced nine testimonials by people of standing both in Bahia and in his home town of Almada, on the Tagus. These certified that not only his father and mother, but also his grandmother, had been Catholics. His most important witness was the sexagenarian Luís Vaz de Paiva, a citizen of Bahia, and the official recorder of the Jews and New Christians who had come from Portugal to settle in Bahia. He swore that the parents of Francisco Ferreira had not been among these emigrants. This was confirmed by reference to the lists of Jewish émigrés in the possession of another witness.[1] The final outcome of these enquiries is not mentioned.

[1] 'Luis Vaz de Paiva, m^or nesta cid^e de idade q' disse ser de sesenta annos pouco mais ou menos, t^a a q^m o Provedor deu juram^to dos Sanctos Evangelhos em q' pos sua mão, e prometteu dizer verd^e e do custume dizer nada. E perguntado p^lo

The second case occurred fifty years later and centred on Joanna Leal, a native of Bahia. The Misericórdia was unusual among Bahian brotherhoods in that admission of a brother automatically included the acceptance of his wife who enjoyed the same privileges but was subject to the same regulations as her husband. In 1669 the first husband of Joanna Leal, lieutenant Francisco Rodrigues de Aguiar, was refused entry to the brotherhood because of the alleged impurity of blood of his wife. Ten years later her second husband, the chief officer in the Court of Appeals, Domingos Rodrigues Correia, met with a similar refusal on the same grounds. The higher social position of Domingos Rodrigues Correia demanded a fuller enquiry than had been accorded to his predecessor and the Junta was called for the first time on this issue. Domingos Rodrigues produced testimonials testifying to his wife's purity of blood and a signed statement by the scribe of the Carmelite Order in Bahia, friar António da Trindade, that the brother of Joanna Leal had been accepted into the Order after exhaustive enquiries had established his purity of blood. Nevertheless, the board of guardians of the Misericórdia rejected the petition on the grounds that Joanna Leal's purity of blood was not sufficiently proven. Correia, dissatisfied by this decision, reapplied in March of 1680, supporting his petition by lengthy testimonials ordered specially from Lisbon. Evidently the case had become a key issue with the Misericórdia for in December of 1679 the Mesa had written to its counterpart in Lisbon asking for information on the parentage of Joanna Leal. It was indicative of the importance attached to purity of blood, that it was only after contact had been established with the Misericórdia of Luzã, a village near Coimbra, and evidence had been received from the scribe that the grandparents of Joanna Leal had been members of the brotherhood in Luzã, that Domingos Rodrigues Correia was finally admitted as a brother of the Misericórdia of Bahia.[1]

---

contheudo na petição atras disse: q' conheceo a Ant⁰ Mēdes e a sua mulher, os quais elle tᵃ sempre os teve por Christãos Velhos, e assy o ouvio dizer nesta terra. E q' foi elle tᵃ fintador da gente de nação, e q' veio de Portugal fintados della mᵗᵃ gente, da q' avia nesta cidᵉ; sem o suppᵉ nem seu pay virem na dita finta, nem là os fintarão p elle tᵃ e os mais os terem p Christãos Velhos' (ASCMB, vol. 195, ff. 3–4v).

[1] The scribe of the Carmelites confirmed that 'o Rᵈᵒ Pᵉ Fr. Mᵉˡ Leal, Irmão da sobredita Joanna Leal fora aceito na dᵃ Religião do Carmo pella limpa informação q' se tirou de seu nascimᵗᵒ e sanguinidᵉ, e ser Christão Velho sem rasa algũa pᵃ q'

These two examples confirm that prejudice against Jews or New Christians was present in seventeenth-century Bahia. The publicity given to the case of Domingos Rodrigues Correia was doubtless responsible for the clause, present in all the registers of admissions between 1679 and 1685, that any brother who took for his second wife a woman of Jewish descent would be expelled from the brotherhood.[1] From 1685 to the turn of the century the inclusion of this clause became increasingly rare, and from 1700 candidates for election were simply required to prove their general suitability. Although the strength of the prejudice may have been reduced, it still remained a preoccupation in the minds of the members of the boards of guardians when they came to make the elections. In the first three decades of the eighteenth century there were rare instances of brothers being expelled for this reason, but in all cases they were later re-admitted. There was no further expulsion after 1730. This may have been partly due to a move of the centre of the New Christian population of Brazil to Rio de Janeiro in the eighteenth century. A contributory factor may have been the social acceptance of the business class which has already been discussed. The decreasing mistrust felt towards the business community brought with it, if not acceptance, at least greater tolerance towards those of New Christian descent.

In the testimonial of the purity of faith of the grandparents of Joanna Leal, the scribe of the Misericórdia of Luzã had stated that they were 'Old Christians without taint of Moor or mulatto'. This near equation of a non-Catholic to a person of colour is reminiscent of the attitude of the fifteenth- and sixteenth-century Portuguese chroniclers who had simply dismissed those of other faiths and colours as infidels and pagans. In Brazil the native, be he Indian or Negro, was regarded as inferior, but the extent of miscegenation compelled the authorities to adopt some policy. In this they were far from uniform and much depended on the nature of the inter-marriage. In general, the *mamelucos* and *caboclos*, offspring of white-Amerindian parent-

---

necessitasse de escripto algũ Apostolico q' não ouve pella grande limpeza q' se achou em seu sangue'. The scribe of the Misericórdia of Luzã stated that the grandparents were 'Christãos Velhos sem rasa de mouro ou mulato' (ASCMB, vol. 195, ff. 12v, 16v–17 and 21–2). Domingos Rodrigues Correia was admitted as a brother of 'major' standing on 15 April 1680 (ASCMB, vol. 2, f. 156).

[1] 'com declaração q' casando-se segunda vez com mulher de nação hebrea, seria logo expulso e excluido da dita Irmandade' (ASCMB, vol. 2, ff. 144v, 263, *inter alia*).

age, came off rather better in the eyes of the Portuguese authorities than the *mestiços* and mulattos, products of black and white sexual unions. The reason for the more tolerant attitude to the former was that once the Tupís had been driven from the urban areas, they no longer troubled the administrative machinery or social structure. Moreover, they were far less common in Bahia than in Maranhão or the region of São Paulo, where the colonists mated with the local Amerindian women. On the rare occasions in Bahia when a white person of good social position took an Amerindian as his wife, the offspring married into good families in the capital.[1] But such cases were exceptional. Despite a royal decree in 1755 giving such marriages the royal blessing and assuring that no loss of social position would result, the majority of such unions were temporary and unsanctified by the Church.[2] The Indian remained in the interior of the Captaincy of Bahia and consequently played no part in the urban life of the capital. The same cannot be said of Negroes and mulattos who achieved a sufficiently high degree of social consolidation to found brotherhoods and provide a disrupting element in urban life by their aspirations.

In theory a Negro was either a freed man or a slave but in practice such a distinction was often forgotten and a Negro was simply a chattel at the disposal of a white person. Well aware of this disregard, a slave in Lisbon who had been granted his freedom by a clause of his master's will, took good care to bring this fact to the notice of Dom João V before undertaking a journey back to Bahia. The king ordered the viceroy to ensure that this new-found liberty was respected.[3] The accessibility of the monarch to the coloured subjects was again shown by the appeal of a Negro slave, António Fernandes, to Dom João V, alleging that he had been unjustly tortured. An enquiry was held and representatives of the Misericórdia gave evidence (pp. 256–7). The Crown was not deaf to these appeals and fully realised the appalling conditions in which the slaves were brought from Africa and then employed on the sugar plantations. Numerous decrees were issued to protect the Negro, such as those aimed at reducing the mortality in the slaving ships (appropriately enough known as *tumbeiros* or pall-bearers) by lessening the numbers of slaves crowded below decks, punishment for slave owners found

---

[1] Jaboatão, *Catalogo genealógico*, p. 165, cf. p. 51.
[2] *Alvará* of 4 April 1755 (APB, *Ordens régias*, vol. 55, ff. 129–30).
[3] King to viceroy, 26 November 1746 (APB, *Ordens régias*, vol. 44, doc. 10).

guilty of cruelty, as well as measures to ensure that every slave received a decent burial. Although such decrees bore witness to the good intentions of the Crown, they were largely ineffective in reality, and the Brazilians went their own way and exploited the slaves as far as possible.

Although theoretically protecting the Negro in these decrees, there can be no doubt that the Portuguese authorities practised a policy of racial discrimination.[1] When administrative appointments were made, the Crown stipulated that those selected should be 'all white men free of infected blood'.[2] Nor did the attempts of Dom João V to achieve closer harmony between the coloured and white elements in Bahia meet with any more success than his decrees. In 1733 he ordered the amalgamation of the militia regiments of Bahia composed of *pardos* and Negroes with those regiments of white soldiers, 'and trust that the *pardos* will serve me as well as white men'. Within three years the viceroy was obliged to re-establish the coloured regiments because the white soldiers refused to serve alongside coloured soldiers.[3] No order from a monarch some three thousand miles away could remove the ingrained prejudice of the white Bahians, already illustrated in

---

[1] For a full discussion of the racial situation in colonial Brazil see C. R. Boxer, *Race Relations in the Portuguese Colonial Empire, 1415–1825* (Oxford, 1963), pp. 86–121.

[2] The king stipulated that four appointees to the Treasury in Bahia in 1715 should be 'todos homens brancos livres de infecta nação' (APB, *Ordens régias*, vol. 53, f. 267). In 1712 Dom João V asked the Commissioner of the Treasury to report on the 'limpeza de sangue' of an applicant for the post of Guarda dos Contos because anybody with a 'stain' could not be accepted in public office (ANRJ, *Códice* 539, vol. 2, f. 71).

[3] Decision of the Overseas Council of 15 December 1732 communicated to the viceroy by the king in a letter of 12 January 1733. The viceroy reported that he had begun to carry out this order in a letter of 13 April 1733 (APB, *Ordens régias*, vol. 29, docs. 62 and 62a). In a report of 20 June 1736 the viceroy informed the king of the necessity to revert to the former situation. Approving this action the king quoted from this report '. . . q' de nenhũa maneira convem a meu serviço, que os mulatos forros se anexem âs companhias dos brancos porque estes os não querem admitir nem servir com elles por cuja cauza os separarão os Governadores vossos antecessores em comp^as com off^es da mesma cor, e assim servirão sempre sugeitos aos Coroneis da Ordenança com boa satisfação, sem haver as dezordens que antes se experimentavão e prezentemente se tinhão observado e que da mesma sorte me servião os prettos forros, cujo prestimo e fidelidade de huns e outros era notoria' (APB, *Ordens régias*, vol. 40, doc. 54).

the defence of their bell-tower by the tertiaries of St Francis and in the refusal by the noble soldiers to accompany their superiors' chairs 'side by side with the negro bearers'. The scorn felt by white Bahians towards the coloured peoples, even in positions in which they were on a par with their white fellows, as in the garrison where pay increases to white soldiers were not matched by similar increases to coloured soldiers, led the coloured population either to direct revolt or to establishing representative bodies to plead their case.[1]

In Minas Gerais in the eighteenth century the rebellious tendencies of the slaves had on more than one occasion caused apprehension among the local authorities. In 1725 Dom João V, fearing that the total white force of Brazil would not be capable of suppressing such a general revolt, suggested to the viceroy that only Angolan slaves be sent to the mines as those from the Mina coast were disruptive elements. Open revolt had only been averted because the two nations had been unable to agree on the selection of a king to head both groups.[2] In the early nineteenth century in Bahia slave revolts of the Hausa and Nagô were to occur, but previous outbreaks were easily put down by the authorities. Flight offered a degree of freedom to the slave. Groups of slaves known as *calhambolas* formed *quilombos* in the interior and were often joined by freed slaves. Such bodies of unrest challenged the national security and severe penalties were enforced against offenders — branding on the shoulder on the first occasion and the cutting off of an ear on the second. In neither case was there any possibility of appeal.[3] The unrealistic manner in which the Crown contemplated the problem was exemplified by the orders for an attack on a *quilombo* of 1,000 Negroes at S. João del Rei in 1747. Dom João V ordered the white force of 400 to

[1] Gregório da Silva, a *pardo* with eighteen years' service as an artillery man in the Bahia garrison, asked Dom João V to grant him permission to leave the force 'porque por ser pardo se lhe não dá, nem o Supplicante espera acrescimento algum'. The matter was referred to the viceroy who approved his retirement in a letter to the king of 23 March 1747 (APB, *Ordens régias*, vol. 44, doc. 6).

[2] King to viceroy, 18 June 1725. In his reply of 23 February 1726 the Count of Sabugosa reported that Angolans were totally unsuitable for anything but domestic work and suggested that closer supervision would stop the unrest (APB, *Ordens régias*, vol. 20, docs. 105 and 105a).

[3] *Provisão* of 3 March 1741 (ANRJ, *Códice 952*, vol. 30, f. 264 and accompanying documents).

attempt to bring the unruly Negroes to order, not by massacre as had been the case on previous occasions, but by capture followed by fair trial. The king hoped this would be an example to others of similar inclination.[1] A fine example of royal idealism perhaps, but unlikely to be heeded by the colonisers in the mining region.

The urban counterpart of the *quilombo* was the brotherhood. Many coloured brotherhoods were established in Bahia in the seventeenth and eighteenth centuries — there were some five for mulattos and six for Negroes dedicated to the Virgin Mary alone — and testified to the social consolidation achieved by the coloured populace. In some cases the brotherhood was founded with the object of freeing its members from bondage: once free, a member contributed to the liberation of his brothers.[2] The majority had wider terms of reference to protect the interests of their members during life and to give them a decent burial at death. The most powerful coloured brotherhood of Bahia was that of Our Lady of the Rosary, the only brotherhood to hold annual elections of a king and queen which were to intrigue the nineteenth-century artist Maurice Rugendas. In Bahia the *Compromisso* of this brotherhood was confirmed in 1685. Other branches of the same dedication, in addition to that in the Pelourinho, were in the parishes of the Conceição da Praia, Sant' Ana, Sto António além do Carmo and S. Pedro Velho. In its early years membership was limited to Angolan Negroes but later it admitted Brazilian Negroes, mulattos and even white people. It was the initially exclusive nature of the Rosary which resulted in the foundation of brotherhoods with more flexible terms of entry. One of these was the Brotherhood of St Anthony of Catagerona, founded in 1699 by a group of creole Negroes and Angolan Negroes. This brotherhood admitted anybody, irrespective of state or sex, but maintained the equal representation of Angolans and creoles on its board of

---

[1] After this recommendation in the use of peaceful methods, the *aviso* continued 'tendo porem entendido VS^a que não he da Real intensão de S. Mag^e prohibir o procedimento mais violento, e executivo nos termos em que não possa ter lugar o das prisões, pela rezistencia, e obstinação dos mesmos negros, os quaes, ou por hum, ou por outro modo devem experimentar hum castigo exemplar, que sirva de escarmento aos mais' (ANRJ, *Códice 952*, vol. 33, f. 390).

[2] Such was the Brotherhood of Our Lady of the Rosary and Ransom (*N. Sra. do Rosário e Resgate*) in Rio de Janeiro which had to obtain royal permission before a slave could be freed (ANRJ, *Códice 952*, vol. 3, f. 202).

guardians.[1] Such was the profusion of these coloured brotherhoods that any person of colour, a slave or a freed man, African or Brazilian, could find a brotherhood to suit his condition.

The ethnic groups of white, Negro and mulatto founded brotherhoods in this chronological order. Once social consolidation had been achieved the conditions of entry to the respective brotherhoods were gradually relaxed. This is well exemplified in the attitudes of the black and white brotherhoods to Jews and those of other ethnic groups. The Rosary, initially exclusive, became more tolerant to the extent of admitting white people. Never did its statutes, or those of any other coloured brotherhood, discriminate against New Christians. There was a similar move towards greater tolerance among several of the white brotherhoods. As mulattos achieved social standing and even administrative positions if they were not of too dusky a hue, and the Negroes gained their independence in increasing numbers, the white brotherhoods relaxed their conditions of entry. In fact, the Negro was well enough provided for by his own brotherhoods and did not need to apply to a white brotherhood for membership: but this tolerance enabled the light-skinned mulatto, the *branco da Bahia*, to gain entry to a society previously closed to him.[2]

The Third Orders and the Misericórdia did not follow this tolerant trend. They were the most privileged of the Bahian brotherhoods and as a result felt the encroachments on their rights more than the other white brotherhoods. They preserved their statutory provisions for purity of blood and the self-imposed condition of whiteness and maintained themselves as exclusive social bodies for the white élite. Not only was entry barred to anyone of dubious racial origin, but a brother or tertiary who married such a person was automatically expelled. In this stipulation there was the tacit equating of racial inferiority and social inferiority. 'A person of infected blood' (*pessoa de sangue infecta*) or with a 'defect in the blood' (*defeito de sangue*) — terms applying equally to New Christians and coloured people — was automatically a 'person of the basest condition' (*pessoa de ínfima condição*) socially. The legacy of this equation has survived to the present day in Brazil.

---

[1] This *Compromisso* is discussed in detail in Manoel S. Cardozo, 'The lay brotherhoods of colonial Bahia', in the *Catholic Historical Review*, vol. 33 (1947), pp. 12–30.

[2] Thales de Azevedo, *Ensaios de antropologia social* (Bahia, 1959), p. 99.

F

This attitude of racial exclusiveness possibly explains the comparative absence of any references to a racial problem within the Misericórdia. In 1679 the petition of a pastry cook, Domingos Rodrigues Lisboa, for membership was rejected because he was married to a mulatta. Four years later both he and his wife were admitted, and it would be interesting to know what change of circumstance brought about this acceptance.[1] The Mesa was not so charitable in the outright rejection of the petition of José Baptista Lemos in 1713 because he and his wife were *pardos*.[2]

When dealing with colour and anti-semitic prejudices there is the difficulty of 'pinning down' attitudes existing in the minds of the officials who laid down the law, but which were modified, strengthened, or weakened in the reality of everyday life. If the prejudice against New Christians in Bahia declined in the eighteenth century, there was no decline in the antipathy to coloured people who tried to obtain privileges regarded as the right of white citizens. The Misericórdia fought throughout the eighteenth century against Negro brotherhoods who asked for permission to own funeral biers for the burial of their members. Although admitting slaves to the hospital, only girls of pure white parentage were admitted to the retirement house. The Misericórdia's preservation of white exclusivism was linked, in the final analysis, to a question of pride. The Mesa could look the other way when the seventeenth-century satirical poet, Gregório de Mattos, frolicked with the slave girls of the sugar plantations of the Recôncavo, or when the illegitimate offspring of a *parda* and Cristóvão Cavalcante was admitted to the hospital. It acted severely if a decision involving racial discrimination was forced on it by a brother openly marrying a coloured woman.

Prejudices of class, creed and colour were present in colonial Bahia. Nobody felt these more strongly than the aristocratic, Catholic and white brothers of the Misericórdia. There is strong evidence that class barriers were being broken down in the course of the first half of the eighteenth century. Anti-semitic and racial prejudices lingered on. To be white and of Old Christian stock implied honesty and integrity. A 'white girl of Old Christian descent' was, by implication, 'a virtuous girl'. A scribe who was 'white and an Old Christian' was similarly 'a good scribe, sincere and

---

1 ASCMB, vol. 195, f. 17v, and vol. 2, ff. 189–90.
2 'por ter color de pardo e sua mulher' (ASCMB, vol. 195, f. 48v).

truthful'. Only in 1773 did discrimination against New Christians end officially in the Portuguese empire. Acting on the advice of the Marquis of Pombal, Dom José I issued a decree on 25 May 1773 ordering that the distinction between Old Christian and New Christian be abolished. Use of the term New Christian was prohibited on pain of severe penalties, and so ended 275 years of religious, bureaucratic and social persecution. The tolerance shown by the Marquis of Pombal towards the Indians was not matched by similar decrees favouring the Negro population. The lot of the slave did not improve. The freedman was regarded as socially inferior and bureaucratic office remained closed to all but very light mulattos. In their prejudices the brothers of the Misericórdia reflected the prevailing stresses and strains present in colonial Bahia.

7

Charity in Bahia

A. THE PERSONALITY OF CHARITY

THE social and economic changes which occurred in Bahia in the late seventeenth and early eighteenth centuries had repercussions on the charitable activities of the Misericórdia. The Misericórdia depended on private charity for its main source of income. Although the brotherhood fulfilled a semi-bureaucratic rôle in providing hospital services, aid for prisoners and care for foundlings, official sources were singularly unreceptive to pleas by boards of guardians for financial assistance to meet the cost of these benefits to the community. Royal protection was little more than nominal. The municipal council was constantly in debt and unable and unwilling to make any financial grant to the brotherhood. It was left to the Bahian public to finance the charitable works of the brotherhood by bequests and gifts. The archives of the Misericórdia provide information on the various benefactors who constituted this general public and enable an assessment to be made of the extent to which different social classes reacted to the need for charity in colonial Bahia.

Wills in the archives of the brotherhood constitute the chief source of information for such an analysis. A brief description of their content is necessary because the nature of the clauses limits the conclusions which can be drawn. A Bahian who wished to make a bequest to the Misericórdia could choose one of three courses of action. First, he could make the Misericórdia his heir. Secondly, he could merely nominate the brotherhood as his executor, granting a sum of money to the Misericórdia to cover the costs of administration of the will. Thirdly, he could nominate a relation or even another brotherhood as his heir or executor, ordering that a legacy be paid to the Misericórdia. There was also a choice in the manner in which a donation could be made. The testator could endow the brotherhood with a substantial sum of money which was to be placed on loan and the interest of 6¼ per cent applied to a stipulated end, or he could make a bequest on a once-and-for-all basis. The decision finally reached by a testator confronted by these different possibilities governs the extent of the material available in the records of the Misericórdia.

When the Misericórdia was heir or executor, a complete copy of the will was made by the scribe of the brotherhood. The drafting of a will followed a standard procedure. The will began with a declaration of faith and biographical details of the testator — place of birth, parentage, civil state and present place of residence. These opening details were followed by clauses making arrangements for the funeral and providing for the saying of masses. The third part of the will was devoted to the granting of legacies to friends, relations and brotherhoods, and to the manner in which the possessions of the testator in kind and in cash should be disposed of by the executor. The scribe made a statement certifying the authenticity of the will and the board of guardians signified its approval and undertook to fulfil all the clauses. As heir or executor the Misericórdia made an inventory of all the worldly possessions of the testator. In some few cases the records of financial settlements of legacies and debts are still extant. When the Misericórdia was merely the recipient of a bequest administered by a relation of the testator or by another brotherhood, the information is sparse. The scribe of the Misericórdia did no more than record the name of the testator, the value of the bequest and the cause to which the money was to be applied.

Both types of legacy offer certain difficulties. The first difficulty concerns the validity of wills as documentary evidence. Faced with the awe-inspiring prospect of the Hereafter and 'in fear of death', the Bahians were unusually frank in their wills, acknowledging illegitimate offspring, and even admitting some petty crime which had gone undiscovered at the time. This frankness was often tempered by delusions of grandeur or simply by exaggeration. It is difficult to establish the degree of misrepresentation because the physical extent of an estate and its market value often varied greatly in the interim between the date of the will and the time when probate was granted. A single example will illustrate this. Domingos da Silveira, a parishioner of the Desterro, who had died in 1661, estimated his possessions at 50 head of cattle, 150 horses, five slaves and several small plots of land in Rio das

Pedras and Praia do Rio Real. When an inventory was made the 'herd' was found to consist of six thin cows worth 14$700, a dead cow whose hide fetched 480 rs., a jade for which no buyer could be found, and two slaves valued at 70$000: debts due to the dead man amounted to 28$000.[1] It is quite possible that the figures quoted in his will were completely accurate. Smallholders were the constant victims of fortune. No less so were the great plantation owners and cattle ranchers. Heavy rain often ruined the sugar and tobacco crops, drought killed oxen and epidemic killed slaves. From one season to the next the prosperous owner of a plantation or a herd of cattle could be plunged into penury. The wills recorded by the scribes of the Misericórdia make no reference to such changes of fortune and calculations based on figures quoted in the wills would be totally misleading.

The second difficulty arises from the question of whether or not the clauses of a will were fulfilled. A son, after a lifetime spent in the tropics and loss of contact with kith and kin, often satisfied pangs of conscience by making a legacy to a mother, brother or sister in a remote village in Portugal. If they were still alive the money was to be sent to the nearest Misericórdia in Portugal for delivery to these relations. If they were dead the money was to be retained by the Misericórdia of Bahia. Such dispositions were frequent but rarely was the outcome mentioned. Similarly imprecise were those wills in which a testator, after making certain legacies, airily granted to the Misericórdia any residue remaining after all legacies and debts had been settled. Whether the Misericórdia received 10$000 or 100$000 was not stated. A third difficulty concerns those bequests for which the Misericórdia was neither heir nor executor. The name of a testator, the sum of his legacy and the charitable purpose to which this was to be applied indicate nothing of the social status or economic position of the donor.

Finally, changes of economic circumstance make valuations of property totally unrealistic. Inflation and rising costs are inconstant (but ever present) factors in an essentially agrarian community and estimates of the value of property over even comparatively short historical periods are impossible. Nor is inflation uniform in its effects. Different social classes in different regions are diversely affected. In the eighteenth century in Bahia the viceroy reported to the Crown that the migration of slaves to the mines had raised the price of slaves in Bahia to such a degree that the already hard-hit sugar

[1] ASCMB, vol. 41, ff. 59v–62v.

plantation owners faced ruin. The cause of ruin for many of the landed gentry brought temporary prosperity to some members of the business class of the city who exploited the demand for slaves. Even within the rural area, the choice of a sugar plantation or a cattle corral as the means of gaining a livelihood was something of a gamble. Landowners who possessed sugar plantations in the 1680s and 1690s struggled against a fall in demand for this commodity while their cattle-owning counterparts could view with optimism the increased market for hides in Europe.

The social structure of Bahia was reflected in the personality of the donors to the Misericórdia. Sugar plantations and cattle ranches had offered the only means of achieving real wealth in Bahia during the seventeenth century. The principal donors of the Misericórdia came exclusively from the land-owning class of the Recôncavo and the Sertão. They, and only they, could afford to endow the brotherhood with legacies sufficiently large to finance charitable undertakings or the saying of masses from the interest alone. In the seventeenth century the Misericórdia had received 133,785$820 in charitable bequests with recurring obligations: 90,269$000 of this total amount (at the most conservative estimate) had been directly attributable to the landowning class. These legacies had provided a theoretically secure patrimony to be preserved in its entirety by the boards of guardians of the brotherhood and offered a constant return on the capital invested.

The sugar nabobs had been, by tradition, brothers of the Misericórdia and tertiaries of St Francis or the Carmelites. At death they had endowed the brotherhoods of Bahia generously. The following were the more prominent of these donors to the Misericórdia in the seventeenth century. Felippe Correia, owner of a sugar plantation in Pituba, had been one of the first Bahians to realise that money could alleviate social hardship as well as providing masses for the salvation of his soul. In his will of 1650 he had allocated almost half of his 9,250$000 legacy to hospital assistance and dowries.[1] On two occasions in the seventeenth century the brotherhood had found itself the temporary owner of a plantation. Bento de Araújo Soares, who had died in 1653, had left his sugar plantation in Patatiba to the Misericórdia. In pursuance of the policy that money placed on loan offered a surer return than the proceeds of the cane crop, the brotherhood had sold

---

[1] ASCMB, vol. 40, ff. 198–210v.

this property and placed 5,650$000 on loan.[1] The vain António de Sá Doria, who had died in the last days of 1662 or on New Year's Day 1663, had made a similar legacy. Married, but without descendants, he had made the Misericórdia the heir to a sugar mill and plantation with forty-one slaves on the Island of Itaparica. This legacy offers a rare instance of a complete inventory of a property received by the Misericórdia. This inventory, made by the treasurer of the Misericórdia and a public notary, gives details of the sugar mill down to the smallest *repartideira* (a copper pan used in the manufacture of sugar), and describes the slave quarter with its ten tiled houses and the plantation house in the shade of a young coconut grove. The estate had consisted of twenty-one acres of land suitable for sugar cultivation, 3,000 tobacco plants, twenty fruit-bearing coconut palms, sixteen horses to work the mill, twenty cows, fourteen calves, two sows and eight suckling pigs in addition to farm implements such as brush-hooks, saws and axes.[2] The Misericórdia had reaped the benefit of the sugar crop in April and then had sold the entire estate, placing the proceeds of 5,771$730 on loan. The interest on this capital had been applied to the saying of masses for the souls of the benefactor and his spouse. One of the last Bahians to make a fortune in sugar before the slump in the 1680s and 1690s had been João de Mattos. He had indulged successfully in land speculation. At the time of his death in 1685 he was the owner of extensive sugar plantations in Patatiba and employed fifty-five slaves.[3] The Misericórdia had received a legacy of 5,200$000 from this testator and a fortune from his nephew, João de Mattos de Aguiar.

Whereas the sugar plantation owners had usually been the descendants of families of the lesser nobility who had emigrated to Bahia, the cattle ranchers had achieved social acceptance by hard work and financial success. Social acceptance had meant involvement in municipal matters and in the life of the brotherhoods of Bahia. The Misericórdia of Bahia had acknowledged the prestige of these pioneers by electing them Provedors: Francisco Dias d'Avila, of the House of Tôrre; Pedro Barbosa Leal, one of the 'Big Five' landowners of Bahia in the early eighteenth century; Domingos Affonso Sertão, named after the region he had explored. Wealth derived from the raising of cattle and a religious sentiment born of a lifetime in constant

---

[1] ASCMB, vol. 41, ff. 18–23.   [2] ASCMB, vol. 41, ff. 70–9.
[3] ASCMB, vol. 41, ff. 239v–244.

contact with the elements, had found a common outlet in the building of convents and the making of bequests to brotherhoods. The Misericórdia of Bahia had greatly benefited from these benefactors. Mecia Rodrigues, wife of the founder of the House of Tôrre, had made a bequest to the Misericórdia of 3,420$000, a fortune in those early days. In 1650 a priest, Francisco de Araújo, who had inherited cattle ranches in Saubara, had passed this inheritance of four corrals with some 120 head of cattle on to the Misericórdia. The dismay of the brotherhood on finding itself owner of an unwanted property, whose sale had been forbidden by the testator, must have been lessened by the receipt of a legacy of 5,000$000 which had accompanied the donation. Pedro Barbosa Leal, a founder of several townships in the interior, had granted 2,800$000 to the brotherhood in 1684 for the saying of masses.[1] Pride of place among the cattle-owning benefactors of the Misericórdia must go to Domingos Fernandes de Freitas. A native of the archbishopric of Braga, he had emigrated to Bahia and by the time of his death in the 1690s was the owner of four cattle ranches on the lands of Francisco Dias d'Avila in the area of the São Francisco River. These ranches comprised some 850 head of cattle worth from 1$800 to 2$000 per head, 270 mares valued at 3$000 each, 55 stallions worth 10$000 each, and a small stock of some 500 goats and sheep worth 300 rs. each. The small labour force consisted of twelve Negro slaves and seven Indians. After legacies (including 4,000$000 to the Misericórdia of Braga) had been made, the Misericórdia of Bahia had received 18,733$058, to be applied to the saying of masses and the establishment of dowries.[2]

During the eighteenth century merchants and businessmen featured in the lists of testators to the Misericórdia. The legacies made by this class never rivalled those made by the landowning aristocracy in monetary value. There were two reasons for this. The first was the shortage of currency in Bahia in the eighteenth century. The second was the change in the manner of making bequests. No longer were bequests made with recurring obligations to be fulfilled by the brotherhood from the interest received on a capital loan. Instead, the characteristic manner of giving in the eighteenth century consisted of legacies to be directly applied to a specific charitable purpose. The

---

[1] ASCMB, vol. 41, f. 232v.

[2] The copy of this will in the archives of the Misericórdia (ASCMB, vol. 192) is in extremely bad condition.

major legacy received by the Misericórdia from a member of the business
class was that of João de Mattos de Aguiar in 1700. His will contained the
following clauses: 100,000 *cruzados* for the saying of 11,000 masses at 200 *rs.*
each for his soul and those of his parents and grandparents; 16,000 *cruzados*
to be placed on loan and the interest to finance gifts of 1$000 to each poor
person leaving the hospital; 80,000 *cruzados* to be applied to the building of
a retirement house; 134,500 *cruzados* and 14$406 to be placed on loan and
the interest to finance dowries of 100$000 each.[1]

The contents of the will of João de Mattos de Aguiar illustrate to the full
the changing attitude towards wealth. The wills of the seventeenth century
had been characterised by details of plantations, house properties and slaves,
couched in somewhat vague terms. The dispositions of the will of João de
Mattos de Aguiar were characterised by exact lists of borrowers. No longer
was wealth hoarded in a small box or buried among the roots of the cane
crop. Wealth was being used to finance undertakings — the purchase of
houses, a loan to a plantation owner to buy slaves, or to a humble smith
to enlarge his business. The success story of João de Mattos de Aguiar
represented the first break with the economic tradition of the seventeenth
century. It also represented an increasing social conscience which appeared
in the eighteenth century. This replaced the religiosity of the landowners
of the seventeenth century who had left entire fortunes for the purchase of
their salvation by the saying of masses. João de Mattos de Aguiar was still
bound by tradition in this respect, providing for 11,000 masses. This
provision was enormous in comparison with the legacies of other testators
but the financial sum involved merely represented a sixth of the total legacy
of this benefactor. A conservative in religious practice, a liberal in financial
outlook, João de Mattos de Aguiar's foundation of a retirement house was
symbolic of the break with the tradition of economic stagnation and self-
centred righteousness.

Sugar planters and cattle ranchers, whose legacies had formed the patrimony of the Misericórdia in the seventeenth century, had been the most
seriously affected by the economic crisis of the 1680s and 1690s. A series

---

[1] ASCMB, vol. 199. The amounts of the legacies made in his will differ from
the sums received by the treasurer of the Misericórdia, sometimes only after
protracted and expensive litigation (see Table III, on p. 170, calculated on vol.
211).

of bad harvests and hard winters in the eighteenth century had made recovery impossible for all but the most fortunate who had sufficient capital to sustain these setbacks. The more humble forms of agriculture — the cultivation of tobacco and manioc — had been affected by the adverse weather conditions, but to a lesser degree. The cultivation of these two crops had necessitated only a small capital outlay and the labour force had rarely exceeded four or five slaves. The Misericórdia continued to receive small legacies from such donors in the eighteenth century. The combination of barren white wives, high infant mortality, and the severance of all family ties with Portugal made the brotherhoods the most obvious beneficiaries for the wills of such smallholders. Legacies of 200$000 or 400$000 were received by the Misericórdia from this source and provided a small but constant revenue.

The exploitation of gold and diamonds was a major event in the Brazilian economy in the first half of the eighteenth century. Bahia was one of the official outlets for gold (Rio de Janeiro was the other) and it would have been reasonable to suppose that the Misericórdia would have benefited from this new source of wealth. This was not the case. There was but a single instance of a substantial legacy to the Misericórdia being derived from speculation in gold. This was the legacy of Manuel Fernandes Costa. A native of Vila do Conde, a fishing town in the north of Portugal, Manuel Fernandes had been drawn to Brazil in the hope of gaining enough quick wealth from the new Potosí rumoured to exist in the hills of Minas Gerais, to be able to finance a small company in Lisbon. Materialistic ends had brought him to Brazil, but even the most die-hard materialist possessed a lively fear of the Hereafter and had premonitions of the small value attached to life in a gold boom community. The precarious nature of life in Minas Gerais at this time is dramatically illustrated by an ex-voto in the church of Mont'Serrat in Bahia (see Plate). This painting was offered by one Agostinho Pereira da Silva in 1749 to Our Lady of Graces as a token of gratitude for her protection. Like Manuel Fernandes Costa, Agostinho Pereira had been drawn to Brazil in search of gold and had commended his body and soul to Our Lady of Graces before leaving for the mining area. By her intercession he was saved from snake bites, hunger and thirst, and death at the hands of bandits. On his return to Portugal he took holy orders in fulfilment of a vow made to his protector. Manuel Fernandes Costa made a will providing

for the salvation of his soul before leaving Bahia in 1710. Then he left for
the interior with a small party of eleven slaves, six horses, a set of mining
tools, and two additional slaves whom he had been commissioned to take
out to the mines. He did not survive long in Minas Gerais, but the
collection of debts due to him and proceeds from the sale of gold in Lisbon
realised 7,644$263. The Misericórdia of Bahia benefited to the tune of
5,600$000 with the obligation of saying two daily masses for his soul.[1]
This was the only substantial legacy, directly attributable to the new discoveries, received by the Misericórdia of Bahia.

The Misericórdia did receive some small legacies from testators in the
mining areas. A Negro, António de Freitas, had amassed 100 *oitavas* of gold
— probably illicitly — in his lifetime and left it in his will to the proposed
hospital of the mining camp of Trahiras. No hospital was built and the
money was sent to the Misericórdia of Bahia for its hospital.[2] An inhabitant
of Congonhas de Sabará, António Gomes Oliveira, left a small donation of
100$000 in 1751 to the Misericórdia for the sustenance of prisoners.[3] The
gold strikes in the Captaincy of Bahia benefited the Misericórdia no more
than had those in Minas Gerais. The only records of legacies from this area
were of 100$000 left for the hospital by Francisco Pires Lima who died in
Jacobina in 1750 and of 800$000 left in the same year by Manuel Valério de
Nis, a miner of Arassúahy, for dowries.[4]

The gold and diamonds of Minas Gerais which dazzled the eyes of
European potentates and businessmen enriched the Misericórdia of Bahia but
little. An official exit point and a centre for the minting of false coin and for
an illicit trade in gold and diamonds, Bahia should have been the very city
in which the brotherhoods could have expected to replenish their coffers to
overflowing from this source. Yet one of the foremost brotherhoods of
Bahia — the Misericórdia — was scarcely affected by this traffic, official and
illicit. There were two reasons for this neglect of the Misericórdia in the
wills of the gold miners and diamond prospectors. The first reason was
that the majority of early migrants from Bahia to Minas Gerais possessed no
social standing and could never have aspired to membership of a brotherhood

[1] ASCMB, vol. 42, ff. 171–5.   [2] ASCMB. vol. 42, f. 208.
[3] ASCMB, vol. 42, f. 215v.
[4] ASCMB, vol. 42, ff. 221v and 215 respectively. I have found no record of the
second legacy being received by the Misericórdia.

such as the Misericórdia. There were some few exceptions, the supreme case being Manuel Nunes Viana who was one of the major personalities in Minas Gerais in the early eighteenth century.[1] The second reason, of greater importance, was the raising of the mining encampment of Ouro Prêto to the status of a township in 1711. Born a boom town with all the problems of law and order, Vila Rica de Ouro Prêto rapidly formed its own bourgeoisie and social hierarchy. Simão Ferreira Machado, a native of Lisbon who had lived in Minas Gerais and was the first to describe the profane religious festivities of this region in his *Triunfo Eucharistico* of 1734, referred to the social standing of the inhabitants of Ouro Prêto:

> In this town live the chief merchants, whose trade and importance incomparably exceed the most thriving of the leading merchants of Portugal. Hither, as to a port, are directed and collected in the Royal Mint the grandiose amounts of gold from all the Mines. Here dwell the best educated men, both lay and ecclesiastic. Here is the seat of all the nobility and the strength of the military.[2]

A eulogistic description perhaps but the fact remained that from vagrant and *garimpeiro*, or illicit diamond speculator, there had developed a corporate cultured society. By 1720 there were some twenty brotherhoods in the mining area. These were not only in Ouro Prêto but also in the neighbouring towns of Mariana, São João del Rei and Sabará, and catered for blacks, whites and *pardos*.[3] There was no inducement for intending testators in the mining areas to risk loss by sending their money to Bahia for the saying of masses or the care of a hospital in a city where they were themselves unknown and where their generosity would be accorded no posthumous social accolades.

The changing personalities of the testators to the Misericórdia reflected these major developments in the Bahian economy in the seventeenth century.

[1] An outline of the life of Manuel Nunes Viana is in C. R. Boxer, *The Golden Age of Brazil*, pp. 364–5.

[2] This work was dedicated to Our Lady of the Rosary by the Negro brothers and commemorated the moving of the Eucharist from the Church of Our Lady of the Rosary to the new church of the Pilar on 24 May 1733. For a description of this book see Rubens Borba de Moraes, *Bibliographia brasiliana*, vol. 2. I have here followed the translation of C. R. Boxer, *The Golden Age of Brazil*, pp. 162–3.

[3] Fritz Teixeira de Salles, *Associações religiosas no Ciclo do Ouro* (Belo Horizonte, 1963), pp. 31–3.

In the eighteenth century there was a redistribution of wealth. As far as can be judged from casual references, the majority of testators came from the city, owning houses in the districts of São Bento or the Ajuda as an investment and engaging in some form of commerce. If they did have landed interests, these were not mentioned and less frequently was the place of residence one of the townships of the Recôncavo. The bourgeoisie of the city reacted to the charitable impulse in a manner no less praiseworthy than had the rural landowners, but the economic decline of Bahia made their legacies less substantial.

The rise of the artisan class has already been apparent in connection with the social structure of Bahia in the eighteenth century. Greater representation on the city council and ennoblement as the result of temporary commissions in the local garrison were indicative of the social ascent of this class. The appointment of Manuel Antunes Lima to be treasurer of the Misericórdia indicated that a member of a trade could achieve financial success. This latter aspect was well documented by the presence of members of the mechanical trades among testators to the Misericórdia. I have chosen the representatives of four trades — a tinsmith, a saddler, a stonemason and a wax-chandler — to exemplify this aspect.

The tinsmith was João Ribeiro, born of a French father and a Portuguese mother. In his will of 1674 he had made elaborate provisions for his funeral procession. This was to be accompanied by six brotherhoods of which he was a member, and by seven more of which he was not a member, on payment of a small donation. In addition, the priests of the cathedral and the chaplain of the Misericórdia were to accompany the bier. An inventory of his possessions showed that his vanity had a solid financial basis. The sale of four slaves, old brass and tools, realised 566$067 — a notable sum for a mere tinsmith to have accumulated.[1] A saddler, João da Costa, had made less elaborate funeral provisions in his will of 1677, but his financial position had been no less secure. He had left to the Misericórdia houses of an estimated value of 900$000 with the sole obligation that a weekly mass should be said for his soul and that of his wife.[2] The most remarkable instance of an artisan 'making good' was afforded by Manuel João who had died in 1686. A stonemason by calling, he had left his native village of Salvador de Valadares in the bishopric of Oporto and come to Brazil in

[1] ASCMB, vol. 41, ff. 122v–124.   [2] ASCMB, vol. 41, f. 150v.

search of fortune. He had rapidly become integrated in the social life of Bahia and belonged to some seven brotherhoods. Probate had revealed him as the owner of eleven slaves, ten houses and assets to the tune of 4,056$340 in debts due to him.[1] The Misericórdia had received 2,800$000 of this sum for the saying of a daily mass. Finally the wax-chandler, Manuel Baptista Ferreira, illustrated how a craftsman could achieve financial stability. He nominated the Misericórdia as his heir and executor in a will of 1748. His possessions included 200$000 of gold, seven slaves (of which one was a licensed chandler and himself the owner of two slaves), a house in São Bento with 400$000 worth of furniture and personal effects and a chandler's shop fully equipped with copper pans and ladles.[2]

Such 'success stories' must have been few and far between. For every artisan who succeeded, many died in poverty in the Misericórdia hospital, leaving a small donation to the brotherhood to cover the costs of burial and masses. The members of the artisan classes never made a large contribution to the overall revenue of the Misericórdia. Nevertheless, the fact that a tin-smith or stonemason could emulate the lesser gentry in their funerals and in their legacies showed that humble social standing did not bar the way to financial success.

The clergy of Brazil fit into no social hierarchy, nor were they always associated with an urban way of life. I include them here in the belief that, for every one who did follow the trail of fortune to Minas Gerais, many hundreds remained in the city of Bahia.[3] The popular respect accorded to those who took the tonsure was often unjustified. Inquisitorial enquiries and viceroyal correspondence dwelt on the unedifying aspects of a vocation more materialistic than spiritual — love nests in villages of the Recôncavo or dubious business dealings in smuggled gold.[4] Whether the money which

[1] ASCMB, vol. 42, ff. 11AV–14v and ff. 16v–20v.

[2] ASCMB, vol. 42, ff. 210–212v.

[3] In a letter of 18 September 1723 the Count of Sabugosa recommended to the king the prohibition of 'a passagem dos Religiozos, e clerigos ao Brazil, que para esse effeito como selhes nega os Passaportes, procurão vir com praça de Capellaens nos Navios mercantes, e tanto que chegão, se encaminhão para as Minas, Certão, e Ryo de São Francisco, vivendo tão escandalozamente em todas estas partes, que mais parecem infieis, que Catholicos' (APB, *Ordens régias*, vol. 17, doc. 93a).

[4] A rousing account of clerical concubinage in Sergipe in 1748 is contained in APB, *Ordens régias*, vol. 47, ff. 96–100.

these clerics accumulated was made honestly or not, the fact remained that the priestly class was notable for its generosity. The archdeacon, Gonçalo Rodrigues, canon of the cathedral of Bahia for thirty years, left 223$000 to the Misericórdia in 1648 for the saying of masses.[1] Two eighteenth-century canons, Manuel Ramos Pacheco and Manuel Ribeiro Penha, made legacies to the Misericórdia of 800$000 and 1,600$000 for prison care and masses respectively.[2] Parish priests in the city remembered the Misericórdia in their wills and arranged for collections to be taken among their parishioners for specified charitable purposes provided for by the Misericórdia. A priest of Ilhéus, Henrique Luís d'Espendola, who had died in the hospital of Bahia in 1682, had been of the number who had dabbled in small trade. He bequeathed 400$000 for the saying of masses.[3] If sometimes an unusually generous legacy to a slave girl and her offspring arouses one's scepticism as to the degree of adherence to the priestly vows, nevertheless, one can only admire those minor clerics who eked out an existence based on alms of 320 *rs.* for the saying of masses — a far from lucrative source of income. Canon or cleric, saint or sodomite, the priests of colonial Bahia contributed generously to the coffers of the Misericórdia.

Finally, there were those unfortunates who died in the hospital of the Misericórdia and who left their small worldly possessions to the brotherhood. Sickness levelled classes in colonial Brazil. The Misericórdia maintained the only general hospital in the city of Bahia. Destitute priest, impoverished cobbler and slave were all jostled together in cramped conditions. As death approached, the scribe of the Misericórdia drew up the will of the dying man and a priest of the Misericórdia prayed for his soul. Inevitably at such a moment the brotherhood appeared to the dying man as the most suitable executor and heir. The Misericórdia was prevented by statute from keeping legacies in kind and monthly sales were held of clothes and *bric-à-brac* left by the dead. The inventories make interesting reading and a sample may be quoted. A saintly priest, João Lopes, who had died in 1691, had left some clothes, a book of universal history, a breviary, a copy of the decrees of the Council of Trent, a Book of Hours, and an ink pot.[4] The worldly posses-

---

[1] ASCMB, vol. 40, ff. 181–183v.

[2] They died on 5 July 1720 and 18 May 1728 respectively (ASCMB, vol. 42, f. 166v and ff. 179v–180).   [3] ASCMB, vol. 41, ff. 204–207v.

[4] ASCMB, vol. 42, ff. 60v–61.

sions of a common soldier comprised a box containing 34$000, a sword, a gold locket, buckles, a tortoiseshell box and some clothes. A mulatta who died intestate possessed no more than the clothes she had been wearing on arrival at the hospital. The hospital also catered for the sick off the Indiamen and the trading ships from Angola. The bounty-chest of a sailor of an Indiaman included such luxuries and curiosities as silk counterpanes, ivory crucifixes, pepper, spices, fine cloths and china. António Ribeiro Briozo seems to have belonged to rather a different class, that of a small businessman who was returning from the East with merchandise for sale in Portugal. His death in the hospital of Bahia in 1702 denied him the opportunity of dazzling the eyes of relations in a distant Portuguese village with the riches of the Orient. His possessions included china teacups and saucers, lacquered boxes, fans, silver braid, crystal rosaries and large quantities of textiles. The Bahians spent freely to acquire such luxuries. Two peacock plumes fetched 1$600 and the Misericórdia benefited.[1] In comparison, the wills of the sailors and merchants from Angola make dull reading — a slave, or various pieces of gold and silver.

The personalities of donors to the Misericórdia changed in the course of the seventeenth and eighteenth centuries. In the seventeenth century cattle ranchers and sugar planters had formed the majority of the donors both in quality and in quantity. The legacy of João de Mattos de Aguiar was indicative of a still embryonic business community, the extent of whose donations was restricted by economic necessity. Smaller legacies were provided by tobacco cultivators and manioc growers in the rural areas. With increasing urbanisation and the social and financial ascent of the small bourgeoisie, members of the mechanical trades and those gaining their livelihood as middlemen were among the benefactors of the Misericórdia.

B. THE CHARITABLE IMPULSE

The economic and social factors which influenced the type of donor to the Misericórdia in the seventeenth and eighteenth centuries also determined the character, form and purpose of bequests made to the brotherhood. Once again the wills copied in the registers of the Misericórdia constitute the

[1] ASCMB, vol. 42, ff. 135–138v.

principal source of information. These have been complemented by a survey of all legacies received by the brotherhood, conducted by the scribe in 1754 in response to a royal enquiry, and the account ledgers. These records provide a fairly complete picture of legacies received by the brotherhood between 1600 and 1750 and make possible a statistical analysis of the mechanism of charity. A brief note is necessary on these statistics. In 1700 the Misericórdia received the mammoth legacy of 217,092$475 from João de Mattos de Aguiar. This sum completely distorts all tables and graphs showing the general charitable trends in colonial Bahia and has been omitted except where stated.

There were two courses open to a testator wishing to make a bequest to the Misericórdia. The possible alternatives were legacies with recurring obligations to be fulfilled by the brotherhood, and legacies making a donation once-and-for-all with no further commitment. The choice made by testators when faced by these alternatives was significant and revealed a gradual change in the type of donation made to the Misericórdia in the seventeenth and eighteenth centuries. The first type of legacy consisted of a donation to the Misericórdia, which the board of guardians then offered on loan at an interest rate of $6\frac{1}{4}$ per cent. The interest was then applied to the charitable end specified by the testator in his will. From the time of the earliest records of the financial affairs of the Misericórdia, some half-dozen of which pre-date the Dutch invasion of Bahia in 1624, up to 1750 the Misericórdia received legacies of this type to a total value of 187,409$454 from 116 testators.[1] If this total is divided up into historical periods of twenty-five years a gradual pattern emerges:

Years	No. testators	Value of legacies
Pre–1625	15	13,620$000
1625–1650	20	12,785$632
1650–1675	27	54,747$130
1675–1700	34	52,633$058
1700–1725	14	41,623$634
1725–1750	6	12,000$000
	116	187,409$454

[1] These figures are compiled from ASCMB, vol. 211. My table excludes João de Mattos de Aguiar and his legacy.

If the period before 1625 is regarded as something of an unknown entity, the period 1625–50 must be considered as years of restoration after the Dutch invasion and the destruction of numerous sugar plantations in the Recôncavo. The years 1650–75 bore the fruit of this period of reconstruction and represented the period of greatest economic stability in the history of Bahia. The gradual decline which has already been discussed is shown in the lessening of the value of legacies in the last quarter of the seventeenth century. The period of economic transition in the first half of the eighteenth century is reflected in the decrease in revenue derived by the Misericórdia from this type of legacy. Even more revealing than the figures for the amounts of money received are those of the number of testators who chose this type of legacy — a mere twenty in the years 1700–50 compared with sixty-one in the preceding half century. The decline in monetary values of this type of legacy may be explained in financial terms but this does not account for the abrupt change in the manner of giving in the eighteenth century. A consideration of the other type of legacy will provide an answer to this problem and will explain how it was that the Misericórdia managed to survive, albeit in increasingly difficult financial circumstances, until the 'moment of truth' in 1754, when a royal enquiry was held into the affairs of the brotherhood.

Legacies given to the Misericórdia on a once-and-for-all basis placed no obligation on the brotherhood beyond the immediate allocation of the bequest. Therefore the figures quoted do not include alms granted to the brotherhood for accompanying the funeral bier, for attending the burial of a testator, or for the saying of masses over an extended period. The total number of legacies granted to the Misericórdia on a once-and-for-all basis in the whole of the seventeenth century did not exceed a score with an approximate monetary value of 1,000$000.[1] During the half century 1700–50, for which the records are practically complete, there were some 140 references in the account ledgers to legacies of this type received by the treasurer of the Misericórdia. These legacies amounted to the sum of 24,681$290. The enormous difference between the number of testators making this type of legacy and those leaving bequests with recurring obligations is sufficient indication that financial circumstances alone did not determine the manner of giving.

[1] This figure includes a rough estimate of the proceeds derived from the sale of houses and slaves where the prices of these are not stated in the inventories.

The changing character of the bequests received by the Misericórdia was due to a combination of economic and social factors. The sums of money recorded in the ledgers and the calculations made by the accountants of the Misericórdia should not be accepted blindly. They demand interpretation. The basic fact is that there was a marked decrease in the number of legacies made to the Misericórdia of the type where commitments were met from interest, and a marked increase in the number of legacies on a once-and-for-all basis. Financial reasons provide a partial answer. Lessening opportunities for accumulating sufficient capital to finance charitable works from the interest alone might explain the increase in the number of legacies given on a single occasion. Such an explanation is not entirely satisfactory because it does not take into account that testators frequently left comparatively small sums of money, such as 200$000, to the brotherhood with obligations to be fulfilled annually. Conversely some of the single legacies were of substantial sums of money of as much as 600$000.

Reasons of a social nature provide a more satisfactory explanation for the change. The first reason lies in the different social standing of the donors. On the one hand was a landed aristocracy, God-fearing and prestige-seeking. On the other hand was an urban community, secular in outlook, many of whose members were immigrants who had rubbed shoulders with penury on their way to financial success. The former gave to the Misericórdia out of a feeling of obligation to their class and sought to enhance their own social standing by the provisions made in their wills, often dedicated to the saying of masses. The latter preferred that their money should provide immediate relief of the social suffering of the community. The second reason concerns the attitude of mind of the testators towards the Misericórdia. The position of Provedor and membership of the board of guardians had been the prerogative of certain landowning families of the Recôncavo and Sertão in the seventeenth century. The Misericórdia meant far more to these families than a mere mediaeval brotherhood founded in Lisbon in 1498. It was a club where they could expect to meet others of the same financial interests and of the same social standing. The urban bourgeoisie did not appreciate the wealth of tradition embodied by the Misericórdia. They looked at the brotherhood with harder eyes than the aristocratic plantation owners and regarded the Misericórdia as an administrator of social philanthropy in a dubiously effective manner. Whereas the landowning class automatically chose the Misericórdia or a Third Order as their executors and heirs, the bourgeoisie maintained a lively distrust for the brotherhoods and preferred to nominate a relation or neighbour as their executor.

These two attitudes contributed to the change in the manner of giving. The Misericórdia suffered from this change. It lost the patrimony which, although it might have been expected to decrease as a result of the economic decline of the eighteenth century, nevertheless did represent a solid financial basis. Legacies given without recurring obligations were all too easily dissipated in meeting the every-day costs of a policy of social philanthropy which had become too ambitious and bore no relation to the financial resources of the brotherhood. The burghers of the eighteenth century felt the charitable impulse no less strongly than had the landowners of the seventeenth century. They simply attached less importance to posthumous social accolades such as ceremonial funerals and were more conscious of the immediate social benefits which wealth could bestow on a community. They were also less institutionally minded and were reluctant to be involved in the administrative machinations of a brotherhood which had been a family tradition for their predecessors.

The form of bequests made to the Misericórdia in the seventeenth century differed from those made in the eighteenth century. The legacies made to the Misericórdia can be divided into the two categories of those given in kind and those given in cash. The financial policy of the Misericórdia up to the mid-1650s had been based on property. Houses within the city limits had been believed to offer the best form of investment both because of their security and because of the return on capital. With some few exceptions all the legacies made to the brotherhood before 1660 with recurring obligations had consisted of houses whose rentals would meet the costs of the saying of masses or would provide for some charitable purpose. The brotherhood, in pursuance of this policy, had even acquired properties at public auctions. The board of guardians of 1652 had been the first to doubt the wisdom of this form of investment and several properties had been sold to meet the immediate needs of the hospital. The doubts of later Mesas had been strengthened by demands from dissatisfied tenants that extensive repairs should be undertaken because many of the houses were in a derelict state. The cost of these repairs had left the boards of guardians in doubt no longer. In 1663 the Mesa had decided to implement fully a royal privilege of 1657 granting the brotherhood the right to sell all properties on which no restriction had been placed by the testator. All monies derived from such sales were to be placed on loan.[1] This decision on policy and the changing attitude towards the making of bequests had meant that the Misericórdia rarely received legacies of properties after 1660. The only exception of a property being retained by the Misericórdia was the estate of the priest Francisco de Araújo. A clause of the testator's will had forbidden the sale of this property. Despite the small return, the Misericórdia remained the owner of this property until the early nineteenth century.

As an executor of legacies the Misericórdia often found itself in temporary custody of a heterogeneous collection of goods. By statutory requirement these were sold and the proceeds sent to the heirs after the payment of all debts had been made, except when the testator ordered that the money should be applied by the Misericórdia to some charitable purpose or to the saying of masses. There were two exceptions to this rule. The first was when a slave was left to the Misericórdia on the understanding that after working for a certain time in the service of the brotherhood he should be granted his freedom. An example of this practice was Cipriano, left to the Misericórdia by Matheus de Araújo in the eighteenth century, who earned two *patacas* a week for the brotherhood by the sweat of his brow. The second exception was gifts in kind to the hospital. In 1668 the Master of the Field, João de Araújo, had ordered his executors to send to Portugal for twelve beds for the hospital of the Misericórdia of Bahia. These had duly arrived, each complete with a mattress containing about thirty pounds of wool, two sheets, two pillows and a blanket.[2] Other testators gave bed clothing to the hospital. In 1664 the lawyer, Jerónimo de Burgos, had ordered that a hundred yards of linen be given to the Misericórdia every two years by his executors, and similar amounts were given by other benefactors.[3]

Legacies in cash became more common after 1660. The increasing practice of making legacies on a once-and-for-all basis to the Misericórdia meant that

[1] Minute of 30 September 1663 (ASCMB, vol. 41, f. 88). Royal privilege of 11 December 1657 (ASCMB, vol. 209, f. 48).

[2] ASCMB, vol. 41, ff. 109v–110. Each mattress contained one *arrôba* of wool. In Brazil the weight of the *arrôba* varied at different times and from region to region, but was the Portuguese equivalent of the English quarter.

[3] ASCMB, vol. 41, ff. 97v–98v. The legacy was of 100 *varas* of linen. The *vara* varied regionally but was the approximate equivalent of the yard.

cash offered a more suitable form of donation. Alms to cover the administrative costs of a legacy or to pay funeral expenses were always in money. On other occasions it was only after the properties had been sold and legacies and debts settled that the Misericórdia received its due. Frequently the brotherhood was a temporary owner of slaves before these were sold at the door of the church. Another form of indirect cash legacies were bequests of debts to the brotherhood. For example, in 1650, João Gonçalves, the boatman of the landowner Lourenço Cavalcante, left a debt of 18$190 to be collected by the Misericórdia.[1] Frequently, sailors who died in the hospital left the pay packets due to them to the Misericórdia.

The change in the kind of legacy received by the Misericórdia was partly the result of a decision on policy and partly the result of a change in attitude towards bequests. With the increasing dearth of ready money in the eighteenth century, the brotherhood must often have had cause to regret its earlier decision and a half-hearted attempt was made to reintroduce an investment policy based on property rentals.

The shift in importance in the social structure and changing attitudes towards bequests played a large rôle in determining the purpose for which a donation was given. Examination of the various purposes for which legacies were left to the Misericórdia shows the changing aspirations of Bahian society in the seventeenth and eighteenth centuries. Wills reveal the spirit of an epoch by the very nature of their clauses. A characteristic of the seventeenth century had been religious fervour mingled with a lively fear of the Hereafter. The main characteristic of the eighteenth century was a preoccupation with alleviating social distress. An analysis of these two characteristics indicates the extent to which an increasing tendency toward secularisation was allied to the social changes already described.

Religious sentiment could be expressed in two forms. The first was by making elaborate arrangements for the funeral cortège. The second was by ordering that masses should be said for the soul of the benefactor and his relations. Funeral cortèges embodied a mixture of pious sentiment and pompous egoism. The testator usually ordered that he should be buried in the habit of St Francis and that he should be carried to his grave on the bier of the Misericórdia. Small alms were granted to the Third Order and the Misericórdia for both these services. Foreign visitors to Bahia in the

[1] ASCMB, vol. 40, ff. 193v–197.

seventeenth and eighteenth centuries commented on the popular religious fervour which was manifested in processions. Even the staunchly Protestant Mrs Kindersley was constrained to regard this aspect of Bahian life with a greater degree of favour than she usually accorded to Popery. The religious fervour of the slave particularly impressed her, especially in public ceremonies.[1] If devotion was mingled with a love of ceremony among the Negroes, no less was religious sentiment tempered by sanctimony among the white population. This sanctimony took the form of mundane aspirations to a posthumous prestige: 'Religion had not merely to be done; it had to be seen to be done.' António de Sá Doria, the wealthy seventeenth-century landowner, had commanded his executor to ensure that his funeral be conducted 'with all the pomp customary in the funerals of noble people of substance'.[2] The success of such a spectacle had been measured by the number of brotherhoods attending the funeral. Often the testator was a member of one or two of the major brotherhoods — the Misericórdia, the Third Order of St Francis or the Third Order of the Carmelites, and three or four parochial brotherhoods. These attended the funeral of a brother by statutory obligation and the donation of a small sum for this service was customary but voluntary. Other brotherhoods to which the testator did not belong sent representatives to funerals on payment of a small sum to their coffers. It was here that wealth could buy the ceremonial indicative of social standing, and ensure the posthumous prestige of the dead man. António Dias de Ottões, a brother of the Misericórdia and the owner of a sugar plantation in Jucuruna, had ordered in his will of 1653 that all the priests of the cathedral chapter, the friars of the Carmelite monastery, and representatives of all the brotherhoods and religious orders of the city and its environs should attend his funeral. The priests were to receive a candle and the brotherhoods 4$000 each for this service.[3] Other testators often specified by name as many as twenty brotherhoods to attend their funerals. This love of ceremony was by no means limited to the upper class. It has already been seen that the tinsmith João Ribeiro made provision for the attendance of some thirteen brotherhoods at his funeral.

[1] Mrs Nathaniel Edward Kindersley, *Letters from the Island of Teneriffe, Brazil, the Cape of Good Hope, and the East Indies* (London, 1777), p. 50.

[2] 'com toda a mais pompa, que se costuma fazer às pessoas nobres e de qualidade' (ASCMB, vol. 41, ff. 37–38v).   [3] ASCMB, vol. 41, ff. 24–9.

The cost of this pomp and piety was considerable. The satirist Gregório de Mattos had chided the extravagance of the Vieira Ravasco family at the Feast of the 11,000 Virgins:

> Gastou com liberal mão
> Nesta festa sem cautelas.[1]

In the early eighteenth century the French traveller Le Gentil de la Barbinais commented that the Portuguese would be rich but for their weakness for saints and mistresses.[2] Even the modest funeral provisions of a small cattle owner, Domingos da Silveira, cost 47$560 in 1661.[3] The costs of the funeral of the wealthy João de Mattos in 1685 came to a sum in the region of 1,000$000. This included a donation of 40$000 to the Third Order of St Francis for a habit of the Order, alms to all the clergy and brotherhoods, 30$000 each to the monastery of St Theresa and the convent of the Desterro for masses, and provided for the saying of 200 masses at 240 *rs.* each over his coffin, and a further 2,000 masses at 200 *rs.* each as soon as possible after his burial.[4]

The second manner of showing religious fervour was by catering for the salvation of the soul by the saying of masses. These masses fell into three categories — those said over the coffin *de corpo presente*, those said a week after death and those for which the brotherhood had a recurring obligation. The first two categories provided the Misericórdia with small alms. Revenues derived from the third type, known as *capelas de missas*, formed the patrimony of the brotherhood.

There were various methods of instituting a *capela de missas* and the only common point was that all such obligations were financed by a bequest whose capital was placed on loan. The most modest *capela de missas* was for masses to be said on the four principal festivals of the year. A variation was for masses to be said on certain saints' days. Other *capelas de missas* ranged from monthly masses to those said daily for the souls of a testator and his relations. The capital outlay necessary to provide sufficient interest to finance the saying of a mass daily meant that only the richest members of Bahian society could afford this luxury. Only fifteen of the 117 testators to

[1] Gregório de Mattos, *Obras completas*, vol. 4, p. 42.
[2] Le Gentil de la Barbinais, *Nouveau Voyage au tour du monde par Monsieur Le Gentil. Enrichi de plusieurs Plans, Vüës et Perspectives des principales Villes & Ports du Pérou, Chily, Bresil & de la Chine etc* (3 vols., Paris, 1727), vol. 3, p. 193.
[3] ASCMB, vol 41, ff. 59v–62v. [4] ASCMB, vol. 41, ff. 239v–244.

the Misericórdia between about 1610 and 1750 stipulated the saying of a daily mass in their wills and their names read as a *Who's Who* of the social élite of Bahia. The only exception was the stonemason Manuel João who died in 1686, to whom reference has already been made. An élite within an élite was formed by those who could afford two masses daily — António de Sá Doria, João de Mattos and Manuel Fernandes Costa were such people. The cattle owner, Domingos Fernandes de Freitas, went one better by ordering that three masses should be said daily for his soul. The financial giant of colonial Bahia, João de Mattos de Aguiar, made provision in his will for the saying of 11,000 masses each year at 200 *rs*. each for the salvation of his soul and those of his parents and grandparents. This commitment was financed from the interest of 2,200$000 on a capital outlay of 40,000$000. The obligation of meeting these commitments weighed heavily on the Misericórdia. Increased salaries for the priests who said these masses and the loss of the capital originally donated, led the Misericórdia to petition for the reduction in the number of these masses in the eighteenth century. Only after this had been granted could the Misericórdia contemplate providing for social services which were less well endowed.

The Misericórdia practised social philanthropy by maintaining a hospital, a retirement house and a 'turning wheel' for foundlings. It also assisted prisoners and distributed alms to the needy. Only in 1734 did the Misericórdia receive a royal contribution towards the cost of the hospital and the care of foundlings and this amounted to no more than a token contribution towards the enormous expenditure made by the Misericórdia in these two charitable enterprises. The Misericórdia was dependent on the charity of the Bahian public for the financing of social services.

The changing aspirations of Bahian society and the gradual trend towards secularisation are reflected in the benefactions received by the Misericórdia. In the seventeenth century the bulk of legacies was directed toward the saying of masses and any social preoccupation was limited to the granting of a dowry to a niece of the testator. In the eighteenth century a redistribution of wealth and the assumption of civic reponsibilities by an urban bourgeoisie resulted in greater attention being paid to public welfare. This growing social conscience can be fully documented in the registers of wills and ledgers of receipts of the brotherhood. A comparison of those legacies with recurring obligations received by the Misericórdia for charitable heads with legacies for masses will indicate this secular trend and is best represented graphically (Table II).[1] Legacies to the Misericórdia for charitable purposes

II. Legacies left to the Misericórdia for the saying of masses or for charitable purposes, 1600–1750

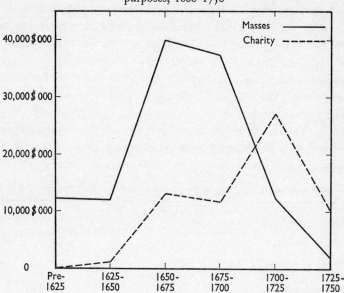

provided a steadily increasing proportion of the number of bequests received by the brotherhood. Perhaps the greatest confirmation of this swing from the religious to the secular is that in the seventeenth century there had been but a single instance of a donation to the Misericórdia without a commitment for the saying of masses. This had been the bequest of Jerónimo de Burgos in 1664 for 100 yards of linen to be given to the hospital every two years.

[1] The actual figures are as follows:

Years	Masses	Charity
Pre–1625	13,620$000	—
1625–1650	12,069$000	716$632
1650–1675	40,226$730	14,520$400
1675–1700	38,465$000	13,368$058
1700–1725	13,600$000	27,023$634
1725–1750	1,600$000	10,400$000

These figures do not include the legacy of João de Mattos de Aguiar.

In the half-century 1700–50, eleven of the twenty-one testators made no provision for the saying of masses in their legacies to the Misericórdia. The secular trend apparent in these legacies with recurring obligations is even more in evidence in the legacies received by the brotherhood on a once-and-for-all basis. Between 1700 and 1750 the Misericórdia received approximately 24,681 $290 from legacies of this type, of which only 600$000 was to be applied to masses.

The charitable purposes for which legacies were left to the Misericórdia ranged from the enormous bequest of João de Mattos de Aguiar in 1700 for the building of a retirement house to a small donation by a sailor to buy sheets for the hospital. The charitable applications of legacies made to the brotherhood between 1600 and 1750 with recurring obligations are shown in Table III. These include the money collected on the legacy of João de Mattos de Aguiar of 40,015 $300 for the retirement house, 135,470 $280 for dowries and 6,400$000 for alms. The Misericórdia also received single alms

III. Legacies left to the Misericórdia for charitable purposes, 1600–1750

Years	Hospital	Foundlings	Prisoners	Retirement house	Dowries	Alms
			Charitable purposes			
1600–1625	—	—	—	—	—	—
1625–1650	316$632	—	—	—	400$000	—
1650–1675	2,420$000	—	—	—	12,100$400	—
1675–1700	100$000	—	300$000	—	12,268$058	700$000
1700–1725	11,207$332	1,000$000	9,816$302	40,615$300	139,870$280	6,400$000
1725–1750	5,800$000	4,400$000	200$000	—	—	—
	19,843$964	5,400$000	10,316$302	40,615$300	164,638$738	7,100$000

for charitable works. These were insignificant in the seventeenth century, but the amounts donated in the half-century 1700–50 were as follows:

Hospital	10,894$145
Prisoners	3,419$405
Foundlings	1,951$610
Visits to the needy	700$000
Dowries	500$000
Poor	360$040
Unspecified	4,590$470
	22,415$670

Both sets of figures must be interpreted because the statistics alone do not

explain why, for example, legacies were only made to the Misericórdia for
the care of foundlings in the eighteenth century. The hospital of the
Misericórdia was the only general hospital of Bahia in the seventeenth and
early eighteenth centuries to offer medical aid to all, irrespective of colour,
class or creed. As such, it had been an obvious charitable object for the
legacies of Bahians from the earliest times. Bahians always adopted an
attitude of strait-laced morality towards white girls, and the granting of
dowries ensured that these girls would not be forced by penury into positions
of dubious respectability. In fact a condition governing the granting of
many dowries was that the recipient should be of good repute. The legacy
of João de Mattos de Aguiar in 1700 for the foundation of a retirement house
and the establishment of thirty-eight dowries of 100$000 each catered for
such girls quite adequately and later testators directed their legacies to other
charitable purposes. It is curious that prisoners, foundlings and the poor
should only be provided for in the legacies of the later seventeenth and
eighteenth centuries. The state of prisoners had always been lamentable and
the discarding of unwanted products of illicit sexual relationships had been
a constant feature of Bahian life. The reason why testators had not given
legacies to alleviate these social problems earlier was simply because the
landowners of the Recôncavo and the Sertão had not come into contact with
these essentially urban problems. An escaped prisoner had always been
assured of hospitality on any sugar plantation and an illegitimate child had
been easily assimilated in an agricultural community. Dom João de Lencastre had rebuilt the city prison during his governorship from 1694 to 1702
and the Count of Sabugosa (Viceroy 1720–35) had induced the Misericórdia
to establish a turning wheel for foundlings in 1726. These two facts and
increasing urbanisation possibly explain the increase in the number of donations for these two charitable purposes.

There was also an increasing tendency in the eighteenth century to spread
the provisions of a will over a wider variety of charitable enterprises. If the
benefactor of the seventeenth century had provided for social philanthropy
at all, he had tended to direct the entire legacy to a single charitable end.
António Dias de Ottões had left 1,700$400 to the Misericórdia exclusively
for dowries, and the cattle magnate Domingos Fernandes de Freitas had
left 10,268$058 for the same purpose. The only two instances of a legacy
being distributed over more than one charitable head had been Felippe

Correia (400$000 to the hospital and 4,000$000 for dowries) and Francisco
Fernandes do Sim (900$000 for the hospital and 6,400$000 for dowries).
In the eighteenth century it was customary for testators to spread their
legacies over several charitable heads. In 1713 Miguel Carvalho Mascarenhas, a Familiar of the Holy Office, divided his legacy to the Misericórdia of
9,134$000 between masses (3,200$000), the hospital (600$000), foundlings
(600$000), prisoners (1,134$000), the retirement house (600$000), dowries
(2,000$000) and the fabric of the church (1,000$000). Even the comparatively modest legacy of 1,200$000 made by Paschoal da Silva Moreira in 1712
was split equally between the hospital, foundlings and prisoners.[1]

Changes in the personalities of testators and in the nature of their bequests
to the Misericórdia were allied to the economic and social transformations
which occurred in Bahia of the seventeenth and eighteenth centuries. On
the one hand was a rural aristocracy whose wealth was invested in real
estate and whose vanity found an outlet in providing for sumptuous funeral
processions and the saying of masses. On the other hand was an urban
bourgeoisie whose wealth had been gained by speculation and commerce.
This social and economic shift in importance was accompanied by increased
secularisation and a greater awareness of social problems. The immediate
results of these changing attitudes towards charity and the brotherhoods
affected the Misericórdia primarily in the administrative field. The custom
of giving legacies on a once-and-for-all basis and in cash cast a heavy burden
on the integrity of the Misericórdia as an administrator. All too easily could
the monies of a legacy be completely lost or misplaced and the purpose for
which the bequest had been made totally forgotten. The increasing tendency
in the eighteenth century to nominate a person rather than an institution as
executor also meant that the Misericórdia was denied even the small alms
given for fulfilling this service. Finally, the growth of an urban population
created its own social problems. The Misericórdia attempted without financial assistance from official sources to meet the needs of this populace by providing a retirement house, a turning wheel and increased aid to prisoners. In the
following chapters each of the charitable services operated by the Misericórdia
will be described in detail, making possible an appreciation of the rôle played
by the Misericórdia in the practice of social philanthropy in colonial Bahia.

[1] ASCMB, vol. 42, f. 176.

8

Dowries

S o c i a l philanthropy can take two forms. The first consists of a programme of social rehabilitation spread over a period of months, or even years. The second is by means of outright relief, financial or in kind. The most suitable form of assistance varies from case to case and is determined by the social, physical and economic circumstances of the person in distress. Generally speaking, social rehabilitation is necessary when the victims of poverty or misfortune have already reached an advanced state of moral and physical degeneration. Assistance, usually of an institutional nature, helps them to regain their former position in society. Outright relief is directed at the causes of poverty at a stage when medical, financial or domestic assistance can prevent a person from slipping into endemic poverty or chronic illness. Such temporary relief can tide a family over the death of the breadwinner, sudden illness insufficiently serious to merit hospital treatment, the collapse of a home or the blight of a crop. It takes the form of alms, medical supplies and clothing.

The Misericórdia of Bahia in the seventeenth and eighteenth centuries was active in both fields. In the practice of social rehabilitation the action of the Misericórdia was without parallel in colonial Bahia. The brotherhood maintained a hospital, a retirement house and a foundling wheel and its members visited the prison regularly. The Misericórdia also strove to assist people in modest circumstances by outright alms. Brothers were supplied with the names of needy citizens by parish priests and these were visited and assisted in so far as the resources of the brotherhood permitted. Dowries were granted to girls to enable them to preserve their honour and contract suitable marriages. In colonial Brazil even a girl of respectable parentage found difficulty in marrying unless she had a dowry. Without this aid from the Misericórdia there was a very real danger that she would slip into a life of prostitution. In the concession of dowries the Misericórdia was contributing on a private level to a national policy. A brief outline of the set of political and social circumstances which made the granting of dowries a part of Portuguese colonial policy will help to place in greater perspective the action of the Misericórdia of Bahia in this charitable field.

The concession of dowries had been regarded as politically expedient since the earliest days of the Portuguese expansion. Portugal, one of the smallest countries of Europe, had undertaken the task of establishing an overseas empire whose outposts had extended from Gôa to the Mina fort as early as 1510, and which were to extend from Nagasaki to Bahia by the mid-sixteenth century. The outposts founded by the Portuguese had served a dual purpose: primarily they had been trading posts, secondarily they had been garrison stations. Continental Portugal had lacked the man-power necessary to maintain these garrisons at even moderate strength and in the early sixteenth century Affonso de Albuquerque had repeatedly complained that fortresses on the Indian coast were under-manned. Both he and his predecessor, Dom Francisco de Almeida, had attempted to remedy this situation by advocating a 'marriage policy'. Portuguese soldiers and traders had been offered the command of a fortress or the stewardship of a factory if they married selected local brides of good social position and undoubted respectability. Financial and mercantile privileges had been offered as further inducement. Nevertheless, the response had been small for two reasons: first, because the dowries had been badly administered and not paid promptly; secondly, because the prospect of some isolated fortress or factory had not been sufficiently attractive to entice the soldiers and traders away from their mistresses.

This second factor of a social nature had been decisive in the failure of any policy seeking to increase the small numbers of Portuguese in the East by planned marriages. Anthropologist and historian alike have noted the 'assimilating powers' of the Portuguese in their contact with other ethnic groups. It has often been suggested that this facility was born of contact with the Arabs during the Moorish invasions of the Iberian peninsula. The fact of the matter was that there were few Portuguese women in Asia or Brazil in the sixteenth century. The sex-starved Portuguese simply took any woman available, be she a Kaffir girl of East Africa, an Indian girl of Gôa or a Chinese *bicha* of Macao. In Gôa, Albuquerque had attempted to curb this enthusiasm by hanging a young nobleman who was having a love-affair with a Moorish girl. In Macao, the unrestrained libertinage had brought sharp rebuke from the civil and ecclesiastical authorities. In Brazil, the early Jesuits had lamented this aspect of the Portuguese colonisation. Within six months of landing at Bahia in 1549, the Jesuit Manoel da Nóbrega had written to Portugal stressing the urgent need for white women in Brazil. He had suggested that prostitutes be sent out to the new city where there was no doubt that they could marry well. Rather optimistically, he had added that such examples of sanctified unions might induce those at present living in sin to marry their concubines.[1] There had been nothing new in this proposal. Similar requests had been made in India and were to be made in Macao. In all cases the Portuguese Crown had complied by sending out from Portugal white orphan girls of marriageable age, known as 'orphans of the king'. These had been too few in numbers to make any real difference. Many of those who had married had died soon afterwards either in child-birth or as a result of their inability to adapt themselves to the tropics.

The problem of the lack of white women and the unbridled enthusiasm of the Portuguese for local girls was common to Portuguese Asia and to Brazil. But the circumstances were slightly different in the two continents. Whereas in Asia the Portuguese had never seriously advanced a policy of imperialism or colonisation which would have brought them into conflict with local potentates, in Brazil there had been a concerted effort at colonisa-tion from the outset. This had been readily apparent from the instructions given to Tomé de Sousa which had made provision, not only for the establishment of Bahia as a seat of government, but for the agricultural development of the Recôncavo and the encouragement of commerce. In Asia the Portuguese had usually settled in the immediate vicinities of the fortresses and trading posts. There had been exceptions such as villages in Ceylon and on the islands of Gôa, or the *Provincia do Norte* near Bassein, but these had been rare. In Brazil, there had been an immediate attempt at colonisation away from the cities. In Asia, the Portuguese was either a soldier who regarded his stay in Gôa as a posting, or a merchant who had come out to the East to enrich himself as rapidly as possible and then return to Portugal to enjoy an early retirement. In Brazil, the Portuguese was

[1] Manoel da Nóbrega, *Cartas*, pp. 79–80. Letter of 9 August 1549 to Pe. Mestre Simão.

G

often an emigrant from the north of Portugal who hoped that his agricultural skills or mechanical trade would find a more rewarding outlet in the littoral regions of Bahia, Pernambuco or São Vicente than in the rocky valleys of the Alto Douro or the mountainous Trás-os-Montes. The same problems were common to Asia and Brazil, but the phrasing of them was different.

The Misericórdia of Bahia played a valuable rôle in advancing the national policy of marriages and in affording some degree of protection to girls who might otherwise have been unable to marry or whose precarious financial position would have rendered them susceptible to prostitution. All records in the Misericórdia archives for the sixteenth century were destroyed by the Dutch, but for the seventeenth and eighteenth centuries the registers afford a complete record of bequests made to the brotherhood for the provision of dowries.

The dowries for which testators provided in their wills fell into three categories. First, there were dowries granted by the testator to the daughters of a relative or of a friend. In such cases the Misericórdia was merely the executor of the will and passed on the dowry to the nominee after the estate of the testator had been settled. Secondly, there were dowries left to the Misericórdia for immediate distribution to orphan girls without the brotherhood incurring any further obligation. Thirdly, there were dowries left by the testator for administration by the Misericórdia. These were financed from the interest on capital placed on loan and were granted annually. Before discussing the last two types of dowry, I wish to dwell briefly on the attitudes of mind revealed by the terms of these wills towards the position of women in colonial Brazil because frequently these attitudes show social, religious and racial preoccupations.

Wills making legacies for the allocation of dowries have certain features in common. The testator was usually of the upper class and the main beneficiaries were his nieces. In all cases the concession of a dowry, be it to a relative or not, depended on the undoubted virtue of the nominee. These aspects have implications in the wider social context of colonial ideology.

Testators who provided dowries for their relatives were not all of the landed aristocracy of Bahia. Nevertheless they were sufficiently prominent in the social life of the city to be very conscious of class distinction. This preoccupation with social standing is very apparent in the clauses of a will stipulating the terms for the concession of a dowry. Jorge Ferreira, who had died in 1641 leaving 2,450$000 to the Misericórdia for the saying of masses, was of the landowning class and had just such a preoccupation. The owner of a sugar plantation in Sergipe, a provision farm in the Serra, a smallholding in Rio Vermelho and houses in the city of Bahia, he was not one to wish that his niece should marry below her station. Thus he had bequeathed the results of his sixty-three years' labour to his niece, Jerónima Ferreira, as a dowry 'so that her husband may be ennobled thereby'.[1]

Jorge Ferreira had possessed the ready wealth to guarantee the respected position of his niece and her future husband in society. Colonel José Pires de Carvalho, a Familiar of the Holy Office, was not so fortunate. He was of good birth, had married well into the landowning Cavalcante e Albuquerque family, and was sufficiently prominent in Bahian society to be elected Provedor of the Misericórdia in 1719.[2] His wealth was tied up in real estate and he did not possess the ready cash to provide dowries for his daughters to marry 'with people of equal social standing'. He proposed to solve this difficulty by placing his daughters in the Desterro convent and appealed to the king to authorise this action because there was no vacancy in the convent. Dom João V refused to do this. Sweeping aside all affirmations of alleged nobility and faithful service which might justify the royal intervention, he commented tartly that if the potential value of the estate of José Pires was so high, there should be no lack of members of the nobility willing to marry his daughters in the expectation of future benefits. In a tongue-in-cheek closing phrase Dom João V commended such action to José Pires as thereby he would extend the nobility (previously rejected by the king as insufficient to justify royal assistance) of his own house.[3] Dom João V evidently had little time for the upstart nobility of his colonies.

Preoccupation with the maintaining of social prestige and with the hazards of marrying 'below one's station' led many families of Bahia to send their daughters to convents in Portugal rather than risk the possibility of

[1] 'pᵃ que o marido com quem cazar fique mais enobresido' (ASCMB, vol. 40, ff. 143v–153).

[2] He had married Theresa de Cavalcante e Albuquerque (ASCMB, vol. 3, f. 50v).

[3] In a letter to the viceroy of 15 February 1718, Dom João V commented, 'convem que sendo a caza deste Coronel tam opulenta caze suas filhas, porque não faltarão na esperança dos dotes pessoas de toda a nobreza que lhas procurem emnobrecendose por este caminho a sua familia, e tambem ajudando a extenderse mais a sua calidade' (APB, *Ordens régias*, vol. 12, doc. 12).

their contracting socially undesirable marriages in Bahia. Young girls and boxes of currency were constant features of any fleet from Bahia to Portugal in the late seventeenth and early eighteenth centuries. Dom João de Lencastre (Governor-General, 1694–1702) told the king of the social and economic evils of this practice. No longer were there any society marriages in Bahia, and large sums of money were being sent to the convents of Lisbon, Oporto and Viana to provide for the expenses of these girls. The governor-general had strongly recommended the total prohibition of this practice in a letter of 1695, but Dom Pedro II had rejected such a measure on the grounds of possible inconvenience.[1] It is difficult to account for this decision by the king when faced by a state of affairs so manifestly prejudicial to Bahia, except by the fact that pressure was exerted on him by powerful courtiers. Possibly he still believed that the Desterro convent was adequate for the needs of those Bahian families who wished to withdraw their daughters from society. At the time of the foundation of this convent (1677) the number of places had been limited to fifty so that marriages would not be prejudiced. This measure had failed because, once the fifty places had been allocated, the richer families had simply sent their daughters to Portugal. The increase in population in the forty years following the foundation of the Desterro, estimated by the municipal council at two-thirds, owed nothing to the upper class families. As many as eight to ten women of the cream of Bahian society left Brazil by each fleet. In 1717 the councillors suggested that the number of places in the Desterro be increased by another fifty since this would mean that both money and girls would be kept in Bahia.[2]

Not only was the practice of sending girls to Portugal prejudicial to the

---

[1] 'Dom João de Lancastro. Am⁰. Eu ElRey vos envio mᵗᵒ saudar. Viosse a vossa Carta de 18 de Junho deste anno, em q' me reprezentais os inconvenientes q' se seguem as familias desse Estado, com a rezolução que os moradores delle tem tomado de mandar para este Reynno suas filhas a serem Relligiozas nos Conventos delle, por estar cheyo o numero dos lugares do dessa cidade, parecendovos justo o prohibirselhes mandarem suas filhas para esta corte, ou para as Ilhas a serem Relligiozas, para asy se evitar a falta que ahy ha de cazamentos e de cabedais, pello muito q' gastão em as recolherem, e sustentarem nos Conventos deste Reynno. E pareceume dizervos q' este vosso arbitrio não he admiçivel por muitas rezões e inconvenientes que nelle se conciderarão. Escritta em Lisboa a 19 de Novembro de 1965' (APB, *Ordens régias*, vol. 3, doc. 108).

[2] City council to king, 25 August 1717 (AMB, vol. 176, ff. 119v–120).

society and economy of Bahia. Frequently the girls themselves were the victims of parents who compelled their daughters to take the veil against their will. It was this human aspect rather than the financial and social well-being of Bahia which induced Dom João V to act. In a decree of 1 March 1732, he ordered that in future no girl should be sent from Brazil to Portugal without the royal consent having been previously obtained. Before such permission would be granted, the viceroy and governors were to hold a full enquiry to determine all the circumstances of the petition made by a girl wishing to go to Portugal. In addition to this civil enquiry, there was to be an ecclesiastical report. The archbishop or bishop was to interview the girl and ensure that the petition was born of true religious vocation and not of parental intimidation. The penalties for non-observance of this decree were severe. The captain of a ship found carrying a girl against her will was liable to a fine of 2,000 *cruzados* and two months' imprisonment.[1] This measure effectively curtailed the traffic in girls from Bahia to the convents of Portugal because the royal consent was granted on few occasions. It could not stop the traffic in coin from Bahia to Portugal for dowries for nieces and relatives of testators in Brazil.

There can be no doubt that the principal reason which induced so many families to send their daughters to Portugal was class prejudice. A secondary and even subconscious influence may have been the idealism felt by many Brazilians towards the religious life. Although the respect for the tonsure was often unjustified and the frolickings of the nuns of the Desterro brought viceroyal rebuke, the attitude of the populace to priest or nun was one of reverence. Testators made special provisions in their wills for descendants who wished to enter the religious life. A widow of Cotegipe, Isabel da Costa, had made a will in 1675 allocating dowries of 100$000 to certain girls. In the event of any male relative wishing to enter the Church all such dowries

---

[1] 'Eu ElRei faço saber aos que este meu Alvara virem, que sendo-me prezentes os motivos, porque no Brasil não há mais crescimento de gente em grave prejuizo do augmento, e povoação daquelle Estado, sendo a principal causa desta falta o grande excesso, que ha em virem para este Reyno muytas mulheres com o pretexto de serem Religiosas, violentadas por seus pays, ou mays, constragendolhes as vontades, que devião ser livres para elegerem estado, de que resulta faltarem estas mulheres para os matrimonios, que convèm augmentar no Brasil, e ellas viverem sempre desgostosas com a vida que não querião tomar ...' (ANRJ, *Códice* 952, vol. 26, ff. 398–401).

were to be suspended for four years and the 400$000 was to cover the costs of his training.[1] The miner of Arassúahy, Manuel Valério de Nis, allocated two dowries of 400$000 to orphans of a retirement house of either Rio de Janeiro or Bahia: any girl wishing to become a nun was to receive a further 100$000.[2] The dowries administered by the Misericórdia were intended to enable young girls to marry. When a girl expressed the wish to enter a convent, it represented a partial failure in the policy of the brotherhood. On the rare occasions when this did occur the Mesa advanced the money willingly and commended the girl for her desire to enter a 'more perfect state'. All testators insisted on the good repute of their nieces or any other girls who received their dowries: any dishonour automatically rendered the legacy invalid.

Religious feeling may have contributed on a sub-conscious level to the decision of many families to send their daughters to the convents of Portugal. The other characteristic of the wills recorded in the registers of the Misericórdia — that legacies to relatives were frequently confined to the nieces of the testator — had a purely physical basis. Barrenness among white women and infant mortality were frequent in the tropics. On the one hand was the case of the businessman Gaspar dos Réis Pinto who had been married three times but was still without offspring. On the other was Luzia Freire, widow of a brother of the Misericórdia, who had produced eight children of whom only two had survived. In his will of 1643 Gaspar dos Réis Pinto ordered his executor to sell his plantations in Sergipe and Rio Vermelho and distribute as many dowries as possible from the proceeds.[3] For her part Luzia Freire stipulated in her will of 1685 that monies derived from the sale of her sugar plantation in Patatiba and her cattle ranches on the S. Francisco river be applied to the saying of masses for her soul.[4] These purely physical factors obviously led many testators to send to distant relatives in Portugal the fruits of a lifetime's labour in the tropics.

Bahians who made legacies to nieces and the daughters of relatives in Brazil were guided by a different set of reasons. All testators were obsessed by the possibility of spurious claimants challenging their wills in an attempt to inherit lands or possessions. The wills of married couples and bachelors alike often began with the categorical statement that the testators had no

[1] ASCMB, vol. 42, ff. 24–6.
[2] ASCMB, vol. 42, f. 215.
[3] ASCMB, vol. 40, ff. 160–166v.
[4] ASCMB, vol. 41, ff. 248–51.

offspring 'natural or spurious'. Such was the extent of this fear that many testators adopted a matrilineal attitude when making their legacies. Two Bahian bachelors of the early seventeenth century, Francisco Dias Baião and Diogo Fernandes, stipulated that only the daughters of their relatives could benefit from their wills. In no circumstances was a male relative to inherit.[1] The philanthropist Felippe Correia, after making numerous legacies to the Misericórdia in his will of 1650, left his plantations in Pituba to his sister on the condition that in no way was her husband to enjoy part ownership of these properties. Possibly this condition may have been the result of personal animosity; if so, there was no reference to it, and Correia gave as his reason that he wished the property to remain in the Correia family.[2] Other testators founded trusts to be enjoyed by the distaff side only. In the event of there being no more female descendants the trust was to be administered by a brotherhood for charitable purposes.

The attitude towards what might be called the 'legitimacy of the womb' and even the practice of sending daughters to Portugal may have been influenced by the multi-racial nature of Bahian society. There was always the fear that a daughter might have an affair with a coloured man. In this there was one law for males and quite another for females. It was considered rather *macho*, or masculine, for a teenage son of a white family to have a coloured mistress: if she did conceive, so much the worse for her. On the other hand, for a white girl to have a coloured *amigo*, or lover, was tantamout to demanding social ostracism.[3] This fear on the part of parents was rarely expressed but strongly felt. When the lawyer Jerónimo de Burgos and his wife had established a trust in 1664 for the saying of masses and charitable purposes, they had stipulated that after the terms of the trust had been fulfilled any additional income should be given to their heirs provided that 'they do not marry anyone tainted with the blood of the forbidden races'.[4] In an age when race and creed were often equated, such a clause effectively ruled out coloured or New Christian partners.

[1] ASCMB, vol. 40, ff. 23v–28v and ff. 28v–33v.

[2] ASCMB, vol. 40, ff. 198–210v.

[3] For a study of attitudes towards mixed marriages in modern Bahia, many of which coincide with the colonial standpoint, see Donald Pierson, *Brancos e pretos na Bahia. Estudo de contacto racial* (São Paulo–Rio de Janeiro–Bahia, 1945), chapter 6.

[4] 'contanto que não cazem com gente que tenha algũa raça das prohibidas (ASCMB, vol. 41, ff. 97v–98v).

The attitudes of Bahians towards the distaff side of their families have shown that many of the conditions attached to legacies were prompted by racial, religious and social prejudices. Bahia was a multi-racial society and the coloured population was infinitely larger than the white population. The enthusiasm felt by the early settlers for the Amerindian girls and Negresses continued even after there had been an increase in the number of white women available for marriage. The so-called *Minas* (probably Fulahs or Ashantis) were especially favoured because of their good appearance, dignified carriage, and their fame as mistresses of the culinary skills. The attitudes shown by testators in their wills towards their coloured slaves reveal the complexity of the racial issue.

Historians and anthropologists alike have dwelt on the manner in which the white masters exploited their female slaves. It is undeniable that the girls of the *senzalas*, or slave quarters, were often the concubines of the masters, the butts for the anger of jealous wives, and the playthings of adolescent sons. But there was another side to the picture of inter-racial contact which is usually forgotten. Many slave owners appear to have taken a genuine interest in the welfare of their slaves. The receipt ledgers of the Misericórdia frequently recorded payments of up to 50$000 made by a plantation owner for the cure of a slave in the hospital of the brotherhood. João de Mattos referred in his will, with evident pride, to how he had arranged the marriage of one of his slave girls and had given her a dowry and some household possessions.[1] Many slaves were granted their freedom as a reward for years of faithful service. A wealthy widow, Theodora de Góis, who died in 1693, granted her slave Luiza her freedom and ordered that a dowry of 100$000, clothing and gold trinkets be given her on marriage.[2] This paternal attitude on the part of the white ruling classes towards the coloured population was not limited to slaves. Many families adopted coloured children. Pedro Viegas Giraldes and Felippe Correia, both benefactors of the Misericórdia in the seventeenth century, brought up mulatto children in their homes.[3] The history of the relationships between masters and slaves, white and black, was not always a chronicle of cruelty and exploitation. There was often an undercurrent of Christian idealism

[1] He died on the last day of February, 1685 (ASCMB, vol. 41, ff. 239v–244).
[2] ASCMB, vol. 42, ff. 88–91.
[3] ASCMB, vol. 40, ff. 122v–129 and ff. 198–210v.

among the authoritarian and domineering plantation owners of colonial Bahia.

On other occasions the attitude of the white man to his slaves was not paternal, but uxorious. One slave owner, Pedro Domingues, was consumed by jealousy at the prospect of his concubine marrying. In his will of 1676 he granted her her freedom, the ownership of his house, and three slaves on the condition that she should stay single.[1] Other slave owners had had children by their slave girls and made generous provision for both mother and child. A smallholder, Diogo Fernandes, left detailed instructions in his will for the care and education of his son by a Negress: he was to be taught the Bible and trained as an apprentice in a mechanical trade.[2] The bachelor Joseph Lopes, who had established a 'chapel of masses' in the Misericórdia in 1656, also regarded his favourite crioula as more than a mere *peça de Indias* ('piece of the Indies'). He granted the mother and her son and daughter their freedom. The little girl was to be placed in an honourable home and on marriage was to receive a dowry of 100$000 and furniture. Evidently the family of Joseph Lopes had opposed his recognition of paternity, because he stipulated that his daughter should not be boarded in the house of any of his relatives.[3] This respect for the Negro slave was based largely on her rôle as the mother of the white man's children. The glorification of the wife in her maternal rôle still persists in Brazil and although a fickle husband may indulge in the enchantments of his concubine to the full, he will rarely leave his wife, simply because she is the 'mother of my son'.

Preoccupations of class, creed and colour were constant factors in the minds of Bahians of the seventeenth and eighteenth centuries. Anxiety for the preservation of class status was allied to an obsession with the maintaining of purity of blood. Members of an essentially male-dominated society were influenced by these two factors into adopting matrilineal attitudes when making their wills. The position of women in Portuguese colonial society is usually presented as insignificant. Travellers to colonial Brazil commented on the seclusion of females. The seclusion of women in colonial times has been considered by historians as indicative of the insignificant position they enjoyed, but it seems likely that the womanhood of colonial Bahia was a good deal more influential than is generally realised.

[1] ASCMB, vol. 41, ff. 134v–140v.   [2] ASCMB, vol. 40, ff. 28v–33v.
[3] ASCMB, vol. 41, ff. 42v–44v.

The attitudes to women and slaves illustrate to the full the almost paradoxical variety of outlook in colonial Brazil. The apparent contradiction of a male-dominated society adopting matrilineal attitudes had its counterpart in the attitude towards the coloured population. On the one hand was the brutality of the slave ships and slave markets. On the other hand was the Christian charity shown in the adoption of a coloured orphan, the emancipation of a slave, or the granting of dowries. A modern visitor to Bahia referred to the 'Bay of all saints and of all devils'.[1] This would have been an accurate epigram for Bahia in colonial times when idealism and materialism, virtue and vice were so closely interwoven.

Dowries for relatives or the illegitimate offspring of slave girls only involved the Misericórdia in its rôle of executor. The main interest of the brotherhood lay in legacies which granted dowries to orphans, and nominated the Misericórdia as the administrator of these dowries. Just as charitable bequests to the Misericórdia fell into the two categories of single legacies and legacies with recurring obligations, so also did dowries. Some bequests were made for the provision of dowries on a single occasion, whereas other bequests were *in perpetuum*. In the latter instance the interest derived from capital placed on loan financed a certain number of dowries each year.

Dowries of the first type rarely exceeded 50$000. They were given by testators unable to afford the large capital outlay necessary to finance an annual dowry from the interest alone. Even an annual dowry of 50$000 demanded an outlay of 800$000 at the interest rate of 6¼ per cent, whereas a single bequest of 150$000 could provide three dowries of 50$000 for orphans for a small outlay. This was well illustrated by the legacy of Maria Lopes Oleira. The wife of João de Valensa Pereira, she had lived apart from her husband for twelve years and was financially independent with a small holding of manioc. The sale of her possessions in 1678 realised 486$750 — too small a sum to finance even one annual dowry — of which the Misericórdia received 282$834 for six dowries of 40$000 and one of 25$000.[2]

---

[1] Giménez Caballero, *Bahia de todos os santos e de todos os demônios* (Bahia, 1958), a variation on Gilberto Freyre's *Baía de Todos os Santos e de quase todos os pecados* (Recife, 1926).

[2] The remaining 17$834 was kept by the Misericórdia to cover administrative costs (ASCMB, vol. 41, ff. 151–159v and f. 210).

The legacy was modest, but was enough to enable seven orphan girls to get married. The number of legacies of this type was small and no more than half a dozen orphans benefited in the average year. Greater range was offered by those bequests which instituted a trust for the distribution of dowries annually. The financial administration of this second type of legacy was the responsibility of the Misericórdia who selected the girls, arranged their marriage ceremonies and paid their dowries.

The rôle of the Misericórdia as an administrator of dowries had not been envisaged in the *Compromisso* of 1516. It had been only in 1618 that statutes had been drawn up to govern the administration of this type of legacy. The Misericórdia of Bahia followed the *Compromisso* of Lisbon and candidates for dowries had to fulfil certain conditions. Any applicant for a dowry administered by the Misericórdia had to present a petition to the Mesa with the following information: first, the names of her parents, their place of birth and present residence; secondly, the financial and social circumstances of her parents; thirdly, the age of the applicant and a statement of the reasons why she needed a dowry; fourthly, the applicant had to consent to a full enquiry by the Mesa and agree to honour all the conditions stipulated in the *Compromisso*. The Provedor then appointed a panel of brothers not on the Mesa to verify the truth of the statements contained in the petition, and to establish that the girl was of good repute. If the report was favourable the girl's name was placed on a list and votes were cast by the Mesa for the most deserving.

The dowries administered by the Misericórdia of Lisbon were not limited to girls from Lisbon, nor even to Portugal. Applications were accepted from girls in fortresses on the African coast. Such applications had to be accompanied by a testimonial of good character from the captain of the fortress or from the local branch of the Misericórdia if this existed. Dowries granted to such girls had to be re-registered every two years with the Misericórdia of Lisbon.[1] Each branch of the Misericórdia was autonomous. Although the Misericórdia of Gôa was recognised as the chief branch in Asia, its dowries were granted only to local girls. Orphan girls in Malacca or Macao applied to their own *Santas Casas*. This was also the case in Brazil. The Misericórdia of Bahia was acknowledged as the most important branch, but it did not offer dowries to girls from other captaincies. Testators leaving legacies

---

[1] *Compromisso* of 1618, chapter xxix, §18.

for dowries to be administered by the Misericórdia of Bahia came from the city or the Recôncavo and intended that girls from these regions should benefit.

In the years 1620–1750 nine testators left bequests to the Misericórdia in order that a certain number of dowries could be financed from the interest on capital. These testators had little in common and I will simply enumerate them, commenting briefly on their social position, the extent of the legacy and the number of dowries for which it provided:

1. Joanna Fernandes (1649) was the owner of some houses in the city and illiterate. She left 400$000 for an annual dowry of 25$000, augmented to 40$000 by the Misericórdia.[1]

2. Felippe Correia (1650). The wealthy owner of a sugar plantation in Pituba, he left 4,000$000 to the Misericórdia for dowries. 3,200$000 was devoted to dowries for daughters of friends and relatives, and the remaining 800$000 was retained by the Misericórdia to provide an annual dowry of 40$000.[2]

3. António Dias de Ottões (1653). A plantation owner in Jucuruna, he ordered that the income derived from the plantation (about 1,700$400 annually) should provide two dowries of 50$000 each yearly.[3]

4. Francisco Fernandes do Sim (1664). The owner of several plantations in Patatiba and Sto Amaro, he was Provedor of the Misericórdia on several occasions. He left 6,400$000 for eight dowries each year of 40$000 each.[4]

5. Isabel da Costa (1688). The owner of a sugar plantation in Cotegipe, she left 2,000$000 to the Misericórdia for dowries. This legacy remained under litigation.[5]

6. Domingos Fernandes de Freitas (1688) was the owner of extensive cattle ranches on the S. Francisco river. The residue of his estate realised 10,268$058 and provided for five dowries each year of 100$000.[6]

[1] ASCMB, vol. 40, ff. 167–8.   [2] ASCMB, vol. 40, ff. 198–210v.
[3] ASCMB, vol. 41, ff. 24–9.   [4] ASCMB, vol. 41, ff, 91v–97.
[5] ASCMB, vol. 42, ff. 24–6.
[6] The copy of his will and the inventory made on 5 August 1696 are in very bad condition (ASCMB, vol. 192), but the minute books of the brotherhood contain details of his legacy (ASCMB, vol. 14, ff. 249v–250v).

7. João de Mattos de Aguiar (1700). The philanthropic leviathan of colonial Bahia, he left houses and 135,470$280 for thirty-eight dowries each year of 100$000 each.[1]

8. Miguel Carvalho Mascarenhas (1713). A Familiar of the Holy Office who served the Misericórdia as scribe in 1710, he left 2,000$000 for an annual dowry of 100$000.

9. Francisco Coque (1722). He left 1,600$000 for one dowry of 100$000 each year, and 400$000 to the Misericórdia for administration. The brotherhood refused this legacy and only accepted in 1724 when the administrative fee was raised to 800$000.[2]

Thus the Misericórdia was the administrator of legacies to a total value of 164,638$738. The interest on this capital provided for forty-five dowries of 100$000, two dowries of 50$000, and ten dowries of 40$000.

These legacies had been left to the Misericórdia with certain conditions made by the testators for their administration. All testators stipulated that the recipients should be honourable, poor and orphans. The last designation demands some clarification. Whereas an orphan is usually regarded as a child who has lost both parents, in present-day Brazil this is not the case. It is sufficient for a child to have lost one of its parents to qualify as an orphan; it will be an *orfão de pai* or an *orfão de mãe*, depending on the parent it has lost. Should it have lost both parents it will then be referred to as an *orfão de pai e mãe*. This was also the custom in colonial Brazil and an 'orphan' girl whose mother or father was still living was considered a proper applicant for a dowry of the Misericórdia. Joanna Fernandes placed a geographical limitation — that girls receiving her dowries should be either of the city or

---

[1] The amounts mentioned in the copy of the will of João de Mattos de Aguiar (ASCMB, vol. 199) differ from those given in the account ledgers of the brotherhood, based on the actual receipts, but in both cases the number of dowries is the same.

[2] In 1699 William Dampier met 'one *Mr. Cock* an *English* Merchant, a very civil Gentleman and of good Repute. He had a Patent to be our *English* Consul, but did not care to take upon him any Publick Character, because *English* Ships seldom come hither' (*A Voyage to New Holland*, p. 53). I have been unable to establish if he was also the benefactor of the Misericórdia, but the scarcity of foreigners in colonial Bahia makes the presence of two different gentlemen of such similar names unlikely. For details of his legacy see ASCMB, vol. 42, f. 167 and vol. 14, ff. 134v–135v.

the Recôncavo. João de Mattos de Aguiar was the only testator to demand 'purity of blood' of the applicants for the dowries of his legacy. He stipulated that his dowries should be allocated only to 'girls of good repute, poor, white and of Old Christian parentage'.

The Misericórdia laid down further conditions to be satisfied by an applicant for a dowry. She was to be between fourteen and thirty years of age, previously unmarried and of financial circumstances sufficiently precarious to place her honour in jeopardy. In the event of her receiving a dowry, she agreed to register this annually in the Misericórdia and to be married in the church of the brotherhood. If she did not marry within the six years stipulated by the *Compromisso*, the dowry automatically lapsed and was re-allocated by the Mesa. In these conditions the Misericórdia of Bahia was following the *Compromisso* of Lisbon, but it differed from the parent body in the manner of selecting those girls most fitted to receive dowries.

The Misericórdia of Bahia followed the example of Lisbon in enquiring fully into the circumstances of an applicant. It was in the process of selection that Bahia differed from Lisbon. In Lisbon the Provedor proposed three candidates for each dowry of a set amount, and the board of guardians voted for the most suitable. Preference was given to girls in the retirement house, to those whose good looks would make them more susceptible to temptation, to daughters of brothers, to daughters of people receiving alms from the brotherhood and finally to girls of the city of Lisbon and its environs. In Bahia the administration of charity was less impartial and was based on influential contacts. Until 1725 the dowries available were distributed among the members of the board of guardians. Each member then allocated the dowries at his disposal according to his personal whim. Inevitably such a process meant that the daughters of relatives and friends received all the dowries. An orphan girl without influential sponsors had no chance of obtaining a dowry from the Misericórdia. The system brought the brotherhood into disrepute. There were quarrels among the officers as to the number of dowries each should receive for distribution and the good name of the Misericórdia as an administrator of legacies was called in question.

This situation was remedied by the Mesa of 1725 under the Provedor António Gonçalves da Rocha. Within its first week of office the Mesa totally reformed the process of allocating dowries. All petitions would in future receive a number. Slips of paper similarly numbered with the additional figure of the value of the dowry (100$000, 50$000 or 40$000) were to be placed in an urn. On 13 June each year these slips were to be drawn and matched off with the petitions. An order of precedence was established: first, girls in the retirement house; secondly, daughters of poor brothers; thirdly, girls who had been foundlings of the Misericórdia. This resolution of the Mesa was sent to Lisbon for royal approval.[1] After Dom João V had sounded out the opinion of the Count of Sabugosa, who was favourable to reform, the king approved this decree of the Mesa and ordered that it should not be amended by any future board of guardians.[2]

Reforming zeal of this type was looked at askance in colonial Bahia. The two folios of the minute book (*Livro de Acórdãos*) registering the decree were surreptitiously removed and the Mesa was obliged to write to Lisbon for a transcript of the copy sent to the king. Although succeeding Mesas observed this decree, they did not always respect one of the prime conditions stipulated by all the testators, namely that the applicant for a dowry should be poor. The Mesas of 1728–9 and 1729–30 granted dowries of 100$000 to each of the three daughters of the Master of the Field (*Mestre do Campo*) António Ferrão Castelo Branco and further dowries to the two daughters of Paulo Franco and the two daughters of Joseph Moreira. All were brothers of the Misericórdia but in no way could they be regarded as poor. Conscience-ridden, the Mesa of 1729–30 revoked its own decision and that of its predecessor and ruled that the dowries had been erroneously conceded.[3] This annulment was not by unanimous approval and one member of the Mesa was expelled for refusing to sign the decree. The most violent reaction came from the former Provedor of the Misericórdia and future Governor of S. Tomé, António Ferrão Castelo Branco. He had been sent to Lisbon by the Count of Sabugosa to report to the king on the mutiny of the garrison of Bahia. He had taken advantage of this opportunity to take his daughters to Lisbon to be nuns, presumably relying on the dowries of the Misericórdia.[4] When the news of the Mesa's decision reached him, he fought the annulment

[1] ASCMB, vol. 14, ff. 172–173v.

[2] King to viceroy, 18 February 1726 and the reply of the Count of Sabugosa, 7 June 1726 (APB, *Ordens régias*, vol. 20, docs. 32 and 32a). The royal approval was granted by a decree of 22 March 1729 (APB, *Ordens régias*, vol. 24, doc. 42).

[3] Decree of 12 March 1730 (ASCMB, vol. 14, f. 159).

[4] APB, *Ordens régias*, vol. 23, doc. 116.

order with the same violence with which he had contested the office of
Provedor ten years earlier. He immediately protested to the Supreme Court
of Appeals in Lisbon. Such was his influence that his appeal was upheld and
all embargoes brought by the Misericórdia were rejected.[1] It was ironical
that it was a decree made to safeguard the interests of the brotherhood —
that a Mesa could not revoke an act passed by its predecessors — which was
the key issue of the successful appeal by António Ferrão Castelo Branco. All
action by the Misericórdia of Bahia was in vain and the brotherhood had to
pay the dowries.

The importance of the rôle played by the Misericórdia in the administration of dowries can be gauged by the number of endowed girls who did get
married. I have chosen the dowries conceded during the years 1710–20 for
detailed analysis. This choice is arbitrary but this decade recommends
itself for several reasons. The documentary evidence is most complete for
this period. The first two books with records of dowries on the legacies of
various testators have been lost and volumes three, four and five cover the
period 1708–24, 1725–34 and 1750–71. The records of dowries on the
legacy of João de Mattos de Aguiar are complete for the years 1700–50, but
some of the bound volumes of this series are in such an appalling condition
because of the effects of ants and humidity that they cannot even be opened.
Moreover, with the exception of the single dowry of 100$000 of Francisco
Coque in 1722, the Misericórdia had received all those legacies providing for
dowries. The legal wrangles surrounding the legacy of João de Mattos de
Aguiar had been settled by 1710 and the administration of his dowries was
operating smoothly. Finally, the Misericórdia had not yet been severely
affected by its own precarious financial position which was to lead to a
reduction in the number of dowries granted by the brotherhood.

The number of dowries conceded by the Misericórdia varied from year
to year for different reasons. Although all dowries were conceded for six
years in the first instance, many were taken up before the six years had
expired. Others were extended for anything from one to three years. Sometimes the Mesa ruled that the concession of a dowry be terminated because
of the changing circumstances of the girl or as a result of additional information received by the board of guardians. On some rare occasions a dowry

[1] ASCMB, vol. 14, ff. 161–2.

was suspended because of the *desmancho da dotada*, or dishonour of the girl.[1] Although the Misericórdia possessed a theoretically constant number of dowries at its disposal, in practice the number varied greatly from year to year. In the decade 1710–20 the following dowries were granted: João de Mattos de Aguiar, 509; Domingos Fernandes de Freitas, 93; António Dias de Ottões, 31; Francisco Fernandes do Sim, 164; Felippe Correia, 15; Joanna Fernandes, 21.

In addition to the irregular nature of the cycle itself, some Mesas allowed their generosity to get the better of them and conceded far more dowries than actually were available. As early as 1653 when the Misericórdia had only had to contend with the legacies of Joanna Fernandes and Felippe Correia, the Mesa had been faced with social and financial embarrassment because it had granted dowries in anticipation of the legacies falling due. Many girls had transferred from one dowry to another and it had been impossible to observe conditions as to age.[2] The bequest of António Dias de Ottões in 1653 had forced the Mesa to rule that in future no dowries should be granted in anticipation and no dowry could be exchanged for another. This ruling was not observed. In the eighteenth century several Mesas over-allocated. Their successors were compelled to annul the dowries they had themselves granted in the belief that the full number of dowries was available for distribution.[3] The evil of this practice was the very real danger that the scribe would forget to annul a dowry conceded a second time and that the Misericórdia would be morally (and sometimes legally) obliged to honour two dowries instead of one.

It is difficult to judge the social background of the girls who received dowries from the Misericórdia. They came from a wide social spectrum ranging from the daughters of a brother of the Misericórdia to the illegitimate offspring of a free Negress. Allegations that the brotherhood reserved dowries for the convenience of its members were not justified. Certainly if the daughter of a brother did receive a dowry this was always of 100$000 on

[1] A dowry conceded in 1733 was annulled in 1736 'por constar de pessoas fidedignas q' a dotada Clemencia do Nascim^to q' consta deste termo asima se tinha deshonestada e vivia do estado de meretriz' (ASCMB, vol. 1174, f. 132v).

[2] ASCMB, vol. 13, f. 42.

[3] The Mesa of 1710 was guilty of severe over-allocation of dowries. For examples of girls transferring dowries in the eighteenth century, see ASCMB, vol. 1173, f. 45 and vol. 14, ff. 192v–193v.

the legacy of João de Mattos de Aguiar. But within the first twenty years of the administration of this legacy only 9.7 per cent of these dowries were allocated to the offspring of brothers — a modest proportion considering that these did enjoy some preference over other applicants.[1] Many of the recipients had been foundlings in the care of the Misericórdia or were given regular alms by the brotherhood. In other cases the girl was working in the house of an uncle or brother-in-law because of the death of her own parents. Dowries enabled such girls to contract decent marriages. After the founding of the retirement house in 1716 the Misericórdia was able to provide protection for those girls too old to be helped as foundlings, but too young to be granted dowries. In such cases the concession of a dowry provided the final point of several years of social assistance afforded by the brotherhood.

The impartiality shown by the Misericórdia in selecting girls from all walks of life is also illustrated by its attitude towards coloured applicants. João de Mattos de Aguiar had been the only testator to stipulate that the dowries on his legacy be given only to white girls. This condition was entirely respected by the brotherhood. Indeed instances of a coloured girl receiving one of the larger dowries of 100$000 or 50$000 were very rare. It is quite possible that not very many coloured girls applied to the Misericórdia. The Negro brotherhoods offered some assistance in the form of small dowries to the daughters of their poorer brothers. There was also less likelihood of a Negro girl being able to contend with the bureaucratic problems surrounding a petition to the Misericórdia. Finally, the whole concept of the giving of dowries was based on a wider range of social stratification than existed among the coloured population of Bahia, and a Negro would not have demanded that his future wife should be endowed. Thus, the number of coloured girls who received dowries from the Misericórdia was small: between 1708 and 1725 only nineteen received dowries and the average was one or two yearly. Although the Misericórdia did not provide many dowries to girls of coloured parentage, it did not discriminate against them. Some years no coloured girl featured in the records of dowries granted. In other years there were several and in 1732–3 the Mesa conceded twenty-seven dowries to coloured girls out of a total of fifty-two

---

[1] Of 914 dowries conceded in these years from this legacy only 89 were given to daughters of brothers of the Misericórdia.

dowries. Such girls were the offspring of freed slaves and usually illegitimate, *de pai incerto*. The most remarkable instance of illegitimate offspring receiving dowries concerned the two daughters of Theresa de Jesú who each received dowries of 40$000 in 1712. Perhaps the Mesa was overcome by the pious ring of the mother's name because it made no comment on the fact that each girl had a different father![1]

The Misericórdia did not permit racial prejudice to influence the granting of dowries, nor did it limit the area of its charity to the city and its immediate environs. It was only natural that girls from the parishes of the city should predominate in the lists of those receiving dowries. In the decade 1710–20, Mesas granted 833 dowries. The place of origin of 229 of the recipients is uncertain. Of the remaining 604 girls, 398 came from the city and 206 from the Recôncavo and the interior of the Captaincy of Bahia.[2] The disposition of these 206 girls indicates the area of greatest demographic density, which was along the coast. The fertile region of the Recôncavo was heavily populated and the majority of girls came from the townships of Cachoeira, Maragogipe, Jaguaripe and the villages of Paripe and Pirajá. The importance to the city of Bahia of the wheat-growing area to the south of the Recôncavo was illustrated by the large number of girls from Camamú and Cairú who received dowries from the Misericórdia. The position of Itaparica opposite the city, and its importance as a fishing centre, made it a comparatively heavily populated island, and it was to be expected that many girls from there should receive dowries from the brotherhood. The presence of a few girls from the more distant and less populated islands in the Bay of All Saints, such as the Ilha dos Frades and Madre de Deus, on the lists of candidates for dowries is more surprising. A few girls came from Mata de S. João and the mining area of the Rio de Contas. All these townships and villages were within the Captaincy of Bahia, and came under the

---

[1] ASCMB, vol. 1173, f. 63v and f. 64.

[2] These 206 girls came from the following townships or villages: Boipeba, 3; Cachoeira, 31; Cairú, 12; Camamú, 21; Caruragipe, 1; Cotegipe, 2; Cotenguiba, 2; Iguape, 1; Itaparica, 22; Itaporocas, 2; Ilha dos Frades, 2; Itapicurú, 1; Jucuruna, 1; Jaguaripe, 15; River Joannes, 1; Madre de Deus, 7; Maragogipe, 20; Mata de S. João, 4; Patiba, 1; Pirajá, 4; Paripe, 10; Passé, 8; Patatiba, 4; Paramirim, 3; Pitinga, 5; Pituba, 1; Rio de Contas, 3; Saubara, 3; Sergipe, 11; Rio Vermelho, 2; Vᵃ S. Francisco, 3. These are based on the records of dowries in the Misericórdia archives, vols. 1164, 1165 and 1173.

general jurisdiction of the municipal council of Bahia and were served by the Misericórdia of Bahia.[1] To the north of Bahia was Sergipe do Conde with its own city council and Misericórdia. Evidently this branch of the brotherhood referred all petitions for dowries to the capital because there were references to girls not only from Sergipe itself, but also from Cotinguiba, nowadays a centre for the extraction of rock salt. Thus the charitable rôle of the Misericórdia was recognised not only beyond the villages of the Recôncavo, but in the backlands of the interior and in more distant Sergipe.[2]

There were many physical and bureaucratic hazards between the concession of a dowry and final payment being made to the girl on marriage. Of the 833 dowries granted in the years 1710–20, 571 were paid to girls on the occasion of their getting married and 258 lapsed, either due to the failure on the part of the girl to re-register annually or because the six years had expired. The remaining four dowries were paid to girls who wished to go to Portugal to become nuns. The payment of dowries to girls who wished to take the veil ran counter to the whole object of this type of charity which was to enable girls of humble state to contract worthy marriages. Nevertheless, the phrase *tomar estado* ('to take state'), used by testators in drawing up their wills, did have this duality of meaning. Dowries were paid to such girls once the Misericórdia had been assured of a guarantor for the amount of the dowry and on condition that evidence be submitted to the brotherhood within two years showing that the girl had carried out her intention and had entered a convent in Portugal.

The manner in which the girls received their dowries led to certain abuses. Although the statutes expressly forbade the transfer of dowries, this was done with the full sanction of the Mesa. Frequently a girl in a village distant from the capital would nominate an attorney to receive payment of her dowry. These two factors meant that often the Misericórdia officials were unaware of which girl did have the dowry and whether she was married or not. A brother was expelled for having exploited this situation and receiving payment for a girl who had not married.[3] Another brother, Manuel de Sousa

---

[1] The first branch of the Misericórdia to be founded in the Recôncavo was at Cachoeira in the eighteenth century, but its archive only dates from the nineteenth century.

[2] The Misericórdia of Sergipe had been founded in the late sixteenth century.

[3] ASCMB, vol. 195, f. 120.

Salgado, showed how somebody of audacity and imagination could profit from such doubt as to the true holder of a dowry. In 1726 a dowry of 100$000 had been granted to Maria de Valansuela. In 1732 a petition was received by the Mesa, purporting to be from her, saying that she was ill and incapable of marrying and asking the Misericórdia to transfer the dowry to her sister Francisca. The petition had been authenticated by a public notary in the city and was accompanied by a document in which Maria renounced all further right to the dowry. The Mesa authorised the transfer of the dowry. In May of the following year the Mesa received a letter from Maria saying that she was on the point of marrying and wished to claim her dowry of 100$000. She was in perfect health and had been living in the house of her brother-in-law in Saboara for many years. During these years she had never come to the city of Bahia and had never drawn up the document renouncing all claims to her dowry. It emerged that Manuel de Sousa Salgado was the culprit. In the hope of gaining a dowry for his own sister Francisca he had forged the petition asking for the transfer of the dowry. Then one night he had gone to a public notary accompanied by two women, his mother and his sister. His mother signed the document renouncing the dowry and the notary public witnessed the forged signature.[1]

The majority of girls receiving dowries from the Misericórdia married within the six years stipulated by the statutes. Even this culminating act brought the brotherhood into conflict with the ecclesiastical authorities. The *Compromisso* ruled that all girls receiving dowries be married in the church of the Misericórdia. The chaplains of the Misericórdia did not have authority to conduct marriage ceremonies. Thus, the marriage service was conducted by the priest of the girl's parish, in the church of the Misericórdia. The privileged position of the Misericórdia had always been a point of conflict with the clergy. The Mesa resented the intrusion of the parish priests, considering that they were challenging the exemption of the brotherhood from all ecclesiastical jurisdiction. No payment was made to the parish priests for this service so there was no question of the chaplains of the Misericórdia losing their due. It was simply a matter of pride. In the eighteenth century many appeals were made to Lisbon for the granting of permission to the principal chaplain of the Misericórdia so that he could

---

[1] Manuel de Sousa Salgado was expelled in 1733 but re-admitted in 1735 (ASCMB, vol. 195, ff. 93v–96).

conduct the marriage ceremonies, but in vain.[1] Finally the brotherhood acted against the terms of the *Compromisso* and permitted girls who had received dowries to be married in their local parishes.[2] This was an extreme case of the brotherhood defending its privileges. Although at least one brother had resigned over this issue when the practice of girls marrying outside the Misericórdia was still new, by the mid-eighteenth century it had become accepted.[3]

In addition to the social implications of the concession of dowries, there was also the financial aspect. In 1682 the Misericórdia had appointed two brothers, one 'major' and the other 'minor', to be responsible for all legacies left to the Misericórdia for providing dowries from the interest on capital. In 1700 the enormous legacy of João de Mattos de Aguiar was entrusted to their care and from this date all such legacies were referred to generally as of the 'deposit of João de Mattos de Aguiar'. The legacy of João de Mattos de Aguiar made the treasurers of these bequests more important than the treasurer of the Misericórdia in terms of money at their disposal. There was an essential difference between the two deposits. The capital of the Misericórdia had been derived from general legacies: once the conditions of a legacy had been fulfilled, the residue could be used for the day-to-day expenses of the hospital, prison or turning wheel. All the legacies of the 'deposit of João de Mattos de Aguiar' had been left to the brotherhood for a specific purpose — the granting of dowries. For the administration of legacies the Misericórdia received a fee depending on the extent of the legacy, e.g. for the administration of the thirty-three dowries of João de Mattos de Aguiar (excluding the five dowries financed from the income derived from properties) the Misericórdia received the interest on 24,767$294 which amounted to 1,547$790 annually.[4]

The administration of dowries was the first charitable service of the Misericórdia to be affected by the disruption of the economic *status quo* of Bahia. For their successful administration, dowries depended on a stable

1 ASCMB, vol. 52, ff. 178–81 and ff. 220–221v.
2 ASCMB, vol. 53, ff. 155v–156v.
3 João Godinho da Maia had been expelled in 1705 for opposing this practice. He was re-admitted in 1720 because of his 'grande utilidade' to the Misericórdia (ASCMB, vol. 195, ff. 34v–35).
4 ASCMB, vol. 199, ff. 10v–11 and ff. 14v–16v.

economy consisting of a steady cycle of loan and repayment, with a guaranteed annual income from interest. The whole financial system of Bahia was based on the needs of the sugar plantation owners. These borrowed money from the Misericórdia in October and November to cover the costs of the cultivation, reaping and grinding of the sugar cane. Securities of property were offered for the capital and guarantors were provided for the payment of interest. All such loans were made on the understanding that, with the arrival of the fleet and the sale of the crop, they would be repaid with all interest due. This financial cycle was disrupted in the eighteenth century. The Misericórdia was often obliged to accept payment in sugar, for which there was no ready market, rather than no payment at all. The Misericórdia was also the victim of a fall in land values in the early eighteenth century. The securities demanded by the Misericórdia on loans usually took the form of plantations. Although the value of a plantation might have been considerable when accepted as security, by the time that legal wrangles had been overcome and the Misericórdia could claim the property in lieu of payment, the value would often have decreased. The administration of dowries was severely affected by this situation.

The Misericórdia was compelled to reduce the number of dowries granted annually. In 1732 the brotherhood cancelled eleven of the dowries of João de Mattos de Aguiar financed from the interest on the residue of his fortune. It also reduced from five to four the dowries granted on the income from property.[1] In 1738 the Misericórdia asked the Jesuits in Bahia to decide whether the brotherhood could alter the terms of clauses made by a testator so that the number of dowries could be further reduced. The ecclesiastical and moral issue was the same as that which had governed the reduction in the number of masses and the Misericórdia was referred to the Roman Curia or its representative in Bahia.[2] In the same year the Misericórdia tried to woo new borrowers in the form of other brotherhoods and religious orders by offering loans at an interest rate of 5 per cent instead of $6\frac{1}{4}$ per cent.[3] This had little effect and the Mesa tried to restore financial stability by petty economies. In 1739 the subsidy of 15$000 paid by the Misericórdia to augment the dowry of 25$000 given by Joanna Fernandes was stopped.

---

[1] Decree of Mesa of 9 April 1732 (ASCMB, vol. 14, ff. 170v–171v).
[2] ASCMB, vol. 14, ff. 243v–245.
[3] Decree of 12 June 1738 (ASCMB, vol. 14, ff. 242v–243v).

The situation deteriorated. In 1739 the Misericórdia owed dowries to some fifty girls who had married but to whom payment of their dowries had not been made. Law suits and continual protests compelled the brotherhood to take 10,000 *cruzados* from capital to make good its promises and preserve its damaged reputation.[1] This could be no more than a temporary measure. In 1751 the Misericórdia wrote to one of its debtors that his refusal to pay was prejudicing an orphan girl to whom a dowry was due rather than the brotherhood itself. The Mesa asked that payment of this debt be made directly to the girl because the brotherhood had no money with which to pay dowries.[2] This was no mere pretence to wring a debt out of a stubborn man. In the following year the Mesa exhorted its attorney in Sergipe to make a supreme effort to collect all debts as the Misericórdia faced financial ruin. The wages of employees were nine months overdue; the wet-nurses of the foundlings had not been paid for eighteen months; large numbers of dowries were unpaid.[3] This estimate of the Misericórdia's financial position was accurate. When Simão Gomes Monteiro drew up the balance sheet for the Misericórdia for the years 1744–54 to satisfy a royal enquiry, it was revealed that eighty-three dowries to the value of 13,260$000 were still unpaid to girls who had married in the belief that their dowries would be paid. There were a further 268 dowries which had been granted and which, if claimed by the girls, would deplete the slender resources of the brotherhood by another 20,840$000.[4]

The final blow to the administration of dowries came in 1757. From the time of the earliest records in the archives of the Misericórdia up to 1757, the interest rate had been $6\frac{1}{4}$ per cent for private loans. All legacies of a perpetual nature were based on this interest rate for the fulfilment of their terms, be it for the saying of masses or the granting of dowries. By a decree of 17 January 1757, Dom José I ordered that the rate of interest be lowered to 5 per cent. The administration of masses was thrown into chaos; the administration of dowries no less so. The Misericórdia tried to honour the terms of the legacies but this became increasingly difficult. In 1763, the Provedor Jerónimo Sodré Pereira proposed to the Mesa that rather than

[1] Decree of 11 October 1739 (ASCMB, vol. 14, ff. 248–249v).

[2] ASCMB, vol. 53, f. 76v.

[3] The Mesa wrote, 'q' na verdade achamos esta Sta Caza em hũa total decadencia' (ASCMB, vol. 53, f. 97r).   [4] ASCMB, vol. 210, ff. 60v–62v.

attempt to fulfil the last wishes of a testator by granting the full number of dowries stipulated in the will, and which the Misericórdia was unable to pay, it would be infinitely better to give no dowries at all. After all, as he pointed out to a reluctant Mesa, why pay forty or fifty dowries if a further eighty or ninety remained unpaid? Only thus would much suffering and financial distress be spared those girls who had married trusting in the payment of a dowry which was never made.

The Misericórdia was in a cleft stick. No longer could loss of capital and interest be hidden by raids on the coffers of the brotherhood in order to satisfy the pride of successive Mesas who continued distributing dowries generously. There were two courses of action: a reduction in the number of dowries or a reduction in the value of the dowries, e.g. those at 100$000 could be reduced to 80$000. In both cases the charge would be levelled that the brotherhood had failed to comply with the wishes of the testators. The solution proposed by Jerónimo Sodré Pereira was ingenious. It saved the Misericórdia from all such accusations. If properly executed it might even have turned deficit into credit. He suggested that all dowries which lapsed, because of failure to register on the part of the girl or for other reasons, should not be re-allocated. In this manner the Misericórdia could recuperate its past losses and, when this had been done, resume the full allocation of dowries.[1]

The administration of dowries by the Misericórdia exemplifies all that was good and all that was bad in the brotherhood. Dowries were given to coloured girls as well as white girls, to girls of the city and to girls of the surrounding region. By so doing, the Misericórdia offered a social service without parallel in Bahia of the eighteenth century. Many girls who would otherwise not have married, or would have been degraded, were able to marry honourably. By this action the Misericórdia was to a small degree responsible for reducing the domestic instability, illegitimacy and prostitution for which Bahia was notorious. Unfortunately its powers of administration did not equal its idealism. Loans were placed on poor securities and lost. Legal disputes made others impossible to collect. Small sums were lost through the dishonesty of brothers or employees. The Misericórdia was affected by external factors: disruption of the economy; the decrease in the value of

[1] Decree of 7 June 1763 (ASCMB, vol. 15, ff. 165–71).

properties; lack of co-operation from the judiciary in law suits brought against debtors. It was pride which prompted the Mesas to continue granting dowries for as long as they did, without consideration for hard financial realities. Although it is easy to condemn the administrative deficiencies of the brotherhood, the important rôle played by the Misericórdia in the distribution of dowries can only command respect.

9

Burials

BURIAL is always a problem in a tropical climate. Deterioration is rapid and the risk of infection is high. Any visitor to modern Bahia who has seen the bizarre spectacle of a cortège trotting through the streets, in the late afternoon, coffin bouncing on the carriers' shoulders, is aware of this problem. Nowadays a law decrees that burial must take place on the same day as death, before the cemetery closes at 5 o'clock in the afternoon. In colonial Brazil there were no such laws. Burials were unhygienic and superficial. In 1832 a commission on public health in Rio reported that on premature exhumation 'the bones would come out with the ligaments and membranes still clinging to them, and the soft and rotting tissues would adhere like mire to the mattocks'.[1]

Conditions in colonial Bahia were equally appalling. The monopoly on all burials in colonial Bahia was held by the Misericórdia. This monopoly frequently brought the Misericórdia into conflict with other brotherhoods and the ecclesiastical authorities. The statutes of the Misericórdia stipulated that each brother should be accompanied to his grave by a ceremonial cortège of the brotherhood. In addition to this statutory obligation, the Misericórdia operated a variety of funeral services, both for payment and charitably. In this service the Misericórdia was continuing a tradition of co-operative burial present among the brotherhoods of western Europe since the early Roman Empire. The legacy of this tradition had been preserved in the statutes of the mediaeval brotherhoods and in the *Compromisso* of the Misericórdia of Lisbon.

In ancient Rome the funerary ceremonies had varied according to the rank and wealth of the dead person. The scion of a noble family, a successful

---

[1] Gilberto Freyre, *The Masters and the Slaves. A Study in the Development of Brazilian Civilisation* (English ed., New York, 1946), p. 441, n. 92.

general, or a rich business man could have expected to be buried with all due pomp and circumstance. The middle and lower classes could not have expected similar posthumous recognition. Unless they had made provision for burial during their lives, their bodies had been buried in the 'potter's field', a cemetery reserved for slaves and poor people. To provide against this eventuality the middle and lower classes had formed co-operative funeral associations known as _collegia funeraticia_. These associations had flourished in the early Roman Empire, assuring their members a decent burial in the columbarium of the brotherhood on payment of an annual subscription during their lives. The early Christians in Rome had formed such a co-operative society, burying their dead in the catacombs.

This tradition of co-operative burial had continued in western Europe. The mediaeval brotherhoods of France, Germany and Italy had included a clause in their statutes concerning the burial of brothers and their families. These brotherhoods had demanded annual dues of their members. Failure to pay had often resulted in the loss of privileges. The poorer members of the community had not even been able to afford the cost of membership of such associations. It had been these lower classes whose precarious financial position and squalid living conditions had rendered them most susceptible to sudden misfortune such as plague and famine. Thus there had been a pressing need for associations willing to undertake the burial of the poor without payment. One of the first of such associations had been the Misericòrdia of Florence, to which reference has already been made (pp. 3–4), founded with the express object of burying those who had died suddenly on the streets. In Portugal the brotherhoods of the thirteenth and fourteenth centuries had provided for the burial of their members and their families. Few had contained a clause in their statutes providing for charitable burials. In this aspect, as in so many others, the Misericòrdia had represented a considerable advance on its predecessors. The _Compromisso_ of 1516 had included detailed instructions for the ceremonial at the funerals of brothers. Provision had also been made for the saying of masses for the soul of a dead brother. The _Compromisso_ had also stipulated that a litter should be maintained for the funerals of the poor.[1]

The brotherhoods of the Portuguese colonial empire followed the statutes of the parent bodies in Lisbon. The brotherhoods of colonial Bahia had

---

[1] _Compromisso_ of Lisbon of 1516, chapters 3 and 14.

preserved the traditional clause as to the burial of members. Even the coloured brotherhoods had followed the example of their white counterparts and had included this clause in their statutes. The statutes of two brotherhoods well illustrate the similarity of the clauses dealing with burials. The first was a white brotherhood, many of whose members would have been conscious of the European tradition of co-operative burials. The second was a coloured brotherhood whose members had drawn up statutes closely modelled on those of the white brotherhoods.

The white Brotherhood of Our Lady of the Immaculate Conception had been founded in 1645 in the parish of that name on the narrow strip of shore between the cliff and the sea. It had been founded primarily for the propagation of the doctrine and ceremonial of Catholicism and exerted little influence in the field of social philanthropy. Its *Juízes*, or presidents of the board of guardians, in the seventeenth and eighteenth centuries included several prominent Bahians such as the Governor of Angola, Francisco de Tavora, the landowner António Guedes de Brito, Francisco Dias d'Avila of the House of Tôrre and the Secretary of State, José Pires de Carvalho e Albuquerque.[1] The coloured brotherhood was that of St Anthony of Catagerona. This had been founded in 1699 by a group of free and captive Angolans and creoles. Despite the disparity of social standing between the two brotherhoods and of the financial resources available to their members, the similarity of the clause on burials in the respective *Compromissos* is remarkable.

The statutes of the Brotherhood of Our Lady of the Immaculate Conception ordered that the whole brotherhood should attend the funeral of a brother, his wife, and his children if they were over ten years of age and still under parental jurisdiction. Should a brother be too impoverished to provide for his shroud and grave, the brotherhood undertook to meet these expenses. At the funeral the priest of the brotherhood was to say ten masses for the soul of the dead man, and each brother was constrained to say fifteen Hail Marys and fifteen Our Fathers. Once a year the brotherhood attended a solemn mass for the souls of former members. These privileges, both physical and spiritual, were dependent on regular payment of the annual subscription of one *tostão*: failure to pay for three successive years meant the

[1] *Memórias e mais papéis pertencentes às Irmandades do SS^{mo} Sacramento e de N. S^{ra} da Conceição da Praia* (BNRJ, 11–33, 26, 13, doc. 35).

loss of rights of membership.[1] The statutes of the Negro brotherhood contained similar clauses and conditions. Attendance at the funeral of a brother was obligatory and each member was to say a chaplet (a third of the rosary) for the intention of the deceased. The brotherhood commissioned a priest to say eight masses for his soul, and once a year the brotherhood congregated for a solemn mass for all brothers. As had been the case of the white brotherhood these benefits were conditional and failure to pay the dues for two years meant the withdrawal of all privileges.[2] The only difference between the clauses on the burial of brothers was in the ceremonial. The white brotherhood could afford a more ornate cortège and the saying of more masses. In this respect even the Brotherhood of the Immaculate Conception, a parochial brotherhood, could not compare with the urban brotherhoods such as the Misericórdia and the Third Orders. These brotherhoods placed great importance on the ceremonial perfection of the cortèges of their brothers as indicative of the prestige and financial standing of the brotherhood. The Misericórdia of Bahia even went so far as to appoint a priest specifically to ensure that there should be no fault in the ceremonial of the public functions of the brotherhood.

As soon as news was received of the death of a brother, the Provedor was informed. He convoked the Mesa to make all arrangements for the funeral. An employee of the brotherhood was dispatched to summmon all the members by the ringing of a handbell through the streets. All the brothers were obliged by statute to attend the funeral, wearing their cloaks. Once the brotherhood had assembled at the Misericórdia, the cortège went to the house of the dead brother and his body was placed on the bier, which was then carried to the place of burial stipulated in the will of the dead man. The order of ceremony was laid down in detail in the *Compromisso*. The cortège was headed by an employee, known as the *homem de azul* because of his blue cloak, ringing a handbell. He was followed by the brother elected monthly to supervise the funerals, and known as the *irmão da vara*, or 'brother of the

---

[1] *Compromisso da Irmandade da immaculada e sacratissima Virgem Nossa Senhora da Conceição instituida e confirmada em a praia desta Bahia. Anno MDCXLV* (ANRJ, *Códice 824*, vol. 1). A *tostão* was worth 100 *rs.*

[2] The statutes of this brotherhood are described by Manoel S. Cardozo, 'The lay brotherhoods of colonial Bahia', in *The Catholic Historical Review*, vol. 33, no. 1 (April 1947), pp. 12–30.

staff'. He, in turn, was followed by a 'noble' brother bearing the banner of the brotherhood and flanked by two brothers, one of each class, carrying large ceremonial candles. Then came the brothers of the Misericórdia and the Provedor with his staff of office. Six members of the board of guardians carried the bier, and the remaining four bore torches on either side of it. The composition of the rest of the cortège depended on the importance of the dead man. The more eminent he had been in the social life of Bahia, the more brotherhoods, religious orders, priests and poor people there would be in the cortège. At the rear came another employee of the Misericórdia asking for alms for the charitable works of the brotherhood. Prayers were said over the grave and each brother had the personal obligation of saying four-teen Hail Marys and fourteen Our Fathers for the soul of the dead man. On the following day an office of nine lessons was said in the church of the Misericórdia. Once a year there was a mass attended by the brotherhood for the souls of all dead brothers and their families. These privileges were extended to the wives of brothers on condition that they should not be married again to somebody who was not a brother. They also applied to children of brothers between the ages of eighteen and twenty-five.[1]

The clauses of the *Compromisso* of 1618 for the burial of brothers were respected by the Misericórdia of Bahia. The conditions regarding the wives of brothers were strictly enforced. The Misericórdia of Bahia ruled that a brother, before marrying, should inform the Mesa of his intention and an enquiry as to the 'purity of blood' of the prospective bride was held. Failure to inform the Mesa before marriage meant that the wife forfeited the privileges of a ceremonial funeral by the brotherhood.[2] In such cases there was always the suspicion among those not in the brotherhood that the refusal to grant this favour was founded on the grounds of her being a New Christian. In some cases this was true, but the Mesas were firm in their

---

[1] *Compromisso* of Lisbon of 1618, chapter 35.

[2] A rare instance of this clause being invoked was in September 1751. The Mesa refused to permit lieutenant Francisco Nunes Ferreira to use the bier reserved for funerals of brothers and their families for the funeral of his second wife, Hilária Francisca Soares. The Mesa also refused the ceremonial cortège attended by the brotherhood, as was usual in such cases. The scribe insisted that the only reason for this refusal was that Francisco Nunes Ferreira had not informed the Mesa before marrying a second time, and that there was no question of any 'defect' on his part or that of his wife (ASCMB, vol. 1252, f. 355).

refusal to permit anyone of 'infected blood' to enjoy the privileges of burial by the brotherhood. This anti-semitic prejudice often went to extremes. In 1679 António de Brito de Sousa had been refused admittance to the brotherhood, although he was a Knight of the Order of Santiago. He was a widower and his wife had been a New Christian, but it was not this fact which had influenced the Mesa. His application had been rejected because, if he had been admitted, the children of this marriage could have demanded to be carried to their graves on the bier of the brotherhood, as was their right. The Mesa refused to countenance such a possibility.[1]

The only modification by the Misericórdia of Bahia of the clauses of the *Compromisso* concerned the saying of masses for a dead brother. The brotherhood was obliged by statute to say an office of nine lessons for a dead brother. This had not been observed in Bahia because of the precarious nature of the brotherhood's finances. In 1704 an improvement in the financial situation led the Provedor Pedro Barbosa Leal to propose that an office be said in addition to the ten masses which had been celebrated for the soul of a dead brother before this date.[2] These masses had been said by the priests of the brotherhood who received 200 *rs.* for each mass. In 1723 no priest could be found to say a mass for this small sum and the rate was increased to 320 *rs.*[3] In the 1750s the office and masses for each brother cost the Misericórdia 11$600 and over a year this amounted to some 350$000, excluding the cost of candles lit in the church. Although this only represented about 2 per cent of the annual expenditure, the Mesa of 1759 ordered that fifteen masses should be said instead of the office, thus making a total of twenty-five.[4] This spirit of petty economy, already apparent in the administration of dowries, did not enhance the reputation of the Misericórdia. The Mesa of 1760 revoked the decision of its predecessor as unworthy of so illustrious a brotherhood.[5] During the next decade successive Mesas were swayed by financial necessity and the preservation of prestige. Mammon

[1] ASCMB, vol. 195, f. 19.
[2] Minute of 15 June 1704 (ASCMB, vol. 14, f. 74).
[3] Minute of 21 February 1723 (ASCMB, vol. 14, f. 131).
[4] The Mesa had consulted the Jesuits in Bahia on the theological implications of this change before reaching a decision on 2 September 1759 (ASCMB, vol. 15, ff. 115–116v).
[5] Minute of 23 October 1760 (ASCMB, vol. 15, ff. 125v–126v).

Compromisso of 1516 of the Misericórdia of Lisbon

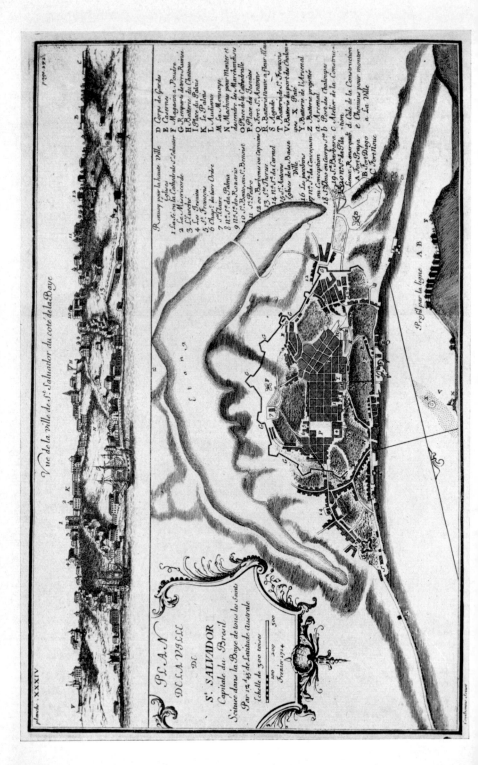

planche XXXIV

1790-1791.

Vue de la ville de St Salvador du cote de la Baye

PLAN
DE LA VILLE
DE
St SALVADOR
Capitale du Bresil
Scitue dans la Baye de tous les saints
Par 12.d 45' de Latitude Australe
Echelle de 300 toises
100   200   300   500

Fevrier 1714

R emuy pour la haute Ville
Eglises
1 La St ou la Cathedrale St Saluator
2 la Misericorde
3 L'Euechi
4 Les Jesuites
5 St François
6 Chap. du hors Ordre
7 Marie
8 N.t St de Palma
9 N.t St du Rozario
10 St Bento ou St Benoit
11 St Pedro
12 ou Barthemi ou Capucins
13 Ste Theresa
14 N.t St du Carmel
15 St Antoine
Eglises de la Basse
Ville
16 Le pilorine
17 N.t St la Conception
ou Conception
18 Santo ou Santa St
de la Pita   tion.
Lieux Remarquables
A Fort Praya
B St Diego
C Fortifious

D Corps de Garde
E Caserne
F Magasin a Poudre
G Rempart devers Riviere
H Batterie du Chateau
I Place du Palais
K Le Palais
L Audience
M La Mousque
N Machinne pour Monter et
descendre Les Marchandises
O Place de la Cathedrale
P Place du Iesuites
Q Fort St Antoine
R Batterie Vieux à Fleur Haut
S Agatte
T Batterie de St François
V Batterie du port du chalou-
pes   X Pai
Y Batterie de l'Arsenal
Z Batterie projettée
1 Arsenal
b Porte des Chaloupes
c Atelier de la Construction

d Cale de la Construction
e Chemin pour monter
a La Ville

Profil par la ligne A B

*An ex-voto of the
eighteenth century
in the church of
Mont'Serrat, Bahia*

João de Mattos de Aguiar, a painting in the Misericórdia of Bahia

Francisco Fernandes do Sim, also in the Misericórdia of Bahia

*The Misericórdia of Bahia taking part in the Maundy Thursday procession.
Tiles in the church of the brotherhood in Bahia*

The 'procession of the bones'

The funeral cortège of a brother of the Misericórdia

Punishment of a Negro at Feira de Santana

A foundling wheel, in the
convent of Sta Clara do
Desterro, Bahia

The Santa Casa da Misericórdia
of Bahia in 1958

finally won the day and the Mesa of 1768 decreed that a total of twenty-five masses be said at 240 *rs.* each. This decree was referred to the viceroy, the second Marquis of Lavradio, for approval and sent to the king for royal ratification.[1]

This apparently trifling question of the number of masses is highly significant as illustrating the struggle experienced by boards of guardians. On the one hand they were faced with decreased revenue. On the other they were the guardians of the prestige of a brotherhood whose name had become synonymous with high social standing, purity of blood and financial wealth. It was this consciousness of the reputation of the Misericórdia which led Mesas to deal severely with those who brought the name of the brotherhood into ill repute on public occasions. Funerals provided an excellent opportunity for the brotherhood to 'show off': the saying of masses with due pomp and lavish ceremonial cortèges were inducements to potential members. Frequently the brothers and the paid priests of the brotherhood forgot the illustrious past of the Misericórdia and were negligent in obeying the clauses as to attendance at funerals and the saying of masses.

The brothers often sought to evade their obligations. The monthly duty as 'brother of the staff' was unpopular and many brothers were expelled because of their refusal to hold this post.[2] Others refused to carry the bier. Not only did such refusals constitute a personal affront to the brother on duty, but publicly discredited the Misericórdia. All brothers were required to be part of the official cortège. Many refused and joined the crowd of miscellaneous followers where their presence was all the more apparent because of their long cloaks. In 1737, so common had this practice become that the Mesa decreed that in future any brother attending a funeral and not taking part in the official cortège would be expelled. In the 1730s some brothers even went so far as to boycott the funerals entirely.[3]

The chaplains employed by the Misericórdia did little to enhance the standing of the brotherhood. Relations between the Mesa and the priests of the choir were always acrimonious. The main reason for this situation was the exemption of all clerics from civil jurisdiction. Confident in this immunity, they made outrageous demands as to terms of employment.

[1] ASCMB, vol. 85, ff. 135–7.
[2] ASCMB, vol. 195, ff. 46, 98–100, 111, 115v–116v, 117.
[3] ASCMB, vol. 195, f. 103 and vol. 14, f. 239.

H

Although one Mesa in a fit of pique might dismiss the entire choir, the next was compelled to reinstate the priests if masses were to be said and brothers buried. Masses and funerals provided the main bones of contention. In 1671 all but one of the chaplains had been dismissed, after they had refused outright to say masses.[1] An important factor in the decision of 1760 to revert to saying an office for each brother was the complaint of the clergy that they had lost alms because of the reduction.[2] Funerals were the other source of disagreement. Each priest served spells of duty of two weeks accompanying the biers and attending the funerals of those people buried by the Misericórdia. The priests were negligent in their duty, claiming payment for funerals at which they had not officiated, or sending another priest not of the Misericórdia in their place.[3] One even sent his nephew who had not taken the tonsure! Such actions brought the name of the Misericórdia into ill repute. Testators ordered that the masses for their souls should be said in churches other than the Misericórdia and did not give alms as generously to the brotherhood for accompanying their funerals.

Prestige was of supreme importance to the brotherhoods of Bahia. The most influential brotherhoods of colonial Bahia in the seventeenth and eighteenth centuries were the Misericórdia and the Third Orders. Brothers of the Misericórdia were often tertiaries. Membership of the one was a passport to the others and to a position on the city council. Relations between the Misericórdia and the Third Orders were good. The Third Orders did not attempt to rival the Misericórdia in the field of social philanthropy, and the Misericórdia respected their privileges. The only point of disagreement was over the funerals of those brothers of the Misericórdia who were also tertiaries of St Francis. The issue resulted in discord and even physical violence between the brothers of the Misericórdia and the tertiaries. This dispute affords the only instance of the Misericórdia coming into direct conflict with another white brotherhood of equal social standing and also

---

[1] ASCMB, vol. 195, f. 14.

[2] ASCMB, vol. 15, ff. 125v–126v. A choir of a president and six chaplains had been formally established in 1672. By 1683 this had grown to a president, a sacristan, twelve chaplains and three choir boys. In 1683 the number was fixed at one president, eight chaplains and two choir boys (ASCMB, vol. 14, ff. 11–12v). In 1717 the entire choir was dismissed because of its refusal to say masses for the intention of brothers (ASCMB, vol. 14, f. 13).

[3] ASCMB, vol. 14, ff. 143v–144.

illustrates the susceptibility of the brotherhoods to any infringements of their privileges.

The Misericórdia and the Third Order of St Francis were required by statute to bury their members. It had been customary for the brothers of the Misericórdia to carry the body of the dead man on their bier to the chapel of the Third Order. Here a friar of the Franciscan Order had officiated at the burial. In 1654 this arrangement had ceased. Both brotherhoods had suddenly adopted an attitude of unusually stubborn adherence to their statutes. The Misericórdia had stated that only the brothers of the Misericórdia should carry the body of a fellow, even if he were also a tertiary. The Third Order had countered that their members had a similar statutory obligation to be present at the funeral of any tertiary and a Franciscan friar should officiate at the graveside. The common object of both brotherhoods — to honour the dead man by burial with all due reverence — was forgotten.

It is not clear who did instigate the dispute. There are no records in the archives of the Third Order to clarify the position of the tertiaries. The decrees taken by successive Mesas of the Misericórdia provide the only source of information. Ostensibly the dispute had been started by the friars of the Franciscan Order. They had incited the tertiaries to demonstrate publicly against the Misericórdia.[1] The alacrity with which the Third Order had leapt to the defence of the friars cast doubts on the true nature of its rôle. The Third Order, founded less than twenty years before, had already become a powerful brotherhood. It drew its members from the same social classes as did the Misericórdia, but did not enjoy the privileges of that brotherhood. It was inevitable that at some stage it should tilt against the Misericórdia. If this was the case, the Third Order was prudent in its choice of instruments. The friars were not employees of the Third Order and the board of guardians could dissociate itself from their opinions and actions if

---

[1] A minute of 26 June 1654 recorded: 'pelo dito Prov^or foi proposto q' a todos os Irmãos era patente a novid^e com q' os Rev^os P^es de S. Fran^co desta cidade fazião força e violencia a esta Santa Irmand^e nos enterramentos dos Irmãos q' se mandão enterrar no seu mosteiro, querendo e mandando q' os Irmãos terceiros tirem da tumba da Irmand^e e levem a sepultura o corpo do defunto, q' em sua vida tendo sido Irmão da Miz^a o foi tambem terceiro . . .' (ASCMB, vol. 13, ff. 50–51v).

necessary. The friars were also exempt from civil jurisdiction, should the Misericórdia wish to seek legal redress.

Whatever the rôle of the Third Order initially, its members had become actively involved in the dispute. Several brothers of the Misericórdia, who were also tertiaries, had openly supported the cause of the Third Order. They had been expelled from the Misericórdia.[1] The Franciscan friars had over-reached themselves in 1654. On 26 June the Misericórdia was accompanying the funeral of the son of a brother who was not a tertiary. The friars had attacked the bier of the Misericórdia, opened the grille, seized the corpse, and had carried it away for burial in the cloister of their monastery. Protests by the Misericórdia had been frustrated by the immunity of the friars. Incensed, the Mesa had decreed that in future the privilege of a ceremonial funeral, accompanied by the brotherhood of the Misericórdia, be withdrawn from all those brothers who were also tertiaries of St Francis. No longer would such brothers be carried to their graves on the bier of the Misericórdia reserved for brothers and their families, but on the bier used for charitable burials of the poor.[2]

These were strong measures indeed. The loss of the impressive cortège and the stigma of being carried on the bier usually used for people who had died in the hospital or for those who could not afford the alms of the more expensive bier, did not go unremarked by the Third Order. The friars were induced to come to terms with the Misericórdia in an attempt to save the honour of the Third Order. Agreement was reached at a meeting between the Mesa of the Misericórdia and the Franciscans, represented by the Provincial of the Order and the Prelate of the monastery in Bahia. It had been decided that, pending a decision from Lisbon deciding the issue, two brothers of the Misericórdia and two Franciscan friars should carry the body from the bier to the grave.

This agreement had been short-lived. In 1655 the Misericórdia had suffered the humiliation of the funeral cortège of a brother being brought to a halt at the door of the chapel of the Third Order. The way had been barred by the lawyer, Domingos Ferraz de Sousa, brandishing pistols and other

[1] On 31 May 1654 three brothers of the Misericórdia had been expelled for openly supporting the claims of the tertiaries at the funeral of the wife of a brother of the Misericórdia, who was a tertiary (ASCMB, vol. 195, ff. 8v–9v).

[2] Minute of 26 June 1654 (ASCMB, vol. 13, ff. 50–51v).

small arms. Chastened, the Misericórdia had preserved some semblance of dignity by simply retiring and had buried the body in the cathedral.[1] By the fleet of this year the Misericórdia had received a royal decree upholding its complaint of interference by the friars and tertiaries of St Francis. The king had ordered that the privileges of the Misericórdia in the matter of burials be respected.[2] This had not been the end of the matter. Nor was the pious hope of a document entitled 'Proposal much in the service of God Our Lord', that Christian unity should triumph, fulfilled. This unsigned and undated document is in the archives of the Desterro convent in Bahia. After giving both sides of the dispute over burials, it draws a biblical parallel reminiscent of the sermons of the great Jesuit preacher António Vieira. The burial of Christ was compared to the burial of a tertiary who was also a brother of the Misericórdia. Joseph of Arimathea and Nicodemus, 'true brothers of the most noble Brotherhood of Holy Mercy', had carried the body of Christ to the tomb, but had allowed Mary Magdalene to anoint the body. This had simply been an act of respect and veneration. In the same way, the action of the Franciscan friars in receiving the body of a brother or tertiary at the graveside, did not detract from the action of the Misericórdia in accompanying the bier. The document ended with an exhortation to Our Lady of Mercy to lead the erring brothers and tertiaries back to the paths of righteousness.[3]

Royal decrees and pious exhortations were ineffective. What had started as a dispute over the rôle of the Franciscan friars at the burial services, developed into a conflict between the Third Order and the Misericórdia. The Misericórdia stood firm by its decision and refused to allow the friars to participate in the burial service. This action was supported by an affidavit of 1698, signed by the Count of Assumar as scribe of the Misericórdia of Lisbon, confirming that such was the practice in the metropolis.[4] The only

[1] This incident was on 24 June 1655 (ASCMB, vol. 195, f. 10).

[2] 'Alvará p^a q' os terceiros de S. Fr^{co} não se entrometão com a Irmand^e da Mizericórdia em tirar os defuntos da tumba', dated 19 December 1654 (ASCMB, vol. 207, f. 19).

[3] ACDB, *Caixa I, pasta* 43.

[4] Affidavit of 15 February 1698 (ASCMB, vol. 42, f. 124). This had been requested because of an incident in 1696 involving the friars, tertiaries and the brothers of the Misericórdia. A minute of the Mesa of 17 November 1696 recorded the decision of the Mesa to adhere to the resolution of 1654 (ASCMB, vol. 14, f. 47).

concession made by the Misericórdia was to lend to the Third Order the cloth used to drape the bier of the brotherhood.[1] The Third Order even appealed to the Bahian judiciary but dropped the case.[2] In the eighteenth century the cause of the dispute was forgotten and the two brotherhoods bickered over trivial issues. During the viceroyalty of the Count of Galvêas (1735–49) the Third Order appealed to the king, alleging that the Misericórdia refused burial in the chapel of the Third Order to any brother who died intestate. Moreover, the tertiaries complained that the Misericórdia demanded fees for the use of the bier, and refused to allow the tertiaries to carry it. All these charges were refuted by the Misericórdia, but relations remained strained between the two brotherhoods throughout the colonical period.[3]

The dispute between the Misericórdia and the Third Order of St Francis had its roots in the privileged position of the Misericórdia. The Third Order could not hope to gain all the privileges conceded to the Misericórdia by successive monarchs. Nor indeed did it need those privileges facilitating the practice of social philanthropy. The one privilege coveted by the Third Order concerned funerals. This was the privilege conceding to the Misericórdia the sole right to possess biers for the funerals of its brothers and other people. This privilege had been granted to the Misericórdia on 30 June 1593 by the Cardinal Archduke Albert of Austria as governor of Portugal under Philip II of Spain. The success of the Misericórdia of Lisbon during its first century of activity had encouraged many imitators. These had copied the ceremonial of the Misericórdia, undertaken burials for payment, and even adopted the name of 'Misericórdia'. The Misericórdia itself had suffered from these spurious imitators and had lost the income derived from burials. Recognising the importance of the charitable acts of the Misericórdia, the cardinal archduke had ruled that no other brotherhood of the city of Lisbon should imitate the ceremonial followed by the Misericórdia, nor should it practise those charitable works already undertaken by the Misericórdia, nor

[1] Minute of 14 July 1699 (ASCMB, vol. 14, f. 50v).

[2] In an undated letter of October or November 1702 the Mesa of the Misericórdia thanked the Third Order for not pursuing the dispute over burials and renouncing its appeal to the *Casa da Suplicação* in Lisbon (ASCMB, vol. 52, f. 6v).

[3] In September 1742 Dom João V asked the Chancellor of the High Court in Bahia to investigate the allegations of the Third Order (ASCMB, vol. 52, ff. 214v–219). Disputes over payment continued up to 1765 (ASCMB, vol. 85, ff. 97v–98v).

should it possess a bier for the funerals of its own members or for hire. A penalty of excommunication and a fine of 1,000 *cruzados* had been levied for infringement of this privilege. When the privileges of the Misericórdia of Lisbon had been extended to Bahia, the Misericórdia had enjoyed the same monopoly. The Provedor had ordered the publication of this privilege throughout the city of Bahia in 1627.[1]

The Third Order resented this monopoly exercised by the Misericórdia. The financial benefits were small, the social prestige enormous. At the death of a tertiary, the Third Order had to request permission of the Misericórdia for the use of its bier. All petitions by the Third Order to the Crown for a similar privilege were referred to the viceroy. The viceroy consulted the Mesa of the Misericórdia and the petitions were rejected. The Third Order was fully conscious of the opportunity provided by funerals for a display of the wealth of the brotherhood. In the 1740s it sought to evade the jurisdiction of the prelate and erect a bell tower: the construction was halted by Dom João V in 1743 pending an enquiry. Defending its actions the Third Order gave as one of its reasons the need for a bell to celebrate the burials of tertiaries with due solemnity. It cited other brotherhoods with bell towers. As final justification it referred to the coloured Brotherhood of Our Lady of the Rosary:

> Even the Brotherhood of the niggers of Our Lady of the Rosary built their own church near to the cathedral of this city. This church has bells and towers on either side. Perchance it is the intent of Your Majesty that the tertiaries should be buried with less solemnity than the blacks of the Rosary.[2]

This fine display of racial scorn for the 'niggers' of the Brotherhood of the Rosary did not crush opposition and the construction was halted permanently. If the tertiaries begrudged a coloured brotherhood a bell tower, how much more painful to the white élite of the Third Order must have been the fact that these same 'niggers' had been granted permission by the Misericórdia to

[1] The only exceptions to this ruling in Lisbon had been the national brotherhoods of Our Lady of Loreto of the Italians and St Bartholomew of the Germans (BNRJ, 11–33, 24, 45, doc. 24).

[2] 'E até a Irmandade dos pretinhos de N. S^ra do Rozario, que sahindo-se da Sé desta cidade, fizerão sua Igreja separada, tem nelle sinos, e torres aos lados. Por ventura pode ser vontade de VMag^de que os Terceyros sejão sepultados com menos solemnidade que os pretos do Rozario' (APB, *Ordens régias*, vol. 41, doc. 9c).

use a bier for the funerals of their brothers. Nor was the Rosary alone in this privilege. Three other coloured brotherhoods and two white brotherhoods also enjoyed this concession from the Misericórdia. The conditions governing the granting of this permission throw light on the relations between the Misericórdia and the lesser brotherhoods of colonial Bahia. They also present another aspect of the attitude of the Misericórdia towards the racial question, and the increasing rôle played by the coloured brotherhoods in eighteenth-century Bahia.

The white brotherhoods of colonial Bahia who used biers for the funerals of their members were the clerical Brotherhood of St Peter and the Brotherhood of the Holy Cross of the paid soldiers of the two regiments of the garrison. The circumstances in which these two brotherhoods gained this privilege differed. It has already been seen that the relations between the Misericórdia and its paid priests were bad. This acrimony may well have been born of an infringement of the privileges of the Misericórdia in 1656. In this year the clerics had decided to inaugurate a bier for the funerals of their brothers. The Misericórdia had not been consulted. All protests by the Mesa had been ignored. The clerics had simply proceeded to carry two of their dead brothers to the place of burial on their own bier. The fact that one of these was a brother of the Misericórdia had added salt to the Misericórdia's wounds. The only action open to the Misericórdia had been the expulsion of all clerics who were members of the Misericórdia.[1] Later boards of guardians had relented and accepted clerical members, but up to the mid-1680s this had been only on condition that they renounced membership of the Brotherhood of St Peter. In the eighteenth century this condition was omitted from the terms of entry and several clerics were accompanied by the Misericórdia to their graves but carried on the bier of their own brotherhood.[2]

[1] Minute of 22 October 1656: 'Detriminou o d⁰ Prov⁰ʳ com os Irmãos Concelheiros da Meza q' se riscassem todos e quais quer clerigos q' fossem Irmãos desta S. Irmandᵉ e q' se puzesse verba em seus assentos pᵃ não averem de ser mais Irmãos; e a razão está p q' o clero desta cidᵉ de seu poder absoluto levãtara hum esquiffe em q' querem enterrar todos os clerigos, como com effeito enterrarão dous clerigos, e hum delles Irmão desta S. Caza, sem terem poder pᵃ isto, nem privilegio, nem bula, e somᵗᵉ se atreverão nisto fiados em serem clerigos, e q' não são da jurisdição secular' . . . (ASCMB, vol. 195, ff. 10v–11).

[2] 'com declaração que não será Irmão da Irmandade de S. Pedro dos Clerigos da Santa Sé desta cidade, porque sendo será logo expulso da Santa Misericór-

Whereas the clergy of Bahia had openly flaunted the authority of the Misericórdia, confident in their immunity from legal redress, the soldiers had adopted a more conventional approach and petitioned the Misericórdia for the right to use a bier for the funerals of the members of their brotherhood. I have been unable to establish the exact date of the granting of this privilege. It had become normal practice by 1675, because in this year one Salvador Rodrigues, a carpenter by trade and a soldier in the regiment of the Master of the Field João Furtado de Mendonça, had made a will making the Misericórdia his legal executor and heir, and ordering that his body should be carried to the place of burial on the bier of the brotherhood of the soldiers.[1] The conditions surrounding the concession of this privilege led to misunderstandings between the soldiers and the Misericórdia. In 1722 Dom João V asked the Count of Sabugosa to enquire into the complaint by the soldiers that the Misericórdia was infringing their privileges in this respect. The soldiers alleged that they had always carried their fellows and their families on their own bier. The Provedor of the Misericórdia now refused to permit this for their families and claimed payment for the use of the bier of the Misericórdia for the funerals of all dependents. The soldiers alleged that they could not afford the fee of 4$480 for this service. The Misericórdia defended itself against these charges. It showed that the privilege had been granted for the funerals of soldiers only, and not of their families. Allegations of poverty were unfounded because in such cases the Misericórdia buried people without payment.[2] In the eighteenth century the Misericórdia was to regret having authorised the use of this bier by the soldiers. At a time when the costs of the hospital were rising, the income from biers offset

---

dia'. This was included in all registers admitting clerics from 1675–9 (ASCMB, vol. 2, ff. 106v, 116, 138v, 142v) but omitted in similar elections in 1685 (ASCMB, vol. 2, ff. 248v–249, 254, 255 and 262). There had been a similar clash between the Misericórdia and clergy in Gôa in 1600, but it appears an amicable settlement was reached (J. F. Ferreira Martins, *Historia da Misericordia de Goa*, vol. 1, pp. 475–476 and vol. 2, p. 21). [1] ASCMB, vol. 41, ff. 130v–132.

[2] APB, *Ordens régias*, vol. 16, docs. 19, 19a and 19b. In a letter of 15 June 1723, Dom João V asked the Governor of Rio de Janeiro to enquire into a petition by the soldiers' Brotherhood of the Holy Cross and the sailors' Brotherhood of St Peter asking royal permission for them to possess their own bier. They alleged the Misericórdia levied exorbitant fees for the hire of its bier (ANRJ, *Códice 952*, vol. 22 (1st part) f. 52).

H 2

the expenditure to some degree. The soldiers received treatment at cheap rates and they did not contribute to the income derived from biers.[1] Possibly the soldiers scored the final point. In 1760 the first Marquis of Lavradio died in Bahia after serving as viceroy for a mere six months. He was a brother of the Misericórdia and had been Provedor of the branches in Elvas and later in Luanda. The Misericórdia of Bahia decided to honour him with masses and the ceremonial cortège accorded to a brother. The soldiers refused to allow any participation of the Misericórdia and the body was buried in the ossuary of the Third Order of St Francis.[2] Possibly this was a case of the tertiaries and the soldiers 'ganging up' on the Misericórdia from fear that if it did participate it would steal the limelight.

The brotherhood of the soldiers was the only white brotherhood to receive official authorisation from the Misericórdia for the use of a bier. Thus it is rather surprising to find that four coloured brotherhoods were accorded this privilege before 1750. The first coloured brotherhood to enjoy the privilege of using a bier had been the Brotherhood of Our Lady of Succour (*Irmandade de Nossa Senhora do Amparo*) of free and captive mulattos. In 1649 the Misericórdia had granted them this privilege on two conditions. The first had been that only slaves should be carried on this bier: all freed members of the brotherhood should be buried by the Misericórdia. The second condition had been that permission to use the bier did not imply possession, and the Misericórdia maintained the right to withdraw this privilege at any time.[3] In 1656 the privilege of the Brotherhood of Our Lady of Succour had been challenged by the Brotherhood of Our Lady of Guadalupe of mulatto slaves. They had claimed that there were no longer any slaves belonging to the Brotherhood of Our Lady of Succour, and that the privilege of using a bier should be transferred to their brotherhood. The board of guardians of the Brotherhood of Our Lady of Succour had vigorously denied this and produced lists of slave members. Indeed, with the exception of the three officers (Judge, scribe and treasurer), the remaining eight members of the board of guardians were all slaves. The Misericórdia had confirmed the privilege of the Brotherhood of Our Lady of Succour to use the bier, and reached a compromise with the Brotherhood of Our Lady

---

[1] ASCMB, vol. 15, ff. 49–51. [2] ASCMB, vol. 15, f. 119.

[3] The concession had been for the use of an 'esquife raso', in effect little more than a bare board. Minute of Mesa of 25 July 1649 (ASCMB, vol. 13, ff. 9–10).

of Guadalupe. The former was to permit the brothers of the latter to use the bier, which would be carried by two members of each brotherhood. Should the Brotherhood of Our Lady of Succour fail to comply with the conditions laid down by the Misericórdia and bury freed members, the bier would pass to their rivals.[1] These two brotherhoods were both small and exerted little influence in the city. The most powerful coloured brotherhood of Bahia was the Brotherhood of Our Lady of the Rosary. This brotherhood had branches in most of the parishes but its most vocal group was in the Pelourinho.

The Brotherhood of Our Lady of the Rosary also enjoyed the privilege granted by the Misericórdia of using a bier for the funerals of its brothers. Although the majority of its members were slaves, it was also allowed to bury its freed brothers. The only restriction imposed by the Misericórdia was that only brothers should be carried on its bier. In 1693 the Misericórdia had established a litter for the funerals of slaves, known as the *banguê*. A charge, payable by the masters, had been levied for this service. All licences granted to coloured brotherhoods had been withdrawn but renewed on formal application to the Misericórdia.[2] Greater vigilance had been exercised by the Misericórdia to ensure that the conditions stipulated in the privileges were observed. It had been discovered that the Rosary was an offender in this respect. It was burying people who were not brothers, but for whom the scribe made false entries in the registers of members. Moreover it was also charging for the use of its bier. The Misericórdia had brought legal charges against the Rosary. The case had been undefended and in 1694 the Rosary had lost the privilege of using a bier. The plea by the Rosary to the governor that it had been in possession of the bier had been rejected. The following year the Misericórdia had relented and had granted the right of using a bier for the funerals of brothers of the Rosary only. The Rosary had agreed to this condition and renounced all claims to possession of the bier.[3]

[1] Minute of 18 October 1656 (ASCMB, vol. 13, ff. 67v–71v).
[2] The licences had been withdrawn on 20 October 1693 (ASCMB, vol. 14, f. 35). Authorisation to use biers was granted again to the Guadalupe and the Rosary on 1 July 1695 (ASCMB, vol. 14, f. 43 and f. 44). Either the Brotherhood of Our Lady of Succour had lost this privilege or been incorporated into the Guadalupe because there is no further reference to it.
[3] APB, *Ordens régias*, vol. 15, doc. 16 and accompanying documents.

In the eighteenth century an increasing number of slaves gained their freedom. The Negro became a more vocal element in urban society, although the majority of administrative positions were still barred to all except those of light hue. The Brotherhood of the Rosary was the mouth-piece for Negro rights. In 1720 the Rosary addressed a petition to Dom João V for the privilege to possess a *tumba de arco*: this was a covered bier and represented an advance on the mere litter, or *esquife*, they had been permitted to use. The challenge to the Misericórdia was two-fold: first, for possession of a bier, a privilege of the Misericórdia; secondly, for a covered bier, whose use had previously been regarded as the exclusive prerogative of the white population. This petition represented a demand by the leading coloured brotherhood to the leading white brotherhood for equal privileges. The Misericórdia, to whom the petition was referred by the king, rejected it outright. The attitude adopted by the Misericórdia and the wording of its rejection reveal the socio-racial prejudice felt by white Bahians towards the coloured population.

The Misericórdia dismissed the petition of the Rosary on four counts. The first was on grounds of social distinction: only the Misericórdia was permitted to possess covered biers, because of the nobility and distinction of the people it buried. The petition of the brothers of the Rosary was un-worthy of further attention 'because they are blacks and of the most servile of this city since the majority of them are bondsmen'. This is a fine example of the equating of colour to class, to which reference has already been made. The second issue concerned the allegations by the Rosary that the soldiers of the coloured regiment of the garrison, called 'the regiment of Henrique Dias', served without pay and were brothers of the Rosary.[1] The Rosary proposed that in the same way as the soldiers of the white regiments had a bier, so should the coloured soldiers enjoy the same benefits. The Miseri-

---

[1] A Bahian by birth, Henrique Dias had spent much of his life in Pernambuco where he had been active as a guerrilla leader against the Dutch in 1636. He had returned to Bahia in 1639 and the Count of Tôrre had conferred on him the title of Governor-in-Chief of all creoles, Negroes and mulattos in the royal service. He had returned to Pernambuco, leaving Matheus Fernandes Vieira in charge in Bahia. Henrique Dias was the only Negro leader to hold the title of Governor. His successor in this position held the rank of Master of the Field and the commanding officer of the coloured troops in Bahia was a Captain-Major (APB, *Ordens régias*, vol. 54, f. 88).

córdia quashed this allegation. First, the coloured soldiers rarely did guard duty and when they did they received payment. Secondly, the comparison between the coloured and white regiments was nothing short of ridiculous. Whereas the white soldiers, popularly known as *Infantes*, gained prestige and nobility by military service, the soldiers of the regiment of Henrique Dias were no more than soldiers in name. Thirdly, the Misericórdia denied all rights of ownership of a bier by the Rosary. Finally, the Misericórdia cited its privileges in the matter of burials, concluding that the 'blacks of the Rosary' should think themselves lucky to be able to use even a rough litter. The Misericórdia was supported by the viceroy and the petition of the Rosary rejected.[1]

The Brotherhood of the Rosary had lost its case for equal privileges, but it had succeeded in bringing to the notice of the Crown that the burial of coloured people, especially slaves, was a real problem. The *banguê* of the Misericórdia was inadequate. This had been recognised by the Misericórdia. After a trial period of a year, licences for burials had been renewed to the brotherhoods of the Rosary and Guadalupe. In 1736 Dom João V authorised the coloured Brotherhood of St Benedict, whose seat was in the Franciscan monastery, to use a bier for the funerals of its brothers. The brotherhood had sent a petition direct to the king, representing that the cost of burial by the Misericórdia was beyond the means of its members and that the brotherhood had been obliged to resort to the practice of abandoning the bodies of brothers in church porches in the hope that they would receive a charitable burial. Dom João V referred the petition to Bahia. The Misericórdia rejected the petition as prejudicial to its own interests: if slaves had been left in the porches of churches this was because of the lack of human feeling of their masters. The Misericórdia also gave financial reasons for its refusal of the petition, listing at great length its charitable commitments and showing that the income derived from burials helped to defray costs.[2] Despite this strong recommendation by the Misericórdia against the concession of a bier to the Brotherhood of St Benedict, Dom João V granted

---

[1] The document of the Mesa of the Misericórdia was dated 15 February 1722. The two copies are in APB, *Ordens régias*, vol. 15, doc. 16b–d and ASCMB, vol. 162, ff. 3–5v, both being in an appalling condition.

[2] Letter of the Mesa of 25 July 1734 to the High Court judge enquiring into the petition (ASCMB, vol. 52, ff. 143–145v).

this favour in 1736. There were two conditions: first, that a certificate of membership of the brotherhood be forwarded to the Misericórdia before the funeral of a brother; secondly, that this privilege only applied to the funerals of brothers.[1] Similar petitions were made by other coloured brotherhoods in the eighteenth century. The Misericórdia rejected each one. The manner in which Dom João V failed to support the Misericórdia in the case of the Brotherhood of St Benedict was significant. We will return to this later (pp. 270–1) in connection with the hospital of the Misericórdia when there was a similar hardening of attitude on the part of the Portuguese Crown towards the Misericórdia.

The circumstances surrounding the granting of biers to coloured brotherhoods permit a clearer understanding of the reasons why the Misericórdia denied a similar privilege to the tertiaries of St Francis. The Brotherhoods of Our Lady of Succour and of Our Lady of Guadalupe had been granted the use of a bier for the funerals of slave members only. The majority of the brothers of the Rosary and St Benedict were also slaves. By granting privileges to these brotherhoods, the Misericórdia was relieved of a moral responsibility to bury all the slaves of Bahia — clearly an impossible task. The stipulation that all emancipated Negroes and mulattos should be buried by the Misericórdia was dictated by financial considerations since these would have been in a position to afford the cost of burial using the Misericórdia bier. By sharing the moral obligation for the burial of slaves the Misericórdia was providing itself with a line of defence against criticism of inadequate facilities for the burial of slaves. In short, the Misericórdia had little to lose by granting biers to the coloured brotherhoods, and the number of priests and soldiers buried annually would not have affected the income of the Misericórdia. This would not have been the case if the Third Order had also possessed a bier. The brothers of the Misericórdia were drawn from the same social class as those of the Third Order. Many testators ordered that they should be carried on the bier of the Misericórdia and buried in the habit of St Francis, often in the chapel of the Third Order. Alms were granted for these services. If the Third Order had possessed a bier the Misericórdia would have received nothing, and the alms for the bier were often substantial. One seventeenth-century Provedor, Bernardim Fernandes Barros, had left 100$000 to the brotherhood for this last act and benefactors

---

[1] Royal *provisão* of 13 January 1736 (BNRJ, 11–33, 32, 12; index no. 166).

such as António Dias de Ottões and António de Sá Doria made similar bequests.[1] Pride of privilege and economic considerations led the Misericórdia to deny vigorously the repeated petitions of the Third Order.

The Misericórdia offered complete facilities for funerals and burials. The brotherhood possessed three covered biers, known as *tumbas*. The best bier was reserved for the funerals of brothers. The other two were granted according to the social and financial position of the person to be buried. One was for the funerals of brothers whose cortèges were not accompanied by the Misericórdia. It was also on hire to people willing to pay the fee of 8$480. The other bier was for the funerals of those of modest circumstances on payment of a fee of 4$480. It was also used for charitable funerals of the poor of the city and suburbs. The Misericórdia regarded its biers as symbols of prestige. They were kept in perfect condition and replaced frequently. In 1735 the brotherhood commissioned an embroiderer to make a new cloth to cover the biers. The cloth was to be of black velvet, fringed with gold brocade, and with floral decorations also of the best brocade available. The cost to the Misericórdia was 1,000$000 — the total average income from burials in any year.[2] The Misericórdia took less care in the maintenance of its litters, known as *esquifes*: these were little more than boards. The Misericórdia possessed three such litters. One, known as the *banguê*, was for the funerals of slaves at a cost of 800 *rs.* to their masters, a charge reduced to 400 *rs.* in 1695. The other two were first used in 1726 for the funerals of *anjinhos* ('little angels'), or babies. Fees of 3$200 and 2$560 were levied for the use of these litters and they could be hired by anybody, irrespective of colour or status. The Misericórdia buried slaves and children charitably if the master or the parents were too poor to pay these fees.

Before 1693 the Misericórdia had maintained three biers, two of which were for hire. In 1693 it had inaugurated a litter for the funerals of slaves. In 1726 two more litters were provided for the funerals of infants. In a country with a large slave population and notorious for its high infant

[1] ASCMB, vol. 40, ff. 118–22.
[2] Pride dictated this extravagance. Condemning the old cloth as unfit for further use, the Mesa noted that 'se fazia de todos reparavel nos actos publicos em q' sahia a Rua, ao q' muito se devia de attender e olhar, tanto por ser credito da Miz.ª quanto por ser lustre da d.ª Irman.de' (ASCMB, vol. 14, ff. 217v–218v, cf. p. 229).

mortality rate, it was surprising that the Misericórdia should not have possessed litters for such funerals at a much earlier date. The reason why it did not cater for the burial of slaves and children earlier than these dates is not clear. The circumstances which induced the brotherhood to establish these three litters are similar and throw light on the changing attitudes of the authorities towards the Misericórdia.

Dom Pedro II had been much concerned about the conditions of the Negro in Brazil. In 1684 he had introduced a law to reduce the mortality of slaves on the crossing from West Africa to Brazil in the slave ships.[1] In 1688 he had ordered the Governor of Rio de Janeiro to investigate all allegations of cruelty by the masters against their slaves, and to take legal action against the masters if these allegations were shown to be true.[2] In 1693 he had written to the Chapter of the cathedral of Rio that measures should be enforced to ensure that the last sacraments were administered to all slaves on the point of death. It had been brought to the royal attention that this was not the case, partly because the priests demanded exorbitant fees, partly because the masters of the slaves refused to call a priest to a dying slave.[3] Letters from the king to his governors and archbishops rarely produced practical results. Nevertheless, they were evidence of strong royal concern for the living conditions of slaves in Brazil. On 4 October 1693, the Mesa of the Misericórdia of Bahia had established the *banguê* for the burial of slaves.[4] Possibly the brotherhood had hoped to augment its income from this source. Certainly the charge originally levied of 800 *rs*. offered some profit, although the Mesa had said that it would barely cover the costs of priests and the slaves to carry the litters. The archbishop had thought otherwise and instructed his flock to pay no more than 400 *rs*. for the use of the bier.[5] Possibly the Mesa had been moved by pious sentiments to provide for the burial of slaves. It is more likely that official pressure was exerted on the Misericórdia to bury slaves. If the Mesa failed to comply, the burial monopoly of the Misericórdia would end. The circumstances surrounding

---

[1] *Documentos historicos*, vol. 79, pp. 379–88.
[2] Letter of 20 March 1688 (ANRJ, *Códice 952*, vol. 4, f. 168).
[3] Letter of 17 March 1693 (ANRJ, *Códice 952*, vol. 6, f. 225).
[4] ASCMB, vol. 14, ff. 33v–34.
[5] The Mesa had appealed to the king in 1695 against this ruling of the archbishop (ASCMB, vol. 14, f. 45).

the establishment of a litter for the burial of slaves by the Misericórdia of Rio de Janeiro in May 1694 support this suggestion.

In January of 1694 Dom Pedro had ordered the Governor of Rio to ensure that all slaves received decent burial.[1] The king had suggested that he should enlist the help of the abbot of the Carmelites and that approaches be made to the Misericórdia to provide this service. The overtures had been successful and the Misericórdia had agreed in May 1694 to bury all slaves at a charge of 960 *rs.* each. Of this sum, 320 *rs.* were allocated to the saying of two masses, and the remaining 640 *rs.* were to cover the cost of expenses by the Misericórdia. This was exorbitant and in January 1695 the king had told the governor to reach a more reasonable agreement with the Misericórdia, on the basis of the fee of 400 *rs.* which had been levied in Bahia. The king had reminded his representative to observe the privileges granted to other brotherhoods for the use of biers. This broad hint had had the desired effect. On 25 May 1695 the Governor of Rio had reported to the king that the Misericórdia had agreed to bury slaves for 400 *rs.* only.[2] There can be no doubt that royal pressure had induced the Misericórdia of Rio to bury slaves and it is more than possible that this had also been the case in Bahia.

There is a similar degree of coincidence between official suggestion and Misericórdia action in the establishment of the two litters for the burial of children on 20 June 1726.[3] In this year the Misericórdia of Bahia inaugurated a turning wheel for foundlings. There can be no doubt that the motivator of the scheme was the Count of Sabugosa. The Mesa was far from unanimous in its approval of the motion supporting the foundation. No official threat could be made in this case because the *Compromisso* contained no clause for the care of foundlings. Nevertheless the Misericórdia established the turning wheel without any official financial aid and without any bequest for this purpose. The Count of Sabugosa did not mince words with those

---

[1] 'Vos encomendo muito especialmente a do meio q' se entendeo conveniente para q' os escravos possão ser enterrados com a decencia de Christãos; sobre o q' obrareis tudo o q' for necessr⁰ para q' se não continue mais tempo algum, hũa acção tão impropria, e tão contraria a carid^e q' para com todos, negros e brancos, deve ser igual'. King to governor 23 January 1694 (ANRJ, *Códice 952*, vol. 7, f. 18).   [2] ANRJ, *Códice 952*, vol. 7, f. 148 and vol. 8, f. 7.

[3] ASCMB, vol. 846, f. 130.

who did not fall in with his plans and the Misericórdia acquiesced meekly. Whether his proposals extended to litters for burials of children is not mentioned. Possibly the Mesa itself suggested this service in the hope of recovering some of the expenses incurred in the care of foundlings.[1]

By the eighteenth century the Misericórdia provided biers and litters for the funerals of people of all social classes, from the prosperous landowner to the impoverished slave. The Misericórdia was the only Bahian brotherhood to offer such funeral services to those who were not members of a brotherhood. Although the priests and soldiers and certain coloured brotherhoods could bury their own members, they were forbidden to make any charge for the use of a bier. Only the Misericórdia could derive income from burials, and only the Misericórdia (in theory) could undertake charitable burials. The records of the archives of the Misericórdia provide only partial evidence on the number of burials undertaken by the brotherhood. Burials using the biers of the Misericórdia were registered in the *Livros das tumbas*, of which the first (1685–1709), sixth (1735–53) and seventh (1753–8) are extant. All are in poor condition. The records of slave burials using the *banguê* are more deficient: the first register covers the years 1741–3, the second 1746–9, the third 1749–53 and the fourth has been lost. No separate record appears to have been kept for infant burials before 1753. The deficiencies of the burial registers can be remedied to some degree by reference to the account ledgers. By using information derived from a variety of sources an estimate can be made of the number of free people and slaves buried by the Misericórdia and the extent of this action of the Misericórdia in relation to the population of Bahia.

The Misericórdia carried some 300 free people annually on its biers to their graves. The majority of these were white citizens from within the urban area. With the exception of the priests and soldiers, the Misericórdia maintained a burial monopoly for white people. Thus the burials of white people recorded in the burial registers indicate the approximate mortality rate among the white urban population. The registers of the Misericórdia

---

[1] In 1656 the Misericórdia had authorised the cathedral sacristan to use an 'esquifezinho' he had built for the burial of children under six years old. The Mesa had ruled that the bier should be kept in the building of the Misericórdia and children over six could only be carried on it to their graves with the permission of the Mesa (ASCMB, vol. 13, ff. 75–6).

are sufficiently complete to provide total statistics for two periods, 1690–1704 and 1738–52. These are as follows:

Years	No. women buried	No. men buried	Total white burials
1690–94	407	1,098	1,505
1695–99	444	846	1,290
1700–04	478	738	1,216
	1,329	2,682	4,011
1738–42	569	805	1,374
1743–47	566	781	1,347
1748–52	427	706	1,133
	1,562	2,292	3,854

A comparison between the two periods, each of fifteen years, suggests two facts. First, the mortality rate among the white urban population remained approximately constant during the period 1690–1750 despite a population increase. There are two possible reasons for this: first, more effective sanitary measures for the inspection of all boats from Europe or Africa arriving at Bahia; secondly, the lesser number of outbreaks of plague in the eighteenth century. These two factors are inter-related because many of the epidemics of Bahia had originated in Africa and were transmitted by the transport of infected slaves. The second fact to emerge is the increase in the number of white women. In the earlier period 33.1 per cent of the total white burials were of women. In the later period there was an increase of 7.4 per cent, and 40.5 per cent of the total white burials were of women. Possible reasons for this significant increase may have been the drain of manpower to the mining areas in the early eighteenth century, the effectiveness of a royal decree of 1732 preventing the sending of women to Portugal, or simply that more families were emigrating to Brazil. Regulations concerning passports for immigrants were frequently not observed. Until more detailed statistics are available on immigration no definitive conclusions can be reached on white mortality or on the increase in the white female population of Bahia in the first half of the eighteenth century.

The lack of statistics bedevils the hope of relating accurately the figures quoted from the burial registers of the Misericórdia to the urban population of Bahia. The first censuses were ecclesiastical, based on parochial records of people of communicable age within each parish. In 1706 an archiepiscopal estimate for the city of Salvador, consisting of six parishes, calculated the number of communicants at 21,601. A similar count made in 1755 for the nine urban parishes placed the number of those of communicable age at 37,543.[1] The relationship of these estimates to the total population of the city cannot be ascertained. They excluded children who had not reached the age of puberty, adults who had not been baptised, and people without homes (*fogos*). Lay estimates were equally imprecise. A census of 1757 calculated the urban population at 37,323. Another census two years later by the engineer José António Caldas arrived at the slightly higher figure of 40,263 for the urban population. His estimate, based on parochial returns, did not include children under seven years of age, Indians, nuns or clerics. No reference is made to the proportion of slaves included in these totals. In 1714 the French engineer Frézier estimated that for every score of people in the streets of Bahia, nineteen were slaves.[2] Caldas, in 1759, estimated that every second person in Bahia was a slave. Although Frézier's estimate was more in the nature of a casual observation, it is likely that the proportion of black to white did decrease in the eighteenth century because of the migration of many slaves to the mines. Probably an estimate of the total population of the urban area at 80,000 in 1700, increasing by about two-fifths during the next half century, would not be too far wrong. About a quarter of this total population was adult and of fixed address in the city, and about a half (a conservative estimate for the earlier period) were coloured. A comparison of the statistics for the white people buried by the Misericórdia with these archiepiscopal estimates would suggest an approximate mortality coefficient per annum for the adult white urban population of 25/1,000 for the earlier period and 14/1,000 for the later years.[3]

The Misericórdia records for the burial of slaves do not permit even

---

[1] Accioli–Amaral, *Memorias historicas*, vol. 5, p. 503. Thales de Azevedo examines the difficulties surrounding demographic statistics in colonial Bahia in his *Povoamento da cidade do Salvador* (2nd ed., São Paulo, 1955), pp. 184–206. For the later part of the century see Dauril Alden, 'The Population of Brazil in the Late Eighteenth Century: a Preliminary Survey', in *Hispanic American Historical Review*, vol. 43 (1963), pp. 173–205.   [2] Frézier, *Relation du voyage*, p. 275.

[3] These may be compared with mortality estimates for the parish of the Passo (Bahia) at the end of the century. Thales de Azevedo has deduced mortality coefficients of 37.2/1,000 in 1798; 31.3/1,000 in 1799; 43.3/1,000 in 1800. The

approximate calculations for slave mortality. This was notoriously high, and the average working life of a slave on a plantation did not exceed ten years. Slaves in domestic service in the city could probably have expected a longer life span. Many achieved a degree of liberty. The women sold sweetmeats on the streets or acted as washerwomen or cooks. Some male slaves were qualified as masons, carpenters or painters and were themselves employers of slaves. The average number of slaves buried each year by the Misericórdia in the eighteenth century was in the region of 600.[1] This represented only a small proportion of the number of slaves who died annually, but it must be remembered that the Negro brotherhoods had assumed responsibility for the burial of their own members, many of whom were slaves.

The Misericórdia also carried children to their burials, from 1726, on two litters made for this purpose. Here again, there are no natality figures for the earlier part of the eighteenth century, nor are there figures for the infant mortality among coloured and white families respectively.[2] Nor are the registers of the Misericórdia any more informative as to the number of infant burials made annually by the brotherhood. The account ledgers suggest some eighty to a hundred burials annually in the 1730s. This number dropped sharply in the next two decades, because of a change of custom in the burial of the 'angels of Heaven'. Instead of being carried to their graves on litters, they were carried on *tabuleiros*, or trays.[3] In 1754 the Misericórdia buried twenty children, and in 1755 only sixteen.[4]

The Misericórdia collected fees for the use of its biers and litters. It also buried all classes of the population charitably. No charges were levied for

---

approximate mortality coefficient for the parish of Sto António além do Carmo was 32.5/1,000 in 1776 and for the parish of the Sé 21.3/1,000 in 1785. These figures are based on the total population for these parishes (*Povoamento*, p. 205, n. 225).

[1] This is based on the accounts ledgers for receipts. Detailed records are only available for 1709–11 when 1,273 slaves were buried by the Misericórdia and 1715–17 when 1,363 slaves were buried. From July 1741 to December 1743 there were 1,369 burials and in the years 1744–5 there were 1,275 (ASCMB, vol. 846 and vol. 15, ff. 22v–23).

[2] Estimates of infant mortality and natality for the latter part of the century are in Thales de Azevedo, *Povoamento*, pp. 204–6. Cf. Gilberto Freyre, *The Masters and the Slaves*, p. 382, n. 288 for the early nineteenth century in Pernambuco.

[3] BNRJ, 11–33, 24, 45, doc. 31.   [4] ASCMB, vol. 1256.

such burials, although frequently the Misericórdia had to admonish its priests for demanding payment from the relatives of poor people. The charitable burials recorded in the registers of the Misericórdia were of free people. These represent some 21 per cent of all funerals using the biers of the Misericórdia. The fact that only a tenth of such burials were of coloured people indicates the high proportion of 'poor whites' in colonial Bahia. The effect of this charitable action of the Misericórdia on the total population must have been small. Nevertheless that a fifth of the burials undertaken by the Misericórdia were charitable, representing a financial loss to the brotherhood, awakes respect rather than censure. In the months of May and June 1686, when an outbreak of plague struck the city, the Misericórdia made over 200 charitable burials.[1] With regard to the number of slaves buried charitably by the Misericórdia in the eighteenth century this was some 5 per cent of the total number of slaves carried on the *banguê* of the brotherhood. Whether this low figure was because the Misericórdia tended to ignore poor slaves, or whether the coloured brotherhoods provided adequately for their burial, is not known.

The manner of burial depended on the financial resources of the person to be buried. All those people who could afford to pay the fee for the biers of the Misericórdia could afford coffins. The poor people were buried in shrouds supplied by the Misericórdia for charitable burials. The great fear of the poor was that their bodies should simply be thrown into an earth grave. Some went so far to guard against this eventuality as to buy a coffin with their life savings. Others asked that their bodies should be wrapped in carpets, hammocks or straw mats. This fear was well founded. The Misericórdia cemetery was little more than such in name. Communal graves barely below ground level were the burial places for the very poor and slaves. Luís dos Santos Vilhena severely criticised the superficiality of the act of interment in the cemetery of the Misericórdia towards the end of the eighteenth century.[2] In the nineteenth century, the English traveller Maria

---

[1] ASCMB, vol. 1251.

[2] Luiz dos Santos Vilhena, *Recopilação de noticias soteropolitanas e brasilicas contidas em XX cartas, que da cidade do Salvador Bahia de Todos os Santos escreve hum a outro amigo em Lisboa, debaixo de nomes alusivos, noticiando-o do estado daquella cidade, sua capitania, e algumas outras do Brasil* (2 vols., Bahia 1922), vol. 1, pp. 154–5.

Graham saw the arm of a Negro sticking out of the sand on the shore of Recife. The conditions in Bahia a century earlier cannot have been any better, and the presence of dogs prowling round the city and living off corpses lent some weight to the fears of the poorer people.

The place of burial depended to a lesser degree on financial position. On the plantations of the Recôncavo the patriarchal spirit of family cohesion had led to the custom of burying the dead under the house or chapel. Slaves of long service with the family were similarly buried, and there was a small cemetery for other slaves near to the chapel.[1] In the city there was greater social distinction and greater socio-racial prejudice. The common practice in colonial Bahia was for all free people to be buried in churches. This was the practice in the Misericórdia for all burials, including those of brothers who wished to be buried there. The Third Orders of St Francis and the Carmelites had ossuaries for their members. These aroused the envy of the Misericórdia and in 1775 a stonemason was appointed to convert the old female ward of the hospital below the sacristy into a place for the burial of brothers.[2] Citizens of Bahia who were not brothers were carried on the bier of the Misericórdia to be buried in one of the parish churches. This practice was very unhygienic. In the Misericórdia itself people who died in the hospital were buried in the cloister very near to a water cistern built under the cloister in 1702 to supply water to the hospital.

The Misericórdia also maintained a cemetery at the Campo da Pólvora. This was in use in the eighteenth century, but whether it had been founded earlier is not mentioned in the records of the Misericórdia. The situation of this cemetery was heavily censured by Vilhena, because the daily breezes passed over it before arriving at the city. Moreover, it was too small for the number of bodies buried, measuring only thirty-two yards by forty-eight yards with no room for expansion.[3] This cemetery was reserved primarily for the burial of slaves carried on the *banguê* of the Misericórdia. Many slaves did not even receive this burial. As late as 1814 the Count of Arcos

---

[1] Gilberto Freyre, *The Masters*, pp. 439–40.

[2] Pride dictated this construction: 'Foi proposto pelo dito Irmão Provedor, que sendo esta Irmandade da Santa Mizericórdia tão ilustre, e principal entre todas as mais desta Cidade, se achava sem hum cemiterio ou carneiro, em que se sepultassem os corpos dos seus Irmãos defuntos . . .'. Minute of 19 March 1775 (ASCMB, vol. 15, f. 239). [3] António Joaquim Damázio, *Tombamento*, chapter 7.

issued a decree that the practice of leaving the bodies of slaves at the doors of churches must cease. He ordered that the night watchmen be especially vigilant in arresting any Negro found depositing a body in this manner, and that the carrier be imprisoned until the cost of a decent burial was paid by the owner of the dead slave.[1] The wording of the petition of the Brotherhood of St Benedict is sufficient evidence that this practice was common in the previous century. Some owners of dead slaves disposed of their bodies by binding them to pieces of wood and sending them out on the tide.[2] At the other end of the scale were those owners who went so far as to commission a bier of the Misericórdia for the funeral of a slave. Esteem for the slave was tempered by the vanity of the master. This practice increased in the eighteenth century and it cannot have been mere chance that the majority of slaves so honoured were female![3] Some masters even ordered the *tumba boa* at a cost of 8$480 for a favourite. In such cases the Misericórdia renounced ethnic pride for financial gain. A male slave to be so honoured was Chinese with the very Portuguese name of Carlos, buried in the cathedral of Bahia in 1747.[4]

In the rejection of petitions by other brotherhoods for biers, the Misericórdia alleged that it would sustain severe financial loss if such petitions were granted. The ledgers of receipt and expenditure are sufficiently complete to give a full picture of the income derived by the Misericórdia from burials and the proportion of such income to the total income received by the

[1] 'Devendo em fim acabar huma vez nesta Capital Costumes barbaros e desconhecidos de todos os outros homens; e sendo hum delles o de conduzir de noite, e abandonar Cadáveres junto ás Portas das Igrejas com escandalo da Natureza, e de tudo o q' há de mais sagrado na Sociedade humana; Ordeno q' os Capitães da Ronda da Cidade, e os Officiaes inferiores Comm^es das Patrulhas nocturnas vigiem com a maior attenção nas immediações dos Adros das Igrejas de tal maneira q' infalivelm^te sejão prezos os Conductôres, depois de ser obrigados a conduzir os cadáveres q' levavão até o lugar q' para esse fim foi destinado pela Meza da St^a Caza da Mizericórdia . . .'. Decree of 26 July 1814. (ASCMB, vol. 162, f. 126).

[2] Gilberto Freyre, *The Masters*, p. 441.

[3] From 1685 to 1709 only two female slaves were carried on the biers of the Misericórdia on payment by their masters. In the period 1735–55 a total of 137 slaves received this treatment, of which eighty were female.

[4] This was in March 1747: 'Em 2º do dº faleceo Carlos china de nação escravo de Faustino Pires Chaves morador na freg^a da Sê sepultado na d^a Sê na Tumba da Charid^e de q' se deu de esmolla 4$480' (ASCMB, vol. 1252, f. 260).

brotherhood. The Misericórdia charged 4$480 and 8$480 for the use of a bier. These fees were variable on some rare occasions.[1] In an average year the Misericórdia received 1,000$000 from the hire of biers. The charge for slave burials had been established initially at 800 *rs.*, reduced to 400 *rs.* in the 1690s, and later restored. The average income received annually by the Misericórdia from this source was 200$000. The bier for the funerals of infants earned 485$840 in its first year of operation.[2] This source of income decreased and in the five years 1750–5, the Misericórdia received a total of only 230$520 for the funerals of children. The allegation by boards of guardians that the concession of burial privileges to other brotherhoods would be prejudicial to the Misericórdia does not appear to have been justi-fied. The evidence available only provides an answer with regard to the extension of this privilege to the Brotherhood of St Benedict in 1736. In the fifteen years 1716–31 the Misericórdia received 3,089$120 for slave burials. In the period 1736–51 it received practically the same amount, 2,988$780. The income derived from funerals and burials was remarkably constant for each year. The average total annual income of the Misericórdia in the first half of the eighteenth century was in the region of 16,000$000. The income from biers and the *bangué* represented about 8 per cent of this total annual income.[3] The income from the burials of babies after 1726 raised this to about 10 per cent. Although comparatively small financially, this income was of great importance to the Misericórdia. Whereas the hospital, prison aid, the turning wheel and even dowries were liabilities, the money received by the Misericórdia for funerals and burials bore no further commitment and placed the brotherhood under no obligation.

The income derived by the Misericórdia from burials was not total profit. Upkeep and replacement of the biers and litters was not costly: a new bier cost 10$080 in 1702 and the *bangué* cost only 3$520 in 1705.[4] The most expensive item of the bier was the cloth: for the *bangué* and the bier for

---

[1] In the seventeenth century the fee had been about 4$000; in the eighteenth century it varied between 3$620 and 8$480 (BNRJ, 11–33, 24, 45, doc. 31).

[2] ASCMB, vol. 846, f. 130.

[3] This was to diminish in the nineteenth century. In the printed account for the year 1814–15, the biers earned 212$560 and the *bangué* 466$400. The total income for this year was 24,667$905 (ANRJ, *Caixa 129*, doc. 32).

[4] ASCMB, vol. 850, f. 227 and f. 255v.

charitable burials even this was not costly, but the vanity of the Mesa led to extravagance on the drape for the best bier. In 1737 the Mesa spent 800$000 on a gold-embroidered cloth. When this had to be replaced in 1762 the board of guardians economised to the extent of omitting the embroidery, but the bill still came to 400$000.[1] The Misericórdia provided the funeral shrouds for those buried charitably, a small but constant expense. The priests of the parishes where the burial was made received 240 *rs.*, and the priest of the Misericórdia who accompanied the bier received a small fee. The cost of opening and closing the grave was also borne by the Misericórdia for charitable burials.

The heaviest expenditure was on salaries. The choir, consisting of a president, master of the chapel and some nine priests, would have to have been maintained by the Misericórdia in any case for the saying of masses and the religious ceremonies of the brotherhood. The cost of saying masses for brothers, amounting to some 350$000 annually, can similarly be regarded as a necessary expenditure implied in the conditions of membership of the Misericórdia. The use of a bier demanded few employees. There were from seven to nine carriers of the biers, known popularly as *gatos pingados* ('spotted cats'). Their annual wages were 16$000, in addition to which they received a quarter of manioc flour every ten days, fish oil for their lamps, and a daily ration of food. These could be promoted to the post of *homem de azul*, a general factotum. The annual salary of the *homem de azul* was 20$000, and he received a blue cloak of office, six pairs of shoes each year and a daily ration of food. All the carriers of the biers and the two *homens de azul* were accommodated in or near the Misericórdia. The *banguê* had no regular carriers. Whereas the carriers of the biers had to be white by statute but were, one suspects, light mulattos, the carriers of the *banguê* were slaves employed by the Misericórdia. There can be no doubt that the general expenditure on masses and burials was high: but if certain items are discounted because they constituted the obligations of the Misericórdia towards its brothers, the actual cost of the service of hiring out biers was small in comparison with the returns.

The burial services of the Misericórdia were comprehensive. It provided burials for its brothers and their families. The Misericórdia also buried charitably those people, free or slave, too poor to afford decent burial. These

[1] ASCMB, vol. 852, f. 67 and vol. 15, ff. 149v–150.

activities were not practised solely by the Misericórdia. The Misericórdia was unique in that it provided a burial service for the general use of the community, jealously preserving the sole right to charge for the hire of biers. The effect of this burial monopoly was that although the Misericórdia provided adequately for the burial of white citizens, it did not cater for the burial of slaves to the same degree. Gilberto Freyre, the Brazilian sociologist, severely censures the Misericórdias and Church for failure in the burial of slaves.[1] It must be realised that the Misericórdia of Bahia never attempted to provide burial for the total slave population. The concessions of biers to the coloured brotherhoods were indicative of the willingness of the Misericórdia to share this burden. The only criticism that can be levelled was that the Misericórdia ought to have delegated total responsibility to the Negro brotherhoods for the burial of slaves. Any assessment of the action of the Misericórdia in providing a burial service for colonial Bahia must take into account the contemporary attitude towards burials. In eighteenth-century Bahia there were no laws dealing with burials. There was only one cemetery. The roads were in poor condition. Communication was difficult. Burials under churches or in a cramped cemetery were unhygienic. The abandonment of bodies under cover of night or the throwing of corpses into the sea was inhumane. But these were common practices in colonial Brazil, and the twentieth-century reader must acknowledge this fact, however distasteful it may be to him. Only then can an appreciation be reached of the positive and even innovatory rôle played by the Misericórdia in providing burial services for the populace of Bahia in the eighteenth century.

[1] Gilberto Freyre, *The Masters*, p. 441.

10

Justice and Charity

CRIME was rampant in the Portuguese empire: crimes committed not by Africans, Indians, Chinese or Amerindians, but by loyal subjects of the Portuguese Crown. In the sixteenth century the Orient had been a happy hunting ground for the dishonest and the unscrupulous. The pickings had been lucrative and easily gained. Brazil had only become an attractive proposition for criminal activities with the discovery of gold and diamonds in Minas Gerais in the 1690s. The difficulties faced by the Portuguese authorities in enforcing law and order in Asia and Brazil were virtually insuperable. The major problem in both cases was the extent of the area to be policed. On the one hand were the expanses of the Indian Ocean and South China Sea with an abundance of islands offering safe havens to any pirate. On the other was a coastline reaching from the jungles of the Amazon to the plains of Rio Grande do Sul, and an interior much of which had only been partially explored and defined even in the nineteenth century.

The enforcement of law and order was less effective in Portuguese Asia than in Portuguese America. This is largely explicable by the different courses taken by the Portuguese expansion in the two continents. In Asia an initial phase of military conquest had given way to an era of mercantile activity. The capture of Gôa by Affonso de Albuquerque in 1510 had been the climax of the first phase. The agreement negotiated by Lionel de Sousa, leading to the Portuguese settlement at Macao in 1555–7, had represented the supreme achievement of the second phase. The settlements of Portuguese, ranging from Sofala to the Moluccas, had been mainly urban. They had been composed of a floating population of opportunists who had come to the Orient in the hope of acquiring wealth quickly and then returning to Portugal. The Portuguese soldier and chronicler, Diogo do Couto, disillusioned by the nature of the Portuguese empire in Asia, wrote at the end

234

of the sixteenth century: 'They have no intent other than to harvest and carry off the fruit of this vineyarde very three years.'[1] Diogo do Couto had been referring here to the viceroys' triennial period of office, but his mordant aphorism was equally applicable to the many Portuguese lured to the East in search of ready profit.

This spirit of opportunism was present in all ranks of officials from the viceroy down to the most humble factor. The members of the judiciary were not immune to the prevailing atmosphere. The *ouvidor geral*, or chief justice, was posted to Gôa for three years and usually made a fortune before his return to Portugal. Even the *desembargadores*, or High Court judges, whose longer term of office was intended to give a degree of stability and continuum to the administration of justice, achieved wealth far in excess of their salaries within a short space of time. Ill-qualified and badly paid, these judges were willing accomplices in embezzlement, bribery and perjury. The principle of 'Dog does not eat dog' characterised the relationship between judge and criminal in the East. Even without the all-prevailing dishonesty among the judiciary, it is doubtful if justice could have been enforced in the Orient. The presence of highly organised crime before the arrival of the Portuguese and the ease with which wealth in gold could be obtained were insuperable obstacles to law and order. Moreover the Portuguese authorities never attempted to establish liaison with local potentates for law enforcement. Once a criminal passed the immediate limits of Gôa, Macao or the smaller settlements, he was to all intents and purposes a free man.

In Brazil the stress from the outset had been on colonisation rather than the establishment of outposts. The hoe had replaced the sword as the instrument for survival. Small sugar plantations had been established in the Recôncavo of Bahia before 1549. Tomé de Sousa had founded the capital of Portuguese America, but the City of The Saviour had been in no way a purely urban settlement. The *Regimento* given to Tomé de Sousa by Dom João III revealed the change of attitude in the royal policy towards the overseas possessions. These instructions had provided for all aspects of administration, be they civil, economic, social, military or juridical.

[1] 'Já se não pretende senão levar, e vindimar cada três anos esta vinha', Diogo do Couto, *O soldado prático* (ed. Rodrigues Lapa, Lisboa, 1937), p. 79. He severely criticised the shortcomings of the judiciary, op. cit., 2ª parte, cena 3ª.

Appointments of officials had been made in Lisbon before the departure of the fleet. These had included the appointment of Dr Pedro Borges as chief justice of Brazil. He had been accompanied by a private secretary and a *meirinho*, or minor court official. Thus the problem of law enforcement in Brazil had been faced even before the foundation of a capital. Within a short time the legal machinery was in full operation. The city of Bahia had been founded to provide an administrative centre for an extra-urban area whose extent had then still to be defined, but over which the authorities had assumed juridical responsibility. Colonisation had increased in the sixteenth and seventeenth centuries. Brazilian-born Portuguese had been sent to Coimbra to study law and had returned to Bahia to practise their profession. A body of native-born Brazilians had come to hold office in the Appeals Court of Bahia. This had assured a degree of continuity in the administration of justice which had been totally absent in the Orient.

If, in some respects, Dom João III had learnt from the experience of Dom Manuel I, there had been one aspect in which the royal attitude had remained unchanged. This had been the function of the new-found territories as dumping grounds for convicts. Throughout the sixteenth, seventeenth and eighteenth centuries Asia, Africa and Brazil were places of exile for convicts. Once these exiles, or *degredados*, reached their destination they received no assistance from the authorities. Many turned to further crime and were imprisoned in the local gaols. Here also the civil authorities ignored their physical welfare and many died of disease and malnutrition in the prisons of Bahia and Gôa. The only organization to provide for the material needs of prisoners was the Misericórdia. In India many prominent Jesuits had praised this action of the brotherhood.[1] The French traveller, Pyrard de Laval, himself a prisoner in the gaol of Cochin in 1608, had had cause to be thankful for the daily ration of cooked rice and fish distributed by the brothers of the Misericórdia.[2] In Bahia, the brotherhood performed similar charitable deeds. In this action the Misericórdia had been practising a European tradition of prison aid, whose final act had been the burial of those condemned to death.

[1] Silva Rêgo, *Documentação*, vol. 3, no. 8; vol. 5, no. 36; vol. 9, no. 71.
[2] Pyrard de Laval, *Voyage de François Pyrard de Laval*, vol. I, chapter 28, p. 464. He also commended the charity of the brothers of the Misericórdia in the Gôa prison (vol. II, chapter 1, p. 22).

In fifteenth-century Italy there had been at least one brotherhood in every city responsible for the removal from the scaffold and burial of the bodies of criminals hanged by justice. For many brotherhoods the interment had represented the final charitable act towards prisoners assisted by the brotherhood during their lives. This assistance had been material and spiritual. In 1497 the Brotherhood of S. Corona in Milan had appointed one of its brothers to visit the prison and distribute food. This brotherhood had also assisted prisoners gaoled for small debts.[1] In Florence, the Brotherhood of S. Giovanni Decollato had been founded in 1488 to attend to the spiritual welfare of prisoners condemned to death. On the day of execution the criminal had been accompanied to the gallows by the entire brotherhood, chanting penitential psalms. After execution the brothers had carried his body back to their private cemetery for burial.[2]

In Portugal the Misericórdia had provided similar assistance for prisoners. Two brothers from the board of guardians, one of each class, had been elected annually to supervise this charitable work. They had been known as the *mordomos dos presos*, or stewards of the prisoners. They had been responsible for the cleanliness of the prisons of Lisbon and their duties had included the distribution of rations to prisoners and arranging for the priests of the brotherhood to hear confessions in the gaols. On the day of an execution the brotherhood had accompanied the condemned man to the scaffold and had buried his body afterwards. In one respect the Misericórdia had progressed beyond the Italian brotherhoods in assisting prisoners. It provided legal counsel for certain criminals and defended their cases in the Appeals Court.

Privileges had been granted to the Misericórdia to facilitate the administration of social aid to prisoners. Dom Manuel I had given the brotherhood the status of a semi-bureaucratic institution to provide for the welfare of prisoners. The privileges granted to the Misericórdia have already been discussed (pp. 17–19) and will be briefly summarised here. They fell into two groups — financial and legal. All legal costs were waived for prisoners defended by the Misericórdia, and gratuities could not be

---

[1] G. M. Monti, *Le confraternite medievali*, vol. I, p. 96. Other brotherhoods assisting prisoners are described in vol. I, chapters 5–7.

[2] Ludwig Pastor, *The History of the Popes* (English trans., 40 vols., London, 1899–1961), vol. 3, p. 32.

claimed by officials before presenting cases to the Appeals Court. The brothers of the Misericórdia enjoyed freedom of access to all prisons and were at liberty to question any criminal. In the city of Lisbon the Misericórdia held the monopoly for the collection of alms for prisoners. The brotherhood also received a free supply of meat for distribution in the prisons. The legal privileges of the Misericórdia were primarily concerned with expediting the sluggish course of justice. Criminal judges visited the prisons weekly to examine cases, the scribe of the Misericórdia had the status of public notary and the stewards of the prisoners had the right to speak first in any session of the courts.

The Misericórdia of Bahia had been granted the use of these privileges by a royal decree of 1622. Local authorities did not always respect these privileges. Nevertheless the Misericórdia did manage to fulfil the conditions of the *Compromisso* providing for the care of prisoners. The problems faced by the judiciary in Brazil differed from those previously encountered in Portugal and Asia. A brief survey of the problems faced by the Portuguese Crown in the maintenance of law and order in Brazil will provide a background for the action of the Misericórdia in the Court of Appeals and prison of colonial Bahia.

Justice in Bahia was administered at two levels. The first was municipal, represented by the city council. The second was higher and represented by the *Relação*, or High Court. The city council was a court of the first instance with two *juízes ordinários*, or Justices of the Peace.[1] These were citizens of social standing and undoubted integrity who were elected annually. They had no legal training and were scornfully treated by the trained Crown lawyers. This contempt gave rise to much ill-feeling between the municipal authorities and the Crown representatives.[2] In 1696, the office of *juíz ordinário* was abolished in Bahia.[3] From this date the senior Crown lawyer, known as the *juíz de fora*, or district magistrate, presided over the city council. The legal powers of the city council were reduced and

---

[1] There was only one *juíz ordinário* in 1550, 1580, 1614, 1683, 1685, 1686, 1688, 1689 and 1690. For a more or less complete list see Affonso Ruy, *Historia da Câmara*, pp. 347–57.

[2] Rivalry between the city council and the judiciary is discussed in C. R. Boxer, *Portuguese Society*, pp. 74–5, 86, 144–5 and 148.

[3] Affonso Ruy, *Historia da Câmara*, p. 357.

municipal affairs were dominated by the judiciary.

The highest Court of Appeals in Brazil was the *Relação*. The *Relação* had been established in Bahia in 1609, suppressed in 1625 because of the Dutch occupation, and re-established in 1652.[1] The senior legal officer was the chancellor, sent out from Lisbon every three years. During the years when the *Relação* was not functioning the *ouvidor geral* headed the judiciary. The chancellor exercised authority over all areas of Brazil and was second only to the governor-general or viceroy in power. Judgements in the Court of Appeals were passed by *desembargadores*, many of whom were sent from Lisbon. The influence exercised by these High Court judges over the city council and brotherhoods was enormous. Their monopoly of the post of Provedor of the Misericórdia during the early eighteenth century was only broken by viceroyal intervention. Lesser posts were those of *juiz de fora* and *corregedor da comarca*, both established in 1696. In 1742 a *juiz do crime* was appointed to deal with criminal cases only. The final court of appeal was the *Casa da Suplicação* in Lisbon. In India, Diogo do Couto had commented bitterly on the arbitrary nature of justice, because the judges had been confident that the victim would have neither time nor money to appeal to Lisbon. This was not the case in Brazil. There were frequent appeals not only to the *Casa da Suplicação* but to the king himself. In the latter case the king ordered enquiries to be made to ensure that justice was done, even if the appellant were a Negro or mulatto.

Although civil and criminal courts existed at Bahia, the administration of justice was often deficient. In Brazil there had not been that same feeling of opportunism which had characterised the judiciary in the Orient, but there had been similar complaints of *falta de justiça*, or lack of justice. It is difficult to estimate how far these complaints were justified. Certainly the repeated complaints by the city councillors of Bahia about the failings of the judges of the High Court can be taken *cum grano salis*. Complaints against judges influenced by family ties were often well founded.

The fact that Brazil had been colonized rather than merely occupied had

---

[1] It was suppressed by a decree of 5 April 1625. Pedro Calmon suggests this was because of the upheaval wrought by the Dutch occupation, *Historia da civilização brasileira* (3rd ed., São Paulo, 1937), p. 151. Sebastião da Rocha Pitta, *Historia da America Portugueza*, livro 5, $110–11, suggests financial motives to save expenditure on salaries for the Crown officials.

I

had a decisive influence on the administration of justice. On the one hand, it had meant the acceptance of juridical responsibility for the territory so vaguely defined by the papal treaty of Tordesillas in 1494. On the other hand, it had meant the creation of a land-owning aristocracy. It had become traditional for at least one of the sons of such families to return to Portugal to study law at Coimbra. On finishing his studies, the son would return to Bahia to practise his profession. His advancement would depend as much on his family background as on his own ability. In such a closely inter-married society as Bahia, it was inevitable that every family of social standing would have some relative in the High Court who could be relied upon to protect the family interests. In response to numerous complaints by the municipal council that family ties were perverting the course of justice, the Crown decreed in 1670 that in future Brazilian-born judges could serve only in Portugal and the colonies but not in Brazil.[1] Such a law was only partially effective. Many judges sent out from Portugal married into the families of the land-owning aristocracy after arriving in Brazil.

One of the most serious murder cases in Portuguese America of the eighteenth century was nullified because of family ties between certain judges and the accused. This *cause célèbre* involved one of the leading land-owning families of colonial Bahia, the Dias d'Avila family of the House of Tôrre. Francisco Dias d'Avila, the third of this name, Knight of the Order of Christ, Familiar of the Holy Office, and Master of the Field of the auxiliaries, died on 1 April 1750. His premature death caused no surprise as he had been in ill health for some time. Shortly afterwards his widow, Catharina Francisca Correia de Aragão, remarried. In 1753 rumours that Francisco Dias had been poisoned led to an investigation by the criminal judge of Bahia. Despite medical evidence testifying to the natural death of Francisco Dias, the goods of his widow and her second husband were confiscated, and both imprisoned. The evidence of witnesses, mostly slaves, was contradictory and the viceroy referred the case to Lisbon. In 1754 the Overseas Council ordered a full enquiry, and in 1755 the criminal judge in Bahia submitted a report directly to Lisbon, by-passing the local High Court. All the enquiries were in vain. At the first suspicions the accused couple had

[1] C. R. Boxer, *Portuguese Society*, pp. 87–8.

been granted a pass of safe conduct (*carta de seguro*) by partisan judges of the High Court in Bahia which had guaranteed their immunity from further charges.[1]

Even in the rare instances when a family had no relative in the judiciary, it was enough to be of the landed aristocracy to ensure immunity from legal action. Local officials in some township of the Recôncavo were unwilling to risk the displeasure of a powerful family by bringing criminal charges against its members. When José Pereira Sodré of a noble Bahian family was murdered in 1732, his brother complained to the viceroy, stating the names of the murderers and the motive of the crime. Local evidence varied. A notary of Jaguaripe swore that the dead man had been wounded once in the head, whereas a doctor of Cachoeira testified to the presence of seventeen wounds. Despite the evidence, albeit conflicting, the Count of Sabugosa refused to act because the accused were 'people of distinction'. The brother appealed to the Crown, enquiries were held, but the murderers were not brought to justice.[2]

Justice in Brazil was also frequently frustrated by the sanctuary offered by the religious orders to criminals. In Rio de Janeiro the Carmelites and Benedictines were constant offenders in the eighteenth century, harbouring escaped slaves, criminals and debtors despite royal orders forbidding this practice. The friars were also receivers of stolen property and hid contraband within the monasteries. The Third Order of St Francis was equally permissive, allowing vagrants and criminals to sleep in its church and sacristy.[3] In Bahia the right of sanctuary was similarly abused. In 1713 Dom João V ordered the religious orders to expel all criminals and debtors, and in the 1740s the king threatened the board of guardians of the Third Order of St Francis with exile to Angola unless they desisted from sheltering criminals.[4] In addition to sheltering criminals, the monasteries of Bahia also

[1] Pedro Calmon, *História da Casa da Tôrre*, pp. 159–60 and the sources there quoted, to which may be added, APB, *Ordens régias*, vol. 49, ff. 37v–38v and vol. 51, ff. 88–90.

[2] APB, *Ordens régias*, vol. 29, docs. 60 and 60a; vol. 30, doc. 63; vol. 32, docs. 113 and 113a.

[3] ANRJ, *Códice 952*, vol. 19, ff. 208 and 278; vol. 23, ff. 1, 26, 46, 63 and 65; vol. 34, ff. 165–7.

[4] King to viceroy, 4 March 1713 (APB, *Ordens régias*, vol. 8, doc. 31). The document threatening deportation is missing from the bound volume of royal

provided hiding places for exiles who escaped from their guards while waiting for ships to take them to Angola.[1] Bahia was one of the outlets for smuggled gold and the monasteries afforded a safe hiding place until shipment could be arranged. In 1730 the Count of Sabugosa wrote in his own hand to the Secretary of State in Lisbon so that no third party should be aware of the contents of his letter, asking for permission to search monasteries which he suspected of hiding gold leaf or bars.[2]

As a lay brotherhood the Misericórdia was subject to civil jurisdiction and could not offer sanctuary in its administrative buildings. In 1704 it paid 8$000 to the Prior of St Theresa for the upkeep of a mulatto slave of the Misericórdia who was a fugitive from justice.[3] The only sanctuary the Misericórdia could offer was its church. The practice was not encouraged by the brotherhood who tried to avoid any civil or ecclesiastical intervention. Occasionally during the eighteenth century a priest was sheltered in the church on payment of 160 *rs*. daily.[4] In 1713 this right of sanctuary was put to the test. Joseph da Costa Ferreira, a brother of the Misericórdia, was escorting a petty criminal in his official capacity as sergeant of the garrison. On passing the Misericórdia the criminal escaped from his escort, dashed to the church of the Misericórdia and clung to the bolts securing the main door. Joseph da Costa Ferreira tore him away and placed him securely under arrest again. For this violation of the right of sanctuary the zealous sergeant was expelled from the brotherhood by the board of guardians.[5]

If family ties and the privilege of sanctuary impeded the course of justice

---

orders, but an index reference gives the substance of this: 'Sobre se passar ordem aos Ministros e ao Escrivão da Ordem 3ª de S. Francisco para que expulsem e não consintão homiziados nella, e constando o contrᵒ sejão prezos, e remettidos para Angola a ordem de S. Magᵉ.' This was probably issued in 1745 (APB, *Ordens régias*, vol. 43, index ref. to f. 91).

[1] BNRJ, 11–33, 32, 11.

[2] He complained of people who possessed gold dust illegally and 'busquem o segredo dos Conventos donde muytos comissarios e mineyros tem cofres particulares em que sem susto depositão os seus cabedaes tanto em dinheyro como em creditos, e escripturas', viceroy to secretary of state, 20 August 1730 (APB, *Ordens régias*, vol. 26, doc. 47).

[3] The expenditure ledger records payment of 8$000 'q' deu ao Prior de Santa Thereza do sustento do mulatto q' lá estava homiziado da Caza' (ASCMB, vol. 850, f. 253v).   [4] ASCMB, vol. 860, f. 51v.   [5] ASCMB, vol. 195, f. 46v.

in the urban area, in the large rural areas beyond the littoral region, the difficulties of maintaining law and order were almost insuperable. Whereas in the Orient the legal authorities had simply closed the dossier on any criminal who escaped beyond the cities, in Brazil the jurisdiction of the High Court of Bahia extended from the Maranhão to São Paulo. In the sixteenth and seventeenth centuries the *hinterland* of Bahia was largely unexplored, except by cattle ranchers. The discovery of gold and diamonds led to the establishment of mining camps in the interior. These were far from the arm of the law and the easy gains attracted many criminals. Even in the 1930s bandits, or *cangaceiros*, dominated the interior of the states of Pernambuco and southern Ceará, without fear of the law. How much more was this the case in the eighteenth century when there were inadequate communications, police or transport. The discovery of mineral deposits in the 1690s led to a wave of lawlessness in the interior. For the first time the authorities in Bahia were faced with the problem of maintaining justice in the interior.

The purely physical problem of maintaining justice over a vast area was aggravated by the transient nature of the criminal population. A criminal 'working' the mining area moved with ease from one encampment to another. A cattle rustler had only to drive his charges into another captaincy to escape all risk of capture. The Crown policy of exiling gypsies to Brazil contributed to the criminal population. These first appear in documents of the early eighteenth century. The families deported to Brazil had multiplied so rapidly that the area provided for them in Bahia in the Bairro da Palma had become too small and they had overflowed into adjoining parishes. By 1755 they had become a serious problem for the legal authorities. In the city they traded in horses and slaves as a cover for criminal activities, spoke their own language which had been forbidden by a law of 1647, and completely took over certain areas of the city. In the Recôncavo the situation was no better. They stole horses, held up travellers and were receivers of stolen goods. Even the tough miners paid for the corralling of their horses in a locked paddock in Cachoeira, when they came to Bahia.[1] Half-hearted suggestions by the Count of Arcos in 1757 that gypsy boys be apprenticed to a trade, the men be enlisted in the garrison, commerce be forbidden, and the families widely dispersed, were not implemented.[2]

---

[1] City council to king, 5 July 1755 (AMB, vol. 182, ff. 48–9).
[2] Viceroy to king, 12 October 1757 (APB, *Ordens régias*, vol. 59, ff. 122–3).

The High Court in Bahia was responsible for maintaining justice and conducting legal enquiries throughout Brazil. A Crown judge was supposed to make triennial visits to the various captaincies and set up local courts of enquiry. In practice this was rarely done. In the first twenty-four years following the re-establishment of a High Court in Bahia in 1652 no judge visited any of the villages even of the Captaincies of Bahia or Pôrto Seguro.[1] This negligence was because all expenses for such journeys were borne by the visiting judges, the travelling was rough and there was considerable risk to life and limb. Even when payments were made, the results were negligible.[2]

Governors and viceroys faced the problems of maintaining law and order with varying success. Dom João de Lencastre (1694–1702) had fought the problem of taking justice to the backlands by the establishment of townships in the Recôncavo. Such were Jaguaripe (1697), Cachoeira (1698) and São Francisco (1698). The Count of Sabugosa (1720–35) continued this policy, raising mining encampments to municipal status with their own Justices of the Peace and prisons. According to his reports to the Crown, the effects on the reduction of crime were spectacular. In the diamond encampment of Jacobina alone there were 532 murders by firearms in the years 1710–21. In 1721 the Count of Sabugosa gave Jacobina municipal status. With justifiable pride he reported to the king in 1725, that in the preceding four years there had only been two murders in Jacobina, both unpremeditated, one with a knife and the other with a sword.[3]

Certainly this policy of establishing municipalities did contribute to the reduction of crime, but the Count of Sabugosa was exaggerating in his suggestions that crime would be abolished by this measure. Jacobina continued as a den of thieves and the High Court in Bahia was no deterrent to the criminals of the interior. In 1732 the Count of Sabugosa himself lamented to the king that 'although many criminals have been executed and

---

[1] ANRJ, *Códice 540, assento* 60.

[2] On 4 February 1662 the Relação in Bahia decided that in addition to their salaries the *juiz ordinário* should receive 1$000 daily and his assistants 500 *rs.* daily as travelling expenses. This was to be collected from those criminals who were convicted (ANRJ, *Códice 540, assento* 33).

[3] Viceroy to king, 20 January 1725 (APB, *Ordens régias*, vol. 19, doc. 40).

hanged during my term of office as governor of this state, nevertheless such is the character of men who live in the most remote regions of the interior, that their freedom and absolute authority make them forgetful of these examples'.[1]

In 1742 an attempt was made to increase the efficiency of the juridical machinery by dividing the Captaincy of Bahia into two zones. The first was *Bahia do Norte* and continued to be administered from Bahia. The second was *Bahia do Sul* and was administered by a chief justice resident in Jacobina. Even with this division of legal responsibilities the southern zone occupied an area larger than the Iberian Peninsula and included the mining areas of Rio de Contas and Arassúahy.[2] The legal loophole afforded by the River S. Francisco which was the border with the Captaincy of Pernambuco was plugged in 1749 when the legal officers of both captaincies were given authority over both banks of the river.[3]

Crimes of all types were committed in colonial Bahia. Premeditated murder seems to have been infrequent. Robbery with violence and knife attacks were common. In 1721 the Count of Sabugosa described an attack by twenty armed men on the house of a wealthy miner. Although the owner and a slave were beaten up, the thieves' haul only amounted to one box containing 14,000 *cruzados* because the miner had deposited the bulk of his wealth in the monastery of St Theresa.[4] Drunken brawls were frequent, despite half-hearted municipal measures to restrict the distillation and sale of *cachaça*, or rum. In the eighteenth century there was a wave of robberies from churches, including that of the Misericórdia from which some candlesticks and gold plate were stolen.[5] After the discovery of gold and the establishment of a mint at Bahia in 1694, the making of false coinage flourished. With the discovery of diamonds, Bahia became the centre for the smuggling

---

[1] 'e não obstante se terem degolado e enforcado muitos, depois que governo este Estado, hé tal o genio dos homens, que vivem no sertão mays remoto, que a sua liberdade, e tirania os fas esquesser destes exemplos', viceroy to king, 16 September 1732 (APB, *Ordens régias*, vol. 28, doc. 78).

[2] APB, *Ordens régias*, vol. 38, docs. 62, 62a, 62b and 62c.

[3] Although a resolution to this effect had been taken in Lisbon on 28 November 1747, the king only informed the viceroy in a letter of 8 August 1749 (APB, *Ordens régias*, vol. 47, f. 112).

[4] APB, *Ordens régias*, vol. 15, doc. 59.

[5] ASCMB, vol. 14, f. 94.

of these jewels. As the distance from the city increased, so also did the number of crimes increase.

A reading of the minutes of the municipal council and the viceroyal correspondence suggests that the majority of offenders were coloured people. This may well have been the case simply because of the predominantly coloured population. Frequently also, a slave was the hired killer for a white person, or was made the scapegoat for a crime involving a prominent family. Escaped slaves were a constant source of disorder in the city. They became drunk and attacked passing citizens for money to buy food or facilitate their escape to the interior. The law also discriminated against Negroes. In the eighteenth century laws were issued forbidding a Negro to wear silk or fine wool, even if he were a free man. Nor was he allowed to carry a sword. This last law was later relaxed for white people of the lower classes, but not for Negroes.[1] Finally it is well to bear in mind that a coloured person would meet with less tolerance than a white offender when he was arrested.

Penalties were severe but curiously distributed. Punishments varied between monetary fines, branding, amputation of an ear, whipping or prison, and the heavier penalties of exile or execution. Social discrimination appeared, e.g. only a slave or freed Negro would be whipped: only a person of some social standing could obtain the privilege of being beheaded rather than hanged.[2] Minor misdemeanours were harshly punished whereas major crimes received comparatively light sentences. A petty official of the Treasury of Bahia who had pilfered public funds was hanged in 1723, whereas abduction and rape of a minor merited a monetary fine and ten years exile to Cape Verde.[3] Offenders were deported to Angola for vagrancy,

---

[1] An *alvará* of 24 May 1749 contained the clause: 'Ordeno que não possão trazer estas armas aprendizes de officios mecanicos, lacayos, mochillas, marinheiros, barqueiros, e fragateiros, negros, e outras pessoas de igual, ou inferior condição' (APB, *Ordens régias*, vol. 50, ff. 28–34). In a letter of 30 May 1753 the king asked the Governor of Rio de Janeiro to give his opinion concerning the petition by the free *pardos* of Rio for a relaxation of this law in their favour (ANRJ, *Códice 952*, vol. 37, ff. 129 and 131–2).

[2] In 1732 Colonel Francisco Dias do Prado, son of a prominent São Paulo family, was sentenced to be hanged for several murders, but 'mostrando nos ultimos embargos a sua nobreza, passou do Patibullo da forca ao Pillourinho donde o degularão' (APB, *Ordens régias*, vol. 28, doc. 78).

[3] APB, *Ordens régias*, vol. 17, doc. 73 and vol. 2, doc. 40.

thefts, or the carrying of weapons prohibited by law, and received sentences similar to criminals convicted of murder.[1]

The Misericórdia assisted the potential victims of this rather arbitrary form of justice. The stewards of the prisoners of the brotherhood visited the gaol of Bahia regularly. They drew up lists of those prisoners most deserving of legal and material assistance. Since it would have been impossible for the Misericórdia to help all the prisoners, certain conditions were stipulated. First, the prisoner had to be destitute. Secondly, the brotherhood was forbidden by statute from helping anyone gaoled for debt, failure to honour pledges, or who was awaiting deportation. Thirdly, only after having spent thirty days in gaol could a prisoner qualify for assistance. The names of prisoners meeting these requirements were entered on a roll kept by the stewards. These prisoners were then entitled to receive a ration of food, medical aid and legal counsel from the brotherhood.

The material aid afforded by the Misericórdia to criminals was centred on the prison of Bahia. The conditions in the prison were appalling. A sentence of imprisonment in the gaol of Bahia was tantamount to a death sentence. The official attitude towards criminals was that once they were under lock and key they ceased to exist. The prison of Bahia was a municipal responsibility. Since the city council was invariably in financial straits, imaginary or otherwise, no money was allocated either for the fabric of the prison or for the sustenance of prisoners. In 1660 cramped and insanitary conditions resulted in so much illness among prisoners, that the city council was compelled to enlarge the prison.[2] By 1681 the prison was in ruins and a petition was sent to the king asking for permission to levy a tax on fish-oil for the reconstruction.[3] During the energetic and popular governor-generalship of Dom João de Lencastre the prison was rebuilt, but within ten years further repairs were necessary and by 1736 the building was a total ruin.[4]

This situation was partly due to a division of responsibilities. The office of gaoler was let out on a contract basis to the *alcaide-mór*, an official responsible for the policing of the city. He nominated the gaoler to the city council and pledged a sum of money as security. The gaoler collected all

[1] A selection of these deportees is in C. R. Boxer, *Portuguese Society*, pp. 197–209.
[2] *Atas da Câmara* (6 vols., Bahia 1944–5?), vol. 4, pp. 50–1.
[3] *Cartas do Senado* (3 vols., Bahia 195?–3), vol. 2, pp. 93–5.
[4] AMB, vol. 176, f. 180.

fees payable by prisoners and forwarded these to the *alcaide-mór*. Faced with financial difficulties in the early eighteenth century the city council exploited this situation. First, the councillors alleged that the *alcaide-mór* was also responsible for the fabric of the prison, because he received prisoners' fees.[1] When this allegation failed to produce results, the councillors resorted to more forceful methods. 'Rigged' charges were brought against any gaoler nominated by the *alcaide-mór*: he was relieved of his duties and replaced by minor officials of the High Court (*meirinhos da Relação*) who paid no fees to the *alcaide-mór*. This was yet another instance of the increased influence of the Crown authorities over the city council, which has already been mentioned. The king upheld the complaints of the *alcaide-mór* in 1717 insisting that the councillors accept his nominees for the post of gaoler.[2] Nevertheless when the post of *alcaide-mór* was abolished both the Count of Sabugosa and the Count of Galvêas refused to allow the city council to use the fees collected from prisoners for repairs to the prison, and all such fees were received by the High Court.[3]

The prisoners were the victims of this administrative sniping. The cramped conditions resulted in epidemics. The sick and dying were ignored. Sanitation was absent. Rations were inadequate. Legal defence was not available. The prisoner was at the mercy of the municipal council and the High Court. The Misericórdia was the only brotherhood of Bahia to assist prisoners. It sought to relieve their discomfort by installing wooden bunks in the prison in 1706.[4] It may have been responsible for the establishment of a small ward for the sick within the prison.[5] The brothers distributed food regularly. The doctors of the Misericórdia visited the prison, treating prisoners and, where necessary, removing them to the hospital of the brotherhood. The lawyers of the Misericórdia undertook the legal defence of a prisoner, availing themselves of their privileged position

---

1 AMB, vol. 26, ff. 92v–93v.

2 APB, *Ordens régias*, vol. 11, doc. 34.

3 In a letter of 5 September 1736 the city council asked the king to permit these fees to be used for the rebuilding of the prison by the municipality (AMB, vol. 176, f. 180).   4 ASCMB, vol. 850, f. 273v.

5 The accounts' ledger for 1750 records expenditure of 12$000 for 'pinturas nas enfermarias da cadeia' (ASCMB, vol. 862, f. 109). I have been unable to establish whether or not this implies that the brotherhood had previously instituted a small ward in the prison, whose construction had been finished in 1750.

to secure an acquittal. The chaplains of the Misericórdia gave spiritual solace to the condemned.

The Misericórdia received no aid, financial or material, from official sources for the welfare of prisoners. The brotherhood was entirely dependent on charity.[1] The only major bequest received by the Misericórdia for the care of prisoners was of 6,282$302 left by João Alves Fontes in 1702. This was to be placed on loan, but it is doubtful if the complete legacy was ever collected. In 1754 the total patrimony existing for the care of prisoners was calculated at 3,424$500, giving an annual return of 214$031.[2] This was totally inadequate to meet the costs of food and medicine. Other testators made small legacies on a once-and-for-all basis. Usually the only instructions accompanying such legacies were that they should be distributed to the most needy prisoners. This was unsatisfactory because the prisoners simply squandered the money on drink or gaming. The Misericórdia tried to overcome this by securing a royal privilege ordering that all legacies for prisoners should be given to the stewards of the prisoners for allocation in the most suitable manner. This suggestion was first made in 1741. Dom João V was more interested in the exotic birds of Brazil than in prisoners and the Misericórdia received no reply before his death in 1750.[3]

On some rare occasions bequests were made for specific purposes. It had been customary for the wealthier citizens of Bahia to provide meals for the prisoners, either annually or on certain saints' days. After their deaths, these benefactors left small legacies to the Misericórdia so that the provision of such meals could be continued. Other testators stipulated that their

---

[1] On 14 October 1754 the king ordered the Governor of Rio de Janeiro to authorise payment by the Treasury of 400$000 annually for three years to the Misericórdia of Rio to provide adequate assistance for prisoners (ANRJ, *Códice 952*, vol. 37, f. 338).

[2] In 1754 the following legacies were administered by the Misericórdia for the welfare of prisoners: João Alves Fontes (1702), 1,790$500; Miguel Carvalho Mascarenhas (1713) 1,434$000; Dr Francisco de Oliveira Pôrto (1748), 200$000 (ASCMB, vol. 210, f. 22). By this time the capital derived from the following legacies made for the same purpose had been lost: João Álvares de Azevedo (1692) 300$000; Paschoal da Silva Moreira (1712) 400$000; Canon Manuel Ramos Pacheco (1720) 800$000; Manuel Coelho Pôrto (1724) 1,200$000; Manuel Simões Lisboa (1750) 100$000. The original legacy by João Alves Fontes (1702) of 6,282$302 had been considerably reduced (ASCMB, vol. 211).

[3] ASCMB, vol. 52, ff. 196, 198v–199v., and vol. 53, ff. 111v–112v.

bequests be used for the clothing of prisoners and convicts. Since the Misericórdia lacked the financial resources to provide for all prisoners, there were many who received no benefit from the brotherhood. These were most to be pitied. Some bequests were intended for the aid of such prisoners who were sustained from the 'general ration' and not by the Misericórdia.

The material aid provided by the Misericórdia consisted of a weekly ration and medical aid. The *Compromisso* of 1618 had specified the nature of the ration. It had consisted of bread on Sundays and Wednesdays, and an additional allowance on Sundays of a bowl of soup and a piece of meat.[1] In Bahia the practice was to provide a daily ration for a smaller number of prisoners. In the year 1700–1 the brotherhood spent 434$020 on feeding the prisoners on its roll. It lacked the funds to provide for more prisoners and in the three years 1733–6 more than seventy prisoners died of starvation.[2] The Misericórdia freely admitted that it could only provide for fifty prisoners and that there were a further two hundred prisoners receiving no aid at all. In 1736 the brotherhood launched an appeal to bring home to the Bahians the plight of the prisoners. The object was to find 366 Bahians, each willing to donate a daily ration for the prisoners. The slogan was 'A Christian a day to keep hunger away'. Initially the appeal faced failure. Then the Count of Galvêas donated twelve meals and the archbishop matched the viceroy's example. Other citizens contributed smaller amounts and the mortality among prisoners due to starvation was cut.[3] In August 1739 the Misericórdia launched a further appeal. Collecting boxes were circulated round all the parishes of the city by brothers making door-to-door collections. This was very successful, the annual receipts from this source sometimes exceeding 200$000, and averaging 140$000.[4] Collections were also made in churches of the Recôncavo for the same purpose, and within the city the Prior of St Theresa also provided small alms for prisoners.[5]

The only occasion on which the Misericórdia received payment for feeding prisoners was when these were runaway slaves. Runaway slaves were common and in the seventeenth century had formed large groups in the interior. The most famous of these had been at Palmares and had only been

---

[1] *Compromisso* of Lisbon of 1618, chapter 11.

[2] ASCMB, vol. 15, f. 3v.　　　　　　[3] ASCMB, vol. 52, f. 196.

[4] It exceeded 200$000 for the years 1740–1 and 1741–2 (ASCMB, vols. 855 and 856).　　　　[5] ASCMB, vol. 858, f. 55 and vol. 863, f. 44.

subdued by an organised military attack. Regular search parties were sent out from Bahia to capture escaped slaves. These slaves were placed in prison and were fed by the Misericórdia. The brotherhood incurred no financial loss by feeding these slaves. In 1703 Dom Pedro II had issued a decree giving full instructions for measures to be taken with such slaves. If a slave refused to reveal the name or address of his master, then proclamations were to be published throughout the city of Bahia and the towns of the Recôncavo. If the master claimed his slave, he was to be liable for all expenses. If not, then the slave was to be sold and the proceeds were to go to the Treasury. Should the owner only appear after the sale of a slave, then the money received was to be paid to him less the expenses of food and imprisonment.[1] In 1711 the Misericórdia was paid the substantial sum of 152$640 for feeding four slaves in prison for more than two years.[2]

Material assistance provided by the Misericórdia for prisoners also took the form of medical care. The small rooms of the prison would have been inadequate for the criminals of urban Bahia alone. The cramped conditions were aggravated by the influx of criminals from all parts of Brazil and of convicts *en route* to their places of exile. Bahia had the only *Relação* of Brazil until 1751 when a High Court was established at Rio de Janeiro.[3] Before this date criminals on serious charges were sent to Bahia and housed in the prison. In addition, prisoners from the interior of the Captaincy of Bahia were brought to the city for trial. In 1685 major criminals had been transferred from Pernambuco to Bahia simply because the walls of the Pernambuco prison were too insecure.[4] Finally there were the large numbers of exiles waiting for transport to India or Angola. It was small wonder that epidemics occurred in the prison and that when an Officer of Health was appointed by the municipality one of his first duties was to check the health of prisoners.

The doctors of the Misericórdia were obliged to visit the prisons once or twice daily and give assistance to the sick.[5] Sometimes all that was necessary

---

[1] *Alvará* of 5 May 1703 (APB, *Ordens régias*, vol. 7, doc. 182).

[2] ASCMB, vol. 846, f. 17.

[3] Later foundations were in the Maranhão in 1812 and Pernambuco in 1821 (Pedro Calmon, *Historia da civilisação brasileira*, p. 151).

[4] ANRJ, *Códice 540, assento 78*.

[5] ASCMB, vol. 14, f. 236.

was a medicament from the apothecary of the Misericórdia. On other occasions a prisoner was moved to the Misericórdia hospital. We will return to this charitable action of the Misericórdia in the following chapter with reference to the hospital of the brotherhood.

The assistance given by the Misericórdia to convicts came into a class by itself. In Lisbon the Misericórdia had enjoyed certain privileges to help those being deported. The duties of the stewards of the prisoners had included biannual visits to the galleys to secure the release of convicts who had fulfilled their sentences.[1] Bahia was a wayport for such convicts but the Misericórdia was forbidden by statute from giving assistance to convicts awaiting deportation. All that the brotherhood could do for these half-naked wretches was to bury them charitably when they succumbed to the rigours of the prison. Some exiles were already on the roll of the brotherhood because the Misericórdia of Lisbon had undertaken their defence before they had been convicted. Frequently convicts had to wait for long periods in Bahia before deportation. The presence of these in the prison caused serious overcrowding. The authorities remedied this to some extent by conscripting able-bodied men for service on the Indiamen which frequently put in to Bahia with half of the crew sick and unable to continue the voyage.[2] Other convicts were used to replenish the garrisons of S. Tomé and outposts in India. The conscription of these convicts for garrisons in India had the additional advantage of making it more difficult for them to return to Brazil, whereas this was frequently the case of convicts deported to Angola.[3] With the decline in the slave trade to the Mina coast in the eighteenth century, there were few ships from Bahia to S. Tomé and Angola. In 1738 there was the fear of epidemic in the prison of Bahia because of the large number of convicts awaiting transportation to Angola. The Count of Galvêas reduced this gross overcrowding by sending many of these convicts to the garrisons of the island of Fernando Noronha and the Rio Grande.[4] Not only convicts

[1] *Compromisso* of Lisbon of 1618, chapter 11.

[2] In 1725 the ship *Jesus Maria Joseph* put into Bahia with only sixty of her crew capable of continuing the voyage, an average of only two to each gun. The viceroy enlisted deportees and jailbirds to make the crew up to 100, the minimum necessary for the vessel to continue her voyage (APB, *Ordens régias*, vol. 20, doc. 35).

[3] APB, *Ordens régias*, vol. 28, doc. 59.

[4] Resolution of 8 November 1738 of the *Relação* of Bahia (ANRJ, *Códice 540*, *assento* 137).

were affected by the lack of ships going to West Africa. In the 1730s the Bishop of S. Tomé waited in Bahia for nine months for a ship. The Governor-elect of S. Tomé, António Ferrão Castelo Branco, had to buy a ship at his own cost in 1740 to take up his appointment.[1]

In Bahia no record was kept of the aid given by the Misericórdia to convicts. The brotherhood certainly did act on behalf of convicts because there are references to disputes between the attorney of the Misericórdia and the scribe in charge of exiles as to the payment to be received by the latter.[2] When a prisoner was condemned to exile, he was often accompanied by his family. On one occasion the Misericórdia paid the passage money of children so that they could accompany their father to Angola.[3]

The legal aid given by the Misericórdia to prisoners was of supreme importance. A situation reminiscent of Kafka's *The Trial* existed. Charges against a prisoner were vague, no legal counsel was available. The dilatory legal machinery often meant that a prisoner remained in gaol for months, and even years, before being brought to trial. One of the actions of Dom João de Lencastre had been to expedite the cases of prisoners in the gaol of Bahia. Dom João V threatened punishment for scribes who ignored the cases of poor prisoners in favour of those which promised better payment.[4] Despite viceroyal and royal intervention, the machinery of the judiciary remained sluggish.

The Misericórdia of Bahia was the most active branch in Brazil in providing legal counsel for prisoners. Until 1751 the *Relação* of Bahia was the only High Court in Brazil and all major criminals were sent to Bahia for trial. In 1709 Dom João V commended to the Misericórdia the legal defence of those prisoners most likely to be ignored by the scribes of the High Court, and consequently those most likely to remain in prison without trial. The royal advice was unnecessary because the Misericórdia already provided legal advice for prisoners admitted to its roll of prisoners.[5] This aid applied not only to prisoners admitted by the Misericórdia of Bahia but to those sent to Bahia by other branches of the Misericórdia in Brazil.

---

[1] APB, *Ordens régias*, vol. 36, doc. 1a.   [2] ASCMB, vol. 52, ff. 88–9.

[3] ASCMB, vol. 850, f. 287v. The Misericórdia also provided clothing for deportees, many of whom arrived at Bahia half naked.

[4] ANRJ, *Códice 952*, vol. 32, ff. 244–6 and vol. 33, f. 193.

[5] ASCMB, vol. 52, f. 40v.

The procedure was as follows. The Misericórdia which had first admitted a prisoner to its roll forwarded to Bahia a certificate stating that the prisoner was receiving assistance from the brotherhood. This certificate was drawn up by the scribe and signed by the board of guardians. Without such a certificate the prisoners did not benefit from the privileged position of the brotherhood and were liable for legal costs and subject to fines.[1] This last privilege — that prisoners on the roll of a Misericórdia could not be sentenced to fines — was of vital importance to the brotherhood because such sentences condemned the criminal to prison until the fine was paid (which he was incapable of doing) and meant that the brotherhood had to bear the costs of sustaining the prisoner. When more evidence was necessary, the Misericórdia of Bahia wrote to the branch concerned which made further enquiries. Such co-operation between the Misericórdia of Bahia and other branches was reciprocal, other branches collecting debts due to the brotherhood in Bahia.

The Misericórdia maintained a qualified legal staff consisting in the eighteenth century of two lawyers, one for civil cases and the other for criminal cases. The most famous of these was Dr Manuel Ribeiro Rocha, appointed in 1742 as the lawyer for civil cases at an annual salary of 110$000.[2] He was an ardent abolitionist and in 1758 published a book entitled *Ethiope resgatado, empenhado, sustentado, corregido, instruido e libertado (The Ethiopian ransomed, indentured, sustained, corrected, educated and liberated).* This advocated the substitution of Negro slavery by a system of indentured labour.[3] The lawyers of the Misericórdia were assisted by clerks employed by the brotherhood. The action of the stewards of the prisoners was limited to presenting the final appeal in the High Court in cases where a criminal faced the death sentence. This in itself was a privilege, because ordinary lawyers were forbidden from entering the High Court. In the same way that the Misericórdia chose a Provedor capable of defending the brotherhood against the municipal and ecclesiastical authorities, so did the brotherhood choose a person of social standing to be the 'noble' steward of the prisoners. This position was a stepping stone to the Provedorship and was occupied by

[1] Details of cases and of the procedure are in ASCMB, vol. 52, ff. 45v–46, 47, 51v–52 and 91.   [2] ASCMB, vol. 14, f. 271v.

[3] A brief summary of this important work is in C. R. Boxer, *Race Relations*, pp. 111–13.

such prominent Bahians as the Master of the Field João Honorato, the land-owner Domingos Affonso Sertão, the future Governor of S. Tomé, António Ferrão Castelo Branco, and the Secretary of State José Pires de Carvalho e Albuquerque. Should the 'noble' steward for the prisoners not be available, the board of guardians appointed a brother of equal social standing. When the steward from the lower class protested against this action in 1709 and attempted to present the final appeals of a criminal himself, he was expelled from the brotherhood for insubordination.[1]

The cost of all legal expenses was borne by the Misericórdia. No bequests were received to offset this cost. The account for an average year was in the region of 120$000 but this sum did not include the salaries of the lawyers and other employees of the Misericórdia. The brotherhood was held in high repute for the efficiency shown by its lawyers in the defence of criminals and frequently was asked to take on a case for a citizen accused of a crime on a purely business basis. In such cases the Misericórdia received full payment for its services.

There are no registers in the archives of the Misericórdia to indicate the extent of the legal activities of the brotherhood. The appointment of a lawyer in the eighteenth century to deal solely with criminal cases suggests that the Misericórdia was increasingly busy in this respect. The brotherhood took on all deserving cases, be the accused white or black, and it was probably in the defence of slaves that the action of the brotherhood was most significant.

The slave was a criminal scapegoat. He was frequently the instrument for the crimes of his master. When captured he received no defence and was unable to present his case. The master disowned him and the law condemned him. Reference has already been made to the concern shown by Dom João V in the protection of the slave from exploitation and cruelty. This preoccupation extended to slaves accused of crimes. In 1710 the Bishop of Rio de Janeiro complained to the king of the impossibility of a slave presenting any defence against his master. Dom João V authorised

---

[1] A footnote to the expulsion order alleged that his wife had a 'defeito de sangue'. This was later proved not to be so and he was readmitted (ASCMB, vol. 195, ff. 41 and 44). This contrasts with the attitude of the Mesa of 1630 who had dismissed a brother because he was married to a Jewess, but had recorded his expulsion as occasioned by negligence in his duties (vol. 195, f. 5).

the appointment of a lawyer, whose salary would be paid by the Crown and whose duties would be limited to the presentation of charges made by slaves against their masters in the Appeals Court.[1]

In Bahia the only case on which there is adequate information concerned the defence of a slave by the Misericórdia. His name was António Fernandes and he was the slave of friar Manuel da Madre de Deus, former Provincial of the Carmelite Order in Bahia. António Fernandes faced a charge of murder. Only two facts were certain: first, that one António Guedes and his slave disappeared in Bahia in 1718; secondly, that shortly afterwards António Fernandes was sent to Rio by friar Manuel to be sold. While in Rio it was alleged that António Fernandes had confessed to the double murder, saying he had acted on his master's orders. The Crown judge in Rio sent him back to Bahia to stand trial on the charge of murder. The charge was unsubstantiated. There was no evidence of the crime and the bodies of the murdered men were not discovered. The witnesses, who claimed to have heard António Fernandes confess to the crime, failed to recognise him in an identity parade. The accused pleaded innocence and the Misericórdia took up his defence. Despite the lack of evidence he was sentenced to be tortured. This sentence was justified by the legal authorities on two dubious grounds. First, that the accused was a 'base person and a slave'. Secondly, that in such a serious case mere hearsay was enough evidence to proceed to torture. One of the judges noted that, in any case, the severity of the punishment received at the hands of the law would have been no greater than the beatings António Fernandes suffered from his master. The lawyer of the Misericórdia appealed to the High Court but the appeal was rejected. A second appeal was also rejected and the lawyer was fined 20$000 for his temerity, whereupon he refused to continue the defence and resigned from his post as lawyer to the Misericórdia. The sentence was carried out and António Fernandes was tortured with brutal severity. The torture lasted four hours and the victim became unconscious twice. On each occasion the doctor and surgeon of the High Court were called to examine the accused to see if the torture could be continued. Only after he had fainted for the second time did the doctor and surgeon forbid further punishment on medical grounds, although the doctor affirmed that there had been no danger of death and the surgeon said that he had treated worse cases who had been sent to the Misericórdia

[1] Royal order of 5 November 1710 (ANRJ, *Códice 952*, vol. 18, f. 23).

hospital after torture. The stewards of the prisoners of the Misericórdia, who had also been called to assist the accused after each fainting, testified ambiguously that 'although he (António Fernandes) was mad with the pain of the torture, nevertheless we cannot be certain if his condition resulted from the torture alone or was simulated'. António Fernandes appealed to Dom João V, complaining of the 'inhuman tribulations and injustices' he had suffered. The king ordered a full enquiry in 1722. The Count of Sabugosa replied that the enquiry had shown that the torture had been justified and that there was no reasonable doubt as to the guilt of the accused. Nevertheless Dom João V, possibly aware that Sabugosa himself had been named unfavourably in the appeal of Fernandes, ordered a second enquiry to be made in 1723. This was to be conducted by the new Crown judge being sent to Bahia, Dr Bernardo de Sousa Estrella. The king ordered that friar Manuel da Madre de Deus be expelled from the captaincy for the duration of the enquiry because his powerful influence might obstruct the course of justice.[1]

The final charitable act of the Misericórdia towards prisoners was to provide spiritual solace for those condemned to death. On the day sentence was passed, a priest of the Misericórdia confessed the condemned man. On the following day a mass was held in the prison. On the day of execution the brotherhood sent a white habit to the prisoner and announced that a hanging was to be held. A procession formed outside the prison, consisting of nine chaplains, the stewards of the prisoners and the brothers of the Misericórdia clothed in black. The condemned man was given the crucifix of the Misericórdia to kiss, thereby receiving full indulgence granted by a papal privilege. At the gallows prayers were chanted and after the hanging the brotherhood returned to the Misericórdia.[2]

A curious tradition existed concerning hanging. It was that, if by any chance the criminal should fall from the gallows and still be alive, no further punishment could be taken against him if he were covered by the flag of the Misericórdia. In 1715 this tradition caused a public scandal, viceroyal action, and a sharp reproach for the Misericórdia from the king. Two Negroes had been condemned to death. One had been hanged and the second was

[1] APB, *Ordens régias*, vol. 16, doc. 23 and accompanying documents; vol. 17, docs. 29a, 37 and 37a.

[2] *Compromisso* of 1618 of Lisbon, chapter 36.

already on the gallows when the cross-bar broke and both bodies fell to the ground. The brothers of the Misericórdia leapt forward and covered the second criminal, who was still barely alive, with the banner of the brother-hood. There was a scuffle. The *meirinho*, or minor court official, believing that the brothers of the Misericórdia were going to carry off the criminal, drew a dagger and killed him. The populace threatened to lynch the official for this action and peace was only restored by the senior city councillor who ordered his arrest. The brothers of the Misericórdia trooped to the governor's palace and publicly demanded that the official be hanged. The Marquis of Angeja called out the palace guard to disperse the restless populace and arrest those brothers who refused to go peacefully. They were only released on the personal appeal of the Provedor to the viceroy. The incident was reported to Dom João V who severely rebuked the brotherhood for inter-vening in the execution of justice.[1]

Once a year, on All Saints' Day, the brotherhood congregated for a solemn procession to the gallows. The brothers collected the bones of all those who had been hanged in the previous year and took them back to the Misericórdia to be buried in holy ground. These processions sometimes occasioned disputes between the Misericórdia and the local clergy. In the eighteenth century the gallows were in the parish of St Peter, beyond the city walls. It had been customary for a priest of the cathedral chapter to accompany the procession as far as the city gates. Here the procession was met by the vicar of the parish of St Peter who accompanied it to the gallows. Both priests received payment for this service, but it was their intervention in a private ceremony of the Misericórdia which led the board of guardians to protest against this practice. The 'procession of the bones' is depicted on tiles in the church of the Misericórdia, showing the brothers bearing the three biers behind the banner of the brotherhood (see Plate). The last occasion on which this procession was held was in 1825.[2]

The need for tempering justice with charity has been amply illustrated. The colonisation of Brazil demanded a higher degree of juridical responsibility than had been shown by the Portuguese authorities in Asia. The problems

---

[1] APB, *Ordens régias*, vol. 10, doc. 40.

[2] ASCMB, vol. 52, ff. 220–221v; Marieta Alves, *A Santa Casa de Misericordia e sua igreja* (Bahia, 1962), p. 8. A description of the order of ceremony is contained in chapter 37 of the *Compromisso* of 1618 of Lisbon.

of maintaining law and order were different in the two continents. The attitude of the judiciaries towards criminals of little social standing or few financial resources was markedly similar. All too frequently the preferment of a charge was tantamount to the passing of a sentence. Once accused, the victim of this arbitrary justice was imprisoned and his case delayed. If the attitude of the juridical authorities was one of disregard, the attitude of the municipal authorities towards the inmates of its prison was no better. They were left to die of starvation or of disease.

The action of the Misericórdia in assisting prisoners was of the greatest importance. Prisoners were sustained by the rations distributed by the brotherhood and the sick received medical treatment. A qualified lawyer examined charges made against a prisoner and strove to secure his acquittal if innocent, or at least a fair trial if guilty. The assistance given by the Misericórdia to prisoners demonstrated the semi-bureaucratic function of the brotherhood. In this instance the Misericórdia of Bahia worked to remedy the shortcomings of a sluggish judiciary and a negligent municipal council, but received no official support or recognition for its labours. Another aspect of the bureaucratic rôle played by the Misericórdia was the provision of hospital services for the community. Here the brotherhood was less willing to give its services without reimbursement as had been the case with its aid to prisoners.

I I

The Hospital of Saint Christopher

THE only general hospital in Bahia during the entire colonial period was administered by the Misericórdia. This hospital had been known as the Hospital of Our Lady of Candles or the Hospital of the City of the Saviour in the sixteenth century. From the late seventeenth century it was always called the Hospital of St Christopher. This single hospital provided for an urban population which had grown from 1,000 settlers in 1549 to some 130,000 residents in 1755. Although the first governor, Tomé de Sousa, had ordered the construction of the hospital in 1549, his successors failed to follow his example in providing hospital services for the city. Governors and viceroys paid scant attention to the peculiar medical problems of a community, the majority of whose members had emigrated to Brazil. The city council was equally remiss. No part of the income derived by the municipality from heavy taxation was ear-marked for medical aid for the community. The councillors failed to enforce even the most rudimentary measures for public hygiene. These two factors — a society composed of three races from three continents and a disregard for urban sanitation — contributed to the high incidence of disease within the City of the Saviour.

Miscegenation in Brazil had involved three races — the Indian, the white and the Negro — from three different continents. This purely ecological factor had been important in making Bahia an unusually fertile breeding ground for disease. This may be explained by two established medical facts. First, each area has a range of diseases peculiar to that area. Secondly, the inhabitants of a given area develop resistance to these diseases by constant contact. A traveller visiting an area for the first time is highly susceptible to infection during the initial phase of his stay. In proportion to the length of time he remains in that region he develops an increasingly diminished response to local diseases. Conversely, if the introduction of an alien group into an area is sufficiently large, then a totally new range of diseases may be imposed on the indigenous population. This has occurred recently in Brazil. The construction of a highway from Brasília to Belém has resulted in contact being made with tribes previously unknown. Bulldozers have broken down physical barriers. The workmen following in the wake of these massive machines have constituted a moving bacteriological frontier of diseases common to the urban areas of Brazil. The result has been the decimation of Indian tribes by whooping cough, measles and the common cold.

There had been an analogous occurrence in the sixteenth century in Brazil. Not two, but three groups of diseases had converged — the American, the African and the European. The Indian had been the victim of this initial contact. Thousands had died of smallpox and tuberculosis in the villages established by the Jesuits. Those who had been enslaved had died of changes of diet, unaccustomed types of work, or alcoholism.[1] The retreat of the survivors from the littoral region and from the Jesuit outposts had only made them all the more susceptible to future contacts. The white coloniser had brought diseases of European origin, such as smallpox, measles and influenza. Although syphilis appears to have originated in America, the dominant transmitter of this and other venereal diseases had been the European coloniser. Nevertheless the white man had been the most susceptible to a whole new range of tropical diseases such as malaria, chagas and yellow fever.

The race least affected by the tri-continental convergence of diseases had been the Negro. Many of the diseases present in Brazil had also been present in Africa. Thus the Negro had already developed a degree of resistance to these diseases and was better equipped to withstand contact with new strains present in Brazil. Also, many Negroes had already been exposed to European diseases brought to the west coast of Africa by Portuguese traders and slavers. When attempting to assess the importance of the slave as a transmitter of disease, two *caveats* must be made. First, contemporary documents such as the viceroyal correspondence must be used with care, because there was a tendency to blame all disease on the *negro*

[1] For the devastating effect of diseases resulting from these early contacts see Thales de Azevedo, *Povoamento*, p. 69 and sources there quoted.

bichado ('bug-ridden Negro'). Secondly, loose medical terminology was often used to describe diseases common among slaves, but which had been already present in Europe. The most evident example was scurvy, referred to as *mal de Luanda* ('evil of Luanda'), but known to sailors centuries before the first carrying of slaves in bulk. Diseases ascribed to African origin included leprosy, dysentery, buboes and nematode worms.[1]

The heavy mortality rate among slaves had been the result less of medical factors than of social conditions. The appalling conditions of the slave ships, hard plantation labour and continual malnutrition reduced the maximum working life of a slave on a plantation to ten years. Ironically enough, the enforced contact of the Negro slave and the white man had benefited both races. The European had gradually developed a resistance to tropical diseases. The African had developed a similar resistance to European diseases. This did not mean that there had emerged a society immune to both European and tropical diseases. There was a continual increase in the numbers of colonists from Europe and slaves from Africa during the sixteenth, seventeenth and eighteenth centuries. These new migrants, slaves or freedmen, succumbed to the new diseases as easily as had their predecessors until they too achieved a degree of resistance. Hybridisation played a major part in overcoming the adverse medical effects of migration. There was some truth in the adage that Brazil was 'A Hell for Blacks, a purgatory for Whites, and a paradise for Mulattoes'.[2]

The problems of urban sanitation in the tropics are many. Nevertheless the task of the municipal council of Bahia should have been facilitated by the geographical situation of the city. Bahia was essentially a healthy city. In 1549, the Jesuit priest Manoel da Nóbrega had commented on the healthy position chosen for the new capital. He had extolled the fresh breezes, the ready supply of fresh water, the uniformity of temperature and the abundance of fresh fruit and game.[3] The natural advantages of Bahia were described in almost identical terms by the Professor of Greek at Bahia, Luís dos Santos Vilhena, in the late eighteenth century.[4] Some three hundred

---

[1] Such diseases are listed by Gilberto Freyre, *The Masters*, p. 475, n. 204, and Thales de Azevedo, *Povoamento*, p. 218, n. 245.

[2] Cited by C. R. Boxer, *The Golden Age*, p. 1.

[3] Manoel da Nóbrega, *Cartas*, p. 89.

[4] Vilhena, *Noticias soteropolitanas*, vol. 1, p. 36.

years after the original settlement, the British doctor, Robert Dundas, reported on the comparative salubrity of Bahia which he ascribed to the uniformity of temperature and the cool nights.[1] Despite enthusiastic testimonials from such different witnesses, the fact was that the city of Bahia was riddled by disease and suffered from severe epidemics in the seventeenth and early eighteenth centuries.

The responsibility for this situation must be laid to the charge of the city council and, to a lesser degree, the Crown authorities. The city council failed to act in three respects. Laws dealing with urban sanitation were not enforced. There were no inspections of shops, butchers, slaughter houses and markets. Foodstuffs and medicines imported from Europe were not examined on arrival in Bahia. Some blame must also be attached to the Crown authorities. Bahia was not only a terminal port for the slave trade but was also a wayport for the Indiamen. Royal decrees concerning hygiene and diet on the slave ships and Indiamen were not implemented. Bahia was swamped by disease-ridden slaves, soldiers and sailors whenever one of these ships put into port. The Crown authorities might well have assisted the municipality in providing a hospital because many of the sick were in the royal service.

The city of Bahia was a filthy place. Those foreign visitors of the seventeenth and eighteenth centuries who lavished praise on the monasteries and churches, decried no less vehemently the insanitary conditions of the city. A distinction must be made between the upper and lower cities. In 1699 the English traveller William Dampier described the upper city in glowing terms. He was most impressed by the strong stone buildings, the broad paved streets, belvederes and gardens. The lower city was the commercial area cramped into a narrow strip of land between the sea and the cliff. It was composed of warehouses, small shops, taverns, brothels and poor houses huddled together in the narrow and dirty alleys. The upper city was comparatively healthy only because of its superior position. The municipality provided only the most primitive of sewage systems and no form of refuse collection. Responsibility for domestic sanitation was left to the individual householder. The *tigres*, or barrels of excrement, piled up in the houses until a slave was finally ordered to carry them down to the waterfront

---

[1] Robert Dundas, M.D., *Sketches of Brazil, including new views on tropical and European fever* (London, 1852), pp. 204–9. Robert Dundas was medical superintendent of the British hospital in Bahia for twenty-three years.

to be emptied. Rubbish was disposed of in the same way or was burnt. The results of this official negligence can well be imagined. The slave simply dumped the excrement and the rubbish in one of the less populous parts of the upper city. The area behind the wall of the Franciscan monastery and the tops of the paths going to the lower city were the most commonly chosen places. These paths, or *ladeiras*, were little more than open drains for the upper city. Herds of pigs rummaged among the piles of dirt and rubbish.[1] The alley between the hospital and the retirement house of the Misericórdia became impassable because of the piles of excrement and dead animals. The odours prejudiced the health of patients in the hospital and girls in the retirement house. In 1742 the brotherhood suggested to the municipal council that a gateway be placed across the entrance to the alley.[2]

The lower city was the cesspool for the upper city. Heavy rains washed the piles of rubbish down the steep slopes of the cliff. The alleys of the lower city became choked and the hot sun caused putrefaction, endangering the health of people already weakened by malnutrition and poor living conditions. It was small wonder that the English lady, Maria Graham (later to be Lady Callcott), during her visit to Bahia in 1821, referred to the 'filthy lower town' of Bahia.[3]

The second failure of the municipal council concerned lack of hygiene in the sale of foodstuffs. The principal causes of infection were meat and manioc flour. Large herds of cattle were brought to the cattle fair at Capoâme, eight leagues from the city.[4] From here they were driven to the city where they were kept in corrals for anything up to a week. During this period they received only water. Frequently the beasts were suffering from infection before being slaughtered. Additionally, hygiene was absent in both the slaughter houses and the butchers' shops. Butchers alleged shortage of supplies in the morning to force up prices. At night they sold off cheaply meat which had been hanging in the sun all day and become infested with flies. Profiteering was also common in the sale of manioc flour.

---

[1] In 1739 the city council announced sentences of up to thirty days imprisonment for owners who allowed their pigs to roam the city (AMB, vol. 30, f. 196).

[2] ASCMB, vol. 14, f. 273v.

[3] Maria Graham, *Journal of a voyage to Brazil and residence there during part of the years 1821, 1822, 1823* (London, 1824), p. 133.

[4] Antonil, *Cultura e Opulencia*, part 4, chapter 3.

This was supplied to Bahia from the townships of Boipeba, Camamú and Cairú in the south of the Captaincy of Bahia. The supplies were superficially inspected on arrival in the city. Unscrupulous merchants hoarded supplies until a lean period of the year and then sold the commodity at extortionate prices.[1] Frequently, the flour as it appeared on the market was not fit for pigs let alone for human consumption.

The municipal council also failed to examine foodstuffs and medicines sent from Europe. Wheat flour, butter, cheeses and wines reached Bahia already in poor condition. Such commodities were rotten when they reached the markets and were bought by poor families and by masters for their slaves. When Frézier, the engineer sent by Louis XIV to make hydrographical observations and plans of ports and fortresses in Portuguese and Spanish America, made his report on Bahia he stressed that it was not a good port because of the lack of fresh provisions.[2] Medicines were also imported from Lisbon. These were not inspected on arrival with sufficient care, nor were periodic inspections made of the chemists' shops to ensure that old stock was destroyed.

The responsibility of the Crown centred on the strategic position of Bahia as a port for slavers and Indiamen. Sanitary conditions on the slave ships were appalling. Before embarkation in Africa many of the slaves had already undergone the hardship of a long trek from the interior in chain gangs known as *alimbambas*. On the ships the slaves received meagre rations, or even nothing at all. The conditions were cramped and the 'heads' inadequate. The mortality rate on the six-week crossing from Luanda was high. Those slaves who did reach Bahia alive were infected, at best with scurvy, at worst with yellow fever. Cursory medical checks and rapid sale meant that infected slaves were the carriers of diseases both in the city and in the plantations of the Recôncavo.

The conditions on the Indiamen were infinitely superior to those on the slave ships. Nevertheless, inadequate supplies of food and fresh water resulted in whole crews falling prey to scurvy and dysentery. On arrival at Bahia many sailors were sent to hospital and their places taken by jail-birds and convicts hastily pressed into the royal service so that the ship would be adequately manned. Not only sailors were affected by disease. Many of the

---

[1] *Atas da Câmara*, vol. 3, pp. 130–4 and p. 197.
[2] Frézier, *Relation du voyage*, part 3, p. 279.

Indiamen carried soldiers for the garrisons of Africa and India, and these too frequently remained in Bahia for long periods of convalescence.

I do not wish to give the impression that legislation did not exist to combat these evils. It did, at both the municipal and Crown levels. In both cases it was ignored by those concerned. A casual glance at the minutes of the municipal council for the seventeenth century reveals the frequency with which laws concerning sanitation and hygiene were issued. This very frequency was indicative of their ineffectiveness. Laws were passed threatening severe penalties for failure to dispose of rubbish at the waterfront, or for failing to keep clean the street outside one's house. Other laws made it compulsory for butchers to wash their counters. Wine-merchants had to clean their measuring cans regularly.[1] The Crown had issued decrees aimed at reducing slave mortality. In 1664 Dom Affonso VI had ordered slave traders to provide adequate supplies of food and water, and ensure that the slaves were not overcrowded in confined spaces. All these laws and decrees were in vain. They were difficult to enforce. Corrupt officials and family connections made a mockery of any municipal or royal order.

A single event had jerked Crown authorities and municipal councillors into more positive action. This had been an outbreak of yellow fever in Bahia in 1686. We will be returning to this later (pp. 288-9). Suffice it to say here that such had been the severity of the outbreak that up to 200 people had died in a single day. The municipal council was compelled to take a firm stand on urban sanitation and the inspection of foodstuffs. Without doubt this was in part due to intervention by governors and viceroys who needled the councillors into action. The first governor-general to act in this respect was Dom João de Lencastre (1694–1702). During his term of office all remaining traces of yellow fever were extinguished, chemists' shops were inspected and laws on urban sanitation were enforced. During the eighteenth century the Count of Sabugosa (Viceroy, 1720–35) continually reminded the councillors of their obligations to the populace.

The most important appointment to emerge from this pressure was the election of a *Provedor da Saúde*, or Officer of Health. Although two sanitary inspectors known as *almotacés da limpeza* had been elected in 1673 to inspect the cattle corrals, slaughter houses, and enforce laws dealing with hygiene

---

[1] *Atas da Câmara*, vol. 1, pp. 5–9, 19, 33, 126; vol. 2, pp. 67–9, 103–4, 154–6, 205, 253–4; vol. 3, pp. 241–3. Affonso Ruy, *Historia da Câmara*, pp. 137–41.

and sanitation, these officials had not been effective.[1] No payment had been made and the only candidates had been 'men of inferior standing'. They had been negligent in their duties and had lacked the authority to command the respect of householders or shopkeepers. Penalties had not been enforced against slaves because of fear of reprisal by their masters against the sanitary inspectors. In 1694 the city council had asked the Crown to approve the appointment of an Officer of Health. The incumbent would not possess any medical training but would be a person of sufficient social standing and nobility to inspire respect.[2]

During the eighteenth century the Officer of Health was a councillor. His duties included the regular inspection of slaughter houses, shops and markets. He was accompanied by a doctor appointed by the city council and from the 1730s by a surgeon, also a municipal appointee. All medical inspections were registered, and penalties were levied against offenders.[3] Medical inspections were also made of all ships arriving from Africa. On more than one occasion in the eighteenth century the inspecting team complained of the 'fetid stench' in the holds of slave ships. In severe cases of infection the ship was quarantined at a place known as the *ponta do curral*.[4]

A closer check was kept on medicines imported from Europe. In 1744 the king ordered that rules for the inspection of chemists' shops in Portugal be applied to Brazil. These inspections were carried out by commissioners appointed by the chief physician. These agents examined medicines arriving on ships and made triennial visits to chemists' shops. Payment was made for the latter service but not for the former. Evidently the agents were over-zealous, possibly to compensate for non-payment for visits to ships. Numerous complaints reached the king from chemists of how the agents were

---

[1] The minute approving these appointments is dated 16 November 1672; the first elections were made on 31 January 1673 (*Atas da Câmara*, vol. 5, pp. 78–81 and pp. 93–4). On 4 March 1673 the city council asked the king to approve these posts and the royal approval was granted on 30 March 1675 (AMB, vol. 173, ff. 150v–151v and vol. 176, f. 12v).

[2] City council to king, 30 July 1694 (AMB, vol. 174, ff. 124v–125).

[3] The earliest extant register of these inspections is AMB, vol. 522.

[4] AMB, vol. 29, ff. 139v–140. As early as 1626 passengers from an infected ship had been quarantined on the Ilha dos Frades (*Atas da Câmara*, vol. 1, pp. 39–40). Thus Vilhena's suggestions for the quarantining of ships in the late eighteenth century had some historical precedent (*Noticias soteropolitanas*, vol. 1, p. 156).

insisting on making 'extraordinary visits' to their shops and claiming payment for these unauthorised inspections.[1]

The Crown authorities were primarily concerned with safeguarding Portugal from disease. On hearing of the yellow fever epidemic of 1686, the king had ordered that all ships from Brazil to Portugal should inform the sanitary authorities in Lisbon of arrival, before anybody disembarked.[2] Bills of health were instituted in 1691. Known as *cartas de saúde*, they registered the prevailing state of health in the city of Bahia at the time of departure of the ship. They were presented to the officer on duty in the tower at Belém at the mouth of the Tagus, who would allow the ship to berth or would order quarantine as was necessary.[3] This information was obviously inadequate. In 1694 the king had ordered that the bills of health should have details of the number of passengers and crew, their state of health, and the exact nature of any sickness on board.[4] On the suggestion of the municipal doctor of Bahia this practice was later extended to all ships arriving from Africa at Bahia and resulted in the inspections already mentioned.[5]

The Crown also took measures to reduce slave mortality. In 1684 Dom Pedro II had issued laws aimed at reducing the chronic over-crowding of the slave ships, which often resulted in actual bodily injury. He had been particularly concerned with ensuring adequate ventilation and had worked out regulations for the number of slaves to be carried, based on tonnage and ventilation. For example: for every two tons, seven slaves could be carried on decks with portholes, whereas only five could be carried in those parts without portholes. The ratio of slaves to tonnage increased in proportion to the height of the decks above sea-level.[6]

Neither royal nor municipal measures had any lasting effect. It is true that Portugal did not suffer from plague in the eighteenth century. Yellow

---

[1] APB, *Ordens régias*, vol. 42, doc. 119. For complaints and royal action to stop abuse see vol. 47, f. 92.

[2] King to governor of Rio de Janeiro, 22 April 1688 (ANRJ, *Códice 952*, vol. 4, f. 210).

[3] Secretary of state to governor-general, 19 January 1691 (APB, *Ordens régias*, vol. 2, doc. 9).

[4] King to governor-general, 30 January 1694 (APB, *Ordens régias*, vol. 3, doc. 6).

[5] APB, *Ordens régias*, vol. 5, docs. 39 and 39a.

[6] Law of 18 March 1684. On 16 May 1744 Dom João V told the viceroy to ensure that this law was observed (APB, *Ordens régias*, vol. 41, docs. 52 and 52a).

fever persisted in Bahia until the 1930s although it never again reached the epidemic proportions of 1686. Slave ship conditions did not improve. A single example will suffice to illustrate this. When the slaver *N. S^r do Rosário e S. Gonçalo* arrived in Bahia in 1724 after the short voyage of twenty-nine days from São Tomé, a medical inspection revealed that over 300 slaves had died during the crossing and that the survivors were in need of hospital treatment.[1] The situation was no better on the Indiamen. Whole crews were placed in hospital in Bahia after contracting scurvy. Urban sanitation may have improved during the viceroyalty of the Count of Sabugosa, but his successors were lax and even opposed certain improvements suggested by the municipal council.[2] The letters of Vilhena written at the end of the eighteenth century present a sordid picture of disease and squalor. He severely censured the Misericórdia for the unhealthy conditions of its cemetery for slaves, but he reserved his harshest criticism for the negligence of the city council.[3]

Vilhena made no reference to the failure on the part of the city council to provide any hospital for the city. Nor did the city council provide even rudimentary medical assistance. The duties of those doctors on the municipal pay-roll were limited to treating the soldiers of the garrison and certain public officers. The fact that Vilhena made no reference to this failure of the municipal authorities is curious in such a severe critic of local government. The reason was simply that hospital services were not then regarded as a municipal responsibility. This had also been the case in Spanish America during the colonial period. The responsibility for social services had been assumed by the Church and religious orders. In Brazil this responsibility had devolved upon the brotherhoods. Because of its privileged position the Misericórdia had been the most prominent brotherhood in this respect. In maintaining public hospitals in cities and townships of Brazil, the Misericórdia had been unique among the brotherhoods of colonial Brazil.

In Bahia the Misericórdia was the sole administrator of the hospital. All expenses were met from the brotherhood's funds. All staff were appointed by the board of guardians. Successive boards of guardians were torn

---

[1] AMB, vol. 29, ff. 139v–140.

[2] Disagreements between the Crown officials and the councillors are described by Affonso Ruy, *Historia da Câmara*, pp. 150–2.

[3] Vilhena, *Noticias soteropolitanas*, letter 4.

between vanity in the preservation of this monopoly and the hard financial reality of insufficient funds. Vanity triumphed. During the eighteenth century the Misericórdia opposed three rival attempts to found hospitals.

The first was in the 1720s. A friar, Bernardo da Conceição, asked Dom João V to grant privileges to a hospital he proposed to build at Peneafou. The request was referred to the Count of Sabugosa who consulted the Misericórdia. The board of guardians of 1724–5 rejected the request on two grounds: first, testators would endow the new hospital instead of that of the Misericórdia; secondly, royal approval for the new foundation would be interpreted as a vote of no confidence in the Misericórdia. The Mesa pointed out that no charge was made for the treatment of the sick in the brother-hood's hospital and that it was totally dependent on charity.[1]

The second case of rivalry concerned the Brotherhood of the Holy Body of Christ. The captains of deep-water ships had approached the board of guardians of this brotherhood with a proposal for the foundation of a hospital for sailors. An agreement had been signed in 1714, the seamen promising to pay dues to the brotherhood calculated on the size of the ship and its port of departure. This agreement had been approved by the Marquis of Angeja in 1715 and the brotherhood received the promised dues.[2] No hospital was built and the brotherhood spent the money on its various private needs. When the brotherhood came to ask for royal confirmation of their privilege in 1736 both the city council and the Misericórdia strongly opposed any such authorisation. The Misericórdia extolled the virtues of its own hospital and suggested that those funds already collected be handed to its treasurer.[3]

The third threat to the monopoly of the Misericórdia came from the viceroy. Bahia was a wayport for Indiamen carrying soldiers to Portuguese garrisons in Asia. Many of these soldiers contracted scurvy and had to remain in the hospital in Bahia. During the governor-generalship of Dom João de Lencastre the soldiers of the garrison of Bahia had mooted the construction of a

---

[1] ASCMB, vol. 14, f. 142.

[2] All ships from Lisbon, Oporto, Angola, Costa da Mina and the Atlantic Islands paid 10$000 per voyage; smacks paid 5$000; each passenger paid 640 rs. Lower charges were levied for vessels arriving at Bahia from Brazilian ports, e.g. 2$000 for a smack from Rio de Janeiro (*Documentos historicos*, vol. 62, pp. 35–8).

[3] ASCMB, vol. 52, ff. 162–3.

military hospital. This proposal had not been implemented because the only funds the Crown had been willing to allocate for this purpose had been the tithes on certain livestock. These tithes had previously been conceded to the Misericórdia. It was indicative of the fickle nature of the royal support for the Misericórdia that Dom Pedro II had been perfectly willing to withdraw this financial benefit.[1] The question of a military hospital fell into abeyance. In 1740 the Count of Galvêas provided limited accommodation in the barracks of the Rosary for sick soldiers from Crown ships, but there was still great pressure on the Misericórdia hospital.[2] During the 1740s the Misericórdia adopted a tough line and insisted on more payment for treating the soldiers of the garrison in its hospital. Dispute over payment to the Misericórdia had dragged on for almost half a century and the attitude of Crown officials to the 'privileged' brotherhood had soured. In 1750 the viceroy, the Count of Atouguia, recommended to the king in no uncertain terms that the claims of the brotherhood be ignored and that a military hospital be built.[3] This suggestion was not followed and an uneasy agreement was reached with the Misericórdia as to payment. Only after the College of the Jesuits fell empty in 1759 following the expulsion of the Order did the city of Bahia have its own military hospital.[4]

The Misericórdia only opposed the foundation of hospitals which would rival its own. The Jesuits and Franciscans both had wards for sick members of their respective orders. In 1746 the Prior of the Capuchins was granted permission to establish a small hospital for sick and convalescent missionaries.[5] The Third Order of St Francis had mooted a hospital for sick tertiaries in the early eighteenth century but construction was only begun in 1802.[6] The Misericórdia did not oppose such foundations by the religious orders. Nor did it oppose the establishment of a leprosery. The hospital of the Misericórdia contained no isolation ward. When the Provedor of the Brotherhood of St Lazarus approached the city council in 1755 for financial

---

[1] King to governor-general, 16 November 1695 (APB, *Ordens régias*, vol. 3, doc. 94).

[2] APB, *Ordens régias*, vol. 47, f. 194.

[3] Viceroy to king, 24 March 1750 (ASCMB, vol. 15, f. 49v).

[4] Carlos Ott, *A Santa Casa*, p. 21 and n. 34.

[5] APB, *Ordens régias*, vol. 43, doc. 35a.

[6] Marieta Alves, *História da Venerável Ordem 3ª da Penitência do Seráfico Pe São Francisco da Congregação da Bahia* (Bahia, 1948), pp. 328–34.

K

aid for such a foundation the Misericórdia did not oppose this move. The petition was supported by the city council and the viceroy.[1] In 1762 the king approved the imposition of a municipal tax known as the *Real de S. Lazaro* and nominated the Provedor of the Misericórdia as one of the three guardians of the funds.[2] The opposition shown by the Misericórdia to the foundation of hospitals by friar Bernardo da Conceição, the Brotherhood of the Holy Body of Christ, and the viceroy, was not born of stubborn resistance to all such proposals. The Misericórdia was simply safeguarding its own interests. Whether these interests coincided with those of the community is debatable.

The hospital of the Misericórdia in Bahia failed to evoke those eulogies lavished on its counterpart in Gôa. In 1584 Gabriel Soares had commented on the smallness of the hospital. He had hastened to point out that this had been because of the absence of official financial support and not due to any negligence on the part of the brotherhood. Visitors to Bahia at the close of the seventeenth century and the beginning of the eighteenth century such as Froger, Dampier and Frézier dismissed it with no more than a reference. Mrs Kindersley did not even mention the Misericórdia in her *Letters*. In the late eighteenth century the caustic Vilhena described the hospital as 'sultry, small and wholly unsuitable'.[3]

There were some grounds for such criticism. There can be no doubt that the Misericórdia's order of priorities was wrong. During the seventeenth century the hospital came a poor second to the church. Boards of guardians adopted the attitude that ceremonies and religious festivities brought more prestige to the brotherhood than the cure of the sick. In this attitude the Mesas were correct. Colonial society followed a scale of values based on superficial appearances. A well organised funeral or glittering mass brought

---

[1] Petition of city council dated 5 July 1755 (AMB, vol. 182, ff. 49–50), supported by the viceroy in a letter of 9 October 1757 (APB, *Ordens régias*, vol. 59, f. 127). The viceroy suggested the imposition of a tax of 20 *rs.* on each householder, to meet the cost of construction which would be higher than for a comparable building in Portugal.

[2] Royal *provisão* of 27 March 1762. Taxes were imposed on a sliding scale depending on the social standing of the householder: plebeians — 20 *rs.* annually; householders enjoying the privileges of the nobility — 40 *rs.* annually; householders with charters of nobility — 80 *rs.* annually (ASCMB, vol. 208, ff. 1–2).

[3] Vilhena, *Noticias soteropolitanas*, vol. 1, p. 98.

more new members and more bequests to the brotherhood than would have the medical treatment of all the ragged beggars and half-starved slaves of the entire Recôncavo. The Misericórdia catered for the society of its time. A proposal for the complete rebuilding of the church was passed in 1653, within three years of the board of guardians itself having admitted that lack of funds was prejudicing its hospital services.[1] During the actual period of construction, involving enormous expenditures, one of the wards of the hospital was in such a state of ruin that it had to be shored up with props.[2] In the 1690s when the Misericórdia's financial resources were weakened by reconstruction of the hospital, an order was placed for a new retablo for the church at a cost of 1,000$000.[3] In the eighteenth century the hospital came a poor second to the other activities of the brotherhood in the field of social philanthropy. Nevertheless, it was the first to be quoted by successive boards of guardians in their protests to the king against infringements of the privileges of the Misericórdia.

The first hospital of Bahia had been built by Tomé de Sousa. This had undergone many changes, many of which are undocumented. During the seventeenth century there had been two major reconstructions. The first had been in 1649 when the 'old ward' had been rebeamed through the generosity of a benefactor.[4] In 1661 the medical ward had been in a state of collapse and the Mesa had decided to sell houses received by the brotherhood under the terms of the legacy of João Jerónimo. The proceeds from this sale had been applied to repairing the ward.[5] These repairs had been a short-term measure. During the next thirty years there had been numerous references in the account ledgers of payments to stonemasons and carpenters for work on the wards. In 1690 or 1691 the Mesa realised that money spent on such patching jobs was money lost. The old hospital was demolished and work begun on a totally new hospital.

There are few references in the Misericórdia archives to the nature of this

---

[1] Minute of 1 November 1653 (ASCMB, vol. 13, f. 41).

[2] 'e outrosy se considerou como a enfermaria das chagas deste Hospital está ja ameaçando sua ruyna, por estar despejada e cõ pontões, e indicando a mesma ruina as mais'; minute of 13 March 1661 (ASCMB, vol. 41, f. 55).

[3] Minute of 22 May 1695. The woodcarver, Manuel Pereira, received 50$000 for the plan and 950$000 for executing the work (ASCMB, vol. 14, f. 41).

[4] ASCMB, vol. 13, f. 13.   [5] ASCMB, vol. 41, f. 55.

reconstruction. Carlos Ott assumes that work began in 1691 but there is no documentary basis for this supposition.[1] The only certain piece of information is an inscription of 1696. This is situated on the corner of the building formed by the Ladeira da Misericórdia and the old Rua Direita, now known as the Rua da Misericórdia. Since this inscription is on the level of the second floor it is reasonable to assume that at least the outer walls of the new hospital had been finished by that date. If this was the case, work on the interior seems to have flagged. This may well have been due to lack of funds. In 1702 the treasurer of the brotherhood borrowed 1,000$000 from the treasurer of dowries to meet the cost of a water cistern constructed under the cloister.[2] In 1703 payments were made for the plastering, whitewashing and tiling of the hospital so it is safe to assume that the interior decoration was completed by this date.[3] The brotherhood then turned its attention to the building of a chemist's shop, finished in June 1704.[4] The hospital was now in its final state.

The new hospital was built on a narrow plot of land between the Rua Direita and the edge of the cliff. It was rectangular and its internal dimensions were sixty-nine feet by thirty-five feet.[5] The longer walls were bordered on the north by the brotherhood's church and on the south by the alley leading to the lower city. The east wall faced the street and the west wall was on the edge of the cliff. The only advantage of the site was that it was contiguous to the main administrative block of the Misericórdia. Otherwise the site was far from ideal for a hospital. It was situated in the busiest street of the city. Noise disturbed the patients and these for their part provided a ready source of infection. The hospital was also subject to the

---

[1] Carlos Ott, *A Santa Casa*, pp. 53–4.

[2] It had been decided to build this in 1701 to reduce the expenditure on slaves carrying water (ASCMB, vol. 14, ff. 59–60). The loan was made on 26 July 1702 (vol. 14, f. 64v).

[3] In April 1703, 69$900 was paid to the stonemason Belchior Ferreira for plastering the wards. In May 4$120 was paid to Ignacio Teixeira Rangel for tiles and whitewash for the hospital (ASCMB, vol. 850, f. 230).

[4] In February 1704, 283$200 was paid for wood and labour on the construction of the pharmacy. In June further payments totalling 121$520 were made for two window panes, iron fittings and painting (ASCMB, vol. 850, ff. 239v and 242).

[5] These were the dimensions given in an inventory made in 1844 and cited by Carlos Ott, *A Santa Casa*, n. 378.

evil-smelling alley leading to the lower city. Most detrimental was the unprotected situation on the edge of the cliff. The hospital was exposed to the rain and winds of the winter months and the scorching heat of the summer sun.

There were two wards, the medical ward (*enfermaria das chagas*) and the fever ward (*enfermaria das febres*). The upper ward came to be known as the ward of St Christopher because of a statue of this saint placed there.[1] This was the better of the two wards and was later chosen by the Count of Atouguia as more suitable for the treatment of soldiers.[2] The interior furnishings were sparse. Each ward had its own altar and masses were said on Sundays and saints' days. It is unlikely that there were beds for all the patients, because bequests of beds and bed-linen were made to the brotherhood. A straw mat brought by the patient on admittance often served as his bed and his shroud. Conditions were cramped and uncomfortable. Vilhena's testimony in this respect has already been quoted. In 1813 a testator left 8,000$000 to the brotherhood to improve the conditions of the sick, because these were often so bad that the health of a patient deteriorated rather than improved while undergoing treatment.[3] In 1816 the Mesa confirmed that this was the case and asked the Crown to authorise a lottery to provide the funds for a new building.[4] A century earlier the conditions had been even worse. At that time the Misericórdia had treated all the soldiers of the garrison and visiting ships in addition to the sick of the city and Recôncavo. Also latrines had only been installed in 1742; previously excrement had piled up during the day until a slave emptied the barrels in the evening.[5]

---

[1] ASCMB, vol. 214, f. 35.   [2] APB, *Ordens régias*, vol. 55, ff. 300–1.

[3] Legacy of Francisco Dias Coelho (ASCMB, vol. 42, f. 295v).

[4] In its petition of 20 September 1816 the Mesa stated: 'O Hospital da Caridade da dita Cidade, onde tantos desgraçados procurão amparo foi situado, talvêz, à mais de 200 annos na crista da montanha fronteira à Bahia, que serve de ancoradouro da mesma Cidade: todas as enfermarias, dispensa, cozinha, e mais arranjos do dito Hospital, são como subterraneos expostos, hũa parte do anno a grandes ardores do sol, e outra parte a ventanias, e humidades, de sorte, que se pode concluir, que os individuos, que procurão remedio às suas molestias no Hospital, encontrão o aumento dellas; acrescendo que o seu espaço he tão diminuto, que malmente poderia acomodar metade dos enfermos, que ora tem...' (ANRJ, *Caixa 288*, doc. 20).   [5] ASCMB, vol. 14, f. 273v.

Additional hospital accommodation was provided in the eighteenth century. This consisted of a madhouse for the insane and a ward for women. The construction of these was only started after the main hospital block contiguous to the church had been finished in 1703. In both cases advantage was taken of the slope of the hillside which permitted building below the level of the church and administrative buildings.

Little is known about the madhouse. Part of the large building programme of the brotherhood at the turn of the eighteenth century had included modifications to the cloister and the construction of a cistern. This cistern had been completed in 1702 and was directly under the cloister. Because of the slope of the hill there still remained some space between the cistern and the edge of the cliff below the level of the cloister. A group of rooms, referred to as the 'casinhas dos doudos', were built here and were completed by 1706.[1] The carriers of the biers were also accommodated in this part of the Misericórdia.[2] These were the unskilled and unpaid guardians of the insane.

The second addition was the female ward. This was also finished by 1706 and was a development of the work on the cloister and cistern.[3] This ward was in a very bad position under the sacristy. Not only was it damp because of its subterranean position but it was totally exposed to the elements, perched as it was on the very edge of the cliff. Ventilation was bad. There were only two windows. These were more of a bane than a boon. During the summer the sun entering the ward through these windows made the interior so hot and stifling that the sick were compelled to leave the windows open at night in order to cool the ward. Many developed respiratory ailments as a result of this. The Provedor himself described it in 1767 as an 'open shed'. It was a fair judgement of the living conditions in this ward that when a charnel-house for brothers was mooted in 1767, the female ward was selected as a suitable place. When the alterations were started the female patients were moved to better accommodation in the lower part of the retirement house.[4]

---

[1] Payment of 27$500 was made to Gabriel Ribeiro in September 1706 for this work (ASCMB, vol. 850, f. 274v).

[2] In May 1713 payment of 4$060 was made for the 'conserto da porta da caza dos homens da tumba e dos doudos' (ASCMB, vol. 851, f. 17).

[3] In November and December 1706 two jacarandá candlesticks and a chasuble were bought for the female ward and the oratory in this ward was painted (ASCMB, vol. 850, ff. 275-6).   [4] ASCMB, vol. 15, ff. 205v–206v and f. 239.

In 1712 it appears that another ward was built. This is something of a mystery. The only reference is payment of 129$000 in November of that year to a stonemason and carpenter for work on the 'new ward'. The place of this ward is not mentioned. During the eighteenth century there were numerous references to the 'ward for the poor' and the 'ward for incurables'. Whether these were alternative names for the medical ward and the fever ward or were alternative names for the new ward, is not clear. The designation of this ward as the 'new ward' presents a further difficulty. It will be recalled that the 'old ward' had been rebeamed in 1649 (pp. 94–5). In 1775 when the charnel-house became a reality the proposed site was mentioned as the 'old ward, formerly for women'. There are two possible explanations. First, that the ward rebeamed in 1649 was the same as the future charnel-house. Secondly, that the female ward was referred to in 1775 as the 'old ward' to differentiate it from the later 'new ward'. These suggest two conclusions. If the ward of 1649 and the charnel-house were in the same place this would suggest that the original hospital was off the street and on the edge of the cliff. There are several objections to this conclusion. Reference in 1661 to a medical ward (p. 273) implies the presence of another ward for which there would not have been room on the edge of the cliff. Moreover, the old church and sacristy had been demolished in 1653 when construction of the new building had been proposed. The work on the high altar had only been commissioned in 1670 and this had been built on the site of the former sacristy. Only in 1674 had work begun on a new wing containing the administrative offices of the brotherhood in the upper part and the sacristy in the lower.[1] Thus the female ward could only have come into existence after the establishment of the sacristy. Finally, there had been the description of the then Rua dos Mercadores made by Gabriel Soares in 1584. He had referred to the wards of the hospital.[2] The second conclusion, which seems the more probable, was that a new ward was built in 1712 and known as the 'new ward' to differentiate it from the female ward constructed some six years earlier which was known as the 'old ward'. By the eighteenth century the hospital of the Misericórdia consisted of three wards and rooms for the insane.

An important subsidiary of the hospital was the pharmacy. In the seven-

---

[1] A fully documented description of the building of the church and sacristy is given by Carlos Ott, *A Santa Casa*, pp. 32–51.

[2] Gabriel Soares de Sousa, *Notícia*, vol. 1, p. 256.

teenth century each ward had had its own pharmacy but these were amalga-
mated in 1704. At that time this pharmacy was one of the few pharmacies of
colonial Bahia. Its main function was to supply medicine to the hospital
but private citizens could also buy medical supplies. Although some of the
supplies for this pharmacy were bought locally, the majority of the medicines
were ordered from Lisbon. This led to abuse. In 1739 the Mesa discovered
that its chemist in Lisbon was making profits of between two and three
hundred per cent.[1] All risks were borne by the supplier against loss by fire,
sea or piracy.[2] The chemist administering the pharmacy in Bahia was an
employee of the Misericórdia. The only stipulation concerning his employment was that he should be an Old Christian.[3] Not surprisingly many of the
incumbents were ill-qualified and during the eighteenth century there were
several instances of chemists deserting this post, often taking the proceeds
of any sales with them.

The Misericórdia employed a paid medical staff for the hospital. These
ranged from well qualified doctors and surgeons to male nurses who had
been promoted from carrying the funeral biers. The number of doctors and
surgeons working in the wards varied. During the seventeenth century one
doctor and one surgeon had sufficed. In the eighteenth century with an
increasing urban population and more soldiers seeking hospital treatment an
increase in staff was necessary. A second doctor was appointed in 1711 and a
second surgeon in 1732.[4] The duties of the medical staff were to visit the
hospital morning and evening, be on call at any hour of the day and night if
summoned to the hospital, and treat the prisoners on the roll of the brotherhood. Although the appointment of two doctors was successful, that of the
two surgeons was not. Disagreements over duties and diagnoses prejudiced
the health of the patients and the Misericórdia reverted to the appointment of
a single surgeon.[5]

There is little information on the medical background of the doctors and
surgeons holding these appointments. The two exceptions are the doctor

---

[1] ASCMB, vol. 14, f. 254.   [2] ASCMB, vol. 52, f. 117.

[3] The minute of the Mesa recording the election of a pharmacist in 1693 noted
that the candidate finally selected was a 'Christão Velho, parte essencial requerida
pelo Compromisso' (ASCMB, vol. 37, f. 58).

[4] ASCMB, vol. 14, f. 95 and ff. 168v–169.

[5] Minute of 27 March 1757 (ASCMB, vol. 15, ff. 89v–91).

Francisco de Araújo e Azevedo and the surgeon Francisco da Costa Franco, both prominent in eighteenth-century Bahia. The first was involved in a disputed election for the post of doctor to the city council. This office fell vacant in 1742 on the retirement of Dr João Álvares de Vasconcellos. The post was not advertised and the councillors simply elected Dr João Nunes Velho, a doctor of established reputation. Francisco de Araújo e Azevedo challenged the method of election and was upheld in the Court of Appeals. The appointment was annulled. When Dr João Álvares de Vasconcellos died in 1745 the city council posted notices in the city inviting applications. There were only two candidates, Francisco de Araújo e Azevedo and João Nunes Velho. This was simply because the other doctors recognised the superiority of these two candidates and did not wish to risk their own reputations. Both candidates fulfilled the conditions governing the appointment. These were the following: first, that the candidates be approved by the University of Coimbra; secondly, that they be competent in their profession; thirdly, that they be Old Christians. The result was decided by the casting vote of the *juiz de fora* as president of the municipal council and João Nunes Velho was elected. Francisco de Araújo e Azevedo challenged the result. His appeal was based on a royal decree of 1585. This decree had ruled that any doctor who was an Old Christian and had received his medical training at Coimbra should be preferred over any other doctor. The viceroy upheld this appeal following an enquiry ordered by Dom João V.[1] In 1749 Francisco de Araújo e Azevedo was elected doctor of the hospital of the Misericórdia.[2] Certainly on this occasion the Mesa could not be accused of making a poor appointment.

The surgeon Francisco da Costa Franco was no less experienced. He had served in the ships of the *carreira da India*, had practised in India, and had been surgeon of the garrison at Mozambique before coming to Brazil.[3] In 1731 he was chosen by the city council as municipal surgeon to inspect ships arriving in Bahia from Africa.[4] Later it was alleged that he owed this

---

[1] This incident is fully documented in AMB, vol. 30, ff. 319v–320v and f. 359v and APB, *Ordens régias*, vol. 43, doc. 59 and accompanying documents.

[2] ASCMB, vol. 37, ff. 218 and 225.

[3] APB, *Ordens régias*, vol. 38, doc. 70 and accompanying documents.

[4] AMB, vol. 176, f. 171. He had first been nominated for this post in 1729 by the Count of Sabugosa at the express wish of the city council. In 1733 Dom João V

K 2

appointment to his skilful portrayal of a lackey in a comedy organised by the municipality to celebrate a royal marriage! Nevertheless he could muster the favourable testimonies of the Count of Galvêas and various Provedors of the Misericórdia. He served in the hospital of the Misericórdia from 1734 to 1751.[1]

The rest of the staff in the hospital held no such claims to a knowledge of medicine. The 'barber' (*barbeiro*) was usually a coloured person with a rudimentary training in his art. In 1727 the Misericórdia even apprenticed the children of one of its slaves to a 'barber', who was himself a slave, to learn the art of bleeding. In so doing the Misericórdia hoped to save the salary a free man would have demanded.[2] It is possible that the situation may have improved in the mid-eighteenth century after the city council instituted examinations for all 'barbers' and midwives as members of the so-called mechanical trades.[3]

The nurses were totally unqualified. During the eighteenth century there were two male nurses and one female nurse. From 1706 these were under the supervision of a chief nurse.[4] The only qualifications demanded by the brotherhood were that nurses be white and without taint of Jewish blood. The nurses were frequently illiterate and gave the wrong medicines to patients. Many of the male nurses had started in the Misericórdia service as carriers of the biers. Their treatment of the sick can be imagined. One was dismissed for playing cards with the soldiers while patients were dying.[5] When the brotherhood appointed a *picardo* of criminal tendencies in 1722, even the viceroy was constrained to remind the brotherhood of its obligations to the sick.[6]

---

excused the council from having a municipal surgeon. In 1744, when the post was re-created, Francisco da Costa Franco was ignored in favour of another candidate. He appealed to the king but his petition was rejected by the viceroy in 1756 (APB, *Ordens régias*, vol. 51, ff. 62–3 and vol. 55, ff. 85–125).

[1] ASCMB, vol. 37, f. 185 and f. 214.

[2] At the end of three years' instruction the *barbeiro* was to receive payment of 12$000 for each child (ASCMB, vol. 14, ff. 153v–154).

[3] The certificate of competence for a *barbeiro* stated 'que ele possa sangrar, sarjar, lançar venosas e sanguessugas'. The first such rudimentary medical examinations are recorded in AMB, vol. 191.

[4] Whereas the annual salary of a nurse in 1706 was 29$200, that of the chief nurse was 45$200 (ASCMB, vol. 850, f. 282). [5] ASCMB, vol. 13, f. 15v.

[6] He had been cured of an illness in the hospital and retained as a nurse. The Count of Sabugosa described him as a 'picador por autonomásia, e não por ofício' and ordered his dismissal in 1722 (*Documentos historicos*, vol. 45, p. 17).

The spiritual needs of the sick were provided for by a priest employed by the Misericórdia. He was appropriately called the *padre da agonia* ('priest of the agony'). He received free accommodation next to the hospital and was obliged to attend to the sick by day and by night. He made an inventory of the clothes and possessions of people entering the hospital. His religious duties consisted of saying masses in the wards, hearing confessions and administering the sacraments to the dying.

There are no registers extant in the archives of the brotherhood which provide information on the identity, place of origin, civil status or colour of the sick treated in the hospital. Nor is there any register of the number treated in the hospital and the nature of their ailments. Lack of documentary evidence rules out a detailed statistical survey of those receiving medical assistance from the Misericórdia, but a general picture can be obtained from a variety of sources. The Misericórdia treated any sick person in its hospital without prejudice of class, colour or creed. It must be remembered that the prime purpose of the Misericórdia was to assist the poor. Any citizen who could afford the services of a doctor received medical attention in his own house. Thus the patients of the Misericórdia were what might be termed nowadays 'second class citizens'. They fell into four groups: first, coloured people and poor whites; secondly, foreigners; thirdly, the soldiers of the garrison; fourthly, soldiers and sailors from the Indiamen and other Crown vessels.

A large part of the population of colonial Bahia was Negro, mulatto or *mestiço*. These coloured people were either slaves or freedmen. The position of the slave was ambiguous. On the one hand he was the object of the sadism and cruelty of his master. He worked long hours and received a meagre ration. On the other hand he represented a financial investment and consequently he was a symbol of the social prestige of his master. Many slaves were treated in the Misericórdia hospital. Sometimes they had been abandoned by their masters at the first sign of infirmity or senility. On other occasions a more benevolent master sent his slave to the hospital to be treated. This was more common in the eighteenth century when the price of slaves rose considerably. It was cheaper to pay for medicines than to replace a good slave.

The position of the slave who had been emancipated was no less ambiguous. The Negro was the butt of a society in which racial inferiority was equated to social inferiority. A slave granted his freedom by a kind master had no cause to be unduly grateful for his emancipation. Some few did achieve financial independence by learning a trade. The majority continued in servile employment or relied on public charity. The freed female slave was better off than the male in this respect: at least she could turn her culinary skills to a profitable end. In the burial records of those dying in the hospital there were numerous references to freed *pardos*. Sometimes there was a comment which casts light on the way of life of the freedman: a beggar from door to door; a prisoner in the gaol; a convict from Oporto. The freedman had no less need of the charity of the Misericórdia than the slave.

Few Indians were treated in the hospital. The indigenous population had retreated from the urban area at an early date and even from the Recôncavo by the eighteenth century. Moreover, few Indians overcame their distrust of medicine as practised by the European. Very occasionally the odd Tupí drifted into the hospital for treatment. More frequently those Indians who were patients had been brought from Jacobina and Rio de Contas under arrest to stand trial in Bahia. They succumbed to the conditions of the prison or the harshness of their punishment and were sent to the hospital of the Misericórdia.

Bahia also contained a large number of 'poor whites'. Brazil was a country of possibility for colonisers with a trade. A peasant of the Minho could adapt his agricultural knowledge to the cultivation of tobacco. A carpenter or stonemason of Lisbon was sought after in colonial Bahia for work on churches and monasteries. But there were many without a trade. They had been attracted to Brazil by stories of fortunes to be made in gold. Brazil was also a place of exile. A convict was left to his own devices after transportation to Bahia. Vilhena noted that a large part of the population was accustomed to hunger, partly as a result of their lack of training, partly because of lethargy and pride.[1] A life of malnutrition and an unhealthy environment led to diseases of a socio-economic nature. The hospital of the Misericórdia offered the only medical treatment for this 'poor white trash'.

Foreigners were not welcome in colonial Brazil. Tales of English captains finding gold in the Amazon region reduced the Portuguese court to

---

[1] Vilhena, *Noticias soteropolitanas*, vol. 2, p. 927.

a state of panic whenever a foreign ship put into a Brazilian port.[1] When a ship of the English East India Company put into Bahia in 1749 for repairs to a broken mast, the pilots were questioned, the charts examined and witnesses interrogated, before she was allowed to berth. A High Court judge carried out an enquiry and the viceroy informed Lisbon of the event.[2] When a foreigner, one Cornelius, was dying in the fort of St Anthony where he was imprisoned in 1719, the viceroy authorised his removal under guard to the hospital of the Misericórdia for treatment; afterwards he was to be replaced in the fort.[3] Thus there are few records of foreigners receiving treatment in the Misericórdia: some sailors off a French ship; Spanish sailors; two natives of Hamburg; even a mad Englishman solemnly recorded as being 130 years old!

Any estimate of the number of civilians treated each year in the hospital can be little more than a guess. The only clues are entries in the account ledgers. In 1700 João de Mattos de Aguiar died leaving a sum of 16,000 *cruzados* to the Misericórdia. The annual interest on this bequest was 500$000 of which the Misericórdia received 100$000 for administration. The other 400$000 was for poor patients leaving the hospital, each patient receiving 1$000.[4] In the first year of operation 400 patients received this bounty.[5] In subsequent years the number fell to some 150 each year. In the quin-quennium 1750–5 only 455 patients received their 1$000.[6] Whether this drop in numbers was due to financial difficulties experienced by the brother-hood, or was the result of improved urban sanitation, it is impossible to say. I am tempted towards the latter explanation. In the years 1757–63 a register

---

[1] One such case was in 1714, when a vague rumour reached Lisbon concerning one Captain Bond. While sailing to the Mina coast, he had been driven off course and had landed on a desolate part of the coast of South America. The natives had shown him samples of gold. He had reported this discovery to Queen Anne, who had made concessions of the new lands to her ministers and authorised the equip-ping of two cargo ships and three frigates to make further exploration. Rumours reaching Lisbon placed the landfall as somewhere between the Amazon and the Island of Sta Catharina! Dom João V alerted the governor in Rio and the viceroy in Bahia to prevent any landing (ANRJ, *Códice* 952, vol. 19, ff. 96–7).

[2] APB, *Ordens régias*, vol. 46, doc. 24.   [3] *Documentos historicos*, vol. 55, p. 204.
[4] ASCMB, vol. 199, ff. 3v–4.   [5] ASCMB, vol. 850, f. 219.
[6] Calculated from the account ledgers for these years (ASCMB, vols. 862, 863, 864, 865 and 866).

of women patients records a total of 179 entries,[1] which suggests that the earlier calculations for both sexes may be accurate.

The soldiers of the garrison of Bahia were also treated in the hospital of the Misericórdia. The garrison consisted of two infantry regiments known as the 'old regiment' and the 'new regiment'. There was also an artillery regiment in the eighteenth century. The garrison was constantly under-manned. Military service was unpopular and the church offered an easy option. A cobbler or smith with a family of boys guaranteed their future by having them ordained. The archbishop co-operated enthusiastically to the fury of the Count of Sabugosa.[2] The conditions of military service were hard. Pay was bad. Soldiers deserted at any opportunity. Only the 'old regiment' had barrack accommodation. Other soldiers were boarded out in the city. Both infantry regiments had their own surgeon, and the surgeon of the 'old regiment' also treated the artillerymen.[3] There was no military hospital and all sick soldiers were sent to the Misericórdia for treatment. The additional numbers placed great pressure on the medical staff of the Misericórdia and on its financial resources. Reference will be made later to the cost of treatment of these soldiers. Suffice it to say here that payment was inadequate and delayed. In these circumstances it was not surprising that the Misericórdia should tend to give priority to the civilian patients of the city and the Recôncavo. Especially in the knowledge that if a soldier deserted after being cured (as frequently happened) the brotherhood would receive no payment for medicines or treatment. Complaints were made by the soldiers of negligence. The Mesas petitioned the Crown for adequate payment. Kings and viceroys ignored both complaints and petitions and relations between the Misericórdia and the soldiers deteriorated.

The Count of Atouguia (Viceroy, 1749–55) took matters in hand. Within

---

[1] ASCMB, vol. 1043, ff. 2–20v.

[2] In a letter of 24 July 1722 to the king, the viceroy complained of how totally unsuitable candidates were being ordained, the archbishop apparently favouring 'os ignorantes e mal procedidos'. Explaining the lack of soldiers he commented: 'Não so nesta cide, mas nem ainda em toda a Capla ha pessoa que se possa fazer soldado, porque o Ferreyro, Sapatro e mais officiaes que se achão com quatro ou cinco filhos, todos se ordenão e todos acha o Arcebispo que devem ser admittidos' (APB, *Ordens régias*, vol. 16, doc. 4a).

[3] He received an additional monthly stipend of 6$000 for this by a royal order of 1738 (APB, *Ordens régias*, vol. 34, doc. 134).

a year of taking office he ordered the reluctant brotherhood to build ten cubicles in one of the wards for soldiers so that they should not be infected by contact with the other sick. He also ordered an infantry lieutenant to visit the hospital each day and ensure that the soldiers were well treated.[1] The viceroy followed up this action by commending to the king in March 1750 the building of a military hospital. Plans had been drawn up and an estimate made. The Count of Atouguia told the king bluntly that this would prove cheaper than paying the Misericórdia. The chief commissioner of the Treasury was more cautious in his report. He advised that adequate financial reimbursement be made to the Misericórdia and that the soldiers should continue to be treated in the hospital.[2] Perhaps the viceroy was embittered by this report. Certainly he offered the brotherhood no quarter. In 1751 he totally rejected in the strongest terms a petition by the Misericórdia to the king for more payment.[3] The king ignored the domineering attitude of his representative and adopted the only reasonable course. He ordered the viceroy to reach an agreement with the Misericórdia over payment.[4] The Count of Atouguia summoned the commissioner and the Provedor of the Misericórdia, José Pires de Carvalho e Albuquerque, and an agreement was signed on 19 February 1754. This was disastrous to the brotherhood. The payment was insufficient. The best ward of the hospital was commandeered for the use of the garrison.[5]

Unfortunately the earliest registers of the numbers of infantrymen and artillerymen treated in the hospital only date from 1757. Thus they can only serve as a rough guide to the earlier period. In the years 1757–63, the following numbers of soldiers received treatment:

> 'Old regiment' (twelve Companies): 595.
> 'New regiment' (twelve Companies): 678.
> Artillery (five Companies): 152.

The number of deaths among these soldiers receiving treatment in the hospital was astonishingly low: twenty-three out of a total of 1,425. It is interesting to note that fifteen of these were among soldiers of the 'new regiment'. This suggests that the barracks did make a significant difference

---

[1] ASCMB, vol. 15, ff. 34v–35v.   [2] ASCMB, vol. 15, ff. 49v–51.
[3] Viceroy to king, 3 May 1751 (APB, *Ordens régias*, vol. 47, ff. 187v–188v).
[4] King to viceroy, 13 September 1753, copied in ASCMB, vol. 15, f. 70.
[5] APB, *Ordens régias*, vol. 55, ff. 307v–308v.

to the numbers of seriously sick. The figures also suggest that the proportion of minor ailments was constant in the two regiments and that complaints by the Misericórdia of malingering were well founded.[1]

The soldiers and sailors of the Indiamen and other Crown vessels did not awake the same antipathy in the Misericórdia as their land-based colleagues. Whereas treatment of the garrison represented a financial loss, the treatment of the sailors and soldiers in transit represented a gain. The spirited opposition by the Misericórdia to the pretensions of the Brotherhood of the Holy Body of Christ was born of purely economic considerations. Ridiculously enough the soldiers of the garrison paid only their paltry daily wage to the Misericórdia. The soldiers and sailors of the Indiamen paid dues calculated on the numbers carried by each ship, irrespective of whether these were sick or not. Thus their treatment was extremely profitable to the brotherhood. The pressure on the hospital was much greater than was the case with the soldiers of the garrison. But it was concentrated into the few weeks following the arrival of the fleet in Bahia.

Conditions on the Indiamen were bad. Sailors were kept at work day and night. Their clothes were no more than rags. Their rations were small and lacking in proteins and vitamins. The basic diet consisted of biscuits, half a pound of salted meat daily, and some water. The biscuits were often rotten. The meat shrank to some four ounces on cooking. The water was putrid. In addition, the kitchen clerk and the mate frequently stole rations of chickens and other foodstuffs put on board for the sick. It was small wonder that the Count of Galvêas commented that 'almost all arrive here more skeletons than men'.[2]

These sick were treated in the Misericórdia hospital. The pressure on the hospital staff can be gauged from some few examples of ships arriving at Bahia riddled with scurvy. In June 1710 the Misericórdia faced the problem of accommodating 300 sick sailors and soldiers from the fleet.[3] In 1738 the medical expenses on the sick of two frigates came to over 5,000 *cruzados*, although there is no mention of the numbers treated.[4] In 1748 the ship *Bom*

---

[1] ASCMB, vols. 1040, 1041 and 1042.

[2] APB, *Ordens régias*, vol. 36, doc. 52 and vol. 45, doc. 34.

[3] ASCMB, vol. 52, ff. 39–40.

[4] When a third ship arrived the viceroy ordered its sick to be taken to the Rosário barracks. Noting that the cost of their treatment there was half that incurred in the

Jesus de Vila Nova berthed at Bahia after a sixty-day crossing from Lisbon: twenty-three sailors had died and eighty were sent to hospital.[1] Victims of scurvy were not limited to Portuguese ships. In 1728 a ship of the Ostend Company homeward-bound from Bengal put into Bahia with half her crew of 110 suffering from scurvy.[2]

The Count of Galvêas was the only viceroy to combat this evil. He tried to remedy dietary deficiencies by planned victualling. Vegetables and fruit formed the basis of this diet. Protein was supplied by cooked beans and fatty meat. Salt meat was reserved for special occasions because it was suspected of causing intestinal troubles.[3] He ordered that ships should carry supplies sufficient to allow the crews to have two meals daily. Sailors were also provided with more substantial clothing to protect them from exposure during the long voyage round the Cape of Good Hope and across the Indian Ocean.[4] No single man could cure such a widespread evil. In 1763 three ships arrived at Bahia with so many sick that they could not be housed in the hospital of the Misericórdia. Many of the 441 sick were placed in the forts of the Barbalho and St Anthony, comfortless prisons. Such was the continual pressure on the hospital that many brothers simply refused to serve in the wards. They were expelled by the Mesa for lack of charity. Expulsion was ineffective. Only after intervention by the acting governors threatening to report all defectors to Lisbon as rebels, were the brothers induced to help in the wards.[5] This was indicative of the

---

Misericórdia hospital, he suggested to Dom João V that this practice be adopted in future (APB, *Ordens régias*, vol. 34, doc. 102).

[1] APB, *Ordens régias*, vol. 45, doc. 34.

[2] APB, *Ordens régias*, vol. 23, doc. 43. In 1724 a French frigate, bound for the Coromandel coast, put into Bahia for repairs to a broken mast. There were only fourteen sick with scurvy out of a complement of 250 (APB, *Ordens régias*, vol. 18, doc. 61).

[3] Viceroy to secretary of state, 28 September 1740 (APB, *Ordens régias*, vol. 36, doc. 44).

[4] In a letter of 22 June 1748 to the Marquis of Alorna, the viceroy observed that many deaths on board were 'porque o estrago q' fez nestes homens a morte, não procedeo tanto das infermidades como da fome que experimentarão na viagem': (APB, *Ordens régias*, vol. 45, doc. 34).

[5] After the death of the Marquis of Lavradio on 4 July 1760 a triumvirate consisting of the Archbishop-elect Manuel Santa Ignez, the Chancellor José Carvalho de Andrade, and Colonel Gonçalo Xavier de Barros Alvim, formed the government.

extent to which the Crown authorities were dependent on the Misericórdia.

The patients treated in the hospital of the Misericórdia came from all walks of life and suffered from a wide variety of diseases. The prevalent diseases in colonial Bahia fell roughly into three groups: first, the so-called 'tropical diseases'; secondly, diseases resulting from climatic conditions; thirdly, diseases of socio-economic origins. It must be realised that such divisions are arbitrary. Many ailments were the result of general reduction rather than of any specific cause. Pulmonary infection in a slave was variously attributable to high humidity, exposure to sudden rains and hot sunshine, or cramped living conditions in water-logged slave quarters.

Certain diseases are more common in tropical than temperate climes. In colonial Bahia malaria, yellow fever and leprosy prevailed. Lepers were not admitted by the Misericórdia but were treated by the Brotherhood of St Lazarus, so will not be discussed here. Malaria was common in colonial Bahia, although disguised as agues and unknown fevers. The low land on the east side of the city between the Benedictine and Carmelite monasteries was very swampy. A small river, the Rio das Tripas, ran along the Baixa dos Sapateiros in the winter months. It dried up in the summer leaving pools of static water. Vilhena referred to the agues and 'mortal fevers' caused by this marshland and static water.

There had been an epidemic of yellow fever in Bahia in May and June of 1686. It had originated in Pernambuco where there had been over 2,000 victims. The first signs in Bahia had been the deaths of two men after having eaten in a brothel in the lower city. Plague had enveloped the city. The contemporary chronicler Sebastião da Rocha Pitta referred to days when there were more than 200 deaths. The hospital was full, houses were crammed with the dying, and the streets were littered with corpses. The action of the brotherhood in treating patients and burying the dying can be gauged from the entries in the burial registers. In May 1686 the Misericórdia buried a total of 288 people. These included 129 charitable burials, and 60 of people who had died in the hospital. In the following month the figures were 186, 73 and 51 respectively.[1] The plague had its hero and heroine. The hero was the governor, the Marquis of Minas, who visited the sick of

---

These three signed the letter of 9 February 1763, threatening to report defectors to the king (ASCMB, vol. 15, ff. 151–2).

[1] Sebastião da Rocha Pitta, *Historia*, Livro 7, §35 and ASCMB, vol. 1251.

the city and sent assistance to the villages of the Recôncavo. The heroine was the widow, Dona Francisca de Sande, who converted her home into wards for the sick. The plague only subsided after the populace had adopted St Francis Xavier as the patron saint of the city. Some cynics would attribute it to the oncoming of the cooler winter months.

Although the climate of Bahia is fairly uniform with a variation of only 6° C. between summer and winter, there is considerable difference in the frequency and intensity of rains in the two seasons. Change of season or heavy rain in summer brought on outbreaks of infections of the pulmonary and respiratory organs. Colds and catarrhs developed into inflammation of the lungs, tuberculosis, rheumatic fevers and agues. The burial record of a patient of the hospital frequently noted that 'he came without speech' which suggests the presence of pulmonary oedema and secondary cardiac failures. Sometimes these illnesses reached epidemic proportions. During November and December of 1742 and the first eight months of 1743 there were over 5,000 deaths in Bahia as the result of such illnesses.[1] These illnesses usually diminished with the cooler winter months of May, June and July.

The third type of disease resulted from socio-economic causes. Seasonal change was often allied to conditions of environment. Flooding resulted in many hovels of the lower city being invaded by swirling waters, carrying faecal waste, typhoid and dysentery. Inferior living standards increased the supply of susceptibles. The Count of Sabugosa noted in 1730 that disease was more prevalent among the lower classes.[2] This was undoubtedly true. Malnutrition was common in colonial Bahia. Many slaves resorted to earth-eating to supply mineral deficiencies. Nor was malnutrition limited to the lower classes. The table of many a plantation owner lacked fresh meat, fish and vegetables. Slave and master alike suffered from ailments of the digestive tracts. Strong seasoning of foods with *dendê* oil and peppers had similarly adverse effects.

Diseases introduced into Bahia by slaves, sailors or colonisers included measles, smallpox, syphilis and scurvy. Measles affected the rural areas of the interior severely. In 1750 the Governor of the Captaincy of Rio de Janeiro, Gomes Freire de Andrada informed the Count of Atouguia of a rumoured

---

[1] APB, *Ordens régias*, vol. 39, doc. 47.   [2] APB, *Ordens régias*, vol. 26, doc. 38.

epidemic of measles in Pará and Maranhão in which 60,000 Indians had died.[1] Smallpox also seems to have moved from the interior to the coastal area. In the sixteenth century the Jesuit missionary José de Anchieta had reported the deaths of some 30,000 Indians in less than three months in the Jesuit villages. An epidemic of smallpox among the slaves of the Recôncavo in the years 1680–4 had reduced the number of labourers so drastically as to affect sugar production severely. In the eighteenth century the disease raged in the city. Some landowners refused to leave their plantations in the Recôncavo to come to the city from fear of catching smallpox. Any criminal sent from the interior to the gaol in Bahia could regard his imprisonment as a death sentence because of this disease.

Syphilis was probably the commonest disease of colonial Bahia. It was the disease of the *casa grande* ('big house') and the *senzala*, or slave quarters: the disease of plantation owner, householder, soldier, priest and slave. In 1717 the city council wrote to Dom João V asking that a French surgeon should be allowed to stay, despite the royal order to expel all foreigners from Bahia, simply because he had developed a successful remedy for the *morbo gallico*.[2] Many sailors and slaves arriving in Bahia were suffering from scurvy. It was often referred to as the *mal de Luanda* ('evil of Luanda') — a fine example of racial prejudice. In fact the white sailors were as much the guilty parties as the slaves. Because of the superficial similarity in the ulcerative signs of scurvy and leprosy, these were frequently confused. When the city council supported the establishment of a leprosery in 1755, reference was made to the 'evil of Luanda' as well as leprosy as diseases introduced into Bahia by slaves. In granting approval Dom José I differentiated between the two diseases, pointing out that scurvy was not contagious and was curable.[3]

The treatment of patients in the hospital was of the most rudimentary. The stock remedies for any ill were bleeding and purging. The abuse of blood-letting in Brazil was even more common than in Europe. During the

---

[1] ANRJ, *Códice 84*, Livro 12, f. 56v.

[2] Letter of 25 August 1717 (AMB, vol. 176, f. 119). Cf. similar requests by the city council of Macao for royal authorisation to employ foreign doctors in *Arquivos de Macau*, vol. 1, no. 1 (1929), p. 21; 3rd series, vol. 2, no. 5 (1964), p. 306; 3rd series, vol. 2, no. 6 (1964), p. 378.

[3] AMB, vol. 182, ff. 49v–50 and ASCMB, vol. 208, ff. 1–2.

yellow fever epidemic many of the sick had been totally debilitated by protracted bleeding. When the future Provedor of the Misericórdia, André Marques, was ill with fever and haemorrhoids in 1736, he was bled daily for a week and almost died as a result.[1] Purgatives featured prominently on any order for the pharmacy of the Misericórdia — 'purgas de batata, purgas de antimónio, conservas purgativas, pilulas purgativas'. Although Gabriel Soares in his *Notícia* of 1584 had mentioned the therapeutic value of plants and medicinal herbs to be found in Brazil, most of the medicines used in colonial Bahia were imported from Portugal. Pharmaceutical lists from Portugal included elixirs, waters of Melissa, pills containing mercury (for syphilis), infusions of valerian, electuaries of opium, syrups of all sorts, ointments, oils of sweet almonds and plasters.[2]

The maintenance of a hospital was a considerable drain on the financial resources of the brotherhood. To a minor degree this was offset by small charges levied by the Misericórdia for medical assistance. On some occasions a patient was able to contribute financially to the cost of his treatment, but would have been unable to afford the expense of a doctor in his own home. The Misericórdia charged 320 *rs.* for each day of treatment. Costs for the cure of slaves were met by their masters at the same rate. The annual income derived was small, rarely exceeding 100$000. The second source of income was the pharmacy. In addition to supplying the hospital, the chemist also sold medicines to the public. In the early years of the eighteenth century the receipts were substantial — 251$360 in 1720.[3] By mid-century the larger numbers of pharmacies in Bahia had spoilt the market for the Misericórdia. Receipts were 105$110 in 1737: 24$140 in 1738; 221$950 in 1740: 92$560 in 1741: 32$300 in 1742. It is readily apparent that the hospital services of the Misericórdia far from paid for themselves. The brotherhood relied on private and public funds for most of its income.

The major part of the money spent by the Misericórdia on medical services came from private sources. Whereas prisoners and foundlings had failed to arouse the sympathy of potential testators in the seventeenth century, the hospital of the Misericórdia had been remembered in numerous wills. In

[1] APB, *Ordens régias*, vol. 55, f. 117.
[2] The two complete lists of orders for the pharmacy of the Misericórdia are of 1660 and 1739 (ASCMB, vol 13, ff 125–6 and vol. 14, f. 254).
[3] ASCMB, vol. 846, f. 84.

1750 the total of bequests left to the brotherhood to be placed on loan for financing the hospital was calculated at 15,843$964.[1] In practice the money available fell far short of this sum. An enquiry of 1754 revealed that only 6,095$530 of such bequests still remained.[2] Most of these legacies were made for general purposes. Some few were for the purchase of beds or bed linen. In the eighteenth century the type of bequests changed to legacies without any administrative commitment. The Misericórdia received single bequests amounting to some 200$000 in an average year to be applied to the hospital.

Public funds provided the second source of income for the Misericórdia. The contribution of the city council towards the expenses of the brotherhood was negligible. No municipal grant was made for the hospital, and only in the face of severe opposition were the councillors persuaded to assist the brotherhood financially in the care of foundlings. The Crown was more forthcoming. The hospital of the Misericórdia catered specifically for men on the royal service. This semi-bureaucratic function of the brotherhood was recognised by the Crown and grants were made to the Misericórdia to lessen the financial burden of maintaining the hospital. This Crown aid took two forms — financial privileges or outright grants, and payment for the treatment of men on the royal service.

The Misericórdia was granted a concession from the tithes collected on livestock, fowls, eggs, suckling pigs and goats. This tithe was known as the *miunça dos dízimos*. This had been granted originally in 1677 or 1678 and was renewed by the Crown for six yearly periods until 1703.[3] In this year it lapsed and was not renewed despite insistent pleas by the brotherhood. The contractors of the tithe simply kept the 130$000 formerly collected by the Misericórdia. Dom João V stopped this practice in 1709 by ordering that the contractor pay this sum to the Treasury.[4] The Misericórdia of Bahia never regained this favour. The other contribution by the Crown to the hospital was in 1734. Boards of guardians had been petitioning the Crown throughout the century for financial aid for the hospital. The brothers had even threatened to refuse to treat the soldiers of the garrison unless a grant were forthcoming, or payment increased for their treatment. In 1734 Dom

---

[1] ASCMB, vol. 211.   [2] ASCMB, vol. 210, f. 21v.

[3] In 1683 the Provedor João Peixoto Viegas had asked that this concession be renewed *in perpetuum*, but this had not been granted (ASCMB, vol. 207, ff. 21v–22).

[4] King to viceroy, 5 July 1709 (APB, *Ordens régias*, vol. 7, doc. 636).

João V yielded to this insistence and issued an order for 200$000 to be paid annually to the brotherhood by the Treasury.[1]

The Misericórdia was paid for the treatment of sailors and soldiers on Crown vessels. Payment for members of the Indiamen varied in the course of the eighteenth century. Until 1712 the cost had been calculated on the general basis of a contribution by each ship arriving in Bahia, at a rate of 4$000 for each ship and 2$000 for each smack. In 1712 an additional charge was levied of 1$000 on each member of the crew, be he sick or not.[2] This method of payment was later replaced by one based on the numbers of soldiers and sailors cured in the hospital. Fees of 320 *rs.* on days when there was chicken, and 200 *rs.* when there was meat, were paid to the brotherhood.[3] Payment for the treatment of soldiers of the garrison was on a different scale. During the seventeenth century 40 *rs.* had been stopped from the pay packet of each soldier; this had amounted to 120 *rs.* over three months and had been known as the *mostra*. In 1704 Dom Pedro II ordered that these contributions be stopped and that any soldier, sick in the hospital of the Misericórdia, should only pay to the brotherhood his earnings during the time he was in hospital. The pay of soldiers was deplorably low. The Misericórdia only received 40 *rs. per diem* for each soldier, totally inadequate to meet the cost of food, medicine and medical attention. Only in 1754 was this payment increased to 200 *rs.* and the brotherhood rapidly discovered that this too was insufficient.[4]

It is impossible to produce a balance-sheet for the expenditure made by the Misericórdia on the hospital. The following are mere indications of expenses incurred, calculated on the average annual costs for the eighteenth century: pharmacy: 500$000; food (including that for prisoners, foundlings, staff, girls of the retirement house): 3,600$000; salaries for medical staff: 520$000; bedclothes: 50$000. If fees for burials, price of slaves and expenses of upkeep are added, the total expenditure by the Misericórdia on the

---

[1] King to viceroy, 28 June 1734 (APB, *Ordens régias*, vol. 31, doc. 6).

[2] Minute of Mesa of 26 May 1712 (ASCMB, vol. 14, ff. 100v–102).

[3] This was established practice by 1738 (ASCMB, vol. 14, ff. 243v–245).

[4] The fee of 200 *rs.* had been settled on 19 February 1754. By September the Mesa realised this was inadequate and asked the king to increase it to 400 *rs.* for each soldier. In 1756 both the commissioner of the Treasury and the viceroy supported this petition (APB, *Ordens régias*, vol. 55, ff. 300–10).

hospital would probably be in the region of 5,000$000 each year. This was one-third of the total expenditure made by the brotherhood in any year and was offset by only a small contribution from the Crown.

By maintaining a hospital the Misericórdia made its greatest contribution to social welfare in colonial Bahia. In a city where sanitation was bad and disease common the Misericórdia alone offered any form of medical attention to the populace. The brotherhood performed a service which would now be the responsibility of the city, if not of the state. In the eighteenth century the responsibility was shirked by the Crown in Lisbon and the municipal council in Bahia. Thus it was that a lay brotherhood came to play a semi-bureaucratic rôle in public life. In this the Misericórdia was unique among the brotherhoods of the Portuguese colonial empire. Not only in Bahia, but in Luanda, Gôa and Macao the Crown and municipal authorities recognised the importance of the Misericórdia and the extent to which they were dependent on the brotherhood in providing social aid for the respective communities.

I2

The Foundling Wheel

FOUNDLINGS had always been an essentially urban problem. Municipal councils, religious orders and charitable brotherhoods had assumed responsibility for the upbringing of babies abandoned by their mothers in alleys or on doorsteps. The first hospice for such children in Europe had been founded in Milan in A.D. 787 by a priest called Datheus. This example had been followed by other European cities — Siena 832, Padua 1000, Montpellier 1070, Einbeck 1200, Florence 1317, Nürnberg 1331 and Paris 1362. In Portugal Dona Isabel, the Queen of Dom Diniz, had founded the home for foundlings in Santarém, known as the Hospital of Saint Mary of the Innocents, in 1321. She had established another hospice for foundlings in Tôrres Novas.[1]

A peculiarly Mediterranean development of care for foundlings had been the 'turning wheel'. This was a cylindrical wooden box placed within the walls of a building. It revolved on a pivot placed through its vertical axis, and was partitioned in the middle. Originally these turning wheels had been common in convents. Food, medicines and messages had been placed in the partition facing the outer part of the wall. The wheel had been turned, thereby transporting the commodities to the inside without the recluses either seeing outside or being seen. Occasionally a poor mother had placed her baby in such a wheel, trusting in the charity of the nuns to rear the child. The first turning wheel to be established specifically for receiving babies had been in the Hospital of the Holy Spirit in Rome in 1198. Installation of such wheels in hospitals had become common practice throughout southern Europe by the fifteenth century. There had been several methods of notifying those inside of the presence of a baby in the wheel. Usually a bell had been placed on the outside wall near the wheel and had been rung by the

---

[1] Vitor Ribeiro, *A Santa Casa*, pp. 21–2.

mother: more refined had been those wheels where the weight of a child had automatically operated a bell inside the hospital.

In Portugal all municipal councils had been obliged by law to provide for the care and upbringing of foundlings. The Hospital of All Saints, founded by Dom João II in Lisbon in 1492, had contained accommodation for such children. All costs had been met by the municipality. The foundation of the Misericórdia had given Portugal its first lay brotherhood to provide for all aspects of charity. Dom Manuel, recognising the immediate popularity of the brotherhood, had granted numerous privileges to the new body. In some cases, e.g. prison aid, these privileges had resulted in the Misericórdia assuming duties formerly fulfilled by the municipality and other official organs. This had happened with foundlings. In 1543 Dom João III had made the Misericórdia responsible for the care of all foundlings in Lisbon, with the exception of those housed in the Hospital of All Saints. This had led to a division of responsibilities between the municipal authorities and the lay brotherhood.

This division of responsibilities had been strengthened by the handing over to the Misericórdia in 1564 of the administration of the Hospital of All Saints. Not unnaturally, the city councillors of Lisbon had interpreted this as releasing them from any further commitments for the care of foundlings. Disputes had developed between the board of guardians of the Misericórdia and the councillors. These had only been settled by the king who had insisted that the care of foundlings *de facto* by the Misericórdia had not implied the end of all the legal obligations of the city council. The city council had been ordered to make an annual financial contribution towards the costs of maintaining the foundlings. In 1590, when there had been a similar transfer of administration from the city council to the Misericórdia in Oporto, it had been stipulated that the cost of feeding and clothing the children should be met by the municipal authorities and not by the brotherhood.[1]

During the seventeenth century there had been frequent misunderstandings between the Misericórdia and the city council as to the precise nature of their respective responsibilities. The continual grievance of the Misericórdia had been that the contribution by the municipality towards the costs of the Hospital of All Saints had been insufficient to cover the additional expenses of providing for foundlings. In 1635 Philip III had placed an

[1] *Alvarás* of 26 May 1590 and 12 June 1592, Vitor Ribeiro, *A Santa Casa*, p. 396.

ultimatum before the councillors: either the municipality should meet its legal obligations and assume full responsibility for all the foundlings of Lisbon, or it should make an annual grant of 689$360 to the Misericórdia for this purpose.[1] After some argument the city council had finally agreed to these terms in 1637.[2] The brotherhood had soon discovered that this contribution was inadequate and in 1646 had attempted to renounce all further obligations for the care of foundlings. In 1657 a foundling home had been founded in Lisbon on the suggestion of the Misericórdia and this had considerably reduced the large expenditure made on boarding out foundlings in private houses.

In the Portuguese overseas empire there was similar confusion, misunderstanding and acrimony as to who was responsible for the care of foundlings. Whether in Gôa, Macao, Luanda or Bahia the city councils were responsible *de jure*. But in all cases it was the respective Misericórdias who received, fed, clothed and housed children deserted by their mothers. These Misericórdias were not obliged by statute to provide for foundlings. The 1516 *Compromisso* of Lisbon (followed by many of the overseas branches) had made no reference to the care of foundlings. Only in the 1618 reform of the *Compromisso* had there been brief mention of the charitable duties of the Misericórdia towards foundlings, and even then it had been stressed that these were no more than the obligations of one Christian to his fellows and not an official function of the brotherhood.[3] In Gôa the locally made *Compromisso* of 1595 had provided for the care of foundlings by the Misericórdia with funds given by the city council.[4] In Macao in the late eighteenth century the Misericórdia appealed to the Crown for financial aid for the care of foundlings, a duty assumed by the brotherhood in their *Compromisso* of 1627.[5] In Brazil, the Governor of the Captaincy of Rio de Janeiro, António Paes de Sande, had written to the king in 1693 deploring the lack of charity shown

---

[1] *Alvará* of 28 March 1635, 'para que a Camara desta Cidade, em cazo que senão queira encarregar da criação dos emgeitados, dê, e entregue, todos os annos ao Thesoureiro do Hospital Real de todos os S^tos seis centos outenta e nove mil trezentos e seçenta reis para o dito effeito' (ASCMB, vol. 207, f. 35v).

[2] Vitor Ribeiro, *A Santa Casa*, p. 116.

[3] *Compromisso* of Lisbon of 1618, chapter 33.

[4] *Compromisso* of Gôa of 1595, chapter 34, cited in Ferreira Martins, *Historia da Misericordia de Goa*, vol. 1, pp. 218–56.

[5] José Caetano Soares, *Macau e a Assistência*, pp. 282–4 and p. 336.

towards foundlings. Although Dom Pedro II had reminded the governor that foundlings were a municipal responsibility and had suggested the levying of a tax for this purpose, the matter had fallen into abeyance.[1] Only in 1738 was a foundling home established in Rio. It was financed by legacies from two benefactors and was administered by the Misericórdia.[2]

In Bahia there was a division of responsibilities between the city council and the Misericórdia. Both institutions adopted the system of placing foundlings in private houses, known as *colocação familiar*. Payment was made to an *ama de leite* (wet-nurse) over a period of three years to provide for milk, food and clothing. The extent and effectiveness of the charitable action of the municipality and the Misericórdia respectively illustrates to the full the semi-bureaucratic rôle adopted by the brotherhood. This has already been apparent in the maintenance of a hospital for the city of Bahia and the Recôncavo. It must be remembered that the municipality was not legally obliged to provide hospital services for the community. In the case of foundlings the municipality did have a legal responsibility and any action by the Misericórdia was only necessary as a result of official failure to honour this obligation.

In the sixteenth and seventeenth centuries the city council of Bahia had made some provision for foundlings. The extent of this charity had been limited by the funds available. Since the city council had been unable to meet the costs of roads, public fountains and sanitation, the number of foundlings housed at municipal expense had been small. The city council had paid 2$50 quarterly at the end of the seventeenth century to those wet-nurses who brought up foundlings. In 1699 a *Livro de Engeitados*, or register of foundlings, had been started. This had given details of the name, age, date of baptism and cost of keeping the foundling and is an indication of the extent to which the municipal authorities did provide for foundlings. In the years 1699–1726 some 121 foundlings were boarded out with wet-nurses at the municipal expense. Over half of these died within the three

---

[1] ANRJ, *Códice 952*, vol. 6, f. 258.

[2] Vivaldo Couracy, *O Rio de Janeiro no século dezessete* (2nd ed., Rio de Janeiro, 1965), pp. 227–8. For a rather general and mainly nineteenth-century history, see Ubaldo Soares, *O passado heróico da Casa dos Expostos* (Rio de Janeiro, 1959).

years during which the city council assumed responsibility for their upkeep. The total cost to the municipality was 2076$161.[1]

The Misericórdia had also provided for the care of foundlings during the sixteenth and seventeenth centuries. This had been no more than an act of charity and no steward had been appointed to deal with foundlings. The brotherhood had followed the same practice as the city council — *colocação familiar* for three years. There had been one difference: the wet-nurses hired by the Misericórdia had been better paid than those appointed by the city council. In 1700 the brotherhood paid for the upkeep of a foundling at the rate of 80 *rs. per diem*. This had two results which were extremely prejudicial to the Misericórdia. First, the municipal authorities found it difficult to hire wet-nurses for 2$500 quarterly when the Misericórdia paid 2$000 for a single month. Rather than raising their own fees the city council tended to leave the care of foundlings to the Misericórdia. Secondly, the higher pay offered by the Misericórdia enabled it to contract more conscientious wet-nurses. Knowing this, a mother wishing to abandon her legitimate or illegitimate offspring naturally chose the steps of the hospital of the brotherhood rather than those of the city council. The earliest extant register of foundlings in the archives of the Misericórdia only dates from 1757. Nevertheless an indication of the extent to which the Misericórdia gradually assumed a municipal obligation is afforded by the ledgers of expenditure. During the years 1700–8 the payments made by the Misericórdia for the care of foundlings increased steadily from 385$980 in 1700 to 1015$220 in 1708.[2] In view of the fact that this last figure represented half of the total payments made by the municipality over twenty-seven years, there can be no doubt as to the importance of the Misericórdia in this field of social philanthropy.

By 1710 the municipality had, to all intents and purposes, 'opted out' of its legal responsibilities for the welfare of foundlings. The care of children abandoned by their mothers had been assumed by the Misericórdia. The municipality made no grant to the brotherhood to meet the ever-increasing costs of this new commitment. For its part, the Misericórdia had no legacies which could be used for this purpose. Two factors finally induced the board

---

[1] AMB, vol. 202; earlier payments to wet-nurses had been registered in the volumes entitled *Registros de pagamentos feitos pelo Senado*.

[2] ASCMB, vol. 850.

of guardians of the Misericórdia to make a stand against this exploitation by the municipal authorities.

The first was the loss of the concession of the *miunça dos dízimos*. This has already been discussed (p. 292). Suffice it to recall here that this privilege, valued at 130$000 *per annum*, lapsed in 1703. It was not renewed despite repeated petitions by the brotherhood and was finally stopped in 1709 by the king. The second factor was the loss of the income derived from a butcher's shop. In colonial Bahia the city council issued licences authorising the slaughter of cattle by butchers. These butchers operated under contract with the municipality. In 1629 the city council had conceded to the Misericórdia the income for one year from a butcher's shop because of the financial straits of the brotherhood.[1] This privilege had been extended to permit the Misericórdia to possess its own butcher's shop.[2] Other bodies enjoying the same privilege were the ecclesiastical authorities, the archbishop, and the city council itself. In 1706 the chief justice challenged the legal right of the Misericórdia and the ecclesiastical authorities to possess their private butchers' shops. The clergy took the case to the Court of Appeals and won. The Misericórdia was less fortunate. Its appeals were rejected and the brotherhood lost a source of income calculated at 200$000 *per annum*.[3] The board of guardians wrote to the Overseas Council in Lisbon pleading that the income from the shop defrayed the cost of the care of foundlings and that the municipality benefited from the transfer of responsibility.[4] Another letter was dispatched direct to the king asking for his protection. The Misericórdia in Lisbon was also asked to further the cause of its Bahian counterpart. The Mesa in Bahia insisted that without the income from the butcher's shop the cost of the care of foundlings would be too great for the limited financial resources of the brotherhood.[5] All appeals were in vain.

[1] Minute of city council of 7 April 1629 in *Atas da Câmara*, vol. 1, pp. 122–3.

[2] On 26 July 1659 the Mesa of the Misericórdia signed a contract with Manuel de Moura to supply meat for 'o açougue q' esta Santa Caza agora abre'. This shop was at the corner of the main building of the Misericórdia on the Rua Direita (ASCMB, vol. 13, ff. 113–14).   [3] ASCMB, vol. 52, f. 27.

[4] 'livrando por este caminho ao Senado dos gastos que fazia com os engeitados que hoje tem tomado asy esta Caza sem ter mais renda que esta consignada para este gasto'; letter of 16 August 1706 (ASCMB, vol. 52, f. 26v).

[5] Misericórdia of Bahia to Misericórdia of Lisbon, 4 August 1707 (ASCMB, vol. 52, ff. 29–30v).

In 1708 Dom João V ruled that the city councillors of Bahia had not had sufficient authority to concede such a privilege in the first place. The king hinted that if he had been consulted, he would probably have confirmed the privilege.[1] Relations between the Crown authorities and the city council of Bahia were strained. In 1696 the Crown had strengthened its hold over the city council by appointing a Crown lawyer to preside over its meetings. The butcher's shop provided another opportunity for the Crown to remind the councillors of their limited jurisdiction. The victim of this bureaucratic bickering was the Misericórdia.

The Misericórdia made a stand against this official lack of co-operation. Successive Mesas cut down drastically on the number of foundlings supported by the brotherhood. In 1713 only 107$520 was spent on the care of foundlings and costs for the financial year 1713–14 were only 130$780.[2] This withdrawal by the Misericórdia threw the moral and financial onus on the city council once again. The municipal authorities refused to fulfil their obligations. There is no sudden increase in the number of foundlings registered in the municipal register of foundlings. The result was that in the early eighteenth century there existed no adequate provision for the care of foundlings in Bahia.

The number of foundlings left on the streets caused a public scandal. Mothers abandoned their children by night in the dirty streets. Frequently they were eaten by dogs and other animals which prowled the streets of the Brazilian capital. On other occasions they simply died of exposure and hunger. Some mothers left their children in the naves of churches or at the door of a convent in the hope that a kindly priest or nun would feed and find a home for them. Other mothers abandoned their children on the shore to be drowned by the incoming tide.

The large number of foundlings was regarded by the authorities as indicative of the moral torpor of the Bahian populace. Foreign travellers were unfavourably impressed by this aspect of the city — the extravagance of dress, the *palanquins* or chairs carried by slaves, and harlots plying their trade without fear of censure. In the eighteenth century Bahia could rival Macao as a city of luxury and vice.[3] Dom João V exhorted archbishop and

---

[1] King to chief justice, 28 March 1708 (AMB, vol. 136, f. 167).

[2] ASCMB, vol. 851.

[3] José Caetano Soares, *Macau e a Assistência*, pp. 231–2, cites a description of

viceroy alike to remedy this slur on the national reputation. The king had lively fears that Bahia would suffer the fate of Sodom. On the night of 19 March 1721 there was a violent electrical storm over Bahia. One lightning bolt split a stone of the verandah of the Third Order of the Carmelites. Another struck the window of the house of a judge. On the following day a minor landslide destroyed some houses in the district of the Preguiça.[1] On hearing of this event Dom João V wrote to the archbishop of Bahia suggesting that the rage of the Almighty be placated by the holding of devotional exercises in all the churches of Bahia. Penitential processions were also held. The redemptive value of the latter was dubious. The viceroy maintained they generated more vice than virtue in the hearts of Bahians because the men simply lay with the women in the streets after the procession had ended late at night. His rather impracticable suggestion that the sexes be divided had met with the realistic reply from the archbishop that such an act 'would chill their devotion'.[2]

In 1726 the archbishop and the viceroy approached the board of guardians of the Misericórdia to suggest that the brotherhood should establish a turning wheel for foundlings. This move on the part of the viceroy recognized the importance of the Misericórdia in providing social services for Bahia. It also accorded to the brotherhood the status of a semi-bureaucratic institution. Pressure was placed on the Count of Sabugosa from three quarters to take this step. The first was the king who regarded foundlings as so many blots on the record of the Portuguese colonisation. The second was the city council whose precarious financial position was well known to the viceroy. The third was the archbishop concerned with the moral and religious significance of foundlings. Finally there was the personal attitude of the viceroy. The Count of Sabugosa took a keen interest in public affairs. He badgered

---

Macao by a Portuguese captain which repeats almost word for word contemporary descriptions of Bahia in the eighteenth century.

[1] The contemporary Bahian historian Sebastião da Rocha Pitta expressed the common fear that these calamities were a divine punishment (*Historia*, Livro 10, § 58–64).

[2] King to archbishop, 17 January 1722; viceroy to king, 24 July 1722 (APB, *Ordens régias*, vol. 16, docs. 4 and 4a), cf. Sebastião da Rocha Pitta: 'Pozeram-se vias-sacras em todas as parochias, correndo-se frequentemente; exercicios que ainda hoje se continuam, de sorte que de Ninive peccadora se viu a Bahia Ninive arrependida' (*Historia*, Livro 10, § 64).

the councillors on public sanitation, finance and greater diligence in dispatching business. The presence of mutilated corpses of babies on the streets was a constant reminder of the deficiencies of the public order. He was also more religious than was superficially apparent. When there was a minor earth tremor on the morning of 4 January 1724, felt in Bahia and the island of Itaparica, the local astrologists regarded this as a sign of drought. In his official report the viceroy pooh-poohed such notions. Nevertheless he described the tremor as lasting 'the length of a Hail Mary' and he ended by saying that if God did not send water the crops would perish and the populace would face starvation.[1]

The overtures of viceroy and archbishop were not well received by the Misericórdia. The brotherhood had itself been the target of scathing criticism by the Count of Sabugosa. But three years previously the viceroy had reported to the Crown that the brotherhood's finances were in a deplorable state because of cliques on the board of guardians and the practice of loaning money on poor securities. The king had ordered a full enquiry in 1724.[2] Thus the Count of Sabugosa found a good deal of reluctance on the part of the Mesa to assume responsibility for what was, after all, a municipal obligation. The Junta and Mesa were convoked on 14 February 1726 to discuss whether or not the brotherhood should establish a turning wheel for foundlings. Seven brothers did not attend. The motion was passed by nineteen votes to seven, a bare two-thirds majority.

It is difficult to understand the motives which led the Misericórdia to accept this additional responsibility. The finances of the brotherhood were in a precarious state. The administration was severely over-taxed by the massive legacy of João de Mattos de Aguiar received in 1700. One of the clauses of this legacy had provided for the building of a retirement house to be governed by the Misericórdia. The pressure on the hospital has already been described. Nevertheless the already harassed Mesa took on a further responsibility in a field of social aid for which it had no obligation.

Possibly by so doing, the Mesa thought that it would have a good bargaining point for negotiations with the city council over payments for the cure of

---

[1] Viceroy to secretary of state, 12 April 1724 (APB, *Ordens régias*, vol. 18, doc. 35).

[2] Viceroy to king, 24 November 1723, and the royal reply of 28 June 1724 (APB, *Ordens régias*, vol. 19, doc. 62).

L

soldiers of the garrison. Possibly the Count of Sabugosa placed pressure on the brotherhood. Possibly the Mesa saw in the turning wheel yet another means of confirming the Misericórdia as the leading brotherhood of colonial Bahia. Pride had often outweighed financial considerations in the past. These can be no more than suggestions and only two motives are certain.

The first was the moral issue involved in the care of foundlings. Although many Bahians chose to ignore the Ten Commandments in their everyday lives, they were fervent Catholics when faced with moral problems. The purely physical factor of the death of children because of desertion on the streets influenced the Mesa and Junta. The over-riding factor resulting in their extraordinary decision was the very Catholic attitude of seeing each dead child not as a mutilated body but as a soul who had not yet received the baptism of the Catholic Church.

The second factor was that certain promises had been made to the Mesa by the viceroy. The Count of Sabugosa had promised financial aid to the brotherhood in money and privileges. The report on the decision of the Mesa and Junta referred to a petition to the king, which the viceroy had agreed to sponsor. This petition contained four clauses. The first was that the privileges granted to the Misericórdia of Lisbon for the administration of a turning wheel be extended to Bahia. These were to include those privileges enjoyed by wet-nurses in the service of the Misericórdia of Lisbon. The Mesa also asked that the butcher's shop be restored to the Misericórdia. The final clause insisted that an annual contribution be made by the Treasury towards the costs of the foundlings.[1] A detailed examination of these clauses reveals the extent to which the outcome of the petition depended more on bureaucratic factors than on its own merits.

In Lisbon the Misericórdia had been granted privileges by various kings to assist the brotherhood in defraying the heavy costs of providing for foundlings. Philip III had ordered the city council to make an annual contribution to the brotherhood for this purpose. The greatest single item of expenditure had been the payments made to the wet-nurses. Low salaries had been offset by royal privileges. Dom Manuel had ordered that wet-nurses who had served the Misericórdia for three consecutive years should be exempt from all municipal taxes. The families of these women had also

---

[1] Minute of 14 February 1726 (ASCMB, vol. 14, ff. 145–6); petition to king of 3 March 1726 (ASCMB, vol. 52, ff. 112–13).

benefited from the royal favour. Decrees of 1654 and 1695 had excused sons and husbands from service in the militia.[1] Because of these privileges the Misericórdia had found it comparatively easy to engage wet-nurses willing to serve the brotherhood for low wages in return for these advantages.

The petition resurrected the issue of the butcher's shop. This had reverted to the municipality following the royal order of 1708. The first reaction of the authorities in Lisbon was simply to grant the Misericórdia the income from the butcher's shop as had first been done in 1629. Enquiry showed that this would be insignificant. During the time in which the *dote de Inglaterra e paz de Holanda* (dowry of Queen Catherine of England and the war indemnity to the United Provinces) was being collected all restrictions on the butchering of cattle had been suspended. Permission had been granted for cattle to be slaughtered outside the licensed butchers' shops. It was indicative of the bureaucratic confusion prevailing in the Portuguese colonial empire that this change of circumstance had escaped the notice of the viceroy, the *procurador da Coroa* (Crown official responsible for assembling all the information and submitting a report) and the ministers of the Overseas Council in Lisbon.[2] Another instance of the same confusion was in 1729. Dom João V asked the Count of Sabugosa to enquire why the Misericórdia no longer possessed a butcher's shop. It must have given the Count of Sabugosa considerable satisfaction to quote the royal order of 1708 with the briefest of covering letters.[3] A royal donation of 400$000 was made in 1732 to the Misericórdia for the hospital and foundlings.[4] This was non-recurring and simply a temporary measure until a report was received from the viceroy on alternative means. The Count of Sabugosa advised the king that an annual grant be made to the Misericórdia from the income derived by the municipality from the cattle corrals. He estimated this at some 200$000.[5]

The final clause of the petition of the Misericórdia asked for an annual grant from the Treasury. This the king refused to concede. Throughout the enquiries he insisted that the financial and legal responsibility lay with

---

[1] Costa Godolphim, *As Misericordias*, pp. 75–6.

[2] *Documentos historicos*, vol. 90, pp. 133–5, doc. 110.

[3] APB, *Ordens régias*, vol. 25, doc. 22a.

[4] Royal approval of 24 January 1732 (*Documentos historicos*, vol. 90, pp. 243–4).

[5] *Documentos historicos*, vol. 91, pp. 23–5, doc. 14.

the municipal authorities.   Pleas by the city councillors protesting poverty
were ignored, although supported by the viceroy.[1]

A decision was taken in 1734.   The Overseas Council rejected outright
any concession of those privileges enjoyed by the Misericórdia in Lisbon.
The refusal was based on the rather curious grounds that the presence of a
privileged person or body in Brazil constituted a threat to the national
security.   The other clauses of the decision represented a bureaucratic
compromise.   The Treasury was to make an annual contribution of 200$000
for the hospital.   The city council was to match this with a similar contribution of 200$000 from income received from the cattle corrals and butchers'
shops.[2]

No party emerged from this bureaucratic wrangling with credit.   The
position of the Count of Sabugosa was ambiguous.   On the one hand he had
to placate the Misericórdia.   On the other he had to support the city council.
In the end he fell between the two.   The Misericórdia was deceived into
establishing the turning wheel for foundlings by vague promises of official
help.   The city council, whose allegations of financial straits the viceroy had
always supported, was finally saddled with a heavy annual contribution.
The king remained adamant in his refusal to accept a municipal responsibility.   This refusal was based on purely bureaucratic motives and had no
relation to the financial reality of the case.   The city council made some
half-hearted efforts at protest.   The councillors stressed the inability of the
municipality to find further funds and that the maintenance of public
works had resulted in heavy debts.   They also pleaded that they were still
willing to provide care for foundlings at an annual payment to wet-nurses of
10$000.[3]   This second allegation was ridiculous because in the ten years
following the establishment of the turning wheel the city council only
provided for seven foundlings.[4]   Dom João V ignored these petitions by
the city councillors and ordered that payment be made to the Misericórdia.

[1] In a letter of 13 July 1726 the king asked the viceroy how much the municipality
could contribute 'por que segundo a ley, a Camera hé que esta obrigada a semel-
hante dispendio' (APB, *Ordens régias*, vol. 21, doc. 83).

[2] Royal approval of 9 June 1734 (*Documentos historicos*, vol. 91, pp. 23–5,
doc. 14).

[3] City council to king, 20 October 1734, supported by the viceroy in a letter
of 17 November 1734 (APB, *Ordens régias*, vol. 31, docs. 6a and 6b).

[4] The total cost was 160$000 (AMB, vol. 202, ff. 67v–71).

Only after repeated complaints by the Misericórdia was payment finally made in June 1740 for the previous five years.[1]

The Misericórdia made two further attempts to augment this meagre contribution from official sources. In 1738 a petition was sent to Dom João V and the Pope asking that legacies not fulfilled within the time stipulated by the testator be applied to the Misericórdia for the care of foundlings.[2] This petition was unsuccessful. The other attempt was in 1741 and once again brought the Misericórdia into conflict with a municipal authority. The River Paraguaçú ran into the Bay of All Saints some sixteen leagues distant from the city of Bahia. The town of Cachoeira was situated on this river and a ferry service operated across the river at this point. In Minas Gerais the king had sold the privilege of collecting tolls for river passages on a contract basis. This had proved a lucrative source of income for the Treasury. The Misericórdia asked the king to grant to the brotherhood the monopoly of all passage rights on the River Paraguaçú to defray the costs made on foundlings. The Mesa pointed out that the main beneficiaries at present were 'captive Negroes and freedmen' who received 10 *rs.* for each person and a smaller sum for each piece of luggage they ferried across the river. The king referred the matter to the viceroy who consulted the town council of Cachoeira. The local councillors strongly opposed the petition of the Misericórdia. They insisted on the freedom of passage to be enjoyed by all. Many sugar plantation owners used their own craft for the transport of sugar and foodstuffs and there was no reason why they should pay tolls to the Misericórdia every time they used the river. Moreover, the river provided a livelihood for many poor people who ferried passengers. The River Paraguaçú was subject to heavy flooding and thirty boats were kept constantly ready. The Misericórdia would be unable to maintain such a fleet. Finally the councillors defended their municipal rights. The townsfolk of Cachoeira had paid for the building of quays, flood barriers and repairs to houses after the floods. A brotherhood in distant Bahia should not reap the benefit of these improvements. In the face of such opposition this petition was also rejected.[3]

---

[1] The Misericórdia received 1,140$520 (ASCMB, vol. 854, f. 48v).

[2] ASCMB, vol. 14, ff. 243v–245.

[3] The town council of Cachoeira replied on 16 June 1742 (BNRJ, 11–33, 24, 45, doc. 1).

The Misericórdia was compelled to rely mainly on private charity to finance the care of foundlings. Foundlings were the least well endowed of all the charitable services of the Misericórdia. During the seventeenth century no legacy had been left to the brotherhood for this purpose. During the years 1700–55 the Misericórdia only received three legacies to be placed on loan and the interest used for the care of foundlings. The total value of these was 1,400$000. When a report was made in 1754 on the financial position of the brotherhood it was discovered that only part of one of these legacies was intact, giving an annual interest of 56$250.[1] The foundation of the turning wheel aroused some interest and several single legacies were made for the care of foundlings. These amounted to some 2,500$000 in the years 1700–55.

The care of foundlings is the least documented of the charitable activities of the Misericórdia. Before the foundation of the turning wheel in 1726 such children were helped under the heading of general charity. No record was kept. Only in 1726 was the first register of foundlings started and both this register and the second volume have been lost. The third volume (1757–63) gives a general picture of the number of foundlings, their colour, ages and possible social backgrounds. The account ledgers give details of the annual cost to the brotherhood for the care of foundlings. Such figures must be treated with caution because frequently the Misericórdia fell behind in its payments to wet-nurses. The minute books of the brotherhood contain few references to the care of foundlings. Once the turning wheel had been established it appears to have functioned smoothly and no modification was made in the administration. Only when the Misericórdia made a petition to the Crown was there stated the number of foundlings placed in the turning wheel each year.

The circumstances which led a mother to abandon her child varied from case to case. The brief descriptions in the registers of foundlings provide a general indication of the background of those children left in the turning wheel. Frequently an explanatory note was left tied to the deserted child.

---

[1] The three legacie were of Paschoal da Silva Moreira (1712) 400$000, Miguel Carvalho Mascarenhas (1713) 600$000 and Bento de Magalhães (1740) 400$000 (ASCMB, vol. 53, ff. 190–191v). In 1754 only 900$000 remained of a legacy of almost 1,800$000 made by Miguel Carvalho Mascarenhas for foundlings and prisoners (ASCMB, vol. 210, f. 21v).

On some occasions the child was accompanied by a bundle of clothes. From such meagre sources it is possible to glean information on the social position of these children and the reasons for desertion. The majority of mothers leaving their children in the turning wheel were led to this action by two series of factors, the one economic and the other social.

A large part of the population of Bahia lived at barely subsistence level. Many whites preferred to live in poverty rather than engage in manual labour which they considered only fit for slaves. Coloured people had no such preoccupations: employment was easy to find but the wages were low. The addition of a child to such families placed an impossible strain on the meagre financial resources. After struggling against starvation a mother might well be induced to place her child in the turning wheel of the Misericórdia. The register of foundlings describes how many children arrived 'sick and naked' or 'with the flesh stretched over their bones'. Their only clothing was a shirt or a piece of old linen in holes. Frequently such children needed hospital treatment before they could be boarded out with a wet-nurse. For such families the placing of a child in the turning wheel was a temporary measure. They hoped that better times would enable them to reclaim the child and bring it up in a normal family life. A small note was left with the child: this gave its name, date of baptism and even the names of its god-parents. In this way it could be all the more easily identified when the father came to reclaim it. Sometimes maternal love overcame economic necessity and the mother appeared at the Misericórdia within a few days of having left the child. On other occasions the child was reclaimed only a year after having been left in the turning wheel. In such cases the parents were liable for all expenses made by the Misericórdia while the child had been in the care of the brotherhood.

Economic factors would also compel a mother who had been deserted by her husband to place her child in the turning wheel. Bahia was a city with a transient population. The point of arrival for many immigrants, it was also the point of departure for the mining area or the cattle ranches of the River São Francisco. Many of the soldiers of the garrison were sent from Portugal and were liable to be transferred to another posting in one of the other Portuguese colonies or fortresses. Many of these men married in Bahia, or lived with a woman in a more or less permanent manner although the union had not been sanctified by the Catholic Church. Frequently the wives or mistresses were coloured women. Certainly these were more likely to be abandoned than a white woman. There were several reasons for this. The shortage of white women placed them at a premium and they were able to marry someone offering greater stability and security, e.g. a store keeper or civil servant. The darker the wife or mistress the more likely was she to be deserted by her husband. It has been suggested that a Negress might marry a totally unsuitable lower class white man for socioracial reasons 'to whiten the race'.[1] There can be no doubt that in colonial Bahia social acceptance depended on the degree of whiteness of skin. A light *mulata* might make a good marriage with a smith, cobbler or stonemason. The slight racial taint of the girl would be matched by the low social standing of the white man. The greater the degree of racial differentiation the greater would be the tension in a mixed marriage. A normal relationship would be replaced by a master-slave relationship. The *negra* would be the lover, cook and housemaid of the white man but never a partner in marriage. Finally, if the man decided to leave Bahia, socio-economic reasons might well induce him to desert his wife. If he were a soldier returning to Portugal he would not wish to undergo the social disadvantages of having a Negress as a wife. If he went to the mines a family would be a severe hindrance to his activities. There were several instances of a coloured woman being compelled by poverty to leave her legitimate child in the turning wheel because her soldier husband had been recalled to Portugal. Sometimes the father attempted to make amends. In 1754 the captain of a ship handed a sum of money to the Misericórdia in Bahia for the upkeep of a child, whose father in Lisbon was suffering from pangs of conscience.[2]

The child who had been left in the turning wheel as the result of economic necessity was usually legitimate. The Misericórdia served the rôle of a foster father until the parents could face the financial burden of bringing up the child themselves. When social factors dictated the desertion of a child

[1] Racial tensions in mixed marriages are discussed by Roger Bastide and Florestan Fernandes, *Brancos e negros em São Paulo* (2nd ed., São Paulo, 1959), pp. 210–15. A more balanced analysis is in Donald Pierson, *Brancos e pretos na Bahia*, pp. 202–18. Much of what he says is equally applicable to the colonial period.

[2] Register of receipt of 72$000 handed to the treasurer by the captain of a ship 'cuja quantia pagou por incumbencia q' trazia da Corte, e Cide de Lisboa pa desencargo da consciencia do Pai do dito exposto' (ASCMB, vol. 866, f. 7).

it was usually illegitimate. The turning wheel offered an alternative to leaving the child on the streets or killing it.

Prostitution was probably no more common in Bahia than in any other port. The presence of pretty coloured girls in exotic dresses made it more evident. Many visitors sided with the French traveller Le Gentil de la Barbinais in condemning the moral laxity of the women of Bahia in the eighteenth century.[1] Others were clearly intrigued by the legendary dorsal flexibility of the *Bahiana* — 'o que é que a Bahiana tem'. Municipal authorities, viceroys and the king acted to curb the extravagant dress of these girls. In 1709 a royal decree forbad the wearing of silk or gold trimmings by slave girls who wandered through the streets at night inciting the men with their 'lascivious dresses'.[2] These orders were not strictly enforced and were re-issued on several occasions in the eighteenth century.[3] The by-blows of casual sexual unions between prostitutes and their customers may have contributed to the number of children left in the turning wheel of the Misericórdia.

The illegitimate child was not always the product of lower-class parentage. Nor was the female partner always coloured. There were scandals among the noblest families of Bahian society. The honour of the white girl had to be preserved at all costs. The stigma of dishonour attached to the unmarried mother was infinitely stronger than the stigma of illegitimacy which would be borne by the child. If paternal threats and herbal 'remedies' were ineffective, the birth of the child was kept secret. The foundlings' registers record numerous cases of white children being left in the foundling wheel. Although without any form of identification, the clothes and alms left with the child suggest good parentage. One such trousseau for a girl included: two new linen chemises, decorated with fine lace and embroidered flowers; six ordinary chemises; five new nappies, also embroidered; a pair of drawers as used in India; ribbon; a length of linen edged with lace. Sometimes alms

---

[1] Le Gentil de la Barbinais, *Nouveau Voyage*, vol. 3, pp. 202–4.

[2] Royal order of 23 September 1709 (APB, *Ordens régias*, vol. 7, doc. 616).

[3] Later prohibitions were not always on moral grounds. An *alvará* of 5 October 1742 was issued against the luxury of Angolan customs (APB, *Ordens régias*, vol. 40, doc. 25a). This was reissued on 24 May 1749, but economic considerations for the effects on Portuguese exports dictated revisions. In 1751 the wearing of buttons, lace and veils was authorised provided these were made in Portugal or Brazil, and were not of foreign manufacture (APB, *Ordens régias*, vol. 50, ff. 28–38).

of as much as 50$000 were left with the child. Prejudice against the un-married mother, increasing in proportion to her social position and whiteness, compelled her to place an illegitimate child in the turning wheel.

On some rare occasions the child may have been the product of conventual loves. The Desterro convent was notorious in this respect. Many parents placed their children in this convent rather than run the risk of their making socially unworthy marriages. These often took the veil. The daughter of Manuel Gonçalves Viana, treasurer of the Misericórdia in 1714, was involved in an affair with a parish priest and was the subject of viceroyal correspond-ence in 1738.[1] On at least one other occasion in the early eighteenth century the viceroy intervened in order to avoid a public scandal. A note attached to a white child left in the turning wheel at 2 o'clock on a July morning in 1758 hinted at the circumstances of his birth:

> I pray and beseech any gentleman who will take this child or offer him shelter under his own roof, for these are deeds practised by men of noble blood, that at a future date we will seek out this child and pay all expenses incurred on his behalf. This we swear on the oath of the confessional. The child is white and his kinsfolk are friars, clerics and nuns. He is flushed because of the many medicines taken by his mother to stay his birth. For the love of God I ask that he be named João Baptista.[2]

The foundling has for long been regarded as one of the less praiseworthy, but inevitable, by-blows of miscegenation. It has been assumed that in a multi-racial community there would be a predominance of foundlings of coloured parentage. This has been attributed to the allegedly higher rate of illegitimacy and greater economic instability present among the coloured sectors of such a community. It has also been taken for granted by sociolo-gists that there would be a higher incidence of foundlings in a multi-racial

---

[1] APB, *Ordens régias*, vol. 34, doc. 97 and accompanying documents. In 1717 Le Gentil de la Barbinais commented on the unseemly postures of the actors in a play he attended at the Desterro, *Nouveau Voyage*, vol. 3, pp. 207–10.

[2] 'Rogo e peço a q^al q^r Snr q' este menino quizer tomar, ou recolher pois são couzas q' sucedem aos homens de bem q' em certo tempo se procurarâ e se pagarâ o seu gasto q' houver feito, e dizerseha debayxo da confissão pois he branco, tem parentes frades, clerigos e freyras, esta vermelho p^las m^tas meyzinhas q' tomou sua may p^a haver demora, peço p^lo amor de Dios q' lhe chame João Bapt^a' (ASCMB vol. 1193, f. 38v).

society than in a predominantly white society. The evidence available does not support these views with reference to colonial Bahia which was the prototype of a 'mixed' community.

Entries made in the registers of foundlings specified the colour of each child left in the turning wheel. These registers only date from October 1757, but there are no reasons to suggest that the racial composition of these foundlings differed markedly from those of an earlier period. In the last three months of this year twenty-three children were left in the turning wheel: only four of these were coloured, the remaining nineteen being white. In 1758, the first year for which there is a complete record, a total of seventy-nine children were placed in the turning wheel: fifty-five of these were white and only twenty-four were coloured.[1] Registers for later years show a similar predominance of white children.

Nor do the figures for the number of foundlings in Bahia bear out the view that these were any higher in a mixed society than in a white society. When the turning wheel was founded in Bahia in 1726 the number of foundlings for which the Misericórdia would have to provide yearly was calculated at fifty.[2] This later turned out to be totally unrealistic. In its petition of 1741 for the Paraguaçú river privileges, the Mesa alleged that the brotherhood provided for more than a hundred foundlings in a year.[3] The Mesa was doubtless guilty of exaggeration to support its case. In the six months July–December 1751 a total of thirty-seven foundlings were left in the turning wheel and the 1754 report placed the average annual number at eighty.[4] The number did not increase in the latter part of the century. Vilhena at the end of the century gave the figures for 1796 as seventy-six, for 1797 as ninety-eight and for 1798 as seventy-four.[5] In Lisbon in 1715 there were 706 entries into the foundlings home, 698 in 1717, and 717 in 1720.[6] When one considers that the population of urban Bahia in 1720 was some 115,000 and that of Lisbon in the region of 200,000 the coefficient of foundling : total population differs enormously between the two capitals. In Bahia it was $0.4/1,000$ whereas in Lisbon it was $3.6/1,000$. These figures are no

---

[1] ASCMB, vol. 1193, ff. 1–51v.   [2] ASCMB, vol. 52, ff. 112–13.
[3] BNRJ, 11–33, 24, 45, doc. 1.
[4] ASCMB, vol. 53, ff. 88–90 and vol. 210, f. 37.
[5] Vilhena, *Noticias soteropolitanas*, vol. 1, p. 126.
[6] Vitor Ribeiro, *A Santa Casa*, p. 398.

more than an indication. It can be argued that the disproportionately high figure for Lisbon was because mothers came from the surrounding villages and left their children in the foundling home in Lisbon.[1] But this explanation does not fully answer the question of why there was such a marked difference between the numbers of foundlings left in Bahia and Lisbon. The low proportion of black to white foundlings in Bahia and the markedly smaller number of foundlings in Bahia can be better explained by a set of social factors unrelated to miscegenation.

Purchase of a female slave gave the master the ownership not only of her body but of any children she might produce. This was known as the *lei da ventre* or 'law of the womb'. Although the capture of slaves in Africa had resulted in the atomisation of families, once these had settled in Brazil there was a considerable degree of family cohesion among slaves on the plantations. A plantation owner often encouraged his slaves to marry. He gained any offspring as slaves and a family provided a more secure social unit on a plantation. If an illegitimate child was born, this too became the property of the master. Thus slavery offered a form of insurance to the child, be he legitimate or illegitimate. In both cases he was fed and housed in return for his potential as a future source of income and social prestige for the owner.

Free coloured people did not benefit from this rather dubious form of protection. They were more at the mercy of external economic factors. They were not so subject to social prejudices as their white counterparts in a correspondingly modest position. An illegitimate child did not dishonour the mother to the same extent as a white woman. Whenever financial means would permit, the illegitimate child was brought up as one of the family. A visitor to modern Bahia cannot fail to notice the ease with which coloured families absorb another child, be he illegitimate or the child of a dead neighbour or relation. Somehow there is always room for yet another child. The Negro seems to regard the family as a more flexible social unit than the white man. Financial considerations are not given such prominence, provided that the family can manage to escape starvation. This attitude towards the child cannot have been so different in colonial Brazil and may explain why so few coloured children were placed in the turning wheel.

[1] In 1780 the Misericórdia of Lisbon asked that the cost of caring for these children be to the respective councils of their towns of origin, Vitor Ribeiro, *A Santa Casa*, p. 401.

The contrast in the overall numbers of foundlings in Bahia and Lisbon may be partly explained by a peculiarly Brazilian custom. This is the *compadrio*. The English equivalent of the *compadre* is the godfather, but the *compadre* plays a more important rôle in the child's upbringing than does the godfather. He is not always of the same social standing as the family of his godchild. In colonial Bahia a slave frequently asked his master to be the *compadre* of his child, even if the child were illegitimate. The *compadre* provided a dowry for a girl or apprenticed a boy to a trade. In the event of the death of the parents the *compadre* adopted the child. Travellers to colonial Bahia were surprised to find a piccaninny at the table of a noble family and even bearing the family name.

Adoption also seems to have been common among the better families of colonial Bahia. Mothers deserted their children at the gateway of some *solar*, or mansion, confident in the knowledge that the child would be brought up in the family. When the mother of two mulatto children died in the prison of Bahia in 1657, the Misericórdia took charge of the children. A brother offered to bring them up and educate them without payment. Reference has already been made to dowries and legacies left to adopted children by wealthy Bahians in their wills. Certainly the strong moral ties of the *compadrio* and the common practice of adoption provided for many children who would otherwise have been foundlings.

Once a child had been placed in the turning wheel it was kept in isolation for a short period to ensure that it had no infectious disease. Then it was given to a wet-nurse who was responsible for its upbringing for three years. The wet-nurse was usually a free coloured woman or a widow. The child remained in her house and every quarter the wet-nurse reported to the Misericórdia to receive her pay. The lack of direct supervision by the Misericórdia led to a certain amount of abuse. On more than one occasion the Misericórdia was compelled to remove a child from a wet-nurse because of ill-treatment. The high mortality rate among foundlings may well have been due to malnutrition and negligence by wet-nurses. In Gôa this led the board of guardians of 1717 to have a certain number of paid wet-nurses living in the hospital so that a closer check could be kept on the health of the child but this practice was not followed in Bahia until the nineteenth century.[1]

[1] Ferreira Martins, *Historia da Misericordia de Goa*, vol. 2, pp. 348–50.

The precarious financial position of the Misericórdia of Bahia often resulted in the wet-nurses being irregularly paid. In 1752 payments were eighteen months overdue.[1] Wet-nurses came from the lower classes and relied on the money paid by the Misericórdia in order to live. When this was not forthcoming the only alternative was to dispose of the child. Some sold the children in their care — the price of a *pardinho* in 1758 was 16$000.[2] Others placed the child in the turning wheel again. Then they reclaimed the child and received payment for two children. No check was kept on the number of children in the care of a wet-nurse at any one time. Sometimes a mother driven by poverty placed her child in the turning wheel and then immediately offered herself as its nurse, thereby being paid to look after her own child. At worst the wet-nurse killed the child. In the late eighteenth century in Lisbon a wet-nurse was found to have killed thirty-three children in order to claim payment and the clothes given by the Misericórdia with each foundling.[3] This may well have happened in Bahia to a lesser extent.

The negligence on the part of the wet-nurses may have contributed to the exceptionally high mortality rate among foundlings. In the last three months of 1757 twelve of the twenty-three children left in the foundling wheel died. In 1758 forty-nine foundlings died out of a total of seventy-nine. Before condemning the Misericórdia and the nurses it employed, it must be realised that many of these children arrived in the turning wheel with little chance of living. Also the mortality rate in Bahia was highest precisely among children under five — the age when they were placed in the turning wheel.

The responsibility of the Misericórdia towards the foundling lasted for three years. After this period, the brotherhood placed the child in a suitable home in the city. This was usually successful and the child was brought up as one of the family. From then on the future of the foundling depended partly on the social and financial position of the family. A boy was apprenticed to a trade, helped in a store, or entered the army. A wealthy family might pay for his training to be a priest. An exceptionally lucky foundling might find himself heir to a sugar plantation on the death of his guardian. Girls often worked in private houses in return for their keep. This was not always satisfactory. Sometimes the Misericórdia re-assumed

---

[1] ASCMB, vol. 53, f. 97. [2] ASCMB, vol. 1193, f. 28v.
[3] Costa Godolphim, *As Misericordias*, p. 77.

responsibility for a girl if it was thought that her honour was in danger.[1] She was moved to another family or placed in the retirement house. Priority was given to girls in the retirement house and foundlings in the granting of dowries.[2] Frequently the final act of charity by the Misericórdia towards a foundling was the payment of her dowry at marriage.

The cost of maintaining a turning wheel was considerable. The Misericórdia paid 2$000 each month to a wet-nurse for the care of a foundling: this amounted to 72$000 over three years. On only two occasions between 1735 and 1755 did the annual payment to wet-nurses amount to less than 1,000$000, and the average annual expenditure for these years was 1,715$000.[3] In addition to paying the wet-nurse the Misericórdia also provided medical attention and clothing for foundlings. This deficit was offset by the annual municipal grant of 200$000, interest of less than 100$000 on legacies, and single legacies which averaged some 100$000 in any one year. Thus the Misericórdia spent on the care of foundlings in a year a sum four times in excess of its income allocated for this charitable purpose. The outlay on foundlings alone represented a large proportion of the overall expenditure for a year made by the brotherhood. In 1754, the scribe of the brotherhood calculated the annual expenditure on foundlings at 1,920$000, out of a total expenditure of 17,502$180.[4]

All petitions by the Misericórdia to the king or the city council for further financial aid towards the upkeep of foundlings were ignored. In 1752 the Mesa wrote to Lisbon that the only remedy for the heavy financial loss incurred in the care of foundlings was to block up the turning wheel. This thinly veiled threat ended with the humanitarian appeal that it would be impossible 'to close our hearts to the sad laments which there will be throughout this city'.[5] Appeals of this nature cut little ice in Lisbon. The

---

[1] In 1741 a foundling Josepha was removed from the house of one Natalia Maria 'pello perigo que corre a sua honra a ser exposta desta Santa Caza' (ASCMB, vol. 1180, f. 14).

[2] ASCMB, vol. 14, ff. 172–173v.

[3] The exceptions were the financial years 1750–1 and 1752–3 (ASCMB, vols. 862 and 864).

[4] ASCMB, vol. 210, f. 37.

[5] 'O remedio será tapar a Roda de Pedra e Cal, ainda q' não podemos tapar os noços coraçoens aos tristes clamores q' haverão nesta cidade'; letter of 5 January 1752 to the attorney of the brotherhood in Lisbon (ASCMB, vol. 53, ff. 88–90).

Overseas Council continued to ignore petitions for privileges or the granting of legacies unfulfilled within a stipulated period.[1]

The royal enquiry of 1754 into the affairs of the Misericórdia provided a solid basis for the petitions of the brotherhood. The Crown judge José de Affonseca Lemos devoted one chapter of his report to the turning wheel. He insisted that the care of foundlings was a municipal responsibility. He stressed that the assumption of this responsibility by the Misericórdia without adequate aid was prejudicing those charitable services for which the brotherhood had a statutory obligation. The Misericórdia had a backlog of payments to wet-nurses amounting to 2,800$000. Thus it was not surprising that the Misericórdia had difficulty in finding nurses willing to look after foundlings. At the time of his report there were a dozen in the hospital waiting for homes. His proposed solution was an additional grant of 400$000 by the city council. From his probings into the municipal finances he had discovered a royal privilege of 1665 granting to the municipality a tax known as the *terças*, without the municipality having any legal right to this source of income.[2] The king asked the councillors of Bahia and the viceroy to comment on this report. The Count of Arcos acknowledged that the care of foundlings was a municipal responsibility. He also agreed that the city council was totally incapable of supporting such a financial burden. He suggested that the Treasury should make an annual grant of 400$000 to the Misericórdia in addition to the grant of 200$000 made since 1734.[3] For their part the councillors alleged that what small funds they did possess were swallowed up in public works.[4]

As had been the case with the hospital these enquiries and reports did not benefit the brotherhood. The Misericórdia received neither privilege nor money to help it in the care of foundlings.[5] At the end of the century the Professor of Greek in Bahia, Luís dos Santos Vilhena, commented critically on the administration of the turning wheel. For once, he praised the

[1] The Mesa was still trying to obtain these privileges in 1754, but I do not know the final outcome (ASCMB, vol. 53, ff. 139v–140).

[2] The report was dated Bahia, 16 May 1755 (BNRJ, 11–33, 24, 45, doc. 10).

[3] Viceroyal report of 18 October 1757 (BNRJ, 11–33, 24, 45, doc. 9).

[4] City council to king, 14 December 1757 (AMB, vol. 182, ff. 78–80).

[5] In 1757 the commissioner of the Treasury, acting on the king's orders, requested the Misericórdia to submit a report on legacies to be applied to the care of foundlings. This was drawn up but without result (ASCMB, vol. 53, ff. 190–191v).

municipality for making an annual grant of 200$000 to the Misericórdia for the care of foundlings. He considered this amount excessive, since the Misericórdia provided for less than a hundred foundlings in any one year. He censured the brotherhood for inefficiency.[1] How unjustified was this criticism can be seen from the account ledger of 1814–15 when the Misericórdia paid 2,239$760 on the care of ninety-two foundlings.[2] The bitter and hypercritical attitude of Vilhena well matched the negligence of the city council and the indifference of the Crown.

The turning wheel contributed towards the financial decline of the Misericórdia in the eighteenth century. The board of guardians of 1726 was deceived by unfounded promises into establishing a turning wheel. Despite official lack of co-operation and financial loss, the brotherhood persevered in providing this charitable service for the city of Bahia. As had been the case of the hospital the brotherhood was the victim of bureaucratic negligence, providing a social service for which it was not responsible. The history of the turning wheel of the Misericórdia in Bahia is a history of bureaucratic self-interest. Spices and gold were dearer to the hearts of Portuguese kings and their ministers than the spirit of Christian charity which they so openly professed.

[1] Vilhena, *Noticias soteropolitanas*, vol. 1, p. 126.
[2] ANRJ, *Caixa 129*, doc. 32.

13

The Retirement House of the Most Holy Name of Jesus

PORTUGUESE women were the most jealously guarded in Europe. A Portuguese writer of the seventeenth century compared female honour with an arithmetical calculation: an error was an error, be it by one or by a thousand.[1] A virtuous woman only left her house thrice in her lifetime — for her christening, her marriage and her funeral: such was the moral ideal for womanhood.[2] In the Portuguese overseas empire the seclusion of the white woman was, if anything, more severe. Travellers of other European nations to the Orient or to Brazil never failed to comment on the seclusion of the Portuguese female, be she wife or daughter. In colonial Bahia the French engineer Froger remarked that the white women only left their homes to attend mass on Sundays.[3] Frézier, also an engineer, who visited Bahia some eighteen years later in 1714, was intrigued rather than dismayed by the strict seclusion of the Portuguese female. Although acknowledging the jealous precautions taken by husbands to guard their wives and daughters, he slyly commented: '... they are almost all of them Libertines, and find means to impose upon the Watchfulness of their Fathers and Husbands'. He continued, 'Whether it be the Effect of the Climate, or of our natural Bent after that which others endeavour to keep from us by Force, there is no need of any extraordinary Efforts to be admitted to the last Familiarity.'[4] Frézier was allowing himself to be carried away by his own romantic hopes in this assessment of Portuguese womanhood. All the evidence points to a

---

[1] 'A honra da mulher comparo eu à conta do algarismo; tanto erra quem errou em um, como quem errou em mil', Francisco Manuel de Melo, *Carta de guia de casados* (ed. Lisboa, 1959), p. 42.

[2] Cited by C. R. Boxer, *The Golden Age of Brazil*, p. 137.

[3] Froger, *Relation d'un voyage*, p. 137.

[4] Frézier, *A Voyage to the South-Sea*, p. 300.

supreme preoccupation with the honour of a daughter and the fidelity of the bride. Any lapse on the part of the woman met with death as a matter of honour. Vilhena stated the case when he said that a *senhora* will act as such: any false impression gained by travellers was based on women of pleasure (*mulheres da tarifa*) who exist the world over.[1]

A convent had been the traditional place of seclusion for the daughters of upper-class white families. Suitably endowed, these girls had been sent to convents in Portugal, often against their will. Sexual honour was allied to social prestige in the minds of the martinets of the Bahian aristocracy. Marriage to an officer of the garrison would have been as disastrous as the defloration of the girl. This was especially true since, in the latter case, some poor noble could be found who would be willing to overlook such a detail in return for a handsome dowry. The cost of sending a daughter to Portugal was heavy. During the seventeenth century the leading families and the city council of Bahia had repeatedly petitioned the king for permission to establish a convent. This had been finally granted and the Convent of Santa Clara de Nossa Senhora do Desterro had been founded in 1677.

The Desterro had been founded by the aristocracy for the aristocracy. Originally there had been places for fifty nuns of the black veil and twenty-five of the white veil. The latter category was inferior; its members had no vote and were responsible for the menial labour of the convent. Although the fifty places of the higher category had been filled rapidly and a waiting list established, there had been no applicants for the inferior category. In 1688 the city council had sent a second petition to the king asking for his authorisation to commute these to the higher status but this had been refused.[2] During the eighteenth century most of the aristocratic families of Bahia could count at least one daughter in the Desterro, although few went to the lengths of Colonel José Pires de Carvalho who placed all five daughters in the Desterro.[3]

The need for social seclusion rather than religious seclusion had led to the foundation of the Desterro. In addition to the nuns, female relatives and

[1] Vilhena, *Noticias soteropolitanas*, vol. 1, pp. 46–7.

[2] Accioli-Amaral, *Memorias historicas e politicas*, vol. 5, pp. 222–3.

[3] ACDB, *Livro I das entradas e profissões das religiosas de Santa Clara do Desterro da cid⁰ da Bahya*, entries nos. 89, 96, 104, 108 and 109.

young girls, known as *educandas*, were also accepted. There was intense secular interest in the internal affairs of the convent. Vacancies were closely scrutinised and on several occasions in the eighteenth century there were complaints of secular canvassing in the elections of abbesses. Vows of abstinence and poverty were often forgotten. Each nun was permitted to have two servants, usually orphan girls, but sometimes slaves. Some nuns continued business enterprises such as the loan of money or sale of lands. Rumours of feasts and amorous frolickings within the convent scandalised the city and occasioned severe reprimands from the Crown.

The foundation of the first convent in Bahia in no way benefited the citizens. The aristocrats continued to send their daughters to Portugal. The middle class families found it impossible to secure a place for a daughter in the Desterro, such was the vigilance of the aristocracy over all entrants. The financial position of the middle class was never sufficiently solid for a family to be able to sustain the loss of the breadwinner. The Misericórdia had assisted the widows and dependants in a small degree. On the recommendation of a parish priest or in response to a petition, the stewards in charge of such visits (*mordomos das visitadas*) had provided clothes, medicine and alms. After extensive enquiries the Mesa had provided dowries to girls of undoubted virtue. The brotherhood lacked the financial means and accommodation to offer more substantial protection to the daughters of such needy families.

There had been an increasingly secular feeling in Bahia in the last decades of the seventeenth century. This had been apparent in the provisions of wills leaving legacies to the Misericórdia. After the initial outburst of civic enthusiasm, the city council had been remarkably disenchanted with the Desterro. This had been in part due to the heavy financial burden of the construction which had been accepted by the municipal authorities when permission had been granted for the foundation. Public funds would have been adequate for one religious foundation, but in addition to the Desterro, work was in progress on the cathedral, the Benedictine monastery and that of the 'barefooted' Carmelites. In 1680 the councillors had protested strongly against royal authorisation for the building of a hospice for eight French Capuchins. The councillors had stressed the number of religious constructions already financed by charity and hinted that these 'deuced foreigners' might form a fifth column and cause unrest.[1] More latent was the attitude that there were already enough religious foundations, which contributed little to Bahia but were supported by the alms of its already overtaxed citizens. A shortage of money, lack of white women and the increased recognition of the social problems of urbanisation coincided with this attitude and resulted in the establishment of the first secular retirement house in Bahia.

João de Mattos de Aguiar, popularly known as João de Mattinhos, was responsible for this foundation. When he died on 26 May 1700 he nominated the Misericórdia as his trustees. From mammoth bequests to the Misericórdia he ordered that 80,000 *cruzados* should be placed on loan and the annual interest of 5,000 *cruzados* be applied to the building of a retirement house. Once the construction had been finished the interest was to be spent on the upkeep of the fabric and the feeding and clothing of the girls housed there.[2] The choice of site, building details, selection of candidates and administration was left to the discretion of the board of guardians of the Misericórdia.

The choice of site aroused great controversy. The issue was whether the new retirement house should be on the outskirts of the city or in the Rua Direita next to the Misericórdia and backing on to the Ladeira da Misericórdia. The latter involved the purchase and demolition of four houses and the moving of the Travessa da Misericórdia to a more southerly position next to the mint. Nevertheless the Mesa of 1700–1 decided on the site next to the hospital for three reasons: economy of labour, ease of administration and the benefit of those privileges already granted to the brotherhood by the Crown.[3] Royal approval was sought and Dom Pedro II referred the request to the Chancellor of the High Court in Bahia for his opinion.

Meanwhile a new Mesa under the chief commissioner of the Treasury Francisco Lamberto had taken office for the year 1701–2. This immediately reversed the decision of its predecessor and voted for a suburban site. It was later to be alleged that the Secretary of State, Gonçalo Ravasco Cavalcante e

---

[1] City council to king, 14 April 1680 (AMB, vol. 174, ff. 19–20v), cf. a similar protest on 4 August 1756 by the council against the proposed foundation of a hospice of St Philip Neri (AMB, vol. 31, ff. 190v–191).

[2] ASCMB, vol. 199, ff. 5v–7. The Misericórdia received 500$000 from a further 20,000 *cruzados* placed on loan to cover the costs of administration (ibid., ff. 7v–8).

[3] Minute of Mesa of 22 July 1700 (ASCMB, vol. 14, f. 54).

Albuquerque, had been responsible for this sudden change of heart by exerting pressure on the Mesa to buy some of his own land in the Preguiça.[1] Nevertheless the reasons advanced in opposition to a site on the Rua Direita were entirely valid: the cost of buying houses on the Ladeira only then to demolish them; the delay in providing alternative accommodation for the occupants; the difficulty of moving the Travessa; the heavy cost of transporting materials from the wharves on the shore; the impossibility of enlarging the building; the lack of a good water supply and the effect on the hospital whose light and ventilation would be severely prejudiced by an adjacent building. The Mesa advocated a suburban site which offered more space, a ready water supply, a healthier position and enabled building to be undertaken more cheaply and quickly.[2] This proposal was supported by the chancellor, João da Rocha Pitta, and received royal approval.[3]

This decision was not final. The Mesa of 1702–3, also under Francisco Lamberto, took no further action. Its successor, under the dynamic leadership of Pedro Barbosa Leal, took up the problem within a fortnight of assuming office. Pedro Barbosa Leal, one of the richest landowners in Bahia, was determined that building should start during his term of office and that it should be next to the Misericórdia in the Rua Direita. He appealed to the feeling of pride and honour of the members of the Mesa and Junta, referring to the 'sumptuous work' which would be the retirement house, with rooms, cloister and a water cistern — a building worthy of the girls sheltered there. The image presented was that of the noble Misericórdia dominating the main street of the city. Any delay in protecting orphans and the needy would prejudice the good name of the brotherhood. This appeal was supported by a plan for the new retirement house, drawn up by one of the best architects of the period, Gabriel Ribeiro. This provided for 106 cells, laundry, cloister and offices and offered the possibility of expansion as far as the mint. The Misericórdia would receive all privileges previously granted and the royal permission could be applied to the new building without amendments. The city council was placated by the fact that the new building would enhance the Rua Direita and would offer commercial benefits

---

[1] The only reference to this alleged intervention is in a letter of 20 October 1703 from the Mesa in Bahia to the Misericórdia in Lisbon (ASCMB, vol. 52, ff. 9–11).

[2] Minute of Mesa of 28 July 1701 (ASCMB, vol. 14, ff. 57–58v).

[3] *Provisão* of 21 May 1702 (ASCMB, vol. 207, ff. 27–8).

in the form of shops to be installed on the ground floor of the new building.[1] Having been bullied into submission, the Mesa and Junta approved the proposal and decided on day labour as being most suitable for the new building.[2]

The city council intervened at this stage and took legal action to forbid further development of the site. The councillors objected on two grounds. First, the transfer of the Travessa da Misericórdia some fifteen yards to the south was not satisfactory because at present it provided a link between the Ladeira on the seaside and the Rua do Tijolo on the other side of the Rua Direita. Secondly, the grandiose plan for the retirement house meant encroaching on the Ladeira da Misericórdia, thereby narrowing the width of one of the main arteries between the upper and lower cities. Once again it was hinted that Gonçalo Ravasco (a councillor for 1703–4) had exerted pressure on his fellow councillors. It is impossible to establish whether this was the case or not. Certainly at a later municipal enquiry over the retirement house, strict impartiality was observed and interested parties were replaced by those having no connection with the brotherhood.[3] The Misericórdia appealed directly to Dom Pedro II and all municipal objections were quashed by a royal order of 2 April 1704.[4]

The Mesa immediately requested tenders for the new building. Seven of the leading stonemasons submitted estimates. Among these was Manuel Quaresma, who had collaborated in the building of the Third Order of St Francis.[5] Such was his reputation that he was commissioned although his tender was considerably higher than those of his competitors. The Provedor, Pedro Barbosa Leal, agreed to meet the difference from his own fortune.[6] The Mesa may also have been influenced in its choice by the fact that Manuel Quaresma was a member of the board of guardians for the year 1703–4 and had previously served on the Mesa and Junta.[1] If the Miseri-

---

[1] Minute of 17 July 1703 (ASCMB, vol. 14, ff. 68–70v).

[2] Minute of 31 July 1703 (ASCMB, vol. 14, f. 71).

[3] At an enquiry held on 26 March 1704 to examine objections raised by the attorney of the city council to the building, both Pedro Barbosa Leal and Miguel Calmon de Almeida were replaced because they were brothers of the Misericórdia (AMB, vol. 25, ff. 126–128).

[4] AMB, vol. 136, ff. 142v–143.

[5] Marieta Alves, *História da Venerável Ordem 3ª*, p. 22.

[6] Minute of 10 September 1704 (ASCMB, vol. 14, ff. 76v–77v).

córdia chose its Provedors with discretion, it also elected as brothers craftsmen whose skills could be placed at the brotherhood's service.

Despite his reputation and record of service, little progress was made on
the retirement house in the next two years. In 1705 the board of guardians
decided to let out the work on a contract basis to Faustino de Almeida and
José Gonçalves Pena.² The new contractors faced difficulties, many of
which had been envisaged by the board of guardians of 1701–2 in its objections to a site next to the Misericórdia. Work on the hospital would
effectively delay that on the retirement house and meanwhile there was the
problem of where to accommodate the displaced sick. The old issue of the
purchase of houses for demolition was raised again. The city council
objected to the narrowing of the Ladeira and suggested the Misericórdia
should buy the houses on the seaside of the Ladeira and demolish them in
order to preserve the width of the street. A compromise was reached.
Gabriel Ribeiro submitted a new plan providing for fifty-eight cells and all
necessary offices. This new building would be connected to the hospital by
a passageway over the Travessa. Should expansion prove necessary this
could be done in the direction of the mint, further storeys could be built on
the hospital and new passages made over the Travessa.³ The councillors
were satisfied by the restoration of the former Travessa and agreed to grant
some three feet of the upper end of the Ladeira to the Misericórdia so that
the new building would be rectangular.⁴

Work on the retirement house took some ten years, and only in 1716 was
it in a fit condition to be inhabited. Apart from the difficulties of changing
contractors, other problems contributed to this delay. The legacy of João
de Mattos de Aguiar involved the Misericórdia in numerous legal disputes
and lawyers were appointed to deal with these alone. The collection of

---

¹ Manuel Quaresma had been admitted to the Misericórdia as a brother of minor
standing on 14 April 1683 (ASCMB, vol. 2, f. 188). He served on the Mesa in
1687, 1691, 1699 and 1703 and on the Junta in 1689, 1692, 1694, 1701 and 1704
(ASCMB, vol. 34). He received an advance payment of 400$000 (ASCMB, vol.
14, f. 77), but he either died or fell out with the Mesa because he did not serve on
the Mesa or Junta after 1704, nor was he invited to be one of the technical con-
sultants for the new plans in December 1705 (ASCMB, vol. 14, ff. 79v–81).

² The contract was dated 21 August 1705 (ASCMB, vol. 14, ff. 78v–79).

³ ASCMB, vol. 14, ff. 79v–81.

⁴ Minute of municipal council of 14 December 1705 (AMB, vol. 25, ff. 251v–254v).

interest and capital lent by the testator during his lifetime proved extremely difficult. Finally, the Misericórdia exceeded the limits envisaged by João de Mattos de Aguiar. The building was only finally concluded in 1739 at a total cost in the region of 130,000 *cruzados*.[1] The number of *porcionistas*, or boarders, never remotely approached expectations and much of the building was unoccupied.[2] Opinions as to the final result varied. The Bahian chronicler Sebastião da Rocha Pitta, who had watched the arduous progress on the building, numbered the finishing of the retirement house among the more significant events of the viceroyalty of the Marquis of Angeja.

> During the viceroyalty of the marquis (the animator of noble under-takings, whose enthusiasm stimulated all aspects of government) work was finished on the retirement house for honourable women. This is a distinguished building in concept and excellence of design. It is exempt from the jurisdiction of the Ordinary and is under the authority of the *Casa da Santa Misericórdia*, next to the seat of the brotherhood whose church will also serve the retirement house. It is a building of three storeys with many rooms, cells, bedrooms and windows affording extensive views over the land and the sea. Its turret can be seen from far out to sea. In the lower part of the building are large rooms sufficient in number to serve many people. This whole edifice presents a nobility of appearance and majesty of execution equal to that of the largest monastery.[3]

Other opinions were less favourable. Vilhena, at the end of the century, commented guardedly that 'the retirement house for girls is adequately spacious' — praise indeed from this carping critic of the Misericórdia.[4] Thus it was surprising that António Joaquim Damázio, nineteenth-century historian of the Misericórdia and its meticulous accountant, should have condemned the retirement house so completely as lacking in architectural elegance, having inadequate lighting and ventilation, cramped accommodation and being totally unsuitable for its purpose.[5]

The Retirement House of the Most Holy Name of Jesus was formally

[1] ASCMB, vol. 14, ff. 248–249v and ff. 249v–250v. At the time of opening in 1716 the cost was 105,000 *cruzados* (ASCMB, vol. 14, ff. 113–15).

[2] In 1767 it was proposed that the lower part of the retirement house be converted into a ward for women because it had remained empty since 1716 (ASCMB, vol. 15, ff. 204v–207v).   [3] Sebastião da Rocha Pitta, *Historia*, livro 10, § 14.

[4] Vilhena, *Noticias soteropolitanas*, vol. 1, p. 98.

[5] Damázio, *Tombamento*, chapter 5.

declared open on 29 June 1716, by the Provedor, the judge of the High Court Dionísio de Azevedo Arvelos.[1] Work still remained to be done on the interior of the retirement house and on the special choir in the church for the girls, but the building was habitable and there was no point in leaving it empty. This was the explanation given by the board of guardians for the premature opening. Two external factors may have influenced their decision: first, a viceroyal report of 1715 alleging gross maladministration by the Misericórdia of its finances; secondly, the fact that Dionísio de Azevedo Arvelos was the fifth successive High Court judge to be elected Provedor and this had caused some scandalised comment in the city, whatever his personal merits. The Marquis of Angeja had also remarked that the delay in the building of the retirement house should be investigated.[2] Its opening proved the integrity of the Provedor and the honest administration of the finances of the Misericórdia. There was some ground for the Mesa's belief that solid achievement would allay suspicion and the enquiry ordered by the king failed to reveal any 'hidden skeletons'.

The retirement house was primarily intended for young girls of middle class families who were of marriageable age and whose honour was endangered by the loss of one or both parents. These were accepted as *recolhidas*, or recluses, and were granted a dowry on marrying. In his letter of approval for the establishment of a retirement house, the king had strongly commended to the Mesa the admittance of two other types of women. The first group were *porcionistas*, widows or spinsters of good repute who would pay for their board and lodging. The second group were wives of men absent from Bahia on business and who would be placed in the retirement house during their husbands' absence.[3] This second suggestion, tantamount to a command, directly contravened the *Compromisso* of 1618 which had stipulated that in no circumstances was a retirement house administered by the Misericórdia to be used as a depository for women.[4] The board of guardians had little option but to agree to these suggestions and may even

¹ ASCMB, vol. 14, ff. 113–15 and f. 115v.

² Viceroy to king 12 July 1715; Dom João V, in a letter of 26 September 1716, ordered a full enquiry by the Crown judge Joseph de Sá e Mendonça (APB, *Ordens régias*, vol. 10, doc. 63).   ³ ASCMB, vol. 207, ff. 27–8.

⁴ *Compromisso* of Lisbon of 1618, chapter 20, § 14. At no time was the retirement house of the Misericórdia in Bahia intended for 'mulheres desvalidas e desviadas que, por imposição das famílias, necessitassem de reclusão para se

have welcomed them as providing a pretext for a larger building than that envisaged for the recluses alone. The first plan of Gabriel Ribeiro had provided for seventy-six boarders and others out of a total of 106; even the amended plan catering for fifty-eight women proved excessive. The fact that the retirement house was regarded from the outset as fulfilling a civic purpose may explain the wholehearted royal support, viceroyal co-operation, and the unusual willingness on the part of the city council to compromise.

The Mesa of the Misericórdia stipulated certain conditions for acceptance of all women, be they recluses or boarders. All had to be virtuous, of Old Christian stock, and white. The last two conditions coincided with the policy of the Third Orders, and were common to the religious orders and to the convents of eighteenth-century Bahia. In 1689 the king had intervened to order the Jesuits to continue to admit coloured pupils (*moços pardos*) to their school in Bahia.[1] In 1736 the city council complained to the king that the Benedictines refused to admit 'sons of Brazil' whatever their colour, and that in the 145 years of the Order's existence on Brazilian soil only a handful of Brazilians had achieved office.[2] With regard to convents there was a total ban on the admittance of coloured girls. As late as 1754, at a time when Bahia could count three convents, the three daughters of a sergeant major of the garrison requested the royal permission to go to Portugal to be nuns: although orphans, they had been well brought up and were well endowed, but had been refused admission to any Bahian convent because they were '*pardas* to the second degree'.[3]

A candidate for the retirement house presented a petition to the board of

---

regenerarem': nor did the city council make any financial contribution towards its upkeep as suggested by Affonso Ruy, *Historia da Câmara*, p. 198.

[1] Royal order of 28 February 1689 (AMB, vol. 136, f. 51).

[2] City council to king 5 September 1736. The councillors also complained that this was the practice of the Capuchins who had brought over thirty friars from Oporto using alms given by the citizens of Bahia (AMB, vol. 176, ff. 178–179v). For a similar situation in Olinda, see C. R. Boxer, *Race Relations*, pp. 118–19.

[3] 'mossas pardas em segundo grao'. In their petition they described the situation in Bahia, 'e como na d^a cidade da B^a não tomam nos Conv^{tos} della p^a religiozas mossas com manchas de pardas, não obstante serem as supp^{tes} não m^{to} trigueiras, e terem sido creadas com toda a estimação e abundancia ...' (APB, *Ordens régias*, vol. 53, ff. 167–72).

guardians. An enquiry was made to establish her age, virtue and necessity.[1]
If favourable the girl was admitted as an *encostada*, or probationer, until a
vacancy should occur among the recluses. The time spent on probation
depended entirely on the number of recluses leaving to get married. During
this period, which could be anything up to two years, all the costs of food
and clothing were met by a guarantor at the rate of 80 *rs*. daily. After promotion to full recluse status the girl was supported by the Misericórdia for
four years and received a dowry of 100$000 on marrying.[2] If she failed to
marry within this period she was returned to the home of her guarantor or
could remain in the retirement house as a boarder.

A boarder also submitted a petition to the Mesa and a similar enquiry was
held. In the case of a boarder the preoccupation of the Mesa was more
financial than moral. Advance payment was demanded, the financial standing of the guarantor(s) was examined, and the Misericórdia reserved the
right to dismiss any boarder if this proved necessary. In 1716 the annual cost
was fixed at 80$000 but this was raised to 100$000 in 1734 in view of the
higher cost of living and 'these hard times'.[3]

In the selection of girls for the retirement house, the boards of guardians
favoured applications from foundlings and the daughters of the poorer
brothers of the Misericórdia. The retirement house provided a place of
refuge for those foundlings who had been supported by the Misericórdia
for three years and had then been boarded out with a family, sometimes with
unsatisfactory results. Whereas in Macao the Misericórdia had simply
ignored any foundling once it was seven years old, in Bahia the Misericórdia
could continue to provide assistance in the form of the retirement house.[4]

---

[1] These enquiries were destroyed, as were those concerning the admission of
brothers. An indication of the severity of the enquiry can be gained from the case
of one girl who submitted three petitions — two to the Mesa and one to the vicar-
general. The scribe of the Misericórdia called for three testimonials from independent witnesses before her petition to be an *encostada* was granted (ASCMB, vol.
1180, ff. 43v–44).

[2] *Recolhidas* had maximum priority in the allocation of dowries as 'filhas da
Casa' (ASCMB, vol. 14, ff. 172–173v and vol. 85, ff. 76v–77v).

[3] Minutes of 1 June 1716 and 10 January 1734 (ASCMB, vol. 14, ff. 113–15 and
ff. 191–2).

[4] In the decade 1740–50 some twelve foundlings were admitted to the retirement
house (ASCMB, vol. 1180).

The retirement house also provided an extension of the social services offered by the Misericórdia to its brothers and their dependents. In the event of the disruption of home life by the death of a parent or financial misfortune, the Misericórdia provided a home for daughters of marriageable age.[1]

The number of girls admitted to the retirement house varied from year to year, depending on the number leaving to be married. It also depended on the progress of the work on the building and money available. In 1716 eight recluses were admitted: a further one was admitted in 1717 when it was discovered there was a balance. After final payment on the construction had been made, the number was increased to eighteen in 1740 and to twenty-one in 1750 as the result of economies in the method of distributing food.[2] The number of places was always filled. In his report of 1755 the High Court judge alleged chronic over-allocation of places with thirty-three recluses.[3]

The number of boarders never came up to the expectations of the king or board of guardians. In the fifteen years 1740–55 (the earliest for which there are records) only ten boarders entered the retirement house. Three of these had been placed there during the absence of their husbands and two were divorced or separated from their husbands. This total lack of response can only be explained by the demand for white women in colonial Bahia and the unlikelihood of a white woman remaining single.

Despite the clauses of the *Compromisso* the Misericórdia was forced to admit women on the orders of the archbishop or viceroy. This offers the only instance of successful intervention by the civil and ecclesiastical authorities in the domestic affairs of the brotherhood in Bahia. By its unquestioning acceptance of the conditions of the royal permission in 1702, the Mesa severely compromised its independence. The archbishop or viceroy ordered the seclusion of women on moral grounds on some half-dozen occasions before 1755. Usually this was when a woman was being ill-treated or prostituted by her husband and was causing a public scandal. In such cases the archbishop ordered the removal of the woman from her home and placed her in the protection of a relative or friend. If this failed, the Misericórdia was ordered to accept her in the retirement house. The

---

[1] ASCMB, vol. 14, ff. 248–249v.
[2] ASCMB, vol. 14, ff. 115, 117v–118 and 261v; vol. 15, f. 42.
[3] BNRJ, 11–33, 24, 45, doc. 10, chapter 29.

most unusual case involved one Dona Helena de Lima and her two daughters. A widow, she had been the concubine of a friar. He induced the archbishop Sebastião Monteiro de Vide (Archbishop of Bahia, 1702–22) to order the seclusion of her two daughters in the Desterro against the will of their mother. After the death of the archbishop and in the absence of the friar, Dona Helena successfully petitioned for the release of her daughters. Two of her relatives informed the viceroy, because they knew of an agreement between Dona Helena and two men (one in Holy Orders) for the young girls to become their concubines. This plan was frustrated by the viceroy. As soon as the girls had left the Desterro and were about to enter the carriages of their prospective lovers, officers of the law intervened and escorted the girls to the retirement house.[1] On several other occasions boarders and divorcees were kept in the retirement house against their will on the royal command.[2]

Although not intended as a prison, life in the retirement house was extremely austere and the rules severe. In the desire to protect the honour of the inmates, boards of governors went to extremes in the matter of seclusion. All visitors had to seek authorisation from the Mesa, and even close relatives were forbidden to speak to any recluse or boarder without the permission of the *regente*, or warden. Even the Provedor could only visit the retirement house when accompanied by the scribe and other brothers were only permitted to visit in pairs with due authorisation.[3] All outside contacts by letters or verbal messages were forbidden. To this end a passage-way had been built to connect the retirement house with the hospital so that the girls would have no pretext for going into the Rua Direita. Even the window-sills were built up so that any view of the street was impossible for the girls in the retirement house.

There are few records of details of life inside the retirement house. One of the few records is a document of 1749 with the everyday costs of food and other domestic items. This document is of sufficient interest to be quoted in full:

[1] Viceroy to king 22 October 1723 (APB, *Ordens régias*, vol. 17, doc. 55a).

[2] The struggle by Theresa de Jesus Maria to leave the retirement house where she had been placed against her will by the archbishop in 1751, supported by the viceroy and king, is described in APB, *Ordens régias*, vol. 58, ff. 315–440, comprising 22 documents.

[3] *Compromisso* of Lisbon of 1618, chapter 20, §13, 14 and 15.

Two pounds of meat for each person, and four for the warden, will be distributed daily by the steward as is the usual practice.

Two pounds of pork fat for each person monthly.

30 *rs.* worth of cabbage for all daily.

200 fagots of wood for all monthly.

Three *quartos* of flour for each person monthly, and six for the warden.

One flask of olive oil on days of abstinence, for all including the servants.

Thirty pints of fish oil monthly for all.

Nine *quartos* of beans monthly for all.

Three *quartilhos* of vinegar monthly for all.

One *quartilho* of oil monthly for the lamp in the oratory.

On days of abstinence 80 *rs.* of fish daily for each person, and a double ration for the warden. The servants will receive a ration of fish costing 40 *rs.* on such days.

Half a bushel of salt monthly for all.

320 *rs.* worth of cotton monthly for all.

Bananas to the value of 320 *rs.* monthly.

Soap to the value of 320 *rs.* monthly.

One pound of wax monthly.

Fowls and chickens for the sick will be distributed by the steward on the orders of the doctor and surgeon.

An allowance of 640 *rs.* each month will be made for domestic necessities such as brooms and pitchers.

Initially foodstuffs were handed over daily to the warden by two stewards. This resulted in wastage and the recluses complained of rotten fish and bad food. In 1749 the system was reformed. Distribution was made monthly, resulting in substantial financial economies to the Mesa and a better planned diet for the recluses.[1]

The menial duties of the retirement house were done by slaves. This was in direct opposition to a royal order forbidding such a practice. When the building of the retirement house had first been mooted, the Governor-General Dom João de Lencastre had written to Dom Pedro II suggesting that Indian girls be taken from the Jesuit villages and admitted to the retirement house as servants. The king totally rejected this proposal, stating that the inmates should provide for themselves as was the case in the convents of Lisbon where even the most noble recluse had no servants.[2] This was yet

[1] ASCMB, vol. 15, ff. 23v–24.

[2] King to governor-general 6 April 1702 (APB, *Ordens régias*, vol. 7, doc. 15).

another instance of the authorities in Lisbon failing to understand the prides
and prejudices of a colonial society based on slavery. After the opening of
the retirement house the Misericórdia followed the royal command and
employed few slaves. The recluses and boarders soon revolted, complaining
that they — 'white women as they are' — were being treated as slaves and
being ordered to wash dishes and scale fish! The warden was dismissed and
the board of guardians discreetly increased the number of slaves.[1]

The severity of the physical conditions in the retirement house was
accentuated by the harshness of the wardens. The all-male board of
guardians was singularly unsuccessful in its appointees to this position. A
succession of spinsters worked out their own jealousies and frustrations by
ill-treating the girls in their care. One was found guilty of lesbianism and
dismissed, the recluse concerned being jailed for a year.[2] The qualifications
demanded of a warden were that she be white, of Old Christian origin,
suitable age, good repute and possess some social standing. The last proved
to be an embarrassment in one instance. The Mesa appointed Dona Maria
Eulalia Villa Lobos da Câmara as warden in 1752 and dismissed her in 1758.[3]
The Mesa was compelled to reinstate her on the order of the Count of Arcos
(Viceroy 1755–60) who was a personal friend of Dona Maria.[4]

In all fairness it must be acknowledged that the task of the warden was
unenviable. On the one hand she had to satisfy the board of guardians and
on the other she had to exert firm control over adult boarders as well as
young recluses. The Mesa elected annually two brothers from the upper
class to serve as the scribe and treasurer of the retirement house. They were
intended to act as liaison officers between the Provedor and the warden, but
failed in this function. Mesas dismissed several wardens who failed to be
sufficiently submissive to their requests. The boarders proved disruptive
elements in the retirement house. They abused the privilege of being
allowed servants and there was a continual flow of slaves in and out of the
retirement house. They also challenged the authority of the warden at
every turn. The Provedor of 1754, Dr Luís da Costa e Faria, was over-
zealous in his desire to reform the retirement house. He forbad slaves not
connected with the Misericórdia from entering the retirement house and built

---

1 Minute of 24 August 1721 (ASCMB, vol. 14, f. 129).

2 ASCMB, vol. 195, ff. 122v–123v.

3 ASCMB, vol. 1180, f. 75.   4 ASCMB, vol. 1180, f. 131.

up the window-sills so that the recluses could not converse with their admirers in the street below. A boarder, whose slaves had been affected by the ruling, threatened the life of the warden and incited the girls to smash windows, bars and window-sills.[1]

The severity of the retirement house ensured its good repute. At no time was the honour of the recluses or boarders questioned. The greatest testimony of this was when the Count of Sabugosa requested the Provedor to admit his two younger sisters to the retirement house.[2] The only serious breach of the rules was with regard to messages. In 1721 and 1722 three priests in the employ of the Misericórdia were dismissed for 'prejudicing the honour and virtue' of the young girls by amorous letters.[3] In the 1750s there was considerable coming and going of servants, and women extraneous to the retirement house used it as a vantage point from which to see processions in the Rua Direita and even slept there.

The financial affairs of the legacy of João de Mattos de Aguiar (which included the retirement house) were entirely independent of those of the Misericórdia. The cost of building the retirement house amounted to 130,000 *cruzados*, a debt finally paid off in 1739. From this date the full annual interest of 5,000 *cruzados* was devoted to the maintenance of the fabric and the care of the recluses. It is impossible to say if the financial crisis which the Misericórdia suffered in the 1740s and 1750s affected the retirement house. From the increase in the number of recluses in 1740 and 1750 it would appear not. Nevertheless, letters from the Mesas to debtors show that difficulty was experienced in enforcing the payment of interest, let alone the return of capital. In 1754 the annual expenditure on the retirement house was estimated as follows: feeding, clothing and housing the warden, mistress, portress, twenty-three recluses and ten slaves cost 2,400$000; repairs were calculated at a further 600$000.[4] Thus the deficit considerably exceeded the balance, even if the Misericórdia succeeded in collecting all the interest due on the capital, some of which may itself have been lost. Thus the increase in the number of recluses in 1750 appears more as an act of vanity than of recognition of the financial situation.

The retirement house of the Misericórdia answered a pressing social need

[1] APB, *Ordens régias*, vol. 55, ff. 266–93 and vol. 73, doc. 49.
[2] Viceroy to Provedor 15 April 1723 (*Documentos historicos*, vol. 45, p. 70).
[3] ASCMB, vol. 195, ff. 64 and 65v.   [4] ASCMB, vol. 210, f. 60.

M

by providing a place of seclusion for girls whose honour was in danger. As such, it received the support of the Crown and city council. It was typical of the official attitude towards social welfare that the initiative for such a foundation should come from an individual and the administration should be provided by a brotherhood. In fact, the retirement house never fulfilled the civic function envisaged by the king and councillors. It merely complemented the social services already provided by the Misericórdia in the care of foundlings and distribution of dowries.

The greatest contribution by the retirement house to eighteenth-century Bahia was its very existence. It was the first occasion on which it had been publicly recognised that the social problems of Bahia were not limited to slaves and gypsies. The gradual increase in the importance of a middle class was accompanied by social difficulties no less severe than those of the lower classes. It also represented the break with the religious tradition of the seventeenth century. Although Catholic in administration, the retirement house was wholly secular in intent. Its example inspired the foundation of similar institutions for social rather than religious ends. The first of these was the Retirement House of Our Lady of Solitude (1739) for repentant prostitutes and young girls.[1] This was followed by the Retirement House of St Raymond (1753) and several privately organised places for the seclusion of young girls.[2] The Retirement House of the Most Holy Name of Jesus not only fulfilled a social function but contributed decisively to the ideology of Bahia in the eighteenth century.

[1] Luiz Monteiro da Costa, *Igreja e convento de Nossa Senhora da Soledade* (Bahia, 1958).

[2] Petitions for the founding of retirement houses were sometimes rejected by the viceroy on the grounds of insufficient financial support (APB, *Ordens régias*, vol. 58, ff. 563v–565v).

14

Conclusion

THE death of Dom João V on 31 June 1750 marked the end of an era in Luso-Brazilian history. The quinquennium 1750–5 was an eventful period, both in the history of the mother nation and in that of her most important colony. It saw the rise to power of Sebastião José de Carvalho e Melo, later to be the Marquis of Pombal. The Minister of State during these years was the ailing Pedro da Mota, but it was Pombal who dominated all sectors of the administration from his post as Minister of Foreign Affairs and War. The new king, Dom José I, left all decisions on policy to his capable minister. Portugal was experiencing a time of economic difficulty. Imports exceeded exports and the influx of low-priced commodities, especially from Britain, was adversely affecting home production. An illicit trade in the re-export of gold from Portugal was flourishing. The system of annual fleets was proving unsatisfactory. Warehouses in Lisbon were flooded with sugar and tobacco for short periods of the year, when prices fell. Pombal enacted a series of measures, replaced lax officials and exercised closer surveillance over the enforcement of dues in an attempt to remedy this situation. The greatest single event in Portugal in these years was the great earthquake of Lisbon on 1 November 1755. This destroyed the centre of the city and was followed by a tidal wave which completed the destruction of those few buildings on the waterfront which had escaped the main shock. A few months later Pedro da Mota died. Pombal was supreme in Portugal and was to remain so for the next twenty-one years. Portugal had exchanged an absolute monarchy for a virtual dictatorship.

The years 1750–5 marked a significant stage in the history of Brazil. They opened with the Treaty of Madrid (1750) between Portugal and Spain. The pioneering era of the *bandeiras paulistas* in Brazil was drawing to a close and territorial expansion had reached its most westerly limits. Based on the principle of *uti possidetis*, the Treaty of Madrid replaced the demarcation line laid down by the Treaty of Tordesillas (1494) and gave to Brazil a boundary which has remained substantially the same to the present day. By the 1750s the gold boom in Minas Gerais had passed and the export of Brazilian gold was on the decline. The energetic economic measures of the Marquis of Pombal extended to Brazil. In 1753 he caused the Crown to decree that the commerce in diamonds would in future be a royal monopoly. In 1755 Pombal founded the state-owned Grão Pará Company. This brought him into conflict with the Jesuits, one of whose main centres of activity was in Pará and Maranhão. Pombal had already faced Jesuit resistance in the demarcation of frontiers in Paraguay with Spain. In Pará the Order strongly opposed the proposed restrictions on its trading interests. In 1755 the first Jesuits were expelled from Pará for voicing their opposition openly, the first victims of the struggle between Pombal and the Jesuits which was to end with the expulsion of the Order from Portugal and Brazil in 1759. In addition to economic measures, during this period Pombal caused to be enacted the first of a series of royal decrees aimed at the secularisation and emancipation of the Amerindian population in Brazil. The first such decree was promulgated on 4 April 1755. It ruled that a Portuguese who married an Indian would suffer no loss of social position thereby. Moreover, it stated that in future the use of the denigratory term *caboclo*, or other insulting epithets applied to Indians or the offspring of such mixed marriages, would be severely punished.

The Misericórdia of Bahia was in a critical condition in the mid-eighteenth century. It had become increasingly apparent to a succession of boards of guardians that only the most draconian measures could restore the brotherhood to its former social eminence and financial stability. No Mesa in the years 1750–5 had the courage to reveal the critical situation of the Misericórdia to the Bahian public or to risk unpopularity among the brothers themselves by taking such measures. The difficulty of finding Provedors was only solved by the intervention of the viceroy and brothers were equally reluctant to accept the post of treasurer. The third register of copies of letters written by Mesas between 1749 and 1755 is a chronicle of despair. It is almost entirely composed of letters to attorneys of the brotherhood, not only in the Recôncavo, but as far afield as Jacobina and Piauí. These were exhorted in frenzied terms to do all in their power to enforce the payment of interest due on loans, ensure that securities were adequate on these loans, and if necessary take legal action against stubborn debtors or urge the sale of property pledged as security on capital loans which had been lost. Many of these pleas verged on the hysterical, but there can be no doubt that at this time the Misericórdia was faced with a backlog in the payments of dowries and the salaries of employees and wet-nurses. It was becoming increasingly difficult for the brotherhood to maintain its social services. This disastrous state of affairs did not escape the notice of the viceroy who brought it to the attention of the king.

By a decree of 17 February 1754 Dom José I ordered a full enquiry to be made into the accounts of the Misericórdia for the previous ten years. The High Court judge José de Affonseca Lemos was dispatched to Bahia for this purpose. At the same time he was to conduct similar investigations into the financial affairs of the Treasury and municipal council. This was not the first time that the Misericórdia had come under the royal scrutiny. In the eighteenth century alone there had been several enquiries, but these had been ineffective. The investigation carried out by José de Affonseca Lemos was characterised by its methodical approach, impartiality, and depth. The causes of the financial decline of the brotherhood were analysed and recommendations were made to remedy this critical situation. On 8 May 1754 the judge ordered the board of guardians of the Misericórdia to supply him with a complete inventory of all properties owned or administered by the brotherhood, the income derived from such properties, and the purposes for which it was used. The Mesa was also to furnish him with complete records of all capital assets, the annual returns on this capital and details of instances when capital had been lost.[1] On 2 June 1754 the Mesa appointed two brothers to draw up this account.[2] Here the matter rested for almost six months. There was a change of Mesa. Only after a further letter from the judge and a forceful reminder from the viceroy was any further attempt made to comply with the judge's order. On 19 November 1754 Simão Gomes Monteiro, scribe for the previous year, was nominated by the Mesa to present the account.[3] He completed this by January of the following year. José de Affonseca Lemos checked this against the ledgers of the brotherhood and made his report on 16 May 1755.[4]

[1] ASCMB, vol. 15, ff. 70v–71. [2] ASCMB, vol. 15, f. 72.
[3] ASCMB, vol. 15, f. 76. [4] BNRJ, 11–33, 24, 45, doc. 10.

All aspects of the financial administration of the Misericórdia came under fire in the thirty chapters of this report. Boards of guardians over the previous ten years were severely censured for mal-administration and inefficiency. The 'great decadence' of the Misericórdia was basically the result of loans having been made, both from the capital resources of the brotherhood and the funds of the legacy of João de Mattos de Aguiar, on poor securities. There had been gross negligence in the collection of interest due on loans, insufficient attention had been paid to the question of placing capital so as to ensure the maximum returns, and in many cases capital had simply been lost. All the other financial and administrative failures of the brotherhood stemmed from this root cause, but four other factors were listed as having contributed to the decline of the brotherhood.

José de Affonseca Lemos criticised boards of guardians for inadequate supervision over their treasurers. Treasurers had been allowed to make expenditures, sometimes of large sums as in the case of salaries, without any specific authorisation from the Mesa. The judge suggested that two items in particular should be under the direct control of the board of guardians. The first was the payment of wet-nurses. These were paid without any attempt being made to verify if they were still looking after a foundling, or indeed if he were alive. The second was the alms of 1$000 given to each convalescent leaving the hospital from the legacy of João de Mattos de Aguiar. In neither case did the treasurer present a list of those to whom payment was made, nor was he required to furnish receipts acknowledging payment. The judge reminded the Mesas of their obligation to audit the accounts of each treasurer at the end of his term of office, which they had failed to do in many cases. He also noted that several Mesas had contravened the clauses of the *Compromisso* by dipping into capital in order to meet everyday expenses: rarely had such 'loans' been repaid.

The judge also criticised the low standard of accountancy shown by the clerks of the Misericórdia. Here too there had been lack of proper supervision. Clerks had simply 'written off' errors or duplicated entries in the account ledgers without authorisation from the treasurer, let alone from the Mesa. In some cases no record had been kept of monies received by the brotherhood. On other occasions items of expenditure had been entered in the appropriate ledger, but the treasurer had not presented any receipts confirming that the payments had in fact been made. José de Affonseca Lemos hinted strongly that such discrepancies in the registers and the total absence of receipts hid the misappropriation of large sums.

Boards of guardians were found guilty of having been unduly extravagant with funds given to the Misericórdia for charitable purposes. The retirement house was a case in point. There was chronic overcrowding and this necessitated the use of funds in addition to the bequest of João de Mattos de Aguiar left to the Misericórdia for this purpose. The judge condemned as extravagant the practice of Provedors giving alms to the staff of the Misericórdia and the poor on the occasion of their election to office. He considered such alms were given 'more from a questing after vain glory than from any charitable sentiment'. He also criticised the perquisites and pickings, known as *propinas*, which were given to the staff and which had amounted to 3,306$500 over the previous ten years. In two instances, the decoration of the sacristy for the festival of the Visitation and the clothing of children for the 'procession of the bones', costs had been met from the funds of the Misericórdia when in reality it was the responsibility of the brothers themselves to pay for such occasions. A contributory factor which had resulted in unnecessary expenditure had been the lack of any clear-cut policy on investments. Whereas one Mesa had invested in property, believing this to show the best return on capital, another had sold houses in order to place the capital on loan at an interest rate of $6\frac{1}{4}$ per cent.

The final point made by the judge was that the Misericórdia was not receiving adequate financial support from the authorities. Municipal and Crown grants towards the foundling wheel and the hospital were totally unrealistic, committing the brotherhood to heavy expenditure on social services for which it had no statutory obligation, and for which it only had a small income from private bequests. José de Affonseca Lemos expressed the opinion that official recognition of the privileges enjoyed by the Misericórdia could do much to remedy the economic straits of the brotherhood. A case in point were some 40,000 *cruzados* owing to the Misericórdia by debtors, who were also in debt to the Treasury. The Treasury had frozen their assets pending legal proceedings, and the Misericórdia had been unable to take steps to enforce payment by invoking privileges permitting the brotherhood to make the compulsory sale of property pledged to the Misericórdia as security on loans.

The High Court judge made recommendations on each of these issues.

His major recommendation was that a judge of the High Court in Bahia should be appointed, together with a private scribe, to protect the interests of the brotherhood in all legal and financial matters. Every three years he was to conduct a thorough investigation into the accounts of the Misericórdia. He was to institute legal proceedings against any brother found guilty of gross negligence, misappropriation of funds, or dishonesty. The report also contained the following more specific suggestions to remedy the financial crisis of the Misericórdia. The maximum loan should be limited to 4,000 *cruzados* and all capital and interest should be repaid within ten years. This ceiling had been suggested because securities usually took the form of slaves or lands, whose value fluctuated considerably from one year to the next. All items of expenditure should be approved by the Mesa and all account ledgers should be examined by the Mesa at the end of the financial year. Treasurers should be obliged to furnish receipts for payments, or would be personally responsible for such sums. All money received by the treasurer should be placed in the coffer of the brotherhood and not kept by the treasurer to meet current expenses. This coffer should be locked with three keys in the possession of the Provedor, scribe and treasurer. No money should be taken by the Mesa from capital in order to meet expenses, unless such expenditure had been specifically authorised by a clause in the will of a testator. All perquisites to the staff should be abolished. The number of women in the retirement house should be reduced to eighteen recluses, three officials, four slaves and a suitable number of paying boarders. A further grant of 400$000 annually by the city council towards the cost of foundlings was suggested. Moreover the report recommended a further municipal grant to be made to the hospital. This grant should be financed from money at present earmarked for perquisites made to the councillors and other municipal officials. José de Affonseca Lemos also recommended that agreement be reached between the Misericórdia and the Treasury to ensure the rapid settlement of outstanding debts still under litigation. His final suggestion was that the royal order of 1740, forbidding the election to the Mesa of any brother in debt to the Misericórdia, should be revoked in the hope that they would be shamed into honouring their obligations to the brotherhood.

This report was submitted to Dom José. The king invited comments from the viceroy and the city council. The Count of Arcos submitted his comments on the report to the king on 18 October 1757, and these are of considerable interest.[1] José de Affonseca Lemos had come to Bahia post-haste from Lisbon and had conducted a thorough investigation into the financial circumstances of the Misericórdia. But he had lacked detailed knowledge of the economic situation in Bahia and the special financial needs of an essentially agricultural economy. Nor had he been in a position to appreciate the social prejudices present in colonial Bahia. The Count of Arcos tried to place the report in its financial and social context. One example will illustrate the differences in attitude between the judge and the viceroy. José de Affonseca Lemos had condemned the perquisites received by the staff of the Misericórdia as a needless extravagance and recommended they be abolished. The Count of Arcos noted that boards of guardians of the Misericórdia were bound by a clause of the *Compromisso* to employ only white people in certain domestic duties. He fully recognised that compliance with this clause was extremely difficult in Brazil where white people were unwilling to serve in menial positions. Thus he regarded such perquisites as essential because unless they could offer such inducements Mesas would find it well nigh impossible to employ white staff.

On the whole the viceroy supported the recommendations made in the report on financial issues, but he expressed strong reservations about those with social implications. Without attempting to whitewash the negligent conduct of boards of guardians, he pointed out that the task of collecting interest due on loans had been impeded by the prevailing economic decline of Bahia. On the major recommendation limiting loans to 4,000 *cruzados*, he thought this sum totally unrealistic in Bahia where most of the borrowers were plantation owners or cattle ranchers who needed capital to replace slaves or stock. Such a sum would be inadequate for this purpose and they would simply borrow from other brotherhoods or the religious orders which had no such restriction. This would severely prejudice the social services of the Misericórdia. The viceroy suggested that a maximum loan of 10,000 *cruzados* would be more in order, depending on the securities offered. The viceroy had already had enough experience of the Bahian judiciary to realise the impracticability of the judge's suggestion that the Misericórdia should take legal action against negligent treasurers or recalcitrant debtors. He recommended that the brotherhood should 'write off' such losses, rather than waste time and money in protracted legal wranglings which might

[1] BNRJ, 11–33, 24, 45, doc. 9.

M 2

prove in vain. He defended the city council on the question of additional municipal grants to the Misericórdia and suggested that the Crown should contribute 400$000 each year to the brotherhood for the upkeep of found-lings.

The Count of Arcos opposed certain recommendations made by José de Affonseca Lemos on purely social grounds. He firmly rejected the proposed triennial investigation into the accounts of the Misericórdia by a judge of the High Court. He pointed out that the brotherhood already found consider-able difficulty in filling the posts of Provedor and treasurer. Such a measure would exacerbate this situation because nobody would willingly suffer the indignity of being subjected to a judicial investigation like a suspected criminal. The viceroy thought that it would be enough for a judge to attend the meeting at which the Mesa examined the accounts presented by the treasurer at the end of the financial year. The Count of Arcos was keenly aware of the desirability of preserving, and if possible enhancing, the social prestige of the Misericórdia. Thus he considered that the practice of the newly-elected Provedor distributing alms should be continued

> because the gift of such alms is voluntary, and prompted by the public nature of the gift. Once this exterior aspect ceases, so also will the action itself. It is readily apparent that not only do the employees of the Misericórdia and the poor of this city benefit from such alms, but the brotherhood itself is held in greater esteem and the office of Provedor gains in distinction thereby.

The viceroy agreed that the royal order of 1740 should be revoked. Whereas the judge had advocated this because of possible financial benefit to the brotherhood, the viceroy advanced social reasons for such a move. He ominously predicted that otherwise the administration of the Misericórdia would soon fall into the hands of 'people of a very different social calibre from those who have governed its affairs up to the present'. The Count of Arcos insisted strongly that people elected to the office of Provedor be compelled to accept, or be able to satisfy the viceroy in person that they had sufficient grounds to be excused. Expulsion from the brotherhood in such cases was totally ineffective because, as he pointed out, 'those people of distinction, who are suitable to serve as Provedors, are firmly convinced that it is they who give honour to the brotherhood by their presence, and they would suffer no loss of face by leaving it'.

The reaction of the city councillors of Bahia was entirely negative, as was to be expected. They explained their position to the king in a letter of 14 December 1757. The councillors rejected completely the possibility of any further municipal grant to the Misericórdia for the care of foundlings. They alleged that they were already committed to heavy expenditure on public works and that the costs of the annual religious festivals and processions swallowed up any surplus from a small annual income of some 6,000$000. They also rejected the proposal that money at present allocated to perquisites for municipal officials should be given to the Misericórdia for the upkeep of the hospital. In this the councillors had their own interests at stake, but they could quote royal decrees in their defence. Decrees of 1686 and 1709 had authorised the payment of perquisites from municipal funds to the district judge, criminal judge, scribe of the city council, attorney of the city council, certain municipal officials as well as to the councillors themselves. The city council reminded the king that these perquisites represented the only payment received by the councillors for their services and afforded a small degree of compensation for the inconvenience of being brought from their plantations in the Recôncavo to the city to attend council meetings. Without such perquisites, many plantation owners would simply refuse to serve as councillors.[1] On the same date the city council dispatched a letter to its attorney in Lisbon telling him to study the position of the city council in the light of the report and to defend its interests to the best of his ability.[2]

The board of guardians of the Misericórdia made a half-hearted attempt to defend itself, and its predecessors, against the charges of negligence contained in the report. It pleaded that the economic decline of the brotherhood merely reflected the prevailing economic situation in the colony. It noted that expenditure had increased, especially in the treatment of the sick and care of foundlings, whereas receipts had remained more or less constant. There can be no doubt that the criticisms contained in the report of José de Affonseca Lemos were fully justified. In the administration of its finances the Misericórdia must stand condemned. It is to the social sphere that we must turn in order to evaluate the positive rôle played by the Misericórdia in colonial Bahia and its relationship to other branches of the brotherhood throughout the Portuguese-speaking world.

The Misericórdia was unique among the brotherhoods of colonial Bahia

[1] AMB, vol. 182, ff. 78–80.　　　　　　　　[2] AMB, vol. 182, ff. 82–3.

in enjoying the patronage of the Crown and extensive royal privileges. These granted certain benefits to the members of the board of guardians during their year of office and were intended to assist the difficult task of administration of legacies and the social services of the brotherhood. The Misericórdia was beyond all ecclesiastical jurisdiction, could not be constrained by the city council to attend municipal functions, and its representatives held privileged positions in the Court of Appeals. The Misericórdia was answerable only to the viceroy or the governor-general as the Crown's representative in Bahia.

The Misericórdia was the only brotherhood in colonial Bahia to provide a comprehensive range of social services, not only for its members but also for the community. It maintained the only general hospital in the city to which anybody was admitted, irrespective of race, social position or religious beliefs. The Misericórdia also provided a funeral service catering for all classes from the sugar nabob down to the most humble slave. The Misericórdia also fed and clothed prisoners and arranged for the defence of deserving cases at the brotherhood's expense. Brothers visited the poor regularly, distributing alms of money and clothing to destitute widows and old people. The Misericórdia administered a large number of dowries and granted these to suitable girls. In 1716 the Retirement House of the Most Holy Name of Jesus was opened and ten years later the brotherhood established a foundling wheel.

The Misericórdia was entirely dependent on private funds for the financing of these social services. Crown and municipal contributions were negligible. Citizens of colonial Bahia regarded social philanthropy as part of the Catholic tradition and contributed generously to the Misericórdia. Bequests were made to the brotherhood on the understanding that the capital would be placed on loan and the interest so derived would be applied to a specific charitable purpose. This resulted in some charitable services being less well endowed than others.

The dependence of the brotherhood on interest derived from loans for the financing of its social services led the Misericórdia to act as a banking organisation. This was common practice among the Third Orders and the monastic orders in Bahia. The monastery of St Theresa was prominent in this respect and afforded a safe hiding place for fortunes made in sugar and cattle, as well as by illicit means. It was common practice for a sugar planter to raise a loan to cover the costs of planting and the purchase of slaves or equipment. This loan was repaid, with interest of 6¼ per cent in the case of the Misericórdia, when the fleet from Europe arrived in Bahia. It has been seen that the boards of guardians of the Misericórdia lacked the ability to administer the financial affairs of the brotherhood to the best advantage, but there is no doubting the importance of the brotherhood within the general context of the Bahian economy.

In providing social services which were the Crown or municipal responsibility, the Misericórdia played a semi-bureaucratic rôle. This again made it unique among the other brotherhoods of colonial Bahia. The importance of the Misericórdia in the social field was grudgingly acknowledged by the Crown and the city council. It would not be too much to say that the authorities depended on the Misericórdia to provide certain public services. The Crown negotiated with the brotherhood over financial terms for the treatment of soldiers in the hospital and the city council contributed towards the upkeep of foundlings by the brotherhood. In both cases the failure on the part of Mesas to insist on adequate compensation was due to their own shortcomings because the Misericórdia was in a sufficiently strong bargaining position to demand total reimbursement for the operation of social services for which the brotherhood had no statutory obligation.

The privileged and semi-bureaucratic position of the Misericórdia brought it into frequent contact with both the ecclesiastical and civil authorities. Instances of conflict with the ecclesiastical authorities usually arose out of infringement of privileges granted to the Misericórdia. This was also the case with the city council. Although the Misericórdia performed social services which were the responsibility of the city council and councillors were invariably brothers of the Misericórdia, there was no official connection between the two bodies. On the whole the Misericórdia and the city council each went their separate ways. On the occasions when the city council was compelled to recognise the brotherhood, the councillors adopted a truculent attitude. There was much vacillation on the part of the city council over the foundation of the retirement house and contributions to the cost of foundlings were made late and only after complaints by the Misericórdia to the Crown. Relations between the Misericórdia and the viceroy or governor-general were based on the fact that he alone could exercise jurisdiction over the brotherhood. Boards of guardians fought shy of official contact and rarely was a governor-general or viceroy elected Provedor. For his part, the governor-general or viceroy only intervened to protect the good name of the Misericórdia when maladministration threatened to bring the brotherhood into disrepute. Royal patronage proved to be a fickle ally. Although the brotherhood had been supported by royal privileges and ready support initially on the part of kings and queens, this interest had waned. Requests made by the Misericórdia to the Crown were ignored. Petitions were delayed and referred back to Bahia for more information. On the matter of treatment of soldiers by the Misericórdia the king was quite prepared to sacrifice the interests of the brotherhood and establish a separate military hospital in Bahia. If, on the whole, the Misericórdia maintained cordial relations with the authorities, they for their part rarely actively co-operated with the brotherhood.

The Misericórdia occupied a prominent position in Bahian society. The brotherhood counted the more eloquent citizens of Bahia among its members. By tradition, the Provedor was of sufficient social and financial standing to defend the brotherhood against the criticism and intervention of the city council, archbishop or even the viceroy. Membership of the board of guardians was hotly disputed. The names of brothers read as a *Who's Who*, not only of the landed aristocracy and senior civil servants, but also of the leading artisans. Whereas the Third Order of St Francis favoured intellectuals, and the Third Order of the Carmelites business men, the Misericórdia showed no such preference in the selection of brothers. In this lies the importance of the brotherhood as being truly representative of Bahian society and colonial ideology.

The Misericórdia of Bahia was in constant communication with branches of the brotherhood in Brazil, Africa, the Atlantic Islands and Portugal. Within Brazil the legal defence of prisoners, collection of debts and the settlement of legacies called for a high degree of co-operation between branches. Until 1751 all prisoners accused of capital crimes were sent to Bahia to stand trial. Their defence fell to the local branch of the brotherhood and has already been described (p. 254). The collection of bad debts and the settlement of legacies were impeded by the transient nature of a large part of the population of colonial Brazil and the difficulty of communications with the interior. The large network of branches of the Misericórdia went some way to offset these difficulties. Boards of guardians in Bahia maintained a steady flow of correspondence with their counterparts in Pernambuco and Sergipe, asking them to trace and take legal action against debtors of the Misericórdia of Bahia who were in their captaincies. Letters between the branch of the brotherhood in Bahia and that in Rio de Janeiro usually concerned the settlement of legacies to be administered by the Misericórdia in Bahia, or for which it was acting as executor.

The position of Bahia made the city a commercial emporium for trade from Europe and Africa, as well as for exports from Brazil. There was a constant triangular traffic in people, as well as merchandise, between Portugal, Brazil and Angola. Soldiers, sailors, merchants, clerics, gypsies and exiles followed the trail of fortune from Lisbon or Oporto or the Atlantic Islands to Bahia and from there to the interior of Brazil or across the Atlantic to S. Tomé or Luanda. These frequently fell ill and died in the hospitals of the Misericórdia in Bahia or Luanda. In their wills they made bequests to friends and relatives in Portugal and the Atlantic Islands, and nominated the Misericórdia as their executor. The Misericórdia then contacted the relatives and forwarded the bequest to them. The Misericórdia of Luanda often sent gold and letters of credit to Bahia, for forwarding to Lisbon, in satisfaction of the terms of a legacy. The Misericórdia of Bahia was in constant contact with branches in the north of Portugal in its rôle as executor. In 1685 João de Mattos left substantial bequests to relatives in the parish of S. Julião de Moreira in the Lima valley in the Minho.[1] The Misericórdia of Bahia sent the appropriate sum to the branch of the brotherhood in Viana do Castelo, who in turn passed it on to the branch in the village of Ponte de Lima for distribution. In 1697 the Misericórdia in Bahia sent 8,000 *cruzados* to the branch of the brotherhood in Braga in fulfilment of the terms of the legacy of Domingos Fernandes de Freitas.[2] The branches of the Misericórdia frequently acted as bureaux to trace missing persons. It was not uncommon for a son, or even a husband, to leave his family in Portugal or Madeira and go to Africa or Brazil, promising to return home once he had made his fortune. Frequently he married and settled in the tropics and severed all ties with home. On his deathbed he made bequests to relatives, if they were still alive. In such cases the Misericórdia in Bahia wrote to the branch of the brotherhood nearest to the last known place of residence of these relatives. The scribe made enquiries and, if the relatives were still alive, furnished proof

[1] ASCMB, vol. 41, ff. 239v–244.   [2] ASCMB, vol. 14, ff. 48–9.

of their identity so that they could claim the legacy. More pitiable were pleas made by a wife or mother, deserted in Lisbon, asking the Misericórdias of Bahia and Luanda to search their burial registers for information on the whereabouts of a missing husband or son.

The most important branch of the Misericórdia was in Lisbon. As such it was consulted by the brotherhood in Bahia on all major issues. The Misericórdia of Bahia employed an attorney in Lisbon to safeguard its interests, be they financial, legal or domestic. His duties ranged from the sale of sugar and the settlement of debts to the purchase of tiles and olive oil. On all matters of policy the board of guardians in Bahia communicated directly with its counterpart in Lisbon. The assistance of the parent body was enlisted in the settlement of the dispute with the Franciscans over funerals, the granting of privileges and petitions to the Crown.

The Misericórdia of Bahia was but one branch of a brotherhood whose members were to be found throughout the Portuguese-speaking world. The common origin of the Misericórdias in Lisbon had ensured that all branches, be they in Asia, Africa or Brazil, preserved many common traits. All branches were governed by the *Compromissos* of Lisbon made in 1516 and 1618. In some cases these were modified to provide for local conditions. The new sets of statutes drawn up by the branches in Gôa and Macao were modelled on those of the parent body and incorporated many of the same clauses. The administrative structure of Mesa and Junta was maintained in all branches, although here again there were local variations in the method of election and composition of the executive bodies. All branches shared the privileges granted to the Misericórdia of Lisbon and many possessed additional privileges to deal with local situations. At one time or another the alleged infringement of these privileges brought all branches into conflict with the local civil and ecclesiastical authorities. All branches had a common banner, preserved the same traditions and celebrated the same festivals. The tradition of a free pardon being granted to any criminal who fell from the gallows and was covered by the banner of the Misericórdia was invoked in Lisbon, Bahia, Luanda, Gôa and Macao with varying degrees of success. The day of the Visitation was the major festival for all branches and all celebrated the Maundy Thursday procession and the 'procession of the bones' on All Saints' Day.

All branches of the Misericórdia represented the best of their respective societies. The Provedor was always a leading member of the community. Positions on the board of guardians were highly prized. Applications for membership were scrutinised to ensure 'purity of blood'. Restrictions on the admission of clerics were common to all branches. Causes of expulsion were similar. Marriage of a brother with a woman of non-white or New Christian parentage, or even if she were socially unacceptable, resulted in his expulsion from the brotherhood. Disobedience or alleged insubordination remained the most common reasons for expulsion.

All branches of the Misericórdia performed similar social services in their respective communities. In every case the most important service was the hospital. Not all branches catered for lepers, as did those in Gôa and Macao, and conditions governing admittance varied from branch to branch. Whereas Gôa and Bahia admitted all sick people, the branch in Macao refused entry to heathen Chinese. Each branch maintained a chemist's shop and this was available to the general public. The larger branches maintained retirement houses. All cared for prisoners and foundlings, provided dowries, visited the poor and distributed alms. The extent of these charitable works depended on the financial resources available and on the demand. Whereas the ransom of captives was an important part of the charitable activities of the Misericórdia in Gôa, there was no need for such assistance in Bahia.

The more important branches of the Misericórdia usually received some form of financial aid from the Crown towards the cost of the treatment of soldiers in the hospitals administered by the brotherhood. There was no hard and fast rule about this. It depended partly on the special needs of each branch and partly on the degree of success of their respective representatives in bringing their petitions to the notice of the Crown. One example will illustrate this. In the early eighteenth century the Misericórdia of Bahia petitioned the Crown for increased financial aid for the hospital. In 1711 the board of guardians in Bahia wrote to the branches in Luanda and Rio de Janeiro to ascertain if they received grants from the Crown to offset expenditure made in the treatment of men on the royal service. Both these branches were considerably more favoured than that of Bahia in this respect. In Luanda the Crown made an annual grant of 400$000 to the brotherhood and paid the salaries of the doctor and surgeon. Moreover each vessel calling at Luanda paid a set fee to the Misericórdia and deductions were made from the pay-packets of soldiers and sailors to cover medical expenses.[1] In 1694 the Misericórdia of Rio de Janeiro had received an annual grant of 200$000 for the hospital. This had been increased to 600$000 in 1702.[2] Royal grants for other charitable purposes were made in an equally haphazard manner. In 1754 the Misericórdia of Rio de Janeiro was allocated 400$000 annually for three years from Crown funds for the care of prisoners.[3]

All branches of the Misericórdia experienced administrative and financial crises similar to that in Bahia. In 1725 in Gôa the board of guardians complained of the difficulty of filling the posts of Provedor and treasurer. In 1730 the *primeira visita*, or alms given by the newly-elected Provedor, was abolished because of the shortage of citizens in Gôa willing to accept office with this financial burden. About the same period the bishop of Macao sent to Lisbon a short list of citizens suitable to serve as Provedors, although lamenting that there was no one ideally suited for the post. In Gôa and Macao there were frequent instances of electoral 'rigging' and the viceroy or governor was compelled to intervene. Maladministration of finances resulted in loss of public confidence in the Misericórdia of Gôa at the end of the seventeenth century and in the branches in Luanda, Macao and Bahia in the eighteenth century. All branches depended on private charity and lent capital on interest. The terms of such loans varied and whereas the Misericórdias of Gôa and Macao made loans to their respective city councils and to the Crown the branch in Bahia did not do so. But in all cases the securities were inadequate, interest was not collected and capital was lost. Royal commissions, similar to that of José de Affonseca Lemos in Bahia, investigated the financial affairs of the branches of the brotherhood in Gôa and Macao.

All branches of the Misericórdia preserved the social distinction of brothers of 'major' standing and brothers of 'minor' standing. This division was maintained in the Mesa and Junta. These executive bodies were composed of the most prominent and influential people in the community, be they plantation owners, merchants, military officers or judges from the upper class, or goldsmiths, painters, masons, carpenters or store keepers from the lower class. Thus, to a certain degree, the minutes of the Mesa and Junta reflect current attitudes and opinions in each community. In them-

---

[1] ASCMB, vol. 52, f. 52v.
[2] ANRJ, *Códice 539*, vol. 2, f. 24v and *Códice 952*, vol. 13, f. 89.
[3] ANRJ, *Códice 952*, vol. 37, f. 338.

selves such records might be regarded as slightly suspect because of their overall institutional bias — hence the reservation. But taken in conjunction with viceregal or gubernatorial correspondence to the Crown and municipal resolutions, the records of the various branches of the Misericórdia provide a detailed and accurate picture of their respective societies. In the case of Bahia the registers of copies of letters from the Crown to its representative and the minutes of the city council are complete for much of the seventeenth and eighteenth centuries. These records permit certain conclusions to be drawn concerning the structure of government and the nature of society in colonial Bahia.

The governor-general or viceroy in Bahia was the Crown's supreme representative in Brazil, but he did not enjoy absolute authority. In all matters he was supposed to report to the Crown or the Overseas Council, although the delay involved in such correspondence often led him to act independently of higher authority. He did not exercise great control over the governors of the various captaincies who reported directly to the Crown. Indeed in the eighteenth century Gomes Freire de Andrada in Rio de Janeiro had jurisdiction over a wider area than the viceroy in Bahia. The viceroy was frequently the victim of *murmuração*, or backbiting, and complaints by governors or even city councils could lead to his decisions being modified or over-ruled by the Crown. The most independent and authoritarian of viceroys was the Count of Sabugosa. He often acted in direct defiance of the wishes of the Crown, as in his defence of the trading rights of the Bahian merchants with the west coast of Africa. During his long viceregency there was a feeling of independence in the air and it can only be a matter of surprise that the final break from the mother country did not occur until a century later.

The city council was extremely powerful in Bahia. Composed of the leading figures of the city and the Recôncavo, it was quite prepared to oppose royal decrees when these ran counter to its own interests. It also maintained a brake on high-handed action by viceroys or governors and in extreme cases exercised its prerogative of direct correspondence with the Crown. Only in 1696 was the authority of the city council diminished by the appointment of a senior Crown lawyer to preside over its meetings, resulting in bitter rivalry between the city council and the High Court. From this date the selection of councillors was made by the viceroy or governor from the electoral rolls.

The social structure of Bahia was in the form of a pyramid. At the top was a small group composed of the nobility of blood, many of whom were descended from the first colonisers. These formed part of a landed aristocracy of plantation owners. Below these were high-ranking Crown officials, ecclesiastical dignitaries and the leading citizens of Bahia who enjoyed certain financial or juridical privileges. The leading artisans and members of the working guilds formed the next stratum of society. These were followed by poor whites and people of mixed parentage, and at the very bottom of the pyramid were the large numbers of slaves.

The concept of a social pyramid grossly oversimplifies the structure of Bahian society. It does not take into account the delicate inter-play of race and economic standing in determining a person's social position. It also suggests a rigid social stratification which was not present in colonial Bahia. Bahian society was characterised by great internal flexibility. At no time was this flexibility more in evidence than in the eighteenth century. Social lines of demarcation between classes became confused. No longer was prestige counted in terms of noble lineage and the possession of plantations or ranches. Wealth was beginning to buy many of the attributes of social equality. A mercantile class gradually emerged and assumed responsibilities formerly considered the monopoly of the landed aristocracy. Wealth alone was not the yardstick of social status. These forerunners of a mercantile patriciate sought public office and the social acceptance this conferred. In Bahia they achieved this in the 1740s when the Crown recognised their suitability to serve as city councillors and the brothers of the Misericórdia elected members of the mercantile class to the office of Provedor. This new sector of the community came to combine many of the functions and values of the nobility with those of the bourgeoisie.

Within the bourgeoisie itself points of contact between the *haute bourgeoisie* and the *petite bourgeoisie* became ill-defined. The possibility of upward and downward mobility within the social structure became easier. In the eighteenth century there were numerous cases of promotion in the Misericórdia of brothers from the lower to the upper class. The reasons varied — municipal office, a royal benefice, a university degree, ordination to the ministry, or a commission in the garrison. Of greatest social significance were those promotions born of financial betterment. As these became more common, so also was there greater social rivalry and increasing bitterness shown by the established members of the *haute bourgeoisie* towards such social upstarts.

Social change was accompanied by increased urbanisation. In the sixteenth and seventeenth centuries the importance of Bahia had been centred on the Recôncavo. Here lay the economic wealth of Bahia and here dwelt the great plantation owners. These visited the city to hold the reins of local government or attend some religious celebration. In the eighteenth century interest was focused on the city itself. This had increased greatly in size during the seventeenth century, but it was only in the eighteenth century that it ousted the Recôncavo as the true social and commercial centre of the captaincy. Many plantation owners moved to the city and left the administration of their plantations in the hands of an overseer.

Economic change differentiated the seventeenth century from the eighteenth century. In the seventeenth century sugar and cattle had afforded the only means of acquiring great wealth. In the eighteenth century financial speculation and the placing of money on loan offered the surest returns on capital. This change resulted in a redistribution of wealth, readily apparent in the changing personalities of the benefactors of the Misericórdia.

The eighteenth century was a period of ideological change in Bahia. The seventeenth century had been an age of traditionalism: traditionalism in business, in religion and in society. The eighteenth century was a time of reaction. Financial speculation replaced agriculture as the major source of income. Personal initiative replaced inherited nobility as a means to social equality. There was increased secularisation. For the first time in Bahia a social conscience was born.

In this era of transition one constant remained. This was the racial prejudice shown by the white population towards Negroes. The white colonists manifested a pathological preoccupation with 'purity of blood', both religious and racial. It has been suggested that in the eighteenth century there may have been a decrease in anti-semitic feeling. It is possible that people of mixed blood could achieve a minimal degree of social acceptance, provided their skin was not too dark. But the Negro remained an 'untouchable' in the eyes of white Bahians. In this attitude they were supported by the Crown and the municipal authorities who denied bureaucratic offices to Negroes.

This description of government and society in colonial Bahia calls for a brief comparison with Spanish America. The Crowns of Spain and Portugal regarded their colonies primarily as sources of revenue for the mother country, but the Spanish Crown kept a much closer hold on the reins of government in its colonies than did the Portuguese. The organs of government were very similar in the two empires. The difference lay in the degree of autonomy they possessed. The viceroys of New Spain and of Peru never enjoyed the independence of action of their counterparts in Brazil. Their authority was limited by the Council of the Indies and by the local *Audiencia*, or High Court. The Royal and Supreme Council of the Indies, to give it its full name, had been founded in 1524. It exercised wider powers and greater jurisdiction than the Portuguese Overseas Council founded in 1642. The second restricting influence on the actions of the viceroys was the *Audiencia*. This fulfilled the same legal functions as the Brazilian *Relação*, but also played a more prominent rôle in local government than its Brazilian counterpart. The *Audiencias* of New Spain and Lima represented supreme authority after the viceroys. They carried out investigations into the conduct of viceroys at the end of their terms of office. High Courts had been established throughout Spanish America, whereas until 1751 there was only one *Relação* in the whole of Brazil. They ensured a higher degree of law enforcement and were obliged to make triennial inspections throughout their respective provinces, not only of legal matters but also into the economy, social conditions and local government. Such commissions had a restraining influence on city councils. By the seventeenth century the city councils had lost their representative nature and had fallen under the direct control of the High Court or viceroy. This resulted in the absence of that dynamic eloquence which so characterised the city council of Bahia which could sway Crown policy by its fierce outbursts.

The attitudes of the Crowns of Spain and Portugal and of the city councils in the two empires coincided in one respect. This was in their policy for social services. There were some rare instances of the Spanish Crown founding a hospital in the New World or taking one under the royal patronage. Similarly there were occasions, for example the Hospital of San Andrés founded in Lima in 1545, when municipal funds were voted for the establishment of a hospital. But, by and large, the provision of social services was not regarded as the responsibility of the authorities. Brotherhoods of lay men and women made some effort in this direction. The Hospital of the Immaculate Conception in Mexico City was founded in the sixteenth century by the Brotherhood of Our Lady. Such private initiative in the founding of hospitals was entirely local and in the Spanish American empire there was no chain of hospitals administered by a single brotherhood as was the case of the Misericórdia in Portuguese America. The part played by the Misericórdias in Brazil in providing social services was fulfilled by the Church in Spanish America. The Church performed an infinitely more important social function in Spanish America than in Brazil. It founded schools, hospitals, retirement houses and hospices for foundlings in addition to distributing alms and dowries. Much such charitable action was stimulated by the personal initiative of local bishops. Juan de Zumárraga, first bishop and archbishop of Mexico, was prominent in the foundation of hospitals. Nevertheless it is worth noting that despite the positive rôle played by the ecclesiastical authorities in the social field, hospital conditions in Spanish America were no better than those in Brazil and in neither case were there ever adequate hospital facilities, even in the cities.

The social structure of colonial Bahia bears comparison with that of New Spain. Here too there had been a white aristocracy. Initially this had been formed of the *conquistadores*, whose military efforts had been rewarded by charters of nobility, and of colonisers who had been granted *encomiendas* by the Crown. This aristocracy remained under the close control of the Crown and its counterpart never existed in Brazil. There also gradually evolved a landed aristocracy of sugar plantation owners and cattle ranchers. This was at its strongest at the end of the seventeenth century and the beginning of the eighteenth century. As had been the case in Bahia a mining boom threatened the foundations of this landed aristocracy and it was on the decline in the nineteenth century. Alongside this landed aristocracy there had developed in the cities a mercantile class whose members had achieved considerable wealth. In the early eighteenth century the abolition of the *encomienda* system compelled the scions of a primitive but impoverished nobility to marry into the rich commercial and mining families of the cities. As had been the case in Bahia, financial wealth began to replace nobility of blood as a yardstick of social status.

Prejudices of class and colour were remarkably similar in New Spain and in colonial Bahia. It was inevitable that colonisers, be they Portuguese or

Spanish, should bring to the new world the legacy of an upbringing which was Iberian rather than peculiar to one nation or the other. There was a common preoccupation with 'purity of blood' in the religious context. In both empires there was an ethnic trichotomy of Negro, white and Indian. In both cases the Crown made a half-hearted official attempt to remedy the shortage of white women but the laws of nature dictated miscegenation. Criteria of social acceptability based on whiteness of skin and Old Christian parentage were common to New Spain and colonial Bahia. The position of the Indian in New Spain differed from his Brazilian counterpart but in general he also got rather a better deal than the Negro. In both cases the Negro was discriminated against by law and was regarded as morally and socially degenerate. In New Spain as in colonial Bahia distinctions of race became confused with economic position and religious beliefs in determining social standing. In both cases it became possible in the eighteenth century for a light-skinned mulatto to achieve minor bureaucratic office, but it appears that whereas in New Spain this was the result of tacit acceptance of racial distinctions, in Brazil it was more the result of the authorities turning a blind eye on minor racial 'blemishes'.[1]

The history of the various branches of the Misericórdia not only casts light on economic and social conditions prevailing in their respective communities, but also contributes to our knowledge of the Portuguese expansion. It is readily apparent that the dominant feature of the Portuguese empire was its administrative conservatism. Institutions of government were modelled on those of the mother country. No new administrative organs were established to deal with the local peculiarities of settlements as diverse as Macao and Bahia. The overseas city councils preserved the same internal organisa-

---

[1] These comparisons are suggested by a reading of the following works: C. H. Haring, *The Spanish Empire in America* (New York, 1947: reprinted with corrections and a new bibliography in 1952 and 1957); J. H. Parry, *The Spanish Seaborne Empire* (London, 1966); François Chevalier, *Land and Society in Colonial Mexico. The Great Hacienda* (Berkeley and Los Angeles, 1963: a translation of a work first published in Paris in 1952 under the title *La Formation des grands domaines au Mexique. Terre et société aux XVIe–XVIIe siècles*); C. E. Marshall, 'The Birth of the Mestizo in New Spain', published in the *Hispanic American Historical Review*, vol. 19 (1939), pp. 161–84; and the challenging article by L. N. McAlister entitled 'Social Structure and Social Change in New Spain' in the *Hispanic American Historical Review*, vol. 43 (1963), pp. 349–70.

tion and enjoyed the same privileges as their counterparts in Lisbon, Évora and Oporto. The High Courts of Portuguese Asia, Africa and America followed the legal codes of Portugal and no attempt was made to accommodate these to local legal practices already in existence. The lay brotherhoods, so characteristic of Portuguese community life, followed the statutes and shared the privileges of the parent bodies in Lisbon.

This administrative conservatism was of considerable positive importance in providing an element of stability in a far-flung empire. Social stability was provided by the different branches of the Misericórdia. A Portuguese in Gôa, Macao, Luanda, Bahia or many of the smaller settlements, could join a brotherhood of which he was already a member in some township of the Minho or Trás-os-Montes. In the event of his death he could rest assured that he would be accorded an honourable burial and that the brotherhood would act as executor for his will. This social stability was accompanied by the administrative stability provided by the city council. The councillors were Portuguese with roots in the various communities. They represented the interests of their fellow countrymen and offered a measure of security against outside pressures by native monarchs.

From the detailed history of the Misericórdia of Bahia and the general references to the principal branches in Africa and Asia, it is clear that the Portuguese Crown, local governors or viceroys, and city councils relied heavily on individual organisations to provide social aid. In Asia and Africa the Jesuits were prominent in this field. In Brazil their contribution to social services was less important and the entire responsibility devolved on the different branches of the Misericórdia. In general the Crown adopted the attitude that the obligations of the authorities were limited to providing an administrative machinery. Problems of social adaptation had to be overcome by the individual. The wide deployment of branches of the Misericórdia illustrates to the full the importance of private initiative in the creation of the Portuguese empire.

The Portuguese empire in Asia remained intact for less than a century and in Brazil was severely threatened in the early seventeenth century. The Dutch and English attacks on Portuguese settlements in Asia after 1600 were major factors contributing to the decline of the Portuguese Asiatic empire. They had severe repercussions on Portugal itself and also on Brazil. The actual internal break-up of the Portuguese overseas empire does not seem to have occurred until the end of the seventeenth century, and was most severely felt during the first half of the eighteenth century. It was no mere coincidence that the branches of the Misericórdia in Bahia, Luanda, Gôa and Macao should all experience financial crises and suffer loss of prestige socially between 1690 and 1750. In 1757 the branch of the brotherhood in Espírito Santo wrote to Bahia lamenting its poverty. In its reply the board of guardians of the Misericórdia of Bahia offered commiseration, but stated that this situation was common to all branches of the brotherhood, especially those in Brazil.[1]

The Misericórdia of Bahia has overcome these, and similar vicissitudes, to survive to the present day. The nineteenth century was a period of drastic reform in all the social services of the brotherhood. The hospital had proved totally unsuitable because of its limited accommodation and bad position. Conditions had been aggravated by the establishment of the Faculty of Medicine in 1816 whose practical instruction was carried out in the hospital. In 1814 a new site for the hospital was mooted in Tororó, but this project failed, partly because of lack of royal support. In 1827 the Mesa decided to acquire a plot of land in Nazaré, and work was begun on the new hospital in the following year. Progress was hampered by numerous delays and finally came to a standstill. As a result, in 1833 the patients still in the old hospital of the Misericórdia were transferred to the former Jesuit College as a temporary measure. This had served as a military hospital from the time of the expulsion of the order up to 1832. The hospital of the Misericórdia was only finished with the aid of funds derived from lotteries and bequests and was inaugurated in 1893 as the Hospital of St Elisabeth.

Aid for foundlings and facilities providing for recluses in the care of the brotherhood underwent modifications in the nineteenth century. In 1832 the turning wheel in the old hospital had been moved to the retirement house. Accommodation for foundlings remained cramped because of additional numbers and the system of employing wet-nurses proved unsatisfactory. In 1844 some cubicles were built in the retirement house for a small number of resident wet-nurses sufficient to look after foundlings who had just been placed in the wheel. In 1847 two rooms were set aside in the old hospital, one for foundlings of each sex, but this accommodation also proved inadequate. This state of affairs was only remedied by an entirely fortuitous

[1] ASCMB, vol. 53, f. 172.

circumstance. In the 1860s the Order of St Vincent de Paul was in financial straits. It possessed a fine building at the Campo da Pólvora, where the Order had intended to found a girls' college. The Misericórdia bought this in 1862 and established a home for foundlings known as the Asylum of Our Lady of Mercy.

This new foundation was linked to developments in the protection of recluses. Many sanitary improvements had been made in the retirement house of the Misericórdia in the first half of the nineteenth century. But the task of administration had proved increasingly difficult. In 1856 the board of guardians had taken the major step of sending to France for a small contingent of the Sisters of Mercy. These had duly arrived and had been invested with the administration of the retirement house and the care of foundlings. This reform met with bitter opposition from the recluses. In this they were supported by the local citizenry. In 1858 the recluses came out in open revolt and the retirement house was stoned by the populace. As a direct result of this, recluses between the ages of six and sixteen were transferred to the Asylum of Our Lady of Mercy. Other recluses and boarders were placed with relatives or found alternative accommodation and the retirement house ceased to function.

The third major reform in the social services of the brotherhood concerned burials. In the nineteenth century there was increased official opposition to the practice of burials in churches and monasteries. In 1805 the Misericórdia decided that no further burials should be made in the cloister of the church, but in the cemetery formerly reserved for the burial of slaves at the Campo da Pólvora. By the 1830s this cemetery was in a deplorable condition. In 1835 the Provincial Assembly took in hand the whole question of burials and cemeteries. It granted the monopoly for the building of cemeteries to a private company for the next thirty years. This company quickly built a cemetery at the Campo Santo and this was consecrated on 23 October 1836. Brotherhoods and Third Orders who had derived income from burial fees felt their livelihood threatened by this action. On 25 October they lodged a formal protest with the authorities and then incited the populace to destroy the new cemetery. The company claimed full compensation and this was granted by the Provincial Assembly. In 1839 the Provincial Assembly offered the administration of the Campo Santo to the Misericórdia or any other brotherhood willing to accept this responsibility. The Misericórdia agreed and financial terms were settled between the Provincial Assembly and the brotherhood in 1840. The Misericórdia agreed to transfer from the Campo da Pólvora to the new cemetery bones of people buried there and then to demolish the old cemetery.

The semi-bureaucratic position of the Misericórdia in colonial Bahia became even more evident after the independence of Brazil. In addition to the above social services, which the Misericórdia maintained from its own funds, the brotherhood administered further institutions for social welfare on behalf of the Provincial Government or city council. These comprised the Hospice of S. João de Deus for mental cases, a cemetery and hospice for lazars, and an asylum for beggars. In 1864 the Provincial Assembly passed a resolution approving the establishment of a mental asylum. It was agreed that it should be administered by the Misericórdia. In 1869 the Provincial Assembly bought the mansion of Boa Vista and in 1874 this was inaugurated and known as the Hospice of S. João de Deus. The Cemetery and Hospice for Lazars had been inaugurated in 1787 by the governor, Dom Rodrigo José de Meneses. In 1850 the cemetery was officially declared a public cemetery and in 1895 the administration of the hospice passed to the Misericórdia. The Beggars' Asylum had been brought into existence by a law passed by the Provincial Assembly in 1862. In 1873 a further law decreed that it should be housed in the same building as the hospice for lepers, and this was enacted in 1876. In 1887 the beggars were transferred to a new building constructed specifically for this purpose in Boa Viagem. The administration of this building was entrusted to the Misericórdia by a municipal order of 1895.[1]

The final change in the affairs of the Misericórdia came almost at the end of the nineteenth century. A new *Compromisso*, replacing that of 1618, was approved by the Mesa and Junta on 31 May 1896. This considerably simplified the *Compromisso* of 1618, reducing the number of chapters from forty-one to eleven. The major differences concerned the election of the Mesa and Junta, stricter financial measures and the appointment of new

[1] The history of the Misericórdia of Bahia for the later eighteenth century and the nineteenth century has yet to be written. The registers for this period are complete and in good condition. This short survey of the brotherhood's activities is based on the *Compromisso* of 1896 published in Bahia in the same year, Joaquim Damázio, *Tombamento*, and occasional gleanings from other sources.

officers to deal with the social responsibilities of the brotherhood. The numerical composition of the Mesa and Junta was maintained, but the social division into classes was officially abolished. The elections of the Mesa and the Junta were moved to the first Sunday in December and their terms of office coincided with the new financial year which started on 1 January. Both executive bodies served two years instead of a single year and the method of voting was altered so that each brother registered his vote for each position on the Mesa and Junta. A much more rigorous surveillance of the brotherhood's finances was introduced and a standing committee of three brothers versed in accountancy was appointed to examine the accounts of the brotherhood. *Mordomos* were elected to assume responsibility for each social service of the brotherhood. The duties of the *mordomo de fora* were assumed by a *mordomo do contencioso*, or steward for litigation, who was responsible for the defence of prisoners, the execution of wills and the legal affairs of the brotherhood. Two new stewardships were created. The first was the *mordomo das locações*, or steward for property, and the second the *mordomo das obras*, or steward in charge of works, who was responsible for the inspection, conservation and building of properties belonging to the Misericórdia.

A visitor to modern Bahia will find the Santa Casa da Misericórdia on the same site as the hospital founded in the time of Tomé de Sousa. The brotherhood has undergone administrative changes and has reduced the range of its social services in the twentieth century. The *Compromisso* of 1896 has been replaced by a new set of statutes approved in 1958. This new *Compromisso* did not radically alter the clauses of its predecessor and also consisted of eleven chapters. The electoral procedure was altered and the Junta was re-named the *Definitório*. The Mesa and the Definitório henceforth composed the *Junta Deliberativa*. The terms of office of the Mesa and the Definitório remained biennial, but started on the first Sunday of February instead of 1 January. Additional financial measures were introduced and new clauses dealt in detail with the terms of employment for the staff of the brotherhood. The stewardships were allocated to members of the board of guardians and one of these was further charged with the surveillance of the patrimony of the Misericórdia.[1]

[1] *Compromisso* of 1958 published in Bahia by the Imprensa Oficial in the same year.

A general picture of the part played by the Misericórdia in providing social services for the community can be obtained from a synopsis of the report presented in February 1965 by the then Provedor at the end of his term of office. Rentals on property constituted the major source of income for the brotherhood. At that time the Misericórdia owned 172 houses and received rent from some 450 tenants and sub-tenants. This income was supplemented by legacies, donations and official financial support for social services provided by the brotherhood. The institutions administered by the brotherhood had been reduced to the hospital, the foundling home and the cemetery. The buildings and equipment of the Hospital of St Elisabeth were greatly improved in the year 1964. A total of 19,986 sick people were treated in the *Ambulatório Silva Lima* and 1,189 were admitted to the wards as patients. Clinics were held regularly in the following fields: paediatrics, surgery, odontology, dermatology, medicine, urology, gynaecology, otorhinolaryngology, ophthalmology, cardiology, protology and orthopaedy. A total of 1,432 operations were performed in the surgical centre during the year. Annexed to the hospital is the *Internato Ernestina Guimarães* founded as a retirement house for widows, poor women and former prostitutes. Ten women were housed there in 1964. The foundling asylum in the Avenida Joana Angélica catered for 178 children in 1964 and had a staff of fifty under the authority of eight Sisters of St Ann. The Misericórdia continues to administer the Cemetery of the Campo Santo. In 1964 a total of 1,830 burials took place there. The report called the attention of the authorities to the exceptionally high rate of infant mortality in the city.[1]

The Jesuit missionary António Vieira commented that God gave his countrymen a small land for their birthplace but all the world in which to die. In the seventeenth century Portugal lost much of its overseas empire at the point of the sword. In the nineteenth century Brazil broke away from the mother country and declared its independence. More recently Portugal's remaining possessions have been reduced by political circumstances. Nevertheless the Brotherhood of Our Lady, Mother of God, Virgin Mary of Mercy, continues to maintain branches in those territories of Africa and Asia where Portuguese is still spoken. In 1967 there were 339 branches of the brotherhood in continental Portugal alone. There were a further four

[1] I am indebted to Dr João da Costa Pinto Dantas Júnior (Provedor, 1963–5), for giving me a copy of this *Relatório*.

branches on the island of Madeira and eighteen in the Azores. Among the overseas territories of Portugal there were branches at Luanda (Angola), Lourenço Marques (Mozambique), Bissau (Portuguese Guinea), S. Tomé, Macao and one in India.[1] Perhaps the greatest testimony to the valuable services performed by the brotherhood is the continuing presence of a large number of branches in Brazil. In 1967 there were 326 branches in Brazil.[2] These enjoy the social prestige and perform those charitable works which characterised the brotherhood during the colonial era. They preserve the positive qualities of personal initiative and Catholic charity which were present in the great Manueline epoch of discovery and expansion.

[1] These figures were supplied to me by the Provedor of the Misericórdia of Lisbon.

[2] I am indebted to the Provedor of the Misericórdia of Rio de Janeiro, Afrânio António da Costa, for information on branches of the brotherhood in Brazil. In many cases the social services of these branches are limited to the administration of a hospital. The continuing need for social assistance in other fields is shown by a note received by a friend of mine in Bahia in 1965. This note had been smuggled out of a small municipal gaol and read as follows (in trans.): 'Dona —, I ask for the love of God for alms because we are three prisoners and we are dying of hunger. Have compassion on us, we who have been without food since yesterday night and with no coffee at all so far. The prisoner —.' The distinction between food and coffee provides an interesting insight into the Brazilian way of life.

APPENDICES

Appendix 1

Dom Manuel I, 1495–1521.
Dom João III, 1521–57.
Dom Sebastião, 1557–78.
Cardinal Dom Henrique, 1578–80.
Dom Felippe I (II of Spain), 1580–98.
Dom Felippe II (III of Spain), 1598–1621.
Dom Felippe III (IV of Spain), 1621–40.
Dom João IV, 1640–56.
Dom Affonso VI, 1656–67 (deposed). Died 1683.
Dom Pedro II, Prince-Regent, 1667–83. King, 1683–1706.
Dom João V, 1706–50.
Dom José I, 1750–77.

b. VICEROYS AND GOVERNORS-GENERAL OF BRAZIL AT BAHIA,
1549–1760

Tomé de Sousa, 1549–53.
Dom Duarte da Costa, 1553–8.
Mem de Sá, 1558–72.
Luís de Brito de Almeida, 1573–8.
Lourenço da Veiga, 1578–81. Died, June 1581.
Interim government of the city council and chief justice, 1581–3.
Manuel Telles Barreto, 1583–7. Died, March 1587.
Interim government of the bishop, chief justice and chief commissioner of the
Treasury, 1587–91.
Dom Francisco de Sousa, 1591–1602.
Diogo Botelho, 1603–7.
Dom Diogo de Meneses, 1608–12.
Gaspar de Sousa, 1613–17.
Dom Luís de Sousa, 1617–21.
Diogo de Mendonça Furtado, 1621–4.
Dutch occupation of Bahia, 1624–5.

Dom Francisco de Moura Rolim, 1625–7 (title of captain-major only).

Diogo Luís de Oliveira, 1627–35.

Pedro da Silva, 1635–9.

Dom Fernando Mascarenhas, Count of Tôrre, 1639.

Dom Vasco Mascarenhas, 1st Count of Óbidos, 1639–40.

Dom Jorge Mascarenhas, Marquis of Montalvão, 1640–1 (1st viceroy).

Interim illegal government of the bishop, chief commissioner of the Treasury and Master of the Field Luís Barbalho Bezerra, 1641–2.

António Telles da Silva, 1642–7.

António Telles de Meneses, Count of Villa-Pouca de Aguiar, 1647–50.

João Rodrigues de Vasconcellos e Sousa, Count of Castelo Melhor, 1650–4.

Dom Jerónimo de Ataíde, 6th Count of Atouguia, 1654–7.

Francisco Barreto de Meneses, 1657–63.

Dom Vasco Mascarenhas, 1st Count of Óbidos, 1663–7 (2nd viceroy).

Alexandre de Sousa Freire, 1667–71.

Dom Affonso Furtado de Castro do Rio de Mendonça, Viscount of Barbacena, 1671–5. Died, November 1675.

Interim government of the Chancellor of the High Court, Master of the Field Alvaro de Azevedo and António Guedes de Brito, 1675–8.

Roque da Costa Barreto, 1678–82.

António de Sousa de Meneses, 1682–4.

Dom António Luís de Sousa Tello de Meneses, 2nd Marquis of Minas, 1684–7.

Mathias da Cunha, 1687–8. Died, October 1688.

Interim government of the Archbishop Dom Fr. Manuel da Resurreição and Chancellor of the High Court, Manuel Carneiro de Sá, 1688–90.

António Luís Gonçalves da Câmara Coutinho, 1690–4.

Dom João de Lencastre, 1694–1702.

Dom Rodrigo da Costa, 1702–5.

Luís Cesar de Meneses, 1705–10.

Dom Lourenço de Almeida, 1710–11.

Pedro de Vasconcellos e Sousa, 3rd Count of Castelo Melhor, 1711–14.

Dom Pedro de Noronha, Count of Villa Verde and Marquis of Angeja, 1714–18 (3rd viceroy).

Dom Sancho de Faro e Sousa, Count of Vimieiro, 1718–19. Died, October 1719.

Interim government of the Archbishop, Dom Sebastião Monteiro da Vide, Chancellor of the High Court, Caetano de Brito de Figueredo, and the Master of the Field João de Araújo e Azevedo, 1719–20.

Vasco Fernandes Cesar de Meneses, Count of Sabugosa, 1720–35 (4th viceroy).

André de Mello e Castro, Count of Galvêas, 1735–49 (5th viceroy).

Dom Luís Pedro Peregrino de Carvalho Meneses de Ataíde, 10th Count of Atouguia, 1749–55 (6th viceroy).

Interim government of the Archbishop, Dom José Botelho de Mattos, Chancellor of the High Court, Manuel António da Cunha Sotto Maior, and Colonel Lourenço Monteiro, 1755.

Dom Marcos de Noronha e Brito, 6th Count of Arcos, 1755–60 (7th viceroy).

Dom António de Almeida Soares e Portugal, first Marquis of Lavradio, 1760 (8th viceroy).

Appendix 2

PROVEDORS OF THE SANTA CASA DA MISERICÓRDIA OF BAHIA, 1560–1755

The earliest extant electoral registers in the archives of the Misericórdia only date from 1667. Names of Provedors before this date have been included in this list for the sake of completeness, but should be regarded as tentative in the absence of conclusive evidence as to their terms of office. Dates refer to the annual terms of office, e.g. 1667 indicates the term of office from 3 July 1667 to 2 July 1668.

1560s. Mem de Sá, Governor-General of Brazil.

1572. Dom Pedro Leitão, bishop of Bahia.

1587. Cristóvão de Barros, chief commissioner of the Treasury.

1613. Henrique Moniz Telles.

1614. Francisco de Barros.

1617. Dom Luís de Sousa, Governor-General of Brazil.

1621. Manuel Pinto da Rocha, High Court judge.

1622. Sebastião Parvi de Brito.

1625. Dom Francisco de Moura Rolim, Captain-Major.

1627. Manuel Ferreira de Figueredo, chief commissioner of the Treasury.

1628. Belchior Brandão.

1629. Dom Vasco Mascarenhas, Master of the Field (later to be Governor-General of Brazil).

1632. Diogo Luís de Oliveira, Governor-General of Brazil.

1633. Diogo Luís de Oliveira, re-elected.

1636. Bernardim Fernandes Barros.

1637. Diogo de Aragão Pereira.

1642. João Álvares de Affonseca.

1643. Sebastião Parvi de Britto.

1644. Felippe de Moura de Albuquerque, Captain.

1646. João Álvares de Affonseca.

1648. Francisco Gil de Araújo.

1649. Pedro Garcia de Aragão.

1650. João Rodrigues de Vasconcellos e Sousa, Count of Castelo Melhor, Governor-General of Brazil.

1651. Balthazar de Aragão de Araújo.

1652. Sebastião Parvi de Brito.

372

1653. António da Silva Pimentel.

1655. Lourenço de Brito Correia.

1656. Francisco Fernandes do Sim, Captain.

1657. Francisco Fernandes do Sim, re-elected.

1658. Francisco Fernandes do Sim, re-elected.

1659. Francisco Fernandes do Sim, re-elected.

1660. Pedro Gomes.

1661. Francisco Fernandes do Sim, Captain.

1662. António Guedes de Brito.

1663. Felippe de Moura de Albuquerque.

1664. Lourenço de Brito Correia.

1665. Cristóvão de Burgos, chief justice for criminal cases in the High Court.

1666. António Guedes de Brito.

1667. Pedro Gomes, Lieutenant-General.

1668. Cosme de Sá Peixoto.

1669. Francisco Gil de Araújo.

1670. António de Brito de Castro, Lieutenant.

1671. Affonso Furtado de Castro do Rio de Mendonça, Viscount of Barbacena, Governor-General of Brazil.

1672. Cristóvão da Cunha de Sá Sottomaior.

1673. Cristóvão da Cunha de Sá Sottomaior, re-elected.

1674. João de Aguiar Villas Boas.

1675. João de Góis de Araújo, High Court judge.

1676. Pedro Camello Pereira de Aragão, Colonel.

1677. Domingos Garcia de Aragão.

1678. António Ferreira de Sousa.

1679. Lourenço Barbosa da Franca.

1680. António de Aragão Pereira, died 21 July 1680. Domingos Garcia de Aragão elected.

1681. Bernardo Vieira Ravasco, Secretary of State for Brazil.

1682. Gaspar de Araújo de Góis.

1683. João Peixoto Viegas.

1684. João de Mattos de Aguiar.

1685. Manuel de Araújo de Aragão.

1686. Pedro Gomes, Master of the Field.

1687. Manuel Pereira de Góis.

1688. Francisco Dias d'Avila, Colonel.

1689. Francisco Dias d'Avila re-elected after both Pedro Garcia Pimentel and Jerónimo Pereira Sodré had refused office.

1690. António Ferreira de Sousa.

1691. Pedro Garcia Pimentel elected after Jerónimo Pereira Sodré refused office.

1692. Domingos Soares da Franca.

1693. Pedro de Unhão Castelo Branco, High Court judge.

1694. João Alves Fontes.

1695. António Maciel Teixeira.

1696. António Rodrigues Banha, High Court judge.

1697. António Guedes de Brito, died before taking office. Colonel António da Silva Pimentel, elected 7 October 1697.

1698. António da Silva Pimentel, re-elected.

1699. Sebastião de Araújo de Góis.

1700. António da Rocha Pitta.

1701. Francisco Lamberto, chief commissioner of the Treasury.

1702. Francisco Lamberto, re-elected.

1703. Pedro Barbosa Leal, Colonel.

1704. Pedro Barbosa Leal, re-elected.

1705. Domingos Affonso Sertão.

1706. Alexandre de Sousa Freire, Master of the Field.

1707. Alexandre de Sousa Freire, re-elected.

1708. Manuel de Araújo de Aragão, Colonel, died in office. Alexandre de Sousa Freire, elected 27 January 1709.

1709. Pedro Fernandes Aranha.

1710. Pedro Fernandes Aranha, re-elected.

1711. João de Sá Sottomaior, chief justice for criminal cases in the High Court.

1712. João de Sá Sottomaior, re-elected.

1713. João de Sá Sottomaior, re-elected.

1714. Joseph de Sá e Mendonça, High Court judge.

1715. Dionísio de Azevedo Arvelos, High Court judge.

1716. José de Araújo Rocha.

1717. Gonçalo Ravasco Cavalcante e Albuquerque, Secretary of State for Brazil.

1718. António Ferrão Castelo Branco, Lieutenant-General.

1719. José Pires de Carvalho.

1720. Gonçalo Ravasco Cavalcante e Albuquerque.

1721. Manuel Ramos Parente, Sergeant Major.

1722. António Ferreira Lisboa.

1723. Balthazar de Vasconcellos Cavalcante.

1724. António Rodrigues Lima, Canon.

1725. António Gonçalves da Rocha, Captain.

1726. Francisco Lopes Villas Boas, Master of the Field.

1727. João Calmon, Rev., cathedral precentor.

1728. João Calmon, re-elected.

1729. Cosme Rolim de Moura.

1730. Miguel de Passos Dias.

1731. Francisco Martins Pereira, Canon and Chancellor of the Ecclesiastical Court.

1733. Francisco Martins Pereira, re-elected.

1734. Francisco Martins Pereira, re-elected.
1735. Simão de Affonseca Pitta.
1736. Francisco de Oliveira Pôrto.
1737. Anselmo Dias, Alcaide-mór.
1738. Anselmo Dias, re-elected.
1739. André Marques, Captain.
1740. António Rodrigues Lima, Rev.
1741. Jerónimo Velho de Araújo, Captain; he resigned on 28 June 1742, and António Rodrigues Lima was elected.
1742. Domingos Lucas de Aguiar.
1743. Custódio da Silva Guimarães.
1744. António Gonçalves Pereira, Archdeacon.
1745. Salvador Pires de Carvalho e Albuquerque.
1746. Salvador Pires de Carvalho e Albuquerque, re-elected after viceroyal intervention. He died on 28 August 1746, and the Archdeacon António Gonçalves Pereira was elected. He resigned on 24 December 1746 and Domingos Lucas de Aguiar was elected on 8 January 1747.
1747. Domingos Lucas de Aguiar, re-elected.
1748. António Álvares Silva, Colonel.
1749. André Marques, Captain.
1750. Domingos Borges de Barros, Captain.
1751. Anselmo Dias. He resigned on 21 September 1751 and Domingos Borges de Barros was re-elected.
1752. Pedro Moniz Barreto de Vasconcellos, Sergeant-Major.
1753. José Pires de Carvalho e Albuquerque, Secretary of State for Brazil.
1754. Luís da Costa e Faria, Rev. He resigned on 9 October and Domingos Borges de Barros was elected on the orders of the viceroy.

Appendix 3

a. CURRENCY IN CIRCULATION IN BRAZIL, 1550–1750

i. 1550–1640

Before the restoration of the Portuguese monarchy in 1640 coins of several foreign nations circulated openly in Brazil, although their use was forbidden officially. During the early period of colonisation wages were frequently paid in merchandise because of the lack of an official currency. A royal *provisão* of 1568 authorised the circulation of the following coins:

SILVER

  1 *Real* to circulate at a reduced value of 1–1½ *Real*
  3 *Réis* to circulate at a reduced value of 3   *Réis*
  5 *Réis* to circulate at a reduced value of ½   *Real*
 10 *Réis* to circulate at a reduced value of 1   *Real*

ii. REIGNS OF DOM JOÃO IV (1640–56), DOM AFFONSO VI (1656–67) AND THE REGENCY OF DOM PEDRO (1667–83)

During this period there were several changes in the value of coins circulating in Portugal and Brazil.

GOLD	Dom João IV	Dom Affonso VI
4 *Cruzados* (*Moeda*)	3$000 *Réis*	3$500 *Réis*
2 *Cruzados* (½ *Moeda*)	1$500 *Réis*	1$750 *Réis*
1 *Cruzado* (¼ *Moeda*)	750 *Réis*	875 *Réis*
Moeda		4$000 *Réis* (1663; 12½ per cent increase)
½ *Moeda*		2$000 *Réis* (1663; 12½ per cent increase)
¼ *Moeda*		1$000 *Réis* (1663; 12½ per cent increase)

SILVER

Portuguese and Spanish coins in circulation in Brazil were withdrawn from circulation and counter-marked with new values in monetary offices established for this purpose in Bahia, Rio de Janeiro, São Vicente and Maranhão.

376

	Basic value	1643–52 (25% increase)	1663 (25% increase)	1679
8 *Reales* (Sp.)		480 *Réis*	600 *Réis*	640 *Réis*
1 *Cruzado*	400 *Réis*		500 *Réis*	
4 *Reales* (Sp.)		240 *Réis*	300 *Réis*	320 *Réis*
½ *Cruzado*	200 *Réis*		250 *Réis*	
1 *Tostão* (1642 minting)	100 *Réis*	circulated in Brazil at 160 *Réis*	200 *Réis*	
1 *Tostão*	100 *Réis*		150 *Réis*	
2 *Reales* (Sp.)		120 *Réis*	150 *Réis*	160 *Réis*
1 *Tostão*	100 *Réis*		125 *Réis*	
4 *Vintens*	80 *Réis*		100 *Réis*	
3 *Vintens* (1642 minting)	60 *Réis*	circulated in Brazil at 80 *Réis*	100 *Réis*	
½ *Tostão*	50 *Réis*		80 *Réis*	
½ *Tostão*	50 *Réis*		75 *Réis*	
1 *Real* (Sp.)		60 *Réis*	75 *Réis*	80 *Réis*
2 *Vintens*	40 *Réis*		60 *Réis*	
1 *Vintem*	20 *Réis*			
10 *Réis*	10 *Réis*			

COPPER

5 *Réis*
3 *Réis*
1½ *Real e Meio*

iii. REIGN OF DOM PEDRO II (1683–1706)

The prevalence of the practice of 'clipping' compelled the authorities to withdraw coins from circulation and impress them with milled edges. This measure proved ineffective because the values of the milled coins by weight now exceeded their face values, e.g. a piece of 2 *Patacas*, with a face value of 640 *Réis*, was worth 750 *Réis* by weight. This difference between the intrinsic and extrinsic values of coins encouraged their export to Portugal from Brazil. A decree ordering that milled coins should circulate at values based on their weights, and not at their face values, proved unworkable in practice. As a final solution colonial mints were established at Bahia (1694), Rio de Janeiro (1699) and Recife (1700). Coins minted in Brazil were valued at 10 per cent less than their counterparts minted in Portugal, and were consequently known as 'weak currency' in distinction to the national 'strong currency'. Although forbidden, the 'strong currency' continued to circulate in Brazil.

GOLD

(struck in Portugal)

Moeda	4$400 *Réis*	*Moeda*	4$000 *Réis*
½ *Moeda*	2$200 *Réis*	½ *Moeda*	2$000 *Réis*
¼ *Moeda*	1$100 *Réis*	¼ *Moeda*	1$000 *Réis*

(struck in Brazil)

Moeda	4$800 *Réis* (Rio)	*Moeda*	4$000 *Réis* ⎫ Rio,
½ *Moeda*	2$400 *Réis* (Rio)	½ *Moeda*	2$000 *Réis* ⎬ Bahia,
¼ *Moeda*	1$200 *Réis* (Rio)	¼ *Moeda*	1$000 *Réis* ⎭ Recife

SILVER

(struck in Portugal)

Cruzado	400 *Réis*	4 *Vintens*	80 *Réis*
12 *Vintens*	240 *Réis*	3 *Vintens*	60 *Réis*
2 *Tostões*	200 *Réis*	½ *Tostão*	50 *Réis*
6 *Vintens*	120 *Réis*	2 *Vintens*	40 *Réis*
Tostão	100 *Réis*	*Vintem*	20 *Réis*

(struck in Brazil)

2 *Patacas*	640 *Réis* (Bahia, Rio, Recife)	4 *Vintens*	80 *Réis* (Bahia, Rio, Recife)
1 *Pataca*	320 *Réis* (Bahia, Rio, Recife)	2 *Vintens*	40 *Réis* (Bahia, Rio, Recife)
½ *Pataca*	160 *Réis* (Bahia, Rio, Recife)	*Vintem*	20 *Réis* (Bahia, Rio, Recife)

COPPER

(struck in Portugal)

20 *Réis*   10 *Réis*   5 *Réis*   3 *Réis*   1½ *Real e Meio*

The circulation of Angolan copper coinage in Brazil was authorised by royal decrees of 1702 and 1704.

iv. REIGN OF DOM JOÃO V (1706–50)

The mints which had been established at Bahia, Rio de Janeiro and Recife had been closed after sufficient coinage had been minted. The mints at Rio and Bahia had started to operate again in 1703 and 1714 respectively. In 1724 a mint was also established in Vila Rica and functioned for ten years. Both systems of currency, the 'weak' and the 'strong', continued to circulate in Brazil. Gold coins of the national ('strong') currency, minted at 1$600 *Réis* the *oitava*, circulated in Brazil at 20 per cent above this value, whereas gold coins of the colonial ('weak') currency, minted at 1$760 *Réis* the *oitava* circulated at this value. Less silver coinage was minted during this reign.

GOLD
(struck in Portugal)

Dobrão (5 *Moedas*)	24$000 *Réis*	½ *Moeda*	2$400 *Réis*
Dobra (8 *Escudos*)	12$800 *Réis*	*Escudo*	1$600 *Réis*
Dobra	12$000 *Réis*	¼ *Moeda*	1$200 *Réis*
Dobra (4 *Escudos*)		½ *Escudo*	800 *Réis*
(Peça)	6$400 *Réis*	*Cruzado Novo*	480 *Réis*
Moeda	4$800 *Réis*	¼ *Escudo* (*Cruzado*)	400 *Réis*
Dobra (2 *Escudos*)			
(½ Peça)	3$200 *Réis*		

(struck in Brazil)

Dobrão	24$000 *Réis*	(Vila Rica)
Dobra	12$800 *Réis*	(Rio, Bahia, Vila Rica)
Dobra	12$000 *Réis*	(Vila Rica)
Dobra	6$400 *Réis*	(Rio, Bahia, Vila Rica)
Dobra	3$200 *Réis*	(Rio, Bahia, Vila Rica)
Escudo	1$600 *Réis*	(Rio, Bahia, Vila Rica)
½ *Escudo*	800 *Réis*	(Rio, Bahia, Vila Rica)
¼ *Escudo*	400 *Réis*	(Rio, Bahia, Vila Rica)

SILVER
(struck in Portugal)

Cruzado	480 *Réis*		(struck in Brazil)	
12 *Vintens*	240 *Réis*	2 *Patacas*	640 *Réis*	(Rio)
6 *Vintens*	120 *Réis*	1 *Pataca*	320 *Réis*	(Rio)
Tostão	100 *Réis*	½ *Pataca*	160 *Réis*	(Rio)
3 *Vintens*	60 *Réis*			
½ *Tostão*	50 *Réis*			
Vintem	20 *Réis*			

COPPER
(struck in Portugal)

Vintem	20 *Réis*	(struck in Brazil)		
10 *Réis*		*Vintem*	20 *Réis*	(Bahia, rarely)
		10 *Réis*		(Bahia, rarely)

During this reign the Lisbon mint produced gold coins of 4$000 *Réis*, 2$000 *Réis* and 1$000 *Réis*, silver coins of 640 *Réis*, 320 *Réis*, 160 *Réis* and 80 *Réis*, and copper coins of 20 *Réis*, 10 *Réis* and 5 *Réis* for the State of Maranhão. It also minted copper coins of 40 *Réis* and 20 *Réis* for circulation in Minas Gerais only.

b. THE PRICE OF LABOUR, 1680–1750

It is not possible to construct a cost-of-living index for the colonial period because of lack of information on the prices of basic commodities at specific times. The following table is intended merely as a general indication of the level of wages between 1680 and 1750, as represented by wages paid to employees of the Misericórdia. It will be noted that in some cases, e.g. lawyers and doctors, the salaries varied according to the numbers employed concurrently.

	1680	1690	1700	1710	1720	1730	1740	1750
'Barber'	—	—	—	20$000 ————————————→				20$000
Carrier of the biers	16$000 ————————————→			20$000 ————————————→				20$000
Chief cook	—	—	29$200	—	—	—	—	—
Choirboy	—	16$000 ————————————————————————→						16$000
Clergy (basic wages) President of choir	—	80$000 ————————————————————→				(1735)100$000→		100$000
Master of choir	—	60$000 ————————————————————→				(1735) 75$000→		75$000
Priest	—	40$000 ————————————————————→				(1735) 50$000→		50$000
Doctor	—	—(1)50$000→(2)40$000 ————————————————————→						(2)40$000
'Homem de azul' (basic)	16$000 ————————→	20$000 ————————————————————————→						20$000
Lawyer	(2)30$000→(1)70$000→80$000→			crime: 50$000→130$000→ 130$000 civil: 40$000→110$000→ 110$000				
Nurse	—	16$000→29$200 ————————————————————→						29$020
Chief nurse	—	—	—	45$200 ————————————————→				45$200
Organist	20$000 ————————————————————→			35$000 ————————————→				50$000
Porter	—	20$000 ————————————————————————→						20$000
Surgeon	—	— (1)50$000 ————————→65$000→(2)50$000→ (1)73$000 / (1)73$000						

Appendix 4

WEIGHTS AND MEASURES

Weights and measures used in Lisbon differed considerably from those used in Brazil and even within Brazil itself there were marked distinctions between regions at different periods. Measures of capacity used in Lisbon were considerably less than their Brazilian counterparts and in Brazil the *Canada* was variously given as 1·375 litres, 2·66 litres and 4·180 litres.

i. WEIGHTS

Quintal	58·982 kilos (= 4 *Arrôbas*). Corresponds to the English hundredweight.
Arrôba	14·745 kilos (= 32 *Arratéis*). Corresponds to the English quarter.
Arrátel or *Libra*	0·46080 kilos (= 2 *Marcos*). Corresponds to the English pound.
Marco	0·23040 kilos (= 8 *Onças*).
Onça	28·800 grammes (= 8 *Oitavas*). Corresponds to the English ounce.
Oitava	3·600 grammes (= 4 *Quilates*). Approximately 2 English drams.
Quilate	0·900 grammes.

ii. MEASURES OF CAPACITY (DRY)

Alqueire	36·27 litres. Approximately 1 English bushel (8 gallons).
½ *Alqueire*	18·135 litres. Approximately 2 English pecks (4 gallons).
¼ *Alqueire* (*Quarta*)	9·07 litres. Approximately 1 English peck (2 gallons).
⅛ *Alqueire* (*Meia Quarta*)	4·535 litres. Corresponds to the English gallon.
Selamin	1·14 litres. Corresponds to the English quart (2 pints).

iii. MEASURES OF CAPACITY (LIQUID)

Tonel	848 litres (= 2 *Pipas Comuns*).
Pipa Comum	424 litres (= 300 *Canadas* in Lisbon).
Pipa de Conta	480 litres (= 180 *Canadas* in Rio de Janeiro). About 2 hogsheads.
Almude	31·944 litres (= 12 *Canadas*). Approximately 7 English gallons.
Canada or *Medida*	2·662 litres in Rio de Janeiro (= 4 *Quartilhos*).
Quartilho	0·665 litres.

iv. MEASURES OF LENGTH

Légua	Varies between 5,555 metres and 6,600 metres.
Braça	2·20 metres (= 2 *Varas*). Corresponds to the English fathom.
Vara	1·10 metres. Corresponds to the English yard.
Côvado	0·66 metres (= 2 *Pés* or 3 *Palmos*).
Pé	0·33 metres. Corresponds to the English foot.
Palmo	0·22 metres. Corresponds to the English span.
Polegada	0·0275 metres. Corresponds to the English inch.

Glossary

Albergaria: a hostelry.

Alcaide: (1) a military governor; (2) official responsible for maintaining public law and order in a municipality.

Almotacé: weights and measures inspector.

Almotacé da limpeƶa: sanitary inspector.

Alvará: royal decree.

Ama de leite: wet-nurse.

Bandeirante: pioneer or explorer.

Banguê: bier used for the funerals of slaves.

Caatinga: scrubland.

Caboclo: (1) cross-breed of white and Amerindian parentage; (2) derogatory term for a low class of person; (3) *Indio manso* (*q.v.*)

Calhambola: group of runaway slaves.

Câmara: municipal council.

Capela de missas: a set number of masses to be said at regular intervals.

Capitania: captaincy (area of territory).

Carreira da India: the sea passage to India.

Carta de examinação: certificate of proficiency in a trade.

Carta régia: a royal letter.

Casa da Suplicação: Supreme Court of Appeals.

Casa grande: house of the owner of a sugar plantation.

Christão Novo: converted or crypto-Jew.

Christão Velho: Catholic.

Colocação familiar: the boarding out of an orphan with a family.

Compadre: approximate equivalent of English god-father: explained on p. 315.

Compromisso: statutes of a brotherhood.

Corregedor: (1) civil governor; (2) judge.

Corregedor da comarca: district judge.

Degredado: exile.

Desembargador: judge of the High Court.

Donatário: land owner with jurisdiction over a *capitania* in Brazil.

Educanda: young girl accepted for instruction in a convent without taking the vows.

Engenho: sugar mill; a plantation, by extension.

Escrivão: scribe.

Esquife: a litter for funerals.

Fazenda: (1) property, usually land; (2) Treasury.

Fidalgo: nobleman.

Fogo: hearth; a home, by extension.

Garimpeiro: illicit diamond prospector.

Homem de azul: 'blue man', an employee of the Misericórdia.

Indio manso: domesticated Indian.

Irmão de maior condição or *Irmão nobre*: brother of higher standing in the Misericórdia.

Irmão de menor condição: brother of lower standing in the Misericórdia.

Juiz de fora: district magistrate.

Juiz do povo: tribune of the people.

Juiz ordinário: justice of the peace.

Junta: a secondary board of guardians of the Misericórdia.

Ladeira: alley or steep path.

Laudémio: transfer fee on the sale of property.

Língua geral: a Tupí dialect spoken by half-breeds and Europeans without any grammatical knowledge of the language.

Lundú: dance of African origin.

Mal de Luanda: scurvy.

Mameluco: cross-breed of white and Amerindian parentage.

Mão de obra: lit: 'working hand', and so a slave.

Mascavado: sugar in the unrefined state.

Meirinho: minor court official.

Mesa: board of guardians of the Misericórdia.

Mesteres: representatives of a trade or group of trades.

Mestiço: half-breed of Negro-white or Amerindian-white parentage.

Mestre do Campo: colonel of an infantry regiment.

Miunça: tithe, paid in kind.

Mordomo: steward, or brother of the Misericórdia with specific duties.

Orfãs del Rei: orphan girls of marriageable age sent from Lisbon to the Orient to be married at the Crown's expense.

Ouvidor da comarca: district judge.

Ouvidor geral: senior Crown judge in a *Relação*.

Palanquim: chair or litter carried on the shoulders of slaves.

Pardo: mulattos and their children.

Pau-a-pique: wattle-and-daub.

Peça de Indias: standard measurement for classification of slaves.

Peste da bicha: yellow fever.

Poderosos do Sertão: powerful, and often tyrannical, landowners in the Sertão.

Porcionista: boarder or lodger.

Procurador: person with powers of attorney.

Procurador da Corôa: Crown official responsible for making the preliminary report on investigations ordered by the king.

Provedor: (1) general term for a bureaucratic office; (2) President of the board of guardians of the Misericórdia.

Provedor-mór da Fazenda: chief commissioner of the Treasury.

Provisão: Crown decree.

Quilombo: community of runaway slaves.

Quinto: royal fifth.

Recolhida: recluse.

Recôncavo: fertile coastal plain around the Bay of All Saints.

Regimento: (1) brief or set of instructions; (2) statutes followed by an association of artisans and approved by the city council or the Crown.

Relação: High Court of Appeals.

Repartideira: small copper pan used in the manufacture of sugar.

Roça: small-holding.

Senhor de engenho: owner of a sugar mill; by extension, the owner of a sugar plantation.

Senzala: slave quarters.

Serpentina: same as a *palanquim* (*q.v.*).

Sertão: semi-barren plateau in the interior of Brazil.

Sesmaria: concession of land.

Tabuleiro: litter used for the funerals of small children.

Terço: infantry regiment.

Tumba: bier.

Tumbeiro: (1) carrier of the bier; (2) slave-ship.

Vereador: municipal councillor.

Bibliography

A. MANUSCRIPT SOURCES

I. SALVADOR

(a) Archives of the Santa Casa da Misericórdia in Bahia
(Abbreviation: ASCMB)

The archives of the brotherhood in Bahia were totally destroyed during the Dutch occupation (1624–5) and many of the codices for the first half of the seventeenth century have been lost. More recent losses include the first register of copies of letters sent by the Mesa and the first register of admissions of brothers, removed from the archives in 1897 to be copied, both of which were consulted by Damázio in 1862. The most important loss is that of the second book of minutes of the Mesa covering the period 1675–80. The majority of the documents are in good condition and quite readable, but a few series have been practically destroyed by damp, corrosive ink, insects, and careless handling. In some cases, such as the first book of minutes of the Mesa, copies of badly damaged documents were made by later scribes and inserted in place of the originals which were destroyed. Both these copies and those made in the late nineteenth century contain many errors and must be used with extreme caution.

The codices and documents for the seventeenth and eighteenth centuries have been generally classified and bound. An attempt has been made to restore some of the more important documents. During binding some folios have been placed in the wrong order and others have been mislaid. This has resulted in discrepancies between the present numeration and the original numeration. The extent of these discrepancies can easily be verified because the majority of the folios were numbered and signed by the scribes. There is no printed catalogue for the archives. The only guide to the contents is a general manuscript index of the titles of the bound volumes made in 1940, which divides the archives into eight sections. This division has been preserved in the bibliography for ease of reference. The first number in each entry corresponds to the number of the bound volume in the archives. All references in footnotes are to these numbers to save needless repetition of the full titles of volumes consulted. This bibliography represents a complete catalogue of pre-1755 documents in these archives.

1. *General administration*

    2. Livro 2º de têrmos dos irmãos, 1663–95 (copy available). The first volume of this series was lost when it was removed from the archives in 1897 to be copied.

3. Livro 3º de têrmos dos irmãos, 1696–1733 (copy available).

4. Livro 4º de têrmos dos irmãos, 1733–72.

13. Livro 1º de acórdãos da Mesa, 1645–74 (copy available).

14. Livro 3º de acórdãos da Mesa e Junta, 1681–1745. The second volume in this series is missing.

15. Livro 4º de acórdãos da Mesa e Junta, 1745–91.

16. Livro 5º de acórdãos da Mesa e Junta, 1791–1834.

34. Livro 2º das eleições das Mesas e Juntas, 1667–1726. The first volume of this series is missing.

35. Livro 3º das eleições das Mesas e Juntas, 1727–91.

37. Livro 4º de têrmos dos capelães e serventuários desta Casa, 1683–1765. The first three volumes of this series are missing.

40. Livro 1º do tombo, 1629–52 (copy available). This includes copies of earlier land leases prior to the Dutch occupation.

41. Livro 2º do tombo, 1652–85 (copy available).

42. Livro 3º do tombo, 1686–1829.

44. Livro 2º de escrituras, 1681–1750. The first volume of this series is missing.

45. Livro 3º de escrituras, 1750–62.

52. Livro 2º do copiador, 1702–49. The first volume of this series is missing.

53. Livro 3º do copiador, 1749–57.

85. Livro 1º do registro, 1760–76.

160. Livro das demandas da Santa Casa, 1747–83.

162. Livro de ordens dos governadores desta província dirigidas à Santa Casa, 1722–1820.

192. Treslado do testamento e inventário dos bens do Capitão Domingos Fernandes de Freitas, 1688–1702.

193. Treslado do testamento e inventário dos bens de Manuel Rodrigues da Silva, 1739.

194. Treslado do testamento e inventário dos bens do Capitão António da Cunha e Andrade, 1742–4.

195. Livro dos segredos, 1679–1809. Contains copies of some earlier documents dating from 1629.

199. Livro das disposições das verbas do testamento do defunto João de Mattos de Aguiar, 1700.

206. Livro das provisões régias que concedem privilégios à Casa da Misericórdia da cidade de Lisboa. Copy of 1720.

207. Livro das provisões dos privilégios concedidos à Santa Casa da Misericórdia de Lisboa e à esta da Bahia. Copy of 1830.

208. Livro das provisões e cartas de Sua Majestade, 1762–65.

209. Livro das provisões e privilégios concedidos à Santa Casa da Misericórdia de Lisboa dos quais uza e goza esta Santa Casa da Misericórdia da Bahia por especial provisão de Sua Majestade.

210. Conta dos patrimónios e rendimento que administra a Casa da Santa Misericórdia da Bahia, 1754.
211. Livro das instituições, 1623–1773.
212. Livro de conta do benfeitor João de Mattos de Aguiar com seus devedores.
213. Livro de inventário da fazenda de Saubara, 1714–60.
214. Livro de todas as cousas pertencentes à igreja e sacristia, 1714–1813.
216. Inventário das cousas pertencentes a Francisco Pereira Ferraz, 1715.
217. Testamento de Pedro Vaz Coutinho, 1747.

2. *Accountancy*

307. Livro de razão e dever e haver de todo dinheiro que está a juros e se deu daqui por diante da consignação da Casa, 1688–1756 (copy available).
309. Livro 2º da consignação da Casa, 1716–50. The first volume of this series is in very bad condition.
310. Livro 3º da consignação da Casa, 1726–1807.
311. Livro 1º de juros da consignação do cofre, 1702–34.
511. Livro de juros e foros da consignação da Casa, 1726–90.
556. Livro de dever e há de haver dos juros que esta Santa Casa tem como legatória de vários defuntos, 1704–35.
748. Livro da consignação da Casa, 1735–1823.
772. Livro das terras foreiras à Misericórdia com as contas dos foreiros respetivos, 1717–68.
778. Registro de juros, 1745–50.
843. Livro de receita e despesa, 1647–53.
844. Livro de receita e despesa, 1669–83.
845. Livro de receita, 1684–1708.
846. Livro de receita, 1709–36.
847. Livro de receita, 1693–4 and 1712–15.
848. Livro de despesa, 1674–81.
849. Livro de despesa, 1683–1700.
850. Livro de despesa, 1700–9.
851. Livro de despesa, 1693–4 and 1712–14.
852. Livro de receita e despesa, 1736–8.
853. Livro de receita e despesa, 1737–8.
854. Livro de receita e despesa, 1739–40.
855. Livro de receita e despesa, 1740–1.
856. Livro de receita e despesa, 1741–2.
857. Livro de receita e despesa, 1742–3.
858. Livro de receita e despesa, 1743–4.
859. Livro de receita e despesa, 1746–7.
860. Livro de receita e despesa, 1747–9.
861. Livro de receita e despesa, 1748–9.

862. Livro de receita e despesa, 1750–1.
863. Livro de receita e despesa, 1751–2.
864. Livro de receita e despesa, 1752–3.
865. Livro de receita e despesa, 1753–4.
866. Livro de receita e despesa, 1754–5.
867. Livro de receita e despesa, 1755–6.
868. Livro de receita e despesa, 1756–7.
869. Livro de receita e despesa, 1757–8.
870. Livro de receita e despesa, 1759–60.
1014. Livro de receita de dinheiro de principaes, 1723–57 (copy available).
1017. Livro de despesa de dinheiro de principaes, 1723–70.
1019. Livro de receita e despesa do dinheiro de principaes pertencentes ao cofre, 1682–1724.
1020. Livro de receita do dinheiro de principaes pertencentes ao cofre, 1731–72.
1022. Livro de despesa de principaes pertencentes ao cofre, 1731–89.
1360. Livro de contas de juros de diversos devedores antigos, 1671–1772.
1366. Livro de receita e despesa da consignação de João de Mattos de Aguiar, 1700–40.

3. *Hospital*

1040. Livro de entradas dos soldados do terço velho da guarnição no hospital, 1757–69.
1041. Livro de entradas dos artilheiros no hospital, 1757–81.
1042. Livro de entradas dos soldados do terço novo no hospital, 1757–69.
1043. Livro de entradas de mulheres no hospital, 1757–76.

4. *Dowries, recluses and foundlings*

1164. Livro 1º dos têrmos e quitações dos dotes de João de Mattos de Aguiar, 1700–13.
1165. Livro 2º dos têrmos e quitações dos dotes de João de Mattos de Aguiar, 1714–25.
1166. Livro 3º dos têrmos e quitações dos dotes de João de Mattos de Aguiar, 1725–31.
1167. Livro 4º dos têrmos e quitações dos dotes de João de Mattos de Aguiar, 1731–48.
1168. Livro 5º dos têrmos e quitações dos dotes de João de Mattos de Aguiar, 1748–58. All the registers of dowries made on this legacy are in an appalling condition and extremely difficult to read.
1173. Livro 3º dos têrmos e quitações dos dotes de vários testadores, 1708–24. The first two volumes of this series are missing.

1174. Livro 4º dos têrmos e quitações dos dotes de vários testadores, 1725–34.
1175. Índice cronológica de todas as dotadas da Casa, 1750–71.
1180. Livro 2º dos têrmos das recolhidas, 1740–59. The first volume of this series is missing.
1193. Livro 3º dos expostos, 1757–63. The first two volumes of this series are missing.

5. Cemetery and burials

1251. Livro 1º das tumbas, 1685–1709.
1252. Livro 6º das tumbas, 1735–53. Volumes 2, 3, 4 and 5 of this series are missing.
1253. Livro 7º das tumbas, 1753–8.
1256. Livro do esquife dos anjos (livres e escravos), 1753–82.
1257. Livro 1º do banguê, 1741–3.
1258. Livro 2º do banguê, 1746–9.
1259. Livro 3º do banguê, 1749–53. The fourth volume of this series is missing.
1336. Livro mestre das contas antigas das instituições, 1662–1773.

6. Chapel and masses

1339. Livro das quitações das missas, 1725–35.
1341. Livro das quitações das missas e mais despesas que se fazem na Irmandade dos Santos Cosme e Damião, 1687–1804.

7. School Eloi Guimarães

1343. Diretório da colegiada da Santa Casa, 1829.
1354. Borrador dos livros das contas de instituições diversas feitas até 1759, contendo particularmente as contas das instituições de missas pelas alunas de diversos benfeitores da Santa Casa, 1623–1759.

8. Hospice São João de Deus

The two volumes consulted from this section, vols. 1360 and 1366, have been wrongly catalogued and should be in the second section comprised of the accounts' ledgers of the brotherhood (*q.v.*).

(b) Public archives of the State of Bahia
(Abbreviation: APB)

A printed catalogue of the contents of these archives is available under the title of *Resenha de manuscritos e documentos outros da secção histórica do Arquivo Público do*

Estado da Bahia (Bahia, 1950). Although forming a useful guide to the material available this catalogue has been rendered obsolete to some degree by the adoption of a new classification of the manuscripts and documents.

Livros de ordens régias. These codices contain copies of the correspondence between the court at Lisbon and the governor-general or viceroy in Bahia. The complete collection consists of 120 volumes covering the colonial period. The documents are in good condition. I have consulted Vols. 1–73 for the period 1648–1760. The volumes for the years 1648–1727 are listed, with subject and onomastic indices, in the *Anais do Arquivo Público da Bahia*, Vols. 31 and 32 (Bahia, 1949 and 1952). These catalogues contain several omissions and errors. The catalogue starts at Vol. 2 of the *Ordens régias*, because the first volume has been lost. This can cause confusion because the bound volumes are numbered from Vol. 1. In all references I have followed the numbers of the bound volumes and not those listed in the *Anais*. Thus my volume 19 will correspond to volume 20 listed in the *Anais*. A new catalogue is in course of preparation and it is to be hoped that this will remove any possibilities of confusion.

Cartas do Govêrno a Sua Majestade, 1664–1780 (Vol. 133).
Cartas do Govêrno a várias autoridades, 1613–63 (Vol. 145).
Cartas do Govêrno a várias autoridades, 1657–66 (Vol. 146).
Cartas do Govêrno a várias autoridades, 1697–1704 (Vol. 147).

(c) Municipal archives of Salvador, Bahia
(Abbreviation: AMB)

Although no printed catalogue of the contents of these archives was available at the time of my visit in 1964–5, a manuscript catalogue lists the general titles of the bound volumes. The documents have been classified and bound and are in reasonable condition. Copies have been made of some series and these are especially valuable, despite faulty transcriptions, in cases where the originals have been lost. The city council of Salvador has done valuable service in publishing several series of documents under the general title *Documentos históricos do Arquivo Municipal*. The most important of these are the minutes of the city council for the years 1625–1700 and the correspondence of the city council to the Crown between 1640 and 1692 (see Printed Sources). The following unpublished collections have been consulted for the present study. The figures in brackets refer to the number of the bound volume in the archives:

Atas da Câmara, 1690–1702. This has been partly published. Original documents (Vol. 22) with copies (Vols. 23–4).
Atas da Câmara, 1702–8. A copy made in 1801 because the original has been lost (Vol. 25).
Atas da Câmara, 1708–11. A copy (Vol. 26).

Atas da Câmara, 1716–18. Original documents (Vol. 27) with copy (Vol. 28).

Atas da Câmara, 1718–31. Original documents (Vol. 29).

Atas da Câmara, 1731–50. Original documents (Vol. 30).

Cartas do Senado a Sua Majestade, 1640–86. Copy of 1805 because the original has been lost (Vol. 173). This series of documents has been partly published but my references are to the manuscript collections and not to the printed volumes.

Cartas do Senado a Sua Majestade, 1678–96. Original documents (Vol. 174). A copy is available for documents of the period 1686–96 (Vol. 175).

Cartas do Senado a Sua Majestade, 1696–1741. Original documents (Vol. 176). A copy is available for documents of the period 1696–1715 (Vol. 177) and 1715–41 (Vol. 178).

Cartas do Senado a Sua Majestade, 1742–1822. Original documents (Vol. 182).

Provisões reais, 1641–80. Original documents (Vol. 135) and copies (Vol. 134).

Provisões reais, 1680–1712. Original documents (Vol. 136).

Provisões reais, 1744–61. Original documents (Vol. 137).

Cartas de ecclesiásticos, 1685–1804 (Vol. 188).

Cartas de examinações de oficiais, 1690–1712 (Vol. 189).

Cartas de examinações de oficiais, 1713–25 (Vol. 190).

Cartas de examinações de oficiais, 1741–70 (Vol. 191).

Livro de engeitados, 1699–1736 (Vol. 202).

Livro de acórdãos, 1711–1828 (Vol. 203).

Livro de condenações por bem da saúde pública, 1750–73 (Vol. 522).

(d) Archives of the convent of Santa Clara do Desterro, Salvador, Bahia
(Abbreviation: ACDB)

There is no catalogue, either printed or manuscript, of the contents of these archives. Although a few of the collections of documents are in bound volumes, for the most part the archives consist of loose folios. These have been classified and placed in folders with a general indication of the contents. Only the following documents were consulted for the present work, but there can be no doubt that these manuscript collections merit a more detailed study:

Livro 1º das entradas e profissões das religiosas de Santa Clara do Desterro da cidade da Bahia.

Caixa 1, pastas 6, 7, 8, 9, 10, 11, 33, 34, 35 and 36. These deal with decrees concerning girls admitted as *educandas* and privileges for the possession of servants within the convent during the period 1679–1750.

Caixa 1, pasta 43. A document entitled 'Proposta mᵗᵒ do serviço de Deus N.S.' dealing with the dispute between the Misericórdia and the Franciscans over funerals.

(e) Documents in private collections in Salvador

Compromisso da Irmandade do SSmo Sacramento da Santa Sé Cathedral desta Cidade da Bahia, 1746. This interesting *Compromisso* is in the possession of the Bahian historian, Dona Marieta Alves, to whom I am indebted for her kindness in showing me this document during my stay in Bahia in 1964–5.

II. RIO DE JANEIRO

(a) The National Archives (Abbreviation: ANRJ)

Correspondência dos Governadores do Rio de Janeiro com diversas autoridades, 1718–63 (Códice 84). The following volumes were consulted: Vol. 5 (1733–6), Vol. 9 (1738–9), Vol. 11 (1743–9) and Vol. 12 (1749–63). An index of the 15 volumes comprising this series is available in the *Publicações do Arquivo Nacional*, Vol. 8.

Registro e indice de ordens régias existentes no Arquivo da Junta da Fazenda da Bahia, 1568–1799 (Códice 539). This series comprises four volumes: Vol. 1 (1584–1769), Vol. 2 (1568–1772), Vol. 3 (1661–1781) and Vol. 4 (1606–1799).

Copia do Livro de Assentamentos da Relação da Bahia, 1658–1764 (Códice 540).

Compromisso da Irmandade da immaculada e sacratissima Virgem Nossa Senhora da Conceição instituida e confirmada em a praia desta Bahia. Anno MDCXLV (Códice 824, Vol. 1).

Cartas régias, provisões, alvarás e avisos, 1662–1821 (Códice 952). The majority of the documents in the 50 volumes of this collection are letters from the Crown to the governor of Rio de Janeiro and, after 1763, to the viceroy of Brazil. Volumes 1–37, covering the period 1662–1754, were consulted. An index is available in the *Publicações do Arquivo Nacional*, Vol. 1 (Rio de Janeiro, 1922).

Mesa do Desembargo do Paço, 1808–28 (Caixas 20–131). The documents in caixas 129 and 130 were consulted. These deal with brotherhoods and charitable associations in Bahia, Alagoas, Ceará, Goiás and Espírito Santo.

Mesa da Consciência e Ordens (Caixa 288). Although consisting mainly of nineteenth-century documents on brotherhoods and the Misericórdia, there are numerous references to the seventeenth and eighteenth centuries.

(b) The National Library (Abbreviation: BNRJ)

All the documents consulted were in the manuscript section of the library.

11–33, 24, 45. A series of documents of the eighteenth century concerning the Misericórdia of Bahia. Several of the letters from the Crown to the viceroy are not in the *Ordens régias* collection of the APB.

11–33, 32, 12. A royal *provisão* of 13 January 1736 permitting the Brotherhood of St Benedict of Salvador to possess a bier.

11–33, 24, 43. A royal letter of 10 June 1716 to the viceroy referring to his proposals for the building of a military hospital in Bahia.

B. PRINTED SOURCES

This is not a bibliography of Portugal and Brazil for the period 1550–1755, nor is it an exhaustive check-list of books and articles written about the various branches of the Misericórdia. It is a list of the full titles of books and articles which have been found relevant to the present work and to which reference has been made. I have added short descriptive and critical notes on works included as primary sources because the titles of many books on Portuguese and Brazilian history give no indication of the true nature of their contents. The titles of books are given here in exactly the same form as they appear on the title-pages, which accounts for minor variations of orthography and accentuation. In those cases where the place of publication is given as 'Bahia', this should be taken as referring to the city of Salvador.

I. PRIMARY SOURCES

ACCIOLI–AMARAL, *Memorias historicas e politicas da Provincia da Bahia do Coronel Ignacio Accioli de Cerqueira e Silva. Annotador Dr. Braz do Amaral* (6 vols., Bahia, 1919–40).

The earlier volumes are especially useful for the colonial period, containing copies of documents in the Bahian archives. The whole series is rather haphazardly arranged and is marred by the lack of an index.

Actas do IV Congresso das Misericórdias (3 vols., Lisboa, 1959).

The first volume contains historical articles on various branches of the Misericórdia and the second provides much interesting information on the hospital services of the brotherhood in the twentieth century.

ALVES, MARIETA, *História da Venerável Ordem 3ª da Penitência do Seráfico Pe. São Francisco da Congregação da Bahia* (Bahia, 1948).

Mainly an architectural and artistic survey of the buildings of the Third Order, but useful for the extensive citation of eighteenth-century documents in the archives of the Order.

Anais do Arquivo Público da Bahia (37 vols., Bahia, 1917–62, in progress: the earlier volumes were entitled *Annaes do Arquivo Publico e do Museu do Estado da Bahia*).

This series publishes documents of archives in the State of Bahia. Volumes 31 (1949) and 32 (1952) contain catalogues of the *Ordens régias*, but must be used with caution because of errors.

Anais da Biblioteca Nacional (79 vols., Rio de Janeiro, 1876–1964, in progress).

The years for which the volumes are announced do not always correspond with the dates of publication, e.g. Vol. 77 (1957) was published in 1964, whereas Vol. 78 (1958) was published in 1963 and Vol. 79 (1959) in 1961. Vol. 68 (1949) contains a catalogue of documents on Bahia existing in the National Library.

Anais do Primeiro Congresso de História da Bahia (5 vols., Bahia, 1950–1).
The second volume was of great relevance to this study.

ANTONIL, ANDRÉ JOÃO (pseudonym of Giovanni Antonio Andreoni, S.J.). *Cultura e Opulencia do Brasil, por suas Drogas, e Minas, com varias noticias curiosas do modo de fazer o Assucar; plantar e beneficiar o Tabaco; tirar Ouro das Minas e descubrir as da Prata* (Lisboa, 1711).
Effectively suppressed by the Portuguese Crown for a century, this book constitutes an excellent survey of the major factors in the economy of colonial Brazil — sugar, tobacco, cattle and gold. Essential reading for the social historian as well as the economist.

Arquivos de Macau (6 vols., Macau, 1929–64, in progress: 1st series, 3 vols., 1929–31; 2nd series, 1 vol., 1941–2; 3rd series, 2 vols., 1964).
Useful publication of local archives, including the *Compromisso* of the Misericórdia of Macao of 1627.

Atas da Câmara (6 vols., Bahia, 1944–5?).
The principal source of information on municipal legislation during the colonial period, these minutes of the city council of Salvador have been published by the Prefecture in the series *Documentos históricos do Arquivo Municipal*. The volumes cover the following years: Vol. 1, 1625–41; Vol. 2, 1641–9; Vol. 3, 1649–59; Vol. 4, 1659–69; Vol. 5, 1669–84; Vol. 6, 1684–1700.

AZEVEDO, THALES DE, *Provoamento da cidade do Salvador* (2nd ed. São Paulo, 1955).
Based on the Bahian archives, this study treats in detail the social and economic problems of colonial Bahia.

BASTO, MAGALHÃES, *História da Santa Casa da Misericórdia do Porto* (Porto, 1934).
A well-documented study of this branch of the Misericórdia, but also analyses the circumstances of the foundation of the brotherhood in Lisbon.

BOXER, C. R., *The Golden Age of Brazil, 1695–1750. Growing Pains of a Colonial Society* (Berkeley and Los Angeles, 1962).
Based on documents in the archives of Lisbon, Rio de Janeiro, Bahia and Belo Horizonte, in addition to extensive published sources, this work is essential reading for anyone interested in colonial Brazil.

—, *Race Relations in the Portuguese Colonial Empire, 1415–1825* (Oxford, 1963).
A comparative study of the racial situation in different parts of the Portuguese empire, including Brazil. This work gives the lie to the much publicised policy of racial tolerance shown by the Portuguese in their contacts with other races.

—, *Portuguese Society in the Tropics. The Municipal Councils of Goa, Macao,*

Bahia, and Luanda, 1510–1800 (Madison and Milwaukee, 1965).

A study in institutional history which reveals much of the social structure of the Portuguese empire and the administrative conflicts between the city councils and local authorities.

BRÁSIO, PE. ANTÓNIO, 'As Misericórdias de Angola', in *Studia*, vol. 4 (Lisboa, 1959, published by the Centro de Estudos Históricos Ultramarinos), pp. 106–49.

A monograph on the branches of the brotherhood in Luanda and Massangano.

CAIO PRADO JÚNIOR, *Formação do Brasil contemporâneo. Colônia* (7th ed., São Paulo, 1963).

An excellent general work, marred only by the lack of an index. It is now available in an English translation.

CALDAS, JOSÉ ANTÓNIO, *Notícia geral de toda esta capitania da Bahia desde o seu descobrimento até o presente ano de 1759* (Bahia, 1951, in a facsimile edition).

A detailed survey of colonial Bahia with numerous diagrams and statistics by this Bahia-born engineer.

CALMON, PEDRO, *Historia do Brasil, 1500–1800* (3 vols., 3rd ed., São Paulo–Rio de Janeiro, 1939–43).

The first 2 volumes give a good general picture of the colonial period in Brazil.

CALMON, PEDRO, *História social do Brasil. 1° Tomo. Espírito da sociedade colonial* (3rd ed., São Paulo–Rio de Janeiro, 1941).

Based primarily on printed sources, this is more a narrative than an analytical history, providing a general interpretation of the colonial period.

CALMON, PEDRO, *História da civilização brasileira* (5th ed., São Paulo–Rio de Janeiro, 1945).

Rather a disjointed account but covers all aspects of colonial society.

CALMON, PEDRO, *História da fundação da Bahia* (Bahia, 1949: Publicações do Museu do Estado — N. 9).

A very general essay on the subject.

CALMON, PEDRO, *História da Casa da Tôrre. Uma dinastia de pioneiros* (2nd ed., Rio de Janeiro, 1958).

A well-documented account of one of the leading Bahian families.

CARDIM, FERNÃO, S.J., *Tratados da terra e gente do Brasil. Introduções e notas de Baptista Caetano, Capistrano de Abreu e Rodolpho Garcia* (Rio de Janeiro, 1925).

Contains interesting details and statistics for the colonial period, as seen by a contemporary historian.

CARDOZO, MANOEL S. 'The lay brotherhoods of colonial Bahia', in *The Catholic Historical Review*, Vol. 33, No. 1 (April 1947), pp. 12–30.

A general description of these brotherhoods with a detailed analysis of the statutes of the coloured Brotherhood of St Anthony of Catagerona.

CARNEIRO, EDISON, *Ladinos e crioulos. Estudos sôbre o negro no Brasil* (Rio de Janeiro, 1964).

A series of essays, including one on the brotherhoods of the Rosary.

Cartas do senado (3 vols., Bahia 195?–3).

Published by the Prefecture of Salvador in the series *Documentos históricos do Arquivo Municipal.* These volumes consist of correspondence from the city council to the Crown and cover the following years: Vol. 1, 1640–73; Vol. 2, 1673–84; Vol. 3, 1684–92.

CASTRO E ALMEIDA, EDUARDO DE, *Inventario dos documentos relativos ao Brasil existentes no Archivo de Marinha e Ultramar de Lisboa* (8 vols., Rio de Janeiro, 1913–36: reprinted from the *Anais da Biblioteca Nacional*, vols. 31, 32, 34, 36, 37, 39, 46 and 50).

The first volume deals with documents relative to Bahia in the period 1613–1762.

Compromisso da Santa Casa da Misericordia da Bahia, approvado na sessão da Junta de 31 de maio de 1896 (Bahia, 1896).

Compromisso da Santa Casa de Misericórdia da Bahia, aprovado em sessão de 28 de março de 1958 (Bahia, 1958).

CORREIA, F. DA SILVA, *Estudos sôbre a história da Assistência. Origens e formação das Misericórdias portuguesas* (Lisboa, 1944).

A survey of charity from antiquity to the sixteenth century. Correia closely follows the thesis of Magalhães Basto (*q.v.*) on the origins of the brotherhood, and corrects Costa Godolphim (*q.v.*) on the dates of foundation of some branches.

DAMÁZIO, ANTÓNIO JOAQUIM, *Tombamento dos bens immoveis da Santa Casa da Misericordia da Bahia em 1862* (Bahia, 1865).

An indispensable record using documents which have since been lost.

DAMPIER, WILLIAM, *A Voyage to New Holland &c. In the year, 1699. Wherein are described the Canary-Islands, the Isles of Mayo and St. Jago. The Bay of All Saints, with the Forts and Town of Bahia in Brasil* (London, 1703).

Dampier visited Bahia in 1699 and described in detail the city, its society, economy and the flora and fauna of the surrounding region.

Documentos historicos da Bibliotheca Nacional do Rio de Janeiro (120 vols., Rio de de Janeiro, 1928–, in progress).

An immense collection of published documents whose value is diminished by the lack of indices to most of the volumes. Vols. 13, 14, 35, 37 and 38 contain documents relevant to the foundation of Bahia; Vols. 33, 34, 56–8, 62, 64–8, 78–80, 86–8 and 89–90 will be found useful for material on the seventeenth century; Vols. 40–55, 59–63, 68–78, 84, 90–2 and 95–8 contain documents on the eighteenth century in Bahia. These volumes contain royal letters, *patentes, provisões, alvarás* and viceroyal correspondence to the Crown and other authorities.

Documentos relativos a Mem de Sá, Governador Geral do Brasil (Rio de Janeiro, 1906; a reprint from Vol. 27 of the *Anais da Biblioteca Nacional*).

Interesting for Mem de Sá's own assessment of his achievements during his term of office.

FERREIRA, FELIX, *A Santa Casa da Misericórdia Fluminense* (Rio de Janeiro, 1898).

A heavily institutional history of the branch of the brotherhood in Rio de Janeiro with detailed analyses of administrative changes in the Misericórdia of Lisbon in the sixteenth century.

FERREIRA MARTINS, J. F., *Historia da Misericordia de Goa (1520–1910)* (3 vols., Nova Goa, 1910–14).

Despite the dates contained in the title Ferreira Martins forces the thesis that Affonso de Albuquerque was the founder of the branch in Gôa. An entirely institutional history with an incoherent narrative and lists of Provedors, regulations and copies of statutes. Primarily useful for the citation of documents. No bibliography or index.

FREYRE, GILBERTO, *Casa-Grande & senzala. Formação da família brasileira sob o regime de economia patriarcal* (11th Brazilian ed., 2 vols., Rio de Janeiro, 1964).

—, *The Masters and the Slaves. A Study in the Development of Brazilian Civilization* (1st Eng. lang. ed., New York, 1946).

A translation by Samuel Putnam from the 4th ed. of *Casa-Grande & Senzala*.

—, *Sobrados e mucambos. Decadencia do patriarcado rural e desenvolvimento do urbano* (3 vols., 2nd ed., Rio de Janeiro-São Paulo, 1951).

—, *The Mansions and the Shanties. The Making of Modern Brazil* (Eng. trans. by Harriet de Onís; New York, 1963).

Both these works by Gilberto Freyre provide an excellent general background to the relationships between the ruling class and slaves in colonial Brazil. The treatment is inter-disciplinary, but with a heavy anthropological bias.

FRÉZIER, AMÉDÉE FRANÇOIS, *Relation du voyage de la mer du Sud aux côtes du Chily et du Perou, fait pendant les années 1712, 1713 & 1714* (Paris, 1716).

—, *A Voyage to the South-Sea and along the Coasts of Chili and Peru in the years 1712, 1713 and 1714* (London, 1717: a translation of the above).

FROGER, F., *Relation d'un voyage fait en 1695, 1696 & 1697 aux Côtes d'Afrique, Détroit de Magellan, Brezil, Cayenne & Isles Antilles* (Paris, 1698).

—, *A Relation of a Voyage Made in the Years 1695, 1696, 1697 on the Coasts of Africa, Streights of Magellan, Brasil, Cayenna, and the Antilles* (London, 1698: a translation of the above).

The accounts of both Frézier and Froger contain interesting descriptions of Bahia in the colonial period.

GAMA BARROS, HENRIQUE DA, *Historia da administração publica em Portugal nos séculos XII a XV* (11 vols., 2nd ed., Lisboa, 1945–54).

The fifth volume is especially useful for the economic situation in Portugal in the thirteenth and fourteenth centuries.

GODOLPHIM, COSTA, *As Misericordias* (Lisboa, 1897).

The first part comprises a general study of the Misericórdia of Lisbon. The second part consists of a list of branches with brief notes. Some of the dates of foundation given by Costa Godolphim have been corrected by Correia (*q.v.*). No index.

História da colonização portuguesa do Brazil. Direcção de Malheiro Dias (3 vols., Porto, 1921–4).

The third volume is useful for Bahia during the early years.

História de Portugal. Edição monumental comemorativa do 8° centenário da fundação da nacionalidade (7 vols. of text and one index volume, Barcelos, 1928–37).

The series is edited by Damião Peres. The fourth volume contains a section on social assistance in Portugal as represented by hospitals, leper houses, inns and the Misericórdias.

JABOATÃO, FR. ANTÓNIO DE SANTA MARIA, *Catalogo genealógico das principaes famílias que procederam de Albuquerques, e Cavalcantes em Pernambuco, e Caramurús na Bahia* (Bahia, 1950: reprinted from Vols. 1–4 (1945–8) of the *Revista do Instituto Genealógico da Bahia*).

Despite several errors, this remains an invaluable guide to the landed aristocracy of colonial Bahia.

LALLEMAND, LÉON, *Histoire de la charité* (4 vols., Paris, 1902–12).

The third and fourth volumes give a useful general survey of charity from the tenth century.

LANDINI, PLACIDO, *Istoria dell'Oratorio e della Venerabile Arciconfraternita di Santa Maria della Misericordia della città di Firenze* (Firenze, 1843).

The first part describes the foundation and administration of the brotherhood.

LAVAL, FRANÇOIS PYRARD DE, *Voyage de François Pyrard de Laval, contenant sa navegation aux Indes Orientales, Maldives, Moluques, Bresil* (2 vols., 3rd ed., Paris, 1619).

—, *The Voyage of François Pyrard of Laval to the East Indies, the Maldives, the Moluccas and Brazil* (2 vols., London, 1887–90; a translation of the above by Albert Gray for the Hakluyt Society).

Contains descriptions of the hospitals of Gôa and the charitable works of that branch of the Misericórdia in addition to a brief description of Bahia in the early seventeenth century.

LEITE, SERAFIM, S.J., *História da Companhia de Jesus no Brasil* (10 vols., Rio de Janeiro–Lisboa, 1938–50).

A fully documented study with complete bibliography and an excellent index. The second and fifth volumes are of interest for the Misericórdias of Bahia and Rio de Janeiro.

o

—, *Artes e ofícios dos Jesuitas no Brasil* (*1549–1760*), (Rio de Janeiro–Lisboa, 1953).
Contains much interesting material on the rôle of the Jesuits in instituting lay brotherhoods for coloured and white people.

Livro do tombo da prefeitura municipal da cidade do Salvador. 1° volume (Bahia, 1953).
Publishes documents of the seventeenth and eighteenth centuries, mainly on land rentals.

Livro velho do tombo do mosteiro de São Bento da cidade do Salvador (Bahia, 1945).
A carefully edited and well produced volume of documents of the seventeenth and eighteenth centuries, many of which concern the Misericórdia.

MARTIN SAINT-LÉON, ÉTIENNE, *Histoire des corporations de métiers depuis leurs origines jusqu'à leur suppression en 1791* (4th ed., Paris, 1941).
Provides points of comparison with the study of Franz-Paul Langhans (*q.v.*) on the social charity undertaken by brotherhoods formed of artisans.

MONTI, G. M., *Le confraternite medievali dell'Alta e Media Italia* (2 vols., Venezia, 1927).
Chapters 4–7 of the first volume are especially relevant to the present study.

NÓBREGA, MANOEL DA, *Cartas do Brasil* (*1549–1560*) (Rio de Janeiro, 1931).
Contains interesting descriptions of the problems faced by the early settlers in Bahia.

OLIVEIRA, EDUARDO FREIRE DE, *Elementos para a historia do municipio de Lisboa* (17 vols. of text, Lisboa, 1885–1911 and 2 index volumes, Lisboa, 1942–1943).
An indispensable guide to the early administration of the city of Lisbon, with numerous references to the Misericórdia.

OTT, CARLOS, *Formação e evolução étnica da cidade do Salvador* (2 vols., Bahia, 1955–7).
A thoroughly documented work with statistical analyses of immigrants and artisans.

—, *A Santa Casa de Misericórdia da cidade do Salvador* (Rio de Janeiro, 1960; published in the series *Publicações da Diretoria do Patrimônio Histórico e Artístico Nacional*, No. 21).
An exhaustive study of the artistic and architectural aspects of the Misericórdia. The second part consists of documents which contain much of importance for the social historian.

PROBER, KURT, *Catálogo das moedas brasileiras* (São Paulo, 1966).
A detailed historical exposition of the complexities of Brazilian currency, with useful illustrations of the coins described. Written by a trained numismatist it is highly technical and corrects Sombra (*q.v.*) on several points.

RIBEIRO, VITOR MAXIMIANO, *A Santa Casa da Misericordia de Lisboa* (*subsídios para a sua historia*) *1498–1898* (*Historia e memorias da Academia Real das Sciencias de Lisboa*, nova serie, 2ª classe, tomo 9, parte 2, Lisboa, 1902).
Although this remains the basic work on the subject, it leaves much to be

desired. Useful for an extensive bibliography on branches of the Misericórdia in Portugal.

ROCHA PITTA, SEBASTIÃO DA, *Historia da America Portugueza desde o anno de mil e quinhentos do seu descobrimento até o de mil e setecentos e vinte e quatro* (2nd ed., Lisboa, 1880).

Second edition of a book first published in Lisbon in 1730. The author belonged to a leading family of colonial Bahia and his work is valuable as it provides an insight into contemporary attitudes towards events in eighteenth-century Bahia.

RUY, AFFONSO, *História política e administrativa da cidade do Salvador* (Bahia, 1949).

—, *Historia da Câmara Municipal da cidade do Salvador* (Bahia, 1953).

Both these detailed works rely heavily on unpublished archival sources, but no references to the precise nature of these sources are made in the footnotes. Both volumes suffer from the lack of an index.

SALLES, FRITZ TEIXEIRA DE, *Associações religiosas no Ciclo do Ouro* (Belo Horizonte, 1963; the first volume in a series published by the Centro de Estudos Mineiros).

A well-balanced study of the brotherhoods of Minas Gerais in the eighteenth century based on the analysis of their *Compromissos*. The relations between the different brotherhoods and racial prejudices are well documented.

SALVADOR, VICENTE (RODRIGUES PALHA) DO, *História do Brasil, 1500–1627. Revista por Capistrano de Abreu e Rodolfo Garcia* (4th ed., São Paulo, 1954).

An early history of Brazil containing some interesting references to the Misericórdia of Bahia.

SAMPAIO, THEODORO, *Historia da fundação da cidade do Salvador* (Bahia, 1949).

Published posthumously, this work contains several errors, and the conclusions have been modified by the subsequent publication of further volumes of the *Documentos historicos* (*q.v.*).

SANTOS FILHO, LYCURGO, *Uma comunidade rural do Brasil antigo. (Aspectos da vida patriarcal no Sertão da Bahia nos séculos XVIII e XIX)* (São Paulo, 1956).

A fascinating narrative of a cattle-ranching family in the interior of the Captaincy of Bahia, told in considerable detail and well illustrated. Evokes interesting points of comparison with the history of the sugar plantation aristocracy of Bahia described by Wanderley Pinho (*q.v.*).

SILVA RÊGO, ANTÓNIO DA, *História das Missões do Padroado Português do Oriente. India, 1500–1542* (Lisboa, 1949).

A missionary history but contains much of more general interest.

—, *Documentação para a história das Missões do Padroado Português do Oriente. India* (12 vols., Lisboa, 1947–58).

Covering the period 1499–1582, these volumes contain numerous references to the branches of the Misericórdia in Africa and Asia.

SIMONSEN, ROBERTO C., *História econômica do Brasil (1500/1820)* (4th ed., São Paulo, 1962).

First published in 1937, this work remains the best general economic history of Brazil.

SOARES, JOSÉ CAETANO, *Macau e a Assistência (Programa médico-social)* (Lisboa, 1950).

The only history of the Misericórdia of Macao, but poorly documented, and with little on the period before 1700.

SOMBRA, SEVERINO, *Historia monetaria do Brasil colonial. Repertorio cronológico com introdução, notas e carta monetária. Edição revista e aumentada* (Rio de Janeiro, 1938).

A good general work, but should be used in conjunction with the more detailed study by Prober (*q.v.*).

SOUSA, GABRIEL SOARES DE, *Notícia do Brasil. Introdução, comentários e notas pelo Professor Pirajá da Silva* (2 vols., 8th ed., São Paulo, 1949).

Contains one of the earliest descriptions of the Misericórdia of Bahia in the late sixteenth century.

SOUSA CAMPOS, ERNESTO DE, 'Santa Casa de Misericórdia da Bahia. Origem e aspectos de seu funcionamento', in the *Revista do Instituto Geográfico e Histórico da Bahia*, Vol. 69 (Bahia, 1943), pp. 213–52.

A compilation of references to the Misericórdia of Bahia culled from various sources, especially Damázio (*q.v.*) and Vilhena (*q.v.*).

VERGER, PIERRE, *Bahia and the West Coast Trade (1549–1851)* (Ibadan, 1964).

An excellent monograph.

VIANNA FILHO, LUIZ, *O negro na Bahia* (Rio de Janeiro–São Paulo, 1946).

A good general study, in part superseded by the work of Pierre Verger (*q.v.*).

VIEIRA, ANTÓNIO, S. J., *Cartas do Padre António Vieira* (3 vols., Coimbra, 1925–8), edited by J. Lúcio de Azevedo.

—, *Obras* (4 vols., Lisboa, 1940), edited by Hernani Cidade, with a biographical study.

A reading of the letters and the sermons of this great missionary is essential for an understanding of the social problems present in seventeenth-century Brazil.

VILHENA, LUIZ DOS SANTOS, *Recopilação de noticias soteropolitanas e brasilicas contidas em XX cartas, que da cidade do Salvador Bahia de Todos os Santos escreve hum a outro amigo em Lisboa, debaixo de nomes alusivos, noticiando-o do estado daquella cidade, sua capitania, e algumas outras do Brasil. Annotadas por Braz do Amaral* (2 vols., Bahia, 1922).

This detailed account of all aspects of Bahian life was written by the Professor of Greek at Bahia at the end of the eighteenth century, and is required reading for any student of Bahian history.

Viollet, Paul, *Histoire des institutions politiques et administratives de la France* (3 vols., Paris, 1890–1903).

The third volume is particularly relevant for the European background to the present study.

Wanderley de Araújo Pinho, José, *História de um engenho do Recôncavo. Matoim–Novo–Caboto–Freguezia. 1552–1944* (Rio de Janeiro, 1946).

A well-documented account of a sugar plantation family, many of whose members were brothers of the Misericórdia.

Wiznitzer, Arnold, *Jews in Colonial Brazil* (New York, 1960).

The basic treatment of the subject.

Zucchi, Maria, 'The Misericordia of Florence', in *The Dublin Review*, No. 229, Vol. 114 (1894) pp. 333–45.

Corrects Landini (*q.v.*) on several points and gives details of the administration of the brotherhood, based on private archives. Numbers 487–502 of *The Dublin Review* were entitled *The Wiseman Review*.

II. SECONDARY SOURCES

Albuquerque, Affonso de, *Cartas* (7 vols., Lisboa, 1884–1935).

Almeida, Fortunato de, *História da igreja em Portugal* (4 vols., Coimbra, 1910–24).

Alves, Marieta, *A Santa Casa de Misericordia e sua igreja. Guia turistico* (Bahia, 1962).

America, being the latest and most accurate description of the New World containing the Original of the Inhabitants, and the Remarkable Voyages thither. The Conquest of the Vast Empires of Mexico and Peru, and other Large Provinces and Territories, with the several European Plantations in those Parts (London, 1671).

Azevedo, Thales de, *Ensaios de antropologia social* (Bahia, 1959).

Barbinais, le Gentil de la, *Nouveau Voyage au tour du monde par Monsieur Le Gentil. Enrichi de plusieurs Plans, Vûës et Perspectives des principales Villes & Ports du Pérou, Chily, Bresil, & de la Chine* (3 vols., Paris, 1727).

Barros, João de, *Ásia. Dos feitos que os portugueses fizeram no descobrimento e conquista dos mares e terras do Oriente* (4 vols., 6th ed., Lisboa, 1945–6).

Bastide, Roger and Fernandes, Florestan, *Brancos e negros em São Paulo* (2nd ed., São Paulo, 1959).

Boxer, C. R., *Fidalgos in the Far East, 1550–1770. Fact and Fancy in the History of Macao* (The Hague, 1948).

—, *The Great Ship from Amacon. Annals of Macao and the Old Japan Trade, 1555–1640* (Lisboa, 1959, reprinted in 1963).

—, *The Christian Century in Japan, 1549–1650* (Berkeley and London, 1951).

—, *Salvador de Sá and the Struggle for Brazil and Angola, 1602–1686* (London, 1952).

BOXER, C. R., *South China in the Sixteenth Century. Being the narratives of Galeote Pereira, Fr. Gaspar da Cruz, O.P., Fr. Martín de Rada, O.E.S.A. (1550–1575)*, edited by C. R. Boxer for The Hakluyt Society (London, 1953).

—, *The Dutch in Brazil, 1624–1654* (Oxford, 1957).

—, *Four Centuries of Portuguese Expansion, 1415–1825: A Succinct Survey* (Johannesburg, 1963).

— and AZEVEDO, CARLOS DE, *Fort Jesus and the Portuguese in Mombasa, 1593–1729* (London, 1960).

—, 'Fidalgos portuguêses e bailadeiras indianas (séculos XVII e XVIII)', in the *Revista de História*, No. 45 (São Paulo, 1961) pp. 83–105.

—, 'Moçambique island and the "carreira da Índia"', in *Studia*, No. 8 (July 1961), pp. 95–132.

BRAAMCAMP FREIRE, A., 'Compromisso de confraria em 1346', in *Archivo Historico Portuguez*, Vol. 1, No. 10 (Lisboa, 1903), pp. 349–55.

CAETANO, MARCELLO, *A administração municipal de Lisboa durante a 1ª dinastia, 1179–1383* (Lisboa, 1951).

CALMON, PEDRO, *História da literatura bahiana* (Bahia, 1949).

CHEVALIER, FRANÇOIS, *Land and Society in Colonial Mexico. The Great Hacienda* (Berkeley and Los Angeles, 1963: translated from *La Formation des grands domaines au Mexique. Terre et société aux XVIᵉ–XVIIᵉ siècles*, published in Paris in 1952).

CORREIA, F. DA SILVA, *Portugal sanitário* (Lisboa, 1937).

COSTA, LUIZ MONTEIRO DA, *Igreja e convento de Nossa Senhora da Soledade* (Bahia, 1958).

COURACY, VIVALDO, *O Rio de Janeiro no século dezessete* (2nd ed., Rio de Janeiro, 1965).

COUTO, DIOGO DO, *O soldado prático*, ed. Rodrigues Lapa (Lisboa, 1937).

Crónica de D. Dinis (Coimbra, 1947).

DUBY, G., *La société aux XIᵉ et XIIᵉ siècles dans la région mâconnaise* (Paris, 1953).

DUNDAS, ROBERT, *Sketches of Brazil, including new views on tropical and European fever* (London, 1852).

FAZENDA, JOZÉ VIEIRA, 'A Santa Casa da Misericórdia do Rio de Janeiro' in the *Revista do Instituto Histórico e Geográfico Brasileiro*, Vol. 69 (Rio de Janeiro, 1908), pp. 7–51.

FRYER, JOHN, *A new account of East India and Persia being nine years' travels, 1672–1681* (3 vols., London, 1909–15), edited by William Crooke for the Hakluyt Society.

GIRAM, JOÃO RODRIGUES, S.J., *Carta anua da Vice-Província do Japão do Ano de 1604*, ed. António Baião (Coimbra, 1933).

GÓIS, DAMIÃO DE, *Crónica do Felicíssimo Rei D. Manuel* (4 vols., Coimbra, 1949–55).

GRAHAM, MARIA, *Journal of a voyage to Brazil and residence there during part of the years 1821, 1822, 1823* (London, 1824).

HARING, C. H., *The Spanish Empire in America* (third printing, New York, 1957).

HERLIHY, DAVID, 'The Agrarian Revolution in Southern France and Italy, 801–1150', in *Speculum*, Vol. 33 (1958), pp. 23–41.

História das artes na cidade do Salvador (Salvador, 1967).

KINDERSLEY, Mrs, *Letters from the Island of Teneriffe, Brazil, the Cape of Good Hope, and the East Indies* (London, 1777).

LAMEGO, ALBERTO, *A Academia Brazileira dos Renascidos. Sua fundação e trabalhos inéditos* (Brussels–Paris, 1923).

LANGHANS, FRANZ-PAUL (DE ALMEIDA), *As corporações dos ofícios mecânicos-subsídios para a sua história* (2 vols., Lisboa, 1943, 1946).

LAWRENCE, A. W., *Trade Castles and Forts of West Africa* (London, 1963).

LOPES, FERNÃO, *Crónica de D. João I* (2 vols., Porto, 1945, 1949).

MARSHALL, C. E., 'The Birth of the Mestizo in New Spain', in the *Hispanic American Historical Review*, Vol. 19 (1939), pp. 161–84.

MARTINS, MÁRIO, S.J., *Peregrinações e livros de milagres na nossa Idade Média* (2nd ed. Lisboa, 1957).

MATOS, GREGORIO DE, *Obras completas* (6 vols., Rio de Janeiro, 1923–33), edited by the Academia Brasileira.

MCALISTER, L. N., 'Social Structure and Social Change in New Spain', in the *Hispanic American Historical Review*, Vol. 43 (1963), pp. 349–70.

MORAES, RUBENS BORBA DE, *Bibliographia brasiliana. A bibliographical essay on rare books about Brazil published from 1504 to 1900 and works of Brazilian authors published abroad before the Independence of Brazil in 1822* (2 vols., Amsterdam–Rio de Janeiro, 1959).

NUNES, DUARTE, 'Notícia da fundação da Santa Casa da Misericórdia', in *Revista do Instituto Histórico e Geográfico Brasileiro*, Vol. 21 (Rio de Janeiro, 1858), pp. 158–60.

PARRY, J. H., *The Spanish Seaborne Empire* (London, 1966).

PIERSON, DONALD, *Brancos e pretos na Bahia. Estudo de contacto racial* (São Paulo–Rio de Janeiro, 1945).

PINA, RUI DE, *Crónica de El-Rei D. João II* (Coimbra, 1950).

PIRENNE, HENRI, *Mediaeval Cities: their origins and the revival of trade* (Princeton, 1946).

ROZMITAL, LEO OF, *The travels of Leo of Rozmital through Germany, Flanders, England, France, Spain, Portugal and Italy, 1465–1467* (Cambridge, 1957), translated and edited by Malcolm Letts for the Hakluyt Society.

SANTOS FILHO, LYCURGO, *História da medicina no Brasil* (2 vols., São Paulo, 1947).

SCHURZ, WILLIAM LYTLE, *The Manila Galleon* (New York, 1959; first published 1939).

SMITH, ROBERT C., *Arquitectura colonial* (Bahia, 1955).

SOARES, UBALDO, *A escravatura na Misericórdia. Subsídios* (Rio de Janeiro, 1958).

SOARES, UBALDO, *O passado heróico da Casa dos Expostos* (Rio de Janeiro, 1959).

SOUSA CAMPOS, ERNESTO DE, *Santa Casa da Misericórdia de Santos* (São Paulo, 1943).

SOUTHEY, ROBERT, *History of Brazil* (3 vols., London, 1810–19).

STRIPLING, G. W. F., *The Ottoman Turks and the Arabs, 1511–1574* (Illinois Studies in the Social Sciences, Vol. 26, No. 4, Urbana, 1942).

TAVERNIER, JEAN BAPTISTE, *Travels in India by Jean Baptiste Tavernier* (2 vols., London, 1889; trans. by V. Ball).

VIEGAS, ARTHUR, *O poeta Santa Rita Durão. Revelações históricas da sua vida e do seu século* (Brussels–Paris, 1914).

ZURARA, GOMES EANNES DE, *Crónica da tomada de Ceuta por El Rei D. João I* (Lisboa, 1915).

Index

Abyssinia, 24
Academy of History, Royal, 76
Academy of the Forgotten, 75-6
Academy of the Re-born, 76-7
Acapulco galleon, 35
Adoption, common in Salvador, 182, 315
Affonseca Lemos, António José de: report
 on *Misericórdia* of Salvador by, 101,
 114n., 318, 339-45; on municipal
 council, 114n., 318
Affonso IV, King Dom, 7, 14
Affonso VI, King Dom, concern for slaves, 266
Affonso Henriques, King Dom, 9, 11, 14
Agriculture: difficulties of, in medieval
 Europe, 1-2; in Portugal, 7; in Bahia,
 65-8, 69, 148, 152-3; lack of royal
 interest in, 70. *See also* Cattle; Manioc;
 Sugar industry; Tobacco
Aguiar, Domingos Lucas de, 109, 121, 123
Aguiar, João de Mattos de, *see* Mattos de
 Aguiar, João de
Albergaria(s), *see* Hostelries
Albergaria de Payo Delgado, 8
Albergaria de Rocamador, 8-9
Albergaria dos Mirléus, 8
Albert, Cardinal Archduke, 212
Albuquerque, Affonso de: capture of Gôa,
 25, 46, 234; mixed-marriage policy, 25-
 26, 174-5
Albuquerque, Felippa de, *see* Cavalcante e
 Albuquerque, Felippa de
Albuquerque, Fernão de, 28-9
Albuquerque, Mathias de, 29
Alcaide-Mór, 82, 247-8
Alcobaça, 10
Alenquer, 18
Alexander VIII, Pope, 103
Algarve, reconquest of, 7; plague in, 7
Alimbamba(s), 265
Aljubarrota, battle of, 7
All Saints, Bay of: physical description of,
 43; origin of name, 45; French pirates

in, 37, 38, 45, 46; early Portuguese
 settlement in, 45-6; visited by Amerigo
 Vespucci, 45; landing of Tomé de
 Sousa in, 47
Almada, 136
Almeida, Faustino de, 326
Almeida, Dom Francisco de, 25; mixed-
 marriage policy, 174
Almeida, Dom Lourenço de, 70
Almeirim, 6
Almotacé(s), elected by *Misericórdia*, 35; in
 Salvador, 132
Almotacé(s) da limpeza, appointed in Salva-
 dor, 266-7
Alms: distributed by corporations of arti-
 sans, 2; by brotherhoods, 3; for ran-
 som of captives, 11; abuse in application
 of, 13. See also *Misericórdia, Santa Casa da*
Alto Douro, hostelries in, 8
Álvares Cabral, Pedro, 37, 44, 45
Álvares Correia (Caramurú), Diogo, 45-6
Álvares da Silva, José, 123
Álvares de Azevedo, João, 249n.
Álvares de Vasconcellos, João, 279
Alves Fontes, João, 249, 249n.
Alvor, Count of, 27
Amadeus III, Count of Maurienne and Savoy, 14
Amazon, River 44, 282
Ambaca, 36
Amboina, see *Misericórdia, Santa Casada*
Amerindians: deployment in Brazil of, 44-5;
 co-operate with French pirates, 37, 45,
 46; conversion of, 39; collaborate in
 building of Salvador, 48; championed
 by António Vieira, S.J., 74; treatises on,
 71; music of, 77; susceptible to disease,
 261, 290; in prison, 282; in hospital,
 282; distrust of European medical treatment, 282; in Jesuit villages, 77, 261,
 290, 333; miscegenation with, 45-
 46, 138-9; Portuguese Crown policy

towards, 138–9, 145, 338; secularisation, of, 338; as slaves, 151, 261, 333; numbers in Salvador of, 50; not included in census, 226; build hospital accommodation in Rio de Janeiro, 40; in New Spain, 358; 'tame Indians', 50

Amsterdam, 55

Anchieta, S.J. José de, 40, 71, 290

Andreoni, S.J., Giovanni Antonio, *see* Antonil, S.J., André João

Angeja (Dom Pedro de Noronha), Count of Villa Verde and Marquis of, 270, 327; and *Misericórdia* of Salvador, 111, 258, 328

Angola : conquest of, 36, 65; garrisons of, 36; slave trade with Brazil, 51, 55, 59, 68, 117, 252; pattern of trade with Brazil and Portugal, 59, 349; deportation of convicts to, 236, 252; Dutch in, 55, 56. See also *Misericórdia, Santa Casa da*, Luanda, Massangano; Luanda; Slaves and Slavery; Bantu

Antonil, S.J., André João, 60; quoted 61, 62

Antunes Lima, Manuel, 132, 156

Arabia, 33

Arassúahy, 70, 154, 245

Araújo, Francisco de, 90, 164

Araújo, Francisco Gil de, 95

Araújo, João de, 164

Araújo, Matheus de, 164

Araújo de Aragão, Manuel de, 118

Araújo de Góis, Gaspar de, 119

Araújo de Góis, Jorge de, 88

Araújo e Azevedo, Francisco de, 279

Araújo Soares, Bento de, 149

Arcos (Dom Marcos de Noronha e Brito), 6th Count of, 334; treatment of gypsy problem, 243; his recommendations on royal enquiry into *Misericórdia* of Salvador, 318, 342–4

Arcos (Dom Marcos de Noronha e Brito), 8th Count of, 229

Aristocracy, landed, in Bahia, *see* Landowners, latifundian

Artisans : corporations in medieval Europe of, 2–3; in Portugal, 12, 19; shortage in East of, 25, 27; representation on municipal council, 126, 156; examinations of, 126, 280; registration of, 126; privileged by commissions, 131, 156; financial prosperity achieved by, 63 156–7; on the fleet of Tomé de Sousa,

47, 48; labour deployment in Salvador of, 130; delusions of grandeur entertained by, 133; donors to the *Misericórdia*, 156–7. See also *Misericórdia, Santa Casa da*, class distinctions

Ashantis, 182

Assumar, Count of, 211

Atlantic Islands, emigration to Brazil from, 50, 60, 129; sugar-cane cultivation, 52. *See also* Madeira, Azores

Atouguia (Dom Luís Pedro Peregrino de Carvalho Meneses de Ataíde), Count of, and *Misericórdia* of Salvador, 109, 271, 275, 284–5

Audiencia, jurisdiction in Spanish America of, 356

Avila, Garcia d', 60, 89

Avila Pereira, Garcia d', 118

Aviz, John of, 7

Azevedo Arvelos, Dionísio de, 111, 328

Azores, see *Misericórdia, Santa Casa da*

Bahia : various meanings of the term, 48 n.; captaincy of, 46; gold strikes in, 70, 154; drought in, 65, 66, 67, 69, 148; climate of, 66–7, 81, 148, 289; smallpox in, 65, 289, 290; Backlands of, 44; townships founded in the Recôncavo of, 244. *See also* Salvador, city of; Recôncavo; Slaves and slavery; Cattle; Cattle ranchers; Sugar planters; Sugar industry

Bandeirantes, 60, 337

Banguê, see *Misericórdia, Santa Casa da*, Salvador, burial of slaves

Bantu slaves, compared with Sudanese, 51, 68, 141 n.

Baptista Carneiro, João, 133

Baptista Ferreira, Manuel, 157

Baptista Lemos, José, 144

Barbados, unrefined sugar of, 59. *See also* West Indies

Barbeiro(s), examinations of, 280

Barbosa, Jacinto, 132

Barbosa Leal, Pedro : holds office in the *Misericórdia*, 118, 121, 125, 150, 206, 324, 325; legacy by, 151; landowner, 118; founder of townships, 151

Barbuda, Francisco de, 88

Barreto, Francisco, 86

Barreto, Roque da Costa, *see* Costa Barreto, Roque da

Barros, Cristóvão de, 87
Barros, João de, quoted, 24 ; donatory, 38
Bassein, 175. See also *Misericórdia, Santa Casa da*
Bay of All Saints, *see* All Saints, Bay of
Beira Alta, 8
Beja, 12
Belém, 268
Belém do Pará, 261. See also *Misericórdia, Santa Casa da*
Benedictines, *see* St Benedict, Order of
Bengal, 287. See also *Misericórdia, Santa Casa da*
Benin, Gulf of, 117. *See also* Angola ; Slaves and slavery
Bissau, see *Misericórdia, Santa Casa da*
Black Death, 5
Boipeba, 265
Bom Jesus de Villa Nova, 286–7
Bond, Captain, 283 n.
Borges, Pedro, 47, 236
Borges de Barros, Domingos, 109–10
Borsi, Piero, 3
Braga, 8, 11. See also *Misericórdia, Santa Casa da*
Brande, Cornelius van den, 57
Brandy, sugar cane, export of, 59 ; restrictions on distillation of, 245
Brasília, 261
Brazil : discovery of, 37 ; early colonisation of, 37–9, 45–6 ; donatory system in, 38–39, 46 ; Portuguese Crown attitude towards, 37, 38, 39, 235, 236, 256 ; colonisation of, compared and contrasted with Portuguese in Orient, 175–6, 234–6, 239–40, 243 ; as place of exile, 236, 282 ; under the Dutch domination, 55–7 ; difficulty of law enforcement in, 239–44 ; foundation of townships in, 39–40, 244 ; development of the interior of, 60
Brazil fleets : irregularity of, 65, 337 ; delayed, 67, 68 ; currency on, 178, 179 ; women on, 178–9
Brazil wood, *see* Dye woods
Brito, António de, 109
Brito de Sousa, António de, 206
Brotherhoods
Our Lady, Mexico City, 357
Our Lady, Mother of God, Virgin Mary of Mercy, Lisbon *et al.*, see *Misericórdia, Santa Casa da*

Brotherhoods—*contd.*
Our Lady of Guadalupe, Salvador, 216–17, 220
Our Lady of the Immaculate Conception, Salvador, 203, 204
Our Lady of the Immaculate Conception, Sintra, 13
Our Lady of Loreto, Lisbon, 213 n.
Our Lady of Mercy, Florence : foundation of, 3 ; class distinctions in, 4 ; governing body of, 4 ; alleged influence on *Misericórdia* of Lisbon, 14 ; undertakes burials, 4, 202
Our Lady of Mercy, Lisbon, 13, 15
Our Lady of the Rosary, Salvador, 142, 143, 213, 217–19, 220
Our Lady of the Rosary and Ransom, Rio de Janeiro, 142 n.
Our Lady of Succour, Salvador, 94, 216–217, 220
St Anthony of the Barra, Salvador, 64
St Anthony of Catagerona, Salvador, 142–143, 203, 204
St Bartholomew, Lisbon, 213 n.
St Benedict, Salvador, 219–20, 230
S. Corona, Milan, 237
S. Giovanni Decollato, Florence, 3, 237
St Lazarus, Salvador, 271–2, 288
St Leonard, Viterbo, 3
St Peter, Rio de Janeiro, 215 n.
St Peter, Salvador, 214
The Chapel of the Cathedral, Salvador, 103
The Holy Body of Christ, Salvador, 270, 272, 286
The Holy Cross, Rio de Janeiro, 215 n.
The Holy Cross, Salvador, 214, 215–16
The Most Holy Sacrament, Salvador, 96
The Worthy Men, Beja, 12–13
Brotherhoods, lay : in Italy, 3–5, 202, 237 ; in Portugal, 12–13, 202 ; in Spanish America, 356–7
Buboes, 262
Buitrago, Caetano, 122
Bungo, see *Misericórdia, Santa Casa da*
Burgos, Jerónimo de, 164, 169, 181

Caatinga, 44, 60
Caboclo : term explained, 138–9 ; use of term banned, 338 ; Portuguese Crown attitude towards, 138–9
Cabral, Pedro Álvares, *see* Álvares Cabral, Pedro

Cachaça, see Brandy, sugar cane

Cachoeira : centre of the tobacco industry, 61 ; raised to township, 244 ; miners leave horses at, 243 ; river port, 44, 307 ; municipal council's rejection of *Misericórdia*'s petition, 307 ; dowries for girls from, 193. See also *Misericórdia, Santa Casa da*

Caetano, Marcello, 12

Cairo, visited by Pero de Covilhã, 24

Cairú, 193, 265

Caldas, 11, 82 n.

Caldas, José António, 77, 226

Calhambola(s), 141

Calicut, 25. See also *Misericórdia, Santa Casa da*

Calmon, João, 104, 120

Calmon, Pedro, 80–1, 82

Calmon de Almeida, Miguel, 325 n.

Camamú, 193, 265

Cambay, King of, 46

Cambembe, 36

Cananéia, Bay of, 38

Cangaceiros, 243

Cannanore, 25. See also *Misericórdia, Santa Casa da*

Capelas de missas, 167–8. See also *Misericórdia, Santa Casa da*, Salvador, legacies for the saying of masses

Capoâme, 60, 264

Capuchin Friars, in Salvador, 271, 322, 329 n.

Caramurú, *see* Álvares Correia, Diogo

Cardim, S.J., Fernão, 50, 71

Cardoso de Barros, António, 47

Carmelite Order : in Salvador, 50, 51, 52, 58, 87 ; insistence on 'purity of blood', 137 ; in Rio, 223 ; harbour criminals, 241

Carmelites, Third Order of, in Salvador ; refusal to admit New Christians, 136, 143 ; refusal to admit coloured person, 143 ; landed aristocracy members of, 63, 149 ; businessmen members of, 348 ; ossuary of, 229 ; not privileged by Crown, 93

Carneiro, Dom Belchior, 34

Carta(s) de examinação, 126. See also Artisans

Carta(s) de saúde, 268

Carta(s) de seguro, 241

Carvalho e Albuquerque, José Pires de, *see* Pires de Carvalho e Albuquerque, José

Carvalho e Melo, José Sebastião de, *see* Pombal, Marquis of

Carvalho Mascarenhas, Miguel, 172, 187, 249 n., 308 n.

Casa da Suplicacação (Supreme Court of Appeals), 75, 190, 239

Castelo Branco, António Ferrão, Provedor of the *Misericórdia*, 112 ; rebuked by João V, 112 ; reports on mutiny of garrison, 112, 189 ; involved in dowry scandal, 189–90 ; Governor of São Tomé, 112, 253, 255

Castelo Melhor (João Rodrigues de Vasconcellos e Sousa), Count of, Provedor of the *Misericórdia*, 91, 94, 116 n.

Castro, António de, 123

Castro, Diogo de, 47

Castro, Francisco de, 88

Castro, Dom Martim Affonso de, 28

Catherine of Braganza, Queen of England, 65, 305

Cattle : raising in Bahia, 60 ; killed by drought, 65, 148 ; precarious livelihood, 148, 149 ; on sugar plantations, 54, 60, 67, 150 ; lack of hygiene in slaughter of, 264 ; as pledges for loans, 63 ; licences for slaughter of, 305

Cattle ranchers in Bahia : compared and contrasted with sugar planters, 61 ; threatened by expropriation of lands, 62, 117 ; religious fervour, 150–1 ; Provedors of the *Misericórdia*, 118, 120, 125, 150, 162 ; legacies to the *Misericórdia* by, 118, 149, 150–1, 159 ; affected by economic crisis, 71, 152–3 ; mobile life of, 61, 69 ; abuse of power in the Backlands by, 62 ; on municipal council, 62–3 ; independence of spirit of, 117 ; in New Spain, 357

Cavalcante e Albuquerque, Cristóvão, 144

Cavalcante e Albuquerque, Felippa de, 119

Cavalcante e Albuquerque, Gonçalo Ravasco : lineage of, 112, 119 ; Provedor of the *Misericórdia*, 112, 119 ; alleged self-interest over siting of retirement house, 105, 324, 325 ; municipal councillor, 325 ; intervention in election of abbess of Desterro, 113 ; expelled from Third Order of the Carmelites, 113 n.

Cavalcante e Albuquerque, Lourenço, 119, 165

Cavalcante e Albuquerque, Theresa de, 177 n.

Ceará : Dutch in, 57 ; cattle ranchers in, 60 ; *cangaceiros* in, 243

Ceballos, Don Pedro de, 78

Ceuta, 7, 24
Ceylon, 28, 175
Chagas disease, 261
Charles II, King of England, 53, 65
Chaul, see *Misericórdia, Santa Casa da*
China : trade in co-operation with Portuguese, 25 ; treatment of sick in, 34
Chinese goods in Salvador, 159
Chinese slave in Salvador, 230
Cistercians, 10
Class distinctions and class discrimination in Salvador, 124–35 ; in the garrison, 133 ; in the Convent of the Desterro, 134, 321 ; in execution of justice, 246 ; in burials, 218, 229 ; in the granting of dowries, 176–7 ; inducement to send girls to Portugal, 177–8 ; allied to sexual honour, 181, 311–12, 321. See also *Misericórdia, Santa Casa da*
Clement XII, Pope, 104
Clergy : popular respect for, 179–80 ; gold smugglers, 157 ; in Minas Gerais, 157 ; non-adherence to vow of celibacy, 157, 158, 332, 335 ; forbidden to hold office in brotherhoods, 109 ; brotherhood of, 214 ; relations with *Misericórdia* of Salvador, 102–3, 195–6, 214, 258 ; hold office in the *Misericórdia*, 94, 104, 109, 120, 123, 127–8 ; employees of the *Misericórdia*, 94, 195–6, 207–8, 281 ; brothers of the *Misericórdia*, 125, 214 ; donors to the *Misericórdia*, 90, 158–9, 164 ; not included in census, 226 ; employees of *Misericórdia* of Lisbon, 22 ; clash with *Misericórdia* of Gôa, 214 n. ; oppose Affonso de Albuquerque's marriage policy, 26
Cochin, 25. See also *Misericórdia, Santa Casa da*
Cock, Mr, 187 n.
Coelho, Duarte, 39
Coelho de Sousa, João, 73
Coelho Pôrto, Manuel, 249 n.
Coimbra, 8, 9, 10, 11, 14, 16, 17, 137 ; University of, 240, 279. See also *Misericórdia, Santa Casa da*
Collegia funeraticia, 202
Colocação familiar, 298, 299
Colombo, 28, 33. See also *Misericórdia, Santa Casa da*
Colour prejudice and discrimination : in brotherhoods and Third Orders of Salvador, 143–4, 329 ; in Jesuit College, 329 ; in convents, 329 ; in garrison, 133 n.; 141, 218–19 ; in militia, 140 ; Portuguese Crown policy of, 140, 246, 355, 357–8 ; present in wills, 181 ; allied to class prejudice, 138, 143, 144, 281–2 ; in execution of justice, 246, 256 ; in New Spain, 357–8. See also Miscegenation ; *Misericórdia, Santa Casa da*
Compadrio, term explained, 315
Compagnia Maggiore di Santa Maria del Bigallo (Florence), 4
Conceição, Fr Bernardo da, 270, 272
Confraternities, see Brotherhoods
Constantinople, 2
Contracts and contractors in Brazil, 37, 307
Contreiras, Fr Miguel, 15–16
Convicts and deportees : in building of Salvador, 47 ; sent to Brazil, 236, 282 ; to Asia, 236 ; to Angola, 236, 252 ; as sailors, 252, 265 ; conscripted to replenish garrisons, 252 ; in prison of Salvador, 251, 252, 253 ; crimes of, 246–247 ; suggested commutation of sentences of, 85. See also *Misericórdia, Santa Casa da*
Coque, Francisco, 187, 190
Coromandel coast, 33
Corregedor da comarca, 239
Correia, Felippe, 94, 149, 171–2, 181, 182, 186, 191
Correia de Aragão, Catharina Francisca, 240
Costa, Dom Duarte da, 85
Costa, Isabel da, 179, 186
Costa, João da, 156
Costa, Sebastião Dionísio da, 132
Costa Barreto, Roque da, 41
Costa e Faria, Luís da, 109, 334
Costa Ferreira, Joseph da, 242
Costa Franco, Francisco da, 279–80
Council of the Indies, 356
Council of Trent, 102
Couto, Diogo do, quoted, 235 ; mentioned, 27 n., 239
Covilhã, Pero de, 24
Crime : in Asia, 234–5 ; in Bahia, 240–6 ; predominance of coloured offenders, 246 ; penalties for, 246–7
Cruz, O.P., Fr Gaspar da, 34 n.
Cubas, Bras, 39
Culto metrico, see Pires de Carvalho e Albuquerque, José

Currency, shortage of, in Salvador, 69–70, 98, 102, 178, 323

Dahomey, 68. *See also* Slaves and slavery
Damao, see *Misericórdia, Santa Casa da*
Damázio, António Joaquim, 80, 88 n., 327
Dampier, William, quoted, 58, 66, 187 n.; mentioned, 63, 65, 263, 272
Datheus, 295
Defeito de sangue, see Colour prejudice and discrimination; Religious prejudice and discrimination
Desembargadores (High Court judges): venality in Portuguese India of, 235; in *Relação* of Salvador, 239–40; rivalry with municipal council, 238–9, 248, 353; Provedors of the *Misericórdia*, 111–12, 120 n., 239, 328
Desterro, Convent of the, see Poor Clares
Diamonds: export from Brazil of, 78, 153, 154; discovery of, 70; smuggling of, 70, 154, 245; Crown monopoly of, 338
Dias, Anselmo, 97, 105, 108, 110, 122
Dias, Bartholomeu, 24
Dias, Henrique, 218–19
Dias, Luís, 47
Dias Baião, Francisco, 181
Dias d'Avila family, 62, 118, 125
Dias d'Avila, Francisco (2nd), 150, 151
Dias d'Avila, Francisco (3rd), 110, 203, 240–241
Dias de Novais, Paulo, 36
Dias de Ottões, António, 95, 166, 171, 186, 191, 221
Dias do Prado, Francisco, 246 n.
Diniz, King Dom, 7, 8, 12; as philanthropist, 9, 11; European contacts of, 14; protector of agriculture, 67
Diseases in Bahia: pattern of, 260–2, 288–290; slaves as carriers of, 225, 261–2, 265, 289–90. *See also* East Indiamen; Slaves and slavery; *Misericórdia, Santa Casa da*, Salvador, hospitals
Diu, see *Misericórdia, Santa Casa da*
'Dog does not eat dog' attitude in Portuguese India, 235
Domingues, Pedro, 183
Donatories in Brazil, 38–9, 46
Dorth, Jan van, 56
Dote de Inglaterra e paz de Holanda, 65, 305
Douro, 8, 129
Dowries: as Portuguese Crown policy, 25–6,

32, 33, 175–6; currency for sent to Portugal from Brazil, 178; class distinctions in legacies for, 176–7; for slave girls, 182–3. See also *Misericórdia, Santa Casa da*
Duarte, Dom, 13
Dundas, Robert, 263
Dutch: trading companies, 55; invasion of Brazil, 55–7; occupation of Salvador, 56–7, 87–8, 239; families in Salvador, 129; in west African ports, 55, 56; destroy archives of *Misericórdia*, Salvador, 80, 88; António Vieira's sermons on relief of Salvador from, 73–4; attacks on Portuguese settlements in Orient, 28, 33, 359; war indemnity to, 65, 305
Dye woods, 37, 52, 59; Portuguese Crown monopoly of, 38
Dysentery, 48, 83, 262, 265, 289

East India Company, Dutch, 55
East India Company, English, 283
East India Company, Ostend, 287
East Indiamen, Portuguese: put into Salvador with sick aboard, 159, 263, 265–6, 269, 270–1, 286–8, 293; diet on, 265, 287; quality of sailors on, 8, 252, 265
Educanda, term explained, 322
Einbeck, 295
Emigration: from Portugal to Brazil, 50, 60–61, 129, 225; from Atlantic Islands, 50, 60, 129; bachelors predominate in, 50, 120, 121, 123; of Jews from Spain and Portugal to Holland, 55; of Jews to Brazil, 136
Encomienda(s), 357
Encostada, term explained, 330
England, exports to Portugal from, 337
English: ships on the Brazilian coast, 282–3; consul in Salvador, 187 n.; residents in Salvador, 129, 283; intervention in the River Plate, 78; attacks on Portuguese in Orient, 359
English Alliance, 78
Ergotism, 10
Espendola, Henrique Luís d', 158
Espírito Santo, see *Misericórdia, Santa Casa da*
Estatística da Bahia, see Oliveira Mendes, Manuel de
Estatística de Lisboa, 16
Ethiope resgatado, etc., *see* Ribeiro Rocha, Manuel

Évora, 6, 8, 9, 11, 14, 16, 359. See also
    Misericórdia, Santa Casa da

Factories (trading posts), Portuguese, 24, 25,
    28, 32, 35, 38, 174
Fado, 78
Falta de justiça, 239
Famine: in western Europe, 1; in Portugal,
    6, 7; in Paraíba, 67
Fanado, 70
Fernandes, António, 139, 256–7
Fernandes, Diogo, 181, 183
Fernandes, Gonçalo, 16
Fernandes, Joanna, 94, 186, 187, 191, 197
Fernandes Barros, Bernardim, 220
Fernandes Costa, Manuel, 153–4, 168
Fernandes de Freitas, Domingos, 151, 168,
    171, 186; 191, 349
Fernandes de Tavora, Estevão, 81, 83
Fernandes do Sim, Francisco, 118, 186, 191
Fernandes Vieira, Matheus, 218 n.
Fernando Noronha, Island of, 252
Ferraz de Sousa, Domingos, 210
Ferreira, Felix, 22, 40
Ferreira, Francisco, 136
Ferreira, Jerónima, 177
Ferreira, Jorge, 89, 92, 94, 176–7
Ferreira de Mattos, José, 113–14
Ferreira Machado, Simão, quoted, 155
Fialho, Hilario dos Santos, 123
Fifths, on gold, 70
Flanders, 37
Fleets, see Brazil fleets
Florence, 3, 4, 14, 295
Flour, see Manioc
Fort Jesus, 25, 36
Forts and fortresses, Portuguese: on Indian
    Ocean, 25, 28, 32, 174; in Salvador, 46,
    58, 283, 287
Foundlings: hospices in western Europe for,
    295; alleged product of miscengenation,
    312–14; responsibility in Portuguese
    Empire for, 296–8. See also *Misericórdia*,
    Santa Casa da
Frades, Ilha dos, 43, 193, 267 n.
Francis I, King of France, 46
Francis Xavier, St, see Xavier, (St) Francis
Franciscans, see St Francis, Order of
Franco, Paulo, 189
Freire, Gomes, 131
Freire, Luzia, 180
Freire, Thomé, 27

Freire de Andrada, Gomes, 78, 289, 353
Freitas, António de, 154
French: pirates in Bay of All Saints, 37–8,
    45–6; Capuchins in Salvador, 322;
    Sisters of Mercy in Salvador, 361;
    surgeon in Salvador, 290; in Seven
    Years War, 78
Freyre, Gilberto, 233
Frézier, Amédée François, 226, 265, 272;
    quoted, 320
Friars, see St Francis, Order of; Capuchin
    friars; St Benedict, Order of; Carme-
    lite Order
Froger, F., 272, 320
Frois, S.J., Luís, 35
Fulahs, 182
Funerals: by brotherhoods in Portugal, 13,
    202; in Roman Empire, 201–2; by
    brotherhoods in Salvador, 203–4, 209–
    213, 214–20; social prestige attached to,
    165–6, 204, 205, 213, 272; extravagance
    of, 167. See also *Misericórdia, Santa
    Casa da*, Salvador
Furtado de Castro do Rio de Mendonça (Vis-
    count of Barbacena), Affonso, 116 n.
Furtado de Mendonça, João, 215

Galvêas (Dom André de Mello e Castro),
    Count of, 271, 280, 286, 287; relations
    with *Misericórdia*, 109, 250; economic
    reports by, 64, 66; and slave trade, 68,
    121
Gama, Vasco da, 25
Gama de Andrade, Simão da, 89
Garimpeiro, 155
Garrisons, Portuguese: undermanned in
    India, 174; manned by convicts, 252;
    in Angola, 36; in São Tomé, 58;
    soldiers of treated by *Misericórdia*:
    Angola, 36–7; Mozambique, 35; Salva-
    dor, 216, 265–6, 270–1, 275, 284–6, 292–
    293, 347; Salvador: treated by municipal
    medical staff, 269, 284; unpopularity of
    service in, 284; barracks of, 271, 284,
    285; military hospital for, 270–1, 285,
    360; brotherhoods of, Salvador, 214,
    215–16; Rio de Janeiro, 215 n.; tem-
    porary marriages by soldiers of, 309–10;
    mutiny of Salvador garrison, 112, 189;
    undermanned, 58; conscription of
    gypsies suggested, 243; pay of, 293;
    class distinctions in, 133; colour dis-

crimination in, 133 n., 141, 218–19;
composition of, 52, 284, 285; coloured
regiment of Henrique Dias in, 218–19
Gôa : capture of, 25, 46, 234; commercial
importance of, 23, 25, 29; defence of,
28; adultery prevalent at, 33; *Relação*
of, 235, 239; lack of white women at,
25–6, 174–5; colonisation of, compared
with Salvador, 117, 175; hospitals of,
29–32; visited by Pyrard de Laval, 29,
33, 51, 87. See also *Misericórdia, Santa
Casa da*
Goch, Michiel van, 57
Godinho da Maia, João, 196 n.
Goiana, 57
Goiás, 60, 78
Góis, Theodora de, 182
Gold : exports from Brazil, 78, 130, 153, 154,
338; discovery in Minas Gerais, 70;
strikes in Bahia, 70, 154; routes to mining areas, 44; repercussions on Bahian
economy, 67–8, 70, 78, 111; royal
fifths on, 70; smuggled, 70, 154, 157,
242; re-exported from Portugal, 337;
African, 24, 59, 159; Portuguese as
carriers of Chinese, 25; legacies to *Miseri-
córdia* of Salvador derived from mining
areas, 153–4; precarious existence in
mining areas, 153–4; difficulty of law
enforcement in mining areas, 234, 243–
245; townships in mining areas, 154,
155; decline of Brazilian gold, 338
Goldsmiths, 126, 130
Gomes, Pedro, 112, 118
Gomes Monteiro, Simão, 198, 339
Gomes Oliveira, António, 154
Gonçalves, João, 165
Gonçalves da Câmara Coutinho, António
Luís, 75
Gonçalves da Rocha, António, 188
Gonçalves de Mattos, Pedro, 91, 92
Gonçalves Pena, José, 326
Gonçalves Pereira, António, 109
Gonçalves Viana, Manuel, 312
Good Hope, Cape of, 24
Governors in Brazil, relations with governor-
general or viceroy, 50, 78, 353
Graham (Lady Callcott), Maria, 228–9, 264
Grão Pará trading company, 338
Guanabara, Bay of, 38, 40
Guedes, António, 256
Guedes de Brito family, 62

Guedes de Brito, António, 118, 203
Guimarães 9, 11
Guinea, 18, 55; slave trade from, 24 n., 50,
59
Guisenrode family, 129
Gypsies in Brazil, 243

Haulthain, Colonel, 57
Hausa, 141
Heeren XIX, 55, 57
Henrique Dias, Regiment of, 218–19
Heyn, Piet, 56
Hides, exported from Bahia, 59, 60. *See also*
Cattle
Historia da America Portugueza, see Rocha
Pitta, Sebastião da
Historia militar do Brasil, see Mirales, José
de
Holland, 55. *See* Dutch
Honorato, João, 255
Hormuz, 25, 28, 29. See also *Misericórdia,
Santa Casa da*
Hospitallers, Order of, 11
Hospitals : of corporations of artisans, 2, 12;
in Portugal, 8–9, 11–12, 13; reformed in
Portugal, 11–12, 13–14, 16–17. See also
Misericórdia, Santa Casa da
Hospitals
All Saints (Gôa), 29
All Saints (Lisbon), 14, 22, 84, 296
Our Lady of Candles (Salvador), 85,
260
Our Lady of Mercy (Gôa), 29
Royal Hospital of the Holy Spirit (Gôa),
29, 84
St Christopher (Salvador), 260 f.
St Elisabeth (Salvador), 360, 364
St Mary of the Innocents (Santarém), 295
San Andrés (Lima), 356
The Holy Spirit (Rome), 295
The Immaculate Conception (Mexico
City), 357
The Poor (Gôa), 29
Hostelries, 8–9, 10, 11

Igarassú, see *Misericórdia, Santa Casa da*
Ilhéus, 158. See also *Misericórdia, Santa
Casa da*
India, Portuguese colonisation of, 25–6, 174–
175, 234–5
Indiamen, *see* East Indiamen
Indians of Brazil, *see* Amerindians

Indios mansos, 50
Influenza and pulmonary ills, in Salvador,
261, 288, 289
Innocent VIII, Pope, 14
Inquisition, not established in Brazil, 50, 52
Interest rates in Salvador, 70, 106, 197, 198
Isabel, Queen of Portugal, 11, 295
Italy : brotherhoods in, 3–5 ; links with
Portugal, 14–15
Itamaracá, 38, 57. See also *Misericórdia,
Santa Casa da*
Itapagipe, 89
Itaparica, Island of, 43, 46, 57, 193
Itapoan, 60, 89
Ivory, 55, 59, 159

Jaboatão, O.S.F., Fr António de S. Maria,
77
Jacobina, 69, 154 ; gold strike at, 70 ; status
of township, 244 ; notorious for crimes,
244 ; chief justice resident at, 245
Jacques, Cristóvão, 37–8
Jaffna, 33. See also *Misericórdia, Santa Casa da*
Jaguaripe, 193, 241, 244
Japan, Portuguese carriers for trade, 25
Jerónimo, João, 273
Jesuits, edifying rôle in Portuguese expansion,
26 ; on fleet of Tomé de Sousa, 47 ; as
intermediaries for ransom of captives,
33 ; persecuted in Oporto, 76 ; expelled
from Brazil, 77, 338 ; missionary villages
of, 77, 261, 290, 333 ; trading interests in
Pará and Maranhão, 338 ; administrators
of Royal Hospital of the Holy Spirit in
Gôa, 29 ; rôle in foundation of *Misericórdias*, 36, 40, 41, 81, 82 ; collaborate
with *Misericórdias* in medical assistance,
41 ; relations with *Misericórdias* : in
Gôa, 29, 33, 236 ; in Mozambique, 35 ;
in Salvador, 89, 90–2, 197 ; Jesuit College of St Antão, Lisbon, 91–2 ; Jesuit
College, Salvador, 49, 50, 51, 52, 58, 71,
77, 87, 271 ; as military hospital, 271,
360 ; admittance of coloured pupils to,
329. *See also* Anchieta, José de ; Cardim, Fernão ; Nóbrega, Manoel da ;
Vieira, António
Jesú, Theresa de, 193
Jesus Maria, Theresa de, 332 n.
Jesus Maria Joseph, 252 n.
Jews, expelled from Castile, 6 ; emigration
from Spain and Portugal to Holland, 55 ;

emigration to Brazil, 136 ; prominent in
Salvador, 50, 52, 135–6. *See also* New
Christians ; Religious prejudice and
discrimination
Joanes, River, 60
João I, King Dom, *see* John of Aviz
João II, King Dom, 7, 11 ; anti-plague
measures, 6 ; hospital reform, 13–14,
296 ; rôle in discoveries, 24, 25
João III, King Dom, 6, 102 ; initiates settlement of Brazil, 38–9, 45–7, 52 ; attitude
to overseas possessions, 235–6
João IV, King Dom, orders relief of Itaparica,
57 ; borrows from *Misericórdia* of Gôa, 28
João V, King Dom, 64, 67, 69, 78, 102, 110,
113, 114, 177, 218, 248, 270, 279, 283 n.,
290 ; concern for slaves, 139–40, 141–2,
219–20, 255–7 ; fear of slave revolt, 141 ;
threatens expropriation of latifundia, 62,
117 ; administrative policy of, 108 ;
Maecenas of arts, 76 ; abolishes *juiz do
povo* in Salvador, 126 ; recognises suitability of business class for municipal
service, 64 ; policy on race relations,
140 ; interest in natural history, 108,
249 ; restricts passage of girls from
Brazil to Portugal, 179 ; shocked by
amorality of Salvador, 301–2 ; order on
laxity in terms of address, 135 ; disregard for Bahian economy, 70 ; his
death as end of an era, 337 ; opposes
Bahian slave-trade monopoly, 117 ;
relations with coloured brotherhoods,
219–20 ; intervention in Third Order of
St Francis, Salvador, 113–14, 213, 241 ;
relations with *Misericórdia*, Salvador,
101, 107, 108, 110, 111–12, 189, 215,
219–20, 249, 253, 257, 258, 292–3, 300–
301, 305–6, 307 ; authorises foundation
of a *Misericórdia* at Vila Rica de Ouro
Prêto, 134
João, Manuel, 156–7, 168
John of Aviz, 7
José I, King Dom, 337, 342 ; prohibits use of
term New Christian, 145 ; encourages
white–Amerindian marriages, 139, 338 ;
orders transfer of Brazilian capital, 79 ;
alters interest rate on loans, 198 ; ap-
proves establishment of a leprosery in
Salvador, 290 ; orders enquiry into
Misericórdia, Treasury and municipal
council of Salvador, 114, 339

Juan I, King of Castile, 7
Juiz de fora, 100, 238, 239, 279
Juiz do crime, 239
Juiz do povo, 126
Juiz ordinário, 238
Justice : effectiveness in the Orient and Brazil
    compared, 234–6, 243 ; right of appeal
    to Crown, 139, 257 ; physical difficulty
    of enforcing law in Brazil, 234, 243, 244–
    245 ; influenced by powerful families,
    100, 239–41 ; hearsay evidence accepted,
    256 ; use of judicial torture, 256–7 ;
    dilatory administration of, 17, 100, 253 ;
    creation of townships improves effective-
    ness, 244. See also *Relação*

Kaffir girls, 26, 34
Kilwa, 25, 35
Kindersley, Mrs Nathaniel Edward, 166, 272

La Barbinais, Le Gentil de, 167, 311
La Pèlerine, 38
Lafões, 9
Lamberto, Francisco, 323, 324
Land values, fall in Bahia of, 197
Landowners, latifundian, in Bahia : nature
    of, 61–2, 117, 134, 354, 357 ; prominent
    in local government, 62–3 ; prominent
    in brotherhoods and Third Orders, 63,
    117–18, 125 ; donors to the *Misericórdia*,
    117–18, 149–51, 162–3 ; intermarried,
    63, 119 ; influence on justice, 100, 239–
    241 ; religious belief of, 152, 162, 165–8 ;
    decline of, 110–11, 119–20 ; compared
    with New Spain, 357. *See also* Cattle
    ranchers ; Sugar planters
Lapa convent, Salvador, 130, 132
Laudémio, term explained, 90
Lavradio (Dom António de Almeida Soares
    e Portugal), 1st Marquis of, 216
Lavradio (Dom Luís António de Almeida
    Portugal), 2nd Marquis of, 207
Leal, Joanna, 137, 138
Leather, *see* Hides
Legal discrimination : against Negroes, 246 ;
    against slave, 246, 255–6, 311
'Legitimacy of the womb' attitude in colonial
    Bahia, 180–1
Lei da ventre, term explained, 314
Leiria, 11, 12
Leitão, Dom Pedro, 94
Leite, S.J., Serafim, 40 n., 80

Lencastre, Dom João de, 75, 270 ; civic
    interests of, 58, 171, 247, 266 ; founds
    townships, 244 ; report to king on girls
    being sent to Portugal, 178 ; interven-
    tion in judiciary, 253 ; advocates use of
    Amerindian girls as servants, 333
Leôa, 81
Leonor, Queen of Portugal, as a philanthro-
    pist, 11–12 ; rôle in foundation of the
    Misericórdia, 1, 15–16
Leproseries : in Portugal, 8, 9–10, 13 ; in
    Salvador, 271–2, 288, 290. See also
    Misericórdia, Santa Casa da, Gôa, Ma-
    cao
Leprosy : in Portugal, 9 ; in Salvador, 262,
    288 ; confused with scurvy, 290
Levant, decline of, 25
Lichthart, Jan Corneliszoon, 57
Lima, 356
Lima, Helena de, 332
Limoeiro prison, Lisbon, 17
Linschoten, J. H. van, 33
Lisbon : population of, 313 ; plague in, 6 ;
    Castilian siege of, 7 ; earthquake, 337 ;
    imports from England, 337 ; position in
    triangular trade with Brazil and Angola,
    59, 117, 349. See also *Misericórdia,
    Santa Casa da* ; Hospitals
Lopes, Fernão, 7
Lopes, João, 158
Lopes, Joseph, 183
Lopes Oleira, Maria, 184
Lourenço Marques, see *Misericórdia, Santa
    Casa da*
Luanda : foundation of, 36 ; slave trade, 51,
    59 ; triangular trade with Brazil and
    Portugal, 59. See also *Misericórdia,
    Santa Casa da* ; Angola
Lundú, 78
Luzã, see *Misericórdia, Santa Casa da*

Macao, Portuguese settlement at, 25, 234 ;
    care of foundlings at, 297 ; shortage of
    white women at, 175 ; vice at, 301. See
    also *Misericórdia, Santa Casa da*
Madeira, 52. See also *Misericórdia, Santa
    Casa da*
Madre de Deus, Island of, 43, 193
Madre de Deus, Fr Manuel da, 256–7
Mafalda, 14
Mafia, 35
Magalhães, Bento de, 308 n.

Mahim, see *Misericórdia, Santa Casa da*
Mal de Luanda, see Scurvy
Malabar, 24
Malacca, 25, 28. See also *Misericórdia Santa Casa da*
Malaria, 261, 288
Mameluco(s), term explained, and Portuguese Crown policy towards, 138–9
Mangalore, see *Misericórdia, Santa Casa da*
Manila, 106. See also *Misericórdia, Santa Casa da*
Manioc, 67, 153, 264–5
Mannar, see *Misericórdia, Santa Casa da*
Manuel I, King Dom, 6, 25, 26, 45, 46, 236; undertakes hospital reform in Portugal, 14, 16–17; title adopted by, 37; encouragement of sugar industry, 52; disinterest in Brazil, 37; rôle in foundation of *Misericórdia*, 1, 16–17; grants privileges to *Misericórdia*, 17–19, 99, 237–8, 296, 304
Mãos de obra, 67. *See also* Slaves and slavery
Maragogipe, 193
Maranhão, 57, 60, 69, 243; measles epidemic in, 290; Jesuits in, 338
Maré, Island of, 43
Mariana, 155
Marques, André, 121, 123, 291
Martins Pereira, Francisco, 104, 120, 127, 129
Mascarenhas, Dom Fr Simão, 36
Mascarenhas Pacheco Pereira Coelho de Melo, José, 76–7
Massangano, see *Misericórdia, Santa Casa da*
Mato Grosso, 60, 78
Mattos, Gregório de, 144; biographical sketch, 74–5; quoted, 167
Mattos, João de, 63, 150, 167, 168, 182, 349
Mattos de Aguiar, João de, biographical sketch of, 63–4; philanthropist, 98, 118, 150, 152, 160, 170, 187, 188, 192, 283, 323, 327; provision for the saying of masses, 104, 152, 168; legacy administered by the *Misericórdia*, 122, 190, 196, 197, 303, 326–7, 335, 340
Mauritsstad, 57
Measles, 261, 289–90
Medici, Cosimo de, 4
Medicines, imported into Brazil, 263, 267–8, 278, 291
Melo, Dom Francisco Manuel de, quoted, 320 n.

Melo e Castro, Francisco de, 34
Mendonça Furtado, Diogo de, 56
Meneses, Dom Aleixo de, 27, 28, 32
Meneses, Dom Rodrigo José de, 362
Merchants and businessmen : prejudice against, in Portuguese world, 120; semitic stigma of, 120–1, 135; achieve financial consolidation in Salvador, 63–4; social acceptance of, 64, 120, 121; hold office in the *Misericórdia*, 121–4, 135, 354; donors to the *Misericórdia*, 151–2, 159, 162–3; brotherhood of, 64; prominent in the Third Order of the Carmelites, 348; on municipal council, 64; relations with sugar planters, 69–70; Board of Business Men, 121; term 'merchant' defined by Dom Pedro II, 125; in Vila Rica de Ouro Prêto, 134–5, 155; in New Spain, 357
Mestiços, Portuguese Crown policy towards, 139
Mexico City, 357
Milan, 3, 295
Military service, *see* Garrisons; Soldiers
Militia, at Salvador, 131, 140–1
Mina (Elmina), S. Jorge da, 24
Mina women, qualities of, 182
Minas (Dom António Luís de Sousa Tello de Meneses), 2nd Marquis of, 288
Minas Gerais, 60, 69, 78; discovery of gold in, 70, 78, 234; slaves in, 67–8, 141–2, 148; emigration from Bahia to, 154–5; townships in, 155; precarious life in, 153–4; clergy in, 157; crime prevalent in, 234, 243; tolls on river passages in, 307; end of gold boom in, 338; routes to, 44
Minho, 8, 129
Mining and miners : townships in Minas Gerais, 155; townships in Bahia, 154, 244; encampments, 154; mobility of miners, 69; outbid planters for slaves, 67–8; leave horses at Cachoeira, 243
Mint at Salvador, 58, 69, 245, 323, 324, 326
Mirales, José de, 77
Miranda Ribeiro, Agostinho de, 130
Miranda Ribeiro, João de, 130, 132
Miscegenation : in India, 25–6, 174–5; Portuguese policy of, 138–9; with Amerindian, 45–6, 138–9; with Negresses, 138–9, 182, 183, 309–10; medical aspects of, 260–2; foundling alleged product of, 312–14

Misericórdia, Santa Casa da, branches of :
Africa, 36–7, 365 ; Far East, 34–5, 365 ;
Brazil, 39–41, 365 ; India, 27–34, 365
Amboina, 35
Azores, 365
Bassein, 34
Belém do Pará, 40
Bengal, 34 n.
Bissau, 365
Braga, 151, 349
Bungo, 35
Cachoeira, 194 n.
Calicut, 34 n.
Cannanore, 34
Chaul, 33
Cochin, 33, 236
Coimbra, 17
Colombo, 33
Damao, 34 n.
Diu, 33, 35
Espírito Santo, 40, 360
Évora, 19
Gôa : foundation, 27 ; *Compromissos*, 27,
116, 297, 350 ; royal privileges, 27 ;
membership numbers, 27 ; class distinc-
tion, 27 ; expulsion, 27 ; threatened
with excommunication, 27 ; 'rigged'
elections, 27, 352 ; loans to official
bodies by, 28–9, 352 ; relations with
Crown, 28, 32, 294 ; relations with
municipal council, 28, 29, 32, 297, 352 ;
relations with viceroys or governors, 27,
28, 29, 32, 107, 116–17, 352 ; relations
with the Jesuits, 29–32, 33 ; relations
with archbishop, 27, 28, 32 ; relations
with ecclesiastical authorities, 27, 29 ;
relations with other branches of the
Misericórdia, 33 ; dispute with clergy,
214 n. ; decline of, 360 ; hospitals administered by, 29–32, 84, 351 ; leper
house, 29, 351 ; retirement houses, 32–3 ;
care for foundlings, 297, 315 ; ransom of
captives, 33, 351 ; *orfãs del Rei*, 32 ;
loans on poor securities, 107, 352 ;
difficulty of filling executive posts, 352 ;
executor of wills, 28, 33 ; aid for prisoners, 33 ; colour discrimination, 32, 33 ;
religious discrimination, 32
Hormuz, 34
Igarassú, 41
Ilhéus, 40
Itamaracá, 40

Misericórdia, Santa Casa da—contd.
Jaffna, 33
Lisbon : foundation, 1, 14–17 ; royal
privileges, 17–19, 99, 237–8, 304–5, 350 ;
class distinction, 1, 20 ; *Compromissos*, 1,
16, 19–22, 96, 124–5, 350 ; alleged
Italian influence in foundation, 14–15 ;
elections, 20, 21 ; duties of *Mesa*, 21–2 ;
executor of wills, 18, 28 ; relations with
municipal council, 18, 19, 296–7 ; relations with judiciary, 18–19 ; relations
with other branches of the *Misericórdia*,
91, 93, 349, 350 ; autonomy from ecclesiastical authorities, 82 ; administers
hospital, 22, 84, 296 ; care for foundlings, 296–7, 304–5, 313–14, 316 ; aid
for prisoners, 17–18, 21–2, 237 ; expulsion, 20–1 ; *mordomos*, 21–2 ; accompanying and burial of condemned, 20,
237 ; official functions, 20
Lourenço Marques, 365. *See also* Mozambique
Luanda, 365 ; foundation, 36 ; membership, 36 ; hospital, 36, 349, 351–2 ;
Crown financial aid, 36, 351–2 ; aid for
prisoners, 36 ; care for foundlings, 297 ;
preference on sale of slaves, 36 ; relations with other branches of the *Misericórdia*, 33, 36–7, 349, 351 ; decline, 36,
360; relations with municipal council, 297
Luzã, 137
Macao, 294, 365 ; foundation, 34 ; hospital,
34 ; *Compromisso*, 34, 35, 116, 350 ;
royal privileges, 34–5 ; 'rigged' elections, 35, 352 ; loans on poor securities,
35 ; care for foundlings, 34, 297, 330 ;
orphanage, 34 ; leper house, 34, 351 ;
dowries, 34 ; finances Japan voyages, 35 ;
relations with municipal council, 297,
352 ; relations with governor-general,
34, 352 ; difficulty of filling executive
posts, 352 ; relations with other branches of the *Misericórdia*, 33 ; religious
discrimination, 34
Madeira, 23, 365
Mahim, 34 n.
Malacca, 33
Mangalore, 34 n.
Manila, 34 n., 35
Mannar, 34
Massangano, 36–7
Mombasa, 36

Misericórdia, Santa Casa da—contd.

Mozambique, 35. *See also* Lourenço Marques

Muscat, 34 n.

Nagasaki, 35

Negapattinam, 34 n.

Olinda, 40, 349

Oporto, 16, 19, 296

Paraíba, 40

Ponte de Lima, 349

Pôrto Seguro, 40

Rio de Janeiro : foundation, 40 ; burial of slaves, 223 ; care for foundlings, 298 ; hospital, 351–2 ; aid for prisoners, 352 ; Crown financial aid, 351–2 ; relations with governor, 223 ; governor as Provedor mooted, 117 n. ; relations with *Misericórdia* of Salvador, 349, 351

Salvador : foundation, 80–6 ; *Compromissos*, 96, 97–8, 104, 362–3 ; royal privileges, 93–4, 99–103, 163–4, 212–13, 237–238, 249, 252, 254, 345–6 ; infringement of privileges, 99–103, 208–12, 214, 215–216, 217–18, 341, 347 ; Papal privileges, 103–4, 257 ; archives destroyed by Dutch, 80, 88 ; official functions, 105, 133, 258, 341 ; described by Gabriel Soares de Sousa, 87 ; membership numbers, 88, 127–9 ; *irmão de maior condição*, term defined, 20, 125 ; *irmão de menor condição*, term defined, 20, 125–6 ; *irmão da vara*, 204, 207 ; *homem de azul*, 204, 232 ; class distinctions, 104, 106, 124–135, 144, 254–5, 363 ; expulsion of brothers, 122, 133–4, 135, 138, 194, 195 n., 207, 210, 214, 242, 255, 287 ; professions of brothers, 129–30 ; place of origin of brothers, 129 ; election of *Mesa*, procedure, 105–6, 363 ; 'rigged' elections, 97, 106–10, 111–12, 342 ; *Junta*, 97, 104–5, 137, 363 ; *Junta Deliberativa*, 363 ; *Definitório*, 363 ; *mordomo das obras*, 363 ; *mordomo das locações*, 363 ; *mordomo do contencioso*, 363 ; *mordomo de fora*, 363 ; *mordomo(s) dos presos*, 100, 103, 237, 247, 252, 254–5 ; *mordomo(s) das visitadas*, 322 ; viceroys or governors-general as Provedors, 86, 88, 91, 94, 116–17 ; High Court judges as Provedors, 111–12, 120 n., 239, 328 ; ecclesiastics as Provedors, 94, 104, 109, 120, 120 n. ; difficulty of filling executive

Misericórdia, Santa Casa da—contd.

posts, 108, 109, 121–3, 338, 344 ; landowners as Provedors, 63, 117–20, 125, 150, 162 ; business class holding office, 121–4, 135, 354

Relations with the Portguese Crown, 100, 107, 108, 110, 111–12, 146, 189, 211, 215, 219–20, 249, 253, 257–8, 271, 294, 300–301, 307, 317–18, 323, 324, 325, 328–9, 332, 333, 347–8 ; subject of royal enquiries, 100–1, 114, 129, 318, 328 n., 339–45 ; Crown financial aid, 84, 87, 168, 271, 292–3, 300, 305–6, 341, 346, 347, 351 ; relations with Jesuits, 89, 90–2, 197 ; relations with municipal council, 101–2, 132, 294, 298–301, 324–5, 326, 329, 347 ; municipal aid, 146, 292, 306–7, 317, 341, 342, 344, 345, 346 ; relations with viceroys or governors-general, 107, 108, 109–10, 111, 120, 171, 189, 207, 216, 219, 222–4, 239, 258, 271, 275, 283, 284–285, 302–6, 318, 328, 329, 331–2, 333, 334, 338, 342–4, 347–8 ; relations with other brotherhoods and Third Orders, 93–4, 144, 208–21, 270, 286 ; relations with judiciary, 99–101 ; relations with ecclesiastical authorities and clergy, 102–103, 125, 195–6, 214, 258, 302–3, 331, 346, 347 ; relations with other branches of the *Misericórdia*, 91, 93, 148, 253–4, 348–50, 351, 360 ; relations with religious orders, 89, 90, 209–212.

Colour prejudice and discrimination, 125, 143–4, 188, 218, 232, 280, 329, 334, 343 ; religious prejudice and discrimination, 124, 136–8, 144, 188, 205–6, 278, 280, 329, 334 ; legal staff, 254, 255–6 ; medical staff, 94, 278–80 ; clergy, 94, 195–6, 207–8, 281 ; *propinas*, 341, 342, 343 ; status and obligations of the Provedor, 109–10, 111–12, 116, 118, 341, 344 treasurer, 121–4, 340, 342, 344

Financial policy, 90, 92–3, 98, 149–50, 163–165, 197, 341 ; maladministration and misappropriation of funds, 106–7, 114, 122–123, 198, 199–200, 274, 340–2 ; property-owner, 88, 89, 90, 149–50, 163–4, 341, 364 ; involvement in law-suits, 90–2, 100–2, 198, 300–1, 339, 341 ; affected by Bahian economic situation, 98, 106, 110–11, 123, 146, 151, 159–72, 196–200,

Misericórdia, Santa Casa da—contd.

343, 345; social background of benefactors, 118–19, 149–59; form of legacies, 163–5; financial extent of legacies, 149, 160–1, 169–70; legacies for the saying of masses, 88–9, 90, 103–104, 107, 120, 149, 150–1, 152, 154, 156–157, 158, 162, 167–70, 172; legacies for charitable purposes, 94, 103, 118–19, 149, 151–2, 154, 158, 164, 168–72, 186–187, 249–50, 275, 291–2, 308, 317, 323; character of legacies, 159–63

Church, 86, 87, 94–5, 102, 103, 118, 129, 133, 172, 195, 229, 245, 272, 273, 277; charnel-house, 229, 276, 277; cemeteries: for lazars, 362; Campo da Pólvora, 228, 229, 269, 362; Campo Santo, 361–2, 364; Beggars' Asylum, 362; Hospice for Lazars, 362; Hospice of S. João de Deus, 362; Asylum of Our Lady of Mercy, 361, 364; Internato Ernestina Guimarães, 364; pharmacy, 274, 277–8, 291, 293; water cistern, 229, 274, 276

Hospitals and medical care, 260–94; foundation, 81–6; St Christopher: structure, 94–5, 273–7; bad conditions, 264, 274–5, 276; cost of maintenance, 269–70, 291–4; madhouse, 276; treatment of soldiers, 216, 265–6, 270–1, 275, 284–8, 292–3, 347; treatment of sailors, 159, 265, 270, 286–8, 293; treatment of civilians, 281–4; treatment of slaves, 182, 269, 281; treatment of Amerindians, 282; poor quality of care, 94, 280, 290–291; alms for convalescents, 152, 283; diseases treated, 288–90; St Elisabeth, 275, 360, 364

Foundling wheel and care for foundlings, 295–319; establishment of foundling wheel, 98, 302–7, 360; cost of maintenance, 299–301, 305–8, 317–19; numbers, 313, 319; wet-nurses, 298, 299, 304–5, 315–16, 317, 318, 339, 340, 360; after-care, 316–17; mortality rate, 315–316; colour of foundlings, 313; Asylum of Our Lady of Mercy, 361, 364

Retirement house, 320–36; construction, 105, 323–8; cost of building and maintenance, 323, 327, 335; living conditions, 264, 327, 332–4; conditions of

Misericórdia, Santa Casa da—contd.

acceptance, 329–30; recluses, 328, 329–330; boarders, 328, 330, 331, 334, 335; fees, 330; slaves employed, 333–4, 334–335; revolt, 334–5; staff, 334, 335; numbers of inhabitants, 324, 326, 329, 331, 335, 341, 342; used as hospital ward, 276; foundling wheel transferred to, 360. *See also* Relations with the Portuguese Crown; Relations with municipal council; Relations with viceroys; etc.

Funerals and burials, 201–33; of brothers and their families, 204–6, 229; symbols of prestige, 165–6, 207, 208; privileges challenged, 208–20; facilities for, 221–222; of slaves, 217, 219, 220, 221, 222–3, 224, 226–7; of children, 223–4, 227; of soldiers, 215–16; charitable, 227–8, 288; numbers of, 224–5, 227, 288; of condemned, 257, 258; staff employed, 232; financial aspects of, 93, 165–6, 215–16, 219, 220–1, 222, 230–2

Prison aid, 234–59; for convicts, 252–3; medical aid, 247, 248, 251–2; legal assistance, 94, 247, 248–9, 253–7; rations distributed, 247, 248, 249–51; feeding slaves, 250–1; accompanying condemned, 86, 257–8. *See also* Royal privileges

Dowries, 173–200; selection for, 188–9; conditions for candidates, 187–8, 190–1; numbers of, 186–7, 191, 193–4, 197; for prospective nuns, 194; for coloured girls, 192–3; places of origin of applicants, 193–4; priorities in allocation of, 189, 191–2, 317; maladministration of, 94, 188, 189–90, 191, 194–5, 198–9. *See also* Religious prejudice; Colour prejudice; Relations with Portuguese Crown; Relations with viceroys; etc.

Santos, 39
São Luís de Maranhão, 41
São Paulo, 40
São Tomé, 34, 365
São Tomé de Meliapor, 33
Sena, 34 n.
Sergipe, 40, 194, 349
Tapuytapera, abolishes class distinction, 131
Tarapur, 34 n.
Tidor, 35
Viana do Castelo, 349

Misericordia, Santa Casa da—contd.
Vila Rica de Ouro Prêto, abolishes class distinction, 134–5
Miunça dos dízimos, 271, 292, 300
Modinha, 78
Moluccas, 25, 35
Mombasa, 25, 28, 35–6. See also *Misericórdia, Santa Casa da*
Moniz Barreto, Diogo, 81, 82, 83, 84
Monomotapa, 35, 86
Monopoly contracts in Brazil: on dye woods, 37, 38; on diamonds, 338
Monteiro de Vide, Sebastião, 332
Montpellier, 295
Mont'Serrat, Church of, 153
Moreira, Joseph, 189
Morgade, Gonçalo de, 90
Mota, Pedro da, 337
Moura Rolim, Dom Francisco de, 88, 116 n.
Mozambique, 25, 35, 279. See also *Misericórdia, Santa Casa da*
Mulattos: Portuguese Crown policy towards, 138–9, 358; social rise of, 139, 143, 358; brotherhoods of, 142–3; in New Spain, 358. *See also* Colour prejudice and discrimination
Municipal councils: in Portugal, impose sumptuary laws, 6; establish leper houses, 9; legally responsible for care of foundlings, 296–7; in Portuguese empire, 269, 358–9; in Spanish America, 269, 356
Cachoeira, 307
Coimbra, 17
Gôa, 28, 29, 32, 297, 352, 359
Lisbon, 9, 18, 19, 296–7, 359
Luanda, 297, 359
Macao, 297, 352, 359
Oporto, 16, 296, 359
Rio de Janeiro, 114
Salvador, monopolised by landed aristocracy, 62–3, 66; reluctance to serve on, 64, 110–11; mercantile class serving on, 64, 354; 'rigged' elections, 114; royal enquiry into, 114, 339; alleged impecuniosity of, 114, 306, 345; valuation of sugar by, 101; perquisites of, 342, 345; responsibility for prison, 247–8; inaugurates examinations of artisans, 126, 280; rivalry with *Relação*, 238–9, 248, 301, 353; measures concerned with urban sanitation, 260, 263–9; medical

Muncipal councils—*contd.*
staff of, 267, 268, 279–80, 284; comedies organised by, 77, 279–80; artisans represented on, 126; judicial function of, 238–39; care for foundlings by, 298–300, 305–6; taxation by, 65–6, 272, 318; plan for slave trade with east Africa, 68; representation to Crown to close gold mines, 67; attitude to foundation of convents and monasteries, 321, 322–3; encourages establishment of leprosery, 271–2; restricts distillation of brandy, 245; concern with economic situation, 65–6, 67; relations with viceroy or governor-general, 266, 269, 302–6, 353; relations with Crown, 65–6, 301, 353. See also *Misericórdia, Santa Casa da*, Salvador
Muscat, see *Misericórdia, Santa Casa da*
Music, in Salvador, 77–8
Muxima, 36

Nagasaki, 23, 25. See also *Misericórdia, Santa Casa da*
Nagô, 141
Nascimento, Clemencia do, 191 n.
Nassau-Siegen, Johan Maurits van, 57
Negapattinam, see *Misericórdia, Santa Casa da*
Negroes: legal discrimination against, 246; social inferiority of, 138, 143, 144–5, 218, 281–2; brotherhoods of, 142–3, 144, 155, 216–20; music of, 78. *See also* Bantu slaves; Colour prejudice and discrimination; Slaves and slavery
Nematode worms, 262
New Christians: term explained, 135; emigration from Spain and Portugal to Holland, 55; emigration to Brazil, 136; prominent in Salvador, 50, 52, 135–6, 138; as contractors in Brazil, 37; in Rio de Janeiro, 138. *See also* Religious prejudice and discrimination
New Spain, society and administration compared and contrasted with those of Portuguese America, 269, 356–8
Ngola, King of Mbundu kingdom, 36
Niger, River, 24
Nis, Manuel Valério de, 154, 180
Nobiliarquia paulista, see Taques, Pedro
Nóbrega, S.J., Manoel da, 47, 71, 81, 82, 85, 175, 262; quoted, 48, 80

Noronha, Fernão de, 37
Nossa S^{ra} do Rosário e S. Gonçalo, 269
Notícia do Brasil, *see* Soares de Sousa,
    Gabriel
Notícia geral desta capitania da Bahia, *see*
    Caldas, José António
Novo Orbe Serafico Brasileiro, *see* Jaboatão,
    O.S.F., Fr António de S. Maria
Nun, Cape, 24
Nunes da Cunha, João, 122 n.
Nunes de Figueredo, João, 132
Nunes Ferreira, Francisco, 205 n.
Nunes Velho, João, 279
Nunes Viana, Manuel, 155
Nuns : in Salvador, 226, 321–2 ; dowries for
    intending, 179–80, 194 ; passage of girls
    from Brazil to Portugal to be, 177–81,
    194, 321, 322, 329. *See also* Poor Clares
Nürnberg, 295

Oficiais mecânicos, term explained, 20, 125.
    See also *Misericórdia, Santa Casa da,
    irmão de menor condição*
Ogilby, John, quoted, 53–4
Old Christian, 138, 144–5, 278, 279. See also
    Misericórdia, Santa Casa da, Salvador,
    religious prejudice and discrimination ;
    Religious prejudice and discrimination
Olinda, 57. See also *Misericórdia, Santa
    Casa da*
Olive oil, 59, 333
Oliveira, Diogo Luís de, 71, 91, 94, 116 n.
Oliveira Correia, Manuel de, 127 n.
Oliveira Mendes, Manuel de, 77
Oliveira Pôrto, Francisco de, 249 n.
Oporto, 8, 9, 11, 16, 76, 296, 359. See also
    Misericórdia, Santa Casa da
Ordenações Affonsinas, 13
Orfãs del Rei, 32, 175
Orphanages : at Macao, 34, 35 ; at Salvador,
    80, 187. See *Orfãs del Rei*
Ostend East India Company, 287
Ott, Carlos, 80, 81, 129, 274
Ouro Prêto, *see* Vila Rica de Ouro Prêto
Ouvidor da comarca, 100
Ouvidor geral : at Gôa, 235 ; at Salvador,
    239
Overseas Council (*Conselho Ultramarino*), 99,
    356

Padre da agonia, 281
Padua, 295

Paes de Azevedo, Aleixo, 119
Paes de Sande, António, 297
Palmares, 250–1
Pampilhosa, 8
Papal bulls, 13–14, 17, 18, 50
Pará, 290, 338
Paraguaçú, River, 38, 44, 307, 313
Paraguaçú, Catharina de, 45
Paraguay, 338
Paraíba, 57, 60, 67. See also *Misericórdia,
    Santa Casa da*
Paripe, 193
Paris, 295
Passports, 157 n., 225
Patatiba, 63
Patta, 35
Peçanha, Manuel, 14
Pederneira, 10
Pedro I, King Dom, 13, 14
Pedro II, King Dom, defines term 'merchant',
    125 ; concern for slaves, 139–40, 222–3,
    251, 268 ; relations with *Misericórdia* of
    Salvador, 100, 271, 293, 323, 325, 333 ;
    protection for *Misericórdias*, 41
Pegu, 33
Peru, 56, 356
Peixoto Viegas, João, 125, 292 n.
Pemba, 35
Pepper, 28, 159, 289
Pereira, Galeote, 34 n.
Pereira, Nuno, 28
Pereira Coutinho, Francisco, 46, 47, 83
Pereira da Silva, Agostinho, 153
Pereira Sodré, José, 241
Pernambuco : captaincy of, 39 ; gallo-
    Portuguese trading rivalry, 37, 38 ;
    sugar cultivation, 39, 52, 60, 111 ; de-
    fence of, 65 ; drought in, 67 ; Dutch
    invasions of, 55, 57 ; *cangaceiros* in, 243 ;
    bandeirantes in, 60 ; boundary with
    Bahia of, 44, 245
Persian Gulf, 24, 25
Peste da bicha, *see* Yellow fever
Pharmacies : at Alcobaça, 10 ; at Salvador,
    inspections of, 265, 266, 267–8 ; of
    Misericórdia, 274, 277–8, 291, 293
Philip I, King of Portugal (II of Spain), 99
Philip III, King of Portugal (IV of Spain),
    99, 296–7
Phlebotomy, excessive practice of, 32, 290–1
Piauí, 60, 69
Pinto de Freitas, Gonçalo, 88, 89

Pirajá, 193
Pirates : French and Breton 45, 46 ; Dutch, 55
Piratininga, Plateau of, 38
Pires de Carvalho, José, 177, 321
Pires de Carvalho e Albuquerque, José, 77, 203, 255, 285
Pires de Carvalho e Albuquerque, Salvador, 109
Pires Lima, Francisco, 154
Plague : in western Europe, 1 ; in Florence, 4 ; Portugal, 5–6, 7 ; Salvador, 225, 228, 268
Plate, River, 38, 78
Poderosos do sertão, 62
Pombal (Sebastião José de Carvalho e Melo), Marquis of : dictator of Portugal, 337 ; establishes trading companies, 338 ; officially ends religious discrimination, 145 ; promises social equality for Amerindians, 139, 145, 338 ; organises Crown diamond monopoly, 338 ; anti-Jesuit, 76–7, 338 ; invokes English Alliance, 78
Ponta do Padrão, 46
Ponte, House of, *see* Guedes de Brito
Ponte de Lima, 63. See also *Misericórdia, Santa Casa da*
Poor Clares at Salvador : convent of, 134, 177, 332 ; foundation, 58, 178, 321 ; secular intervention in, 113, 322 ; amorous reputation of, 179, 312, 322 ; viceroyal intervention in, 179, 312, 322 ; class distinctions in, 134, 321
'Poor whites', 228, 282
Population : western Europe, 1 ; Portugal, affected by overseas colonisation, 7 ; Lisbon, 313 ; Salvador, 47, 50, 178, 225–226, 260, 309, 313
Pôrto Seguro, 44, 45, 46. See also *Misericórdia, Santa Casa da*
Portugal : emigration to Brazil from, 50, 60–1, 129, 136, 229 ; plague in, 5–6, 7 ; depopulation of, 7 ; famine in, 6 ; Spanish invasions of, 7, 78 ; social philanthropy in, 8–13 ; agriculture in, 7 ; corporations of artisans in, 12, 19 ; lay brotherhoods in, 12–13, 202 ; monastic orders in, 10–11 ; military orders in, 11 ; economic interest in trade with west Africa and Brazil, 59, 60, 61, 117 ; trade with England, 337 ; diplomatic relations with France, 37 ; overseas expansion : Asia,

25–6 ; Africa, 35–6 ; Brazil, 37–9 ; administration of overseas empire, 108, 234–6, 358–9 ; decline of overseas empire, 359–60
Portuguese : scorn for manual labour, 282, 309 ; weakness for mistresses and saints, 167 ; alleged 'assimilating powers' of, 26, 175 ; chronic xenophobia, 129, 282–283, 290, 322–3 ; excessive practice of phlebotomy, 32, 290–1 ; entertain delusions of grandeur, 133, 134, 147
Praia do Rio Real, 148
Prester John, 24
Price fluctuations : of property, 92–3, 342 ; of slaves, 68, 148, 342 ; of cattle, 148 ; of sugar, 64–5, 66 ; of manioc flour, 67, 264–5 ; prevalent in an agrarian economy, 148–9 ; sugar plantations, 102
Príncipe, Island of, 17, 51
Prisons : Lisbon, 17 ; Cochin, 236 ; Pernambuco, 251 ; Salvador, 49, 58, 171, 247–8, 250–3, 290
Prison aid, by brotherhoods in Italy, 3, 237 ; in Portugal, 13. See also *Misericórdia, Santa Casa da*
Privileges : of municipal council of Salvador, 318, 345 ; of Cistercians at Alcobaça, 10 ; offered by Affonso de Albuquerque to encourage marriages, 25–6, 174 ; of holders of commissions in militia, 131 ; of soldiers' brotherhood in Salvador, 215. See also *Misericórdia, Santa Casa da*
Prostitution : in Macao, 34 ; in Salvador, 301, 311, 336
Provedor, term explained, 82
Provedor da Saúde, 266–7
Provincia do Norte, 175
Pulmonary infections, 288, 289
Pureza de sangue, term explained, 124–5. See also *Misericórdia, Santa Casa da* ; Colour prejudice and discrimination ; Religious prejudice and discrimination
Purgatives, 290, 291
Pyrard de Laval, François, 29, 33, 43, 87, 236 ; description of Salvador by, 51–2

Quarantine of ships : at Lisbon, 268 ; at Salvador, 267
Quaresma, Manuel, 118, 325–6
Quilombos, in Minas Gerais, 141–2 ; in Bahia, 250–1
Quintos, see Fifths

Race relations, *see* Miscegenation ; Colour prejudice and discrimination

Ramos, Maria, 94

Ramos Pacheco, Manuel, 158, 249 n.

Rangel, Francisco, 34

Ransom of captives, 11, 33, 351

Real de São Lazaro, 272

Recife, 57, 75

Recôncavo, of Bahia : *sesmarias* granted in, 38, 39, 46, 61, 83 ; topography of, 44 ; Amerindians in, 44 ; visited by Vespucci, 45 ; ravaged by Dutch, 57 ; gypsies in, 243 ; yellow fever in, 127 ; shift in importance from Recôncavo to city, 111 ; centre of sugar-cane cultivation, 39, 44, 46, 52–4, 59–60, 61 ; cultivation of tobacco, 44, 61. *See also* Bahia ; All Saints, Bay of ; Salvador, city of

Red Sea, 24, 25

Regimento : of corporations of artisans, 12 ; of Tomé de Sousa, 39, 47, 235–6

Réis Duarte, Belchior dos, 122 n.

Réis Pinto, Gaspar dos, 180

Relação (High Court) : at Gôa, 235 ; at Rio de Janeiro, 78, 251 ; at Salvador, 58, 78 ; jurisdiction of, 78, 243, 244, 251 ; rivalry with municipal council, 238–9, 248, 301, 353 ; family ties in, 240–1 ; administrative structure of, 239 ; compared with Spanish *Audiencia*, 356 ; in Portuguese empire, 359

Religious observance and fervour : characterises brotherhoods and corporations in Europe, 2, 12, 13 ; in Salvador compared with East Indies, 52 ; of landed aristocracy, 150–1, 152 ; outward display of, 165–8, 204, 207 ; of slave, 166

Religious Orders : in Portugal, social philanthropy by, 8, 10–11 ; in Brazil, establish houses in Salvador, 50, 58 ; harbour criminals, 241–2 ; social services by, 84 ; in Spanish America, 269. *See also* Jesuits ; Orders of St Francis, of St Benedict, etc.

Religious prejudice and discrimination : in convents, 329 ; in religious orders, 137, 329 ; in Third Orders and brotherhoods, 136, 143, 329 ; in clauses of legacies, 181, 188 ; in official administrative appointments, 140 ; against mercantile class, 120–1, 135, 138 ; ended officially in Portuguese empire, 145 ; in Spanish

America, 358. See also *Misericórdia, Santa Casa da*, Gôa, Macao, Salvador

Retirement houses

Mary Magdalene (Gôa), 32–3

Our Lady of the Mountain (Gôa), 32

Our Lady of Solitude (Salvador), 336

St Raymond (Salvador), 336

The Most Holy Name of Jesus (Salvador), see *Misericórdia, Santa Casa da*, Salvador

Ribatejo, 18

Ribeiro, Gabriel, 324, 326, 329

Ribeiro, João, 156, 166

Ribeiro Briozo, António, 159

Ribeiro do Valle, Paulo, 123

Ribeiro Penha, Manuel, 158

Ribeiro Rocha, Manuel, 254

Rio das Pedras, 147–8

Rio de Contas, 70, 245

Rio de Janeiro : defence of, 65 ; centre of New Christian population, 138 ; transfer of capital to, 79 ; ousts Salvador in importance, 78 ; outlet for gold and diamonds, 78, 153 ; *Relação* of, 78, 251 ; Religious Orders at, 113, 223, 241 ; Third Orders at, 113, 241. See also *Misericórdia, Santa Casa da* ; Municipal councils

Rio Grande do Norte, 57, 60

Rio Grande do Sul, 78, 252

Rocha Pitta family, 125

Rocha Pitta, António da, 110, 118–19

Rocha Pitta, João da, 324

Rocha Pitta, Sebastião da, 288 ; biographical sketch, 76 ; quoted, 63–4, 302 n., 327

Rodrigues, Gonçalo, 158

Rodrigues, João, 16

Rodrigues, Mecia, 89, 151

Rodrigues, Salvador, 215

Rodrigues Correia, Domingos, 105 n., 137, 138

Rodrigues da Costa, António, 131

Rodrigues de Aguiar, Francisco, 137

Rodrigues Lima, António, 109

Rodrigues Lisboa, Domingos, 144

Rodrigues Pinheiro, José, 122

Rodrigues Ronca, João, 16

Rodrigues Velloso, João, 131

Rolim de Moura, Cosme, 107

Rome, 104, 201–2, 295

Royal Academy of History, 76

Rozmital, Leo of, 5

Rugendas, Maurice, 142

Rum, 59, 245

Sá, Estácio de, 40
Sá, Felippa de, 91
Sá, Francisco de, 91
Sá, Mem de, 82, 86, 91–2, 94, 116 n.
Sá Doria, António de, 150, 166, 168, 221
Sá e Benavides, Salvador Correia de, 75, 92
Sá e Mendonça, Joseph de, 328 n.
Sabará, 155
Sabugosa (Vasco Fernandes Cesar de Meneses), Count of: founds townships, 244; founds theatre, 77; encourages arts, 75–76; defends Bahian business community, 117; relations with *Misericórdia* of Gôa, 107, 117; relations with *Misericórdia* of Salvador, 107–8, 171, 189, 219, 223–4, 257, 270, 302–6, 335; relations with the municipal council, Salvador, 266, 269, 302–3; authoritarian, 353; and execution of justice, 241, 244, 257; reports on Bahian economy, 66, 102; complains of lack of co-operation from archbishop, 284; measures to discover smuggled gold, 242; sisters of, 335
Sacramento, Colonia do, 58, 78
Sailors: low quality of Portuguese, 8; convicts as, 252, 265; brotherhood of, in Rio, 215 n.; pay fines to hospital, Salvador, 81, 84; carriers of disease, 289, 290; hospital proposed in Salvador for, 270; treated by *Misericórdia*, Salvador, 159, 265, 270, 286–8, 293
St Antão, Jesuit College of, 91–2; Order of, 10
St Benedict, Order of: in Salvador, 50, 51, 52, 58, 87, 322; as landowners, 89, 90; refusal to admit Brazilian-born, 329; in Rio de Janeiro, criminal activities of, 241
St Dominic, 3; Order of, in Salvador, 58
St Francis, 3; Order of, in Salvador, 50, 51, 52, 58, 89, 271; relations with Third Order, 113, 209–11, 213; chronicle of Order, 77; in Rio, 113
St Francis, Third Order of, 3; in Salvador, membership of, 63, 149, 220, 348; lack of royal patronage, 93; 'rigged' elections in, 113–14; relations with friars, see above; Crown intervention in, 113–114, 213, 241; hospital of, 271; bell-tower of, 113, 141, 213; ossuary of, 229; harbour criminals, 241; building of, 325; relations with the *Misericórdia*, 208–12; demands 'purity of blood', 136, 143; in Rio de Janeiro, harbour criminals, 241; dispute with friars, 113
St James, 8
St Mary of Rocamadour, Order of, 10–11
St Peter, basilica of, Rome, 104
St Philip Neri, Order of, 323 n.
St Theresa, monastery of, 242, 245, 250, 346
St Vincent de Paul, Order of, 361
Salitre, River, 73
Salt, riot over price increase in, 126
Salvador, city of: foundation of, 47–50, 83, 235–6; name defined, 48 n.; Dampier's description of, 58, 263; Pyrard de Laval's description of, 51–2; population of, 47, 50, 178, 225–6, 260, 309, 313; mortality rate of, 153, 180, 224–7, 315–316; prison of, 49, 58, 171, 247–8, 250–253, 290; presence of 'poor whites', 228, 282; Dutch invasion of, 56–7, 87–88, 239; mint at, 58, 69, 245, 323, 324, 326; Faculty of Medicine at, 360; healthy position of, 47–8, 262–3; lack of hygiene at, 228–9, 260, 263–9, 274; garrison of, see Garrisons; unpopularity of military service at, 284; shortage of currency at, 69–70, 98, 102, 178, 323; militia in, 131, 140–1; patron saint of, 67; school of military engineering at, 77; High Court at, see *Relação*; taxation at, 65–6, 126, 247, 272 318; Jesuit College at, see Jesuits; literary academies at, 75–7; theatre at, 77; counterfeiting of coins at, 154, 245; centre of diamond and gold smuggling, 70, 154, 242, 245; leprosery at, 271–2, 288, 290; centre of New Christian population, 50, 52, 135–6, 138; seclusion of white women at, 183, 320–1; foreign residents at, 129, 187 n., 263, 290; earth tremor at, 66, 303; lotteries in, 275, 360; prostitution in, 301, 311, 336; processions at, 67, 102–3, 258, 302, 335; dogs roam at night in, 229, 301; bishopric instituted, 50; raised to metropolitanate, 58; electrical storm at, 302; position in triangular trade with Africa and Portugal, 59, 117, 349; secular feeling at, 168–70, 322, 336, 355; way-port for East Indiamen, see East Indiamen; cemeteries at, 228, 229, 269, 361–

362, 364; civic pride after restoration, 88, 94–5; forts at, 46, 58, 283, 287; windlass at, 51–2; shortage of white women at, 175, 178 n., 310, 323, 331; yellow fever at, 127, 266, 268–9, 288–9; European visitors to, 43, 51–2, 58, 63, 65, 66, 87, 166, 167, 226, 228–9, 236, 263, 264, 265, 272, 301, 311, 320. See also *Misericórdia, Santa Casa da*; Municipal councils; Religious Orders; Colour prejudice and discrimination; Religious prejudice and discrimination; Brotherhoods; etc.

Salvador, O.S.F., Fr Vicente do, 71

Salvador de Valadares, 156

Sampaio, Theodoro, 80

Sancho I, King Dom, 11, 67

Sanctuary, right of, 241–2

Sande, Francisca de, 289

Santa Catharina, 77, 78

Santa Clara do Desterro, Convent of, *see* Poor Clares

Santarém, 7, 9, 11, 14, 16, 295

Santiago de Compostela, 8

Santos, see *Misericórdia, Santa Casa da*

São Francisco, River, 44, 60, 73

São Francisco do Conde, 244

São João, Fr Macário de, 95

São João del Rei, 141–2, 155

São Jorge da Mina (Elmina), 24

São Julião de Moreira, 349

São Luís de Maranhão, 131. See also *Misericórdia, Santa Casa da*

São Paulo, 86

São Paulo, captaincy of, 78. See also *Misericórdia, Santa Casa da*

São Roque, Cape of, 45

São Sebastião, city of, *see* Rio de Janeiro

São Tomé, sugar in, 52; slave trade to Brazil from, 50, 252–3, 269; garrison of, 58; convicts sent to, 17; Dutch traders at, 55; António Ferrão Castelo Branco, Governor of, 112, 253, 255. See also *Misericórdia, Santa Casa da*

São Tomé de Meliapor, see *Misericórdia, Santa Casa da*

São Vicente, 38, 44, 60; sugar-cane cultivation in, 39, 52

Schoppe, Sigismund von, 57

Schouten, Albert and Willem, 56

Scurvy, 262, 265, 269, 270, 286–7, 289, 290

Segovia, 15

Sena, see *Misericórdia, Santa Casa da*

Senegal, River, 24

Senhoria, abuse of title, 135

Senzala (slave quarters), 61–2, 150

Sergipe, 57. See also *Misericórdia, Santa Casa da*

Serra do Espinhaço, 44

Sertão: topography of, 44; development of, 60, 117–18; justice in, 244–5

Sertão, Domingos Affonso, 118, 125, 150, 255

Sesmarias (concessions of land), 38, 39, 46, 61, 83

Seven Years War, 78

Siena, 295

Silks, 25, 59, 159

Silva, Gregório da, 141 n.

Silva, Pedro da, 91

Silva Alva, Pedro da, 27

Silva Moreira, Paschoal da, 172, 249 n., 308 n.

Silva Pimentel family, 125

Silva Pimental, António da (father), 95, 118 119

Silva Pimental, António da (son), 119

Silveira, Domingos da, 147–8, 167

Silver, Peruvian, 56; Japanese, 25; currency at Bahia, 69

Simões S.J., Garcia, 36

Simões Lisboa, Manuel, 249 n.

Sintra, 6, 13

Sisters of Mercy, French, 361

Slaves and slavery, Amerindian, 151, 261, 333

Slaves and slavery, Chinese, 230

Slaves and slavery, Negro: essential in Bahia, 59, 61, 67–8; trade with Angola, 51, 55, 59, 68, 117, 252; with Guinea, 24 n., 50, 59; with Príncipe, 51; with São Tomé, 50, 252–3, 269; plan of Count of Galvêas for, 121; with east African ports proposed, 68; relative merits of Sudanese and Bantu, 51, 68, 141 n.; musical tradition of, 77–8; numbers in Bahia, 50, 226; shortage in Bahia, 67–8; mortality rate, 226–7, 262; tribal distinctions among, 51, 68, 141; religious fervour of, 166; rebellious in Minas Gerais, 141–2; revolts in Bahia, 141; life on sugar plantations, 54, 61–2, 74, 262, 314; brotherhoods in Salvador, 94, 142–3, 203, 204, 213, 216–20, 230; in Rio de Janeiro, 142 n.; runaway slaves, 141–2, 246, 250–1; sexual appeal of slave girls, 311; dowries for slave girls,

182–3 ; legal defence of, 255–7 ; legal discrimination against, 246, 255–6, 311 ; burial of, 94, 203, 204, 213–14, 216–20, 221–3, 224, 226–7, 228–30 ; as financial investment and symbols of social prestige, 281, 314 ; as pledges for loans, 63, 342 ; price in Salvador of, 68 ; cemetery for slaves in Salvador, 229, 269, 361 ; migration to Minas Gerais from Bahia, 67–8, 148 ; defended by António Vieira, 74 ; treated in hospital of the *Misericórdia*, 182, 269, 281 ; left to the *Misericórdia* as legacies, 89, 164, 165 ; appeals to Crown by, 139, 257 ; royal concern, for, 139–40, 141–2, 219–20, 222–3, 251 255–7, 266, 268 ; epidemics among, 65, 67, 148, 290 ; attitude to female slave, 182–3 ; punishment of, 141, 246, 256–7 ; cohesion of slave families, 314 ; ambiguous position of freed slave, 139, 281–2, 314 ; scapegoat for crimes, 246, 255 ; in convents and retirement house of Salvador, 322, 333–4 ; emancipation of, 143, 182, 218 ; carriers of diseases, 225, 261–2, 263, 265, 289–90 ; slave-breeding in West Indies, 71

Slave ships : conditions on, 262, 265, 269 ; quarantined at Salvador, 267 ; inspections of, at Salvador, 265, 267, 268, 279 ; Crown measures concerning, 139, 222, 266, 268

Smallpox, 65, 261, 289, 290

Smuggling : of gold and diamonds, 70, 154, 157, 242, 245 ; of tobacco, 61

Soares, Hilária Francisca, 205 n.

Soares, Lopo, 27

Soares de Sousa, Gabriel, biographical sketch of, 73 ; quoted, 87 ; mentioned, 85, 272, 277, 291

Social welfare, Portuguese Crown policy on, 13–14, 84, 269 ; Spanish Crown policy on, 356–7

Socotra, Island of, 25

Sodré Pereira, Jerónimo, 198–9

Sofala, 24, 25

Soldiers : as civilian administrators, 38 ; on fleet of Tomé de Sousa, 47 ; dearth in East of, 25, 174 ; sexual alliances by, 26, 32, 174–5, 309–10. *See also* Garrisons

Sousa, Lionel de, 234

Sousa, Luís de, 116 n.

Sousa, Martim Affonso de, 38, 39

Sousa, Tomé de : brief as governor-general of Brazil, 39, 47, 175, 235–6 ; fleet of, 47 ; founder of Salvador, 47–50, 83–4, 260, 273

Sousa Campos, Ernesto de, 80

Sousa de Meneses, António de, 75

Sousa Estrella, Bernardo de, 257

Sousa Ferraz, Constantino de, 131

Sousa Salgado, Manuel de, 194–5

Sousa-a-Velha, 11

Soveral, Dom Francisco do, 36

Spain : invasion of Portugal, 78 ; of Colonia do Sacramento, 78

Spanish America, social and administrative structure compared with Portuguese, 269, 356–8

Spice trade, East Indian, 24, 25

Sudanese slaves, compared with Bantu, 51, 68, 141 n.

Sugar and sugar industry : in Pernambuco, 39, 52, 60, 111 ; in São Vicente, 39, 52, 60 ; in Madeira and São Tomé, 52 ; in West Indies, compared with Bahia, 59, 64–5, 70–1 ; in Recôncavo of Bahia, 39, 44, 46, 57, 61 ; difficulties of, 65–8, 70, 148–9 ; technical aspect of refining, 53–54, 59 ; dependent on slaves, 59, 61, 67–8 ; affected by mineral discoveries, 67–8, 70, 78, 111, 148–9 ; cattle employed in, 54, 60, 67, 150 ; industry protected by Crown, 101 ; sugar mills destroyed by Dutch, 57 ; number and output of sugar mills, 52–3, 57, 67 ; transportation of sugar, 44, 60, 67, 307 ; scarcity of, 66 ; high quality of Bahian sugar, 59, 65, 66 ; valuation of sugar crop, 101 ; price of, 65, 66, 69 ; tax on, 65 ; sugar as form of currency, 98, 110, 122, 123 ; crop as security for loans, 63, 106, 197 ; secondary products, 59 ; inventory of a plantation, 150 ; fall in prices of plantations, 102 ; decline in demand for Bahian sugar, 64–5

Sugar planters : prestige of, 62 ; compared and contrasted with cattle ranchers, 61 ; on municipal council, 62, 66 ; influence at court, 62 ; prominent in brotherhoods, 63, 149 ; Provedors of the *Misericórdia*, 118, 120, 125 ; benefactors of the *Misericórdia*, 118, 149–50, 159 ; relations with mercantile class, 69–70 ; petition Crown for delay in departure of fleet, 67 ; interfere in course of justice, 100, 239–41 ; decline in prestige of, 111, 119–20 ; in New Spain, 357. *See also* Landowners, latifundian

Surgeons : at Macao, 290 n. ; at Salvador, 131, 267, 278, 279–80, 284, 290

Swahili coast, 35–6

Syphilis, 261, 289, 290, 291

Tagus, River, 6, 268

Tapuya(s), 44–5

Tapuytapera, see *Misericórdia, Santa Casa da*

Taques, Pedro, 77

Tarapur, see *Misericórdia, Santa Casa da*

Tatuapara, 60

Tavernier, Jean-Baptiste, 29, 32

Tavora, Francisco de, 203

Taxes and taxation, in Portugal, 6 ; in Bahia by donatories, 38 ; Crown prerogative on export taxes, 38 ; in Salvador : for leprosery, 272 ; on fish-oil, 247 ; on sugar, 65 ; on tobacco, 65 ; proposed on imported goods, 126 ; complaints to Crown on excess of, 65–6

Teixeira, Dom Marcos, 56

Templars, 11

Terças, privilege of, 318

Theatre at Salvador, 77

Third Orders, *see* St Francis, Third Order of ; Carmelites, Third Order of

Tidor, see *Misericórdia, Santa Casa da*

Tithes, 271, 292, 300

Tobacco in Bahia : fame of, 61 ; tax on, 65 ; cultivation of, 44, 60–1, 66, 153 ; trade, 55, 59, 61, 337 ; smuggled, 61

Toledo y Osorio, Don Fadrique de, 56, 87

Tôrre, House of, *see* Dias d'Avila family

Tôrres, Mathias, 108

Tôrres Novas, 295

Tôrres Vedras, 11

Torture, judicial, 256–7

Trahiras, 154

Treasury : at Gôa, 28, 32, 33 ; at Salvador, 47, 49, 51 ; subject of royal enquiry, 114–115, 339 ; relations with *Misericórdia*, 341, 342 ; privilege of ordering compulsory sale of properties, 100. See also *Misericórdia, Santa Casa da*, Crown financial aid

Treaty of Madrid, 337–8

Treaty of Tordesillas, 37, 240, 338

Trindade, Fr António da, 137

Trinitarians, Order of, 10–11, 15

Triunfo Eucharistico, see Ferreira Machado, Simão

Tumbeiro, term explained, 139

Tupí Indians, distinction between Tupinambás and Tupiniquins, 44. *See also* Amerindians

'Turning wheel' described, 295–6. See also *Misericórdia, Santa Casa da*

Typhoid, 289

Unhão Castelo Branco, Pedro de, 112

Union of Utrecht, 55

Vahia Monteiro, Luís, 113

Valadares, Jorge de, 47, 83

Valansuela, Maria de, 195

Valdés, Diogo Flores, 40

Valencia, 15

Valensa Pereira, João de 184

Vasconcellos, Francisca de, 119

Vasconcellos Cavalcante, Balthazar de, 67, 119 n.

Vaz de Caminha, Pedro, 44

Vaz de Paiva, Luís, 136

Velho de Araújo, Jerónimo, 109, 122

Venice, 2, 3

Vespucci, Amerigo, 37, 45

Viana do Castelo, 178. See also *Misericórdia, Santa Casa da*

Vicente, Gil, 8

Viceroys : in Portuguese India, opportunism of, 235 ; in Brazil, extent of authority, 50, 78, 353, 356 ; in Spanish America, 356

Viegas Giraldes, Pedro, 90, 182

Vieira, S.J., António, 41, 73–4, 112, 211, 364

Vieira Ravasco family, 167

Vieira Ravasco, Bernardo, 93, 112, 119

Vila do Conde, 153

Vila Rica de Ouro Prêto, 155. See also *Misericórdia, Santa Casa da*

Vilhena, Luís dos Santos, 228, 229, 262, 267 n., 269, 272, 275, 282, 288, 313, 318–319, 321, 327

Villa Lobos da Câmara, Maria Eulalia, 334

Villa-Pouca de Aguiar (António Telles de Meneses), Count of, 57

Vitória, 40

West India Company, Dutch, 55

West Indies, 64–5, 70–1

Wet-nurses : at Macao, 34 ; at Salvador, 298, 299, 306, 315–16, 317, 318, 339, 340, 360 ; at Gôa, 315 ; at Lisbon, 316 ; privileges of, 304–5
Whale oil, 59
Willekens, Jacob, 56
Wills, clauses of, 146–8 ; reveal social attitudes, 165, 176–81
Women : alleged amorality of Indo-Portuguese, 33 ; shortage of white, in Portuguese Asia, 174–5 ; shortage of white, in Spanish America, 358; shortage of white, in Salvador, 175, 178 n., 310, 323, 331 ; prohibited from leaving Brazil, 179, 225 ; many sent to convents in Portugal, 177–81, 194, 321, 322, 329 ; seclusion of Luso-Brazilian white women, 183, 320–322 ; increase in number of white, in Salvador, 225 ; barrenness of white, 153, 180 ; attitudes towards white, in Salvador, 171, 176–81, 183–4 ; attitude to coloured, 309–10 ; attitude to slave, 182–183 ; honour of, 171, 187, 311, 321

Xavier, S.J., (St) Francis, 41, 67, 289

Yellow fever, 127, 261, 266, 268–9, 288–9

Zanzibar, 35
Zumárraga, Juan de, 357
Zurara, Gomes Eannes de, 7